D1591210

MICAH JENKINS, SHOWN HERE SHORTLY BEFORE HIS PROMOTION TO
BRIGADIER GENERAL AT AGE **26** IN JULY **1862.**
(LIBRARY OF CONGRESS, NEGATIVE REVERSED)

THE STRUCK EAGLE

A BIOGRAPHY OF
BRIGADIER GENERAL MICAH JENKINS,
AND A HISTORY OF
THE FIFTH SOUTH CAROLINA VOLUNTEERS
AND THE PALMETTO SHARPSHOOTERS

James J. Baldwin, III

 Burd Street Press

Copyright © 1996 by James J. Baldwin, III

This Burd Street Press publication was printed by
    Beidel Printing House, Inc.
    63 West Burd Street
    Shippensburg, PA 17257

In respect for the scholarship contained herein, the acid-free paper used in this book meets the guidelines for permanence and durability of the Committee on Production Guidelines for Book Longevity of the Council on Library Resources.

For a complete list of available publications please write:
    Burd Street Press
    Division of White Mane Publishing Company, Inc.
    P.O. Box 152
    Shippensburg, PA 17257

Library of Congress Cataloging-in-Publication Data

Baldwin, James J., 1941-
    The struck eagle : a biography of Brigadier General Micah Jenkins, and a history of the Fifth South Carolina Volunteers and the Palmetto Sharpshooters / James J. Baldwin, III.
        p.   cm.
    Includes bibliographical references and index.
    ISBN 1-57249-017-9
    1. Jenkins, Micah, 1835-1864. 2. Generals--Confederate States of America--Biography. 3. Confederate States of America. Army--Biography. 4. Confederate States of America. Army. Palmetto Sharpshooters--History. 5. Confederate States of America. Army. South Carolina Infantry Regiment, 5th--History. 6. United States--History--Civil War, 1861-1865--Regimental histories. I. Title.
E467.1.J4B35 1996
973.7'3'092--dc20
[B]
                                        96-14115
                                          CIP

PRINTED IN THE UNITED STATES OF AMERICA

So the struck eagle, stretch'd upon the plain,
No more through rolling clouds to soar again,
View'd his own feather on the fatal dart,
And wing'd the shaft that quiver'd in his heart;
Keen were his pangs, but keener far to feel,
He nursed the pinion which impell'd the steel;
While the same plumage that had warmed his nest,
Drank the last life-drop of his bleeding breast.

From "English Bards and Scotch Reviewers, a Satire" by George Gordon, Lord Byron.

CONTENTS

LIST Of ORGANIZATION CHARTS

LIST OF MAPS

Note: Maps not drawn exactly to scale.

Preface

The bloody American Civil War, and the unparalleled set of circumstances which led to it, had a profound effect on the character of our nation and our history. Viewed from a broad historical perspective, this period of turmoil is both captivating and revealing: it shows what we as a nation have become in the more than two hundred years since its birth.

Perhaps this spirit was best demonstrated on July 3, 1913, during a reenactment of Pickett's famous charge by the surviving veterans of the battle, as part of a reunion at Gettysburg. The aging Confederates advanced steadily toward Cemetery Ridge just as they had so courageously done on that bloody third day of July, fifty years before. Finally, they charged the Union veterans who were positioned behind the stone wall along the ridge. Before the old Confederates reached the wall, however, their former foes rose to meet them; not in mortal combat, but to embrace them in mutual respect and admiration. As this reenactment symbolizes, the war had ultimately created bonds of unity among a once bitterly divided people.

But the Civil War also had a profound effect on the soldiers and their families, and it is this aspect that is often neglected. It is too easy to view the war with a kind of detached reverence, thinking of it mostly in terms of statistics and dates. It is true that some of the numbers are worth remembering: more than 600,000 participants on both sides lost their lives during the conflict, a staggering number by any standard. The statistics have a tendency, however, to anesthetize us, causing great events to appear impersonal and colorless. The Battle of Sharpsburg (Antietam), for example, is now remembered by too many of us simply as the day nearly 23,000 Americans fell, the bloodiest single day of the war.

Approaching the Civil War from too impersonal a perspective, or from merely a detached consideration of dates and numbers, has its disadvantages. By taking such a limited approach, we fail to grasp the horrible, day-to-day reality of the conflict, and we cannot fully appreciate the individual sacrifices made both by the fighting men and by their families. The civilians who were swept along by the tidal wave of events which propelled the states into such violent combat, and those who fought each other for four long and gruelling years, were men and women with families and communities not so unlike our own. It is in studying the fascinating and compelling stories of these individuals that we can begin to appreciate the effects of the war on the soldiers and on the wives and children they left behind. Only by understanding some of what they endured, can we properly honor them, which is the primary reason for this book.

The political and social issues which led to such bitter sectionalism and antagonism between the states have been exhaustively debated. It is not the purpose of this work to consider the merits of those issues, nor is it to apologize for the Southern demand for independence. The problems of that period should be considered in the context of those times and not judged entirely by today's standards. Whatever we may now know about those issues and problems, the fact is that the war killed over six hundred thousand fathers, sons, and brothers, on both sides, who fought for reasons in which they deeply believed. One of the dead was Micah Jenkins, my great-great-grandfather, who left behind a young widow and four young sons.

Micah Jenkins' family was more heavily involved than most in the events which led South Carolina to secede. His uncle and his brother were delegates to the Secession Convention of 1860 presided over by his father-in-law, David F. Jamison. Jamison later served briefly as South Carolina's secretary of war. After the war began, Jenkins and his two brothers served in the Confederate Army. One was a surgeon, another a cavalry major on the coast of South Carolina; Micah Jenkins rose to the rank of brigadier general in the famous Army of Northern Virginia under the command of General Robert E. Lee.

Jenkins seemed destined for military service from the time he entered the Citadel as a freshman in 1851. Even as a young student, he appeared to be preparing himself for the command of men in battle, which, in fact, he would do only ten years later. When the war finally erupted in April 1861, Jenkins was well-respected in the upper part of South Carolina for his military leadership abilities. At age twenty-five he was elected the commanding officer of the Fifth Regiment of South Carolina Volunteers, one of ten infantry regiments formed in the state at the time it seceded from the Union.

As the Battle of Fort Sumter raged in Charleston Harbor, Jenkins and his men were ordered into service. They boarded trains in the upstate and assembled in Columbia for the trip to Charleston. At that time, the events in Jenkins' life began to parallel those of the men under his command. Thus, in describing the events in his life during the war, one must necessarily recount the story of the men in the Fifth South Carolina Volunteers as well as of those in the new regiment organized by Jenkins in April 1862, the Palmetto Sharpshooters. When Jenkins was promoted to brigadier general in July 1862, these two fine regiments were part of his brigade, and they fought continuously in it until the surrender of Lee's army at Appomattox.

Research into Jenkins' early years has been hampered by the fact that some of the relevant records were destroyed during Sherman's devastating march through South Carolina in early 1865. When Columbia was burned in February 1865, for example, Jenkins' and other pre-war Citadel graduates' records, stored at the Arsenal Academy, were destroyed. In spite of such losses, however, much material has been preserved. Large collections of Micah Jenkins' letters and papers, as well as those of his brother, John, are at the South Caroliniana Library in Columbia, South Carolina. Articles and letters from the Yorkville *Enquirer*, a newspaper published weekly in Yorkville, South Carolina, during the 1850's and 1860's, are filled with relevant information, and letters and recollections written by soldiers who served under Jenkins have been relied upon extensively. Post-war memoirs, most notably those of Asbury Coward, Jenkins' closest friend and business partner and later colonel of the Fifth South Carolina Volunteers, also provided a wealth of information, not only on Jenkins, but also on that regiment.

Jenkins seems to have matured early, and his letters show him to be highly idealistic. In his war correspondence he speaks repeatedly of fighting for his country, for the liberty of his children and for independence. No doubt the ideals of the Revolutionary War days were etched into Jenkins' mind from his boyhood. Once the Civil War began, he developed into a man who General Wade Hampton later said was, "the finest soldier I ever saw." Jenkins proved himself absolutely fearless in battle, and early in the war even displayed a boyish eagerness for the fighting to begin. He loved his men, and he was known to have dismounted to walk with them, sometimes allowing an older soldier to ride in his place. He became a devout Christian who regularly read the Bible and discussed the scriptures with his men. By his final year, Jenkins had become disappointed by the harsh reality of politics in the Confederate military system. He failed to win promotion to major general, in part because of his close ties to General James Longstreet who had fallen into disfavor with Jefferson Davis.

Jenkins' men were clearly worthy of his devotion to them. In late 1861, General Longstreet was delighted to learn that the Fifth South Carolina Volunteers had been assigned to his division. His aide-de-camp described the Fifth as "one of the finest, if not the finest, regiments in the Army." By June of 1862, following their courageous performance during the Battle of Seven Pines, Jenkins' newly-organized Palmetto Sharpshooters were receiving similar accolades. Except for Chancellorsville, Gettysburg, and the Battle of the Crater, these two South Carolina regiments participated in most of the major infantry engagements fought by Lee's Army of Northern Virginia. The Fifth South Carolina Volunteers began fighting at First Manassas in July 1861, and finished near Appomattox Court House in April 1865. The Palmetto Sharpshooters, beginning with the Battle of Williamsburg in May 1862, also fought to Appomattox, and was the largest single regiment to be surrendered there, a fact which to this day stands in tribute to its members' devotion, determination, and tenacity. The story of the courageous men who served in these two regiments must be preserved so that they may be honored for their deeds and sacrifices by future generations.

Finally, one comment should be made on the method I have chosen to present this history. Certain events in the lives of the major characters in this work are of prime importance in understanding their part in the overall story. Available records, however, often have not described these events fully enough. In several of those instances, therefore, I have taken the factual event and added certain minor details based on my best estimate of how the event reasonably would have occurred. This has been done solely to make the event come to life for the reader.

J.J.B.

ACKNOWLEDGMENTS

Without the unpublished letters and papers of Micah Jenkins, this work would have not been possible. I am especially indebted to Allen Stokes and Henry G. Fulmer at the South Caroliniana Library, Robert H. Mackintosh at the South Carolina Department of Archives and History, and William R. Erwin in the Special Collections Library at Duke University for their assistance to me regarding these and other relevant letters and papers.

I also express my appreciation to those kind persons who have generously allowed me access to their private manuscript collections, especially Elmer O. Parker and Emily Wilson Taylor. Mr. Parker's advice and counsel have been invaluable to me, as has his friendship.

My secretary, Lynn Stewart, deserves credit for remaining with this project from start to finish. She has handled my numerous re-writes with commendable patience, and her cheerful spirit made working with her a pleasure. David J. Rutledge, my friend and consultant, was always willing to assist me on a wide range of matters. On the photographs included in this book, his work was invaluable.

Finally, I am grateful to my family who for five years have had to endure the preparation of this book. For that entire time my wife, Nancy, has acted as counselor, critic, research assistant, proofreader, and editor and has been a constant and welcome source of encouragement.

LIST OF ABBREVIATIONS

D.U.L.   Duke University (Special Collections) Library, Duke
            University, Durham, North Carolina

E.U.L.   Emory University (Woodruff) Library, Emory University
            Atlanta, Georgia

G.D.A.H.   Georgia Department of Archives and History,
            Atlanta, Georgia

S.C.D.A.H. South Carolina Department of Archives and History,
            Columbia, South Carolina

S.C.L.   South Caroliniana Library, University of South Carolina,
            Columbia, South Carolina

U.V.L.   University of Virginia Library, University of Virginia,
            Charlottesville, Virginia

W.U.L.   Winthrop University Library, Winthrop University,
            Rock Hill, South Carolina

Chapter 1

A Boy On Edisto

I t seemed to the boy's mother that it had taken the doctor hours to respond to her urgent summons. There were some disadvantages to living on Edisto Island, one of which was the painfully long time it took the few doctors there to respond to an emergency at one of the planters' homes.

As the doctor's carriage turned into the far end of the long, oak-lined driveway leading up to the plantation house, the horse was at a full gallop, and the wheels crunched as they rumbled along the white surface of crushed oyster shells. An expensively dressed woman stood at the top of the steps on the long front veranda, displaying the kind of wide-eyed anxiety which only a mother can show when her child is hurting.

The doctor was out of the carriage and bounding up the porch steps almost before the carriage had come to a full stop. As he was ushered inside, his horse, well lathered and still hitched to the carriage, was taken by a servant to the stable at a slow walk.

Inside the house, the doctor found young Micah Jenkins, a handsome, blue-eyed twelve-year-old, with a large fishhook imbedded deeply in his wrist. Micah seemed concerned, but he was calmer than his mother. The hook's rusty barb would have ripped the flesh had it been pulled out, and the doctor immediately saw that he would need his scalpel. Anticipating the pain that Micah was about to endure, the doctor reached into his bag, removed a bottle of whiskey, and handed it to him. When Micah realized what it was, he politely returned it without unscrewing the top. Explaining that the whiskey was only to dull the pain, the doctor urged him to drink it for his own good. Micah steadfastly refused, however, and said he could not break a vow he had made to his mother that he would never drink whiskey. Keeping that promise, even in the face of painful surgery, was a matter of honor for the boy.

The scalpel blade sliced deeply into his swollen wrist, and Micah winced while he bled. As the doctor wondered how one so young could endure such pain, Micah's eyes rolled back and he lost consciousness. The doctor immediately took this opportunity to complete the surgery with ease and speed, his patient now oblivious to the pain.[1]

As is usually the case with young boys, it took little time for Micah to recover, and he quickly resumed the wonderful life of growing up on one of South Carolina's most beautiful coastal islands. In the mid-1800's, Edisto Island, about thirty-five miles south of Charleston, was a kind of "small kingdom unto itself" with boats as its only access to the outside world.[2] There were no bridges across the surrounding rivers to link the island to the mainland, and its inhabitants were isolated from the rest of the state. News and mail were regularly delivered to the island by steamers which made scheduled stops at the island's public landing and transported the planters and their families to and from Charleston, Beaufort and Savannah.

With the Atlantic on the southeast and rivers and bays on its other sides, Edisto's isolation merely added to its charm. The ocean, bays, and surrounding tidal backwaters provided islanders with an abundance of fish, shrimp, oysters, and blue crab.[3] They hunted deer and ducks for food, and most planters' sons grew up learning how to use a shotgun and musket. For a young boy like Micah, old enough to hunt and fish on his own, Edisto was a wildlife paradise.

In the 1790's, the island's planters had begun growing high quality long-staple cotton which became known as sea island cotton. Edisto's cotton was soon in great demand, and it made the planters rich. Their plantation homes were elegant structures, surrounded by well-manicured gardens. Edisto Island planters epitomized the traditions of Southern hospitality, giving dances and dinners in their homes. They also

---

[1] John Peyre Thomas, *The Career and Character of General Micah Jenkins, C.S.A.* (Columbia, South Carolina: The State Company, 1903), 23-24. Minor details have been added to Thomas' account of this incident, based on the author's best estimate of how it probably occurred.

[2] Chalmers S. Murray, "Edisto Island and its Place Names," *Names in South Carolina* 7 (Winter 1960): 74.

[3] David Ramsay, *Ramsay's History of South Carolina, From its First Settlement in 1670 to the Year 1808* (Charleston, South Carolina: Walker, Evans & Co., 1858), 279.

frequently attended social events in Charleston, such as the traditional horse racing week each February.

During the summers the planters and their families left their plantations in the interior of the island to move into houses along the island's beach at Edingsville, a small resort village facing the ocean. This annual move was made not only to escape the oppressive temperatures and mosquitos, but also the deadly diseases that were believed to be caused by the sweltering heat. In September the planter families moved back inland, closer to the land which provided their livelihood. They all owned slaves who were used as house servants, field workers, and skilled craftsmen such as carpenters.

The planters of Edisto, like so many other Southerners, observed a code of honor which provided a formal, deadly method for settling disputes on those few occasions when one insulted another. In the event of such a dispute each man would name a second who would then attempt to resolve the matter. If this proved unsuccessful, a duel with pistols was arranged, the details negotiated by the seconds. These problems occurred frequently enough on Edisto that a special dueling ground, located near the beach and known as "the sands," was used to settle such disputes.[4]

Micah Jenkins was born into this unique island world on December 1, 1835, the fourth of Captain John Jenkins' and Elizabeth Clark Jenkins' six children. Micah's two brothers, John and Edward, were both older, and he also had an older sister, Elizabeth, whom he called "Liz." His two younger sisters were Abigail and Lydia. Both Micah's father and his uncle, Joseph E. Jenkins, were among Edisto Island's respected and wealthy planters, and the family's history on the island could be traced well back into the eighteenth century.

Micah's father, Captain John Jenkins, owned several plantations on, or adjacent to, Edisto Island.[5] Perhaps the best known of these was "Old Hill," which Captain Jenkins acquired on his marriage to Elizabeth Grimball Clark who had inherited it from her father. Old Hill consisted of some three hundred acres in the very heart of the island on the "public road" across from the Episcopal church. Captain Jenkins also owned "Mussleborough," a much larger plantation of some nine hundred and fifty acres on Mussleborough Island across the South Edisto River from Edisto Island. In addition, shortly before he died in 1854, he purchased a third plantation called "Bennett's Point" next to Mussleborough. Upon

---

[4]I. Jenkins Mikell, *Rumbling of the Chariot Wheels* (Columbia, South Carolina: R. L. Bryan Co., 1923), 188. There is no record of Micah Jenkins having engaged in a duel. On the practice of dueling in the antebellum South, and its relationship to the concept of honor, see Bertram Wyatt-Brown, *Southern Honor: Ethics and Behavior in the Old South* (New York: Oxford University Press, 1982), 350-361.

[5]It is unclear exactly why Micah's father was called "Captain," but this was probably due to his service in the South Carolina Militia.

his death, Old Hill had to be sold to enable the estate to pay the debt on Bennett's Point.[6] Micah and his family also spent many hours at "Brick House" Plantation, the home of his uncle, Joseph E. Jenkins, who had inherited it from his father (Micah's grandfather).[7] Throughout his childhood, Micah was well attended by servants; his father owned ninety-eight slaves at the time of his death.[8]

Captain John Jenkins was not only a planter; he was also active in the state's political and civic affairs. He was elected in 1838 to the South Carolina Senate by the people of St. John's Parish, Colleton District, and served as their senator until 1841.[9] While in the Senate he was a member of the Military Committee, which no doubt allowed young Micah to overhear dinner table discussions about military issues and affairs. Micah's father was known for his hospitality and entertained at his home not only his fellow planters, but also the local plantation overseers.[10]

During the year before the death of Captain Jenkins in late 1854, Micah's brother, John, who was twenty-nine, began to assume the role of head of the family. As the oldest son, John stepped into his

CAPTAIN JOHN JENKINS, MICAH JENKINS' FATHER

father's shoes and remained on Edisto Island to manage the family's plantations at Mussleborough and at Bennett's Point. Prior to taking over the family business, John had attended Princeton for a year and had served in the South Carolina General Assembly from 1850 to 1852.[11]

---

[6]Report of J. W. Gray, Master in Equity, June 28, 1855, South Carolina Department of Archives and History (hereafter, S.C.D.A.H.), Charleston District, Court of Equity Records Book, March 6, 1855, to June 16, 1856, 164-165.

[7]John Amasa May and Joan Reynolds Faunt, *South Carolina Secedes* (Columbia, South Carolina: University of South Carolina Press, 1960), 167. Micah's grandfather, Joseph Jenkins, resided on Edisto Island and died in 1828.

[8]Inventory and Appraisement of the Goods and Chattel of (Captain) John Jenkins of Edisto Island, Planter Deceased, May 25, 1855, S.C.D.A.H., Charleston District, Inventory Appraisement and Sales, vol. D (1854-1857), 282-283.

[9]N. Louise Bailey, Mary L. Morgan, and Carolyn R. Taylor, eds., *Biographical Directory of the South Carolina Senate*, vol. 2 (Columbia, South Carolina: University of South Carolina Press, 1986), 811-812.

[10]Thomas, *Career and Character*, 24.

[11]May and Faunt, *South Carolina Secedes*, 166.

Only a few weeks before Micah left home to begin college, John married Marcelline Murray, whose father was also a wealthy Edisto planter.

Edward E. Jenkins, Micah's other brother, called "Ned" by the family, left home to study medicine in Paris in 1853 and remained there until May 1855. When he returned home, he married Isabella Jenkins, his cousin, a practice then not uncommon among either the residents of Edisto or in the South generally.

Micah and his siblings received their early schooling on Edisto from schoolmasters privately employed by the planters. One month after turning fifteen, Micah left Edisto Island to begin college in Charleston. He was about to get his first taste of the real world away from the island of his youth. After college, when he was almost twenty and living far from Edisto, Micah wrote a nostalgic Sunday letter in which he recalled:

> When at home [on Edisto] just about this time in the
> evening, we would be sitting on Uncle Joe's piazza [at]
> his house on the bay . . . near the church.[12]

Micah never again lived on the island, returning only to visit his family and friends; however, there were many times when he looked back on his unique Edisto years with a melancholy longing.

---

[12]Micah Jenkins to Caroline Jamison, November 4, 1855, Micah Jenkins Papers, Duke University Library (hereafter, D.U.L.), Duke University, Durham, North Carolina. It is possible that Jenkins was referring to "Brick House," the plantation home on Edisto owned by his uncle, Joseph Evans Jenkins.

Chapter 2

A Military Career Begins

T he tall upperclassman stood silently, watching the new cadets as they assembled for the first time near the Citadel's sally port. As a member of the First Class, John P. Thomas faced less than a year before graduation; now he reflected quietly, remembering the day he too had entered the Citadel Academy as a member of the Fourth Class. While there was a lull in the activities, he struck up a conversation with a new cadet from Edisto Island, Micah Jenkins. During their brief talk, Thomas listened as Jenkins described how much he wanted to graduate first in his class.[1]

Micah Jenkins entered college at the Citadel Academy in Charleston early in January 1851 and began his military career. Having turned fifteen only a month before, he was barely able to meet the Citadel's minimum age requirement.

During the 1850's there were no athletic teams at the Citadel, and the only school-sanctioned extra-curricular activity for cadets was

---

[1]Thomas, *Career and Character*, 25. John P. Thomas graduated from the Citadel Academy in 1851 at the top of his class. He later served fourteen years on the faculty, three years as superintendent and eight years on the Board of Visitors. In 1897 he became South Carolina's State Historian and Commissioner for Confederate Records. In 1903 Thomas published his short work on the life and death of Micah Jenkins.

membership in one of the academy's two literary societies, the Polytechnic and the Calliopean. When new students arrived, they were selected for membership in one of these societies; most of the lowcountry cadets, including Micah Jenkins, became members of the Calliopean Society.[2] There were spirited debates between these two societies, and the members periodically delivered orations.[3] A bitter rivalry existed between the two organizations, and an occasional fight resulted from this acrimony.[4] Each society had its own meeting room, or hall, decorated with trophies and banners and containing a small library, and female guests were permitted to visit these halls only during debates or orations.[5]

The Citadel Academy, along with the Arsenal Academy in Columbia, had been created as part of the South Carolina Military Academy in 1842 by an act of the South Carolina General Assembly. The Act was introduced by Micah Jenkins' future father-in-law, David F. Jamison, the chairman of the House Military Committee, who became one of the original members of the Academy's Board of Visitors.[6]

Jenkins' life as a Citadel cadet in the 1850's was highly regimented. There were daily drills, periodic dress parades, weekly inspections, and delinquencies which were read out to the cadets each Friday afternoon. While study hours were strictly observed, the cadets occasionally sought relief from the discipline and routine. A favorite prank was to roll a cannon ball along the floors of the top level of the dormitory late at night, creating a thunderous noise.[7]

The cadets were permitted to visit the private female academies in Charleston, but the academy ladies were always required to be in groups when they were called upon by the young men. Citadel cadets were often invited to march in parades with the city's military organizations to celebrate patriotic occasions such as the anniversary of the Battle of Fort Moultrie.[8]

In November 1852, while Jenkins was a member of the Third Class, the Citadel's Board of Visitors expelled all thirty-four cadets in the Second

---

[2] John Adger Law, ed., *Citadel Cadets, The Journal of Cadet Tom Law* (Clinton, South Carolina: P.C. Press, 1941), 82.

[3] Ibid., 6, 41.

[4] Sylvia McKenzie, "80 Organizations, Societies Open to Cadet Membership," in "1954-1964, A Decade of Growth: The Citadel," special supplement to the Charleston (South Carolina) *News and Courier* and the Charleston *Evening Post*, May 29, 1964, 4H.

[5] Law, ed., *Citadel Cadets*, 96, 115.

[6] John Peyre Thomas, *The History of the South Carolina Military Academy* (Charleston, South Carolina: Walker, Evans and Cogswell Co., 1893; reprint, Columbia, South Carolina: Palmetto Bookworks, 1991), 169.

[7] Howard H. Lindsay, "Early Citadel Regime Had Lighter Side," in "1954-1964, A Decade of Growth: The Citadel," special supplement to the Charleston *News and Courier* and the Charleston *Evening Post*, May 29, 1964, 8G.

[8] Ibid.

Class, which resulted in no graduations in 1853. This was caused by a group protest of the Second Class over the suspension of one of their classmates which they believed to be unfair.[9] Their action was deemed a prohibited "combination" of cadets under the school's regulations.[10] While Jenkins and the members of his class were not involved, the extremely firm manner with which the protest was handled by the Board of Visitors no doubt taught him a memorable lesson in military discipline.

During his third year at the Citadel in 1853, Jenkins and several other cadets in his class were involved in a scrape which landed them in trouble with the school's officials. While the cause and nature of this incident are unknown, Jenkins was so concerned about its potential effect on his record that he wrote to his father asking permission to resign. The matter was resolved, however, and he remained a Citadel cadet.[11]

During their senior year, Jenkins and a classmate, Asbury Coward, began making plans to establish a military academy after their graduation from the Citadel.[12] Coward, the same age as Jenkins, was born in Charleston District, and their days together in college led to an enduring friendship.[13]

In January 1854, his final year at the Citadel, Jenkins was promoted to second lieutenant of Company B, his first real position of military leadership.[14] At that time, the Citadel's Cadet Corps was made up of two companies, each under the command of a cadet captain.[15] While Jenkins was never promoted to captain, he was nevertheless one of the highest-ranking officers in the Cadet Corps during his graduating year, and he soon became aware that leading other men came quite naturally to him.

In April and May of 1854, the Cadet Corps conducted a sort of public relations "march" through the upcountry of South Carolina. The cadets

[9]Law, ed., *Citadel Cadets*, 38.
[10]O. J. Bond, *The Story of the Citadel* (Richmond, Virginia: Garrett and Massie, Publishers, 1936), 38-39.
[11]Micah Jenkins to his father, Captain John Jenkins, March 22, 1853, Micah Jenkins Papers, South Caroliniana Library (hereafter, S.C.L.), University of South Carolina, Columbia, South Carolina.
[12]Micah Jenkins' brother, John, to Micah Jenkins, undated, apparently sent in 1853, Micah Jenkins Papers, S.C.L. This letter discusses Micah's request for funds to start the proposed school and expresses John's reservations concerning the project.
[13]Marion Salley, "Sixty-seven Years of Married Life," *Confederate Veteran*, 32 (July 1924): 259; Thomas, *History of the South Carolina Military Academy*, 263, 471.
[14]Micah Jenkins' Commission, January 7, 1854, signed by Citadel Superintendent F. W. Capers, Micah Jenkins Papers, S.C.L.
[15]Official Register of the Officers and Cadets, First (Graduating) Class of 1854, Citadel Archives, The Citadel, Charleston, South Carolina.

first went to Columbia by train. On his arrival there, Jenkins wrote his brother, John:

> [T]he entire military (I believe) of Columbia awaited our arrival and escorted us to the Arsenal. The papers too have taken very flattering notice of us.[16]

From Columbia the cadets, accompanied by a brass band, made a two-day march to Winnsboro. From there they proceeded through Chester to Yorkville, a small village close to the North Carolina state line, where they staged a parade and were rewarded with picnics and dances given by the local residents. It was on this upcountry march that Jenkins and Coward decided that Yorkville would be an ideal location for the military school they were planning. When the cadets left Yorkville, they went to Limestone Springs, and one cadet later wrote:

> At Limestone there was a girls' college which, even in that day of greater strictness than young folk now can picture, entertained the "brass button boys" and brought fluttering to many a heart.[17]

The "brass button boys" then proceeded to Spartanburg, Greenville, Laurens and Newberry, their final stop. The entire upcountry tour was a great success and enhanced the image of the Citadel throughout South Carolina.[18]

Shortly after the cadets returned to the Citadel to resume their studies, Jenkins was appointed an assistant professor of belles-lettres. While he again was in a position of leadership, this new responsibility caused him to feel pressured while preparing to graduate. He was, however, gaining valuable teaching experience which he would turn to his advantage less than a year later.[19]

Because of an epidemic of yellow fever in Charleston during the summer of 1854, most Citadel cadets were sent home. Those in the First Class, however, including Jenkins, were sent to the Arsenal Academy in Columbia to continue their studies.[20] Shortly before

---

[16]Micah Jenkins to John Jenkins, April 23, 1854, John Jenkins Papers, S.C.L.

[17]Theodore DuBose Bratton, *An Apostle of Reality, The Life and Thought of Reverend William Porcher DuBose* (New York: Longmans, Green and Co., 1936), 28. The school is now Limestone College, located in Gaffney, South Carolina.

[18]DeWitt Nicholson, "Buildings Tell History of the Citadel," in "1954-1964, A Decade of Growth: The Citadel," special supplement to the Charleston *News and Courier* and the Charleston *Evening Post*, May 29, 1964, 2G.

[19]Official Register of Officers and Cadets, First Class (Graduating) of 1854, Citadel Archives; Micah Jenkins to John Jenkins, June 22, 1854, John Jenkins Papers, S.C.L.

[20]Thomas, *History of the South Carolina Military Academy*, 81.

graduation they returned to Charleston and on Friday, November 24, the Citadel staged commencement exercises for its Class of 1854. The procession of cadets, escorts, dignitaries, and guests began on Calhoun Street at the Citadel Square and wound its way down Meeting Street to Hibernian Hall where selected cadets delivered addresses to a large audience. Micah's friend and future business partner, Asbury Coward, spoke on "Women's Rights."[21] Jenkins graduated at the top of his class and was given the honor of delivering the valedictory address.[22]

Captain Jenkins, Micah's father, had not lived to see his son receive the valedictory honors he had worked so hard to achieve; he died on Edisto Island shortly before Micah graduated.[23] Upon his death, the captain's "goods and chattel" were valued at almost $62,000, and his three plantations contained almost twenty-three hundred acres.[24] John, the captain's oldest son, had already assumed the role as head of the family and had the final say on all its financial matters. Micah began to consult John on many issues, and although there was an eleven year age difference, the two brothers were drawn closer by their father's death.

---

[21]Charleston *Daily Courier*, November 23, 1854.
[22]Ibid., November 25, 1854. A copy of this address has not been located.
[23]Charleston *Mercury*, December 2, 1854.
[24]Inventory and Appraisement of the Goods and Chattel of (Captain) John Jenkins of Edisto Island, Planter Deceased, 25 May 1855, S.C.D.A.H., Charleston District, Inventory Appraisement and Sales, vol. D (1854-1857), 282-283. Bennett's Point and Mussleborough Plantations consisted of approximately one-thousand acres each, and Old Hill Plantation consisted of about three hundred acres.

Chapter 3

On To Yorkville

Micah Jenkins arrived in Orangeburg, South Carolina, around noon on the Columbia train. He was met by a carriage and driver provided by his host, David F. Jamison, and was taken to Jamison's home in the village. There he was greeted by a well-dressed servant who took Jenkins' bag and ushered him into his host's large, impressive library. At the time of Jenkins' visit, shortly before the end of 1854, Jamison had just begun writing his book, *The Life and Times of Bertrand du Guesclin*, a French military leader in the fourteenth century.

Jamison had practiced law in the early 1830's, but had left the profession after only two years to devote his time to politics and managing his plantation, Turkey Hill. He had served in the South Carolina General Assembly from 1838 to 1848, and in 1842 had been instrumental in the creation of the South Carolina Military Academy. Jamison was still a member of the Board of Visitors of the Academy, which was the reason for Jenkins' visit. Jenkins and Asbury Coward were in the process of beginning their military school in Yorkville, and Jenkins had come to Orangeburg to get Jamison's advice on how to set up the new school's curriculum so that its graduates might be accepted as cadets at either the Arsenal or the Citadel. Jamison and Jenkins discussed his plans for the military school most of the afternoon, and he was then shown to his room.

Jamison hosted a dance at his home that evening, and Jenkins was invited to attend. Jamison's oldest daughter, Caroline, was also there, along with several of her friends who attended the female academy in Orangeburg. According to one account, when Jenkins entered the long drawing room after the first waltz with "the gold braid and brass buttons of his uniform gleaming in the candlelight," everyone noticed the handsome young man.[1]

Seventeen-year-old Caroline Harper Jamison was the constant companion of her father, and much of her childhood had been spent learning in his library. In fact, Jamison himself had educated her from the time she was ten.[2] He still thought of her as his little girl, but she had quietly grown into a beautiful woman, and the moment Micah Jenkins saw her he was immediately and completely smitten.

Following the highly successful "march through the upstate" by the Citadel cadets in the spring of 1854, Jenkins and Coward had decided to locate their military school on the outskirts of Yorkville, South Carolina. During their stay in the village, the cadets had been warmly received by the local citizens. They had camped outside the town on the road to Kings Mountain, and Jenkins and Coward had been so impressed with a site near this encampment that they later selected it as the location for their new school.[3]

In the mid-1850's, Yorkville was known as "the Charleston of the upcountry." Incorporated in 1850 and located between Columbia and Charlotte, North Carolina, the village already had a population of about eight hundred people. The new Rose Hotel had been built in 1852, and the Yorkville Female Academy began accepting students two years later. The Kings Mountain Railroad, linking Yorkville with the main railway line at Chester, South Carolina, had only been in operation for about three years.[4] Yorkville may have been only a small village, but Coward and Jenkins felt that it had great promise.

During the fall of 1854, Jenkins and Coward finalized their plans for the opening of the "Kings Mountain Military School" and arranged for the printing of a prospectus.[5] They also agreed that Coward would be in

---

[1]Nell S. Graydon, *Tales of Edisto* (Columbia, South Carolina: R. L. Bryan Co., 1955), 48. Minor details have been added to Graydon's account of this incident, based on the author's best estimate of how it probably occurred.

[2]Thomas, *Career and Character*, 24.

[3]A. S. Salley, "A Career Built in Friendship," *The State Magazine*, a supplement to the Columbia *State*, August 5, 1951, 14-15.

[4]Joseph E. Hart, Jr., *The Church of the Good Shepherd, York, South Carolina: A Centennial History, 1855-1955* (York, South Carolina: Privately printed, 1955), 1-2.

[5]Micah Jenkins to John Jenkins, October 26, 1854, John Jenkins Papers, S.C.L.

charge of the school's business matters, while Jenkins was to have responsibility for its "organization, regulation and discipline."[6]

A few days before the beginning of the first session of the school in early January 1855, Jenkins' first three students arrived in Yorkville by train from Charleston.[7] Classes began with only twelve students in an old rented mansion in the village; those cadets who were not from Yorkville boarded with local families.[8] After the mansion burned later in the year, classes were held on the upper floors of a building on the town square, and the students ate their meals at the nearby Rose Hotel.[9] Tuition for the Kings Mountain Military School was set at twenty-five dollars per session, plus a boarding fee of ten dollars per month, and all cadets were required to furnish their own uniforms.[10]

The pace of events in Jenkins' life had clearly begun to accelerate. In April 1855, only months after meeting her in Orangeburg, Jenkins became engaged to Caroline Jamison, although they set no date for a wedding.[11] By the end of that month, Coward and Jenkins had purchased a large lot on the outskirts of the village on the road from Yorkville to Kings Mountain, where they planned to build their new school.[12] About fifteen miles from the site of the new lot, the famous Battle of Kings Mountain, for which the school was named, had been fought during the Revolutionary War on October 7, 1780. During the school's second term, local citizens of York District staged a celebration, lasting several days, of the seventy-fifth anniversary of the battle. William Gilmore Simms, the noted South Carolina novelist, lecturer, and historian, played a major role in planning the festivities, and he delivered a series of lectures in the village as part of the celebration. The cadets of the Kings Mountain Military School also took part, marching from Yorkville to the battlefield where they camped with military units from around the state. Simms wrote to the Charleston *Mercury*, prior to the celebration:

> I rode up [to Kings Mountain] today in company with . . . the very clever and promising young Principals of the Military Academy of Yorkville, Messers. Coward and Jenkins. . . . [The cadets of the Military Academy], this fine body of young men, about fifty in number, (several

[6]Contract between Coward and Jenkins, signed January 5, 1855, Micah Jenkins Papers, S.C.L.

[7]Micah Jenkins to John Jenkins, December 28, 1854, John Jenkins Papers, S.C.L.

[8]E. T. Crowson, "Jenkins, Coward and the Yorkville Boys," *Sandlapper Magazine* 7 (December 1974): 34.

[9]John Gettys Smith, "K.M.M.S., A York Institution," Columbia (South Carolina) *State*, May 3, 1959, 2C.

[10]Yorkville (South Carolina) *Enquirer*, August 9, 1855.

[11]Elizabeth Jenkins LaRoche to Micah Jenkins, April 23, 1855, Micah Jenkins Papers, S.C.L.

[12]Micah Jenkins to Caroline Jamison, April 20, 1855, Micah Jenkins Papers, S.C.L.

of them are small boys of twelve or fourteen) *will march [here] on foot.*[13]

During this first year in Yorkville, Jenkins did not limit his time and energies solely to his new school. Shortly after his arrival, he and a small group of other men met to organize an Episcopal church in the village. This meeting led to the founding of The Church of the Good Shepherd; Jenkins became its first secretary-treasurer, and Asbury Coward served on the vestry and as junior warden.[14] The founders constructed a church building in the village, and services were held there starting in October 1855. That November, Jenkins was confirmed in the new church by the Bishop of the Diocese of South Carolina.[15]

By the close of its first year of operations, the Kings Mountain Military School had added a new faculty member, Cato A. Seabrook of Edisto Island, and had introduced a "Preparatory Collegiate Course."[16] The decision to add the new course was undoubtedly made on the advice of D. F. Jamison; it was designed to qualify the school's graduating cadets for admittance to the Arsenal and the Citadel.

In April 1856, Jenkins and Coward announced that they had decided to begin the construction of a school barracks on the lot they had purchased outside the village.[17] Later that month, they held a formal dedication at the site and laid the cornerstone. The ceremony was begun by a procession of the cadets, local citizens, and visiting dignitaries, escorted by a brass band, from the village to the site of the new building. Some twelve hundred people attended the dedication.[18] By then the Kings Mountain Military School had an enrollment of eighty cadets, and it was well on its way to becoming a respected upcountry institution.[19]

Meanwhile, Micah Jenkins' brother, Edward, had finished his medical studies in Paris and had returned from Europe. After practicing medicine for a short while on Edisto Island, he moved to Yorkville with his wife, Isabella, in early 1856. By that March, he had become part owner of a retail drug store in the village and wrote that he had "already cut out the tonsils for two persons."[20]

---

[13]William Gilmore Simms to the Charleston *Mercury*, September 15, 1855, in Mary Simms Oliphant, Alfred Taylor O'dell and T. C. Duncan Eaves, eds., *The Letters of William Gilmore Simms* (Columbia, South Carolina: University of South Carolina Press, 1954), 3:396 (emphasis in original).

[14]Hart, *The Church of the Good Shepherd*, 3-4.

[15]Episcopal Church confirmation certificate of Micah Jenkins, November 18, 1855, Micah Jenkins Papers, S.C.L.

[16]Yorkville *Enquirer*, December 20, 1855.

[17]Ibid., April 10, 1856.

[18]Ibid., April 24, 1856.

[19]Ibid.

[20]Edward Jenkins to John Jenkins, March 11, 1856, John Jenkins Papers, S.C.L.

On July 3, 1856, Micah Jenkins and Caroline Jamison married in Orangeburg in a Presbyterian ceremony conducted by Reverend Benjamin M. Palmer. She was eighteen and he twenty, and they looked forward to a happy and prosperous future. The only cloud on their otherwise clear horizon was the possibility of a civil war. Jenkins first mentioned the danger of war in a letter he wrote only five weeks before his wedding. In it he said, "[o]nly let there be no war, and this year pass quietly, and God willing we will be sailing in smooth water soon."[21] No doubt Jenkins was alluding to the so-called "Brooks-Sumner incident" in Washington, and the effect it was having throughout South Carolina.

Only a week before Jenkins penned his letter, South Carolina Congressman Preston S. Brooks had severely beaten Senator Charles Sumner of Massachusetts with a cane on the floor of the United States Senate.[22] Brooks had acted in response to Sumner's vitriolic speech in which he insulted Brooks' aged cousin, Senator Andrew Pickens Butler. Sumner claimed permanent injuries from the beating, but many Southerners suspected that he was only attempting to further his political cause.[23] Northern newspapers praised Sumner as a martyr for abolitionism, an innocent victim beaten almost senseless and nearly killed for the sake of his noble ideals. Rallies denouncing Brooks were held in Boston and other Northern cities, while counter-rallies were held throughout South Carolina in his support.[24] It was at the height of the furor in South Carolina over the Brooks-Sumner incident that Micah and Caroline were married.

Upon his return to Yorkville, Jenkins was officially appointed "Major of the Kings Mountain Cadet Battalion" by the governor of South Carolina.[25] For the next four-and-a-half years, he would be known to all as "Major" Jenkins.

The Kings Mountain Military School's new building outside Yorkville was completed in the fall of 1856, and the school's staff and ninety cadets had moved into it by the beginning of October.[26] It was called "The Garrison," and the main building, three stories high, had twenty-six rooms (with fireplaces). It was described in one newspaper as "a perfect model of college architecture."[27]

---

[21]Micah Jenkins to John Jenkins, May 25, 1856, John Jenkins Papers, S.C.L.

[22]As for the reason Brooks elected to cane Sumner, rather than challenging him to a duel, see Kenneth S. Greenberg, *Masters and Statesmen: The Political Culture of American Slavery* (Baltimore: The Johns Hopkins University Press, 1985), 145-146.

[23]Roy McBee Smith, *Vardy McBee, 1775-1864: Man of Reason in an Age of Extremes* (Columbia, South Carolina: R. L. Bryan Co., 1992), 243-244.

[24]Yorkville *Enquirer*, May 19, 1856.

[25]Certificate of Appointment, August 22, 1856, Micah Jenkins Papers, S.C.L.

[26]Micah Jenkins to John Jenkins, October 4, 1856, John Jenkins Papers, S.C.L.

[27]Smith, "K.M.M.S., A York Institution," 2C.

By the end of 1856, its second year of operation, the school had hired another new faculty member, Evander M. Law, from Darlington, South Carolina, who had just graduated from the Citadel.[28] Jenkins and Law had a cordial relationship in the beginning when Law was employed on the faculty. Over the next few years, however, Law apparently began to resent Jenkins' authority, and relations between the two men eventually became quite bitter.

The Kings Mountain Military School entered its third year in 1857 and was rapidly becoming a tremendous success, its enrollment now rivaling that of South Carolina's colleges. It had grown from twelve students in 1855 to almost one hundred cadets in only two years, and they had an impressive brick headquarters in the Garrison.[29]

Following the York District tradition, the anniversary of the Battle of Kings Mountain was again elaborately celebrated on October 7, 1857, and this time the main ceremonies took place on the school's grounds. Featured were the Columbia Brass Band and the officers of the Thirty-fourth and Forty-sixth militia regiments, which gave the affair a thoroughly military tone.[30] Not only was this a wonderful day for the Kings Mountain Military School, it was especially memorable for Micah and Caroline Jenkins; it was her twentieth birthday.

On Christmas Day in 1857, Asbury Coward married Elise Blum of Charleston and brought her to Yorkville where they lived in one of the wings of the Garrison. Micah and Caroline lived in the other wing with their new baby boy, Micah John, who had been born one year after they were married.

On the last Saturday in March 1858, there was a fire in the kitchen attached to the Garrison. The kitchen, along with most of the school's provisions, burned to the ground, but the cadets, with the help of local citizens, fought the blaze and kept it from spreading. Jenkins and Coward later publicly expressed their gratitude to "the Yorkville Fire Engine Company, and to the citizens of Yorkville, for [their] prompt and zealous assistance."[31]

On July 4 of that year, the success and value of the Kings Mountain Military School was recognized during the village's Independence Day celebration. One local citizen offered a flattering toast to the academy, calling it "the glory and pride of our District." Faculty member E. M. Law responded with a speech, but one who heard it wrote that "of [Law's] address propriety demands that the writer should forbear to speak."[32] Jenkins was undoubtedly in attendance, and perhaps his hearing this

[28]Yorkville *Enquirer*, December 11, 1856.
[29]Micah Jenkins to John Jenkins, January 10, 1857, John Jenkins Papers, S.C.L.
[30]Yorkville *Enquirer*, September 24, October 1, and October 8, 1857.
[31]Ibid., April 1, 1858.
[32]Ibid., July 8, 1858. The exact wording of Law's speech has not been located.

apparently inappropriate speech by Law caused the relationship between the two men to begin to deteriorate. Jenkins wrote to his brother, John, from Yorkville on that date, but his letter contains no mention of Law's remarks.[33]

In September 1859, "annual review" was held for the state militia units in the Yorkville area. The members of the local militia formed part of the South Battalion of the state's Thirty-fourth Militia Regiment. The Cadet Corps of the Kings Mountain Military School took an active part in the review ceremony, and an article in the Yorkville *Enquirer* stated:

> Much of the effect of the day's performance, however, was contributed by Major Jenkins' beautifully trained Corps of Cadets. Nothing can exceed the order, the regularity of movement, the exact discipline, in a word, the thorough military bearing of the King's Mountain [Cadet] Corps. We imagine their training is as perfect as the science can make it, and we would look for nothing superior in the ranks of a veteran company. These young soldiers are to us, for their age and opportunity, a veritable wonder.[34]

The results of the cadets' constant drilling and training, however, served to highlight a serious problem with the state's antiquated militia system; it only rarely required its citizen-soldiers to assemble for training. With the storm clouds of civil war slowly gathering, the press had begun to demand reforms of that system.[35]

By the end of 1859, after serving on the faculty of the Kings Mountain Military School for three years, E. M. Law had resigned his position and moved to Alabama.[36] Early the next year, the school found a replacement for Law in John W. Jamison, Jenkins' brother-in-law, who was hired to teach French. He was well-qualified for the position since he had previously studied the language in Paris.[37] By this time, the school's reputation had grown to the point that its graduates could enter the Citadel as members of the Second Class.[38]

Meanwhile, Jenkins expanded his real estate holdings in York District. In late 1859, he bought three hundred acres outside Yorkville,

---

[33]Micah Jenkins to John Jenkins, July 4, 1858, John Jenkins Papers, S.C.L. Perhaps this letter was composed before Jenkins had heard Law's remarks, which would explain why Jenkins failed to mention the incident to his brother.

[34]Yorkville *Enquirer*, September 8, 1859.

[35]Ibid.

[36]Ibid., June 4, 1868. The reason for Law's resignation is not known.

[37]Ibid., May 3 and May 17, 1860.

[38]Ibid., May 31, 1860.

"The Garrison," the main building at the Kings Mountain Military School in Yorkville, South Carolina, completed in October 1856. Micah Jenkins and Asbury Coward lived with their families in the apartments on opposite wings of the building. (The exact date of this photograph is not known, but it was probably taken about 1858-1859.)

at a price of nearly two thousand dollars.[39] He felt a need for a place away from the school so that he could have, in his words,

> somewhere to take my family now and then, where they may breathe the fresh air, far from the restraint of 100 pairs of eyes.[40]

Jenkins also became involved in local politics. In Yorkville's municipal election during February 1860, he was elected the village's intendant, a position he held for only a year until his responsibilities as an officer in the state's volunteer army forced him to relinquish it.[41]

During the traditional celebration of the Battle of Kings Mountain in October 1860, Jenkins' military school cadets performed a "skirmishing drill" before the spectators. It was described in the Yorkville *Enquirer* as,

> something new in this part of the country; and [it] would pay any man who has a taste for such things . . . for a ride of a dozen miles to see it.[42]

Most South Carolinians were in fact beginning to develop a definite "taste for such things." Events on both the state and national level were causing them to renew their interest in all things military, and by the end of 1860, these events had carried the nation to the very brink of war. When war finally did break out, the Kings Mountain Military School was forced to close after its first session in 1861; its faculty and its older cadets had skills that were needed elsewhere.[43]

---

[39]Micah Jenkins to John Jenkins, January 7, 1860, John Jenkins Papers, S.C.L.
[40]Ibid., August 29, 1859.
[41]Yorkville *Enquirer*, February 2, 9, and 16, 1860.
[42]Ibid., October 11, 1860.
[43]Thomas, *History of the South Carolina Military Academy*, 525; Crowson, "Jenkins, Coward and the Yorkville Boys," 36. See also, Yorkville *Enquirer*, June 4, 1868.

Chapter 4

The Jasper Light Infantry

S ome five years before Micah Jenkins' birth in 1835, his uncle, Joseph E. Jenkins, had made a speech to the Agricultural Society of Edisto Island. In it he stated that the actions of certain leading men in the North "had struck the first wedge which would split this country into two parts."[1] This "wedge" involved tariffs imposed by the Federal government.

The secession movement did not climax in South Carolina until December 1860, but its seeds had been planted more than thirty years earlier in opposition to the Tariff Act of 1828. Southerners complained that the Act was unfair to them because it raised the prices on imported manufactured goods, as a protection for the North, at a time when the prices of the South's agricultural goods (especially cotton) were declining.[2]

Not surprisingly, this so-called "Tariff of Abominations" was extremely unpopular in the South. Many eminent South Carolinians, including John C. Calhoun, took the position that an individual state could declare such an act of the Federal government null and void within the

---

[1]Joseph E. Jenkins to Micah Jenkins, January 22, 1856, Micah Jenkins Papers, S.C.L.
[2]John B. Edmunds, Jr., *Francis W. Pickens and the Politics of Destruction* (Chapel Hill, North Carolina: University of North Carolina Press, 1986), 11.

borders of that state. Thus was born South Carolina's "nullification movement," and with it the very real possibility of the state's secession.[3] During the early stage of this movement, Dr. Thomas Cooper, President of South Carolina College, took the public position that it was "time to calculate the value of the Union."[4] For many, the notion of secession was merely a logical extension of the doctrine of nullification.

By 1832, any substantial reduction of the hated tariff appeared unlikely, and in November a special convention was called by the South Carolina General Assembly. Its delegates deemed the tariff "unconstitutional, unequal and oppressive," and declared that, after a certain date, it would no longer be effective in South Carolina.[5] As part of this "Nullification Ordinance," Federal officials were to be forbidden to collect customs duties within the state. Governor Robert Y. Hayne even recommended that the General Assembly create a "state guard" of twelve thousand men to defend the state from Federal troops, in the event they were sent in to enforce the tariff. Civil war appeared a distinct possibility.[6]

This crisis was averted in February 1833, when Congress passed a compromise tariff act which gradually lowered duties. South Carolina responded by repealing its Nullification Ordinance, but the idea of secession from the Union had now been planted in the intellectual soil of the state where it began to grow deep roots. In addition, the military preparations which South Carolina had made during 1832, in anticipation of armed Federal intervention, became a kind of training exercise for the mobilization that occurred when that threat became a reality three decades later.[7]

Another serious problem arose in 1846 when the United States House of Representatives appropriated two million dollars to purchase territory from Mexico. When an amendment to the bill was proposed to include the "Wilmot Proviso," prohibiting slavery in the new territory, talk of disunion and secession revived almost immediately in South Carolina and other Southern states. Indeed, the South Carolina General Assembly unanimously adopted a resolution in 1848 that the state was

---

[3]Ibid.

[4]Charles Edward Cauthen, *South Carolina Goes to War, 1860-1865* (Chapel Hill, North Carolina: University of North Carolina Press, 1950), 2.

[5]Edmunds, *Politics of Destruction*, 15.

[6]Ibid., 17. Indeed, in 1832 it appeared that President Andrew Jackson fully intended to use force against South Carolina, and many people felt that this would result in civil war. Richard E. Ellis, *The Union at Risk: Jacksonian Democracy, State's Rights, and the Nullification Crisis* (New York: Oxford University Press, 1987), 91. In addition, Jackson officially declared that secession by South Carolinians would be considered treason. Ibid., 179.

[7]Edmunds, *Politics of Destruction*, 18. While Congress compromised on the tariff, it also passed the "Force Act" allowing the Federal government to use force to collect the duties in the states. South Carolina promptly "nullified" the Force Act. For the political ramifications in South Carolina of the manner in which the nullification crisis was resolved, see Ellis, *The Union at Risk*, 180-181.

ready to cooperate with its neighboring states in opposing passage of the Wilmot Proviso "at any and every hazard."[8]   Finally, Henry Clay introduced in the United States Senate the "Compromise of 1850," a proposal that did not include the Wilmot Proviso, which was passed by Congress and signed by the president.   The immediate threat of secession by a confederacy of the Southern states was averted. The Compromise of 1850, however, did not reduce the intense desire of many South Carolinians to secede from the Union. In fact, the heated debate in the state concerning the compromise and over how best to defend the state's rights against the Federal government almost took South Carolina out of the Union in 1851.[9]   When it became clear, however, that she would not be joined in such a move by the other Southern states, South Carolina decided not to attempt the move alone.[10] This ended the first real secession crisis in South Carolina since the nullification movement almost twenty years earlier.

While the Compromise of 1850 helped ease the growing animosity between the Northern and Southern states, the effect was only temporary. In 1852, emotions were again aroused when Harriet Beecher Stowe's *Uncle Tom's Cabin* was published in Boston. Two years later Congress passed the Kansas-Nebraska Act of 1854 which provided that the question of whether either territory would permit slavery would be decided by the settlers. As a result, many in the North were encouraged to move to the Kansas Territory and settle there to help assure that it would become a free state. In response, South Carolina and other Southern states sent their own volunteer immigrants to Kansas, which soon became the geographical focus of the antagonism developing between North and South. Money was raised in several districts of South Carolina, including York District, and sent to the Southern immigrants in Kansas for their support.[11]   By the end of 1855, the opposing factions were clashing in Kansas; the bitter sectionalism had finally turned bloody.

In a January 1856 letter to his nephew, Micah, Joseph E. Jenkins recalled his anti-tariff "struck the first wedge" speech delivered some twenty-five years earlier and wrote that he feared coming events would make him "somewhat of a prophet."[12]   He penned this letter only four months before the next major incident of antagonism between the North and South: the caning of Senator Charles Sumner on the Senate floor in Washington, by South Carolina Congressman Preston Brooks. In

[8]Cauthen, *South Carolina Goes to War*, 3.
[9]Lacy K. Ford, Jr., *Origins of Southern Radicalism: The South Carolina Upcountry, 1800-1860* (New York: Oxford University Press, 1988), 184.
[10]Ibid., 212; Steven A. Channing, *Crisis of Fear: Secession in South Carolina* (New York: Simon and Schuster, Inc., 1970), 145.
[11]Ford, *Origins of Southern Radicalism*, 343-345.
[12]Joseph E. Jenkins to Micah Jenkins, January 22, 1856, Micah Jenkins Papers, S.C.L.

response to meetings held in the North to condemn Brooks, the Yorkville *Enquirer* praised him and stated:

> [W]e earnestly trust that, along with [similar gatherings
> across the state], a meeting will be called in Yorkville to
> give expression to like sentiments [in support of Brooks]
> on the part of the people of our District. The battle
> waxes hot and strong, and if we expect our champions to
> wage it bravely and effectually, we must be prompt to
> lend them a hearty support.[13]

The flames of animosity were being fanned to new heights and there was talk of secession and war, but tempers gradually cooled as the fury of the event died down. There remained a lingering feeling, however, in both North and South that some fresh incident might occur at any time which could cause the still-glowing embers of sectionalism to burst into a full-blown conflagration.

The Brooks-Sumner incident in Washington was followed only three years later by an event in Virginia which proved far more serious. In October 1859, John Brown led eighteen men on a raid against the United States Arsenal at Harper's Ferry, Virginia. Brown, a radical abolitionist, had hoped by his actions to incite a slave rebellion throughout the South,[14] and it was later revealed that Brown's attack had been financed by certain wealthy Northerners.[15] The Brown raid, and especially the fact that many in the North apparently endorsed it, sent shockwaves throughout the South. In South Carolina, the position of moderates was immediately undermined,[16] and many were driven toward a more radical position on secession.[17]

Amid this ever-increasing tension between the two rival sections of the nation, delegates to the Democratic National Convention gathered in Charleston, South Carolina, on April 23, 1860, to nominate the party's candidates for president and vice-president of the United States. A leading contender for the presidential nomination was Stephen A. Douglas who had debated Abraham Lincoln during 1858 on several issues, including slavery. Jefferson Davis, a United States senator from Mississippi, was among the delegates in Charleston, as was William L. Yancey, a "fire eating" secessionist from Alabama. Yancey and other

---

[13]Yorkville *Enquirer*, May 19, 1856.
[14]Shelby Foote, *The Civil War, A Narrative*, vol. 1, *Fort Sumter to Perryville* (New York: Random House, 1958), 31.
[15]Ford, *Origins of Southern Radicalism*, 367.
[16]For the impact of Brown's raid at Harper's Ferry on South Carolina's politics, see Channing, *Crisis of Fear*, 92-93.
[17]Cauthen, *South Carolina Goes to War*, 11, 13.

secessionist delegates demanded the inclusion of a "slave code" in the platform of the party, which would have required it to formally accept the institution of slavery. Robert Barnwell Rhett, the publisher of the Charleston *Mercury,* urged the party's Southern delegates to walk out of the convention as a group if the slave code was not made a part of the platform.[18] When the convention majority refused to adopt the slave code, some fifty Southern delegates did walk out, and the convention adjourned without nominating a candidate.[19] The walkout effectively split the Democratic Party in two, as the country was split, along sectional lines.

Shortly after the breakup of the Charleston convention, the Southern Democrats arranged for a separate convention in Richmond to nominate their own candidates. In South Carolina, local meetings were held to elect persons to attend a state convention in Columbia for the purpose of selecting the state's delegates to the Richmond convention. One of those elected to attend the Columbia convention was Micah Jenkins, representing York District.[20]

The delegates selected in Columbia to attend the Richmond convention included Jenkins' father-in-law, David F. Jamison, as well as the outspoken secessionist, Robert Barnwell Rhett of Charleston. Jamison, Rhett and the other members of this delegation were clearly in favor of secession and desired that South Carolina would lead such a movement.[21] Prior to his departure for Richmond, Jamison expressed little hope that he could achieve anything there, except to protect South Carolina "from the humiliating position of knocking for admission at the door of the [Northern Democrats'] Baltimore convention."[22]

Stephen Douglas was nominated for president by the Northern Democrats at their convention, while the Southern Democrats in Richmond chose John C. Breckinridge. With the party split along sectional lines, it was unlikely that either candidate could receive enough votes to defeat the Republican nominee, Abraham Lincoln.

Micah Jenkins had not awaited the tumultuous political developments of 1860 before he acted. In 1859, it had already become apparent to him that South Carolina's militia system was not adequately preparing its citizen-soldiers for an armed conflict. Many of the state's militia units were more like social clubs than trained military organizations, drilling

---

[18]Bruce Catton, *The Centennial History of the Civil War,* vol. 1, *The Coming Fury* (Garden City, New York: Doubleday & Co., 1961), 26-27.

[19]Ibid., 38-39.

[20]Yorkville *Enquirer,* May 24, 1860.

[21]Channing, *Crisis of Fear,* 223.

[22]David F. Jamison to John Jenkins, June 8, 1860, John Jenkins Papers, S.C.L. (duplicate of original). Jamison was referring to the convention in Baltimore, scheduled by the Northern democrats, after the Charleston convention broke up in disarray.

only on rare occasions.[23] Jenkins decided to form a company of local "volunteers" who could drill regularly and receive intensive military training.

During September 1859, about a month before John Brown's raid at Harper's Ferry, Jenkins held a meeting at the district courthouse in Yorkville to organize "a new Volunteer Uniform Company . . . to be styled the 'Jasper Rifle Guards.'"[24] Jenkins was elected captain; Cato A. Seabrook, still a professor of the Kings Mountain Military School, became first lieutenant; J. Newton Withers was named second lieutenant; and W. B. Metts was chosen third lieutenant.[25]

The Jasper Rifle Guards held their initial drill at the Yorkville parade ground on the first Saturday in October 1859,[26] and drilled on several other Saturdays before the end of the year.[27] The company's name was changed in October, and the Yorkville *Enquirer* later reported:

> [P]erhaps the most notable feature in Yorkville is the organization of the "Jasper Light Infantry." It is emphatically a *volunteer* corps, being made up in most part of men not liable to ordinary military, and of officers in the Militia. . . . Captain Jenkins . . . is in command. The uniform is very neat, though not expensive.[28]

Jenkins' volunteer company was named in honor of Sergeant William Jasper, who became famous during the defense of Charleston in 1776 at the Battle of Fort Moultrie. When British warships shot down the fort's colors, Jasper risked his life to retrieve and restore them to their proper position over the fort walls. His courage was legendary in South Carolina.[29]

In January 1860, the Jasper Light Infantry was formally authorized and incorporated by an act of the South Carolina General Assembly. The act called for the company to be attached to the South Battalion of the Thirty-fourth Regiment of the South Carolina Militia.[30] By April 1860, the ranks of Jenkins' volunteers had swelled to at least 197 men.[31]

The men in the Jasper Light Infantry chose to celebrate the formation of their company every June 28, the same date as the anniversary of the Battle of Fort Moultrie. On the company's first

---

[23]Cauthen, *South Carolina Goes to War*, 110.
[24]Yorkville *Enquirer*, September 15, 1859.
[25]Ibid.
[26]Ibid., September 29, 1859.
[27]Ibid., November 10, 1859.
[28]Ibid., December 8, 1859 (emphasis in original).
[29]Ibid., July 5, 1860.
[30]Ibid., January 5, 1860.
[31]Ibid., April 5, 1860.

anniversary in 1860, the citizens of Yorkville turned out to celebrate. After several speeches, the Jasper Light Infantry and the Cadet Corps from the Kings Mountain Military School were drilled jointly for the assembled guests by Micah Jenkins, and they practiced firing with blank cartridges.[32] By November 1860, Jenkins' company had begun taking target practice with live ammunition.[33]

The Jasper Light Infantry again assembled for parade and target practice a few days before the end of the turbulent year 1860. The Yorkville *Enquirer* noted:

> Before the parade was dismissed, a vote was taken relative to the tender of their services to the Governor of the State in the present emergency, which was almost unanimously resolved on. These, though a beautifully uniformed corps, are not mere holiday soldiers.[34]

Only eight days before this vote was taken by Jenkins' company in Yorkville, delegates to the Secession Convention had met in Charleston and decided to take South Carolina out of the Union. That the men in the Jasper Light Infantry were not destined to be "mere holiday soldiers" was being made abundantly clear by events quickly unfolding in South Carolina.

HERO OF THE BATTLE OF FORT MOULTRIE FOUGHT IN 1776 AT CHARLESTON, SOUTH CAROLINA, SERGEANT WILLIAM JASPER IS DEPICTED HERE RAISING THE SOUTH CAROLINA FLAG OVER THE FORT'S WALLS WHILE UNDER FIRE FROM BRITISH WARSHIPS. IN 1859 MICAH JENKINS NAMED HIS VOLUNTEER COMPANY, THE "JASPER LIGHT INFANTRY," IN HONOR OF SERGEANT JASPER.

---

[32]Ibid., July 5, 1860.
[33]Ibid., November 22, 1860.
[34]Ibid., January 3, 1861.

Chapter 5

South Carolina Secedes

The First Baptist Church of Columbia was filled to overflowing, and delegates from all over South Carolina watched as a distinguished fifty-year-old gentleman was escorted to the podium. As he walked down the long aisle, with all eyes fixed upon him, David F. Jamison undoubtedly thought of many things: of his wife and their new plantation home, "Burwood"; of his oldest daughter, Caroline, now in Yorkville with her young husband and their three baby boys; and of his three oldest sons, David, William, and John, each of whom would no doubt volunteer for military service should a civil war erupt. All of Jamison's family would be placed at risk by the action that South Carolina was about to take, and he realized it.

Jamison's thoughts also drifted back to the 1850 Nashville Convention, when he and other delegates from the Southern states had met in a failed attempt to forge an alliance to protect the rights of their states from the powers of the Federal government. When no concrete solution had emerged from Nashville, he returned to South Carolina, pessimistic that any bold, concerted action would ever be taken by the Southern states. Indeed, Jamison later derisively described that convention as a "spectacle . . . of bravado and submission."[1] Still fresh in his mind was the "rump" Democratic National Convention which he had attended only six months earlier in Richmond to select Southern candidates for president and vice president; candidates who could never be elected because the party was as divided as the country.

When he was almost to the front of the church, Jamison thought of his beloved South Carolina and felt a vague sense of misgiving. He wondered whether the Federal government could be successfully defied by such a small state in the event the other Southern states failed to follow her lead. But he knew as he reached the podium that this was a time for courage; now the risk had to be taken. He waited for the hush of silence from the delegates and then began his speech. At the conclusion of his address, he said:

> We have entered on a great work, and God, who holds
> in His hands the destinies of nations, only knows what
> may be the result.[2]

Micah Jenkins' father-in-law thus accepted the presidency of South Carolina's Secession Convention and sat down while the other delegates cheered. Later that evening, with Jamison presiding, the Convention adopted the resolution "that the State of South Carolina should forthwith secede from the Federal Union. . . ."[3]

Much had happened in South Carolina in the last six months leading to the Secession Convention. After the breakup of the Democratic National Convention in Charleston in April 1860, the secession movement had steadily gained steam. A group called the "1860 Association" published a series of pamphlets in the state; the Association's "Tract No. 1," a kind of handbook on secession, enjoyed the widest circulation.[4] South Carolina leaders began to face the reality that Lincoln, whose election they firmly believed would signal the end of Southern rights, could not be defeated by a divided Democratic Party.

The issue of South Carolina's secession began to dominate the state's politics as the November election approached. Finally, Governor William H. Gist, a respected secessionist from Union District, called for

---

[1]D. F. Jamison to John Jenkins, June 8, 1860, John Jenkins Papers, S.C.L. (duplicate of original).

[2]May and Faunt, *South Carolina Secedes*, 9. Minor details have been added to accounts of Jamison's acceptance of the presidency of the Secession Convention, based on the author's best estimate of how it probably occurred.

[3]Ibid.

[4]Cauthen, *South Carolina Goes to War*, 34; Channing, *Crisis of Fear*, 262 n.18.

DAVID FLAVEL JAMISON, PRESIDENT OF SOUTH CAROLINA'S SECESSION CONVENTION AND FATHER-IN-LAW OF MICAH JENKINS. JAMISON ALSO SERVED BRIEFLY AS SOUTH CAROLINA'S SECRETARY OF WAR.

a special statewide convention for the purpose of considering whether South Carolina should secede from the Union, to be held after what he was certain would be Lincoln's election. Gist also wrote the governors of the other Southern states, urging them to do the same because he felt joint action was essential.[5] Regardless of what her sister states elected to do, however, South Carolina was moving inevitably toward disunion, and the tension increased daily. Micah Jenkins, still in Yorkville at his military academy, alluded to this tension when, two days before the presidential election, he wrote to his oldest brother, saying, "I am most anxious to see you all [on Edisto Island], but political outlooks make it prudent that I stay here."[6]

When Lincoln indeed won the election on November 6, it was felt by many in the South that the secession of the Southern states was assured. For this reason, Charlestonians celebrated the election result as though it were a holiday, and the Charleston *Mercury* boldly proclaimed: "The tea has been thrown overboard, the revolution of 1860 has been initiated."[7] Both of South Carolina's United States Senators, James Chesnut and James Drummond, abruptly resigned from the Senate. As Governor Gist had requested, the South Carolina General Assembly immediately called a "Convention of the People of the State of South Carolina" to meet in Columbia on December 17.[8] A state-wide election was set for December 6 for the selection of delegates to what became known as the "Secession Convention." Among those delegates elected on December 6, three were closely related to Micah Jenkins: his father-in-law, David F. Jamison; his older brother, John Jenkins; and his uncle, Joseph E. Jenkins.

Even though the convention was scheduled to convene in Columbia, some expected it would quickly move to Charleston. Micah Jenkins wrote his sister and said:

> If the times were not so very, very, hard, I would feel much tempted to run down to Charleston, if the Convention adjourns to that place from Columbia, which I suppose it will do on account of the small pox.[9]

He obviously was frustrated at being forced to remain in Yorkville while history was being made only a day's train ride away.

---

[5]Catton, *Centennial History*, 1:105-108; Channing, *Crisis of Fear*, 246 n.34.
[6]Micah Jenkins to John Jenkins, November 4, 1860, John Jenkins Papers, S.C.L.
[7]Catton, *Centennial History*, 1:111, quoting from the Charleston *Mercury*, November 8, 1860.
[8]May and Faunt, *South Carolina Secedes*, 3-4.
[9]Micah Jenkins to Elizabeth Jenkins LaRoche, December 16, 1860, Jenkins and LaRoche Letters, Private Collection, Emily Wilson Taylor, Fountain Inn, South Carolina.

The delegates convened in Columbia at noon on December 17 in the First Baptist Church on Hampton Street. The State House could not be used because it was occupied by the General Assembly which was in session. David F. Jamison was elected president of the convention on the fourth ballot, and the delegates then adopted the resolution that an Ordinance of Secession be drafted which would remove South Carolina from the Union. As Jenkins had predicted, they agreed to reconvene in Charleston the next day because of smallpox in Columbia and then adjourned at about ten that night.[10]

On Tuesday, December 18, the convention's delegates made the journey to Charleston by train. When they arrived at the depot there, Citadel cadets stood in line to meet them and escorted D. F. Jamison to a waiting carriage. He then rode to the Mills House on Meeting Street where he and most of the other out-of-town delegates were quartered.[11] The convention met that afternoon, when Jamison announced that a committee had been appointed to draft the Ordinance of Secession; the delegates gathered again the following day to take up various resolutions.[12]

On December 20, the convention delegates assembled in St. Andrews Hall to consider the committee's proposed draft of an Ordinance of Secession. They adopted the Ordinance by a vote of one hundred and sixty-nine to zero, and afterwards the building was renamed "Secession Hall."[13] When the wording of the Ordinance had been approved, the convention adjourned. It met again that evening in Institute Hall, which was large enough to accommodate members of the General Assembly and a number of distinguished guests, for the signing ceremony. The tedious procedure lasted almost two hours since all the delegates signed the Ordinance. President Jamison then announced that South Carolina was now an independent country, and the celebrating began. The streets of Charleston filled with people elated at the bold action their state had just taken.[14] They watched the explosion of fireworks and listened to brass bands and orations; the euphoria was contagious. The front page of the Yorkville *Enquirer* noted:

> To describe the enthusiasm with which [Jamison's] announcement [of South Carolina's secession] was greeted, is beyond the power of the pen.[15]

---

[10]May and Faunt, *South Carolina Secedes*, 5-10.
[11]Catton, *Centennial History*, 1:132.
[12]May and Faunt, *South Carolina Secedes*, 11-14.
[13]Catton, *Centennial History*, 1:133-134.
[14]Cauthen, *South Carolina Goes to War*, 71.
[15]Yorkville *Enquirer*, December 27, 1860.

It was unfortunate that Jenkins had not gone to Charleston as he had been tempted to do; the celebration there on the night of December 20 was one never to be forgotten.

Micah Jenkins and his young family enjoyed a quiet Christmas five days later in his apartment at the Kings Mountain Military School in Yorkville. He was twenty-five years old, and his delicate and beautiful wife, whom he called "Carrie," was only twenty-three. They had three small sons: Micah John, a three-year-old; Robert Flavel, aged one and a half; and William Edward, only eight months old. But the tranquility of this Christmas of 1860 in Yorkville was only temporary. South Carolina was now on a collision course, and Micah Jenkins was about to become what he had been trained to be since he was fifteen years old: a professional soldier.

Chapter 6

Call To Active Duty

T he cadets of the Kings Mountain Military School watched intently as the mounted messenger rode up the long driveway toward the Garrison. He drew his reins, quickly dismounted, and went inside. A young man dressed in a major's uniform signed for the message and gave him a half-dollar for making the cold ride from the village. It was the last week of February 1861, two months after South Carolina had seceded from the Union.

As Micah Jenkins opened the envelope and removed the document, he quietly prayed that it was the appointment he had so anxiously been awaiting. He first noticed the signature by Governor Pickens; then, as he read the text, Jenkins began to smile broadly. He drew his wife, Carrie, close to him, embraced her affectionately, and announced that he was now officially the colonel of the newly-formed Fifth Regiment of South Carolina Volunteers.[1]

As happy as he was to receive this appointment, Micah could not suppress a corresponding sense of foreboding. He knew this meant that

---

[1]Commission and appointment of Micah Jenkins as colonel of the Fifth Regiment of South Carolina Volunteers, signed by Governor Francis W. Pickens and accepted by Micah Jenkins on February 26, 1861, Micah Jenkins Papers, S.C.L. Minor details have been added to Jenkins' acceptance of the appointment, based on the author's best estimate of how it probably occurred.

he would be separated from his wife and three little boys, perhaps for a long time. He also owed over six thousand dollars on his half of the Garrison debt. If the school had to close, as now seemed likely, he would have difficulty repaying that debt. But he quickly turned to more cheerful thoughts as his old friend, Asbury Coward, congratulated him warmly.

Francis W. Pickens had taken office as Governor of South Carolina about ten weeks earlier, while the Secession Convention met for the first time in Columbia. Shortly before his inaugural address on December 17, 1860, Pickens had spoken to the South Carolina General Assembly advocating the state's secession. In his speech he stated that he "would be willing to appeal to the god of battles – if need be, cover the state with ruin, conflagration and blood, rather than submit."[2]

ASBURY COWARD,
THE BUSINESS PARTNER AND
CLOSEST FRIEND OF MICAH JENKINS.

After the Ordinance of Secession was adopted by the convention in Charleston, the South Carolina General Assembly in Columbia had promptly passed an "Act to Provide an Armed Military Force," calling for the formation of volunteer companies into ten regiments across the state.[3] D. F. Jamison, who had been appointed by the governor as South Carolina's secretary of war, ordered the state's adjutant general to organize the ten regiments, each with ten companies of men volunteering for twelve month enlistments. Jamison also ordered elections within each regiment for the positions of colonel, lieutenant colonel, and major.[4]

One of the infantry regiments was to be raised from York, Union, and Spartanburg Districts, and Micah Jenkins was immediately nominated to be its colonel.[5] He was invited to Spartanburg to address a meeting of the Thirty-sixth Militia Regiment and to drill the volunteer companies of Spartanburg District. In January 1861, the *Carolina Spartan* then

---

[2]Edmunds, *Politics of Destruction*, 152, quoting from Charleston *Mercury*, December 4, 1860, and Charleston *Daily Courier*, December 3, 1860.
[3]Cauthen, *South Carolina Goes to War*, 115.
[4]Yorkville *Enquirer*, February 28, 1861.
[5]Ibid., January 24, 1861.

endorsed his candidacy for colonel of the new volunteer regiment.[6] Jenkins wrote his wife from Spartanburg, saying, "my prospects are very good," but he added that the horse he had hired from the livery stable for the trip had drowned when it jumped off the flat as they crossed the Broad River.[7]

Jenkins' Jasper Light Infantry had by this time become a well-drilled company, and its members had already voted in Yorkville to volunteer their services to the state's defense.[8] They placed a "Call for Volunteers" in the Yorkville *Enquirer*, asking other local men to join them "in the earnest spirit of resistance to tyranny, and . . . to stand forward as champions of Southern rights."[9] Jenkins traveled to Charleston in the middle of January, both to offer the services of his company to the state and to purchase knapsacks, haversacks, canteens, and fatigue suits for his men with $1,300 donated by the citizens of Yorkville.[10]

By the end of January 1861, the men in the Jasper Light Infantry had received their new "service uniforms" which they wore at a ceremony in which they were presented with a flag made by the ladies of Yorkville. Accepting the banner on behalf of his men, Jenkins said:

> Dear as the colors won on [Fort] Moultrie's walls [were] to the heart of [Sergeant] Jasper, will this flag be to us. We will cherish and defend it to the last extremity; and if its folds should ever droop, they shall only droop over the bodies of its defenders.[11]

Meanwhile, tension was mounting in South Carolina over the problem of forts and other Federal installations in Charleston.[12] Upon assuming office, Governor Pickens had immediately been faced with how he should deal with these threats to the state's security. On December 22, 1860, the Secession Convention had adopted a resolution that Fort Moultrie, Fort Sumter, Castle Pinckney, and the Federal Arsenal, all manned by Federal troops in Charleston, should be turned over to the state of South Carolina.[13]

On December 26 the problem of the forts became vastly more complicated. Major Robert Anderson, the commander of the Federal forces in Charleston, evacuated Fort Moultrie on Sullivan's Island, and

[6]Ibid., January 31, 1861; *Carolina Spartan*, January 24, 1861.
[7]Micah Jenkins to Caroline Jenkins, January 18, 1861, Micah Jenkins Papers, S.C.L.
[8]Yorkville *Enquirer*, January 3, 1861.
[9]Ibid.
[10]Ibid., January 17, 1861.
[11]Ibid., January 31, 1861.
[12]May and Faunt, *South Carolina Secedes*, 10-11.
[13]Ibid., 19.

moved his men out to Fort Sumter in the middle of Charleston Harbor. He had feared that South Carolina would try to take the forts by force, and Fort Sumter was more easily defended than Fort Moultrie.

Anderson's action was considered highly provocative throughout South Carolina, especially in Charleston, and Governor Pickens immediately demanded that the major and his men return to Fort Moultrie. Anderson, however, refused to move, and Governor Pickens responded by ordering state troops to occupy both Fort Moultrie and Castle Pinckney, a small installation of little military value in Charleston Harbor. Pickens also ordered the erection of gun emplacements on Sullivan's and Morris Islands and authorized the use of force, if necessary, to prevent the reinforcement of Major Anderson's troops at Fort Sumter.[14] On December 29, South Carolina troops seized the United States Arsenal in Charleston, confiscating over twenty-two thousand rifles and pistols.[15] By the end of December 1860, military developments in Charleston were beginning to spin out of control.

The tension reached new heights on January 9, 1861, when the Federal steamer *Star of the West* arrived in Charleston Harbor in an attempt to reinforce and resupply Major Anderson's garrison at Fort Sumter. The battery of guns on Morris Island, manned by Citadel cadets, promptly fired on the steamer and prevented it from reaching Fort Sumter, although the ship was undamaged. The next day, the Charleston *Mercury* proclaimed:

> The first gun of the new struggle for independence (if struggle there is to be) has been fired, and Federal power has received its first repulse.[16]

Fortunately, this confrontation did not escalate into an immediate battle in Charleston Harbor, as the South Carolinians had only enough gunpowder on hand to keep firing for about three hours.[17]

Two days after the *Star of the West* incident, Governor Pickens sent Secretary of War Jamison and Secretary of State A. G. Magrath out to Fort Sumter in an attempt to persuade Major Anderson to evacuate his position. Anderson refused to move unless ordered to do so by his superiors in Washington[18] where representatives of South Carolina were concurrently attempting to negotiate the transfer of the Federal installations to the state. By the middle of February 1861, the state's

---

[14]Cauthen, *South Carolina Goes to War*, 95.
[15]Ibid., 116-117.
[16]Yorkville *Enquirer*, January 17, 1861, quoting from the Charleston *Mercury*, January 10, 1861.
[17]Cauthen, *South Carolina Goes To War*, 116.
[18]Catton, *Centennial History*, 1:183.

representatives in Washington had concluded that President Buchanan was not going to turn Fort Sumter over to Governor Pickens as he had demanded. Pickens then declared martial law on Sullivan's Island and areas adjacent to it.[19]

By this time, enough volunteer companies had been raised in York, Spartanburg and Union Districts to form a regiment, and the election of its top three officers was scheduled for February 18, 1861. The members of each of the regiment's companies cast ballots in their respective districts. Jenkins ran unopposed for colonel, as did George W. H. Legg for lieutenant colonel; W. T. Thompson defeated Joseph Walker for the position of major.[20] The state's ten new regiments were organized in separate geographical districts throughout South Carolina; Jenkins' regiment was designated the Fifth Regiment of South Carolina Volunteers.

When Jenkins was appointed colonel of his regiment by Governor Pickens, this created a vacancy in the Jasper Light Infantry for the position of company commander. Cato A. Seabrook, still on the faculty at the King's Mountain Military School, was then elected by the men in the company to replace Jenkins as captain.[21]

Meanwhile, during January and February 1861, six other Southern states seceded from the Union, and their representatives met in Montgomery, Alabama, to form a provisional government. On February 18, Jefferson Davis, whose native Mississippi had seceded the previous month, was sworn in as president of the newly-formed Confederate States of America.

Two days later, D. F. Jamison wrote from Charleston to his son-in-law, Micah Jenkins:

> The political unrest [bodes] war. We have enlarged our works for the reduction of [Fort] Sumter, but they are not yet complete.[22]

One of the problems facing Jamison was that Governor Pickens strongly favored attacking Fort Sumter before Abraham Lincoln was inaugurated in early March. When Pickens suggested this plan to Jefferson Davis, however, Davis informed him that the Confederate government in Montgomery would decide if and when the fort should be attacked.[23]

---

[19]Yorkville *Enquirer*, February 14, 1861.
[20]Ibid., February 28, 1861. Legg and Walker were both from Spartanburg and Thompson was from Union, South Carolina.
[21]Ibid., March 7, 1861. Also elected were J. Newton Withers as first lieutenant, Edward B. Clinton as second lieutenant, and Samuel B. Meacham, third lieutenant.
[22]D. F. Jamison to Micah Jenkins, February 20, 1861, Micah Jenkins Papers, S.C.L.
[23]Catton, *Centennial History*, 1:249-250.

Davis then dispatched General P. T. G. Beauregard to Charleston on behalf of the Provisional Army of the Confederate States to take command of the military preparations for the battle everyone believed would soon occur there.

On March 4, 1861, the day after Beauregard arrived in Charleston, Lincoln delivered his inaugural address in Washington. In it he firmly declared that he would "hold, occupy and possess the property . . . belonging to the [Federal] government. . . ."[24] Most South Carolinians interpreted Lincoln's statement as a flat refusal to yield Fort Sumter and as a clear sign that war was imminent. The Charleston *Mercury* criticized Lincoln's speech and his "feeble inability to grasp the circumstances of this momentous emergency."[25] By April 4, Lincoln had decided to reinforce Fort Sumter by a naval expedition.[26] He then notified Governor Pickens that Federal ships were being sent to Fort Sumter to supply "provisions only."[27]

With Federal ships on the way to Charleston, the pace of events in South Carolina suddenly began to accelerate. On April 7, Charleston officials ceased supplying Fort Sumter with food.[28] The next day, 5,000 of the state's new volunteer troops were ordered to Charleston, as one newspaper accurately reported, "in anticipation that an attempt is about to be made to reinforce Fort Sumter."[29] Two days later, on April 10, 1861, the Confederate secretary of war, L. P. Walker, ordered General Beauregard in Charleston to

> at once demand [Fort Sumter's] evacuation; and if this is refused, proceed in such a manner as you may determine, to reduce it.[30]

The nation now tottered on the brink of war. The following day, General Beauregard presented his formal demand to Major Anderson, and the discussions at the fort lasted well into the evening, but still Major Anderson refused to evacuate. Finally he was informed that if he did not evacuate, the bombardment of Fort Sumter would begin at four-thirty the next morning, April 12. At midnight, alarm guns in Citadel Square fired the signal to assemble the Charleston reserve troops. About this same

[24]Ibid., 1:265.
[25]Ibid., 1:268, quoting from the Charleston *Mercury*, March 5, 1861.
[26]Cauthen, *South Carolina Goes to War*, 119.
[27]Ibid., 130.
[28]Ibid.
[29]Yorkville *Enquirer*, April 11, 1861.
[30]Walker to Beauregard, April 10, 1861, in Yorkville *Enquirer*, April 25, 1861. Once L. P. Walker was appointed as the provisional government's secretary of war, this made the position of South Carolina's secretary of war superfluous, and D. F. Jamison apparently gave up the title at that point.

time, it was learned that the Federal fleet had arrived and was anchored outside the harbor, waiting to move in towards Fort Sumter.[31]

James Chesnut, who had resigned as one of South Carolina's United States senators, served as General Beauregard's aide-de-camp during the negotiations with Major Anderson. Chesnut's wife, Mary, who was in Charleston with her husband, recorded the events in her diary. She noted that as the week progressed Charleston's streets became filled with soldiers and ammunition wagons. At four o'clock in the morning of Friday, April 12, she heard the bells toll in the steeple of St. Michael's Church. Half an hour later the shore batteries began firing on Fort Sumter, and she knew that the war had finally begun. Like many others in Charleston, she went to the housetop to watch the bombardment as exploding shells lit up the waterfront.[32]

Only a few hours before the bombardment of Fort Sumter began, Colonel Jenkins received orders in Yorkville to have all of the men in his regiment board trains and "rendezvous in Columbia forthwith."[33] On Friday, April 12, as the battle raged in Charleston Harbor, Jenkins wrote to his brother, "I am ordered into service and leave [Yorkville] tomorrow morning for Columbia."[34]

Most of the regiment's men from York District, including those in the Jasper Light Infantry, the Catawba Light Infantry and some of the Kings Mountain Guards, left Yorkville by train for Columbia on the morning of April 13.[35] The editor-in-chief of the Yorkville *Enquirer*, William East, was among those on that train; he had volunteered and was a corporal in the Jasper Light Infantry. East planned to keep the people of York District well-informed on the movements of the Fifth Regiment by sending regular letters home to Yorkville, to be printed in the *Enquirer* under the by-line of "Our Corporal."[36]

That Saturday morning, as the Fifth South Carolina Volunteers changed trains in Chester en route to Columbia, they were honored with a seven-gun salute.[37] While he was in Chester, Jenkins wrote to his wife:

> Bear up bravely for one who loves you more than life.
> The fighting has commenced in Charleston. The fort is
> partly breached.[38]

---

[31]Catton, *Centennial History*, 1:307.
[32]C. Vann Woodward, ed., *Mary Chesnut's Civil War* (New Haven: Yale University Press, 1981), 46.
[33]Yorkville *Enquirer*, April 18, 1861.
[34]Micah Jenkins to John Jenkins, April 12, 1861, John Jenkins Papers, S.C.L.
[35]Yorkville *Enquirer*, April 18, 1861.
[36]Ibid.
[37]Ibid.
[38]Micah Jenkins to Caroline Jenkins, undated, but written from Chester, South Carolina, on April 13, 1861, Micah Jenkins Papers, S.C.L.

From Columbia that evening, Corporal East sent his first report to the Yorkville *Enquirer*. He described the train trip as "a continued ovation" and said that Jenkins and his men had been heartily cheered at every town along the route.[39] After unloading in Columbia, they marched first to another station to meet the trains carrying their comrades from Spartanburg and Union Districts. Then the entire regiment went to the Columbia Fair Grounds where the men encamped for two nights.[40]

That Sunday, April 14, while Jenkins and his men prepared to leave Columbia for Charleston the next morning, Major Anderson formally surrendered Fort Sumter to General Beauregard. D. F. Jamison, who had been hard at work in Charleston since December, attended the surrender ceremony. That night he wrote to Caroline Jenkins in Yorkville:

> Dear me! What a week the last has been. I have had cares and anxieties all the winter, but during Thursday night, all day Friday [April 12] and during the greater part of Saturday, it was at its culminating point.[41]

Jamison explained how the barracks inside Fort Sumter had caught fire the previous day from the Confederate shells and how Major Anderson had finally agreed to surrender. Then he described for Caroline the surrender ceremony which had taken place at Fort Sumter earlier that same day:

> I went over [to the Fort] with the Governor, General Beauregard and [others] to witness it, and it happened that in a foolish ceremony of saluting his flag, Major Anderson lost two of his men killed by the explosion of some loose powder near one of the guns. . . .
> I do not know whether this letter will find you at home, as Colonel Jenkins is ordered here with his regiment.[42]

In that last sentence, Caroline Jenkins' father was expressing much the same kind of anxiety for the safety of his family as was felt by so many parents, husbands, and wives in South Carolina on that second Sunday in April 1861.

Micah Jenkins and the 1,200 other men of the Fifth South Carolina Volunteers rose very early in the morning on Monday, April 15, and

---

[39]Yorkville *Enquirer*, April 18, 1861.
[40]Ibid.
[41]D. F. Jamison to Caroline Jenkins, April 14, 1861, Micah Jenkins Papers, S.C.L.
[42]Ibid.

prepared to board trains for Charleston. They looked forward to confronting the invaders in the event the Federals attempted to retake the fort. Jenkins' men left Columbia later that morning and arrived in Charleston that evening to the sound of cannon fire from the harbor and amid the rumor that 3,000 Federal troops had landed. Jenkins hurried his men from the train depot to the United States Arsenal, now under state control, where several of his companies were issued muskets and ammunition during a driving rain. It was soon discovered, however, that no enemy troops had come ashore; the cannon fire they had heard was from a Federal ship outside the harbor merely firing a salute to Major Anderson's men as they set sail for the North.[43] The regiment then marched from the arsenal to the race course on the outskirts of Charleston where the rain-soaked men, in "good health, better order and the best spirits," set up camp at about ten o'clock that evening.[44]

The men in Jenkins' Fifth Regiment were by no means the first volunteers to arrive in Charleston. Colonel Maxcy Gregg's regiment of six-month volunteers had been in the city since the beginning of January, long before the arrival of any of the other volunteer regiments.[45] The Charleston *Mercury* reported that three other regiments of volunteers arrived in the city on April 12, the day the Battle of Fort Sumter began.[46] The Fifth Regiment had entered Charleston three days later, the day after Major Anderson's formal surrender ceremony.

At this time, the Fifth South Carolina Volunteers consisted of twelve companies. Three were from Union District: the Johnson Rifles, under Captain John W. Goss; the Pea Ridge Volunteers, under Captain W. J. Thomas Glenn; and the Tyger Volunteers, under Captain Jacob W. Sartor. There were five companies from Spartanburg District: the Batesville Volunteers, under Captain J. J. Brown; the Pacolet Guards, under Captain J. Q. Carpenter; the Lawson Fork Volunteers, under Captain Ryal B. Seay; the Morgan Light Infantry, under Captain J. M. Benson; and the Spartan Rifles, under Captain Joseph Walker. York District contributed four companies: the Jasper Light Infantry, under Captain Cato A. Seabrook; the Kings Mountain Guards, under Captain Andrew Jackson; the Catawba Light Infantry, under Captain R. H. Glenn; and the Whyte Guards, under Captain A. E. Hutchinson.[47]

The regiment remained camped at the race course outside Charleston from Monday night until the morning of Friday, April 19. Then

---

[43]Yorkville *Enquirer*, April 18, 1861.

[44]Ibid.

[45]Cauthen, *South Carolina Goes to War*, 114 n.26.

[46]Charleston *Mercury*, April 12, 1861.

[47]For a list of officers in each company of the Fifth South Carolina and the companies' popular names, at the time they left for Charleston, see the Yorkville *Enquirer*, April 18, 1861. For the rosters of officers and men in each company, see the *Carolina Spartan*, May 16, 1861.

the men broke camp and marched through the city to a wharf near the end of Broad Street. There they began boarding the steamer *Planter* about noon and were ferried in groups across the harbor to Sullivan's Island. Upon arrival, the Jasper Light Infantry was quartered in the Moultrie House, a well-known resort hotel which had been heavily damaged by the guns of Fort Sumter during the battle the previous week. The rest of the men were quartered in private homes in Moultrieville, a small resort village at the southern tip of the island, near Fort Moultrie.[48] It was their third encampment in two weeks, but at least now they did not have to sleep in tents.

Their first Sunday on Sullivan's Island, Jenkins and his men attended church services in the dining room of the Moultrie House. Some of the soldiers suffered from colds and sore throats "caused by the change of climate and the exposure of camp life."[49]

As April came to an end, it appeared that the most serious military threat to the Confederacy was no longer in Charleston but in Virginia, which by then had joined the other Confederate states. Federal troops were gathering in Washington, and a worried Jefferson Davis requested that the governors of the Confederate states send troops to defend Virginia from an expected invasion. Governor Pickens responded immediately. On April 22, Colonel Maxcy Gregg's First Regiment of six-month volunteers, which had been on duty in the Charleston area since January, boarded trains for Virginia.[50]

Meanwhile, the men of the Fifth Regiment remained on Sullivan's Island, and Jenkins wasted no time in imposing a vigorous training program. One soldier wrote to the *Carolina Spartan*, describing in detail their daily routine:

> At 5 o'clock a.m., reveille [and] roll call; 5½, (morning) squad drill, one hour; 6½, breakfast call; 7, Surgeon's call; 7½, Sergeant's call and reports; 8, guard mounting; 8 to 9, Colonel's [Jenkins'] office hours; 9, officers' drill, one hour; 10½, squad drill, one hour; I p.m., dinner call; 2, company drill, one hour, [and] roll call; [3 to 5, leisure time]; 5, battalion drill, one hour and dress parade; 6, retreat and supper, roll call; 9, tatoo [and] roll call; 9½, taps [and] lights out; all of which are strictly enforced and performed.[51]

---

[48]Yorkville *Enquirer*, April 25, 1861.
[49]Ibid.
[50]Ibid., May 2, 1861.
[51]*Carolina Spartan*, May 9, 1861.

MICAH JENKINS, SHOWN HERE AS COLONEL OF THE FIFTH SOUTH CAROLINA VOLUN-
TEERS. THIS PHOTOGRAPH WAS TAKEN IN THE SPRING OF 1861 WHILE JENKINS AND
HIS MEN WERE STATIONED ON SULLIVAN'S ISLAND NEAR CHARLESTON, SOUTH CARO-
LINA.

Even with this demanding schedule, the men did manage to find ways to amuse themselves, and one of them said that in spite of "all our drilling, marching, etc., we are living a pleasant, a merry life."[52] In the evenings after dress parade, they enjoyed the fine spring weather and the island's wide beach where they fished, swam, wrestled and ran foot races.[53] They even enjoyed the music of the "Ebony Band" which had been with the regiment since it left Yorkville. Mr. William Latta, a prominent York District citizen, provided the band at his own expense.[54]

At the end of April, one of Jenkins' soldiers on the beach spotted a capsized sailboat in the main channel, with several people clinging to it, being taken out to sea by the tide. He immediately summoned help, launched a small boat from the beach, and saved the lives of four men. For his decisive action, Corporal Edward J. Dean of the Spartan Rifles received a commendation for gallantry from Colonel Jenkins.[55]

By early May, the men had been issued army muskets, but Colonel Jenkins was attempting to acquire the improved rifle musket for them instead. He was also trying to find a supply of Enfield rifles for his two rifle companies.[56] His duties occasionally took him into Charleston, where he preferred staying at the Mills House on the corner of Queen and Meeting Streets.[57]

While on Sullivan's Island, Jenkins' men assisted in the repair and rebuilding of Fort Moultrie, which had been heavily damaged during the battle in April. The regiment supplied about one hundred men each day to work on the fort and its grounds.[58]

The only serious complaint from Jenkins' men about their duty on Sullivan's Island involved their drinking water. It contained what the men called "little wiggle tails" which they could see swimming in it. According to one man, they finally learned to "pass [the water] through a cloth [before drinking it], which puts the wiggle tails in a quandary."[59]

Despite "wiggle tails" in their water and the monotony of constant drilling, the men of the Fifth Regiment were coming to respect and

---

[52]Yorkville *Enquirer*, April 25, 1861.
[53]*Carolina Spartan*, May 9, 1861.
[54]Yorkville *Enquirer*, April 25, 1861.
[55]*Carolina Spartan*, May 9, 1861.
[56]Ibid. The two companies were the Johnson Rifles and the Spartan Rifles.
[57]Micah Jenkins to Caroline Jenkins, May 4, 1861, Micah Jenkins Papers, S.C.L.
[58]Yorkville *Enquirer*, May 9, 1861.
[59]Yorkville *Enquirer*, May 21, 1861.

admire their commanding officer. Corporal East wrote to the Yorkville *Enquirer* from Sullivan's Island:

> Colonel Jenkins is the same affable, sociable and earnest-spirited gentlemen he is at home. He labors incessantly for our welfare. . . .[60]

On May 12, while still on Sullivan's Island, Jenkins wrote to his wife about a new strategy he saw developing in the young war:

> Yesterday our monotonous camp life was enlivened by the appearance off the "Bar" [outside the harbor] of the steamship Niagra, sent as a blockading ship. She has since been busy chasing ships and sending them away from the Harbor. She stopped three merchant vessels coming in this morning and sent them away.[61]

The Federal naval blockade was just beginning to have an effect on Charleston.

Meanwhile, the need for additional troops in Virginia had become a major topic of conversation among the men of the Fifth Regiment. On May 23, Governor Pickens reviewed the regiment on Sullivan's Island and afterwards addressed the men. He implored them to convert their twelve-month state enlistments into enlistments in the Provisional Army of the Confederacy. It was understood that those who did so would be sent to Virginia for the remainder of their twelve-month enlistments which would not expire until April 13, 1862. Following Governor Pickens' speech, about 900 of the 1200 men in the Fifth Regiment volunteered to convert their enlistments and go to Virginia. Those volunteers were then given time to visit their homes before leaving South Carolina; their furloughs lasted from May 28 until June 3, 1861. Those who chose not to go to Virginia were required to continue their duty in Charleston until early June when they were disbanded by Governor Pickens and sent home.[62]

When Jenkins arrived in Yorkville on his furlough before departing for Virginia, he found that most of the cadets of the Kings Mountain Military School had either already left or were planning not to return for the second session on June 1.[63] Jenkins' war duties meant that solving

---

[60]Ibid.

[61]Micah Jenkins to Caroline Jenkins, May 12, 1861, Micah Jenkins Papers, D.U.L.

[62]Yorkville *Enquirer*, May 30, 1861, and June 13, 1861.

[63]John W. Jamison to his sister, Caroline Jenkins, May 11, 1861, Micah Jenkins Papers, S.C.L. John Jamison wrote: "I fear the school will be exceedingly small, if not altogether broken up by the commencement of the next session." Ibid.

this problem must be left to his partner, Asbury Coward, who had not yet
enlisted. As long as the school had a substantial number of students,
Jenkins and Coward could continue to pay off the mortgage on the
Garrison. If they were forced to close the school, however, Jenkins knew
he would have to contribute his share of the mortgage payments out of
his colonel's salary of $175 a month.[64]

On June 3, 1861, after only five days at home with their families, the
men of the Fifth Regiment who had volunteered for service in Virginia
reassembled in Orangeburg where they camped by the Edisto River.[65]
The next day they were mustered into the Provisional Army of the
Confederate States of America at the Orangeburg Courthouse and
received their new uniforms "of dark Rock Island goods, with red facings,
and gilt S. C. buttons."[66] On June 5 they boarded trains and headed for
the Old Dominion, under orders from Governor Pickens "to report
forthwith to President Davis or the General in command of Richmond."[67]
There they would join the men of four other South Carolina Regiments
already in Virginia.[68]

They were off to fight in what many in the South viewed as the
second American Revolution, but a conflict which some feared might
become protracted.[69] Yet such somber ideas were almost entirely
drowned in an overwhelming exuberance. The Charleston *Mercury*, on
the day after Major Anderson's surrender of Fort Sumter, had exclaimed,
"Thank God the war is open . . . we will [now] conquer or perish."[70]
Whether the Southern states would conquer or perish, however, would
no longer be determined in South Carolina. The focus of the conflict had
shifted to Virginia, where it would remain for four long years.

---

[64]Yorkville *Enquirer*, June 27, 1861. At this time lieutenant colonels earned $170 per month; majors, $150; and captains, $108.

[65]J. D. McConnell, "Recollections of the Civil War," Winthrop University Archives and Special Collections, Winthrop University, Rock Hill, South Carolina, typescript copy, 1.

[66]James B. Steedman, "Pea Ridge Volunteers," in *Recollections and Reminiscences 1861-1865 Through World War One*, vol. 1, (South Carolina Division of the United Daughters of the Confederacy, privately printed, 1990), 219. When the Fifth South Carolina was mustered into Confederate service, it was no longer made up of twelve companies, but had been reduced to ten, the maximum number allowed by law. Charleston *Daily Courier*, January 27, 1862.

[67]Copy of the Order of Governor Pickens to Colonel Micah Jenkins, June 2, 1861, E. M. Law Papers, Southern Historical Collection, University of North Carolina, Chapel Hill, North Carolina.

[68]Cauthen, *South Carolina Goes to War*, 136. Maxcy Gregg's regiment of six-month volunteers had been sent to Virginia on April 22; Joseph Kershaw's Second South Carolina left for Richmond on April 25, followed by T. G. Bacon's Seventh and E. B. Cash's Eighth.

[69]Yorkville *Enquirer*, June 13, 1861.

[70]Cauthen, *South Carolina Goes to War*, 133, quoting from the Charleston *Mercury*, April 15, 1861.

Chapter 7

The First Battle Of Manassas

I t was after midnight on June 6, 1861, when the troop train hit something on the tracks and came to a sudden, screeching stop. The jolt threw sleeping soldiers from their seats, and for a few moments no one knew what had happened. It was soon discovered that the rear wheels of the engine had been knocked loose and that some of the cars behind it had been damaged; only one man had been injured. The men started to get out of the cars but found they were stopped on an extremely elevated section of track with steep embankments dropping off on both sides. Suddenly they heard the distant moan of a whistle from an approaching train loaded with more soldiers of the Fifth South Carolina Volunteers. Unless this second troop train could be warned and stopped, it would smash into the first, injuring or killing many of Jenkins' men.

A young lieutenant, Frederick G. Latham of Captain Jacob Q. Carpenter's Pacolet Guards, alertly grabbed a lantern from one of the cars and ran down the track toward the approaching train, which had begun to build up steam after leaving Columbia. Its engineer caught a glimpse of the dim, moving light on the track ahead and immediately pulled back on the throttle. As his locomotive slowly steamed forward, he saw Latham standing on the tracks and waving a lantern. When the engineer finally brought his train to a stop, the lieutenant told him of the accident a few hundred yards ahead.[1]

The two trains were stopped near Killian's Station, about seven miles from Columbia on the main rail line to Charlotte, North Carolina. Fortunately, none of the damaged cars had plummeted down the steep embankment, and the second train had been warned in time. Lieutenant E. B. Clinton wrote: "It seems almost miraculous that we were not all killed."[2]

EDWARD BYERS CLINTON,
ADJUTANT OF THE FIFTH SOUTH
CAROLINA VOLUNTEERS

Micah Jenkins and the Fifth South Carolina Volunteers had left Orangeburg for Richmond, Virginia, on three separate trains earlier that afternoon, June 5, 1861. Because of the accident, the men were forced to return to Columbia while the lead train was being repaired. The next day some of the men of the Fifth Regiment passed the time by visiting their comrades in Colonel J. H. Williams' Third Regiment which was camped in Columbia. The people of York District, however, had expected the men of the Fifth Regiment to pass through Chester during the morning of June 6 on their way to Charlotte. Families and friends of the soldiers gathered at the depot there to wish them well and say good-bye, but, unfortunately, Jenkins' men were still delayed in Columbia. By the time they finally passed through Chester late that Thursday night, they had missed seeing their friends and relatives who had given up and returned home.[3]

On Friday, June 7, the men finally reached Charlotte: the first train, under the command of Lieutenant Colonel G. W. H. Legg, arrived at eight in the morning, the second at three in the afternoon, and the third right after sunset. That night Jenkins' men camped at the Fair Grounds

---

[1]Yorkville *Enquirer*, June 13, 1861. Minor details have been added to the Yorkville *Enquirer* account of the accident, based on the author's best estimate of how it probably occurred. At this time, Frederick G. Latham was first lieutenant in Company G of the Fifth South Carolina Volunteers. He was later captain of Company M, Jenkins' Palmetto Sharpshooters.

[2]E. B. Clinton to his stepfather, Samuel G. Brown, June 10, 1861, E. B. Clinton Letters, Private Collection, Elmer Oris Parker, Columbia, South Carolina. Edward Byers Clinton was initially second lieutenant of Company I (Jasper Light Infantry) of the Fifth South Carolina. He became the regiment's adjutant on July 1, 1861, but died of natural causes on December 24, 1861.

[3]Yorkville *Enquirer*, June 13, 1861.

and were treated to "the generous hospitalities of beautiful Charlotte."[4] Corporal East wrote from that city:

> [W]herever you go . . . the glorious cause of Southern independence – of the Second Revolution, hallowed by recollections of the First . . . [is met by] a support so pervading and enthusiastic, that it knits all together, as a band of brothers. . . .[5]

Early on Saturday they reboarded their trains, which were well behind schedule because of the accident near Columbia, and resumed their trip to Virginia. From Charlotte the trains went to Petersburg, Virginia, with an intermediate stop at Raleigh, where the soldiers were again treated to picnics by local citizens.

On Monday, June 10, five days after their odyssey began in Orangeburg, South Carolina, Jenkins' men arrived in Richmond, the new capital of the Confederacy. They were dirty from the dust and smoke of their long trip in open cars, and some bathed in the James River as soon as they arrived. During their first day in Richmond, they were temporarily quartered in "several large and filthy tobacco warehouses . . . on the very banks of [the] James River."[6]

Late that afternoon Jenkins marched his regiment, led by a brass band, through the streets of the capital to "Camp Davis" just outside the city. Along the march route they were cheered and showered with bouquets of flowers by the ladies of Richmond. At Camp Davis, near the city's reservoir, they pitched their tents next to those of several other regiments, including two from South Carolina: E. B. Cash's Eighth and Thomas G. Bacon's Seventh South Carolina Volunteers. That night the 830 soldiers of the Fifth Regiment slept soundly, worn out by their long, tiring journey from South Carolina.[7]

Jenkins and his men experienced a memorable event the next day when President Jefferson Davis reviewed them. Addressing them simply as "South Carolinians," his short speech thrilled the soldiers, and they gave Davis a rousing cheer when he had finished.[8] Then they settled into their camp routine in a beautiful village of white tents scattered among the green rolling hills overlooking the Confederate capital.

Two days later, the men of Cash's and Bacon's South Carolina regiments broke camp, loaded their equipment, and marched to the depot. There they boarded trains for Manassas Junction, Virginia, a

---

[4]Ibid. See also, *Carolina Spartan*, June 13, 1861.
[5]Yorkville *Enquirer*, June 13, 1861.
[6]Ibid., June 20, 1861.
[7]*Carolina Spartan*, June 20, 1861; Charleston *Daily Courier*, January 27, 1862.
[8]Yorkville *Enquirer*, June 20, 1861.

strategic rail junction some thirty-five miles southwest of Washington. As their fellow South Carolinians marched past, the men of the Fifth Regiment shouted their encouragement, knowing they would soon be headed in the same direction.[9] That same day, Colonel Jenkins wrote to his wife saying that his brother, Edward, was with the regiment in Richmond, acting as a volunteer medical aid. Jenkins added confidently, "[t]he war seems less to be feared as we draw near to [the] scene of action."[10]

While still camped in Richmond, Jenkins' men learned of the fight at Bethel Church, near Yorktown, the first battle of the war to take place in eastern Virginia. Although it was more of a skirmish than a battle, the Confederates were the clear victors, and this encouraging news buoyed the spirits of Jenkins and his men.[11]

On June 17, four days after the departure of Cash's and Bacon's South Carolina regiments, the Confederate adjutant and inspector general's office issued an order stating:

> Colonel Jenkins' Fifth Regiment [of] South Carolina Volunteers will proceed to Manassas Junction, Va., and report to Brigadier General Beauregard, commanding.[12]

Before leaving Richmond, the regiment was reviewed one final time by the president of the Confederacy. The next day, the men left Camp Davis and marched through Richmond to the Virginia Central Railroad depot where they boarded trains for Manassas Junction. There they would join the four other South Carolina regiments that had preceded them and be placed under General Beauregard's overall command.[13]

During the last week of May, Lincoln had sent eight regiments of Federal troops across the Potomac River to Alexandria and Arlington to establish a bridgehead in northern Virginia.[14] At about the same time, General Beauregard had been transferred from Charleston to Virginia where he began preparing to meet the threat of any further Federal incursions. He had set up his headquarters at Manassas Junction and begun massing his troops there.

---

[9]*Carolina Spartan*, June 20, 1861.

[10]Micah Jenkins to Caroline Jenkins, June 13, 1861, Micah Jenkins Papers, S.C.L.

[11]Yorkville *Enquirer*, June 20, 1861. The battle (or skirmish) took place on June 10, 1861.

[12]United States War Department, *The War of the Rebellion: A Compilation of the Official Records in the Union and Confederate Armies*, 4 ser., 70 vols. in 128 parts (Washington, D. C.: Government Printing Office, 1880-1901), Special Orders No. 73, June 17, 1861, O.R., vol. 51, part 2, p. 141. All references are to Series 1 and are hereafter begun with the abbreviation "O.R.," followed by the applicable volume, part, and page numbers.

[13]Yorkville *Enquirer*, June 27, 1861; *Carolina Spartan*, June 27, 1861.

[14]Catton, *Centennial History*, 1:390.

When they arrived at Manassas Junction early on June 19, Jenkins' men marched to Camp Walker, about two miles north of the depot.[15] There they set up their tents near those of other volunteers from Alabama and Mississippi and began to settle into their new camp. They were located less than thirty miles from similar Federal encampments in Alexandria across the Potomac from Washington. The day after Jenkins' troops had set up their tents, a local belle sent a bouquet of flowers to each captain in the regiment "to be given to the most gallant and handsome private in his company, to be decided by vote."[16]

Camp Walker had previously been occupied by the men in Colonel Bacon's Seventh South Carolina Volunteers who had just recently been moved closer to Alexandria. Before they vacated the camp, Bacon's troops had built some "umbrageous arbors . . . for their protection against the sunbeams," which the men of the Fifth Regiment now gratefully inherited.[17] They also drilled and took daily target practice, firing from distances of 100 and 300 yards.[18]

A few days after its arrival at Manassas Junction, Jenkins' regiment was assigned to the Third Brigade in Beauregard's Army of the Potomac. This brigade was under the command of Brigadier General David R. Jones and included two other regiments: W. S. Featherston's Seventeenth and E. R. Burt's Eighteenth Mississippi Volunteers.[19] General Jones, a relative of Micah Jenkins' wife, had been born in South Carolina but had later moved to Georgia. He had graduated from the United States Military Academy at West Point in the same class with Thomas Jonathan Jackson, an obscure former professor at the Virginia Military Institute who was now a brigadier general in the Confederate Army.[20] In another month, Jackson would be known to all Confederates by his unforgettable nickname.

Jenkins' men had plenty to eat, including crackers, bacon, coffee, sugar, and sometimes, rice and flour. They complained about the crackers, however, and one soldier quipped that "they require a hammer to break them."[21] They also found the bacon quite inferior, and it was said that the dirty brown sugar "would spoil the best cup of coffee ever made."[22] The water was considered tolerable enough, but good water could be had only if one was willing to walk a half mile to get it. Camp

---

[15]Yorkville *Enquirer*, June 27, 1861.
[16]Ibid. The men in the Jasper Light Infantry selected Private C. Knox Williams to receive this award.
[17]Yorkville *Enquirer*, June 27, 1861.
[18]*Carolina Spartan*, July 4, 1861.
[19]Ibid.; Yorkville *Enquirer*, July 4, 1861.
[20]Clement A. Evans, ed., *Confederate Military History*, vol. 6, *South Carolina*, by Brigadier General Ellison Capers (extended edition; Wilmington, North Carolina: Broadfoot Publishing Co., 1987), 406-407.
[21]*Carolina Spartan*, July 4, 1861.
[22]Yorkville *Enquirer*, July 4, 1861.

Walker was situated in a large field of clover beside the railroad, with plenty of large, flat rocks which the men used as seats and tables. Jenkins was getting along well with his men, and one soldier described him as

> an officer and a gentlemen [who] fills his position with promptness and ability [and] answers the demands upon his time and patience with great satisfaction to the Regiment.[23]

The normal routine of camp life at Manassas Junction was abruptly interrupted at daybreak on Sunday, June 23, when Jones' Third Brigade received word that Federal troops were finally making an advance. Jenkins had his regiment "beat to arms," and the men formed up, with muskets loaded, to meet the threat.[24] It turned out, however, to be a false alarm. Federal troops had attempted to burn a bridge about a mile and a half from Camp Walker and had been fired on by Confederate soldiers on picket duty. Jenkins welcomed this opportunity as a "dry run" for his men, and he wrote his wife:

> I was much pleased with the coolness of my officers and men and I am inclined to believe we will march to the fight as cooly as [if] to a parade.[25]

When the alarm had sounded, several members of the Fifth Regiment were in the guard house, under arrest for a variety of minor offenses. They responded to the supposed emergency with such an eagerness to fight, however, that Colonel Jenkins pardoned them in a gesture of appreciation.[26]

At about ten o'clock that same Sunday evening, as Jenkins' men were settling down for the night, they were startled by a rifle shot fired by one of their sentinels, Private Calvin Cook. He had seen something moving in the darkness near his post, and there was no response when he yelled, "Halt!" As the shape continued toward him, Cook leveled his musket, took aim and fired, and the object dropped to the ground with a thud. He then found he had "put a ball right through the head of a large and likely milch cow."[27] Cook was arrested, but insisted to Colonel Jenkins that he had believed the intruder "was a Yankee in a cow skin"

---

[23]*Carolina Spartan*, July 4, 1861.
[24]Ibid.
[25]Micah Jenkins to Caroline Jenkins, June 23, 1861, Micah Jenkins Papers, D.U.L.
[26]E. B. Clinton to S. G. Brown, June 26, 1861, E. B. Clinton Letters.
[27]Yorkville *Enquirer*, July 4, 1861; *Carolina Spartan*, July 4, 1861. Calvin Cook was a private in Captain Ryal B. Seay's Company, the Lawson Fork Volunteers.

and was quickly released.[28] Jenkins' men were delighted with Cook's "mistake," as it meant beef on their table, but Jenkins did pay the owner of the cow for his loss.

By the end of June 1861, Asbury Coward was forced to close the Kings Mountain Military School due to a lack of students, and he promptly left for Virginia to join Jenkins' regiment.[29] Coward arrived at Manassas Junction with no arms and no horse, fully expecting to serve as a private.[30] But on the morning after Coward's arrival, Jenkins took him to meet General Jones who immediately invited Coward to serve as his volunteer aide-de-camp. A few days later, General Jones made an application for Coward to become the Third Brigade's adjutant-in-the-field and sent him to Richmond to personally present the request. The request was approved, and as a member of General Jones' staff, Coward was appointed to the same brigade with his friends and neighbors in the Fifth Regiment.[31]

Meanwhile, Jenkins' brother, Edward, who had been serving in Virginia as a volunteer surgeon for the Fifth Regiment, returned to South Carolina for reasons that are not now clear. Remaining at Manassas Junction was Micah Jenkins' trusted man-servant, "Old Ben" Jones, who cooked the colonel's meals and cared for his horse and uniforms.[32] After spending a month in Virginia, Jenkins still had lingering hopes that negotiations between the governments in Washington and Richmond would result in an "honorable peace."[33] Caroline was pregnant with their fourth child, and Micah was homesick for his growing family.[34]

By the first week in July, Jenkins' regiment had been on active duty for not quite three months, but already he was becoming respected for his military ability by his men. One of them wrote: "Our gallant Colonel is conceded on all sides to be one of the best, if not the very best in the field. . . ."[35] The Fifth South Carolina was itself gaining a fine reputation. On July 4, the regiment was reviewed by Generals Jones and Beauregard and their full staffs. After the review, Jenkins was asked to tell his men that Beauregard was "not only entirely pleased, but actually surprised at [their] performance."[36] Although their morale was high, they did have a problem: an outbreak of measles in the camp. At one point,

---

[28]E. B. Clinton to S. G. Brown, June 26, 1861, E. B. Clinton Letters.

[29]Micah Jenkins to Caroline Jenkins, June 23, 1861, Micah Jenkins Papers, D.U.L.

[30]Natalie Jenkins Bond and Osmun Latrobe Coward, eds., *The South Carolinians: Colonel Asbury Coward's Memoirs* (New York: Vantage Press, 1968), 13.

[31]Ibid., 13-14.

[32]Ibid.

[33]Micah Jenkins to Caroline Jenkins, July 5, 1861, Micah Jenkins Papers, S.C.L.

[34]Micah Jenkins to Caroline Jenkins, June 27, 1861, Micah Jenkins Papers, S.C.L. Whitemarsh, Jenkins' fourth son, was born about a month later.

[35]Yorkville *Enquirer*, July 11, 1861.

[36]Ibid., July 18, 1861.

for example, Captain Goss' Johnson Rifles (Company A) had some fifty men unavailable for active duty as a result of the disease.[37]

By early July, Brigadier General Irvin McDowell, the commander of the Federal troops massed in Arlington and Alexandria, had come under increasing pressure from Washington politicians to take the offensive.[38] The timing appeared to favor McDowell because the Confederate forces in Virginia were split into two parts. General Beauregard's soldiers were at Manassas Junction, guarding the Washington approach to Richmond, while General Joe Johnston's army was stationed in the Shenandoah Valley. The two Confederate armies would have to quickly be combined to even the odds, once McDowell made his move.[39]

Jenkins' men thought the battle was about to begin when they heard heavy firing coming from the direction of Fairfax Court House on the morning of July 8, but the expected Federal advance did not materialize. By then they were fully prepared to fight at a moment's notice. Still camped near Manassas Junction, they had been issued five days' provisions and the regimental quota of thirteen baggage wagons.[40]

McDowell's Federal army of some 34,000 men finally began to advance from Alexandria toward Beauregard's force on July 16. In response, General Johnston immediately started moving his troops from the Shenandoah Valley toward Manassas Junction to reinforce Beauregard.[41]

On the morning of July 17, General Jones' brigade, including Jenkins' regiment, moved out of Camp Walker at about nine o'clock. They marched a short distance to Bull Run, a wide creek that meandered between Manassas Junction and Centreville, a village about six miles northwest of the junction. On the south bank of Bull Run, at McLean's Ford, the two Mississippi regiments in Jones' brigade went into bivouac, while the Fifth South Carolina Volunteers waded across and marched northward toward Centreville, roughly three miles away. Jenkins halted his men on the road about two miles south of Centreville and formed them into a line of battle to slow any Union advance from that village towards McLean's Ford.[42]

---

[37]E. B. Clinton to S. G. Brown, July 13, 1861, E. B. Clinton Letters.

[38]Catton, *Centennial History*, 1:439.

[39]Ibid., 1:444-445.

[40]Yorkville *Enquirer*, July 18, 1861.

[41]Catton, *Centennial History*, 1:445.

[42]National Archives, Compiled Service Records (and Company Record of Events Cards) of the Confederate Soldiers Who Served in Organizations From the State of South Carolina, R.G. 109, series M267, Record of Events Cards for Companies B and C of the Fifth South Carolina Volunteers, July/August 1861 (referred to hereafter as "Record of Events Cards for the Fifth S.C.V.," followed by the appropriate company designations and dates).

That night they could hear Federal troops and equipment moving along the other roads between Bull Run and Centreville.[43] At sunrise the next morning, Jenkins withdrew his men and moved them back down the road to McLean's Ford. This was a timely move because they had been in danger of being cut off from the rest of the Confederate forces by McDowell's advancing Federal army. In fact, as they pulled back towards Bull Run on July 18, some of Jenkins' men could see the Federal advance guard approaching. One officer said that they watched as the Federals "opened their battery upon us."[44] The Fifth Regiment crossed the run in safety, however, and rejoined the rest of the Third Brigade on the south bank at McLean's Ford. Jones' three regiments then dug a line of trenches parallel to Bull Run, about 75 yards from its south bank, and a detachment of the Washington Artillery was deployed on the hill behind them.[45] In this strong defensive position, Jenkins' men could only wait for McDowell's army to attempt to cross Bull Run.

Later that day, a large body of Union troops, conducting a reconnaissance in force, advanced from Centreville towards the run.[46] Three times the Federals attempted to cross at Blackburn's Ford, about a mile west of McLean's Ford, and each time they were driven back by a Confederate brigade under the command of forty-year-old Brigadier General James Longstreet.[47] This limited action at Blackburn's Ford on July 18, however, was merely a prelude to the far more serious general engagement which took place on the south side of the run three days later.

Bull Run, although called a creek, actually resembled a small river; it had banks five feet high in places, and it formed a natural barrier to the advancing Federal army. General Beauregard had strategically placed his brigades along the south bank of the run at likely crossings, in a line stretching some five miles. On the extreme left of the line, South Carolinian Colonel Nathan Evans commanded the brigade which defended the important Stone Bridge where the Warrenton Turnpike crossed Bull Run en route to Centreville. Colonel Philip St. George Cocke's brigade guarded the first three fords downstream from the bridge; General Milledge L. Bonham's brigade of four South Carolina

---

[43]E. B. Clinton to S. G. Brown, July 19, 1861, E. B. Clinton Letters.
[44]Ibid. There is nothing to indicate that the Union troops pursued Jenkins' men as they fell back toward McLean's Ford.
[45]Ibid.
[46]Catton, *Centennial History*, 1:447.
[47]Yorkville *Enquirer*, August 1, 1861; *Carolina Spartan*, August 22, 1861. Born in Edgefield District, South Carolina, Longstreet had graduated from the United States Military Academy in its class of 1842. After fighting in the Mexican War, he served as a major in the U.S. Army's Paymaster Department in Albuquerque, New Mexico Territory, a position he resigned following the outbreak of the Civil War. He was appointed a brigadier general in the Provisional Army of the Confederate States on June 17, 1861, one month before his brigade saw action at Blackburn's Ford.

regiments was posted to Cocke's right at Mitchell's Ford. On Bonham's right, General James Longstreet's brigade was positioned at Blackburn's Ford, the site of the skirmish on July 18. General D. R. Jones' three regiments, including Jenkins' Fifth South Carolina, were to Longstreet's right, at McLean's Ford. On the extreme right of the Confederate line, Richard S. Ewell's brigade guarded the Union Mills Ford as well as the nearby railroad bridge. Beauregard had massed his men at these crossings at and below the Stone Bridge for more than merely defensive reasons. He wanted to advance across the fords toward Centreville and with some luck cut the Union army off from Washington, assuming McDowell would attack where Beauregard expected.[48]

Joe Johnston's four brigades began arriving from the Shenandoah Valley early on the afternoon of July 20 to reinforce a surprised but delighted General Beauregard. He expected McDowell's attack at any time and had feared that Johnston would arrive too late.[49] Beauregard received more good news: the "Hampton Legion," led by Colonel Wade Hampton of South Carolina, had also arrived in time to fight.

Late on Saturday afternoon, July 20, the men in Beauregard's brigades along Bull Run began to hear Federal drums beating in "high style" as McDowell's brigades began moving southwest out of Centreville toward the Stone Bridge.[50] One soldier in Jenkins' regiment reported that

> [e]very movement of their infantry, cavalry, artillery, and immense baggage trains, marching and moving over the various roads . . . until daylight were distinctly heard. From the tremendous noise . . . it seemed as if the whole earth was in motion. . . .[51]

At dawn on July 21, McDowell's troops began crossing Bull Run, but not at or below the Stone Bridge where Beauregard had expected. Instead, they came across at Sudley Ford, about a mile and a half upstream from the bridge where no Confederate troops were positioned to contest their passage. Once across Bull Run, McDowell's regiments then moved down the south bank to engage the Confederate left flank in the vicinity of the Stone Bridge and the Warrenton Turnpike. It was in this general area that the major part of the fighting occurred that day, some four or five miles west of McLean's Ford where Jenkins' regiment was positioned.

---

[48]Douglas Southall Freeman, *Lee's Lieutenants, A Study in Command*, vol. 1, *Manassas to Malvern Hill* (New York: Charles Scribner's Sons, 1942), 46-47; Foote, *Civil War*, 1:76.

[49]Foote, *Civil War*, 1:72.

[50]Yorkville *Enquirer*, August 1, 1861.

[51]*Carolina Spartan*, August 22, 1861.

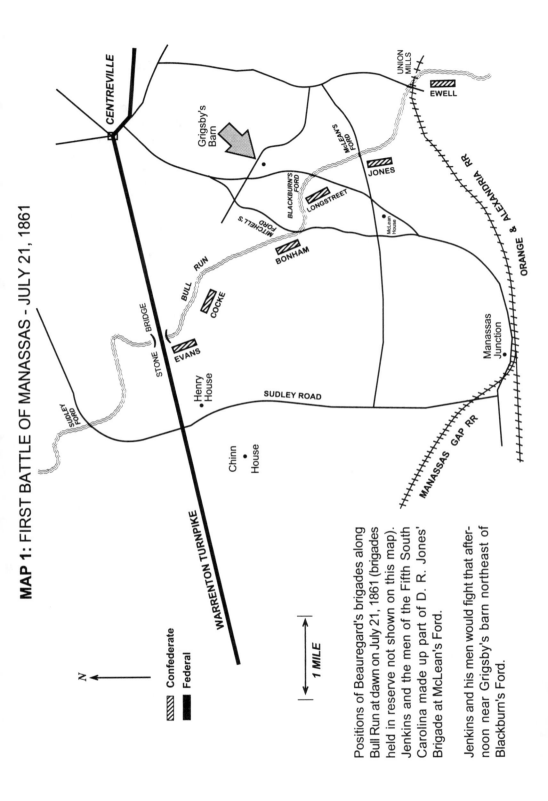

MAP 1: FIRST BATTLE OF MANASSAS - JULY 21, 1861

N

1 MILE

CENTREVILLE

WARRENTON TURNPIKE

Confederate
Federal

SUDLEY FORD

STONE BRIDGE

BULL RUN

EVANS

COCKE

BONHAM

Henry House

Chinn House

SUDLEY ROAD

MITCHELL'S FORD

BLACKBURN'S FORD

LONGSTREET

McLean House

Grigsby's Barn

McLEAN'S FORD

JONES

UNION MILLS

EWELL

ORANGE & ALEXANDRIA RR

Manassas Junction

MANASSAS GAP RR

Positions of Beauregard's brigades along Bull Run at dawn on July 21, 1861 (brigades held in reserve not shown on this map). Jenkins and the men of the Fifth South Carolina made up part of D. R. Jones' Brigade at McLean's Ford.

Jenkins and his men would fight that afternoon near Grigsby's barn northeast of Blackburn's Ford.

Early that Sunday morning, before he had become fully aware of the Federal crossing at Sudley Ford, General Beauregard ordered several of his brigades below the Stone Bridge to advance against the Federal left flank, across Bull Run.[52] Pursuant to those orders, the men in D. R. Jones' brigade waded across the run at McLean's Ford and marched north for about a mile to the road linking Centreville with the Union Mills Ford. There they formed a line of battle and remained in position until about noon. After the fighting had focused near the turnpike on the other side of the run, Beauregard recalled Jones and his three regiments. They then retraced their steps to McLean's Ford, waded back across and awaited further orders.[53] Jenkins' men and the two Mississippi regiments in Jones' brigade remained there only long enough to gulp down some crackers and bacon before they were on the march again.[54] Their new orders gave them a specific objective: they were to silence a battery of eight Federal cannons.

Several hundred yards to the right front of General Longstreet's brigade, on the north bank of Bull Run at Blackburn's Ford, were two brigades of Union troops being held in reserve. The left flank of this force was made up of four Federal regiments supporting eight artillery pieces. Each of these guns had been strategically placed at Grigsby's log barn on a hill overlooking the run and had been shelling the Confederate positions at Mitchell's Ford, Blackburn's Ford and McLean's Ford since early that morning.[55] Generals Jones, Longstreet, and Ewell received orders shortly after noon to silence these guns.[56] This order was soon retracted, but General Jones, unaware of the countermand, proceeded to carry out the order without the support of Longstreet's and Ewell's brigades.[57]

Jones' three regiments once again crossed Bull Run at McLean's Ford and duplicated their morning's march north toward the Union Mills Road. When they reached the Kincheloe farm, they turned left and moved west for about a mile through Croson's field and along a narrow lane getting into position to attack the Federal left flank.[58] When his

---

[52]Foote, *Civil War*, 1:76-77.

[53]Record of Events Cards for the Fifth S.C.V., Company C, July/August 1861; *Carolina Spartan*, August 22, 1861.

[54]Yorkville *Enquirer*, August 1, 1861.

[55]W. S. Nye, "Action North of Bull Run An Often Overlooked Phase of Battle of First Manassas," *Civil War Times Illustrated*, 4 (April 1965): 48-49. At least two of these four regiments were in Colonel Thomas A. Davies' brigade. Most of the guns were under the command of Captain Henry J. Hunt, Battery M, 2d U.S. Artillery. Ibid.

[56]*Carolina Spartan*, August 22, 1861.

[57]Micah Jenkins to John Jenkins, July 25, 1861, in Thomas, *Career and Character*, 14.

[58]D. R. Jones' battle report, July 23, 1861, O. R., vol. 2, pp. 537-538.

Figure 1
ORGANIZATION OF BEAUREGARD'S INFANTRY, INCLUDING DAVID R. JONES' BRIGADE, IN MID–JULY 1861, PRIOR TO FIRST BATTLE OF MANASSAS*

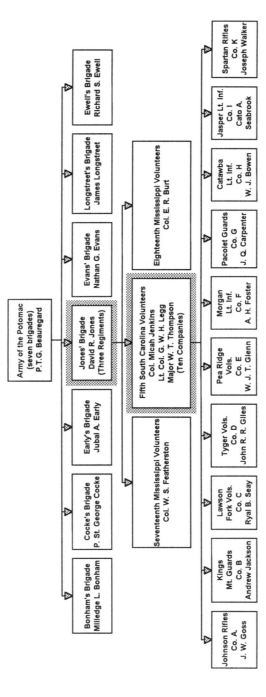

*Does not include those brigades which arrived just prior to the battle to reinforce Beauregard's Army.

brigade was ready to begin its advance, General Jones turned to Colonel Jenkins and said:

> That [Federal] battery has greatly annoyed us; it must be attacked and silenced at all risks and hazards. Lead on to the attack.[59]

Jenkins spoke a few words of encouragement to his men and then gave the commands, "Right face – Forward march." With the Fifth South Carolina in the lead, Jones' brigade approached the Federals' left flank, hoping to take them by surprise. Marching his men through a rough thicket, a ravine, and an almost impassable forest of spruce pines, Jenkins then formed them into a line of battle. His left wing was now plainly visible to the Union soldiers on the hill, who called out, "What troops are you? Are you friend or no?" When they received no response, the bluecoats immediately opened fire with grape shot, shell and musketry.[60]

Once the Eighteenth Mississippi was brought into position in echelon on Jenkins' left rear, he ordered the Fifth South Carolina to advance toward the Union guns some 800 yards ahead. His men moved out, firing as they advanced, crossing fences and descending a steep hill which was thickly covered in laurel to a creek called Little Rocky Run. They had finally reached the bottom of the hill where the Federal artillery was positioned at Grigsby's log barn, and Jenkins halted his men to prepare for the final assault. Describing how this assault began, one soldier in Jenkins' regiment wrote:

> It is truly lamentable to say we were not only exposed to the deadly . . . fire of the enemy in front, but [also to] that of our friends in the rear (the Mississippians) who poured upon our rear a most unfortunate and destructive fire.[61]

The men of the Seventeenth Mississippi had not advanced with Jenkins' troops and were so far to the left rear that some of them had mistaken Jenkins' men for the enemy and fired at them. Then, as the Fifth South Carolina advanced up the hill, the fire from the Federal guns

[59]*Carolina Spartan*, August 22, 1861. This article contains a detailed "account of the . . . daring part taken . . . by the Fifth . . . in the great battle of the . . . 21st of July, 1861 . . ." by a soldier-correspondent in that regiment who wrote using the pseudonym "L." The Yorkville *Enquirer* of August 8, 1861, also contains a similar, but less detailed, account.
[60]Ibid.
[61]Ibid. See also, Nye, "Action North of Bull Run," 49.

MAP 2: FIRST BATTLE OF MANASSAS - JULY 21, 1861

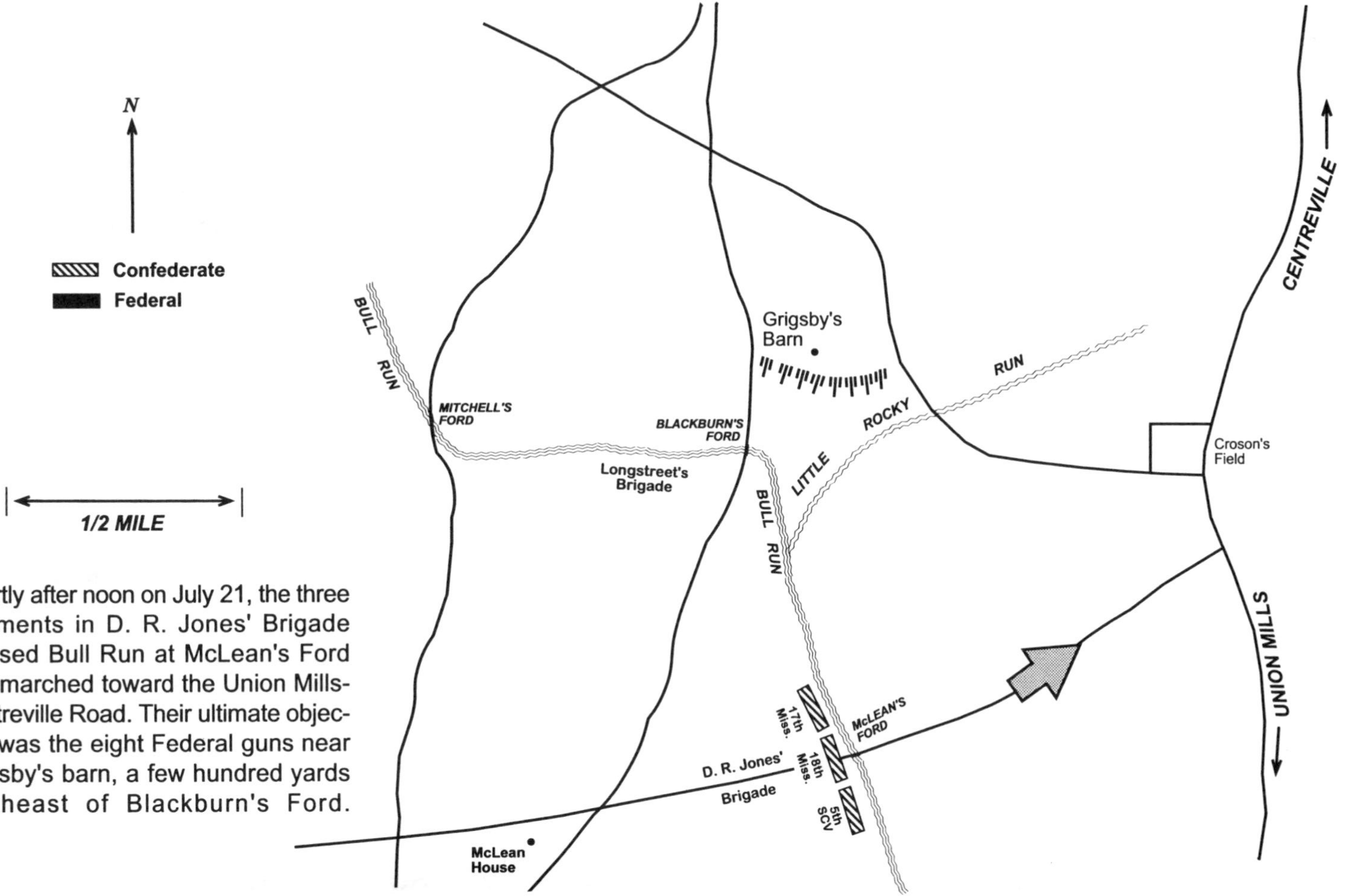

N

Confederate

Federal

1/2 MILE

CENTREVILLE

UNION MILLS

Croson's Field

RUN

ROCKY

LITTLE

Grigsby's Barn

BULL RUN

BLACKBURN'S FORD

Longstreet's Brigade

MITCHELL'S FORD

BULL RUN

McLEAN'S FORD

17th Miss.

18th Miss.

5th SCV

D. R. Jones' Brigade

McLean House

Shortly after noon on July 21, the three regiments in D. R. Jones' Brigade crossed Bull Run at McLean's Ford and marched toward the Union Mills-Centreville Road. Their ultimate objective was the eight Federal guns near Grigsby's barn, a few hundred yards northeast of Blackburn's Ford.

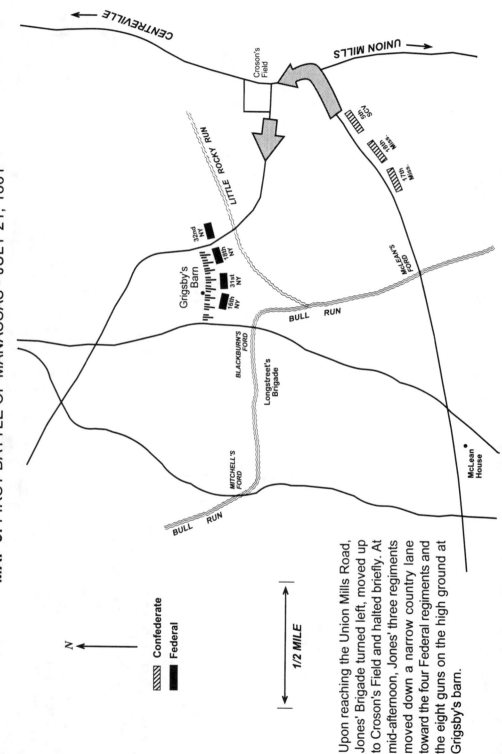

MAP 3: FIRST BATTLE OF MANASSAS - JULY 21, 1861

CENTREVILLE

UNION MILLS

Croson's Field

LITTLE ROCKY RUN

9th S.C.

18th Miss.

17th Miss.

32nd NY

18th NY

31st NY

16th NY

Grigsby's Barn

McLEAN'S FORD

BULL RUN

BLACKBURN'S FORD

Longstreet's Brigade

MITCHELL'S FORD

BULL RUN

McLean House

N

Confederate

Federal

1/2 MILE

Upon reaching the Union Mills Road, Jones' Brigade turned left, moved up to Croson's Field and halted briefly. At mid-afternoon, Jones' three regiments moved down a narrow country lane toward the four Federal regiments and the eight guns on the high ground at Grigsby's barn.

MAP 4: FIRST BATTLE OF MANASSAS - JULY 21, 1861

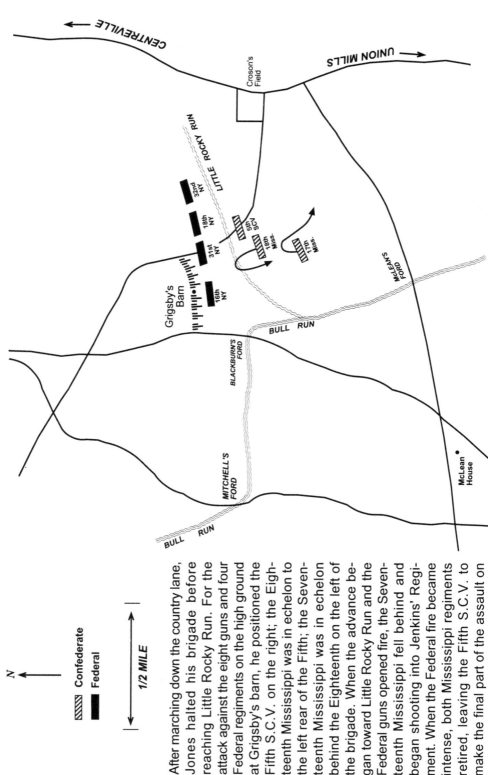

After marching down the country lane, Jones halted his brigade before reaching Little Rocky Run. For the attack against the eight guns and four Federal regiments on the high ground at Grigsby's barn, he positioned the Fifth S.C.V. on the right; the Eighteenth Mississippi was in echelon to the left rear of the Fifth; the Seventeenth Mississippi was in echelon behind the Eighteenth on the left of the brigade. When the advance began toward Little Rocky Run and the Federal guns opened fire, the Seventeenth Mississippi fell behind and began shooting into Jenkins' Regiment. When the Federal fire became intense, both Mississippi regiments retired, leaving the Fifth S.C.V. to make the final part of the assault on its own.

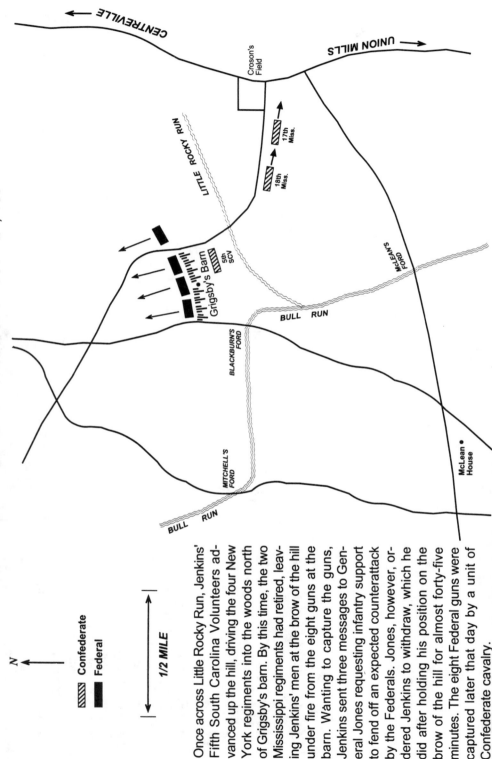

MAP 5: FIRST BATTLE OF MANASSAS - JULY 21, 1861

Once across Little Rocky Run, Jenkins' Fifth South Carolina Volunteers advanced up the hill, driving the four New York regiments into the woods north of Grigsby's barn. By this time, the two Mississippi regiments had retired, leaving Jenkins' men at the brow of the hill under fire from the eight guns at the barn. Wanting to capture the guns, Jenkins sent three messages to General Jones requesting infantry support to fend off an expected counterattack by the Federals. Jones, however, ordered Jenkins to withdraw, which he did after holding his position on the brow of the hill for almost forty-five minutes. The eight Federal guns were captured later that day by a unit of Confederate cavalry.

became so intense it caused the Eighteenth Mississippi to give up.[62] According to one observer, that regiment retired "in confusion, and coming into contact with the 17th Mississippi regiment . . . caused them also to retire."[63] The men of the Fifth Regiment, however, continued their advance, finally almost reaching the crest of the hill. The four Union regiments then retreated into the woods to their rear, leaving their artillery and cavalry to guard their withdrawal.[64]

At this point, Jenkins and his lone Confederate regiment were in position to take the hill and capture the eight guns, but they needed infantry support to defend against a probable Federal counterattack. For forty-five minutes the Fifth South Carolina held its position at the brow of the hill while Jenkins sent messages to General Jones asking for reinforcements. Instead of reinforcements, Jones sent them three separate orders to withdraw, which they finally did, although unwillingly.[65] Jenkins and his men then backed down the hill, recrossed Little Rocky Run, and joined the rest of the brigade which was waiting three-fourths of a mile to the rear.[66]

Even though forced to withdraw, the men of the Fifth South Carolina had passed their first combat test. They had faced a force of superior numbers, supported by artillery, and had not flinched, even when under friendly fire from the Mississippians. Reporting informally to Beauregard after the fight, General Jones modestly stated that Jenkins' Fifth Regiment had played "a little" part in the overall battle. Beauregard replied, "Not a little, [but] a great deal."[67] It was also later reported that even Jefferson Davis had commented upon the "brilliancy and daring of the action."[68]

The turning point in the battle on that hot, dusty Sunday in July occurred between two and three in the afternoon near Henry House Hill on the Confederate side of Bull Run. As the tide of the battle turned, due in no small measure to the gallantry of South Carolinians led by Colonels

---

[62]Jones' battle report, O. R., vol. 2, p. 539. Jones' report indicates that only one company in the Eighteenth Mississippi did not retire with the rest of the regiment: Captain Fontaine's Company H.

[63]*Carolina Spartan*, August 22, 1861. Colonel E. R. Burt later claimed the men in his regiment (Eighteenth Mississippi) had been halted by an impassable gorge. According to an expert on the battle, however, "there are no such ravines in this area; all terrain can readily be negotiated by foot troops." Nye, "Action North of Bull Run," 49.

[64]*Carolina Spartan*, August 22, 1861.

[65]Jenkins' battle report, July 22, 1861, O. R., vol. 2, pp. 541-542; Jones' battle report, O. R., vol. 2, p. 538.

[66]Micah Jenkins to John Jenkins, July 25, 1861, in Thomas, *Career and Character*, 14. Little did General Jones know that the Federal infantry and artillery around Grigsby's barn was about to withdraw back to Centreville, as a result of McDowell's general retreat. Had Jones sent Jenkins the reinforcements, it is likely he could have captured the hill and the guns. Nye, "Action North of Bull Run," 49.

[67]Yorkville *Enquirer*, August 8, 1861.

[68]Ibid. Jenkins and his men had fought what was apparently the only action on the Federals' left flank, north of Bull Run, in the First Battle of Manassas. Nye, "Action North of Bull Run," 49.

Wade Hampton and Nathan Evans, the Federal troops began to fall back in disorder toward the Stone Bridge. They scrambled back across Bull Run toward Centreville in a chaotic and headlong retreat, dropping their haversacks, canteens, and rifles as they fled. Civilians, who had come down from Washington in carriages to witness what they were certain would be a Federal victory, were caught in the panic and confusion on the clogged roads.[69] McDowell's army had been put to rout by a force about equal in size to his own, bringing to a close the first major infantry battle of the war. It was a resounding victory for the Confederate forces of Generals Johnston and Beauregard and a bitter disappointment for the politicians in Washington.

Although not involved in the main part of the battle, Jenkins' regiment had 3 men killed[70] and 23 wounded, some of them by the mistaken fire from Featherston's Seventeenth Mississippi regiment.[71] One of those killed in the attack on the eight guns at Grigsby's barn was Private Thomas W. Fowler from Union District. Earlier that day he had given his knife and thirty dollars to a comrade, saying he had a presentiment that he would be dead by the end of the day.[72] Jenkins himself had narrowly escaped being wounded, and the next day he wrote to Caroline, saying, "three men fell with [sic] five feet of me and a bullet knocked the stirrup from my foot."[73] In this first test of his battlefield leadership, Jenkins had proven himself worthy of his rank. Corporal East, describing the fight to the Yorkville *Enquirer,* wrote:

> Nothing can exceed the devoted love and enthusiastic confidence with which our gallant Colonel inspired his men by his collected, intrepid, prudent and manly conduct during this hour to try his capacity. No colonel has ever had a severer trial . . . in his "maiden effort" and none, we believe, ever acquitted himself more handsomely. Colonel Jenkins has proven himself to be an intrepid, yet rapidly thinking leader.[74]

---

[69]Foote, *Civil War,* 1:77-82.

[70]*Carolina Spartan*, August 1, 1861. The three killed in the Fifth S.C.V. were: Private Hartwell A. McCravy of Captain Walker's company, The Spartan Rifles; Private Thomas W. Fowler of Captain Glenn's company, The Pea Ridge Volunteers; and Private William A. Little of Captain Carpenter's company, The Pacolet Guards.

[71]Micah Jenkins to Caroline Jenkins, July 22, 1861, Micah Jenkins Papers, S.C.L. One officer in the Fifth wrote that the Mississippi soldiers "mistook us for the enemy" and that when their mistake was discovered, "many of them had tears." E. B. Clinton to his half-sister, Mary Elizabeth Brown, August 1, 1861, E. B. Clinton Letters.

[72]Union *Daily Press,* December 9, 1950.

[73]Micah Jenkins to Caroline Jenkins, July 22, 1861, John Jenkins Papers, S.C.L.

[74]Yorkville *Enquirer,* August 1, 1861.

General D. R. Jones was also quite impressed by the fine manner in which Jenkins and his men had handled themselves and wrote in his official battle report:

> Too much cannot be said in praise of the gallantry displayed by Colonel Jenkins and his regiment of South Carolinians.[75]

Although they had failed to capture the eight guns, Jones noted that the Fifth South Carolina had driven the Federals from a "strong position from which [they] completely commanded several fords of Bull Run and the adjacent country for miles around."[76]

After the magnitude of the Manassas victory had set in, many of the Confederate troops, including Jenkins, began to wonder why they were not allowed to pursue McDowell's retreating army on to Alexandria and perhaps into Washington.[77] It was also suggested after the battle that if the Seventeenth and Eighteenth Mississippi regiments had supported the Fifth South Carolina in its attack on the artillery emplacement at Grigsby's barn, a number of retreating Union troops might have been cut off and captured.[78]

When a rumor circulated during the height of the fighting that Jenkins had been killed and his regiment decimated, someone suggested to Jenkins' man-servant, Ben Jones, that he save himself and immediately take the next train back to Warrenton. Ever loyal to Jenkins, however, "Old Ben" refused to even consider such an idea.[79]

Following the battle, Colonel Jenkins was informed that at one point he had been the target of at least four rifles of one of the Mississippi regiments during his advance up the hill toward Grigsby's barn. Just in time, Jenkins' courier rushed up to the Mississippians with two drawn revolvers and yelled that they were aiming at "his colonel." If they shot his colonel, he warned them, he would shoot all four of them. When Jenkins later heard about this, he said there was no doubt that his life had been saved by his young courier, Corporal Joseph R. Witherspoon of Yorkville.[80]

---

[75]Jones' battle report, O. R., vol. 2, p. 539. In his report, General Jones also complimented Jenkins and his men for their "daring advance" and the "coolness with which [they held their] position after [being] completely isolated." Ibid.

[76]Ibid. The eight guns were later captured by a body of Confederate cavalry while in pursuit of the retreating Federals. *Carolina Spartan*, August 22, 1861.

[77]Yorkville *Enquirer*, August 8, 1861; Micah Jenkins to Caroline Jenkins, July 28, 1861, Micah Jenkins Papers, S.C.L.

[78]*Carolina Spartan*, August 1, 1861.

[79]Micah Jenkins to John Jenkins, July 25, 1861, in Thomas, *Career and Character*, 14.

[80]Yorkville *Enquirer*, August 22, 1861. Witherspoon was a theological student and member of Cato Seabrook's Jasper Light Infantry and was acting as Jenkins' messenger to General Jones at the time. W. S. Murray to John Jenkins, August 10, 1861, John Jenkins Papers, S.C.L.

After the battle had ended late that Sunday afternoon, Jenkins' troops, along with the rest of General Jones' brigade, returned to their defensive position on the south bank of Bull Run at McLean's Ford.[81] A day and a half later, two companies of the Fifth South Carolina, along with four companies from the Mississippi regiments, marched to Fairfax Court House, some ten miles north of Centreville. There they were to guard the huge store of arms and supplies which had been abandoned by the retreating Federals. Among the captured supplies were some twenty boxes of the best Harper's Ferry and Springfield muskets, between fifty and one hundred barrels of crackers, and "many barrels of the finest kind of pickled buffalo tongues. . . ."[82]

MAJOR GENERAL
DAVID RUMPH JONES

Four days following the battle, General Beauregard reorganized his army, including General D. R. Jones' Third Brigade. As a result, Jenkins' Fifth Regiment was brigaded with three other South Carolina volunteer regiments: J. B. E. Sloan's Fourth, C. S. Winder's Sixth and J. D. Blanding's Ninth.[83] The Seventeenth and Eighteenth Mississippi regiments were transferred to the Seventh Brigade, under the command of Colonel Nathan G. Evans.[84] Not surprisingly, Jenkins was delighted with these changes and wrote that he had "much more confidence now than before."[85] A private in Jenkins' regiment, Sumter Tarrant, no doubt expressed the sentiment of his fellow soldiers when he wrote:

> Our regiment will [now] be joined with three other S. C. regiments, which I am very glad of – glad to get from those Mississippians – they might shoot us again if we get into another fight.[86]

---

[81]Bond and Coward, eds., *South Carolinians*, 18.

[82]*Carolina Spartan*, August 15, 1861.

[83]Special Orders No. 169, July 25, 1861, O. R., vol. 2, p. 1000. D. R. Jones continued as commander of the Third Brigade after these changes.

[84]Ibid.

[85]Micah Jenkins to Caroline Jenkins, July 30, 1861, Micah Jenkins Papers, S.C.L.

[86]Sumter Tarrant to his brother, Robert Benson Tarrant, July 28, 1861, Papers of the Tarrant, Reese and Radcliffe Families, South Caroliniana Library, University of South Carolina, Columbia, South Carolina. Sumter Tarrant was a private in Company K, Captain Joe Walker's Spartan Rifles.

Figure 2
RESULT OF REORGANIZATION OF BEAUREGARD'S COMMAND (INFANTRY) AND DAVID R. JONES' BRIGADE FOLLOWING THE FIRST BATTLE OF MANASSAS JULY 25, 1861

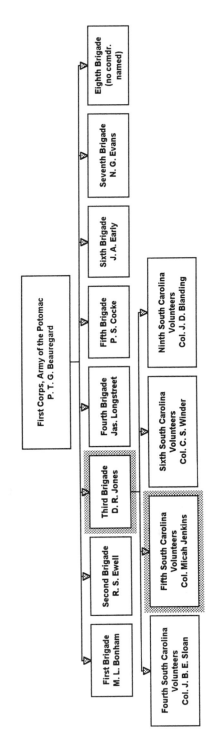

Only days after the First Battle of Manassas, three regiments of South Carolina volunteers were added to the Third Brigade under General David R. Jones: the Fourth, the Sixth and the Ninth. Jones also retained the Fifth South Carolina Volunteers, but he gave up the Seventeenth and Eighteenth Mississippi regiments which were transferred to Nathan G. Evans' Seventh Brigade.

Chapter 8

Expedition To Great Falls

In the afterglow of the momentous Confederate victory at Manassas in July 1861, Micah Jenkins became pensive and melancholy; within a few days of the battle he wrote his wife of how much he longed for peace.[1] He disliked having to remain in Virginia while Caroline was about to give birth, and he was also frustrated by her having to handle business problems back home in his absence. He became furious when he learned that certain Yorkville merchants were pressuring Caroline for payment of overdue bills. He wrote:

> It is cowardly and dishonorable [for] them to be annoying you with bills in my absence, and I will remember them for it when I return.[2]

The idea that able-bodied men would remain at home to make a dollar was bad enough, but for them to pressure a soldier's wife for payment while he was away risking his life for his country was repugnant to Jenkins.

---

[1] Micah Jenkins to Caroline Jenkins, July 26, 1861, Micah Jenkins Papers, D.U.L.; Micah Jenkins to Caroline Jenkins, July 29, 1861, Micah Jenkins Papers, S.C.L.
[2] Micah Jenkins to Caroline Jenkins, July 29, 1861, Micah Jenkins Papers, S.C.L.

Two weeks after the battle, Caroline gave birth to their fourth child, a boy whom they named Whitemarsh. While they had hoped for a daughter, Micah wrote her saying, "perhaps it is better so. In stormy times like these it looks as if the delicate woman should not be ushered into the world."[3] Jenkins longed for his lovely and intelligent wife, and wrote her how much he missed taking walks and riding horses together as they had done so many times in Yorkville before the war.[4]

By the end of the summer of 1861, the military academy in Yorkville had been closed, but Caroline was still living at the school with her baby and three young sons. When she had recovered her strength from the birth of her child, she decided to move temporarily to her father's new plantation, called "Burwood," near Midway, South Carolina. Jenkins urged her to take the carriage and horses with her because if they were left in Yorkville unattended they would "go to ruin."[5] With the school closed, he was also worried about his personal finances. He told Caroline to be careful with the money he sent her, and warned her:

> If I get shot, money will be terribly scarce for you and
> may be anyway: so we must look long at a dollar before
> spending it.[6]

Jenkins' longing for his wife and children, as well as his apprehension concerning his neglected business affairs, was no different from that of most other men in the Fifth Regiment during the summer of 1861. Their willingness to sacrifice by fighting in Virginia was accompanied by the hope that the war would end quickly. In the months that followed the Battle of Manassas, however, as the opposing armies faced each other from their static positions in northern Virginia, it became increasingly apparent that this was not to be a short war.[7]

Three days after the battle of July 21, Jenkins' regiment, with the other three South Carolina regiments in General Jones' newly-structured brigade, moved about eight miles north of Manassas Junction to Fairfax Court House.[8] At Camp Pettus they happily pitched their tents which they had been without for the previous eight days.[9]

In the first week of September, General D. R. Jones ordered Jenkins to make an "armed reconnaissance" some twenty miles beyond the Confederate lines. He was to lead not only his regiment, but also a

---

[3]Ibid., August 9, 1861.
[4]Micah Jenkins to Caroline Jenkins, August 16 and 27, 1861, Micah Jenkins Papers, D.U.L.
[5]Micah Jenkins to Caroline Jenkins, September 8, 1861, Micah Jenkins Papers, S.C.L.
[6]Micah Jenkins to Caroline Jenkins, September 11, 1861, Micah Jenkins Papers, D.U.L.
[7]Catton, *Centennial History*, 1:471-473.
[8]Micah Jenkins to Caroline Jenkins, July 25, 1861, Micah Jenkins Papers, S.C.L.
[9]E. B. Clinton to his half-sister, Mary Elizabeth Brown, August 1, 1861, E. B. Clinton Letters.

squadron of cavalry and a battery of artillery on a night march to Great
Falls, Virginia. A regiment of Union troops in George A. McCall's brigade
was encamped there, on the other side of the Potomac River, guarding
an aqueduct which supplied Washington with water.[10]

Jenkins' troops left Camp Pettus at nine o'clock in the evening on
September 3, and after marching all night, reached Great Falls at seven
the next morning. He carefully positioned his guns and men on the south
bank of the river and at eight o'clock opened fire on the buildings and
troops on the other side.[11] As his artillery shelled a wooden barracks and
the surrounding camp, his sharpshooters picked off confused Union
soldiers. Captain Ryal B. Seay, of the Lawson Fork Volunteers
(Company C), killed two Federals with his "long ranger" rifle.[12] Far in
front of the Confederate advance pickets, and in danger of being cut off
now that his position had been revealed, Jenkins withdrew his men after
an hour of firing. His small force of about 675 men then started the
arduous return march to Camp Pettus after having killed or wounded
some 50 Federal soldiers.[13]

The entire expedition was a success, but the men had marched
almost forty miles in less than twenty hours, and some were simply too
exhausted to make it back to camp on their own. Wagons were quickly
dispatched for the stragglers until all the men had been returned safely
to Camp Pettus. Worn out but proud, one soldier wrote:

> [W]e are the only regiment as yet, in this division, [which
> has] marched to the banks of the Potomac and [which]
> fought the enemy across it.[14]

According to Jenkins, General Jones "expressed himself much
pleased with the manner in which . . . the expedition [was carried out]."[15]
The men in the Fifth South Carolina Volunteers were quickly building a

---

[10]In McCall's report on this skirmish, he identifies the regiment only as the "Seventh Infantry."
McCall's report, September 5, 1861, O. R., vol. 5, p. 127. Based on the make-up of McCall's division on
October 15, 1861, the regiment in question was probably the Seventh Pennsylvania Reserve Infantry. O.
R., vol. 5, p. 17.
[11]Micah Jenkins to Caroline Jenkins, September 6, 1861, Micah Jenkins Papers, D.U.L. See also,
Report of Lt. Charles W. Squires, September 4, 1861, O. R., vol. 51, part 1, p. 39. Squires was in charge
of Jenkins' artillery on the expedition. Regarding the night march to Great Falls, he said that it was so
dark, "we could scarcely see the heads of our horses." Ibid.
[12]Yorkville Enquirer, September 26, 1861.
[13]Ibid., September 19 and 26, 1861; Carolina Spartan, October 3, 1861. McCall's report on the
skirmish did not provide the number of his casualties. He merely said that the Confederates had fired
about "50 shells and shot, mostly too high." McCall's report, September 5, 1861, O. R., vol. 5, p. 127.
[14]Yorkville Enquirer, September 26, 1861.
[15]Micah Jenkins to John Jenkins, September 11, 1861, John Jenkins Papers, S.C.L.

solid reputation, as shown by the opinion of a soldier in another regiment, who wrote:

> [The Fifth] is the best equipped regiment from South Carolina in the Army of the Potomac. They are armed with Enfield rifles and Minnie [*sic*] muskets and know well how to use them with effect upon the enemy.[16]

After the Great Falls expedition, the Fifth Regiment moved forward and began performing picket duty near Munson's Hill, about five miles from Washington, in a schedule of rotation with other regiments.[17] At Munson's Hill they sometimes saw Professor Thaddeus Lowe's military hot-air balloon, sent up by the Federals each day to observe Confederate positions.[18] During one tour of picket duty at Munson's Hill, Colonel Jenkins climbed a tall white oak where he had a clear view of the dome of the Capitol in Washington.[19] Jenkins wrote that his man-servant, Ben, had accompanied him on one such trip and had not only seen Washington but "cooked within rifle shot of the enemy."[20]

The Confederate high command abandoned the advance position at Munson's Hill on September 28, and Jenkins' regiment returned briefly to Camp Pettus near Fairfax Court House.[21] The army's pullback continued into October, and by the middle of the month, Jenkins and his men were once again camped along Bull Run near McLean's Ford where they had fought three months earlier.[22] They had been there only a week, however, when they were on the march once again.

On October 21, a brigade made up of Mississippians and Virginians led by General Nathan Evans of South Carolina soundly defeated a large Union force near Leesburg, Virginia, at Ball's Bluff on the Potomac River.[23] To reinforce Evans against a possible Federal counterattack, Jenkins and his regiment were marched from Bull Run to Leesburg, but they arrived too late to participate in any fighting.[24] The expected counterattack did not occur, but Jenkins and his men remained bivouacked in the woods outside Leesburg for over a week. Finally, they returned to their camp near McLean's Ford, but according to one officer,

[16]Yorkville *Enquirer*, October 10, 1861. The designation "Army of Northern Virginia" did not appear until the spring of 1862.
[17]Micah Jenkins to Caroline Jenkins, September 23, 1861, Micah Jenkins Papers, S.C.L.
[18]*Carolina Spartan*, October 3, 1861.
[19]McConnell, "Recollections," 3.
[20]Micah Jenkins to Caroline Jenkins, September 28, 1861, Micah Jenkins Papers, D.U.L.
[21]Foote, *Civil War*, 1:103; McConnell, "Recollections," 3; Micah Jenkins to Caroline Jenkins, September 28, 1861, Micah Jenkins Papers, S.C.L.
[22]Micah Jenkins to Caroline Jenkins, October 18, 1861, Micah Jenkins Papers, S.C.L.
[23]Foote, *Civil War*, 1:105-108.
[24]Micah Jenkins to Caroline Jenkins, October 29, 1861, Micah Jenkins Papers, S.C.L.; Bond and Coward, eds., *South Carolinians*, 26.

the march, "a distance of 26 miles, was very severe, the weather being so cold and wet. . . ."[25] A war correspondent wrote that, during this long march, Colonel Jenkins,

> [f]requently as he rode along the ranks . . . would discover some old or feeble soldier nearly worn down by fatigue. On these occasions he would dismount from his horse and compel the tired private to take his place and ride till he was thoroughly rested, the Colonel shouldering his musket and marching with the men. Then he would burden himself with an extra knapsack or two, and then trudge along for a few miles [in the ranks]. There are few men in his station who would make such sacrifices . . . [and] still fewer . . . who can lead their regiments into danger with greater reliance upon their devotion to his command. . . .[26]

The most disappointing news of 1861 for Jenkins and his soldiers came when the Federals successfully invaded South Carolina in early November. Within only a few days, both Beaufort and Port Royal were in Union hands, and the entire coast of the South Carolina was threatened, especially the sea islands. Concerned for the safety of his family on Edisto Island and his wife and sons near Orangeburg, Jenkins wrote to Caroline that he could not "recover from the shock of the Yankees' success in South Carolina."[27] All the men in the regiment felt a great concern for "the families [along the coast] who have been driven from their sea island homes. . . ."[28]

Federal troops occupied Edisto Island in late November and found that the plantations had already been abandoned by the planters and their families. According to Jenkins' brother, John, the occupying soldiers sacked the Jenkins' plantation at Bennett's Point, shot the geese and stole the potatoes. Just prior to the Federal occupation of the island, John Jenkins burned some fourteen thousand pounds of the family's cotton, worth a great sum of money, to keep it from falling into Union hands.[29] The Federal occupation of Edisto Island was especially

---

[25]E. B. Clinton to Mary Elizabeth Brown, November 21, 1861, E. B. Clinton Letters. In fact, the march was so severe that it was blamed for two deaths in the regiment, including that of Orderly Sergeant R. E. L. Ewart of the Spartan Rifles, who died on November 21.

[26]Charleston *Daily Courier*, January 27, 1862. This article gives a brief history of the Fifth South Carolina Volunteers and was prepared by the noted Confederate war correspondent F. G. DeFontaine, who wrote using the pseudonym "Personne." The article was later reprinted in its entirety in the *Carolina Spartan* on June 12, 1862.

[27]Micah Jenkins to Caroline Jenkins, November 17, 1861, Micah Jenkins Papers, S.C.L.

[28]Yorkville *Enquirer*, December 5, 1861.

[29]John Jenkins to his wife, Marcelline, December 4, 1861, John Jenkins Papers, S.C.L.

frustrating to Micah Jenkins, who wrote that he and his men were now needed more in South Carolina than in Virginia, because "of our experience and training."[30] For a while it appeared they would be sent back to South Carolina to meet this threat, but in late November they learned that they would spend the winter near Centreville, Virginia.[31]

Meanwhile, the Fifth South Carolina had been assigned two six-pound guns, detached from the Calhoun Artillery, manned by men selected from within the regiment. This battery was under the command of First Lieutenant F. G. Latham, of the Pacolet Guards; the same officer had flagged down the approaching train the previous June preventing a rear-end crash near Columbia. The men in the Fifth Regiment proudly called it the "Star Battery," and its forty men drilled twice a day. Jenkins' troops were equally proud of their fine regimental brass band under the command of Drum Major J. B. Weiss.[32]

During October and November, the army's Department of Northern Virginia, Potomac District, under Beauregard's command, was organized into four divisions.[33] One of the new divisions, the Third, was placed under the command of Major General James Longstreet. D. R. Jones' Second Brigade, still consisting of the Fourth, Fifth, Sixth and Ninth Regiments of South Carolina Volunteers, was assigned to this division.[34] Longstreet was clearly happy to have the Fifth South Carolina in his division and told members of his staff that he considered Jenkins to be "the best colonel in the army."[35] At the same time, Longstreet's aide-de-camp, Thomas J. Goree, described the Fifth South Carolina as "one of the finest, if not the finest, regiments in the army."[36]

Longstreet reviewed his new division for the first time on November 28 in an open field near Centreville. For each of the division's ten regiments, General Beauregard had designed battle flags which he personally presented to each regimental commander during the review. Upon receiving his battle flag from the general, each colonel made a few

---

[30]Micah Jenkins to Caroline Jenkins, November 17, 1861, Micah Jenkins Papers, S.C.L.

[31]Ibid., November 27, 1861.

[32]Yorkville *Enquirer*, November 21, and December 5, 1861. The two six-pound guns were only a temporary addition to the regiment, and the Star Battery no longer existed by the spring of 1862.

[33]General Orders No. 15, October 22, 1861, O. R., vol. 5, pp. 913-914, as modified by General Orders No. 18, November 16, 1861, O. R., vol. 5, pp. 960-961. See also, Yorkville *Enquirer*, December 12, 1861.

[34]Yorkville *Enquirer*, December 12, 1861. Longstreet had been promoted to major general in command of the Third Division, Beauregard's First Corps, on October 7, 1861.

[35]Thomas J. Goree to his Mother, Sarah Williams Kittrell Goree, November 11, 1862, in Thomas W. Cutrer, ed., *Longstreet's Aide: The Civil War Letters of Major Thomas J. Goree* (Charlottesville, Virginia: University Press of Virginia, 1995), 53.

[36]Ibid. In describing Jenkins, Goree, added, "I wish that all the officers of our Army were half so abstemious, but it is not the case." Ibid.

Figure 3
ORGANIZATION OF DEPARTMENT OF NORTHERN VIRGINIA, POTOMAC DISTRICT, FALL 1861

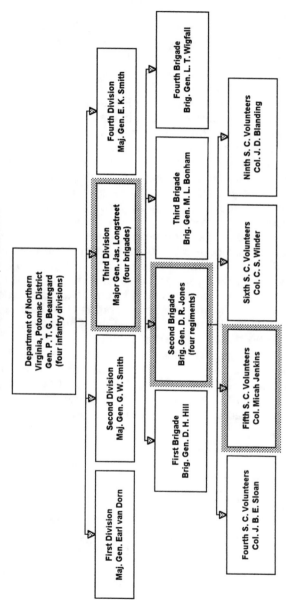

At the reorganization in October–November 1861, Beauregard's command was designated the Potomac District of the Department of Northern Virginia. He was assigned four infantry divisions, including the Third Division commanded by Major General James Longstreet. D. R. Jones' brigade, which included the Fifth South Carolina Volunteers, was designated the Second Brigade and placed in Longstreet's division. The make-up of Jones' brigade did not change at this time. Gen. Orders No. 18, Nov. 16, 1861, O.R., vol. 5, p. 961.

remarks.   Colonel Jenkins, accepting the flag on behalf of the Fifth
Regiment, said:

> Our native soil [in South Carolina] is now impressed with
> the footsteps of the fell invader; his beacon fires are
> lighted upon our headlands. To us a battle flag can only
> be one under which we must conquer or die. As such, I
> accept this.[37]

During this review and presentation, General Longstreet watched
approvingly, mounted "on his dashing bay horse, in his nodding feather
and flowing auburn beard. . . ."[38]

Soon after his brigade had been assigned to Longstreet's division, D.
R. Jones went to Richmond to seek an exchange of commands. As a
result, Longstreet recommended Jenkins for the command of Jones'
brigade, saying:

> [O]ne of the brigades of my division belongs permanently
> to my command – D. R. Jones' brigade, now commanded
> by Colonel Jenkins. . . . I propose [to] make Jenkins a
> brigadier, and let the troops understand that it is to be his
> brigade. . . .   Besides being much liked by his men,
> Colonel Jenkins is one of the finest officers of this army.
> I think him as well worthy and deserving of the position
> of brigadier as any officer in my acquaintance.[39]

General Beauregard enthusiastically endorsed the recommendation,
saying, "Colonel Jenkins . . . has already been warmly recommended by
me as a brigadier general."[40]

In spite of these recommendations, however, Jefferson Davis
refused to approve Jenkins' promotion. When D. R. Jones was later
promoted, vacating the position of brigadier general of the Second

---

[37]Yorkville *Enquirer*, December 12, 1861. Whatever originally motivated Jenkins and his men to
volunteer and fight for the Confederacy, they now had a strong, new reason: the defense of their homes
and families in South Carolina from the invading Federal forces. For a discussion of how this factor
affected the attitudes of Southern soldiers, see James M. McPherson, *What They Fought For: 1861-
1865* (Baton Rouge, Louisiana: Louisiana State University Press, 1994), 18-25.

[38]Yorkville *Enquirer*, December 12, 1861.

[39]Longstreet to William Porcher Miles, December 19, 1861, O. R., vol. 5, pp. 1001-1002.

[40]O. R., vol. 5, pp. 1001-1002. According to Jenkins, General Beauregard also told General D. R.
Jones in October that he had written to Richmond "urging strongly" Jenkins' promotion. Micah Jenkins to
Caroline Jenkins, October 31, 1861, Micah Jenkins Papers, D.U.L. This earlier recommendation by
Beauregard has not been located.

Brigade, it was filled not by Jenkins but by General Richard H. Anderson.[41]   By mid-December, when Beauregard had endorsed Longstreet's recommendation of Jenkins for the command of Jones' Brigade, Beauregard had already fallen out of favor with Jefferson Davis;[42] this may partly explain why Jenkins was not promoted in 1861.

While the organizational changes were taking place throughout the army in Virginia, Asbury Coward became ill and was allowed to return to South Carolina in late November for treatment.   When he arrived in Charleston, he was taken to the home of his wife's parents, where he was nursed back to health. A few nights after his arrival, a fire started in Charleston at the foot of Hasell Street and was quickly spread by a high wind to nearby buildings.[43]   The blaze reached the Gas Works, which exploded, and then destroyed buildings and homes along both sides of Meeting Street. The Mills House at the corner of Queen and Meeting Streets, where General Robert E. Lee had dined earlier that evening, was spared, but the fire continued to spread

LIEUTENANT GENERAL
RICHARD HERON ANDERSON

westward. It destroyed the building where D. F. Jamison and other delegates had signed the Ordinance of Secession, as well as many church buildings and 575 private homes, in a swath of destruction of over 540 acres.[44] Of the attempt to control the blaze, Coward said, "It was like trying to put out Vesuvius with water from a thimble."[45]

At their winter quarters in Centreville, Virginia, the men in the Fifth Regiment were so concerned about the disaster in Charleston that they

---

[41]Richard Heron Anderson was born in South Carolina and had graduated from the United States Military Academy in the class of 1842. He had served as a lieutenant in the war with Mexico and was forty years old. He had just completed his duty at Pensacola, Florida, on the Gulf of Mexico. No person could deny that he was well qualified to command the Second Brigade. Freeman, *Lee's Lieutenants*, 1:157; Bond and Coward, eds., *South Carolinians*, 28. Anderson was ordered to Virginia on February 15, 1862, to assume command of his new brigade. Special Orders No. 48, February 15, 1862, O. R., vol. 5, p. 1074.

[42]Foote, *Civil War*, 1:124-125.

[43]Bond and Coward, eds., *South Carolinians*, 27-28. The fire started on the night of December 11 and burned itself out the next day.

[44]Walter T. Fraser, Jr., *Charleston! Charleston! The History of a Southern City* (Columbia, South Carolina: University of South Carolina Press, 1989), 253-254.

[45]Bond and Coward, eds., *South Carolinians*, 28.

raised money to send to the victims of the fire. Jenkins' men were also saddened by "the destruction of the Institute [Hall] and St. Andrews Hall, consecrated as they were last December to the cause of liberty and State sovereignty."[46]   There was, perhaps, something ominous in the fiery destruction of these buildings only one year after they had been used by the Secession Convention for the meetings which took South Carolina out of the Union.

As the turbulent year of 1861 ended, units of the Fifth Regiment performed picket duty in Germantown, Virginia, near Fairfax Court House on New Year's Eve. On the last night of the year, about a dozen men in Cato Seabrook's Jasper Light Infantry gathered in a small cabin in Germantown and were treated to a "New Year's feast" provided by a generous black resident of the village.[47]

From his cold tent at Centreville, three days before the year came to a close, Jenkins wrote to Caroline:

> I picture myself [at] the cozy fireside at home, with so many loved ones around it, [and] I yearn to be there to sit with my dear wife on my knee . . . your dear head on my shoulder, [and] to see our little ones clustered around us . . . and I pray that my God may not deny the realization to me.[48]

He, like every other man in the Fifth South Carolina, longed to be home with his family, especially during the Christmas season.   But this separation from their loved ones was another hardship of the war that they were forced to endure. Perhaps Corporal East best described the loneliness the men felt at the end of 1861 when he wrote to the Yorkville *Enquirer*:

> Twelve months ago to-day, our little State, all alone, stood out from the breakers on which the old Union had wrecked, to try the dark unknown waters of a mighty revolution. We were then feeling the first thrill of war, wild and deep; now we have grown old in its experiences. Just one year ago this blessed day, we were beneath far-off Southern skies, with long-familiar faces around us; now . . . many, many, long miles lie between us.[49]

---

[46]Yorkville *Enquirer*, January 2, 1862.
[47]Ibid., January 16, 1862.
[48]Micah Jenkins to Caroline Jenkins, December 27, 1861, Micah Jenkins Papers, S.C.L.
[49]Yorkville *Enquirer*, January 16, 1862. This was one of the last letters ever written to the *Enquirer* by Corporal William W. East. He was severely wounded exactly five months later during the Battle of Seven Pines, and died on his way to his father's home in Laurens District, South Carolina. Ibid., July 3, 1862.

Chapter 9

The Confederate Army Reorganizes

As the weather in Northern Virginia began to turn bitter cold, the men of the Fifth South Carolina were still living in tents, which were described by one of the soldiers as "mere apologies for shelter from the rain, snow, sleet and wintry blast."[1] Colonel Jenkins shared this hardship with his men and wrote of how it felt to sit in his tent, "with the bitter cold wind flapping the 'fly' and the comfortless interior. . . ."[2] Finally, in early January of 1862, they got the order to set up their winter quarters on the outskirts of Centreville, Virginia, and happily turned in their flimsy tents.

Jenkins' men combed the countryside for logs and wood to build their winter huts. When they had found enough wood, they would lay out chest-high log walls, filling the open spaces with mud. Some huts had wood roofs, while others used tenting or canvas covered with oilcloth. Many had flues, capped off with flour barrels, while the more substantial ones had brick chimneys with fireplaces.[3] When the men

[1]Yorkville *Enquirer*, January 23, 1862.
[2]Micah Jenkins to Caroline Jenkins, December 27, 1861, Micah Jenkins Papers, S.C.L.
[3]Yorkville *Enquirer*, December 12, 1861.

finally moved into their huts, Private Henry C. Conner wrote his sweetheart:

> [W]e have beene [*sic*] in ours something better than a week and are enjoying our selves finely and I think we will get along first rate if we are allowed to stay in them the balance of the winter.[4]

Picket duty, which was performed in advance of the Confederate lines without tents or shelter, was particularly hard on the men. Private Conner said, "We had to relieve one another onest every hour for it was so could [*sic*] we could not stand [it] any longer. . . ."[5] Even though men on picket duty were instructed not to build fires to cut the chill, this order was not always obeyed.[6]

By February the main topic in camp was reenlistment. Most of the Confederate volunteers in Virginia, including Jenkins' men, had enlisted for only one year, and the great majority of these enlistments were due to expire during April 1862. This created a serious problem for the government in Richmond, which needed to devise a way to keep these experienced soldiers in the service of the Confederacy for the remainder of the war. The main inducement to reenlist was the "Furlough and Bounty Act," passed by the Confederate Congress at the end of 1861. This law promised each soldier who reenlisted for three years, "or for the war," a bounty of fifty dollars and a furlough of up to sixty days, along with free transportation to and from his home.[7] The law, however, also permitted reenlisting soldiers to reorganize into new regiments and to elect their own company and regimental officers.[8] These problems led to a massive reorganization of the Confederate army in Virginia, all of which had to be completed before the Federal forces began their spring offensive toward Richmond.

In one of the most controversial of the organizational changes, Jefferson Davis transferred General Beauregard to Kentucky at the end of January, while General Joe Johnston was retained in Northern Virginia

---

[4]Henry C. Connor to his sweetheart, Ellen O'Leary, January 27, 1862, Henry Calvin Conner Papers, South Caroliniana Library, University of South Carolina, Columbia, South Carolina. For the typed version of these letters, see Katherine Conner Black, comp., "Henry C. Conner Letters," in *Recollections and Reminiscences 1861-1865 through World War I*, vol. 2 (South Carolina Division of the United Daughters of the Confederacy, privately printed, 1991), 2-158. Henry Calvin Conner was a private in the Catawba Light Infantry, Company H of the Fifth South Carolina Volunteers. After the army's reorganization in April 1862, he served as a sergeant in Company G of Jenkins' Palmetto Sharpshooters.
[5]Ibid.
[6]Ibid.
[7]Bruce Catton, *The Centennial History of the Civil War*, vol. 2, *Terrible Swift Sword* (Garden City, New York: Doubleday & Co., Inc., 1963), 175; Foote, *Civil War*, 1:235; Freeman, *Lee's Lieutenants*, 1:130.
[8]Yorkville *Enquirer*, January 2, 1862.

to command the Confederate forces
there. The loss of Beauregard, who
had led them throughout all of 1861,
was difficult for the men of the Fifth
Regiment to accept; one wrote that
"the volunteers regret exceedingly the
necessity for this change. . . ."[9]

By the end of February, Brigadier
General Richard H. Anderson had
arrived at the Second Brigade's winter
quarters near Centreville to replace
D. R. Jones and assume his
command which included Jenkins'
regiment. As soon as he arrived,
Anderson instituted a strict training
schedule for the men, who had been
allowed to relax after going into winter
quarters. A few days after Anderson's
arrival, John W. McLure, an officer in
the Fifth Regiment, wrote:

GENERAL P. T. G. BEAUREGARD

> He is stirring us up considerably [with] roll calls at
> reveille and tattoo to be resumed, regimental guard duty,
> and worse still, four drills daily. . . .[10]

Colonel Jenkins had been on furlough in South Carolina in January,
during which time he pondered the possible effects of the upcoming
reorganization on the Fifth South Carolina. Uncertain of how many men
in his regiment would reenlist, he wrote to his wife on his return to
Richmond:

> I am applying for permission to raise a Legion and have
> the backing of three Representatives to my application,
> but whether it will be granted or not I cannot say.[11]

---

[9]Ibid., February 13, 1862.
[10]J. W. McLure to his wife, Kate McLure, February 26, 1862, McLure Family Papers, South
Caroliniana Library, University of South Carolina, Columbia, South Carolina. John W. McLure was a
lieutenant in the "Pacolet Guards," Company G of the Fifth South Carolina. He later became a member
of the Palmetto Sharpshooters and served as its quartermaster. McLure's wife was Jane Catherine
Poulton McLure, whom he called "Kate."
[11]Micah Jenkins to Caroline Jenkins, February 6, 1862 (the original letter is misdated 1861), Micah
Jenkins Papers, D.U.L. In his letter (or application) to the secretary of war, Jenkins requested the
authority to "raise a Legion for the War, to consist in the initiation of Battalions of Infantry developable
into Regiments and a proportionate cavalry and artillery force." The governor of South Carolina, M. L.
Bonham, endorsed the application and referred to Jenkins as "a gentlemen of superior military
attainment. . . ." Jenkins to the secretary of war (undated), National Archives, Unfiled Papers and Slips

While in Richmond, he submitted this application to the office of the secretary of war, Judah P. Benjamin. Jenkins then traveled by train to Manassas Junction, joined his men in their winter quarters at nearby Centreville, and reported to his new commander, General Anderson.[12] Several weeks later, Jenkins said that he was still having "considerable doubt about [the Fifth South Carolina] volunteering in Virginia" and even wrote of returning to South Carolina with part of the regiment to raise his new legion.[13] His application to the secretary of war, however, was apparently never acted upon, and his idea of a legion was later abandoned.

Meanwhile, in February 1862, Federal troops under General Ambrose Burnside had captured Roanoke Island, North Carolina; this had the effect of opening up a second front which threatened Richmond from the rear.[14] The Confederate commander in Northern Virginia, General Joe Johnston, then advised Jefferson Davis that his army could no longer defend Richmond from its present position in the Manassas area. At the beginning of March, Johnston began withdrawing his army so that it would be closer to Richmond.[15]

As a part of the general withdrawal, Jenkins and his men abandoned their winter quarters in Centreville on March 8 and began a long march south toward the Confederate capital.[16] It took them two weeks to reach Orange Courthouse, some fifty miles south of Manassas Junction, and when they got there, only three companies of reenlistees had been formed in the Fifth Regiment.[17] The men were strongly urged to reenlist as they continued towards Richmond because the expiration of their one-year enlistments was then less than three weeks away. By the first week in April, those companies of the Fifth Regiment in which a sufficient number of men had agreed to reenlist had elected Colonel Jenkins as their commander without opposition. There were, however, only enough reenlistees at that time to form a battalion.[18] At the same time, efforts were under way in Yorkville, South Carolina, to recruit additional

---

Belonging in Confederate Compiled Service Records, R. G. 109, series M347.

[12]Micah Jenkins to Caroline Jenkins, February 6, [1862], Micah Jenkins Papers, D.U.L.

[13]Micah Jenkins to John Jenkins, March 2, 1862, John Jenkins Papers, S.C.L.

[14]Foote, *Civil War*, 1:230.

[15]Catton, *Centennial History*, 2:177.

[16]J. W. McLure to "Doctor," March 25, 1862, McLure Family Papers.

[17]Ibid. A captain in the Fourth South Carolina Volunteers wrote:

> You see, it takes sixty-four men to hold a company, and should they fail to get that number by the 14th of this month, they will be attached to companies who already have the required number to fill them up to their full strength. . . .

Captain William Anderson to his wife, Lucretia McFall Anderson, April 1, 1862, William Anderson Collection, Special Collections Department, University of Virginia Library (hereafter U.V.L.), University of Virginia, Charlottesville, Virginia.

[18]Micah Jenkins to Caroline Jenkins, April 4, 1862, Micah Jenkins Papers, S.C.L.

volunteers to bring the new companies up to their necessary numbers.[19] In order to "encourage" veteran soldiers to reenlist, the Confederate Congress passed a Conscription Act in April 1862.[20] It provided for the conscription of all able-bodied white males between the ages of eighteen and thirty-five, with certain exceptions, for a period of three years or for the war if it ended earlier than that. Thus, most of the Confederate soldiers in Virginia faced the very real possibility of being conscripted unless they voluntarily reenlisted. The threat of the draft no doubt pressured the men in Jenkins' regiment to reenlist, and it was also used to recruit new volunteers at home.[21]

The men of the Fifth Regiment finally reached Richmond on April 14, after what Lieutenant Joseph Banks Lyle described as a "very trying march of more than 100 miles through the rain and snow."[22] Their one-year enlistments had expired the day before, and during the next several days Jenkins continued working to organize a new regiment, having given up his plan to raise a legion. On April 27, he wrote to his wife that he had finally succeeded in organizing his new regiment, which he called "Jenkins' Palmetto Sharpshooters."[23] Consisting of twelve companies, it was made up primarily of reenlistees from three of the original regiments of volunteers from Jenkins' native state. Five of the companies were made up mostly of men who had previously served with Jenkins in the former Fifth South Carolina;[24] four others contained soldiers from the former Fourth South Carolina, and the remaining three

---

[19]Yorkville *Enquirer*, March 27, 1862. Corporal William East, of the Jasper Light Infantry, was sent to Yorkville for twelve days of recruiting on behalf of the Fifth Regiment. This is the same soldier who had written so frequently to the Yorkville *Enquirer* using the pseudonym "Our Corporal."

[20]Many Southerners resented conscription as a Confederate encroachment upon their cherished individualism and states' rights. On the tension between states' rights and the action taken by the Confederate (central) government to implement the draft, see Emory M. Thomas, *The Confederate Nation 1861-1865* (New York: Harper and Row, Publishers, 1979), 152-155.

[21]Yorkville *Enquirer*, March 27, 1862. This article stated, "Now is the time gentlemen; a draft will be upon the District [of York] by the 15th of April, unless you come forward, and meet the just and equal requisition of a bleeding country."

[22]J. Banks Lyle to Dora McArthur, April 16, 1862, J. B. Lyle Letters, Private Collection, Elmer Oris Parker, Columbia, South Carolina. Joseph Banks Lyle, at the time he wrote this letter, was first lieutenant of Company C, Fifth South Carolina Volunteers. He was later promoted to captain of Company C, and at times was in temporary command of the regiment. He writes to Medora McArthur, his fiancee, whom he married in early 1865.

[23]Micah Jenkins to Caroline Jenkins, April 27, 1862, John Jenkins Papers, S.C.L.

[24]The five companies from the former Fifth Regiment, which furnished the majority of men to form Jenkins' Palmetto Sharpshooters at the reorganization, with names of captains as of April 1862, were:

    1. Johnson Rifles, Captain John W. Goss.
    2. Spartan Rifles, Captain John H. Evins.
    3. Jasper Light Infantry, Captain J. Newton Withers.
    4. Morgan Light Infantry, Captain Alfred H. Foster.
    5. Pacolet Guards, Captain Jacob Q. Carpenter.

Yorkville *Enquirer*, May 8, 1862.

Figure 4

FIELD OFFICERS AND COMPANY COMMANDERS OF THE PALMETTO SHARPSHOOTERS WHEN THE REGIMENT WAS FORMED IN APRIL 1862

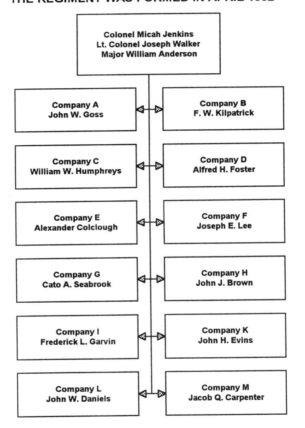

When Jenkins formed the Palmetto Sharpshooters in April 1862, the regiment was made up of twelve companies instead of the customary ten for Confederate regiments at that time. Five of the companies (Goss', Evins', Seabrook's, Foster's and Carpenter's) were made up of men from the former Fifth South Carolina Volunteers. Four of the companies (Kilpatrick's, Daniels', Garvin's and Humphreys') were from the former Fourth South Carolina. The remaining three companies (Colclough's, Lee's and Brown's) were from the former Ninth South Carolina Volunteers. There was no Company J in the Palmetto Sharpshooters.

were men from the former Ninth South Carolina, which was disbanded.[25] The Palmetto Sharpshooters' lieutenant colonel was Joseph Walker,[26] who had been captain of the Spartan Rifles in the Fifth Regiment; the major was William Anderson, who had been a captain in the Fourth Regiment. Major Anderson wrote his wife:

> We are all very much pleased with our new Regiment. Our Colonel [Jenkins] is one of the finest officers I have ever seen and a gentlemen of the first water, besides, everything has to be done in apple pie order about him. Very different from the way things were done in the [former] 4th Regiment.[27]

Another officer in the newly-formed regiment wrote:

> The [Palmetto Sharpshooters] was originally intended for special service as the name indicates, but the exigencies of the army prevented the consummation of this design, and the regiment was thrown into [R. H. Anderson's] brigade as formerly, instead of acting as an independent, separate command, filling the place of sharpshooters, as practiced in the Federal army.[28]

The Fifth Regiment was itself reorganized in April of 1862, and its men elected John R. R. Giles[29] their colonel, Andrew Jackson their

---

[25]Seven of the twelve companies in Jenkins' Palmetto Sharpshooters were made up primarily of men from companies in the former Fourth and Ninth South Carolina Volunteers. As of April 1862, these seven companies with names of captains, were:
1. Calhoun Mountaineers, Captain F. W. Kilpatrick (from the former Fourth S.C.V.).
2. Confederate Guards, Captain John W. Daniels (from the former Fourth S.C.V.).
3. Pickens Guards, Captain F. L. Garvin (from the former Fourth S.C.V.).
4. Palmetto Riflemen, Captain William W. Humphreys (from the former Fourth S.C.V.).
5. Darlington Sentinels, Captain Alexander Colclough (from the former Ninth S.C.V.).
6. Pickens Sentinels, Captain Joseph E. Lee (from the former Ninth S.C.V.).
7. Cowpens Guards, Captain John Brown (from the former Ninth S.C.V.).
Yorkville *Enquirer*, May 8, 1862.
[26]Joseph Walker, the same age as Jenkins, was from Spartanburg, South Carolina. He entered the service as captain of the Spartan Rifles on April 13, 1861, and served in the Fifth South Carolina until the reorganization in April 1862, when he was elected lieutenant colonel of the Palmetto Sharpshooters. He later became colonel of that regiment, which he commanded until the surrender at Appomattox in April 1865. Capers, *South Carolina*, 6:889-890.
[27]William Anderson to Lucretia Anderson, April 24, 1862, William Anderson Collection.
[28]James A. Hoyt, *The Palmetto Rifleman; Co. B, Fourth Regiment S.C. Vols [and] Co. G, Palmetto Sharpshooters: Historical Sketch* (Greenville, South Carolina: Hoyt and Keys, Printers, 1886), 18.
[29]John R. R. Giles was from Union District, South Carolina, and had entered the service on April 13, 1861, as first lieutenant of the Tyger Volunteers in the Fifth Regiment. He was soon promoted to captain of that company, from which he was elected colonel of the Fifth after the reorganization. Capers, *South Carolina*, 6:592. For other regimental and company officers of the newly-organized Fifth Regiment, see A. S. Salley, *South Carolina Troops in Confederate Service*, vol. 3, *Fifth Regiment, South Carolina*

lieutenant colonel, and William M. Foster their major.[30] This reorganized Fifth Regiment contained five of its original companies, while five more were added from other regiments and new enlistees to make up for those companies which had joined the Palmetto Sharpshooters.[31]

In spite of the disruption caused by the army's reorganization, General R. H. Anderson's brigade, still in Longstreet's Division, remained largely intact. Much the same as before the reorganization, Anderson's command now included the reorganized Fifth South Carolina, under Colonel John R. R. Giles; the reorganized Sixth South Carolina, under Colonel John Bratton;[32] and the reorganized Fourth South Carolina Battalion, under Major C. S. Mattison.[33] The major difference in Anderson's brigade, after the reorganization, was that the Ninth South Carolina Volunteers, which had ceased to exist, was replaced by Jenkins' Palmetto Sharpshooters.

After the Confederate retrograde from the Manassas area, the new Federal commander of the Department of the Potomac, General George B. McClellan, recommended to President Lincoln a different strategy for capturing Richmond. McClellan proposed to leave General Irvin McDowell, with a sizeable body of Federal troops, in the Manassas area, while transporting an even larger Federal force by water to Fortress Monroe at the tip of Virginia's peninsula. McClellan planned to then

---

Volunteers (Columbia, South Carolina: The State Company, 1930).

[30]Andrew Jackson, prior to being elected lieutenant colonel of the reorganized Fifth Regiment, had been captain of Company B of the former Fifth S.C.V., the Kings Mountain Guards. William M. Foster, prior to being elected major of the reorganized Fifth, had been a captain in the former Ninth Regiment, which ceased to exist after the reorganization. Yorkville *Enquirer*, May 8, 1862.

[31]The five companies in the former Fifth Regiment, most of whose men remained in that regiment after the reorganization in April 1862, with captains' names, were:
   1. Catawba Light Infantry, Thomas C. Beckham.
   2. Tyger Volunteers, James T. Douglass.
   3. Kings Mountain Guards, Jonathan Fitchett.
   4. Pea Ridge Volunteers, James B. Steedman.
   5. Lawson Fork Volunteers, Ryal B. Seay.
   The five companies in the reorganized Fifth, made up of men from other units, with captains' names, were:
   1. Company A, John D. Wylie.
   2. Company C, Thomas H. Dunn.
   3. Company E, Samuel B. Meacham.
   4. Company G, Thomas P. Whiteside.
   5. Company I, William D. Camp.
See, Salley, *South Carolina Troops, Fifth, S.C.V.*, vol. 3. The five companies of the original Fifth South Carolina which joined the Palmetto Sharpshooters are listed at footnote 24, supra.

[32]John Bratton, from Winnsboro, South Carolina, had initially gone to Virginia as a lieutenant in the former Sixth Regiment of South Carolina Volunteers. After the reorganization of April 1862, he was elected colonel of the reorganized Sixth Regiment. Capers, *South Carolina*, 6:378-379.

[33]Mattison's Fourth Battalion consisted primarily of men from the former Fourth Regiment of South Carolina Volunteers. C. S. Mattison was from Anderson District and had been lieutenant colonel of the Fourth S.C.V., under Colonel J. B. E. Sloan. At the reorganization, many of the men in that regiment opted to join Jenkins' Palmetto Sharpshooters, while most of the remainder chose to form the Fourth Battalion and elected Mattison their major. The four companies of the original Fourth South Carolina which joined the Palmetto Sharpshooters are listed at footnote 25, supra.

Figure 5
FIELD OFFICERS AND COMPANY COMMANDERS OF
THE FIFTH SOUTH CAROLINA VOLUNTEERS
IMMEDIATELY AFTER THE ARMY'S REORGANIZATION
APRIL 1862

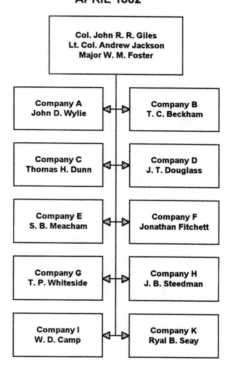

When the Fifth South Carolina was reorganized in April-May 1862, it was formed around five companies of men who had served in the regiment before the reorganization: Beckham's, Douglass', Fitchett's, Steedman's and Seay's. The five remaining companies from the former regiment became part of the Palmetto Sharpshooters at the reorganization. They were replaced in the reoganized Fifth by men from various other units who made up five new companies: Wylie's, Dunn's, Meacham's, Whiteside's, and Camp's. There was no Company J in the reorganized Fifth South Carolina.

march this force of over 140,000 men[34] up the peninsula to Richmond while McDowell's force of 40,000 descended on the Confederate capital from the north, thus mounting a coordinated attack.[35] Once his plan was adopted, McClellan's force began leaving Alexandria, Virginia, by boat on March 17.[36] The arrival of his lead elements at Fortress Monroe was known by the Confederate War Department in Richmond a week later.

Because of this new threat from McClellan, Jefferson Davis ordered General Johnston to position his two strongest divisions so that they could block the expected Federal advance up the peninsula.[37] One of these divisions was Longstreet's, which included R. H. Anderson's brigade of South Carolinians. Along with the other regiments in the brigade, the men in Jenkins' Palmetto Sharpshooters and in the reorganized Fifth South Carolina prepared for the boat trip down the James River to Yorktown where they would be squarely in McClellan's line of advance. Colonel Jenkins knew the odds were not in their favor and wrote to his wife, saying, "I may not live to see you again. If not, take care of my children and remember me."[38] For the gentle and thoughtful Jenkins, these words were surprisingly terse and would have dampened the spirit of even the most courageous soldier's wife.

When General Johnston was put in charge of the Confederate forces on the Virginia peninsula, the name of his command was changed to the "Army of Northern Virginia."[39] This army was soon to become arguably the most famous in American history and its fighting spirit legendary in the annals of war. Except for being detached for a period of about thirteen months, it was in this army that the Fifth South Carolina and the Palmetto Sharpshooters would serve for the rest of the war.

---

[34]Foote, *Civil War*, 1:269.

[35]Catton, *Centennial History*, 2:295.

[36]Stephen W. Sears, *To the Gates of Richmond: The Peninsula Campaign* (New York: Ticknor and Fields, 1992), 22.

[37]Foote, *Civil War*, 1:401.

[38]Micah Jenkins to Caroline Jenkins, April 24, 1862, Micah Jenkins Papers. S.C.L.

[39]Donald Bridgman Sanger and Thomas Robson Hay, *James Longstreet* (Baton Rouge: Louisiana State University Press, 1952), 43; Sears, *Gates of Richmond*, 46.

Chapter 10

The Battle Of Williamsburg

Virginia's peninsula, that narrow neck of land southeast of Richmond lying between the York and James Rivers, was stunningly beautiful in late April 1862. Bird songs seemed to signal the emergence of new life, and the fragrance of springtime was intoxicating. The banks of the James River promised to soon be lush with growth, and the blooms of wild dogwoods dotted the greenery. After rounding a bend in the river, the soldiers aboard the boats might surprise a deer standing at the water's edge, or send wild turkey scurrying into the underbrush. The cruel paradox, so subtly disguised by these scenes of tranquility, is that one of the strongest motives for going to war is the love of peace.

Most of the men in R. H. Anderson's brigade had been away from South Carolina for eleven months, and their romantic feelings about the war were giving way to the stark realization that they now faced protracted service in the field. Within the next three months, they would become battle-hardened soldiers, tempered by the heat of repeated combat. For the moment, however, they enjoyed an all-day ride down the James River and let their minds wander amid thoughts of peace, home, and family.[1]

As General McClellan's Federal army at Fortress Monroe grew in size during April, the Confederate commander in Yorktown, General John B. Magruder, became increasingly concerned. It soon became clear that McClellan's first objective would be to take Yorktown, which was between his army and Richmond.[2] With only 12,000 troops to block McClellan's army, Magruder anxiously awaited the reinforcements being sent to him from Richmond.[3] The quickest way to get them to Yorktown, some fifty miles away, was to send them by steamers down the James River. Being transported to Yorktown was considered quite a luxury by the men in Longstreet's command; after their long march from Centreville to Richmond, they had begun to refer to themselves as the "Walking Division."[4]

The Palmetto Sharpshooters, after having received a tumultuous welcome several days earlier from the citizens of Richmond, left the city by steamer at three in the morning on April 16 and landed near Yorktown that evening.[5] The Fifth Regiment made the same trip two days later and upon arrival marched to a nearby farm where they camped for the night.[6]

By now the predictably cautious McClellan had decided to take Yorktown by siege rather than by assault, and he brought up his big Federal guns.[7] For the latter part of April, he continued this strategy, his siege guns constantly pounding the Confederate defensive works as well as the village.

The Confederate line ran between the York and James Rivers, part of it along the west side of a stream which had been dammed in places

---

[1]Yorkville *Enquirer*, May 8, 1862.

[2]Freeman, *Lee's Lieutenants*, 1:148-151.

[3]Foote, *Civil War*, 1:396.

[4]Ibid., 1:403. Major William Anderson of the Palmetto Sharpshooters wrote to his wife, "We had a very pleasant trip from Richmond here by steam boat down [the] James River. This was much better than marching." William Anderson to Lucretia Anderson, April 18, 1862 (typescript), William Anderson Collection.

[5]National Archives, Compiled Service Records (and Company Record of Events Cards) of the Confederate Soldiers Who Served in Organizations From the State of South Carolina, R.G. 109, series M267, Record of Events Cards for Companies D and G of the Palmetto Sharpshooters, December 31, 1861-April 30, 1862 (referred to hereafter as "Record of Events Cards for the Palmetto Sharpshooters," followed by the appropriate company designation and dates); Diary of Lieutenant William Steele, April 16, 1862, in Richard Lewis, *Camp Life of a Confederate Boy of Bratton's Brigade, Longstreet's Corps, C.S.A., Letters Written by Lieutenant Richard Lewis, of Walker's Regiment, to his Mother, During the War* (Charleston, South Carolina: The News and Courier Book Presses, 1883), 111. William Steele was a second lieutenant in Company B of the Palmetto Sharpshooters.

[6]Record of Events Cards for the Fifth S.C.V., Company H, December 31, 1861 to July 1, 1862. The Sixth South Carolina made the trip on April 17. An assistant surgeon in that regiment wrote that the men were marched to Rockett's Landing in Richmond where they crowded aboard a steamer. He said the trip to Yorktown took a little over six hours. Diary of Dr. James Richmond Boulware, Sixth South Carolina Volunteers, April 17, 1862, typescript, Virginia State Library, Richmond, Virginia.

[7]Foote, *Civil War*, 1:410; Sears, *Gates of Richmond*, 38-39.

to obstruct McClellan's advance.[8]   As soon as the men in R. H. Anderson's brigade arrived, they were put into the rotation with other Confederate units performing picket duty in the trenches east of Yorktown. Being in the trenches for forty-eight hours at a time was rough on the men, and Jenkins described this duty as "anything but a pleasant prospect as the weather has been decidedly against our comfort, and I suppose we will stand in mud and water."[9] While not on picket duty, some of the Palmetto Sharpshooters went into Yorktown, which one described as "scarcely half as large as Yorkville [South Carolina], and a very antiquated looking place."[10] From Yorktown the men could see in the York River eleven Federal gunboats which frequently shelled both the town and the Confederate lines.[11] On May 1 the Palmetto Sharpshooters went into the trenches again, relieving the men of the Fifth Regiment, and had one man killed and one wounded.[12]

     After almost a full month of siege, McClellan, who had been dubbed "the Young Napoleon," finally decided to move against Yorktown. His cautious delay was proved to have been pointless when it was discovered that all Confederate troops had withdrawn only hours before the Federals advanced, leaving behind a deserted town.[13]   The withdrawing Confederate army consisted of four divisions made up of twenty-three brigades; in all, 56,500 men.[14] Longstreet's six brigades left Yorktown on the night of May 3, marched up the peninsula on the Lee's Mill Road, and the next day arrived in Williamsburg, some twelve miles away. Before nightfall, McClellan's advance units had caught up with the Confederate troops there and were preparing to attack. A nasty one-day battle was about to begin, the first for the newly-formed Palmetto Sharpshooters and for the reorganized Fifth Regiment.

     Williamsburg was situated about halfway between the York and James Rivers on a narrow part of the Virginia peninsula, which was only about eight miles wide at that point. The historic village was defended on the east by a series of thirteen earthen redoubts which cut across the width of the peninsula and the roads leading from Yorktown; infantry rifle pits had been dug between some of these redoubts. At the junction of

[8]Yorkville *Enquirer*, May 8, 1862. This stream was the Warwick River, which cut across the peninsula at Yorktown.
[9]Micah Jenkins to Caroline Jenkins, April 27, 1862, Micah Jenkins Papers, S.C.L. Another officer in the Palmetto Sharpshooters wrote, "It rained almost incessantly. The trenches were filled with water. No fires could be allowed." Hoyt, *The Palmetto Riflemen*, 19.
[10]Yorkville *Enquirer*, May 8, 1862.
[11]Ibid.
[12]Diary of Lieutenant William Steele, May 1, 1862, in Lewis, *Camp Life*, 111.
[13]Catton, *Centennial History*, 2:277.
[14]Freeman, *Lee's Lieutenants*, 1:156-160; Sears, *The Gates of Richmond*, 60.

Figure 6

ORGANIZATION OF LONGSTREET'S DIVISION
IN THE ARMY OF NORTHERN VIRGINIA
FOR THE BATTLES OF WILLIAMSBURG, MAY 5, 1862;
SEVEN PINES, MAY 31, 1862; AND THE SEVEN DAYS, JUNE 26–JULY 1, 1862

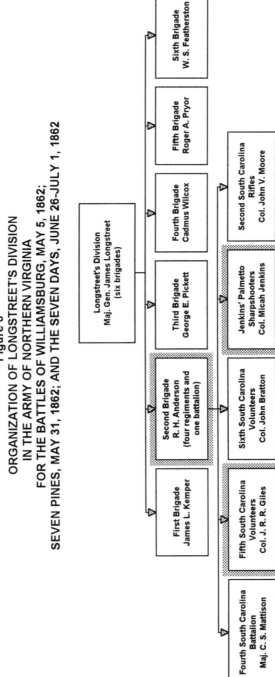

Brigadier General Richard H. Anderson assumed the command of D. R. Jones' brigade in February 1862. When the Provisional Army was reorganized during April–May 1862, Jones' (now R. H. Anderson's) brigade remained in Longstreet's division and was made up of two former South Carolina regiments (the Fifth and the Sixth S.C.V.), and one battalion (the Fourth), which had been completely revamped. Anderson was also assigned Jenkins' Palmetto Sharpshooters, a newly-formed regiment of twelve companies made up of reenlistees from the former Fourth, Fifth and Ninth South Carolina Volunteers. This was the make-up of R. H. Anderson's brigade for the battles of Williamsburg on May 5, Seven Pines on May 31, Gaines' Mill on June 27 and Frayser's Farm on June 30, 1862, except that the Second South Carolina Rifles joined the brigade shortly before Gaines' Mill.

the Lee's Mill and Yorktown roads, facing an open field, was Fort Magruder, the main redoubt. Beyond the open ground in front of the earthwork fort, about 500 yards away, was a dense pine forest where most of McClellan's army assembled for the attack.[15] Longstreet's division had been ordered to hold Fort Magruder and the defensive line at Williamsburg long enough to allow the rest of Johnston's army to continue an orderly withdrawal toward Richmond.[16]

At daybreak on May 5, McClellan's troops opened the Williamsburg engagement by driving in Longstreet's pickets and advancing toward the Confederate works.   General R. H. Anderson was acting division commander, and Colonel Jenkins was acting commander of Anderson's brigade which had been ordered to defend six redoubts along the Williamsburg line. Jenkins' Palmetto Sharpshooters and six companies of the Fifth Regiment, under Colonel John R. R. Giles, occupied the primary redoubt, Fort Magruder. The remaining four companies of the Fifth, under Major William M. Foster, defended the redoubt about 400 yards to the left, and the men in Major C. S. Mattison's Fourth Battalion were deployed as skirmishers in front of Fort Magruder.[17]

At about six in the morning, the skirmishers, led by General Anderson and reinforced by two companies of Palmetto Sharpshooters, drove the advancing Federals back to the woods and then retired to Fort Magruder. Union artillery then began to concentrate on the fort. In Jenkins' regiment, Private Robert L. Hemphill of Company G (Seabrook's Jasper Light Infantry) was shot through the brain.[18]   At ten a.m. a sizeable body of Federal troops attacked Fort Magruder but was repelled by artillery and musket fire from its defenders.[19] It had rained so hard the night before that the men in the fort fought in mud up to their knees.[20] During the morning attack on Fort Magruder, the Union troops also advanced against the redoubt to the left of the fort. The four companies of the Fifth Regiment assigned to defend the redoubt did not fight as well as their comrades inside the fort. John W. Goss,[21] a captain in the Palmetto Sharpshooters, said that the four companies abandoned the redoubt "without firing a gun" when the Federals advanced. According to Goss, the officer who was in command of those companies said later,

---

[15]Ibid. See also, Yorkville *Enquirer*, May 22, 1862.

[16]Foote, *Civil War*, 1:411.

[17]Yorkville *Enquirer*, May 22, 1862; Freeman, *Lee's Lieutenants*, 1:176-179.

[18]Yorkville *Enquirer*, May 22, 1862.

[19]Jenkins' report on the Battle of Williamsburg (undated), O. R., vol. 11, part 1, p. 582.

[20]Diary of Lieutenant William Steele, May 6, 1862, in Lewis, *Camp Life*, 112.

[21]John Wesley Goss, from Union, South Carolina, had been captain of Company A (Johnson Rifles) in the Fifth Regiment. At the reorganization in April of 1862, he became the captain of Company A in the Palmetto Sharpshooters. When Major William Anderson was later killed at Frayser's Farm, Goss was promoted to major of that regiment. When Joe Walker was promoted to colonel, Goss was promoted to lieutenant colonel of the Palmetto Sharpshooters in July 1862.

BATTLE OF WILLIAMSBURG - MAY 5, 1862

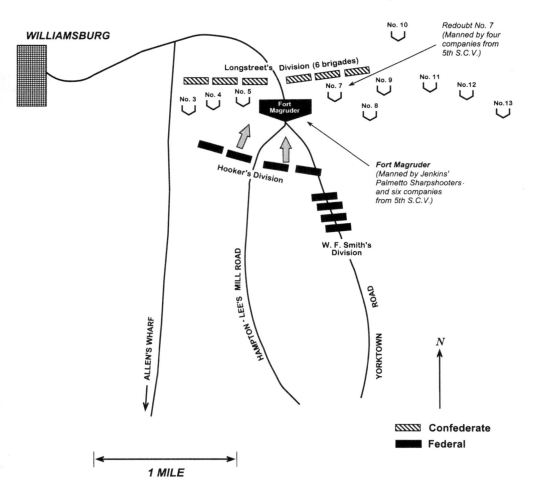

On the morning of May 5, 1862, Hooker's Federal Division attacked Longstreet's Division about two miles east of Williamsburg, Virginia, and the resulting battle raged all day. Colonel Micah Jenkins and his Palmetto Sharpshooters, along with six companies from the Fifth South Carolina Volunteers, successfully defended Fort Magruder, a bastioned earthwork at the intersection of the two main roads leading to Williamsburg from Yorktown. The four remaining companies of the Fifth South Carolina defended Redoubt No. 7 to the left (east) of the fort. The one-day battle bought valuable time for General Joe Johnston to withdraw his outnumbered Confederates toward Richmond.

"he did not want to leave [the redoubt] but the companies all prevailed on him to leave without orders."[22] Fortunately, several other companies of the Fifth Regiment were hurried into the redoubt and were able to hold it.[23]

That afternoon the Federals managed to position a battery of artillery in the redoubt on the extreme left of Longstreet's line, which the Confederates had mistakenly left unmanned. Part of Anderson's brigade, including some companies from the Fifth South Carolina, made a charge to dislodge this Federal battery, which posed a great danger to that part of the line. The charge was unsuccessful because they had too far to advance over open ground and were "all the while exposed to a raking and destructive fire of grape, canister and shell."[24] Later, realizing that the right portion of his line was also endangered, General Longstreet sent a request for assistance to D. H. Hill, whose division had already begun withdrawing from Williamsburg. Hill turned his division around, marched it back to the fighting, and reinforced Longstreet. By late afternoon the battle was over, with each side claiming victory. That night Longstreet's troops resumed their withdrawal toward Richmond, but they had succeeded in their main objective by substantially delaying McClellan's pursuit of Johnston's army.[25]

Jenkins' Palmetto Sharpshooters and most of the men of Giles' Fifth Regiment had fought with tenacity and skill. One account stated that R. H. Anderson's brigade, under Jenkins, had played a "conspicuous part" in the battle, and that the artillery detachment inside Fort Magruder suffered so many casualties that Jenkins' infantry had to help man the guns.[26] His men were credited with doing such effective work that the Union artillery was forced to change locations several times. Jenkins wrote, "One of my men was killed within two feet of me, saving me from the ball, and an artillerist was killed by a shell within a yard of me – I catching him as he fell."[27]

---

[22]John W. Goss to his brother, Laurens Goss, May 20, 1862, South Carolina Confederate Relic Room and Museum, Columbia, South Carolina. The officer in command of the four companies was Major William M. Foster.

[23]Two of the companies of the Fifth Regiment which were sent to salvage the redoubt were James B. Steedman's Pea Ridge Volunteers and Ryal B. Seay's Lawson Fork Volunteers. Ibid.

[24]Yorkville *Enquirer*, May 22, 1862.

[25]Foote, *Civil War*, 1:411.

[26]Capers, *South Carolina*, 6:46. J. W. Reid, a private in Mattison's Fourth South Carolina Battalion, wrote that there were nine pieces of artillery inside Fort Magruder on the day of the battle. J. W. Reid, *History of the Fourth Regiment of S. C. Volunteers from the Commencement of the War Until Lee's Surrender* (Greenville, South Carolina: Shannon and Co., 1892), 81. Jenkins' report indicates that there were only six. O. R., vol. 11, part. 1, p. 582.

[27]Lydia Jenkins to her sister, Elizabeth Jenkins LaRoche, May 23, 1862, Jenkins and LaRoche Letters. This letter describes and quotes from another letter written by Micah Jenkins following the battle, but that letter has not been located.

When it was suggested to him during the thick of the fighting that he was unnecessarily exposing himself to danger, Jenkins responded with an uncharacteristic immaturity, saying, "I feel the bullet has not been molded that is to kill me."[28] One of his men wrote that Jenkins had "exposed himself to great danger all the day" and had handled himself "with perfect self possession."[29] This battle afforded him his first opportunity to command a brigade in battle, and General Jeb Stuart's report praised

> the meritorious conduct of Colonel Jenkins . . . who, under the most trying circumstances, showed all the attributes of the . . . heroic commander.[30]

The Fifth Regiment lost 2 men killed and 19 wounded in the battle on May 5, and the Palmetto Sharpshooters had 4 killed, 22 wounded, and 3 missing.[31] Colonel Jenkins sent a telegram to the Yorkville *Enquirer* including a list of the names of the casualties in his regiment, "to allay all anxiety" of the families back home. He was infuriated when the person in charge of sending the dispatch chose to delete the list of names, and Jenkins immediately sent a new list directly to the Yorkville *Enquirer*. The newspaper then published the list and said that his sending it demonstrated Jenkins' devotion to his men.[32]

After Longstreet and D. H. Hill had bought them some valuable time, General Johnston's weary Confederates continued their retreat up the peninsula toward Richmond. R. H. Anderson's brigade remained at Williamsburg as rear guard until daybreak on May 6, when they joined the withdrawal to the northwest. That day the men marched some twelve miles over roads made nearly impassable by rain and the heavy

---

[28]Ibid. This same letter refers to a verbal account of the battle given to the Jenkins family in Yorkville by Joseph R. Witherspoon, Jenkins' courier, who had fought in the battle and later returned home on furlough. This is the same soldier who had drawn his pistol on the Mississippians during the First Battle of Manassas, to prevent them from shooting at Jenkins.

[29]Yorkville *Enquirer*, May 22, 1862.

[30]O. R., vol. 11, part 1, p. 572. One historian commented that Jenkins had commanded Anderson's brigade and the artillery in Fort Magruder with such enthusiasm and ability that he won much praise. Freeman, *Lee's Lieutenants*, 1:192.

[31]Return of Casualties for the Battle of Williamsburg, O. R., vol. 11, part 1, p. 569. Those killed in the Fifth were Thomas H. Dunn, Captain of Company C, and Nathaniel Hill in Company E. Those killed in the Palmetto Sharpshooters were Z. D. Golightly of Company D, John Kaney of Company F, Robert L. Hemphill of Company G and W. H. Spencer of Company H. Yorkville *Enquirer*, May 15, 1862.

[32]Yorkville *Enquirer*, May 29, 1862, quoting from a May 19, 1862, letter to the *Enquirer* from Micah Jenkins.

retreating traffic. One soldier in Anderson's brigade described this march by saying:

> Of all the mud I ever saw we trudged through it that morning. My overcoat dragged in it. It was about the consistency of fritter batter. . . . There was no way of getting around it.[33]

At some points the mud holes were "belly deep to the horses and mules," and for one hundred yards on either side of the road, the mud was over "half-leg deep."[34] By nightfall Anderson's brigade had stopped and camped in a large, open field some five miles northwest of Smyrna, and the men enjoyed their meager rations – two hard biscuits each. One Palmetto Sharpshooter in Cato Seabrook's company had found a discarded Federal haversack full of peas, beans, and rice; he and his companions then "regaled themselves on a delicious pot full of 'Hopping John.'"[35]

As Longstreet's men marched toward Richmond, they heard frequent rumors that McClellan's troops were close behind, ready to overtake them. Instead of this creating fear, however, the men were ready for the next fight. One soldier in Jenkins' regiment said that if the Federals caught up to them once more, "they will get the best whipping they ever got. . . ."[36]

Two days after leaving Williamsburg, Anderson's brigade was still trudging toward Richmond. At ten o'clock in the evening on May 8, they arrived at a place they called Mill Stream where they spent the night and remained most of the next day "bathing, fishing and resting."[37] This was the first real relaxation they had enjoyed since their boat trip down the James River three weeks earlier.

Longstreet's men had been on short rations since leaving Yorktown, and one soldier in Anderson's brigade described how he and his mess mates shared a single ear of corn for supper. He said that the corn was "duly parched" and served on a clean towel spread on the ground. Due to the gruelling march, most of the men had thrown away their cooking utensils and had devised a way to bake bread by cooking it on barrel staves over a fire. But in spite of the long retreat and the shortage of

---

[33]Reid, *History of the Fourth Regiment of S. C. Volunteers*, 83.

[34]Yorkville *Enquirer*, May 22, 1862. Lieutenant James A. Hoyt, in the Palmetto Sharpshooters, Company C, wrote later that "it was with difficulty that the rear guard could drive before it hundreds of broken down stragglers, who were so perfectly worn-out as to be reckless of all consequences." Hoyt, *The Palmetto Riflemen*, 21.

[35]Yorkville *Enquirer*, May 22, 1862.

[36]Diary of Lieutenant William Steele, May 7, 1862, in Lewis, *Camp Life*, 112.

[37]Steedman, "Pea Ridge Volunteers," 1:233.

food, the men's spirits were high and there was no shortage of camp humor. One man recalled that during the battle on May 5, when it was so cold and rainy, Colonel Jenkins had ordered him to "keep cool." The soldier, who had shivered in his wet clothes that entire day, quipped that it was "the only time [I] ever obeyed an order [so] well in [my] life."[38]

Johnston's army of some 56,000 Confederates was now massed several miles north and east of Richmond. McClellan's Union army of more than twice that number was waiting on the peninsula to combine with Irvin McDowell's 40,000 troops who were expected to march on Richmond from the direction of Fredericksburg. If these two Federal forces were permitted to combine, they would have had nearly a three-to-one numerical advantage over Johnston's Confederates.[39] To make matters worse, it appeared that the Confederates might be unable to prevent Federal gunships from steaming up the James River to Richmond. It was clear that the Confederate capital was now in grave danger, so much so that Jefferson Davis sent his family to North Carolina, the government packed up the archives, and the Confederate Cabinet evacuated the city. There was an element of panic in Richmond.[40]

Meanwhile, Anderson's brigade had crossed the Chickahominy River at Long Bridge and continued toward Richmond. Jenkins' men reached the outskirts of the capital on May 17, but remained there for only a couple of days.[41] They were then sent down to Chafin's Bluff on the north bank of the James River, opposite the Confederate artillery positions on Drewry's Bluff.[42] This was some eight miles due south of Richmond, at a sharp bend in the river where the Confederates had sunk obstructions to prevent the Federal navy from steaming to within shelling range of the Confederate capital. Union gunboats had come up the river and shelled the Confederate batteries at Drewry's Bluff only a week earlier, but had been repulsed.[43] The high ground at Chafin's Bluff, directly across the river, was a likely point of attack for any Federal advance on Richmond, and Jenkins and his regiment were positioned there, in his words, to "resist gunboats and [any] land attack in support. . . ."[44] General McClellan, however, characteristically did not attack; instead he began appealing to Washington for more troops. After

---

[38]Yorkville *Enquirer*, May 29, 1862.

[39]Foote, *Civil War*, 1:440; Sears, *The Gates of Richmond*, 97.

[40]Nancy Scott Anderson and Dwight Anderson, *The Generals, Ulysses S. Grant and Robert E. Lee* (New York: Random House, 1987), 307; Freeman, *Lee's Lieutenants*, 1:209.

[41]Diary of Lieutenant William Steele, May 17, 1862, in Lewis, *Camp Life*, 112.

[42]Micah Jenkins to Caroline Jenkins, May 25, 1862, Micah Jenkins Papers, D.U.L. See also, John W. Goss to his brother Laurens, May 20, 1862, South Carolina Confederate Relic Room and Museum.

[43]Catton, *Centennial History*, 2:288; Foote, *Civil War*, 1:416.

[44]Micah Jenkins to Caroline Jenkins, May 25, 1862, Micah Jenkins Papers, D.U.L.

several days, the men in Anderson's brigade returned to their camps several miles northeast of Richmond, near the Fairfield Race Course.

On the afternoon of May 29, General Longstreet presented a battle flag, commemorating the Williamsburg engagement, to the Palmetto Sharpshooters at their camp outside of Richmond. In making the presentation, he said:

> Colonel, officers and soldiers: I hand you this . . . battle flag. You are honorably mentioned at Williamsburg. I trust that we may be able to mention you in the same way whenever your country calls upon you to do battle.[45]

The men in Jenkins' new regiment had obviously made their division commander proud by their conduct in their first battle.

Most officers were well aware, as the end of May approached, that a massive general engagement near Richmond was imminent. Jenkins was certainly aware of it when he wrote to Caroline, "The great battle is very, very near, I think."[46] Fully cognizant of the Federals' numerical superiority, Jenkins expressed a sense of foreboding in the same letter. He said:

> [T]hough I may fall, yet I hope a blessed peace will [return soon]. . . . Bless my dear little boys, and tell them how many fond hopes I have had for them.[47]

War was turning the young romantic into a somber realist.

---

[45]Yorkville *Enquirer*, June 12, 1862.
[46]Micah Jenkins to Caroline Jenkins, May 28, 1862, John Jenkins Papers, S.C.L.
[47]Ibid.

Chapter 11

The Battle Of Seven Pines

A t dusk on May 31, 1862, with the smoke settling serenely over the field of battle, the South Carolina soldiers in R. H. Anderson's brigade settled down to rest in the camps of their enemy. Colonel Jenkins was emotionally and physically drained from the afternoon's fighting, but he was delighted with the results. On this first day of the Battle of Seven Pines, Jenkins and the fast-moving regiments under his command had overrun four Federal lines and had repulsed a fifth. Following their four hours of very impressive fighting, the men were finally allowed to relax and enjoy the spoils of war as Jenkins rested in his tent.

Shortly after dark a soldier pulled back the young colonel's tent fly and requested permission to speak with the commander. After stepping inside, he presented Colonel Jenkins with a locket he had found belonging to Colonel Henry S. Briggs, the commander of the Tenth Massachusetts Volunteers, who had been wounded in the day's fighting and whose abandoned camp the Palmetto Sharpshooters now occupied. Inside the locket was a likeness of Colonel Briggs' family, and as he studied it, Jenkins' thoughts immediately turned to his own wife and sons in South Carolina. He sat down and composed a letter in which he returned the locket to the Federal colonel. Jenkins' letter said:

> The medallion [locket] was found in your camp, in which my regiment slept the night after the battle of Saturday, the 31st of May. Though willing to meet you ever in the field . . . I do not war with your personal feelings. I, supposing the medallion prized by you, take pleasure in returning it.[1]

Whatever romantic notions he may have lost in the first year of the war, Jenkins' sense of honor was still intact; it was an immutable part of the man's character.

Camped near the Fairfield Race Course on the outskirts of Richmond, Jenkins and his men had expected a major battle all week, but the orders they finally received on the night of May 30 had allowed them little time to prepare. By five o'clock the next morning, they were on the march with the rest of Longstreet's division toward Seven Pines, a small crossroads about five miles due east of Richmond where the Nine Mile Road met the Williamsburg Road.[2]

The weather and other developments during that week had convinced General Joe Johnston that he must take the initiative and attack. McClellan's Federal army was in a vulnerable position, with three of his corps on the north side of the Chickahominy River and the other two on the south side. The river itself was impassable due to the spring rains which would temporarily keep McClellan's army divided. When Johnston finally learned that General Irvin McDowell's troops were not marching to reinforce McClellan, as had originally been feared, the Confederate general decided to strike one of the two Federal corps isolated on the south side of the river. Union General Erasmus D. Keyes' IV Corps, made up of two divisions, was positioned at Seven Pines. Keyes' right flank was near Fair Oaks Station, where the Nine Mile Road crossed the York River Railroad about a mile northwest of Seven Pines. Johnston ordered four Confederate divisions, including Longstreet's, to

---

[1]Micah Jenkins to Colonel Henry S. Briggs (undated), reprinted in the Boston *Journal* and in the Yorkville *Enquirer* of November 12, 1862. By the time Jenkins' letter, with the locket, reached him several months later, Briggs and Jenkins had both been promoted to brigadier general. Briggs responded to Jenkins by writing:

> I beg to assure you of my high appreciation of the generous magnanimity and delicate courtesy of your act, and to thank you with all my heart for the restoration of [the locket]. . . . I cannot without pain contemplate the meeting as a foe . . . one who has performed so honorable an act, and conferred upon me so great a favor.

General H. S. Briggs to Jenkins, October 7, 1862, Micah Jenkins Papers, S.C.L.

[2]H. C. Conner to Ellen O'Leary, June 2, 1862, Henry Calvin Conner Papers.

MAP 1: BATTLE OF SEVEN PINES - MAY 31, 1862

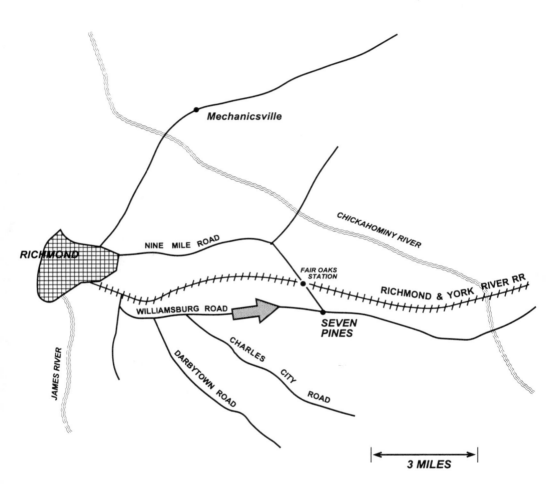

On the afternoon of May 31, 1862, General D. H. Hill's Confederate Division launched an attack against Erasmus Keyes' Federal Corps at Seven Pines, where the Nine Mile Road intersected the Williamsburg Road roughly five miles due east of Richmond. Hill soon requested reinforcements from Longstreet, who sent him Richard H. Anderson's Brigade. Colonel Micah Jenkins was put in command of half of Anderson's Brigade and was ordered to attack northeast toward Fair Oaks Station.

advance toward Seven Pines along three different approaches and to attack Keyes' corps there. General Longstreet was in command of the right wing of the attacking force, which included his own division and the divisions of D. H. Hill and Benjamin Huger. That afternoon the battle was joined when D. H. Hill's division attacked Keyes' Federal corps on the Williamsburg Road, driving the bluecoats back toward Seven Pines.[3]

After Hill's frontal assault began to meet stiff Federal resistance, he requested reinforcements from Longstreet, and one of the brigades he sent was R. H. Anderson's. Anderson divided his brigade by detaching the Palmetto Sharpshooters and the Sixth South Carolina and placing them under Jenkins' command. General Hill then sent Jenkins and his two regiments on a flanking movement in an attempt to turn the Federal right and come in behind the enemy lines. Jenkins' regiments turned off the Williamsburg Road at about three that afternoon and moved northeast toward the railroad crossing about a mile away. After being joined by the Twenty-seventh Georgia, of George B. Anderson's brigade, Jenkins' men attacked east, toward Fair Oaks Station. Within twenty minutes, they had wrecked two Federal regiments in General Darius N. Couch's division and then moved on through their camps. Continuing toward the railroad crossing at Fair Oaks, Jenkins halted to dress his lines and reported to R. H. Anderson, who ordered him to continue his advance. When the adjutant of the Twenty-seventh Georgia reported to Jenkins for further orders, Jenkins yelled, "Come on Georgia; I want you." The three regiments then overran a second line of Union troops near the railroad and went through their camp as well.[4]

By this time, Jenkins and his men had succeeded in turning the right flank of the Union line. He now veered sharply to his right and began driving back down the east side of the Nine Mile Road toward Seven Pines, coming in behind a portion of the Federal corps. Jenkins' three regiments then fought their way over another line of Union troops, forcing them to retreat in a southerly direction. The retreating Federals, however, quickly regrouped and formed a new line in the woods "about 300 yards on the right [south] of the Williamsburg Road."[5]

Jenkins and his half brigade had broken through the middle of three Federal battle lines and were positioned along the Williamsburg Road, facing south toward the Union line which had reformed in the woods.[6]

---

[3]Foote, *Civil War*, 1:442-447.

[4]Colonel Jenkins' report on the Battle of Seven Pines (undated), O. R., vol. 11, part 1, p. 947; Sears, *Gates of Richmond*, 132-133; Report of Lieutenant Colonel Charles T. Zachary, June 5, 1862, O. R., vol. 11, part 1, pp. 953-954. Jenkins' report erroneously indicates the regiment which joined him as the Twenty-eighth Georgia.

[5]O. R., vol. 11, part 1, p. 948.

[6]Clifford Dowdey, *The Seven Days: The Emergence of Lee* (Boston: Little, Brown and Co., 1964), 99. Dowdey says that Jenkins' half brigade cut through the following four Federal divisions: Silas Casey's, Darius Couch's, Philip Kearny's and Joe Hooker's. Ibid.

They were on the eastern side of Seven Pines, well out in front of the main Confederate line and in the rear of some of the Federal units in Keyes' corps.

Just after they had driven the Federals across the Williamsburg Road, Palmetto Sharpshooters Major William Anderson reported that a long column of Union troops was moving west on the Williamsburg Road straight toward Jenkins' position. This meant that he and his three regiments were in serious danger of being counterattacked simultaneously on their front and on their left flank. To make matters worse, they had advanced too far to expect reinforcements from D. H. Hill's division.[7] Colonel Jenkins made his decision without hesitation. In his battle report, he wrote:

> I determined to [first] break the enemy in front before [we] could be reached by this new [Federal] advance [coming up the road], and then, by a change of front, to meet them.[8]

In other words, Jenkins decided to whip the Federal line in the woods to his front first, and then turn his men quickly and take on the Union column coming at them along the Williamsburg Road.

He positioned two companies of the Palmetto Sharpshooters under Major Anderson to hold off the Union column coming up the road. The remainder of his three regiments then charged and routed the Federal line in the woods, driving it back several hundred yards. At this point Jenkins called for Colonel J. R. R. Giles' Fifth South Carolina, which had been fighting in a different area, to lend assistance.[9]

As the Union column on his left drew closer, Jenkins had to disengage with the routed Federals to his front, turn his three regiments to the left, and form them into a line of battle astride the Williamsburg Road. Palmetto Sharpshooter Lieutenant W. B. Smith, in Captain

---

[7]Jenkins had sent one of his officers to General Hill to request reinforcements, but Hill said he had none to send. The officer told Jenkins that Hill refused to believe that Jenkins' force was so far in front of the Confederate line. Hoyt, *The Palmetto Riflemen*, 24-25.

[8]O. R., vol. 11, part 1, p. 948.

[9]Ibid. The two companies which Jenkins sent to hold off the Federal column on the Williamsburg Road were F. W. Kilpatrick's Company B and John Martin's Company H. Since Jenkins was in command of half a brigade, command of the Palmetto Sharpshooters would have normally devolved upon its lieutenant colonel, Joe Walker. Walker, however, was at home sick in Spartanburg, South Carolina, and Major William Anderson was placed in charge of the regiment during this battle. William Anderson to Lucretia McFall Anderson, June 2, 1862, William Anderson Collection.

MAP 2: BATTLE OF SEVEN PINES - MAY 31, 1862

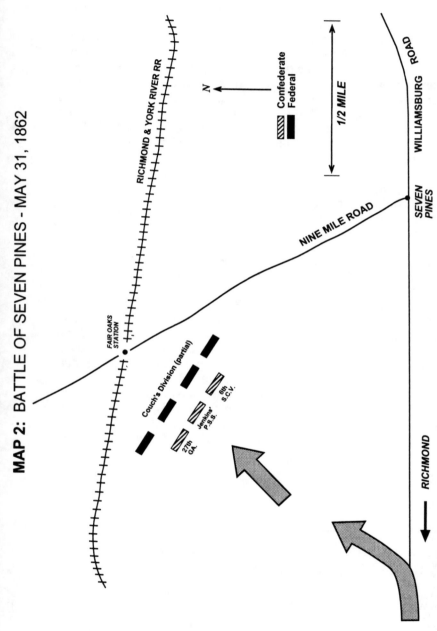

At about 3 p.m. on May 31, Jenkins and his two regiments, the Palmetto Sharpshooters and the Sixth South Carolina Volunteers, turned off the Williamsburg Road and began moving northeast through the woods toward Fair Oaks Station. After being joined by the 27th Georgia Volunteers, Jenkins and his half brigade quickly overran two regiments in Darius Couch's Federal Division and then broke through another line of Union troops. By this time, Jenkins' three regiments were on the right flank of Keyes' Federal IV Corps.

MAP 3: BATTLE OF SEVEN PINES - MAY 31, 1862

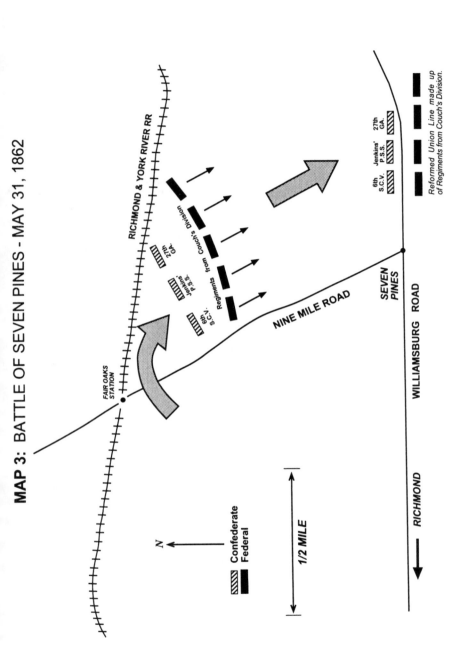

Reformed Union Line made up
of Regiments from Couch's Division.

After breaking the Federal lines west of the Nine Mile Road, Jenkins and his three regiments turned southeast toward Seven Pines. They had succeeded in turning the Federals' right flank near Fair Oaks Station and were in position to move behind the Union troops along the Nine Mile Road. Jenkins' half brigade then moved on toward Seven Pines, breaking another line of Federals. Those Union troops retreated to the southeast and formed a new line about three hundred yards below the Williamsburg Road east of Seven Pines.

MAP 4: BATTLE OF SEVEN PINES - MAY 31, 1862

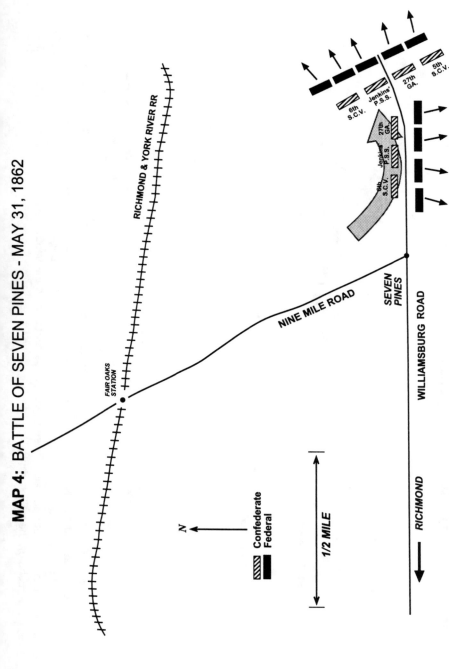

By late afternoon, Jenkins' three regiments attacked the reformed units of Couch's Division south of the Williamsburg Road and broke their line. Jenkins' troops then turned east to meet Federal regiments advancing along the Williamsburg Road. Having been joined by the Fifth South Carolina Volunteers, Jenkins' regiments routed this last Union line. It was then nearly dark, and his men settled down to rest in the abandoned camps of their enemies, about a mile east of Seven Pines. They had penetrated farther than any other Confederate units on May 31.

Seabrook's Jasper Light Infantry, later described how this was accomplished:

> Some one said to [Jenkins]: "Colonel, just look at them coming [toward us] at the double quick." Jenkins replied: "We will meet them at the double quick." He straightened himself up in his stirrups and gave the command to change front on the twelfth company at the double quick, and I never saw on ordinary parade a prettier maneuver. General [then Colonel] Jenkins was magic. He could come nearer making his men work like machinery than any other man I ever saw.[10]

Jenkins' three regiments were drawn up in a line perpendicular to the road and facing the oncoming Federals who had also deployed in a line of battle. The Palmetto Sharpshooters were in the center, the Twenty-seventh Georgia on the right and the Sixth South Carolina on the left. As the fire from the Federal muskets became intense, the Georgia regiment began to fall back. Jenkins then ordered his Palmetto Sharpshooters and the Sixth South Carolina to advance, which they promptly did, "firing full in the face of the foe." They drove the Union troops back "some 200 or 300 yards, the enemy getting more and more disordered and beginning to break badly."[11]

At this point the Fifth South Carolina, under the command of Lieutenant Colonel Andrew Jackson, came up on the right.[12] Seeing this, the troops of the Twenty-seventh Georgia rallied, and the two regiments joined in Jenkins' advance. In short order this last Union line was routed into disordered squads, and Jenkins said that "at 7:40 p.m. we closed our busy day. . . ." That night the Palmetto Sharpshooters slept in the abandoned camp of the Tenth Massachusetts Volunteers, commanded by Colonel H.S. Briggs.[13] It was there that one of Jenkins' men had found the locket belonging to Briggs, which led to the exchange of letters between the two rival commanders.

The first day at Seven Pines had been a brilliant success for the Sixth South Carolina and Jenkins' Palmetto Sharpshooters. The Yorkville

---

[10]Recollection by W. Beaty Smith, quoted in Thomas, *Career and Character*, 15. Smith was then a lieutenant, but later captain, of Company G (Jasper Light Infantry), Palmetto Sharpshooters.
[11]O. R., vol. 11, part 1, p. 949.
[12]Colonel Giles had been killed earlier in the day's fighting, west of Seven Pines. O. R., vol. 11, part 1, p. 949.
[13]Ibid.

Enquirer reported that these two regiments, along with the Twenty-seventh Georgia, had broken

> through four lines of fresh troops and repulsed the fifth – captured four of their pitched camps richly stored with provisions, camp equipment, baggage, stores, etc. – [and taken] three pieces of artillery, three stands of colors, and several hundred prisoners besides dealing death and destruction among the mercenary hirelings of McClellan.[14]

Earlier that day, the men of the Fifth South Carolina, under Colonel Giles, had fought in much the same manner, but in a different sector. The Fifth and several other regiments advanced east towards Seven Pines and broke through two lines, finally facing the Federals in their redoubts behind an abatis of fallen pines. Giles' men then charged into furious musket fire, and he was shot through the heart, but the Union troops were driven out, and their redoubts were immediately occupied by the Confederates. The men in the Fifth Regiment had been holding one of these redoubts for some time that afternoon when Jenkins requested their assistance. They then joined him for his final charge of the day, routing the Federal line advancing toward them along the Williamsburg Road.[15]

During the height of the fighting on the afternoon of May 31, near Fair Oaks Station, Company E of the Palmetto Sharpshooters under Captain Alexander Colclough, had been sent out to "feel the enemy" on Jenkins' left but had become separated from the regiment. They were moving along the railroad when they encountered two companies of Union troops on a similar mission. Colclough and his 47 men promptly captured 139 prisoners, including "1 captain, 5 lieutenants and 133 privates with Enfield rifles in their hands."[16]

---

[14]Yorkville *Enquirer*, June 19, 1862. In addition, the Charleston *Daily Courier* on June 9, 1862, reported that Jenkins and his regiments had routed

> five lines of fresh troops, consisting of the following regiments: 10th Pennsylvania, 52d Pennsylvania, 10th Massachusetts, 56th New York, 11th Maine and 1st Kentucky, as was ascertained from their wounded and prisoners.

For a similar account, see Thomas J. Goree to his sister, Mary Frances Goree Kittrell, June 17, 1862, in Cutrer, ed., *Longstreet's Aide*, 87. Goree wrote:

> [Jenkins] fought 5 separate & distinct lines of the enemy, whipping each one . . . with a little brigade of 1900 men. He passed over several abatis of felled timber, 2 lines of breastworks, captured 3 pieces of artillery, 250 prisoners, & several stands of colors. He whipped the fifth line . . . at about 3 o'clock p.m. At that time he was near two miles in advance of anyone else.

Ibid.

[15]Steedman, "Pea Ridge Volunteers," 1:233-234.

[16]O. R., vol. 11, part 1, p. 950.

In his report on the first day of the battle, General D. H. Hill recounted his request that Longstreet send reinforcements:

> In a few minutes the magnificent brigade of R. H. Anderson came to my support. A portion of this force, under Colonel Jenkins, consisting of the Palmetto Sharpshooters, and the Sixth South Carolina, was sent on the extreme left to scour along the railroad and Nine Mile Road, and thus get in rear of the enemy. . . .[17]

Jenkins and his three regiments had carried out these orders in grand style, fighting their way behind the Federals' right flank and forcing them to retreat east, away from Seven Pines. In fact, Jenkins' regiments had advanced so far ahead of the main Confederate line that, for a while, they were in danger of being isolated and cut to pieces. As darkness ended the fighting, Jenkins' men were still exchanging shots with Union troops retiring from the field.[18] The battered Union brigades, however, regrouped east of Seven Pines, and the Confederates prepared to receive a counterattack at dawn the next day.

Late on the night of May 31, Jenkins and his exhausted men were relieved from their forward position on the Williamsburg Road and brought back to Seven Pines. The following day, the fighting erupted about a mile to the north, close to Fair Oaks Station, but Jenkins and the other men in R. H. Anderson's brigade were not involved. Because of their hard fighting the day before, they were assigned as rear guard to protect D. H. Hill's division. The result of the fighting on June 1 was disappointing for the Confederates; by the end of that day, they had given up almost all of the ground that they had won the day before.[19] The two-day Battle of Seven Pines had ended in a draw, and General Johnston's plan to destroy part of McClellan's army had failed. One thing, however, had been accomplished: the Federal advance on Richmond was temporarily halted.[20]

---

[17]General D. H. Hill's battle report (undated), O. R., vol. 11, part 1, p. 944. General Hill's report also states:

> R. H. Anderson and Jenkins, assisted by portions of G. B. Anderson's brigade . . . swept on the left of the [Nine Mile Road], driving brigade after brigade of the Yankees before them, capturing two more cannon, several camps, with their commissary and quartermaster's stores, and finally, after dark, halting more than a mile beyond the main works of the Yankees at Seven Pines.

Ibid.

[18]Dowdey, *The Seven Days*, 99. Dowdey described Jenkins as a "brilliant" Citadel graduate and "one of the most gifted natural soldiers" to fight for the Confederacy. Ibid. It has also been said that, at Seven Pines, he demonstrated "a pure instinct" for combat. Sears, *Gates of Richmond*, 133.

[19]Gustavus W. Smith, "Two Days of Battle at Seven Pines (Fair Oaks)," *Battles and Leaders of the Civil War*, vol. 2, *The Struggle Intensifies* (reprint; Secaucus, New Jersey: Castle Books, 1982), 261.

[20]Catton, *Centennial History*, 2:313; Foote, *Civil War*, 1:449.

Longstreet's aide-de-camp, Thomas J. Goree, wrote a few days after the battle that Jenkins' half-brigade of only 1,900 men had suffered 700 casualties, but that it had "whipped" Darius Couch's division and had "*immortalized* itself."[21]

Indeed, Jenkins' small force had suffered serious losses. Colonel John Bratton, leading the Sixth South Carolina, was wounded and then captured, and the regiment lost six of its captains. Colonel John R. R. Giles of the Fifth South Carolina was killed, and his major, William M. Foster, was wounded. The Palmetto Sharpshooters lost Captain J. Q. Carpenter of the Pacolet Guards who was shot through the heart. Carpenter, who had served with Jenkins since the war began, said to his men as he was dying, "Boys, I am killed, but you press on!"[22] Out of approximately 600 Palmetto Sharpshooters who went into the fight, 20 were killed and 205 wounded.[23]

JOHN R. R. GILES, ELECTED COLONEL OF THE FIFTH SOUTH CAROLINA VOLUNTEERS DURING THE REGIMENT'S REORGANIZATION IN APRIL 1862.

The two color companies under Captain William W. Humphreys and Captain Carpenter suffered the most. In his battle report Jenkins stated:

> In my two color companies, out of 80 men who entered, 40 were killed and wounded, and out of 11 in the color guard, 10 were shot down, and my colors, pierced by nine balls, passed through four hands without touching the ground.[24]

[21]Thomas J. Goree to his sister, Mary Frances Goree Kittrell, June 17, 1862, in Cutrer, ed., *Longstreet's Aide*, 87 (emphasis in original).

[22]O. R., vol. 11, part 1, p. 950. From Spartanburg, South Carolina, Captain Jacob Quickle Carpenter had entered Confederate service as captain of the Pacolet Guards in the Fifth South Carolina Volunteers. At the army's reorganization in April 1862, he was elected captain of Company M, Jenkins' Palmetto Sharpshooters.

[23]Yorkville *Enquirer*, June 19, 1862. Jenkins gave the casualty figures as 20 killed and 202 wounded. Micah Jenkins to Caroline Jenkins, June 2, 1862, in Thomas, *Career and Character*, 15. Major William Anderson gave the same figures as Jenkins. William Anderson to Lucretia McFall Anderson, June 2, 1862, William Anderson Collection.

[24]O. R., vol. 11, part 1, p. 950.

William Poe, of Humphreys' Company C, was the last man to bear the
Palmetto Sharpshooters' colors on May 31. As the fight was winding
down, he was posted in the middle of Williamsburg Road to separate the
two wings of Jenkins' regiments. He stood alone in the road, proudly
holding the colors, in dangerous defiance of the sporadic firing all around
him. One of Poe's comrades in Company C later wrote that he had
"often heard . . . Jenkins declare that this simple act of the gallant Poe
was the most striking and impressive instance of devotion he had ever
witnessed."[25]

The Fifth Regiment also suffered grievous casualties on May 31. For
example, its color company, under Captain S. B. Meacham, had 38 men
killed or wounded, including every one of its commissioned officers and
3 of its 4 color bearers.[26] One of these officers was Second Lieutenant
J. D. McConnell, who was shot through the calf but managed to limp to
a field hospital after the fight. The surgeon gave him a glass of rye
whisky, and McConnell later wrote:

> A little later [the surgeon] came back and cleaned out
> the wound by sticking a finger in from each side until
> they met in the middle. That hurt worse than the bullet
> which hit [the] numbing blow.[27]

Jenkins had himself been wounded, but not seriously. He was hit in
the knee, drawing blood but doing no other damage except to ruin a good
pair of trousers. A surgeon told him that if the ball had hit another half
inch to one side, it would have been necessary to amputate his leg above
the knee.[28]

In addition to the killed and wounded, some twenty men in the
Palmetto Sharpshooters were captured during the battle and were sent
to Fortress Monroe on the tip of the Virginia peninsula as prisoners of
war.[29]

In spite of all the gallantry displayed by the Palmetto Sharpshooters
during the battle on May 31, not every man in the regiment met the test
of courage. Several days after the fight, four or five soldiers were court-
martialed for abandoning their comrades during the fighting. These men

[25]Hoyt, *The Palmetto Riflemen*, 25-26. Hoyt refers to the color bearer only as "the gallant Poe." This
was William Poe, first corporal in Company C, the Palmetto Riflemen, under Captain William W.
Humphreys. Longstreet's aide-de-camp stated that the Palmetto Sharpshooters flag was hit nine times:
"This flag, at one time, changed hands 4 times in 3 minutes without falling to the ground." Thomas J.
Goree to Mary Frances Goree Kittrell, June 17, 1862, in Cutrer, ed., *Longstreet's Aide*, 89.
[26]McConnell, "Recollections," 4. Samuel B. Meacham was captain of the color company, Company E.
Unfortunately, no overall casualty figures are available for the Fifth South Carolina at Seven Pines.
[27]Ibid.
[28]Micah Jenkins to Caroline Jenkins, June 18, 1862, Micah Jenkins Papers, S.C.L.
[29]H. C. Conner to Ellen O'Leary, June 22, 1862, Henry Calvin Conner Papers.

were singled out at dress parade and sentenced to various punishments, such as being forced to walk on an elevated plank or stand on the head of a barrel for four hours in each of sixteen days, plus giving up one month's wages.[30]

At the end of the first day's fighting, the men in Anderson's brigade had the pleasure of rummaging through several hastily-abandoned Federal camps. A soldier in Company F of the Palmetto Sharpshooters described finding blankets, cheese, honey, tobacco, whiskey, coffee and sugar.[31] Another found "an old fashioned watch, and the photographs of a good many of the [Federal] officers who we have whipped."[32] Jenkins himself sent home some of the trophies he had collected after the battle, including a Union major's overcoat and a drum major's baton. He had a gold head put on the baton and presented it to Mr. William Latta, his friend back in Yorkville, as a gift.[33]

After the Battle of Seven Pines, Jenkins and his regiments received high praise for their part in the first day's fighting. Major William Anderson wrote that the Palmetto Sharpshooters had earned a great measure of respect, and he added:

> We are now pointed out and spoken of by every one here as the heroes of the Battle of Seven Pines, and we are to have the name of the Battle inscribed on our flag.[34]

In his report General Longstreet said that, while D. H. Hill's division had done most of the fighting on May 31,

> the attack of the two brigades under R. H. Anderson – one commanded by . . . Colonel M. Jenkins – was made with such spirit and regularity as to have driven back the most determined foe. This decided the day in our favor.[35]

---

[30]Ibid., June 15, 1862.

[31]J. S. Wingard to his sister, June 11, 1862, Simon P. Wingard Correspondence, D.U.L. This letter was written while J. S. Wingard was a member of Captain Joseph E. Lee's Company F, Palmetto Sharpshooters.

[32]H. C. Conner to Ellen O'Leary, June 2, 1862, Henry Calvin Conner Papers.

[33]Micah Jenkins to Caroline Jenkins, June 14, 1862, Micah Jenkins Papers, S.C.L. Mr. Latta, a prominent businessman from Yorkville, had sent the "Ebony Band" with Jenkins and the Fifth Regiment when they first went into service, in Charleston and on Sullivan's Island, South Carolina, during April 1861. Yorkville *Enquirer*, April 25, 1861.

[34]William Anderson to Lucretia McFall Anderson, June 7, 1862, William Anderson Collection.

[35]Longstreet's battle report, June 10, 1862, O. R., vol. 11, part 1, p. 940.

General Joe Johnston certainly helped Jenkins' chances of promotion by calling attention to the fact that he had acted as a brigadier general commanding several regiments.[36] General Gustavus W. Smith, who had commanded the Confederate left wing during the battle, wrote later:

> It is believed that the annals of war show few, if any, instances of more persistent, skillful and effective "battlefield fighting" than was done by the two South Carolina regiments, under Colonel Jenkins, in the afternoon of May 31.[37]

General D. H. Hill later echoed Smith's praise, saying that Jenkins and his regiments had accomplished a "march to victory, which has had but few parallels in history."[38]

Immediately after the Battle of Seven Pines, it was reported from Richmond that Jenkins' handling of his half of Anderson's brigade was "the theme of praise, from all the old army officers here."[39] There is no question that Jenkins felt he was deserving of promotion to brigadier general. Two weeks after the battle he wrote Caroline, "For various reasons the promotion would be [gratifying], but if it does not suit the President to appoint [me], I am content with my noble regiment."[40] Four days later, he was growing impatient and wrote:

> I am beginning to think I will not be promoted for my conduct in the battle of the "Seven Pines. . . ." If President Davis does not see fit to confer what all seem to think my due, I certainly have no idea of asking that or anything as a favor from him.[41]

He followed that letter with yet another, saying, "I am truly disappointed dear wife on your account, that I have not received promotion. It is highly unjust but cannot be helped."[42] Then he heard a disturbing rumor: General Longstreet had casually remarked that Jenkins could "afford to dispense with promotion [because he] had gotten glory enough."[43] Apparently, Longstreet must have been joking if indeed he ever made

---

[36]Johnston's battle report, June 24, 1862, O. R., vol. 11, part 1, p. 935. Specifically, Johnston stated that colonels Micah Jenkins and James Kemper had exercised "commands above their grades." Ibid.

[37]Gustavus W. Smith, *The Battle of Seven Pines* (New York: C. G. Crawford, Printer, 1891), 63.

[38]Address by General D. H. Hill delivered on October 22, 1885, *Southern Historical Society Papers*, 13 (Jan.-Dec. 1885): 264.

[39]*Carolina Spartan*, June 26, 1862.

[40]Micah Jenkins to Caroline Jenkins, June 14, 1862, Micah Jenkins Papers, S.C.L.

[41]Ibid., June 18, 1862.

[42]Ibid., June 22, 1862.

[43]Ibid.

such a remark. The fact is that on June 7, only one week following the
Battle at Seven Pines, he wrote General Johnston recommending R. H.
Anderson for promotion to major general and Jenkins for promotion to
brigadier general. Longstreet wrote in his letter:

> Colonel Jenkins had the command of General
> Anderson's brigade [at Seven Pines]. The distinguished
> ability and gallantry of this officer, and his brigade on the
> field, far surpasses any conduct of troops during the war.
> He met and drove back in rapid succession three
> brigades. The first . . . was more than double his
> strength, as his morning report of the day shows. The
> other [Federal] brigades fell back in confusion as the
> routed troops rushed [to the rear], closely pursued.[44]

The two-day battle at Seven Pines and Fair Oaks had cost the
Confederates six thousand casualties,[45] one of which would have a
definite impact on the future of
the war. At about sunset on
the first day of the fighting,
the Confederate commander,
General Joe Johnston, was
severely wounded by a rifle
ball and by a shell fragment
and had to be removed from
the field.   Jefferson Davis
responded the following day
by replacing Johnston with the
man who would command the
Army of Northern Virginia for
the remainder of the war –
General Robert E. Lee.

GENERAL JOSEPH E. JOHNSTON

---

[44]Longstreet to General Joseph Johnston, June 7, 1862, National Archives, Letters Received by the
Confederate Adjutant and Inspector General's Office, R.G. 109, series M410. At the end of this letter,
Longstreet added that "Colonel Jenkins was recommended by yourself, General Beauregard, and myself
for [promotion to brigadier general] last winter."
[45]Catton, *Centennial History*, 2:313.

Chapter 12

Gaines' Mill:
The Duel Between Four Regiments

A s a result of the Confederate attack at Seven Pines, General McClellan had held up his advance on Richmond, and his army had assumed a defensive posture a few miles north and east of the city. If allowed to maneuver freely, McClellan might have gotten close enough to Richmond to bring up his massive "siege train," as he had done at Yorktown, to bludgeon the city into submission. General Lee, the new commander of the Army of Northern Virginia, realized that he must prevent this by drawing McClellan's army out into the open, away from the capital. In early June, Lee ordered his troops to begin constructing trenches and earthworks all along their lines outside of Richmond, so that those lines could be held by only a small force. Lee planned to then take the larger part of his army out of the defensive lines in order to draw McClellan into the open for a general engagement.[1]

A daring three-day ride by Jeb Stuart and his Confederate cavalry, completely around the Union army, showed that McClellan's supply line was vulnerable and that his right flank was relatively unprotected. When

---

[1]Dowdey, *The Seven Days*, 133; Catton, *Centennial History*, 2:313-316.

Stuart returned and reported on June 16, 1862, Lee finally had the intelligence he needed to take the offensive. The right wing of the Union army was anchored near Mechanicsville, across the Chickahominy River, only about six or seven miles northeast of Richmond. It was there that Lee would launch his attack. His plan called for leaving General John Magruder and only 25,000 Confederate troops in the defensive lines in front of Richmond. There they were to conduct demonstrations which would deceive McClellan into believing the works were heavily defended. Lee would then use the main part of his army to attack the Federals' exposed right flank, manned by General Fitz-John Porter's V Corps, at Mechanicsville. Lee's strategy called for bringing Stonewall Jackson and his three divisions from the Shenandoah Valley to join in the attack. Underlying the plan was the considerable risk that McClellan might decide on a direct assault against Richmond and shift his forces to attack the lightly-defended Confederate lines east of the city.   Such an audacious attack, however, was not in McClellan's nature, and knowing this, Lee was willing to take the risk. Relying on Stonewall Jackson's own estimate of when his men would arrive at their assigned assault position on the Federals' right flank, General Lee selected June 26 as the date to begin the coordinated attack at Mechanicsville.[2]

Lee ordered Magruder to begin conducting demonstrations along his defensive works outside Richmond beginning on June 25. That same day, McClellan sent one of his corps against Magruder's lines about a mile west of Seven Pines to test their strength, and the Federals were repulsed in the Battle of Oak Grove. As Lee had hoped, these events caused the predictable McClellan to be overly cautious about attacking Richmond, even though the city's defensive works were held by a relatively small force.[3] The fighting along the defensive lines outside Richmond at Oak Grove on June 25 was the first in a series of battles which was destined to continue for a full week. This became known simply as "The Seven Days," and it would prove to be one of the bloodiest one-week military campaigns ever recorded.   In R. H. Anderson's brigade of Longstreet's division, Colonel Jenkins' Palmetto Sharpshooters and the Fifth South Carolina played a conspicuous role during two of the battles that week: Gaines' Mill and Frayser's Farm.

Lee's plan required General A. P. Hill's division to combine with Stonewall Jackson's three divisions near Mechanicsville early on June 26. They were then to turn east and mount a coordinated attack against the Federal right wing along Beaver Dam Creek below the village. After Jackson's divisions failed to arrive outside Mechanicsville as planned, however, A. P. Hill made the assault at Beaver Dam Creek without them

[2]Catton, Centennial History, 2:317-319; Freeman, Lee's Lieutenants, 1:497-498.
[3]Dowdey, The Seven Days, 159-164; Sears, Gates of Richmond, 183-189.

and was repulsed with heavy losses. General Lee had just suffered his first defeat as commander of the Army of Northern Virginia.[4]

Because of the delay caused by Jackson's absence and the resulting Federal repulse of A. P. Hill's assault, Longstreet's division did not become involved in the battle near Mechanicsville on June 26. The night before, Longstreet's men, including those in R. H. Anderson's brigade, had been told to cook three days' rations and were issued "sixty rounds." They fully expected to be in the thick of the next day's battle.[5] At three that morning, they left their camp outside Richmond and marched up the turnpike toward Mechanicsville, following D. H. Hill's division. They reached the Mechanicsville Bridge, where the turnpike crossed the Chickahominy, at about eight o'clock. That afternoon D. H. Hill's division crossed the bridge, and some of his troops joined A. P. Hill in the bloody fight along Beaver Dam Creek. Longstreet's division did not complete its crossing until after dark, and except for two brigades sent to relieve D. H. Hill's troops, went into bivouac near the bridge, well to the rear of the fighting.[6] That same night, aware that Stonewall Jackson's divisions had finally arrived and were prepared to combine with the rest of Lee's army at Mechanicsville, McClellan realized the danger to his right flank and ordered Porter's Federal corps to withdraw from Beaver Dam Creek at dawn the next day.

At daybreak on June 27, with Jackson's divisions in position on his left, Lee advanced against Beaver Dam Creek, but the Federals fell back about three miles to the east, near a five-story structure called Gaines' Mill. After repairing bridges all morning, Longstreet's division joined in the pursuit of the withdrawing Federals, with the brigades of R. H. Anderson and James L. Kemper bringing up the rear.[7]

That afternoon, Lee's army finally caught up with the Union troops who had taken up defensive positions on Turkey Hill, about two miles southeast of Gaines' Mill. On the west side of the hill, McClellan's men had prepared three sets of temporary works, one behind the other, protecting their artillery on the crest. At the foot of Turkey Hill were Boatswain Creek and a boggy swamp, which served as a moat for the Federal position. McClellan had chosen to make his stand here, from an extremely strong and well-defended position. Initial attempts by General A. P. Hill's men to assault Turkey Hill were easily repulsed by the Federals.[8]

---

[4]Catton, *Centennial History*, 2:328; Foote, *Civil War*, 1:481-483.
[5]Foote, *Civil War*, 1:478; Steedman, "Pea Ridge Volunteers," 1:237.
[6]Longstreet's report on the Seven Days' battles around Richmond, July 29, 1862, O. R., vol. 11, part 2, p. 756.
[7]Ibid.
[8]Foote, *Civil War*, 1:486; Freeman, *Lee's Lieutenants*, 1:520.

MAP 1: BATTLE OF GAINES' MILL - JUNE 27, 1862

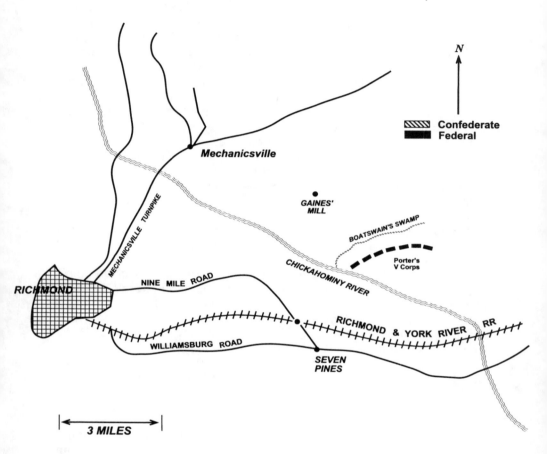

On the afternoon of June 27, 1862, Lee was finally in position to mount a coordinated attack against General Fitz-John Porter's Federal V Corps, which was in a strong defensive position on Turkey Hill, behind Boatswain's Swamp. The battle took place about two miles southeast of a prominent structure known as Gaines' Mill.

At around five o'clock that afternoon, Lee finally brought his divisions in position for a coordinated attack. Longstreet's division was on the far right of Lee's line, with the Chickahominy River a few hundred yards to its right. The initial plan called for that division to make only "a diversion in favor of the attacking columns." Longstreet reported that he quickly determined, however, to "change the feint into an attack, and orders for a general advance were issued."[9]

Longstreet divided R. H. Anderson's brigade, sending part of it, under Anderson, to support George E. Pickett's brigade, and the other part, under Colonel Jenkins, to protect the right flank of the brigades under General Cadmus Wilcox.[10] Anderson took with him the Sixth South Carolina and the Fourth South Carolina Battalion, as well as the Second South Carolina Rifles, a regiment which had just arrived in Virginia to join the brigade.[11] Jenkins took the Palmetto Sharpshooters and the Fifth South Carolina and positioned them on the right of Wilcox's brigade. They were reminded of the several unsuccessful attempts by other units that afternoon to take Turkey Hill, and they were bluntly told:

> [T]his falling back is no part of the General Order of the day – it is not expected that the troops of this command will yield an inch – [but] that they will . . . push steadily forward, driving the enemy before them – that every officer and every man will do his duty.[12]

As they waited to attack, the men in the two regiments under Jenkins' command were concealed from the Federal lines, but many of them were killed or wounded by exploding shells, grape or canister.[13] To most of the men, it was a relief to finally hear the order, "Charge!"[14] When the order came, Jenkins and his two regiments, along with Cadmus Wilcox's men on the left, took off at a full run, yelling and shouting as they crossed Boatswain Creek. First they overran each of the three Union lines of works on the face of the hill; then they charged the Federal guns on its crest. They found, however, that the men in John B. Hood's Texas brigade had narrowly beaten them to the crest and had already taken the guns, but with heavy losses. The Federals were driven from the hill but attempted one counterattack, and Jenkins and his men were sent to

---

[9] O. R., vol. 11, part 2, p. 757.
[10] Ibid.
[11] The Second South Carolina Rifles, *Roll of South Carolina Volunteers in the Confederate States Provisional Army* (Memory Rolls), 3:319, Records of the Confederate Historian, S.C.D.A.H., Columbia, South Carolina. Gaines' Mill was the first engagement in Virginia for the Second South Carolina Rifles.
[12] J. Banks Lyle to M. S. McArthur, July 15, 1862, Joseph Banks Lyle Letters.
[13] *Carolina Spartan*, July 10, 1862.
[14] Ibid.

MAP 2: BATTLE OF GAINES' MILL - JUNE 27, 1862

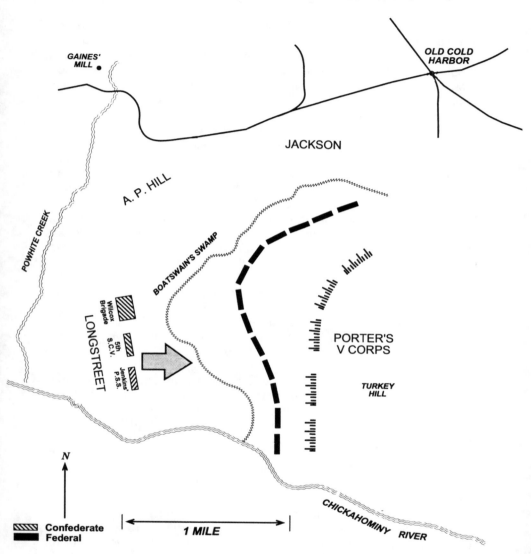

For the attack against Porter's V Corps near Gaines' Mill, Longstreet's brigades were positioned on the right of Lee's army. Longstreet divided R. H. Anderson's brigade and gave Colonel Micah Jenkins command of the Palmetto Sharpshooters and the Fifth South Carolina Volunteers. Jenkins and his men attacked on the right of the brigade commanded by Cadmus Wilcox. They crossed Boatswain's Swamp around five p.m. on June 27 and crashed through three separate lines of Union troops on the west face of Turkey Hill. Jenkins and his two regiments finally joined in the charge against the Federal guns on Turkey Hill, reaching the crest shortly before dark.

meet them. Again the battle opened briefly before the Federal troops gave way in disorder.[15]

Almost at dark, Jenkins and his two regiments were sent off to the right, toward the Chickahominy River, to clear the area of Union stragglers and to protect the right flank of Lee's army. The air was still cloudy and acrid with the smoke of spent gunpowder when the Palmetto Sharpshooters and the Fifth South Carolina Volunteers came upon a large field surrounded by woods. Marching in two separate columns toward the Chickahominy, with the Fifth Regiment in the rear, the men could hear the occasional crack of musket fire behind them. As the two regiments silently moved out into the field, the men in the Fifth South Carolina began to see the shapes of other troops moving in the woods a few hundred feet to the left. As soon as Jenkins received the report of movement in the woods, he stood up in his stirrups and scanned the treeline with his field glasses. In the waning light, a column of men could be seen moving out of the woods toward the river. Unless they changed direction, they would march right by Jenkins and his two regiments. He immediately sensed the danger and, halting his men, faced them to the left and ordered total quiet.[16] With flags furled, the approaching column of two Federal regiments marched stubbornly onward, roughly parallel to the Fifth South Carolina and the Palmetto Sharpshooters. Jenkins made the first move, demanding that the men in the moving column identify themselves. When there was no response, Jenkins gave his troops the command, "Ready," which was repeated all along his line. The column came closer until one Federal regiment was almost directly opposite the Palmetto Sharpshooters, and the other regiment was opposite the Fifth South Carolina. One soldier in Company C of the Palmetto Sharpshooters described what happened then:

> Their column was not more than fifty yards in our front, marching by the flank, while our men were at the ready, and as the head of their column came in front of our color company, the [Federal] officer in command broke the silence by saying, "Halt! Front!" to which Jenkins replied, "Fire!" and our volley made deadly works of their ranks.[17]

---

[15]J. Banks Lyle to M. S. McArthur, July 15, 1862, Joseph Banks Lyle Letters; Dowdey, *The Seven Days*, 239.
[16]*Carolina Spartan*, July 10, 1862; Yorkville *Enquirer*, August 7, 1862.
[17]James A. Hoyt, "Anderson's Brigade at Gaines' Mill," *Confederate Veteran*, 7 (May 1899): 226. Hoyt was a member of Captain Humphreys' Company C, the "Palmetto Riflemen," of the Palmetto Sharpshooters at the time of this incident. For another description of this incident at Gaines' Mill, see Hoyt, *The Palmetto Riflemen*, 28-29.

The Palmetto Sharpshooters had just managed to beat the Sixteenth Michigan to the draw in what has been called "a duel between two regiments."[18]

Actually, the duel turned out to be between four instead of two regiments. The Fifth South Carolina, apparently at some distance to the rear of the Palmetto Sharpshooters, almost simultaneously engaged in a similar shoot-out with the Eighty-third Pennsylvania Volunteers which had been following the Sixteenth Michigan. This other duel, even though it took place on the same field at about the same time, occurred in a manner different from the first. One officer in the Fifth Regiment described how the shooting started between it and the Pennsylvania regiment:

> A white flag advanced towards us from their lines and was met midway by Lieutenant Fross and [Lt.] Colonel Jackson bearing another. To our question, the reply was returned, "We have no orders to surrender," [and] both flags returned to their lines and our boys poured into them at a distance of less than 100 yards a volley which cut them down where they stood by the scores, but they . . . promptly gave us back our fire. The fight was short, but . . . it was very bloody.[19]

After receiving the deadly first volley, each Union regiment was able to return the fire, and several additional volleys were exchanged. Finally, Colonel Jenkins led a charge which broke the opposing line and drove the surviving bluecoats into the swamp along the Chickahominy River.[20] Later it was learned that the two Federal regiments had become separated from their main body during the afternoon's fighting and were trying to make their way back to their retreating comrades. When their attempt to elude Jenkins and his two South Carolina regiments was unsuccessful, and seeing that they were evenly matched, the two Union colonels had decided to confront them. It was a courageous decision, but one which cost both Federal regiments dearly.

---

[18]Thomas, *Career and Character*, 16.

[19]Steedman, "Pea Ridge Volunteers," 2:237. See also, Hoyt, "Anderson's Brigade at Gaines' Mill," 226; *Carolina Spartan*, July 10, 1862; Yorkville *Enquirer*, August 7, 1862; battle report of Lieutenant Colonel Hugh S. Campbell, of the Eighty-third Pennsylvania, July 5, 1862, O. R., vol. 11, part 2, p. 345.

[20]Hoyt, *The Palmetto Riflemen*, 28. In the words of the Eighty-third Pennsylvania historian:
> To retreat in column would be madness. The word was accordingly given to break, and seek the river.

Samuel P. Bates, *History of Pennsylvania Volunteers, 1861-5*, vol. 4 (Harrisburg, Pennsylvania: B. Singerly, State Printer, 1869; reprint, Wilmington, North Carolina: Broadfoot Publishing Co., 1993), 1251.

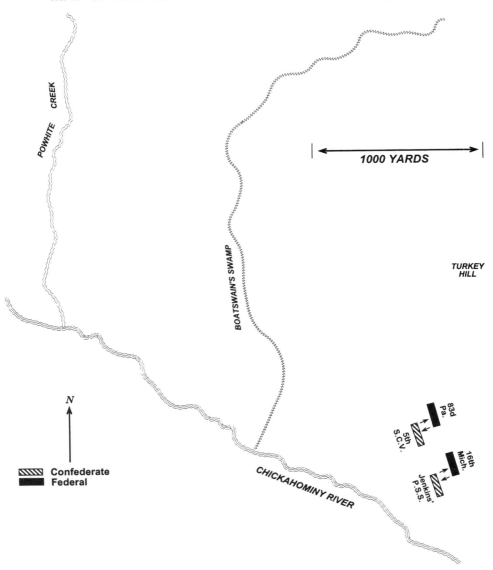

MAP 3: BATTLE OF GAINES' MILL - JUNE 27, 1862

POWHITE CREEK

1000 YARDS

BOATSWAIN'S SWAMP

TURKEY HILL

N

83d Pa.

5th S.C.V.

16th Mich.

Jenkins' P.S.S.

CHICKAHOMINY RIVER

Confederate
Federal

At dusk, after the Battle of Gaines' Mill had sputtered to a halt, Jenkins and his two regiments, the Palmetto Sharpshooters and the Fifth South Carolina, were sent toward the Chickahominy River to clear the army's right flank of Union troops. The two South Carolina regiments surprised two Federal regiments which had become separated from their brigade and were trying to escape across the river. At that time a "duel" occurred between the four regiments in which the Sixteenth Michigan and the Eighty-third Pennsylvania were routed. Jenkins' men captured the colors of the Sixteenth Michigan in the fight.

Unofficially, the Sixteenth Michigan lost 47 killed, including its major, and 114 wounded; the Eighty-third Pennsylvania had 46 killed, including its colonel, and 51 wounded.[21] These figures do not include those Union troops who were taken prisoner or reported missing. In the words of one witness, the two Federal regiments "seemed to have melted away."[22]

The brief and bloody fight was not, however, without great cost to the two Confederate regiments. The Palmetto Sharpshooters had 9 men killed and 74 wounded; the Fifth lost 21 killed and 60 wounded, including Lieutenant Colonel Andrew Jackson. He was wounded in both thighs, and his arm was so badly mangled that it had to be amputated on the field.[23] During the charge that ended the skirmish, the Palmetto Sharpshooters captured the colors of the Sixteenth Michigan. Jenkins formally requested that he be permitted to present those colors to Governor Francis Pickens of South Carolina, and the request was personally approved by General Lee and the secretary of war.[24] In conveying the approval of Jenkins' request, General Longstreet's assistant adjutant general, G. M. Sorrel, wrote Jenkins:

> I am permitted . . . to congratulate you . . . on the possession of these handsome colors, won as they were on the evening of the memorable 27th of June by the conspicuous courage and devotion ever exhibited by your gallant command.[25]

Following the fighting near Gaines' Mill on June 27, General Longstreet wrote in his report:

> There was more individual gallantry displayed upon this field than any I have ever seen. Conspicuous among those gallant officers and men were Brigadier General R. H. Anderson . . . [and] Colonels Jenkins, [and others]. . . .[26]

After the fighting had ended that day, Jenkins and his two regiments slept in the woods among the abandoned Union fortifications near Turkey

---

[21]Hoyt, "Anderson's Brigade at Gaines' Mill," 226.

[22]Yorkville *Enquirer*, August 7, 1862.

[23]Return of Casualties in Confederate Forces, Gaines' Mill, O. R., vol. 11, part 2, p. 979. Jackson's injuries forced him to resign on October 31, 1862.

[24]Lee to Longstreet, July 18, 1862, O. R., vol. 11, part 3, p. 644. In this letter, General Lee stated he was "authorized . . . to comply with the request of Colonel Jenkins, as to retaining the regimental standard of the Sixteenth Michigan for presentation to the Governor of his State."

[25]Sorrel to Jenkins, July 21, 1862, O. R., vol. 51, part 2, p. 595. See also, Yorkville *Enquirer*, August 7, 1862.

[26]O. R., vol. 11, part 2, p. 758.

Hill. According to one soldier, they used discarded Federal knapsacks as pillows, covered themselves with Union blankets, "took a smoke from Yankee cigars . . . and slept soundly amid hundreds of the dead and dying."[27] Before Jenkins turned in for the night, one of the troops in the Sixth South Carolina offered him a metal "breastplate," abandoned by a Union soldier who had worn it for protection against small arms fire. Understanding that his wearing it would convey a negative image to his men, Jenkins declined it and suggested that the soldier use it himself. Fortunately, he took Jenkins' advice; wearing the breastplate, he survived being shot in the chest only three days later.[28]

The morning after the Battle of Gaines' Mill, some of the officers and men in the Sixteenth Michigan, whom the Palmetto Sharpshooters had beaten to the draw the night before, came in to camp and surrendered to Jenkins. They told him that most of the Michigan regiment had either been killed or captured, and they felt they should be with their captured comrades. Their officers said that they had never experienced such a devastating fire as they had in the previous night's skirmish.[29] Later that day, one of the men in R. H. Anderson's brigade wrote:

> Our command is resting a little. I presume that every ambulance in the army is flying to and fro carrying the wounded to Richmond.[30]

During the Battle of Gaines' Mill, General Lee had finally been able to mount a coordinated attack. His army had collapsed the Federal line and taken twenty-two guns and more than 2,000 prisoners. Lee's casualties numbered about 8,500, while McClellan had lost about 6,800, but the new commander of the Army of Northern Virginia had won his first victory.[31]

In spite of his numerical superiority, General McClellan met that night with his corps commanders and announced his plans to retreat to Harrison's Landing on the James River, where his army would be under the protection of Federal gunboats. Uncertain of McClellan's intentions, however, Lee was reluctant to commit his army until he knew more. As a result, he spent all of June 28 trying to determine which way the

---

[27]*Carolina Spartan*, July 10, 1862.

[28]James Lide Coker, *History of Company G, Ninth S.C. Regiment, Infantry, S.C. Army, and of Company E, Sixth S.C. Regiment, Infantry, S.C. Army* (Charleston, South Carolina: Walker, Evans and Cogswell Co., 1899; reprint, Greenwood, South Carolina: The Attic Press, 1979), 75. In the next battle (Frayser's Farm) the soldier was hit in the breastplate, which he was wearing, and the ball glanced off, wounding him in the arm. This soldier is identified only as an "Irishman in Captain Canty's Company" in the Sixth South Carolina Volunteers. Ibid.

[29]*Carolina Spartan*, August 11, 1862.

[30]Reid, *History of the Fourth Regiment of S.C. Volunteers*, 99.

[31]Foote, *Civil War*, 1:490-491.

Federal army was retreating, and McClellan gained a full day's head start.[32]

Finally, on the morning of June 29, Lee became convinced that McClellan's army was indeed withdrawing to the James River, and the Confederate commander saw an opportunity to destroy the massive Federal column as it was in transit. Lee planned to intercept the enemy column as it moved through White Oak Swamp, south of the Chickahominy River, while its maneuverability was severely restricted. He would attack the head of the column as it came out of the swamp, and the tail before it went in, trapping the main Federal body in the middle. To attack the head, Lee sent Longstreet's and A. P. Hill's divisions on a fifteen-mile march to get in position south of the swamp for a combined assault which would be made on Monday, June 30, with Huger's division.[33]

Meanwhile, on June 29, General Magruder's Confederate troops attacked McClellan's rear guard at Savage Station on the Richmond and York Railroad, about a mile below the Chickahominy River. Stonewall Jackson's divisions were expected to join in the assault, but failed to do so, and the Federal rear guard was able to hold fast. The attack at Savage Station did nothing to impede the Federal withdrawal, and McClellan gained another day to move his army toward Harrison's Landing. He was slowly and methodically slipping out of Lee's grasp.[34] The last and best chance to destroy a part of McClellan's army would come the next day, Monday, June 30, as it moved through a crossroads called Glendale, just below White Oak Swamp.[35] A short distance south of that junction was Frayser's Farm, a name that Jenkins and his men would never forget.

---

[32]Freeman, *Lee's Lieutenants*, 1:539-540.
[33]Foote, *Civil War*, 1:495-496.
[34]Sears, *Gates of Richmond*, 269-274.
[35]Ibid., 278-279; Foote, *Civil War*, 1:497-498.

Chapter 13

Carnage At Frayser's Farm

S carcely ten months earlier, Micah Jenkins had written
enthusiastically from Virginia about the war to his brother,
John:

> [S]o ends the first expedition under my command. I wish
> you had been with me to enjoy it. The country was
> beautiful and there was a sufficient sense of danger to
> give spice to it.[1]

That letter was written immediately after the expedition to Great Falls in
September 1861, when Jenkins and his command had successfully
attacked a Federal installation along the Potomac River without suffering
a single casualty. However, on July 3, 1862, he wrote his wife a letter of
an entirely different tone:

> I write with the most saddened feelings. God has been
> merciful, but, oh my God, what terrible trials have we

---

[1]Micah Jenkins to John Jenkins, September 11, 1861, John Jenkins Papers, S.C.L.

been through. Nearly all my best friends, men and officers, killed and wounded.[2]

Clearly shocked by the brutality of the war, Jenkins followed that letter three days later with another in which he promised to tell his wife about the "sad scenes" he had witnessed. In it he said, "I feel so broken up having lost so many of my best officers and men."[3] Both of those letters were composed in the week following the Battle of Frayser's Farm, the next-to-last engagement in the Seven Days. It was a savage one-afternoon fight in which Lee's army failed to carry out his plan for a coordinated attack against McClellan's retreating column.[4] In this battle, the Palmetto Sharpshooters and the Fifth South Carolina played a prominent but bloody role.

By ten o'clock on the morning of June 30, 1862, McClellan's massive Federal column had made an orderly retreat from the Gaines' Mill battlefield through White Oak Swamp and was moving along two roads towards its objective: Harrison's Landing on the James River. McClellan realized, however, that only after his troops and wagon train were safely at Malvern Hill, some six miles south of the swamp, would they be within the protective cover of the Federal gunboats on the James River. About midway between the swamp and Malvern Hill was Glendale, a sleepy crossroads where a blacksmith named Riddell had his shop and where McClellan's two routes of retreat converged into a single road running south to Malvern Hill. As a potential bottleneck for the Federal withdrawal, Glendale provided Lee with a strategic point of attack. On the day before, Lee had started three divisions toward Glendale: General Huger's division by one road, and the divisions of Longstreet and A. P. Hill along the Darbytown Road. For Longstreet and Hill, with some 18,000 soldiers, this was a fifteen-mile march from Gaines' Mill. Lee was hopeful that he could surprise the Federal column the next day as it moved along the Quaker Road from Glendale to Malvern Hill; however, McClellan's generals had fully prepared by posting four divisions at Glendale to protect their withdrawal.[5]

Longstreet's division, including R. H. Anderson's brigade, had marched from Gaines' Mill to a position along the Darbytown Road, and by nightfall on June 29 it was, in Longstreet's words, "within easy striking distance" of the Federal column moving toward Malvern Hill.[6] The next morning the men broke camp, turned left onto the Long Bridge Road and marched northeast to within about a mile of Glendale. There they halted

---

[2]Micah Jenkins to Caroline Jenkins, July 3, 1862, in Thomas, *Career and Character*, 17.
[3]Micah Jenkins to Caroline Jenkins, July 6, 1862, Micah Jenkins Papers, S.C.L.
[4]Foote, *Civil War*, 1:507; Freeman, *Lee's Lieutenants*, 1:587.
[5]Foote, *Civil War*, 506-507.
[6]Longstreet's report on the Battle of Frayser's Farm, July 29, 1862, O. R., vol. 11, part 2, p. 759.

MAP 1: BATTLE OF FRAYSER'S FARM - JUNE 30, 1862

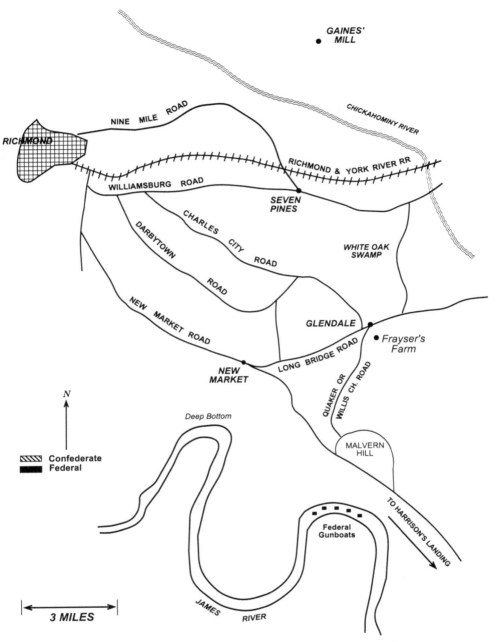

On June 30, 1862, McClellan's Federal army continued its withdrawal south toward Harrison's Landing on the James River. Lee had planned a coordinated attack against the retreating Federal column at Glendale, as the Union troops moved along the Willis Church (or Quaker) Road, toward Malvern Hill. That afternoon Lee sent the divisions of Longstreet and A. P. Hill against four Union Divisions at Glendale. Much of the fighting took place around Frayser's Farm, a two hundred acre tract south of Glendale.

and were joined by General Lee and Jefferson Davis to await the opening of the planned attack by General Huger's Confederate division. The problem was that Huger's division had bogged down short of Glendale on the Charles City Road and was nowhere in sight. When he realized that Huger would not arrive in time to open the engagement, Lee decided to send Longstreet's men, along with Hill's division, against the Federals without further delay. Unknown to Lee, he was sending only two divisions to take on almost twice as many Union troops who also had the advantage of being lodged behind defensive works.[7]

Since he was in charge of the attack, Longstreet had placed his own division under R. H. Anderson, who had in turn given the command of his own brigade to Jenkins, his senior colonel.[8] Anderson's brigade still consisted of the Second South Carolina Rifles, the Fourth South Carolina Battalion, the Fifth South Carolina, the Sixth South Carolina, and the Palmetto Sharpshooters.[9]

Longstreet's men soon located the Union divisions near Frayser's Farm, a two-hundred acre tract less than a mile southwest of Glendale on the Quaker Road. Colonel Jenkins was given orders to determine the size and strength of the Union force, which he did by advancing one of his regiments, the Sixth South Carolina, as skirmishers. The men in that regiment drove the Federal pickets in upon their main body and reported that McClellan's troops were "in force and position, ready for battle."[10] Longstreet then ordered his two divisions brought up for the attack.

At about three that afternoon, Longstreet's artillery began firing, and this fire was immediately returned by the Union batteries west of the Quaker Road. One Federal battery was so close to Longstreet's lines that he ordered Jenkins, with R. H. Anderson's brigade, to silence it. Since the men in the Sixth South Carolina were still deployed as skirmishers, Jenkins advanced the remainder of the brigade toward the battery. Instead of merely silencing the battery, however, Jenkins' brigade attacked it. General Longstreet later recalled:

> I sent orders for Jenkins to silence the battery, under the
> impression that our wait was understood, and that [his]
> sharp-shooters would be pushed forward till they could

---

[7] O. R., vol. 11, part 2, p. 759; Foote, *Civil War*, 1:506-507.

[8] O. R., vol. 11, part 2, p. 759.

[9] Jenkins' report on Frayser's Farm (undated), in Janet B. Hewett, Noah Andre Trudeau and Bryce A. Suderow, eds., *Supplement to the Official Records of the Union and Confederate Armies*, Part One (Battle Reports) in 12 volumes (Wilmington, North Carolina: Broadfoot Publishing Co., 1994 —), 2:442. Jenkins' report states that the units in his brigade were commanded as follows: Second S.C: Rifles, Major Robert A. Thompson; Fourth S.C. Battalion, Captain David L. Hall; Fifth S.C.V., Captain John D. Wylie; Sixth S.C.V., Lt. Colonel J. M. Steedman; and the Palmetto Sharpshooters, Major William Anderson.

[10] O. R., vol. 11, part 2, p. 759.

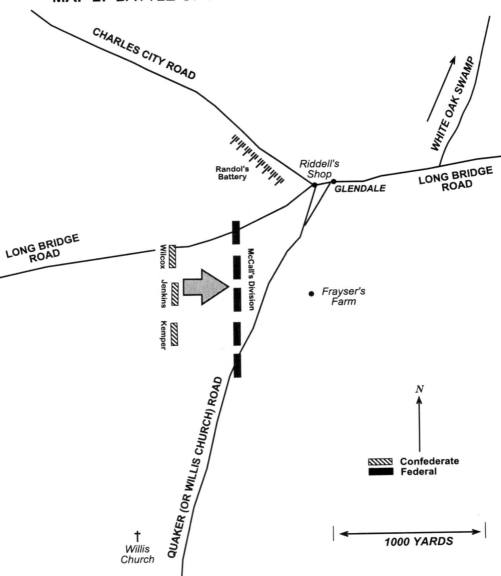

MAP 2: BATTLE OF FRAYSER'S FARM - JUNE 30, 1862

CHARLES CITY ROAD

WHITE OAK SWAMP

Randol's Battery

Riddell's Shop

GLENDALE

LONG BRIDGE ROAD

LONG BRIDGE ROAD

Wilcox

Jenkins

Kemper

McCall's Division

Frayser's Farm

QUAKER (OR WILLIS CHURCH) ROAD

Willis Church

N

Confederate
Federal

1000 YARDS

Shortly after 3 p.m. on June 30, 1862, Longstreet sent his division against the center of the Union lines, manned by troops from George A. McCall's Division, a few hundred yards west of the Quaker (or Willis Church) Road. Jenkins' Brigade drove the gunners from Cooper's Federal Battery and charged McCall's lines which were broken in fierce hand-to-hand fighting. During this charge Randol's Federal Battery, near Riddell's Shop about 300 yards to Jenkins' left, was able to enfilade his lines. Jenkins' men went down by the scores, but they were able to reach and hold a portion of the Willis Church Road until they were compelled to withdraw.

pick off the gunners, thus ridding us of that annoyance; but the gallant Jenkins, only too anxious for a dash at a battery, charged and captured it, thus precipitating battle.[11]

To charge the battery, Jenkins positioned the Second South Carolina Rifles on the right, the Palmetto Sharpshooters on their left, the Fifth South Carolina next, and the Fourth South Carolina Battalion on the left of the brigade. When they advanced, firing at Captain James H. Cooper's Battery B, First Pennsylvania Light Artillery, Cooper's men began limbering their six 10-pounder Parrott rifles and moving them off to the left. Jenkins then yelled, "Shoot down their horses," and as the horses fell, the Federal gunners abandoned their battery. This immediately brought a hailstorm of musketry from General George A. McCall's Federal division, which was protected behind a temporary breastworks in front of Jenkins' brigade. One of McCall's regiments, the Ninth Pennsylvania, then charged and retook Cooper's battery, but with the help of two Alabama regiments, Jenkins' troops rallied and again drove the Federals from the guns.[12]

Jenkins and his men then moved through Cooper's abandoned battery and advanced against the breastworks under a galling frontal fire from General Truman Seymour's Federal brigade. Suddenly, two other Federal batteries opened fire about three hundred yards on the left, and from this position were able "to enfilade [Jenkins'] entire command."[13] At this point, his men were not only taking murderous musket fire in the face, but were being methodically slaughtered by grape, canister and shells from twelve Federal guns on their left flank. Twenty or 30 of Jenkins' South Carolinians fell from each Federal volley of small arms fire, but the twelve guns did even more damage. One soldier described the terrible effectiveness of this artillery fire by writing:

> The sullen "thug" of the grape shot as they bury themselves into the bodies of the men is an appalling sound – one that can never be forgotten. . . . Whole companies are decimated.[14]

---

[11]James Longstreet, *From Manassas to Appomattox, Memoirs of the Civil War in America*, edited by James I. Robertson, Jr. (Bloomington, Indiana: University of Indiana Press, 1960), 135.

[12]Jenkins' report on Frayser's Farm, in Hewett, Trudeau and Suderow, eds., *Supplement to Official Records*, 2:442-443; Sears, *Gates of Richmond*, 295-296.

[13]Yorkville *Enquirer*, August 7, 1862; Jenkins' report on Frayser's Farm, in Hewett, Trudeau and Suderow, eds., *Supplement to Official Records*, 2:442. In his report, Jenkins said, "No support on our left kept us exposed to this terrible enfilade fire during our entire advance. . . ."

[14]Yorkville *Enquirer*, August 7, 1862. A single grape shot was more than an inch in diameter and would leave a gaping wound when it hit a man. James R. Boulware Diary, June 18, 1862, Virginia State Library, Richmond, Virginia.

With "a single wave of his sword [Jenkins pointed] out the path of duty," and even though unsupported on the left by other brigades, his men continued their advance toward the breastworks.[15] Jenkins reported that as they got to within twenty yards of the Union line, many of the Federal soldiers rose and ran, "and our cool, deliberate volleys prostrated them in hundreds."[16] On horseback, Jenkins was the first man over the breastworks, and his horse was shot from under him.[17] Then his men came over behind him and fought the remaining Federal soldiers with bayonets and musket butts. As the Union troops abandoned the breastworks, F. W. Kilpatrick, the captain of Company B of the Palmetto Sharpshooters, along with Lieutenant Robert M. Simms of the Sixth South Carolina, then turned the abandoned guns of Cooper's battery on the fleeing Federals "and handsomely accelerated their 'change of base.'"[18]

After being routed from their works, the Union soldiers of McCall's division retreated for a few hundred yards, but then stopped and regrouped with arriving reinforcements. Although now facing this larger body of Federal troops, Jenkins and his decimated brigade had reached the Quaker Road. In his battle report, Jenkins wrote:

> I had gained command of the "Quaker Road" and [McCall's] reinforcing masses could not advance but in direct fire of our men; I had a very strong position and, with my weakened numbers, could have made it good for some time, but here occurred a painful and disastrous event.[19]

The ability of Jenkins' brigade to hold its strategically important position on the Quaker Road depended entirely on the support he was supposed to have received from Lawrence O. Branch's brigade of A. P. Hill's division. Unfortunately, when they came up on Jenkins' right rear, Branch's men started firing through Jenkins' line at the Federals. In his report, Jenkins stated that Branch's men "threw my right Regiment [the

---

[15]Yorkville *Enquirer*, August 7, 1862.

[16]Jenkins' report on Frayser's Farm, in Hewett, Trudeau and Suderow, eds., *Supplement to Official Records*, 2:442.

[17]Robert F. Jenkins, "Charge of the Carolinians at Frayser's Farm," Charleston *News and Courier*, October 16, 1935, p. 3. This article contains an account of the brigade's charge at Frayser's Farm by W. B. Smith, captain of the Jasper Light Infantry of the Palmetto Sharpshooters, as he gave it to Robert F. Jenkins, Micah Jenkins' son.

[18]Yorkville *Enquirer*, August 7, 1862.

[19]Jenkins report on Frayser's Farm, in Hewett, Trudeau and Suderow, eds., *Supplement to Official Records*, 2:443. The Quaker Road, also known as the Willis Church Road, ran south out of Glendale to Malvern Hill, less than three miles away, and was the Federals' main route of retreat. Dowdey, *The Seven Days*, 283.

Second South Carolina Rifles] into confusion by massing upon it and firing through it," and that Branch's brigade finally "withdrew in great disorder, leaving my few to hold the ground."[20] Eventually, when Federal units had regrouped with reinforcements for a counterattack and had advanced beyond the flanks of Jenkins' brigade, his men were compelled to withdraw from their forward position along the Quaker Road. They then combined with Cadmus Wilcox's brigade in an advance which resulted in the capture of six of the twelve Federal guns on their left. These guns were from Alanson M. Randol's battery, which had killed and wounded so many of Jenkins' men during their charge against McCall's division earlier that afternoon.[21] Again the opposing solders became so mingled that they fought hand-to-hand. General McCall, paying tribute to the combatants on both sides, said in his report:

> It was here my fortune to witness one of the fiercest bayonet fights that perhaps ever occurred on this continent. . . . I saw skulls crushed by the butts of muskets, and every effort made by either party in this life-or-death struggle, proving indeed that here Greek had met Greek.[22]

For Jenkins' brigade, that was the final advance of that bloody June 30, a day in which they had not only "captured [Cooper's] battery in [their] front [and] charged and [driven] back McCall's entire [Federal] division," but had also joined in the capture of the six guns of Randol's battery.[23] They had accomplished all they had been asked to do, and much more, but at a terrible price.

---

[20]Jenkins' report on Frayser's Farm, in Hewett, Trudeau and Suderow, eds., *Supplement to Official Records*, 2:443. In his report, General Longstreet stated that "Branch's brigade . . . did not render the prompt support to our right which was expected. . . ." O. R., vol. 11, part 2, p. 759.

[21]Jenkins' report on Frayser's Farm, in Hewett, Trudeau and Suderow, eds., *Supplement to Official Records*, 2:443. In his report, Jenkins states that the enfilade fire on his left came from twelve guns. Ibid., 2:442. No doubt six of these guns were twelve-pounder Napoleons from Alanson M. Randol's Battery E, United States regulars. Sears, *Gates of Richmond*, 296; Randol's report, July 7, 1862, O. R., vol. 11, part 2, p. 256.

[22]McCall's report on Frayser's Farm, August 12, 1862, O. R., vol. 11, part 2, p. 391. See also, Thomas, *Career and Character*, 17.

[23]Yates Snowden, ed., *History of South Carolina*, vol. 2 (Chicago: The Lewis Publishing Co., 1920), 718; Capers, *South Carolina*, 6:71. Lieutenant Randol reported: "Thirty-eight horses were killed and 8 wounded. I also lost six light 12-pounder guns, four caissons partially packed, and two limbers." Randol's Report, July 7, 1862, O. R., vol. 11, part 2, p. 256.

MAP 3: BATTLE OF FRAYSER'S FARM - JUNE 30, 1862

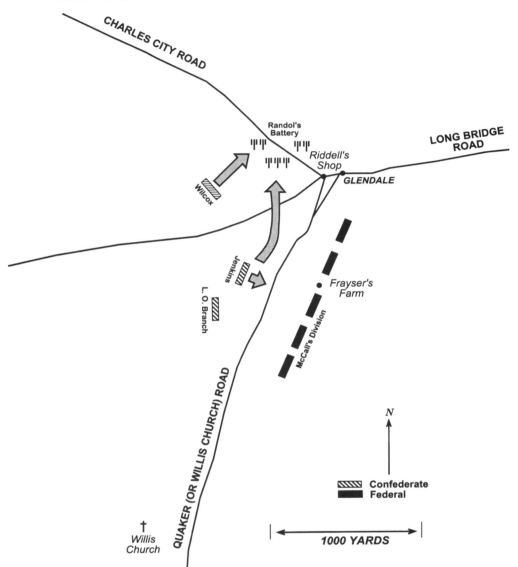

Once Jenkins' Brigade was compelled to withdraw from the Quaker (or Willis Church) Road, it swung left for an attack, with Wilcox's Brigade, against Randol's Battery near Riddell's Shop. Randol's guns, six light 12-pounder Napoleons, were captured, as was Federal General George A. McCall. However, it had been a costly battle for Jenkins' men. The Palmetto Sharpshooters suffered sixty-seven percent casualties in the afternoon's fighting near Frayser's Farm.

One eyewitness to the advance and charge by Jenkins' regiments against Cooper's battery and McCall's division wrote:

> No wonder that tears fill the eyes of some, who have been looking on, as they watch [Jenkins'] devoted band marching through the valley of death.[24]

Some of those tears were shed by Jenkins himself over the death of his young adjutant, John D. Lee. Having just graduated from the Citadel in 1861, the twenty-one-year-old Lee had both legs shot off during the charge. He was able to bandage one leg by himself and partially wrap the other before he died. Upon the close of the day's fighting, Jenkins found Lee on the field and, unable to control his emotions, broke down and wept over the loss of his young friend.[25] In addition, Jenkins' brother-in-law, John W. Jamison, was shot through a lung and was close to death. He had been convinced to leave South Carolina to become Jenkins' aide-de-camp and had only recently arrived in Virginia. While near death and bleeding on the field after the fight, Jamison was robbed of his watch and pistol by "one of the ghouls of the battlefields" who, like vultures, followed the carnage to rob dead and dying soldiers of their personal effects.[26]

The colors of the Palmetto Sharpshooters were borne by several men, all wounded or killed, until the flag was finally carried through the end of the fight by Christopher L. Reid, a private in Captain William Humphrey's Company C.[27] Major William Anderson, who had acted as commander of the Palmetto Sharpshooters, was mortally wounded and died four days later. Jenkins wrote, "I am much aggrieved at the death of my noble Major."[28]

The losses in the Palmetto Sharpshooters were the highest of any Confederate regiment in the battle; 211 wounded (30 of these, mortally) and 49 killed out of 375 who entered the action.[29] No wonder an officer in one of the regiment's color companies, Humphrey's Company C, which

---

[24]Yorkville *Enquirer*, August 7, 1862.

[25]Thomas, *History of the South Carolina Military Academy*, 126-127. John D. Lee was from Sumter, South Carolina, and had served as a lieutenant in Captain Alexander Colclough's Company E of the Palmetto Sharpshooters.

[26]Robert F. Jenkins, "Charge of the Carolinians at Frayser's Farm," 3. Robert Jenkins' version of this incident is based on an account given him by John W. Jamison.

[27]Thomas, *Career and Character*, 17. Christopher L. Reid was from Walhalla, South Carolina.

[28]Micah Jenkins to Caroline Jenkins, July 6, 1862, Micah Jenkins Papers, S.C.L.

[29]Jenkins' report on Frayser's Farm, in Hewett, Trudeau and Suderow, eds., *Supplement to Official Records*, 2:443; Sears, *The Gates of Richmond*, 296, 303. Jenkins also reported 20 killed and 94 wounded in the Second Rifles, out of 275; 14 killed and 65 wounded in the Sixth S.C.V., out of 200; 35 wounded in the Fourth Battalion, out of 70; and 70 killed and 11 wounded in the Fifth S.C.V., out of 175. For slightly different figures, see Return of Casualties of Confederate Forces, Glendale (Frayser's Farm), O. R., vol. 11, part 2, p. 979.

had lost eighty percent of its men, said, "the fight at Frazier's [*sic*] Farm . . . was one of the severest ordeals of fire through which our regiment ever passed."[30] Henry C. Conner, a soldier in Captain J. N. Withers' Company G wrote, several days after being slightly wounded in the battle:

> [W]hat fiew [*sic*] of us who are left . . . in camp we are pretty well played out and our thinned and vacant streets tells terrible of what we have passed through.[31]

Of the approximately 1,000 officers and men who had joined the regiment in April, only about 125 were able to answer the morning roll call on July 1.[32] Colonel Jenkins wrote his wife that the Palmetto Sharpshooters, with a total of 563 casualties since May 30, had "suffered more than any regiment in the service" during the battles around Richmond in May and June of 1862.[33]

The Fifth South Carolina Volunteers lost 70 wounded and 11 killed out of 175 taken into the fight at Frayser's Farm. Like the Palmetto Sharpshooters, the Fifth was now only a shell of what it had been after the reorganization in April. Fewer than 100 men and only 6 commissioned officers were left for duty.[34] Beginning with Seven Pines, all of the regiment's top officers had been killed or wounded, causing a leadership crisis in the regiment.[35] According to the captain of Company C, those few men who remained were so unhappy with the lack of

---

[30]Hoyt, *The Palmetto Riflemen*, 29. Jenkins' brigade suffered 532 casualties at Frayser's Farm, more than any of the other Confederate brigades. Sears, *Gates of Richmond*, 296.

[31]H. C. Conner to Ellen O'Leary, July 10, 1862, Henry Calvin Conner Papers. In Company B (Kilpatrick's) only 1 man was uninjured, and two other companies (including Colclough's Company E) had only 3 men unscathed. Yorkville *Enquirer*, August 7, 1862.

[32]Yorkville *Enquirer*, August 7, 1862; Jenkins' report on Frayser's Farm, in Hewett, Trudeau and Suderow, eds., *Supplement to Official Records*, 2:443. Even some of these remaining 125 men were slightly wounded. One officer recalled:
> Out of 375 who began the charge, 125 reported for duty a few days after, thirty-five of whom [had been] patched up by the surgeons. . . .
Robert F. Jenkins, "Charge of the Carolinians at Frayser's Farm," 3, as later recounted to Robert F. Jenkins by Lieutenant (and later Captain) W. B. Smith, Company G, Palmetto Sharpshooters. Unfortunately, there are no official records available showing the size of the Palmetto Sharpshooters when the regiment was first organized. An unofficial figure of 1,100 was used by a war correspondent. Yorkville *Enquirer*, August 7, 1862.

[33]Micah Jenkins to Caroline Jenkins, July 6, 1862, Micah Jenkins Papers, S.C.L. The Palmetto Sharpshooters had lost, in killed and wounded, 222 at Seven Pines, and 341 at Gaines' Mill and Frayser's Farm. Yorkville *Enquirer*, July 19, 1862; Return of Casualties, Army of Northern Virginia, June 26 through July 1, 1862, O. R., vol. 11, part 2, p. 502. This puts the total number of casualties at 563 men in the regiment in only 31 days (May 31 through June 30, 1862).

[34]Yorkville *Enquirer*, August 7, 1862; Jenkins' report on Frayser's Farm, in Hewett, Trudeau and Suderow, eds., *Supplement to Official Records*, 2:443.

[35]Colonel J. R. R. Giles had been killed, and Major William M. Foster wounded, at Seven Pines on May 31. Lieutenant Colonel Andrew Jackson had been wounded at Gaines' Mill on June 27.

qualified field officers, there was even serious talk of disbanding the regiment altogether.[36]

During the fighting at Frayser's Farm, Colonel Jenkins had found one of his own men cowering behind a fence, afraid to advance with his comrades. Jenkins demanded to know what he was doing. The soldier replied, "It is too hot in there Colonel, and . . . the bullets fly too thick." Jenkins then said to him, "Go back, sir, and don't disgrace yourself."[37] The soldier summoned his courage, obeyed the order and was wounded in the fight. In the Palmetto Sharpshooters, however, such incidents of refusing to fight were remarkably few; only six men had shown the "white feather" since the regiment had been formed.[38]

During the battle, the colors of the Palmetto Sharpshooters had been hit twenty-two times, and those of the Fifth Regiment, thirty times.[39] Miraculously, Jenkins was not seriously injured, but in a letter to his wife he described just how close he had come:

> My sword shot off with a grape, broken again by a ball, the sword knot cut by a ball, my bridle rein cut with a ball, my saddle cloth cut with a ball, my horse shot under me twice, my overcoat, tied behind my saddle, cut in a dozen places with shell, [and] I, hit upon the shoulder with a grape and upon the breast with a shell, am here to praise and bless Him.[40]

A week following the battle, Jenkins wrote, "I have not fully recovered the use of my right arm, the muscles seemingly deadened by the blow of the grape."[41]

Among the prisoners captured by Jenkins' men when they overran the Federal breastworks was the wounded Colonel S. G. Simmons, of General McCall's division.[42] In return for the kindly attention he received for his wounds, he presented an officer in Jenkins' regiment with his sword. Since the tip of Jenkins' sword had been broken off by a ball during the fighting, the officer then gave Colonel Simmons' sword to

---

[36]J. Banks Lyle to M. S. McArthur, July 15, 1862, Joseph Banks Lyle Letters.

[37]Yorkville *Enquirer*, August 7, 1862. This soldier has not been identified.

[38]Ibid.

[39]Ibid.

[40]Micah Jenkins to Caroline Jenkins, July 3, 1862, in Thomas, *Career and Character*, 17.

[41]Micah Jenkins to Caroline Jenkins, July 6, 1862, Micah Jenkins Papers, S.C.L. Apparently, neither the grape shot nor the shell fragment drew Jenkins' blood.

[42]Yorkville *Enquirer*, August 7, 1862. Colonel S. G. Simmons, commander of a brigade in McCall's division, died of his wounds. O. R., vol. 11, part 2, p. 989; James R. Boulware Diary, July 2, 1862; Sears, *The Gates of Richmond*, 295.

Jenkins, who sent his own broken sword home to his wife.[43] He also sent her the rubber overcoat, which had been tied behind his saddle during the battle, because it had been rendered useless with so many holes.[44]

An officer on Longstreet's staff, Thomas J. Goree, sent home a letter three weeks after the battle in which he described the role Jenkins and his men had played. Goree said he had seen Jenkins just at the end of the fight and that he was "weeping like a child" over the loss of so many of his men. Goree also stated that he was told by Jenkins, when so many of his men were falling around him, he had actually prayed that he too would be killed. In this same letter, Goree added:

> Col. Micah Jenkins is a great friend of mine and he is a
> favorite with the army. Gen. Longstreet thinks him the
> best officer he ever saw. He is only 27 years of age and
> is a perfect model of a Christian hero.[45]

In spite of the hard fighting by Longstreet's and A. P. Hill's divisions at Frayser's Farm, the Confederates had not been able to isolate and capture the Federals' massive supply train and their reserve artillery.[46] Lee had been able to bring only two divisions to bear when he needed at least four for the job. Longstreet's and Hill's divisions had, however, fought a magnificent fight.[47] Following the close of the battle, the Federals continued their steady withdrawal to the James River during the night.

By the next day, July 1, McClellan's army firmly controlled the high ground at Malvern Hill, a wide plateau only a mile from the James River and easily within the protection of Federal gunboats. McClellan had been able to mass his artillery on this high ground, and, with the heavy armament of his gunboats, enjoyed position and firepower. Lee attempted to mount a general attack that afternoon, but the Confederates were repulsed with heavy losses.[48] Decimated by the previous day's fighting at Frayser's Farm, R. H. Anderson's brigade did not participate in the fighting on July 1 at Malvern Hill.

---

[43]Micah Jenkins to Caroline Jenkins, July 4, 1862, Micah Jenkins Papers, S.C.L. Jenkins' damaged sword has been on permanent display at the South Carolina Confederate Relic Room and Museum in Columbia, South Carolina.

[44]Ibid.

[45]Thomas J. Goree to his Mother, July 21, 1862, in Cutrer, ed., *Longstreet's Aide*, 95.

[46]Foote, *Civil War*, 1:508.

[47]Freeman, *Lee's Lieutenants*, 1:587.

[48]Foote, *Civil War*, 1:513. Some historians have criticized Lee for attacking at Malvern Hill. It has been suggested that this attack was symptomatic of Lee's costly preference for the tactical offensive, and that it resulted in one of his two "most decisive defeats." Grady McWhiney and Perry D. Jamieson, *Attack and Die: Civil War Military Tactics and the Southern Heritage* (Tuscaloosa, Alabama: University of Alabama Press, 1982), 108.

While McClellan had won the final battle of the Seven Days, his Peninsular Campaign had been a clear failure. By July 2, his army had retreated the final eight miles to Harrison's Landing on the James River, with no further intention of mounting an offensive. Lee's Army of Northern Virginia had succeeded in driving McClellan and his massive army away from Richmond, but the manpower cost to the Confederacy was enormous. During the Seven Days, the Confederates had lost over 19,000 men, killed or wounded, compared to almost 10,000 for the Federals.[49] Lee had not only lost his opportunity to destroy McClellan's army while it was strung out on its retreat to Harrison's Landing, but he had lost more than one-fifth of his army.

After Malvern Hill, there came a temporary lull in the fighting in Virginia. As Asbury Coward later noted, two possible causes of this lull were the terrible losses Lee's army had sustained in the Seven Days and the sickness among the troops.[50]

By July 10, Jenkins and his men had returned to their old camp at the Fairfield Race Course a few miles northeast of Richmond, which they had left only two weeks before on their march to Mechanicsville. Palmetto Sharpshooter Henry C. Conner wrote that the men were "worn out" and said, "I feel as old as the hills, my feet blistered and sore. . . ." He also complained that there were some in the regiment who would "take advantage of every scratch they get to get clear of a fight."[51]

After John Jamison had been wounded in the lung at Frayser's Farm, Colonel Jenkins wrote to D. F. Jamison in South Carolina and suggested he come to Richmond to care for his son who had been sent to one of the city's hospitals. By July 8, Jenkins' father-in-law had arrived, and Jenkins sent his man-servant, Ben Jones, to Richmond to assist the elder Jamison in the care of John.[52]

Two weeks after the Battle of Frayser's Farm, General Lee wrote to President Davis recommending Micah Jenkins for promotion to brigadier general. Lee wanted Jenkins to assume command of the brigade of R. H. Anderson, who was himself recommended for the command of a division. In his letter, Lee wrote:

> Colonel Jenkins has been repeatedly recommended for
> promotion . . . and his conduct at the Battle of the Seven

---

[49]Foote, *Civil War*, 1:516. Lee's losses during the Seven Days were 19,739 of his total force of 95,481, for a percentage of 20.7. McClellan's losses were 9,796 from a total of 91,169 men, for a percentage of 10.7. McWhiney and Jamieson, *Attack and Die*, 19 (table 4). McWhiney and Jamieson use these and other loss-ratio statistics to argue that, since the North could afford the losses but the South could not, the South blundered by taking the tactical offensive in too many engagements. Ibid., 7.
[50]Bond and Coward, eds., *South Carolinians*, 46.
[51]H. C. Conner to Ellen O'Leary, July 10, 1862, Henry Calvin Conner Papers.
[52]Micah Jenkins to Caroline Jenkins, July 8, 1862, Micah Jenkins Papers, D.U.L.

Pines was worthy of all commendation. He has also in the recent battles, shown great skill. Since the battle of the Seven Pines, four Colonels junior to him have been appointed Brigadier Generals. I would therefore suggest if practicable, that Colonel Jenkins' promotion be dated from the Battle of the Seven Pines, 31st May, so as to restore him to his relative rank.[53]

Eleven days later, on July 22, 1862, Jenkins received his appointment to brigadier general, in command of R. H. Anderson's brigade, which he had so ably led during the Seven Days.[54] For unknown reasons, however, Davis refused to follow General Lee's suggestion that the promotion date from May 31. Because of the delay in his promotion, Jenkins' youngest sister said that she had begun to suspect that her brother "must have some secret enemy influencing the President against him."[55]

On July 24 the men in Jenkins' brigade received their pay. This resulted in what one soldier described as "immense gambling" throughout the brigade, and "pie and chicken wagons" appeared around the camps selling food at twice the usual price.[56]

Before the end of the month, General Jenkins was ordered to return to South Carolina to recruit volunteers and enroll conscripts to replenish his depleted regiments. All those soldiers in South Carolina whose furloughs had expired, and who were members of regiments serving in Virginia, were ordered to report to General Jenkins in Columbia. Those who failed to do so were to be dealt with as deserters. While in Columbia, Jenkins presented Governor Pickens with the colors of the Sixteenth Michigan which the Palmetto Sharpshooters had captured after their "duel" at Gaines' Mill on June 27.[57]

Jenkins remained in South Carolina for only two weeks, much of which he spent with his wife, Caroline, and their four young sons. While there, he learned just how severely the Federal occupation of the South Carolina coast below Charleston had affected Edisto Island. His brother,

[53]Lee to Davis, July 11, 1862, in Douglas Southall Freeman, ed., *Lee's Dispatches: Unpublished Letters of Lee to Davis, 1862-1865* (New York: The Knickerbocker Press, 1915), 33-34.

[54]Ibid., 34 n; Micah Jenkins' appointment to brigadier general, July 22, 1862, John Jenkins Papers, S.C.L. The make-up of Anderson's brigade did not change when Jenkins took over command. The secretary of war was later notified that Jenkins' nomination to the rank of brigadier general, along with several other nominations, had been confirmed by the Confederate Senate on September 30, 1862. Burton N. Harrison (Jefferson Davis' private secretary) to the secretary of war, October 22, 1862, National Archives, Letters Received by the Confederate Adjutant and Inspector General's office, R.G.109, series M410.

[55]Abigail Jenkins to Elizabeth Jenkins LaRoche, July 7, 1862, Jenkins and LaRoche Letters.

[56]James R. Boulware Diary, July 24, 1862.

[57]Yorkville *Enquirer*, July 31, 1862.

John, was serving in the Confederate cavalry along the coast and had written a few days earlier:

> The Episcopal Church [on Edisto] has been horribly desecrated, all the church furniture destroyed, horses stalled around the altar, the organ broken to pieces and, worst [of] all, forty Yankees buried in the Churchyard.[58]

Jenkins was saddened that the ravages of the war had finally reached into the very places where he had spent the happy days of this youth.

While Jenkins was recruiting in South Carolina, an unusual incident occurred in the Palmetto Sharpshooters when the regiment was still camped outside of Richmond. A young woman dressed as a soldier, and calling herself Joseph Bell, had been there for over a week and had sought to be mustered into the army as a substitute for D. J. Lemmon, a private in Company E who wanted to go home.[59] In order to enlist, however, a physical exam was required, and her true gender was discovered by the surprised brigade surgeon. He suspected that she might be a spy and promptly had her arrested.[60]

General Jenkins left Yorkville and returned to Richmond on August 11 and learned that Lee had reorganized his Army of Northern Virginia.[61] It had been divided into two "commands," one under Longstreet, the other under Stonewall Jackson.[62] Longstreet's command consisted of five divisions, one of which was his old division. R. H. Anderson had been promoted to major general and put in command of another division in Longstreet's command.[63] Anderson's old brigade, under Jenkins' command since late July and still intact, remained in Longstreet's

---

[58]John Jenkins to his wife, Marcelline Jenkins, July 14, 1862, John Jenkins Papers, S.C.L. John Jenkins had just been put in charge of "The Rebel Troop," a unit of mounted men from Edisto and the neighboring islands. Yorkville *Enquirer*, July 31, 1862. He was later promoted to major of the Third South Carolina Cavalry.

[59]J. W. McLure to Kate McLure, July 27, 1862, McLure Family Papers; Diary of Captain Alexander Colclough, July 24, 25, and 26, 1862, South Caroliniana Library, University of South Carolina, Columbia, South Carolina. Captain Colclough, who was captain of Company E of the Palmetto Sharpshooters, wrote:

> Some persons remark that Joseph Bell looks very much like a woman and
> remark that he is very intelligent. I never dreamt of her being a woman.

Alexander Colclough Diary, July 25, 1862.

[60]H. C. Conner to Ellen O'Leary, July 27, 1862, Henry Calvin Conner Papers. Captain Colclough took the woman to Richmond for investigation and learned that she had previously been imprisoned there as a spy under the name of Mrs. Underwood. Alexander Colclough Diary, July 27, 1862.

[61]Alexander Colclough Diary, August 11, 1862.

[62]Legally at that time there could be no military organization in the Confederacy larger than a division, but Lee had to combine his divisions into informal "wings" or "commands" to solve the problem of his division commanders acting too independently. Freeman, *Lee's Lieutenants*, 1:671.

[63]Joseph Cantey Elliott, *Lieutenant General Richard Heron Anderson: Lee's Noble Soldier* (Dayton, Ohio: Morningside House, Inc., 1985), 55. Anderson was given the command of Benjamin Huger's old division.

division.[64] Replacing Jenkins, Joseph Walker, from Spartanburg, South Carolina, was promoted from lieutenant colonel to colonel of the Palmetto Sharpshooters.[65]

Lincoln and his War Department had made some changes of their own since the unimpressive conclusion of McClellan's Peninsular Campaign. General John Pope was assembling a new Federal force, called the Army of Virginia, in the area of Manassas, while Irvin McDowell's Union forces were still camped near Fredericksburg. At the beginning of August, McClellan had been ordered to evacuate his army from the Virginia peninsula and move it by water to Aquia Landing near Fredericksburg, while Ambrose Burnside's Federal divisions had also been ordered to the same general area a few days before.[66] With all of these Federal forces apparently moving toward a massive combination, General Lee faced the possibility that his army, of less than 70,000 men, would soon be facing twice that many Federal troops, all concentrated for a new southern thrust against Richmond.[67] In August 1862, the focus of the fighting was shifting back to northern Virginia, where it had begun a year earlier.

---

[64]Freeman, *Lee's Lieutenants*, 1:672. Jenkins' brigade continued to consist of the Second South Carolina Rifles (Col. J. V. Moore); the Fifth South Carolina (Lt. Col. Andrew Jackson); the Sixth South Carolina (Col. John Bratton); the Palmetto Sharpshooters (Col. Joseph Walker); and the Fourth South Carolina Battalion (Major C. S. Mattison). O. R., vol. 11, part 3, p. 649.

[65]In addition, John W. Goss, from Union, South Carolina, was promoted to lieutenant colonel and William W. Humphreys, from Anderson, was promoted to major, replacing William Anderson who was killed at Frayser's Farm. Goss had been captain of Company A, and Humphreys, wounded at Frayser's Farm, had been captain of Company C. Goss was replaced by Captain Christopher L. Beaty, and Humphreys was replaced by Captain T. P. Benson.

[66]Foote, *Civil War*, 1:591-596.

[67]Catton, *Centennial History*, 2:388-389.

Chapter 14

Fighting In The Same Place Twice:
Second Manassas

E ach time the wagon hit a bump in the road, the ambulance driver heard his passenger let out a low groan. He had taken many wounded soldiers from the field of battle, especially since the beginning of May, but never a brigadier general. In sympathy with his wounded charge, the driver grimaced with each jolt of the wagon. As he drove his ambulance away from scenes of carnage on this hot August afternoon, he faced his recurring dilemma: ignore the bumps and hurry to the field hospital, where the surgeons could take over, or slow down to ease his passenger's pain. In this case, he determined to get there quickly, even if it meant excruciating pain to the young general; he was bleeding too badly to risk any delay.

As he was being taken from the front lines in the ambulance, twenty-six-year-old Micah Jenkins had no way of knowing that Lee's army had thoroughly defeated John Pope's Federals in the Second Battle of Manassas, in almost the exact place where the first battle had been fought thirteen months earlier. As Jenkins struggled to remain alert, his left side wet with blood, he could still hear sporadic small arms fire and the occasional boom of artillery drifting through the rear opening of the ambulance. Strangely, the thought that he might die never occurred to him as he lay on the wool army blanket, the only cushion between him and the hard wagon bed. No matter how hard he tried, however, he could not move his left arm, causing a nagging fear to creep into his half-consciousness. He closed his eyes and imagined he heard sawing, that terrible rasping sound which came from inside field hospital tents. Jenkins visualized an exhausted Confederate surgeon, wrapped in a bloody apron, amputating his arm at the shoulder. Not once since the war began had he, or anyone else, ever doubted his courage. In each of his five battles he had been too busy leading his men to worry about being wounded or killed, but now he had plenty of time to consider the possible loss of his arm. For the first time, Micah Jenkins understood real fear.

At the field hospital, Jenkins was attended by two surgeons, who after treating him for over an hour, gave him encouraging news. His wounds in the chest and the left arm were serious, and there had been a great loss of blood, but there were no broken bones and no amputation appeared necessary. The wounds were cleaned and dressed, and Jenkins was made to rest, as he silently thanked God for saving his arm. He was in no condition yet to be transferred to one of the Confederate hospitals in Richmond.

The following day, still weak from the loss of blood and in some pain, Jenkins heard an officer of obvious importance and authority being greeted as he entered the far end of the field hospital tent. In a few moments, a tall general in his early fifties, the epitome of dignity and bearing and with a smile of infinite compassion, stood over Jenkins' cot. With genuine kindness, he asked Jenkins if he was being properly treated, and then congratulated him on the part he and his brigade had played in defeating the Federals the day before. Then, with a fatherly affection and his bright eyes shining, General Robert E. Lee looked down at Jenkins, wished him a quick recovery and said, "I hope yet to see you one of my lieutenant generals."[1] This statement, coming from the beloved commander of the Army of Northern Virginia, was not only the finest compliment Jenkins had ever received, it was also the most effective therapy possible to assure his quick return to duty.

The Second Battle of Manassas had come on quickly, only two months after the end of the Seven Days battles around Richmond on July 1, 1862. During the lull which followed those battles, as if playing a massive chess game, the Federals had begun shifting their forces to northern Virginia. The bulk of Pope's Federal Army of Virginia was above Richmond, near Culpepper, some twenty-five miles northeast of

---

[1]Robert Douthat Meade, "Micah Jenkins," in Dumas Malone, ed., *Dictionary of American Biography*, vol. 5, part 2 (New York: Charles Scribners' Sons, 1932), 49; Thomas, *Career and Character*, 26. Minor details have been added to the two accounts of this incident, based on the author's best estimate of how it probably occurred.

Fredericksburg. Burnside's force had been brought from North Carolina to Falmouth, across the river from Fredericksburg, and McClellan's Army of the Potomac had been ordered on August 3 to leave the peninsula by boat and get in position to join Pope. If these Federal forces were allowed to effect a concentration, their sheer numbers could overwhelm the Confederates and take Richmond.[2]

When General Lee learned that Federal troops were leaving the Virginia peninsula on transports, it was obvious to him that McClellan was on the way to join Pope. Lee knew he had to get to Pope before he could be reinforced by McClellan, while the "young Napoleon" and his army were in transit.[3]

With intuitive anticipation of these events, in the middle of July, Lee had sent Stonewall Jackson and his command some sixty miles above Richmond to Gordonsville. On August 9, Jackson attacked two of Pope's divisions at Cedar Mountain, just below Culpepper. In this battle, Jackson's troops, aided by the arrival of A. P. Hill's division, had won the day and then withdrawn to the south side of the Rapidan River.[4]

On August 13, the same day he learned that McClellan's army was beginning to evacuate the peninsula, Lee ordered Longstreet and ten of his brigades to pull out of Richmond and follow Jackson to Gordonsville. Richmond would be left lightly defended, but Lee calculated only a minimal risk that the remainder of McClellan's troops on the peninsula would attack the capital.[5]

As part of Longstreet's division, Jenkins' brigade had camped on the outskirts of Richmond since the second week in July. Jenkins himself had been in South Carolina for part of July and August, attempting to recruit for his brigade, which had suffered so severely at Seven Pines, Gaines' Mill and Frayser's Farm. By the second week of August, the brigade's numbers were improving to the point that one soldier in the Palmetto Sharpshooters wrote:

> Our Regiment and Brigade is in fine health at this time and increasing every day from the wounded coming [back after leave] . . . and the return of many of our prisoners.[6]

The brigade was one of the ten which had been ordered to Gordonsville with General Longstreet, but before leaving Richmond, Jenkins and his men received new uniforms. As a result, a Palmetto

---

[2]Catton, *Centennial History*, 2:389.
[3]Foote, *Civil War*, 1:605.
[4]Catton, *Centennial History*, 2:391.
[5]Foote, *Civil War*, 1:604-605.
[6]H. C. Conner to Ellen O'Leary, August 8, 1862, Henry Calvin Conner Papers.

Sharpshooter said they presented "quite a different [appearance] to what we did a week ago."[7] Perhaps no soldier in the brigade was happier with his new uniform than Jenkins, whose collar now bore the insignia of a brigadier general.

The regiments in Jenkins' brigade left Richmond at various times throughout August 14 and 15 for the one-day train ride to Gordonsville.[8] When they arrived, they camped there for only two or three days and then marched north, crossing the Rapidan River at Raccoon Ford on August 20.[9] During the two previous days, Pope's Federal troops had withdrawn to the north side of the Rappahannock River where they were in a strong defensive position.[10]

By August 24, Jenkins and his brigade were camped at the Orange and Alexandria Railroad crossing of the Rappahannock River. They were two or three miles above Brandy Station and some thirty miles southwest of the enormous Federal supply base at Manassas Junction. Jenkins had arranged for his brother, Edward, to join him as brigade surgeon and was clearly irritated by Edward's last-minute attempts to change these plans.[11]

The two opposing armies were now drawn up along opposite banks of the Rappahannock in an apparent stalemate. But Lee could not afford to be stalemated; he had to hit Pope before McClellan could arrive to reinforce him. Lee decided on a bold maneuver to draw Pope's army out in the open and into a fight before it could be joined by McClellan's force. The Confederate army commander then ordered Stonewall Jackson and his three divisions to pull out of the lines along the south bank of the Rappahannock and march toward the northwest. At Salem they were then to turn east, marching fast so as to get in the rear of Pope's army, where they would cut his supply line: the Orange and Alexandria Railroad. Lee felt that this maneuver would cause Pope to withdraw toward Washington, thus putting more distance between his army and his reinforcements.[12]

Lee's audacious plan was put in motion, and on August 25 Jackson and his 24,000 men started their long march. Longstreet's command, including Jenkins' brigade, remained in defensive positions along the south bank of the Rappahannock River. There they conducted demonstrations to deceive Pope into thinking the Confederates would

---

[7]Ibid., August 17, 1862.

[8]Record of Events Cards for the Palmetto Sharpshooters, Companies A and D, June 30 to October 31, 1862.

[9]Longstreet's report on the Second Battle of Manassas, October 10, 1862, O. R., vol. 12, part 2, p. 563.

[10]Foote, *Civil War*, 1:607-608.

[11]Micah Jenkins to Caroline Jenkins, August 13 and 24, 1862, Micah Jenkins Papers, S.C.L.

[12]Douglas Southall Freeman, *Lee's Lieutenants, A Study in Command*, vol. 2, *Cedar Mountain to Chancellorsville* (New York: Charles Scribner's Sons, 1943), 82-83.

attack from the direction of Culpepper. The next day, after Jackson's force reached Salem, it turned due east and marched through the Thoroughfare Gap to Bristoe Station on the Orange and Alexandria Railroad. There his men destroyed the railroad bridge, cutting Pope's supply line to Washington. Jackson then moved north along the railroad and captured Pope's huge supply base at Manassas Junction. Although Pope's army was cut off from its supplies, Lee's army was split in two parts which were dangerously separated by some twenty miles. Pope was delighted, fully believing that Lee had committed a major tactical blunder.[13]

Lee moved to remedy this problem on August 26 when he pulled most of the men in Longstreet's command out of the lines along the Rappahannock. They were sent on exactly the same circular march which Jackson's men had made thirty-six hours earlier, northwest to Salem, then due east through the Thoroughfare Gap. Because of Longstreet's expanded duties, his old division of six brigades had been split in half, with three of them placed under Cadmus Wilcox. The other three, including Jenkins' brigade, were assigned to General James L. Kemper; these were understood to be temporary assignments.[14]

By August 27, Stonewall Jackson and his three divisions had completely destroyed Pope's supply base at Manassas Junction and had taken up defensive positions on the northwest fringe of the old Manassas battlefield. Meanwhile, Lee was hurrying Longstreet's command toward a link-up with Jackson's divisions. By three o'clock the next afternoon, Longstreet had reached the Thoroughfare Gap, and his men crossed through it after encountering only moderate Federal resistance.[15] One officer in Company K of the Fifth South Carolina said they slept that night in a grassy meadow near the gap and that he "never saw so many grasshoppers."[16]

During this long march to reinforce Stonewall Jackson, an incident occurred in Jenkins' brigade at the end of a long day. The men in one of Jenkins' regiments were walking along a railroad bed after dark while some of the mounted officers of the brigade were riding along an adjacent wagon road. A man on horseback came out of the nearby woods and asked, "What cavalry unit is that?" There was no reply and the question was repeated, but again there was no response. Finally, the

---

[13]Foote, *Civil War*, 1:620-621; Catton, *Centennial History*, 2:423-424.
[14]Freeman, *Lee's Lieutenants*, 2:64.
[15]O. R., vol. 12, part 2, p. 564. Jenkins' brigade was not involved in this skirmish at Thoroughfare Gap.
[16]William Choice, "Memoirs of My Four Years in the War Between the States," Manassas National Battlefield Park Library, Manassas, Virginia, typescript copy, 3. Choice entered the service at Spartanburg, South Carolina, in April 1861, as a sergeant. He remained in the Fifth Regiment after it was reorganized in April 1862 and later became captain of Company K.

Figure 7
ORGANIZATION OF LONGSTREET'S (RIGHT) WING
FOR THE SECOND BATTLE OF MANASSAS, AUGUST 29-30, 1862

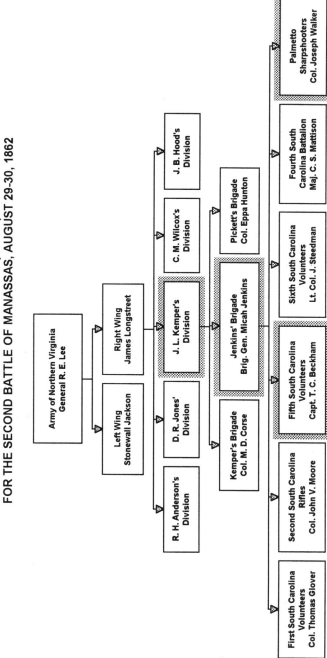

Because of Longstreet's expanded duties as a wing (or corps) commander for the Second Battle of Manassas, his old division of six brigades was split in two parts: Cadmus Wilcox and James Kemper were each given three brigades. Although the assignment was known to be temporary, Jenkins' brigade was assigned to Kemper. A few days before the battle, another regiment, the First South Carolina Volunteers under Colonel Thomas J. Glover, was placed in Jenkins' brigade. This addition brought the strength of Jenkins' brigade up to five South Carolina regiments and one battalion.

questioner rode up to the nearest officer, Palmetto Sharpshooter surgeon Martin Bellinger, grabbed the bridle of his horse and yelled, "I asked you whose company this is. Do you know who I am, sir? I am *General Longstreet*, sir!" The stunned surgeon apologized and explained that they were mounted officers of Jenkins' brigade, not a cavalry company, to which the angry Longstreet replied:

> Doctor, when a civil question is asked you again, don't
> wait to ascertain that your interrogator is a general officer
> before answering it.[17]

On August 28, when Longstreet's men were still near Thoroughfare Gap, Jackson's force attacked a Federal division along the Warrenton Turnpike, resulting in the Battle of Groveton. The battle accomplished little, except that General Pope became mistakenly convinced that Jackson and his Confederates were retreating west to the Shenandoah Valley. Based on this faulty premise, Pope gave chase to Jackson's force. This was a grave miscalculation on Pope's part. By noon on August 29, Longstreet's command had reached Jackson, coming up just behind his right flank. Instead of Jackson trying to escape, as Pope thought, Lee's Army of Northern Virginia was united and ready for battle.[18]

That afternoon, Pope's men attacked Jackson's lines on the north side of the Warrenton Turnpike but were driven back, with A. P. Hill's "light division" repulsing six separate Federal assaults. Except for John B. Hood's division, Longstreet's men, positioned to Jackson's right, did not become engaged on this first day of the Second Battle of Manassas. Jenkins' brigade was marched that afternoon to several locations to meet expected Federal advances which did not materialize. The men were involved only in a minor skirmish when Union troops made an unsuccessful attempt to silence Captain Robert Stribling's battery, the Fauquier Artillery.[19]

Since coming north from Richmond on August 14-15, Jenkins' brigade had been joined by another infantry regiment, the First South Carolina Volunteers, under the command of Colonel Thomas Glover.[20] Glover was the first cousin of Jenkins' wife and had been raised across

---

[17]J. R. Hagood, *Memoirs of the First South Carolina Regiment of Volunteer Infantry*, South Caroliniana Library, University of South Carolina, Columbia, South Carolina, typescript copy, 64 (emphasis in original). Subsequent references to this work will appear as "Hagood, *Memoirs*."

[18]Catton, *Centennial History*, 2:429; Foote, *Civil War*, 1:631.

[19]John J. Hennessy, *Return to Bull Run: The Campaign and Battle of Second Manassas* (New York: Simon and Schuster, 1993), 259.

[20]Hagood, *Memoirs*, 62. The First South Carolina was involved in the minor skirmish on the night of August 29. Ibid., 66-67.

MAP 1: SECOND BATTLE OF MANASSAS - AUGUST 30, 1862

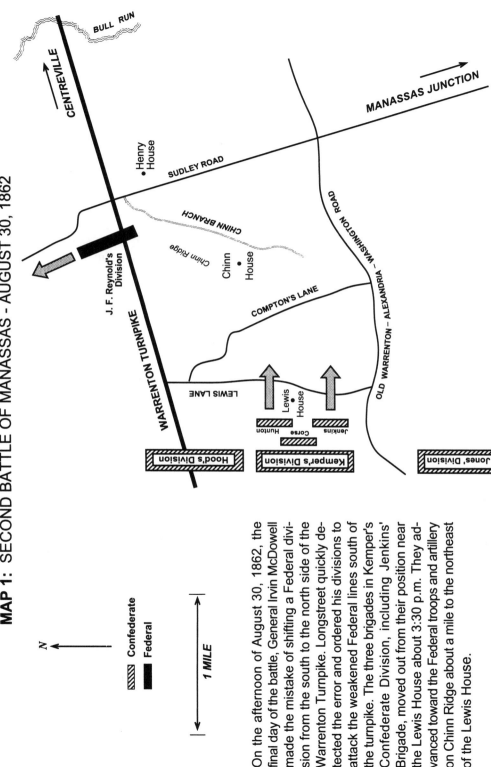

On the afternoon of August 30, 1862, the final day of the battle, General Irvin McDowell made the mistake of shifting a Federal division from the south to the north side of the Warrenton Turnpike. Longstreet quickly detected the error and ordered his divisions to attack the weakened Federal lines south of the turnpike. The three brigades in Kemper's Confederate Division, including Jenkins' Brigade, moved out from their position near the Lewis House about 3:30 p.m. They advanced toward the Federal troops and artillery on Chinn Ridge about a mile to the northeast of the Lewis House.

the street from D. F. Jamison's home in Orangeburg, South Carolina. The addition of Glover's regiment brought the brigade's strength up to five full regiments, along with Mattison's Fourth South Carolina Battalion.

On the night of August 29, Jenkins' men "slept on their guns" in preparation for the coming engagement. The next morning they were formed in a line of battle, where they remained until about three-thirty that afternoon.[21] Along with Kemper's other two brigades, Colonel Eppa Hunton's and General Montgomery Corse's, Jenkins' men were positioned on the William Lewis farm, on the south side of the Warrenton Turnpike, facing northeast toward Centreville. That afternoon, General Irvin McDowell made the mistake of shifting a full Federal division from the south to the north side of the turnpike, adding strength to the attack against Stonewall Jackson, but weakening the Union line in front of Longstreet's command.[22] "Old Pete" Longstreet saw his opportunity and reported later that "my whole line was rushed forward at a charge."[23] A soldier in Jenkins' brigade wrote that they were suddenly taken out of position and double-quicked for about a mile, when they "came fully in contact with the enemy."[24] Jenkins' men and the other two brigades under General Kemper went into the attack at the center of Longstreet's line, which moved steadily forward, parallel to the turnpike. They were headed toward the Federal position on Chinn Ridge, not quite a mile way.

With Hunton's brigade on their left, Jenkins' men advanced first through a field of corn and then through a stand of woods a few hundred yards wide. When they emerged from the woods, in the words of one officer, they beheld "the famous plains of Manassas."[25] In the distance off to their left front, across the Sudley Ford Road, was Henry House Hill, Longstreet's ultimate objective.[26] Before he captured that, however, he had to sweep the Federal troops off Chinn Ridge, about nine hundred yards southwest of Henry Hill.

Jenkins' brigade advanced past the southwest end of Chinn Ridge, all the way down to the creek at the bottom of its eastern slope. By then, Jenkins had "discovered that his line of advance was parallel with the direction of the enemy's left wing."[27] To correct this, he began to pivot his brigade to the left in order to assault the crest of the ridge. With his men

---

[21]*Carolina Spartan*, September 18, 1862.

[22]Hennessy, *Return to Bull Run*, 360-361. The division shifted was that of Brigadier General John F. Reynolds. Ibid.

[23]O. R., vol. 12, part 2, p. 565. A captain in the Palmetto Sharpshooters recorded in his diary that Jenkins' brigade was ordered forward at around three p.m.: Alexander Colclough Diary, August 30, 1862.

[24]*Carolina Spartan*, September 18, 1862.

[25]Hagood, *Memoirs*, 69.

[26]Hennessy, *Return to Bull Run*, 362.

[27]Hagood, *Memoirs*, 69.

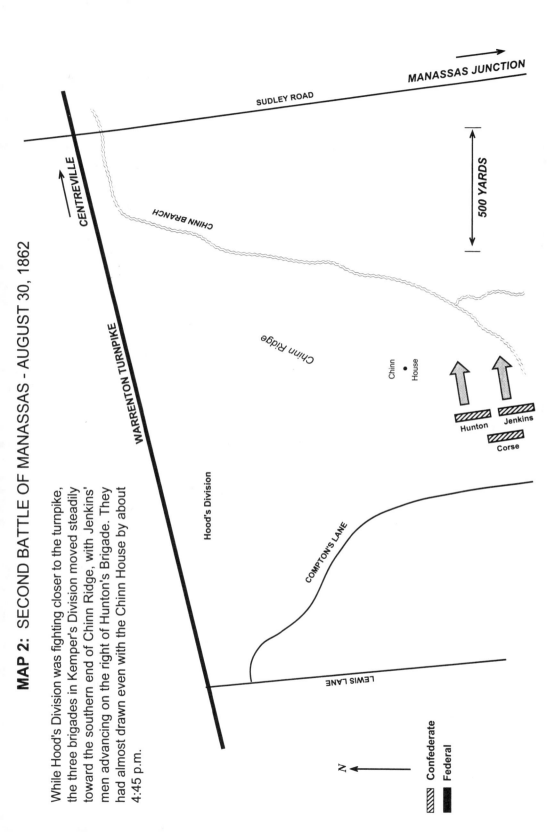

MAP 2: SECOND BATTLE OF MANASSAS - AUGUST 30, 1862

While Hood's Division was fighting closer to the turnpike, the three brigades in Kemper's Division moved steadily toward the southern end of Chinn Ridge, with Jenkins' men advancing on the right of Hunton's Brigade. They had almost drawn even with the Chinn House by about 4:45 p.m.

MANASSAS JUNCTION

SUDLEY ROAD

CENTREVILLE

CHINN BRANCH

500 YARDS

WARRENTON TURNPIKE

Chinn Ridge

Chinn
House

Hunton

Jenkins

Corse

Hood's Division

COMPTON'S LANE

LEWIS LANE

N

Confederate
Federal

straddling Chinn Branch, he ordered the First Regiment to change direction and start the attack; then he began bringing up his other regiments.[28] However, the Federals had begun shifting reinforcements back to the south side of the turnpike, and the Union brigades of John W. Stiles and Zealous B. Tower were positioned on Chinn Ridge. Instead of facing a weakened enemy line, Jenkins and his men charged directly into these Federal reinforcements, and the fighting became especially intense.[29] Lieutenant William Choice, in Company K of the Fifth Regiment, wrote that they fired so fast into the Federals on the ridge that the rifle barrels of the men in his company got extremely hot. He even borrowed a gun in order to keep firing. Choice said that the Union soldiers were "so thick, every shot took effect."[30]

Another soldier in Jenkins brigade described the fighting for Chinn Ridge:

> We took position against an old fence, and here . . . did we perform the hardest labor for the space of 2½ hours that has ever been known to man. It was not until we had repulsed and demoralized column after column of fresh [Federal] troops, as they were hurled upon us from the advance of reinforcements, that we were relieved.[31]

It was during this stage of the fighting for the Chinn Ridge plateau that General Jenkins was severely wounded in the chest and left arm and was taken by ambulance from the battlefield to a field hospital.[32] His men, however, fought on against the fresh reinforcements until the Federals finally yielded Chinn Ridge to the Confederates shortly before dark. One officer in the First South Carolina said that once the ridge was captured, the "ground was strewn with the slain and the debris of the battle."[33]

Other troops from Longstreet's command attempted to take Henry Hill before dark, but were thwarted in this effort by Pope's

---

[28]Ibid.

[29]Hennessy, *Return to Bull Run*, 400-401. Hennessy states that as they assaulted the Federal brigades of Stiles and Tower on the ridge, the Union volleys ripped Jenkins' men. The First and Sixth South Carolina were thrown back temporarily, but they regrouped and came forward again to within less than fifty yards of the Union line. Ibid.

[30]Choice, "Memoirs," 4. At the time, Choice was first lieutenant of Company K, under the command of Captain Ryal B. Seay. Seay resigned shortly after this battle and Choice was promoted to captain of the company.

[31]*Carolina Spartan*, September 18, 1862.

[32]Hagood, *Memoirs*, 70. Colonel Thomas Glover also received a slight wound in this charge but was able to remain on the field in command of the First S.C.V. He was later mortally wounded in the stomach before the battle ended. Ibid.

[33]Ibid., 71.

reinforcements. Jenkins' brigade was not involved in this late-afternoon assault on Henry Hill.[34]

General Pope's last-minute dispatch of reinforcements to Chinn Ridge and Henry Hill had managed to delay Longstreet's advance long enough to give Pope time to withdraw his army in a somewhat orderly retreat up the Warrenton Turnpike to Centreville.[35] Even though Lee's army held the field, a disappointed Longstreet wrote in his report that the Federals had managed to "escape with many of [their] batteries which should have fallen into our hands."[36] The battle finally sputtered to a halt well after dark.

The leadership of Jenkins' brigade suffered severely in the fighting on August 30. Colonel Thomas Glover, of the newly-added First South Carolina Volunteers, was mortally wounded by a shot in the stomach. As he was being removed from the field, he was wounded again in the leg, and before dying he told one of his officers, "*You* can testify that I fell with my face to the enemy."[37] Captain John H. Thompson then took over temporary command of Glover's regiment. Colonel J. V. Moore of the Second South Carolina Rifles was also mortally wounded, and his command was assumed by Lieutenant Colonel Thomas Thomson.[38] After Jenkins was wounded, temporary command of the brigade devolved upon Colonel Joe Walker, commander of the Palmetto Sharpshooters.[39]

The official figures given after the battle showed 16 killed and 52 wounded in the Palmetto Sharpshooters, and 2 killed and 37 wounded in the Fifth Regiment. The First Regiment suffered the most, losing not only its colonel, but 30 killed and 94 wounded.[40]

One of Jenkins' closest friends, Captain Cato Seabrook, of Edisto Island, was killed by a shot in the side.[41] He had become the adjutant of Jenkins' brigade after having served as captain of the Jasper Light Infantry from the time the Fifth Regiment was formed. Lieutenant Choice, in the Fifth South Carolina, lost his orderly sergeant, H. A. Turner, during the fight. Choice wrote that they were fighting side-by-side when Turner was shot in the arm. He stumbled to the rear but could not find a surgeon and bled to death.[42]

---

[34]Hennessy, *Return to Bull Run*, 411, 421.
[35]Foote, *Civil War*, 1:640-642.
[36]O. R., vol. 12, part 2, p. 566.
[37]Hagood, *Memoirs*, 71 (emphasis in original).
[38]Records of the Confederate Historian, S.C.D.A.H., 3:319.
[39]Capers, *South Carolina*, 6:890. John Bratton was senior colonel in the brigade and would have normally taken over in Jenkins' absence, but he had been wounded and captured at Seven Pines.
[40]O. R., vol. 12, part 2, p. 560. In addition, the Sixth South Carolina lost 13 killed and 102 wounded, and the Second South Carolina Rifles lost 9 killed and 49 wounded. Casualty figures for Mattison's Fourth Battalion were not provided.
[41]Yorkville *Enquirer*, September 10, 1862.
[42]Choice, "Memoirs," 3. Turner was fifth sergeant in Captain Ryal B. Seay's Company K.

MAP 3: SECOND BATTLE OF MANASSAS - AUGUST 30, 1862

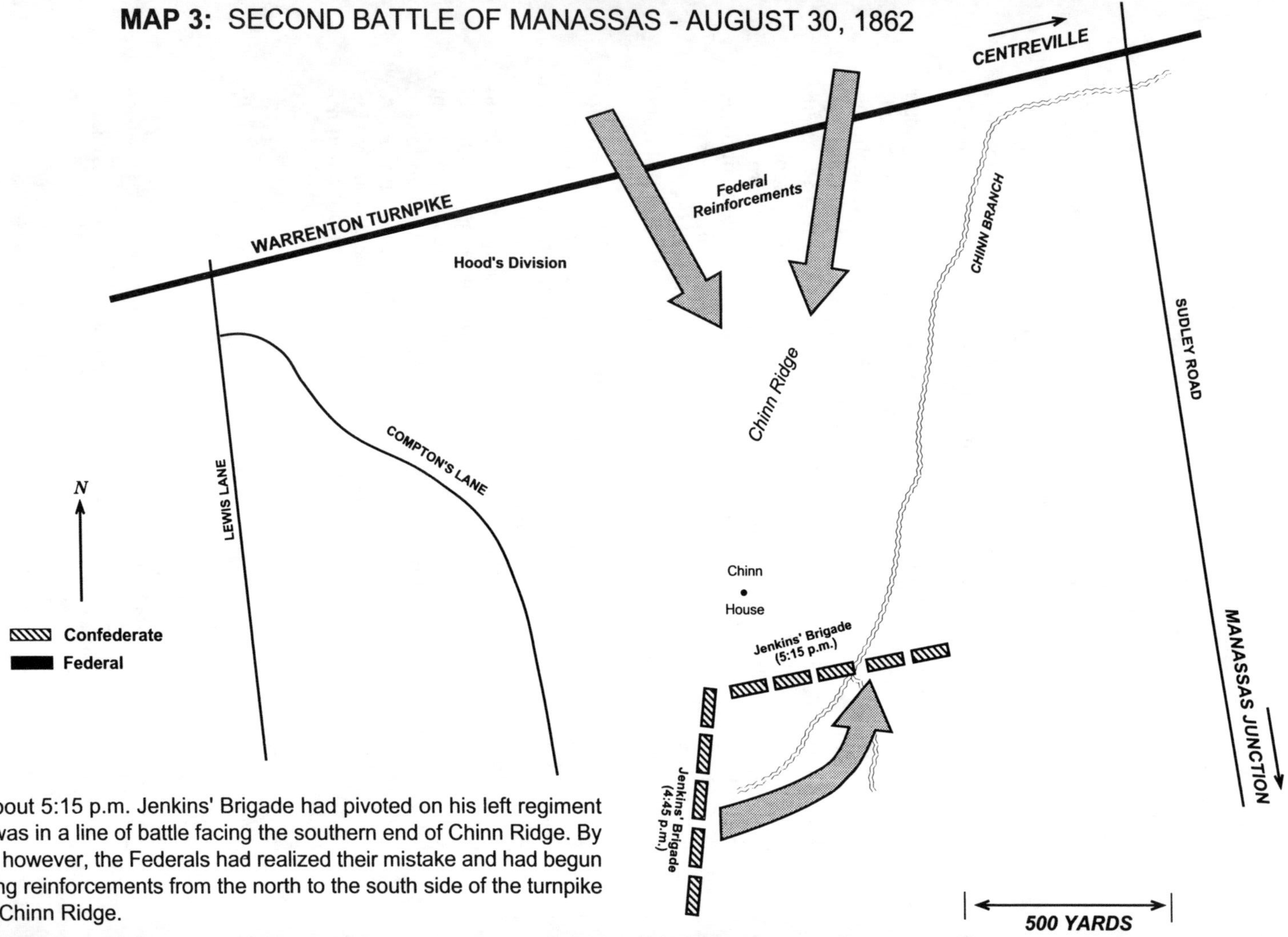

MANASSAS JUNCTION

SUDLEY ROAD

CENTREVILLE

500 YARDS

CHINN BRANCH

Federal Reinforcements

Chinn Ridge

Jenkins' Brigade (5:15 p.m.)

Chinn House

Jenkins' Brigade (4:45 p.m.)

Hood's Division

WARRENTON TURNPIKE

COMPTON'S LANE

LEWIS LANE

N

Confederate

Federal

By about 5:15 p.m. Jenkins' Brigade had pivoted on his left regiment and was in a line of battle facing the southern end of Chinn Ridge. By then, however, the Federals had realized their mistake and had begun shifting reinforcements from the north to the south side of the turnpike onto Chinn Ridge.

MAP 4: SECOND BATTLE OF MANASSAS - AUGUST 30, 1862

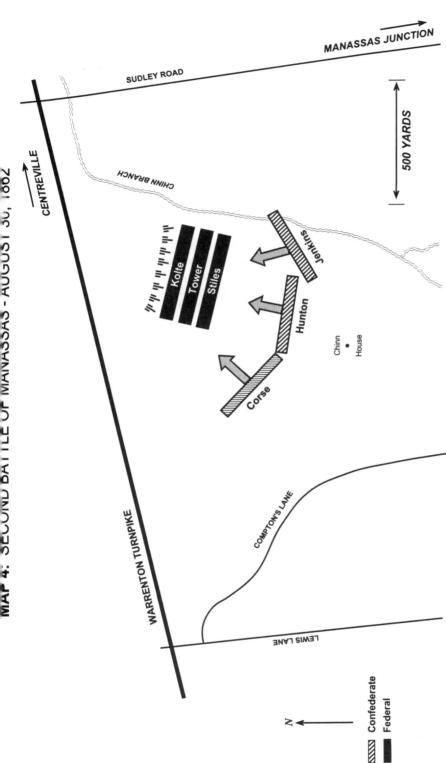

Until well after 6:00 p.m., Kemper's three brigades assaulted the reinforced Federal troops and artillery on the crest of Chinn Ridge. Jenkins' men attacked slightly to the right and rear of the brigades of Hunton and Corse. It was then that the fighting was the heaviest for Jenkins' Brigade and that he was wounded and taken from the field. Chinn Ridge finally fell to the Confederates, and Jenkins' men slept on their guns there after darkness ended the battle.

Company K of the Palmetto Sharpshooters had five men from Wofford College killed by a single artillery shell. The five were mess mates and were resting together when the shell exploded in their midst.[43]

In all, Jenkins' brigade lost approximately 465 men in the one day of fighting on the south side of the Warrenton Turnpike.[44] Lee's army, however, had won a great victory and had rocked Pope's Federal troops back on their heels. Only two months earlier, McClellan's army had been at the very gates of Richmond, but by the end of August the Federals had been pushed back almost to Washington. Lee had finally gained the initiative, and he decided to shift the focus of the fighting to his enemy's territory.

As Lee's Army of Northern Virginia began to move north, toward the Potomac River, Jenkins lay in his hospital bed in Richmond, trying to gain enough strength for the long trip to South Carolina. He was torn between wanting to see his family and his desire to march north with his brigade. But his injuries left him no choice in the matter, and on September 6, he telegraphed his wife, "On my way to Yorkville. Wound doing well."[45] He was going home to recuperate, but his men were going into Maryland, to fight for the first time on Northern soil.

---

[43]Capers, *South Carolina*, 6:134. The five were Theodotus L. Capers, James Palmer, Whiteford Smith, David T. Bearden and Sgt. Horace A. McSwain. See also, Choice, *Memoirs*, 4.

[44]O. R., vol. 12, part 2, p. 568.

[45]Micah Jenkins' to Caroline Jenkins, September 6, 1862, Micah Jenkins Papers, S.C.L.

Chapter 15

Lee Invades Maryland

W hen he finally settled into his seat, General Jenkins was struck with how few civilians were on the train. Almost all the passengers were Confederate soldiers, the majority of them wounded or disfigured. Seeing soldiers with missing limbs was not unusual at this stage of the war, but now he identified with these men. He himself had experienced two brushes with amputation; once with the slight wound in his leg at Seven Pines and again with the injury to his left arm on the plains of Manassas.

The train trip to South Carolina took hours, with stops in Petersburg, Virginia, and Weldon, Raleigh and Charlotte, North Carolina. When he reached Chester, South Carolina, the young general changed trains to the Kings Mountain Railroad which took him to Yorkville. It was late Sunday night, September 6, when he finally arrived home at the Kings Mountain Military School, exactly one week after he had fought with his brigade and been wounded during the Second Battle of Manassas. Earlier that same Sunday, as Jenkins' train rumbled toward South Carolina, his men crossed the Potomac River with other brigades under Longstreet's command to begin General Lee's Maryland campaign.

Jenkins' troops had spent August 31, 1862, the day after the fighting had ended at Manassas, burying the dead and tending to the wounded. Groups of the dead were buried in pits which were usually about thirty feet long and seven feet wide, but only two or three feet deep. Of this grim duty, one officer in Jenkins' brigade wrote that "the spectacle of a hundred detachments doing this work at the same time will always make a forcible impression on the novice's mind."[1]

That same day, Lee sent Jackson and his divisions on another wide circling movement in an attempt to get behind the Union army's right flank. Had this maneuver succeeded, Lee might have been able to cut off the Federal retreat to Washington. General Pope, however, realized the danger and on September 1 he had two of his divisions attack Jackson near Chantilly, a country estate a few miles above Centreville. There was no clear winner in this small battle; however, Pope's troops succeeded in thwarting Jackson's flanking movement.[2] Longstreet's men were in transit from Bull Run to Chantilly when the battle occurred and did not arrive in time to join Jackson's men in the fighting.[3]

The next morning, Longstreet's command headed north to Dranesville and turned northwest toward Leesburg, Virginia.[4] The men in Jenkins' brigade, under the temporary command of Palmetto Sharpshooters colonel Joe Walker, passed through Leesburg on the afternoon of September 3 and marched straight up the main street. The ladies of the town distributed refreshments to the troops and offered encouraging words. Some even entered the ranks of the South Carolina soldiers and placed garlands of roses on the brigade's regimental banners, and miniature Confederate flags were displayed in every window. Jenkins' men "cheered until they were hoarse, and their enthusiasm swelled beyond all bounds."[5] That night, along with other brigades in the Army of Northern Virginia, they camped on the south bank of the Potomac River.

Lee's men were ragged and many lacked shoes; their horses were tired, and food supplies were low. But he had taken the initiative since assuming command of the army in June, and now he sought to press his advantage.[6] He would, however, no longer have to contend with General Pope; following Second Manassas, Lincoln had replaced him with George McClellan. The "Young Napoleon" was to have one more try at destroying the Army of Northern Virginia.[7]

Longstreet's command crossed the Potomac into Maryland at White's Ford, about three miles from Leesburg. The men in Jenkins' brigade

---

[1]Hagood, *Memoirs*, 73.
[2]Catton, *Centennial History*, 2:435. Foote, *Civil War*, 1:644.
[3]Longstreet's report on the Second Battle of Manassas, October 10, 1862, O. R., vol. 12, part 2, p. 566.
[4]Longstreet's report on the Maryland Campaign, October 10, 1862, O. R., vol. 19, part 1, p. 839.
[5]Hagood, *Memoirs*, 74.
[6]Catton, *Centennial History*, 2:436.
[7]Foote, *Civil War*, 1:646.

waded across on September 6, the same day their wounded commander arrived home in Yorkville, South Carolina. After crossing, they marched to Frederick, Maryland, some twenty miles north, arriving there two days later. While there, they saw the army's engineers preparing to destroy the Baltimore and Ohio Railroad bridge across the Monocacy River east of Frederick, to slow the expected Federal advance from Washington.[8] Jenkins' men appeared scruffy to the citizens of Frederick, who were accustomed to seeing well-uniformed Federal soldiers. The townsfolk were not merely indifferent, but openly hostile to the Confederate cause.[9]

Longstreet and his troops remained in Frederick until September 10 when six of his brigades were sent to join in a coordinated attack on the Federal Arsenal at Harper's Ferry. That same day, the remainder of his command, including Jenkins' brigade, was put on the march for Hagerstown, Maryland, with strict orders not to pillage apples or corn from the farms along the road.[10] After leaving Frederick, they marched west through the Boonsboro Pass over South Mountain and continued along the National Turnpike until they reached Hagerstown on September 13. As Jenkins' men passed by Hager's Store, they were taunted by a teenage girl who was waving a Union flag. She yelled, "Why don't you fight under this flag?" One of the soldiers in the First South Carolina shouted back, "Hagerstown, Hager's Store, Hager's daughter – hurrah for Hager!" Then, the rest of his regiment gave her a loud rebel yell.[11]

Meanwhile, McClellan was moving his massive army northwest from Washington in pursuit of Lee, but carefully keeping the Federal divisions between the Confederates and the Northern capital. The day after Longstreet's command left Frederick, lead elements of McClellan's army entered the city. Lee had prepared written orders for his commanders, outlining his Maryland campaign, and a copy was sent to General D. H. Hill. A member of Hill's staff decided to keep a copy as a souvenir and wrapped it around three cigars which he promptly lost. A Federal soldier in one of the forward units of McClellan's army in Frederick found the orders and delivered them to McClellan.[12] Fortuitously, the Union commander had been given a distinct advantage because Lee had divided his army and McClellan was now aware of the dispositions of the Confederate divisions. Learning that Longstreet's men were marching

[8]Record of Events Cards of the Palmetto Sharpshooters, Company L, September-October 1862.
[9]Coker, *History of Company E, Sixth S.C. Regiment*, 103.
[10]O. R., vol. 19, part 1, p. 839; James R. Boulware Diary, September 10 and 11, 1862.
[11]Frank M. Mixson, *Reminiscences of a Private: Company "E", 1st S.C. Vols. (Hagood's), Jenkins' Brigade, Lee's Army, 1861-1865* (Columbia, South Carolina: The State Company, 1910), 27. See also, Record of Events Cards of the Palmetto Sharpshooters, Company L, September-October 1862.
[12]Foote, *Civil War*, 1:667-671. These were the now famous "Special Orders No. 191" which fully outlined Lee's plans for his Maryland campaign.

towards Hagerstown, McClellan dispatched four Federal corps to pursue them. Lee had left General D. H. Hill's division at the Boonsboro Pass to block McClellan's pursuit, but it quickly became evident that Hill was vastly outnumbered and in danger of being overwhelmed.[13] Lee then ordered Longstreet at Hagerstown to countermarch his brigades the fourteen miles down the National Turnpike, back to the Boonsboro Pass. There, according to Longstreet, they were to assist Hill in holding the Federal "army in check, so as to give time for the reduction of Harper's Ferry."[14]

When Longstreet arrived at the Boonsboro Pass at around three on the afternoon of September 14, he found D. H. Hill's division already heavily engaged. Longstreet hurried his reinforcements into defensive positions along the mountain, facing east toward the Union columns attacking from the direction of Frederick.

Colonel Joe Walker and Jenkins' exhausted brigade arrived at Boonsboro about four that afternoon, after a difficult six-hour march in the hot Maryland sun. Upon their arrival, they were ordered to the right of the turnpike on the Pleasant Valley Road for about a mile, along the base of the west side of South Mountain.[15] These orders were then changed, and they were hurried back to the turnpike, then to the top of the mountain, at double time. It was almost dark when Walker and the men in Jenkins' brigade finally reached the top of the pass, and by then they were completely worn out. Longstreet wrote that as they arrived, "the men dropped along the road, as rapidly as if under severe skirmish."[16]

After reaching the top of the mountain, Colonel Walker first moved Jenkins' brigade to a position near the White House Hotel on the turnpike, at the summit of the pass. At about seven o'clock, the brigade, which had been temporarily assigned to D. R. Jones' division for the Maryland campaign, was sent into action. On orders from General Jones, Walker moved the men north, across the turnpike, and onto the Frosttown Road. They weaved around a sharp bend in the road and formed into a line of battle at the foot of a hill where a rough fight was in progress.[17] In this position on the east slope of the mountain, and a short distance to the north of the turnpike, Walker and the brigade immediately

[13]Boonsboro Pass, where the National Turnpike crosses South Mountain on its route from Frederick to Hagerstown, is also referred to as Turner's Gap. Foote, *Civil War*, 1:674.

[14]O. R., vol. 19, part 1, p. 839. According to Captain Colclough in the Palmetto Sharpshooters, Jenkins' brigade began its march back toward the Boonsboro Pass at about ten a.m. on September 14. Alexander Colclough Diary, September 14, 1862.

[15]John Michael Priest, *Before Antietam: The Battle for South Mountain* (Shippensburg, Pennsylvania: White Mane Publishing Co., 1992), 184-188.

[16]Longstreet, *From Manassas to Appomattox*, 224-225.

[17]Priest, *Before Antietam*, 261; Colonel Joseph Walker's report on the Battle of South Mountain, October 24, 1862, O. R., vol. 19, part 1, p. 906; Coker, *History of Company E, Sixth S.C. Regiment*, 109.

Figure 8
ORGANIZATION OF LONGSTREET'S WING FOR THE BATTLES OF SOUTH MOUNTAIN, SEPTEMBER 14, AND SHARPSBURG, SEPTEMER 17, 1862

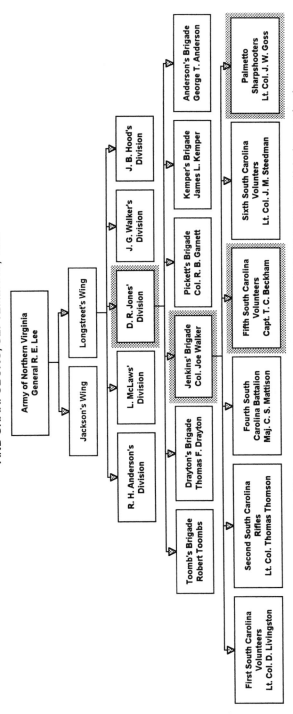

For the Maryland Campaign in September 1862, temporary assignments were again made in Longstreet's command. Jenkins' brigade was assigned to Major General David R. Jones' division. In that division, the men in Jenkins' brigade fought both at South Mountain on September 14 and at Sharpsburg on September 17, 1862. In Jenkins' absence his brigade was under the temporary command of Colonel Joe Walker of the Palmetto Sharpshooters, the only colonel available for duty with the brigade at the time. The others had been either killed, wounded or captured. Thomas Glover of the First S.C.V. had been killed at Second Manassas; John V. Moore of the Second S. C. Rifles had been killed in the same battle; John R. R. Giles of the Fifth S.C.V. had been killed at Seven Pines; and John Bratton of the Sixth S.C.V. had been wounded and captured at Seven Pines.

came under a furious artillery attack which hurled jagged rock fragments in every direction.[18] Walker reported that, before eight o'clock, he advanced the First, Fifth, and Sixth Regiments about 200 yards through a cornfield to a stone fence where "they engaged in a desultory fire with the enemy until dark. . . ."[19] This advance drove the Union troops, who had gotten to within twenty yards of the lines of the Sixth Regiment, back across a ravine. According to one officer in the First South Carolina, the Federals then rallied across the ravine, and

> [our] line was ordered to lay down, and then for two hours an incessant fusillade was kept up between the opposing forces. The distance which separated them could not have been more than fifteen or twenty paces and this deadly proximity lasted until the enemy could only be seen by the flashes of his rifles.[20]

Well after dark Colonel Walker withdrew his regiments to a field near the hotel, and the men were finally permitted to rest. One officer in the brigade remembered the men finally relaxing, "with arms in hand . . . after as fatiguing a day as we ever experienced."[21] The casualties for both the Fifth Regiment and the Palmetto Sharpshooters, in this Battle for South Mountain, were light; 6 men wounded in the Fifth, and only 2 in the Sharpshooters.[22] In the darkness from the mountain top, Jenkins' men looked east, toward Frederick, and saw the camp fires of McClellan's army dotting the landscape "as far as the eye could reach."[23] Concluding that his outnumbered troops could not continue to hold off the Federals for another day, General Lee ordered Longstreet and D. H. Hill to withdraw from South Mountain before dawn the next morning. Their destination was the village of Sharpsburg, about six miles southwest of Boonsboro, where Lee had decided to concentrate his forces and make a stand.[24]

The men in Jenkins' brigade were ordered to cover the Confederate withdrawal from that portion of the mountain near the hotel. Colonel

[18]Hagood, *Memoirs*, 80.

[19]O. R., vol. 19, part 1, p. 906. The First Regiment was under command of Lieutenant Colonel Daniel Livingston; the Fifth under Captain Thomas C. Beckham; and the Sixth under Lieutenant Colonel J. M. Steedman. The Second Rifles, Palmetto Sharpshooters and Fourth Battalion were apparently held back to provide close support.

[20]Hagood, *Memoirs*, 80. Walker's men had engaged the Federal brigades of Colonel William A. Christian and General George L. Hartsuff. Priest, *Before Antietam*, 261. See also, McClellan's report, October 15, 1862, O. R., vol. 19, part 1, p. 52.

[21]Coker, *History of Company E, Sixth S.C. Regiment*, 107.

[22]Priest, *Before Antietam*, 324; Capers, *South Carolina*, 6:145-146. Of 562 men present for the battle, Jenkins' brigade lost 3 men killed and 29 wounded. Ibid.

[23]Hagood, *Memoirs*, 81.

[24]Longstreet's report on the Maryland Campaign, October 10, 1862, O. R., vol. 19, part 1, p. 839.

Walker posted the Second Rifles on the turnpike as a rear guard, and he put out a heavy force of skirmishers. The brigade held this position on South Mountain, protecting the withdrawal, until around four the next morning when it was relieved by a cavalry brigade.[25]

Before dawn on September 15, Jenkins' brigade finally withdrew down the turnpike toward Boonsboro, on the west side of the mountain. Captain James L. Coker, in the Sixth South Carolina, wrote:

> At sunrise we passed through the little village of Boonsboro, and a little beyond were brought across the road in line of battle to receive a threatened cavalry attack.[26]

The attack did not materialize, however, and the men turned southwest, heading for Sharpsburg a few miles away. Coker said that they halted briefly at Keedysville, a small hamlet, where they got a clear view of McClellan's army in hot pursuit "with bright guns and well disciplined ranks."[27] Later that morning they crossed Antietam Creek which meandered to within less than a mile of Sharpsburg. When the last of Longstreet's column had crossed the creek, the advanced elements of McClellan's cavalry "galloped into sight and fired their carbines at the Confederates who still lingered at the bridge."[28]

Shortly before noon, Jenkins' brigade was put into the line to the right of Richard B. Garnett's brigade on Cemetery Hill, "an eminence in front of [Sharpsburg] and to the right of the [Boonsboro] turnpike."[29] The men were glad to finally settle down in one place; they had been marching almost constantly for two weeks, since they left Manassas. Having been issued no rations, they had depended almost entirely on apples and green corn for food, which caused many of them to have diarrhea.[30] Soon after they took up their position, the men heard the sound of cheering moving steadily toward them as regiment by regiment received the exhilarating news that Stonewall Jackson's force had captured Harper's Ferry.[31] This meant that the bulk of Jackson's troops would

---

[25]O. R., vol. 19, part 1, p. 906.

[26]Coker, *History of Company E, Sixth S.C. Regiment*, 107. James Lide Coker was captain of Company E, Sixth S.C.V. He was in temporary command of the regiment for a brief time at Sharpsburg. He was later promoted to major of the regiment. Capers, *South Carolina*, 6:509.

[27]Coker, *History of Company E, Sixth S.C. Regiment*, 107.

[28]Hagood, *Memoirs*, 81.

[29]O. R., vol. 19, part 1, p. 907. The brigade was located on the right of the turnpike, looking back toward Boonsboro, on Cemetery Hill. Stephen W. Sears, *Landscape Turned Red: The Battle of Antietam* (New York: Ticknor and Fields, 1983), 277-278.

[30]Foote, *Civil War*, 1:664; Hagood, *Memoirs*, 83. One man in the Sixth South Carolina wrote that the men spent the night of September 15 in an apple orchard, and the next morning all they had to eat was apples. James R. Boulware Diary, September 15 and 16, 1862.

[31]Coker, *History of Company E, Sixth S.C. Regiment*, 108.

MAP 1: BATTLE OF SHARPSBURG - SEPTEMBER 17, 1862
Third (or Afternoon) Phase

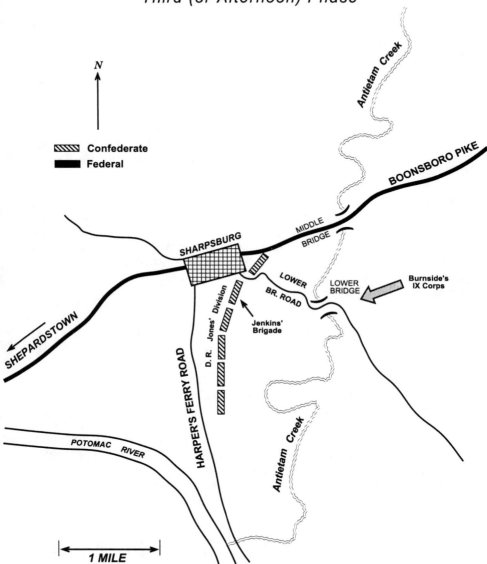

When the Federal attack on September 17, 1862, shifted to Lee's right, the focal point became the Lower Bridge (later renamed Burnside Bridge) across Antietam Creek. Confederate efforts to hold the bridge finally failed and Federal troops from Burnside's IX Corps poured across to begin their assault against Jenkins' Brigade and the other brigades in D. R. Jones' Confederate Division.

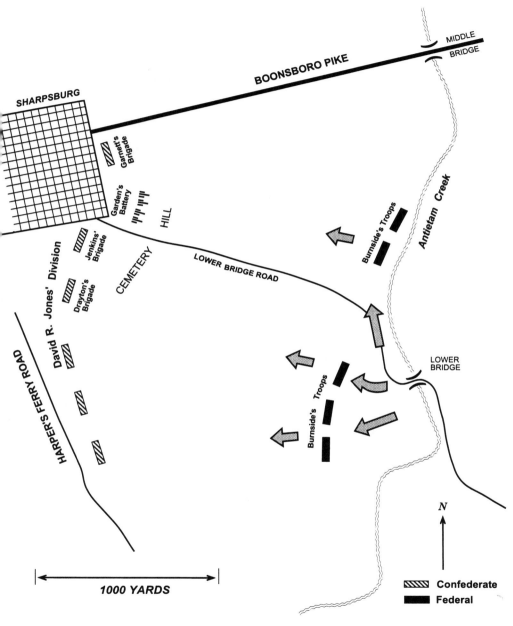

MAP 2: BATTLE OF SHARPSBURG - SEPTEMBER 17, 1862

MIDDLE
BRIDGE

BOONSBORO PIKE

SHARPSBURG

Garnett's Brigade

Garden's Battery

CEMETERY HILL

Jenkins' Brigade

Drayton's Brigade

David R. Jones' Division

HARPER'S FERRY ROAD

LOWER BRIDGE ROAD

Antietam Creek

Burnside's Troops

Burnside's Troops

LOWER BRIDGE

N

1000 YARDS

Confederate
Federal

When Burnside's Federals crossed the Lower Bridge, Jenkins' Brigade, under the command of Colonel Joe Walker, was one of three which made up the left part of D. R. Jones' Confederate Division. Jenkins' men were positioned on Cemetery Hill, near the southeast corner of Sharpsburg. On their left was the brigade of Richard B. Garnett, and on the right were troops from Thomas F. Drayton's Brigade.

soon be on the march for Sharpsburg to help Lee take on McClellan's army.

Late that afternoon, General Jones moved Jenkins' brigade across a ravine and a short distance to the right. According to Walker's report, it remained there "under a heavy fire of shot and shell until 3 o'clock in the evening of the 17th" when it was moved back to its original position in front of the town.[32]

Stonewall Jackson had finally arrived at Sharpsburg with three divisions on September 16, after leaving A. P. Hill's division to hold Harper's Ferry. On the morning of September 17, McClellan launched his attack across Antietam Creek against Jackson's corps along the left of the Confederate line. In vicious fighting, Jackson's men repulsed the Federal attack, but the battle then shifted to the center of Lee's lines. This second phase of the battle raged until about two o'clock that afternoon when the focus of McClellan's attack was shifted again, against the Confederate right held by Longstreet's corps.[33]

The most important feature in front of Longstreet's corps was the lower bridge across Antietam Creek. Brigadier General Robert Toombs' Confederates held the bridge against repeated attacks, but were finally forced to yield by overwhelming numbers.

General Ambrose Burnside's Federal troops fought their way across the lower bridge at about four that afternoon. They then made a desperate attack against Longstreet's right but were met by General D. R. Jones' division of six brigades, including Jenkins' men.[34]

On the extreme left of Jones' division, next to the turnpike, was Garnett's brigade. To its right, on Cemetery Hill, was Jenkins' brigade which Colonel Walker quickly moved forward some 400 yards to an apple orchard, "under a heavy fire of artillery and small arms."[35] He put the First, Fifth and Sixth Regiments in line on the left, and the Palmetto Sharpshooters and Second Rifles in the center and on the right. One officer in the brigade wrote that, as Burnside's Union troops advanced up toward the village from Antietam Creek,

> Colonel Walker . . . ordered a charge to meet the force in our front, [which first] . . . hesitated, and then halted, [and began] firing on us from behind a fence. Our men went boldly forward, down the hill, through an orchard,

[32]O. R., vol. 19, part 1, p. 907.
[33]Foote, *Civil War*, 1:692-697.
[34]Longstreet's report, O. R., vol. 19, part 1, p. 840.
[35]O. R., vol. 19, part 1, p. 907.

to a good stone fence, where [we] were halted and began firing.[36]

This charge temporarily halted the advance in Walker's front and drove the Federal troops back into the woodline along the creek. His men were able to hold the stone fence for only about twenty minutes, however, before the bluecoats regrouped for another advance.

On Walker's right, the pressure of the renewed Federal advance was so great that two of D. R. Jones' other brigades began to give ground, forcing Jenkins' men to begin falling back from the stone wall.[37] Colonel Walker had seen the two other brigades being pushed back, and the pursuing Federals now appeared on his right flank, across a ravine. He then repositioned the brigade in a line parallel with the ravine and opened a destructive enfilade fire upon the advancing Union troops on the other side which helped stop them and send them back toward Antietam Creek. Walker then changed the brigade's front, again facing the creek. Parallel to it ran the stone fence along which he put out a line of skirmishers to await the next Federal charge.[38]

One officer in Jenkins' brigade described waiting anxiously for the next wave of attack:

> As we . . . faced the enemy in our front . . . [suddenly] we saw a thrilling scene being enacted on the right. Somebody had struck Burnside on his left flank. It was A. P. Hill, just arrived from Harper's Ferry.[39]

Hill's division, just in time to keep Longstreet's men from being overwhelmed, crashed into Burnside's troops, throwing them into confusion. As the Union soldiers withdrew back toward the creek, Jenkins' men poured their fire into the retreating blue columns.[40] The last minute appearance of Hill's division had saved the day for

---

[36]Coker, *History of Company E, Sixth S.C. Regiment*, 111. The Federal troops advancing toward Jenkins' men belonged to Colonel Benjamin C. Christ's brigade in the IX Corps division of Brigadier General Orlando B. Willcox. Christ's brigade advanced on the north side of the road leading to Sharpsburg form the lower bridge (Lower Bridge Road) and consisted of the following regiments: 28th Massachusetts, 17th Michigan, 79th New York and 50th Pennsylvania. John M. Priest, *Antietam: The Soldiers' Battle* (New York: Oxford University Press, 1989), 339; Sears, *Landscape Turned Red*, 279.
[37]Hagood, *Memoirs*, 86.
[38]O. R., vol. 19, part 1, p. 907. The ravine which Walker describes in his report is a depression which ran from Antietam Creek up to Sharpsburg. In this depression was the Lower Bridge Road (also called Rohrbach Bridge Road), which ran from the lower bridge up the hill and into Sharpsburg. Sears, *Landscape Turned Red*, 279. Some of the wounded men in Walker's brigade took shelter in this ravine and were captured when the Federals advanced. Coker, *History of Company E, Sixth S.C. Regiment*, 111.
[39]Coker, *History of Company E, Sixth S.C. Regiment*, 112.
[40]Ibid.

MAP 3: BATTLE OF SHARPSBURG - SEPTEMBER 17, 1862

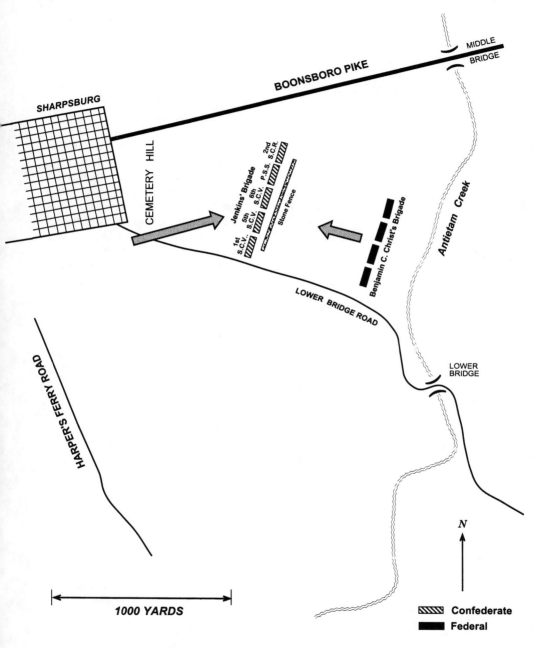

At around 4 p.m. troops in Benjamin C. Christ's Federal Brigade (of Burnside's IX Corps) began their advance from Antietam Creek up toward Cemetery Hill. Christ's men advanced on the north side of the Lower Bridge Road. To meet this advance, Colonel Walker pushed Jenkins' Brigade forward for about 400 yards, through an orchard to a solid stone fence, and managed to repulse Christ's initial thrust.

MAP 4: BATTLE OF SHARPSBURG - SEPTEMBER 17, 1862

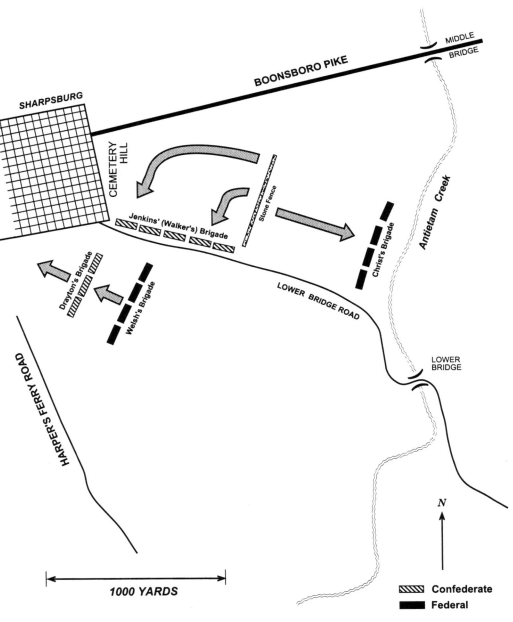

After repulsing the initial advance of Christ's Federal Brigade, Walker's right flank was threatened by the advance of Thomas Welsh's Federal Brigade on the south side of the Lower Bridge Road. As Welsh's men were pushing back Drayton's Brigade, Colonel Walker pivoted Jenkins' Brigade around and positioned his line parallel with the Lower Bridge Road. From here Walker's men were able to enfilade Welsh's lines, greatly impeding their advance. Shortly afterwards, A. P. Hill's Division arrived from Harper's Ferry, just in time to repulse the Union assault, effectively ending the Battle of Sharpsburg.

Longstreet's corps and for Lee's army.[41] An officer in Jenkins' brigade
wrote:

> A. P. Hill's division . . . came up at the double quick and,
> cheering enthusiastically, fell upon the astonished
> Federals with indescribable fury. The fate of the day was
> at once reversed.[42]

Night finally brought an end to the bloodiest single day of the war, but
Lee's men still held the field. McClellan had wasted his golden
opportunity to destroy the Army of Northern Virginia.

That night, Jenkins' brigade bivouacked in the same position it held
at the close of the battle. In the day's fighting, the Palmetto
Sharpshooters, led by Captain F. W. Kilpatrick, had the highest number
of casualties in the brigade: 8 men killed and 57 wounded.[43] Two of
those killed were captains: Joseph E. Lee, Company F, and Nathaniel
W. Harbin, Company B. The Fifth Regiment, under the temporary
command of Captain Thomas C. Beckham, had 6 killed and 27
wounded.[44]

When the stories of the battle were being told by Jenkins' troops as
they bedded down for the night, perhaps the men in Company E of the
Sixth Regiment heard the most interesting tale. During the thick of the
fight, several men in the company were using haystacks for cover while
firing at the enemy. According to an officer in the regiment, at one point
the Union troops advanced past the haystacks, and

> [t]o avoid capture [the men] buried themselves in the
> hay, and managed to escape observation, and after
> Burnside's repulse, rejoined the company.[45]

Following the battle, Colonel Walker had harsh words for some of
the officers in the First Regiment who had not remained with their men
when the fighting intensified. He said in his report:

> Such officers are a disgrace to the service and unworthy
> to wear a sword, for I must believe that their desertions

---

[41]Capers, *South Carolina*, 6:159.

[42]Hagood, *Memoirs*, 87.

[43]Coker, *History of Company E, Sixth S.C. Regiment*, 112; O. R., vol. 19, part 1, p. 907.

[44]O. R., vol. 19, part 1, pp. 907-908. Jenkins' brigade lost a total of 26 killed and 184 wounded. The First South Carolina lost a total of 40; the Second Rifles lost 21; and the Sixth lost 51. Ibid. The brigade took 530 officers and men into the fight. Priest, *Antietam*, 321.

[45]Coker, *History of Company E, Sixth S.C. Regiment*, 113.

of their companies alone induced such conduct upon the part of their privates.[46]

The morning after the battle there was sporadic sharpshooting across Antietam Creek, but McClellan gave up the offensive and massed his artillery on the north bank to defend against a possible attack by Lee's army. Such an attack was not considered advisable, however, because the Confederate ranks had been severely thinned by the previous day's fighting. At about two that afternoon, with neither army having made any effort to renew the conflict, Longstreet addressed a note to General Lee suggesting that the army be withdrawn to the south side of the Potomac. Before the message was delivered, however, Lee met with Longstreet and expressed the same opinion.[47]

The men in Jenkins' brigade spent the entire day after the battle burying the dead and caring for the wounded, and also received their first mail in three weeks.[48] After dark, Colonel Walker received orders from General Jones for the brigade to act as a rear guard for the withdrawal of the division across the Potomac. Walker strengthened his picket line, extending it both right and left, and held the brigade in position until almost daylight on September 19. Jenkins' men were finally relieved by a cavalry brigade, and Colonel Walker reported that they then withdrew "across the Potomac, effecting the passage a little after sunrise, in perfect safety."[49]

Lee's Maryland campaign was over, and while he had held his own against a foe of superior numbers, he had been forced off Maryland soil after having lost more than one fourth of the Army of Northern Virginia.[50] Captain Coker, in the Sixth South Carolina, later wrote that the Battle of Sharpsburg had been "remarkable" for two reasons: first, the disparity in the numbers between Lee's and McClellan's forces; second, the poor condition of Lee's men due to lack of provisions and clothes. Coker found it incredible that Lee's men had fought so well since the "army was

---

[46]O. R., vol. 19, part 1, p. 908. For a full explanation of this incident, see Hagood, *Memoirs*, 88-90.

[47]Longstreet's report, October 10, 1862, O. R., vol. 19, part 1, p. 841. Major Thomas J. Goree, Longstreet's aide-de-camp, noted that Micah Jenkins had missed the battle and wrote: "South Carolina has four (4) brigadiers here. Jenkins is one of the best in the army." Goree to his Mother, October 10, 1862, in Cutrer, ed., *Longstreet's Aide*, 100.

[48]O. R., vol. 19, part 1, p. 907; James R. Boulware Diary, September 18, 1862.

[49]O. R., vol. 19, part 1, p. 907.

[50]Foote, *Civil War*, 1:700-701. The total losses in Jenkins' brigade at South Mountain on September 14, and at Sharpsburg on September 17, were reported as 235, killed, wounded or missing. O. R., vol. 19, part 1, p. 843. The brigade had 562 officers and men present at South Mountain on September 14. Priest, *Before Antietam*, 324.

literally in rags, and their suffering, from actual hunger, more than can now be realized."[51]

Jenkins' brigade crossed the Potomac at a ford some three miles below Shepardstown, Virginia, about fifteen miles above Harper's Ferry. Then they marched "into a clover field west of Shepardstown and [were] given rations . . . and told to rest."[52] During the next few days, the brigade, along with the remainder of Longstreet's command, marched to Martinsburg and then down to Winchester, Virginia. By the end of September, Jenkins' men were comfortably camped within six miles of Winchester where they were to remain for a little more than a month. One soldier in the Palmetto Sharpshooters, happy with the lull in the fighting, wrote:

> [B]adly did they need [the rest] for I never saw men so
> thoroughly exausted [*sic*] from marching, hard fighting,
> and loss of sleep, besides little to eat.[53]

While in Winchester, examination boards were convened to review cases of incompetent officers, and some soldiers were court-martialed for misconduct in Maryland. Lee's troops began daily drilling again and dress parades were reintroduced. The regiments in Jenkins' brigade were soon being strengthened by the "return of convalescents and those who were slightly wounded in the early part of the campaign."[54] G. L. Strait, a captain in the Sixth South Carolina, wrote from Winchester:

> The only excitement at present is a report that our
> Brigade is going to S. C. this winter. Whether there is
> any truth in the report or not I cannot say. Nevertheless,
> I know Genl. Jenkins designs taking us there if he can do
> so.[55]

Before the middle of October, while still camped at Winchester, the men in Jenkins' brigade received word that they were being assigned to

[51]Coker, *History of Company E, Sixth S.C. Regiment*, 114. According to one source, McClellan had almost 54,000 troops engaged as compared to about 30,000 for Lee. Of those engaged, McClellan lost 12,882 (24%) and Lee lost 11,530 (38%). Priest, *Antietam*, 343.

[52]Coker, *History of Company E, Sixth S.C. Regiment*, 114.

[53]H. C. Conner to Ellen O'Leary, October 10, 1862, Henry Calvin Conner Papers.

[54]Hagood, *Memoirs*, 90.

[55]G. M. Lafayette Strait to his mother, Isabella Strait, October 26, 1862, G. L. Strait Letters, Private Collection, Dr. W. Frank Strait, III, Rock Hill, South Carolina. At the time he wrote this letter, Lafayette Strait was captain of Company A, Sixth South Carolina Volunteers. He later became assistant surgeon for the Palmetto Sharpshooters and died of natural causes in October, 1863.

Major General George E. Pickett's division, in Longstreet's command.[56] General D. R. Jones' health was such that he was no longer able to remain in the field, and his brigades were divided among the divisions of John B. Hood and Pickett.[57] The disbanding of Jones' staff had the effect of throwing Jenkins' good friend, Asbury Coward, out of a job.[58]

All of the time that Lee's army was drawn up around Winchester, Lincoln was pressuring General McClellan to cross the Potomac and mount a new campaign to take Richmond. The cautious McClellan delayed, however, and Lee took advantage of the lull to shift half of his army to Culpepper, Virginia, to block any Federal advance toward Richmond.[59] For allowing this to happen, McClellan was relieved of command and replaced by General Ambrose Burnside who, Lincoln hoped, would be more aggressive.

As part of Lee's strategy to block the Union army's path to Richmond, Jenkins' brigade left Winchester on October 27 and began its long march to Culpepper. It took the men three and a half days to reach their destination, some sixty miles away, and one of them wrote that they arrived "much fatigued and sore-footed."[60]

When word of McClellan's firing reached General Jenkins, he wrote Caroline and predicted:

> The disposition of McLellan [*sic*] because of his unwillingness to advance, and the appointment of another commander [Burnside] will, it is thought, lead to a forward movement of the Yankee army. If so, a terrible battle must be fought. . . .[61]

Jenkins was quite correct. The year 1862 was fast coming to a close, but Lee's Army of Northern Virginia had one more battle to fight before year's end, at a picturesque Virginia village at the river's edge called Fredericksburg.

---

[56]J. W. McLure to Kate McLure, October 10, 1862, McLure Family Papers. Jenkins and his brigade were officially assigned to George E. Pickett's division (Third Division, Longstreet's First Corps) on October 27, 1862. Freeman, *Lee's Lieutenants*, 2:269; O. R., vol. 19, part 2, p. 683.

[57]Freeman, *Lee's Lieutenants*, 2:269; O. R., vol. 19, part 2, p. 683. General Jones had a serious heart condition.

[58]Bond and Coward, eds., *South Carolinians*, 66.

[59]Foote, *Civil War*, 1:752-753.

[60]H. C. Conner to Ellen O'Leary, November 1, 1862, Henry Calvin Conner Papers.

[61]Micah Jenkins to Caroline Jenkins, November 18, 1862, Micah Jenkins Papers, S.C.L.

Chapter 16

Fredericksburg And Winter Quarters

T en months had passed since the great Charleston fire, but as he walked through the once-beautiful city, Micah Jenkins was still shocked by the devastation. When he looked down Meeting Street toward Broad, one of the few structures he saw still standing was the Mills House, where he had stayed so many times. The Circular Congregational Church, the Institute Hall where the Ordinance of Secession had been signed, the Arts Association building, the Apprentices' Library and the Charleston Theatre were gone. Charred ruins marked both sides of what had been one of Charleston's busiest streets.[1]

It was late October 1862, and Jenkins was still in South Carolina recuperating from his wounds received at Second Manassas. He and Caroline happened to be in Charleston attending a wedding at Saint Philips Church, which had somehow been spared by the fire. At the wedding reception, Jenkins talked at length with his old friend Asbury Coward, who had recently returned from Virginia after General D. R. Jones' staff was disbanded. Since Coward was in need of a new military assignment, Jenkins suggested that he take the command of the Fifth

---

[1] Fraser, *Charleston*, 253-254.

Regiment of South Carolina Volunteers. The regiment had been without a colonel since the death of John R. R. Giles at Seven Pines. Coward had been offered this appointment two months before, but he had turned it down in deference to the regiment's lieutenant colonel, Andrew Jackson, who would normally have been promoted to the position. Jenkins, however, informed Coward that Jackson had resigned his commission because of wounds he had received at Gaines' Mill, and that the position of colonel was still vacant. Jenkins then offered to visit the War Department in Richmond and have his friend's appointment renewed. Coward jumped at the opportunity to command the Fifth Regiment and asked Jenkins to do what he could to help.[2] The next day, having finally recovered enough to return to duty, Jenkins left for Virginia. Less than a week later, after receiving Jenkins' letter saying that the War Department had accepted his recommendation, Coward quickly began to prepare for his return to the Army of Northern Virginia.[3]

After helping to secure Coward's promotion, Jenkins boarded a train in Richmond and headed north. He finally caught up with his brigade at Culpepper, Virginia, and was received warmly by his men.[4] In the middle of November, he received good news: the infantry companies of the Hampton Legion were assigned to Jenkins' command and were combined with the companies of the Fourth South Carolina Battalion to create a full regiment. While the Fourth Battalion ceased to exist, the merger gave Jenkins' brigade six full regiments.[5] As one member of the Hampton Legion later recalled, "Think of it! Six regiments of South Carolinians, the flower of the old Palmetto State. . . ."[6]

The same day that the Hampton Legion joined Jenkins' brigade, Colonel Asbury Coward arrived in the brigade's camp at Culpepper to assume command of the Fifth Regiment. Some members of the regiment had requested his appointment, as one captain wrote, "to

---

[2]Bond and Coward, eds., *South Carolinians*, 66.

[3]Ibid., 67. Coward's appointment as colonel of the Fifth S.C.V. was dated August 12, 1861, the original date it had been issued and turned down by Coward.

[4]Hagood, *Memoirs*, 92.

[5]Micah Jenkins to Caroline Jenkins, November 18, 1862, Micah Jenkins Papers, S.C.L.. Jenkins' brigade now included the following six South Carolina regiments of volunteers: the First, the Second Rifles, the Fifth, the Sixth, the Palmetto Sharpshooters and the newly-added Hampton Legion (infantry). The Hampton Legion joined the brigade on November 16, 1862. J. Banks Lyle to Dora McArthur, November 16, 1862, Joseph Banks Lyle Letters. The Legion was under the command of Colonel Martin W. Gary, of Cokesbury in Abbeville District, South Carolina. Capers, *South Carolina*, 6:395.

[6]E. Scott Carson, "Hampton's Legion and Hood's Brigade," *Confederate Veteran*, 16 (July 1908):342. The combining of the Hampton Legion (infantry) and Mattison's Fourth South Carolina Battalion was ordered on November 11, 1862. Special Orders No. 239, O. R., vol. 19, part 2, p. 714. These orders called for the new Hampton Legion to remain in J. B. Hood's old brigade, where it had been assigned prior to the merger with Mattison's Battalion. For some reason, this was quickly changed and the Hampton Legion (now including the Fourth Battalion) was placed in Jenkins' brigade.

prevent the promotion of officers whom they considered unworthy."[7] A soldier in the brigade recalled the day Coward reported:

> He was dressed in a brand new suit, polished high top boots, shining spurs and bright sword. He did not weigh over one hundred and twenty pounds, but he looked game.[8]

The well-respected Coward, short in stature, but long on courage and tenacity, was not prepared for what he found. His new regiment, which had taken 560 enlisted men and officers into the Battle of Williamsburg six months earlier, now had only 260 in camp. He was the only field officer present with the regiment, and he had no adjutant and no chaplain. Beginning work immediately, Coward met in his tent with his captains and informed them that the regiment was going to be improved. He said that soon it would be known as the "Old Reliable Fifth," rather than the "Ragged Fifth." He began by establishing a night school in tactics for his officers and random bugle calls for skirmish drills. Morale steadily improved, and some of the vacancies on Coward's regimental staff began to be filled. John N. Craig from Lancaster, South Carolina, was named chaplain and Dr. Joseph H. Foster, of the same place, the regiment's surgeon.[9] Coward worked fast, knowing he had only a short time to whip the regiment into shape before the coming engagement.

The Fifth Regiment was not the only one in Jenkins' brigade to undergo changes during the October and November lull in the fighting. In the Palmetto Sharpshooters, Captain John Wesley Goss, of Company A, was promoted to lieutenant colonel, reporting to Colonel Joe Walker; Captain F. W. Kilpatrick, of Company

JOHN WESLEY GOSS, WHO BECAME LIEUTENANT COLONEL OF THE PALMETTO SHARPSHOOTERS AFTER JOSEPH WALKER WAS PROMOTED TO COLONEL OF THE REGIMENT.

[7] J. Banks Lyle to Dora McArthur, November 16, 1862, Joseph Banks Lyle Letters.
[8] Mixson, *Reminiscences of a Private*, 36.
[9] Bond and Coward, eds., *South Carolinians*, 68-70.

B, was promoted to major.[10] In the Sixth Regiment, Colonel John Bratton, who had been wounded and captured at Seven Pines, was released in a prisoner exchange and had returned to his command.[11]

Jenkins' main problem now was sickness among his troops; without tents and shoes, many were suffering from pneumonia. Each day many of these ailing soldiers left camp at Culpepper on the "sick train;" some died before they reached the hospitals in Richmond.[12]

While Jenkins did see signs of improvement in the strength of his brigade, he wrote that "it would require several months to produce entirely satisfactory results."[13] By the end of November, however, it had become extremely unlikely that he would be given that much time.

After Lincoln replaced McClellan for lack of aggressiveness, General Ambrose Burnside took over command of the Army of the Potomac. He immediately shifted seven corps of Union troops to Falmouth, directly across the Rappahannock River from Fredericksburg. This was the opening phase of a new drive for Richmond, and Lee reacted quickly to counter Burnside's move; he ordered both Longstreet and Jackson to shift their two corps to Fredericksburg.[14]

Jenkins and his men left Culpepper on November 21, along with other brigades in Longstreet's First Corps, and arrived outside of Fredericksburg two days later. Without their tents or baggage, they camped two miles southwest of the town. One soldier in the Palmetto Sharpshooters wrote that it was rumored Burnside had as many as 110,000 troops on the other side of the river.[15] This estimate was surprisingly accurate; at that time there were in fact 113,000 Union soldiers waiting to cross the river into Fredericksburg.[16]

By the first of December, the quaint river town had become nearly deserted. Some of the women and children who had evacuated their homes were living in a church near the camps of Jenkins' brigade.[17] The next week it snowed several inches while his men were still without tents. In spite of the bad weather, the brigade's examining board met with

---

[10]*Carolina Spartan*, December 11, 1862. Joe Walker, formerly the regiment's lieutenant colonel, had replaced Jenkins when he was promoted to brigadier; John Wesley Goss was promoted from major to lieutenant colonel, replacing Walker; Kilpatrick replaced Major William Anderson, who had been wounded at Frayser's Farm and died of his wounds on July 4, 1862.

[11]Coker, *History of Company E, Sixth S.C. Regiment*, 116.

[12]Hagood, *Memoirs*, 92.

[13]Micah Jenkins to Caroline Jenkins, November 18, 1862, John Jenkins Papers, S.C.L.

[14]Freeman, *Lee's Lieutenants*, 2:325. In the fall of 1862, the Confederate Congress decided to permit its armies to be organized into "corps." The Army of Northern Virginia was formally reorganized into two corps on November 6, 1862. Stonewall Jackson's Second Corps was made up of four divisions. Longstreet's First Corps was made up of five divisions. The brigades in Longstreet's old division were split up between John B. Hood and George E. Pickett. Jenkins' brigade was assigned to Pickett's Division on October 27, 1862. Freeman, *Lee's Lieutenants*, 2:269; O. R., vol. 19, part 2, p. 683.

[15]H. C. Conner to Ellen O'Leary, November 25, 1862, Henry Calvin Conner Papers.

[16]Foote, *Civil War*, 1:767.

[17]J. W. McLure to Kate McLure, November 29, 1862, McLure Family Papers.

newly-elected officers and candidates for promotion to determine their qualifications.[18]

Meanwhile, Burnside's army was poised along Stafford Heights, on the east bank of the river across from Fredericksburg, waiting for pontoon bridges to be laid. On the opposite side of the river, Longstreet had posted Lafayette McLaws' division on Marye's Heights, the high ground several hundred yards west of the town. Pickett's division, to which Jenkins' brigade had been assigned since the end of October, was positioned on Telegraph Hill (later renamed Lee's Hill) on McLaws' right, out of range of the Federal artillery across the river.[19]

On December 11, Burnside's troops finally began laying pontoon bridges and by late afternoon were shelling the town from across the river. After dark, long columns of Union soldiers began crossing the bridges into town. The next day, even more bluecoats crossed the river and continued massing in the village for the attack.

A heavy fog shrouded the town and river valley as the opposing armies awoke on the morning of December 13. When the fog finally lifted at around ten o'clock, the Federals advanced first against Jackson's corps south of the town. Pickett's division, including Jenkins' brigade, remained on Telegraph Hill all morning and did not become involved in the fighting in Jackson's sector. By noon, Longstreet's batteries opened fire from the heights west of the town, and the focus of the fight shifted toward the village. Union troops then began a series of costly and futile assaults against the Confederate center on Marye's Heights. They were completely repulsed six times by Thomas R. R. Cobb's brigade of Georgians and Joseph B. Kershaw's South Carolinians who were positioned along "the sunken road" at the bottom of Marye's Heights.[20]

At two that afternoon, Pickett was ordered to send Kemper's and Jenkins' brigades to Marye's Heights to strengthen the Confederate center. Upon their arrival there, Jenkins' men were put in the line in place of Kershaw's brigade, which had already been sent down to the sunken road where the fighting was heaviest.[21] After Jenkins' brigade took its new position in the trenches on Marye's Heights, it was subjected to severe shelling, causing some casualties. Jenkins reported that during

---

[18]J. Banks Lyle to Dora McArthur, December 8, 1862, Joseph Banks Lyle Letters. The brigade's examining board consisted of General Jenkins, Colonel Coward, Major F. W. Kilpatrick of the Palmetto Sharpshooters, and Captain G. L. Strait of the Sixth Regiment. *Carolina Spartan*, December 18, 1862.

[19]Lieutenant General James Longstreet, "The Battle of Fredericksburg," *Battles and Leaders of the Civil War*, vol. 3, *The Tide Shifts* (reprint; Secaucus, New Jersey: Castle Books, 1982), 72-73; Freeman, *Lee's Lieutenants*, 2:330.

[20]Longstreet, "The Battle of Fredericksburg," 3:78-79; Foote, *Civil War*, 2:39-40; Freeman, *Lee's Lieutenants*, 2:359.

[21]Freeman, *Lee's Lieutenants*, 2:365. One of Jenkins' officers wrote, "we thought we were going in" when they were moved to the left to take Kershaw's place on Marye's Heights. Coker, *History of Company E, Sixth S.C. Regiment*, 117.

the shelling, one of his regiments, Colonel Walker's Palmetto Sharpshooters,

> was advanced to meet a threatened flank movement of the enemy and engaged in a skirmishing fight which was highly successful in regard to the objects in view. While on this duty . . . was mortally wounded the very promising Sergeant Major [W. F.] McKeown.[22]

None of the other regiments of the brigade, however, was actively engaged on the day of the battle.

That night, when darkness had halted the fighting, Colonel Coward met Jenkins at eight o'clock in front of his tent before a small fire. He ordered Coward to take the Fifth Regiment down to the sunken road at the bottom of Marye's Heights and relieve some of Kershaw's exhausted troops who had been fighting there most of the day. By dawn, Coward and his men were in position along the sunken road, fully expecting a renewal of the attack by the Union troops.[23] When the sun arose that December 14, the men in Jenkins' brigade were able to view first-hand the deadly results of the Federals' repeated assaults at the foot of Marye's Heights the day before. What they saw shocked them; one veteran soldier in the Palmetto Sharpshooters wrote:

> I have seen several battlefields, but I have never seen the Yankee dead thicker than they are here. There is one piece of ground I suppose about four acres that there is about four hundred and fifty lying dead.[24]

Colonel Coward recalled later that those horrible scenes near the sunken road were forever etched into his memory.[25] Another officer in the brigade described how dead animals, killed during the fighting, littered the town and how the wooden buildings were "thickly perforated with shot."[26] All day Lee's troops waited for an attack which never came; the Federals remained quietly behind their lines in the town.

That night Jenkins' brigade was relieved from duty in the trenches and moved back to a position near the Marye House at the top of the

---

[22]Jenkins' report on the Battle of Fredericksburg, December 25, 1862, in Hewett, Trudeau and Suderow, eds., *Supplement to the Official Records*, 3:806. W. F. McKeown, sergeant major of the Palmetto Sharpshooters, had been promoted from sergeant in Company E only weeks before. He was wounded in the bowels at Fredericksburg and died a few days later.

[23]Bond and Coward, eds., *South Carolinians*, 72-73.

[24]H. C. Conner to Ellen O'Leary, December 18, 1862, Henry Calvin Conner Papers.

[25]Bond and Coward, eds., *South Carolinians*, 73.

[26]Hagood, *Memoirs*, 98.

heights. The next morning, the men again anxiously awaited the renewal of the Federal attack, but all remained quiet. By then the freezing Confederate troops had stripped many of the bodies of the dead Union soldiers, lying thick on the plain in front of Marye's Heights, of needed clothing and shoes. That afternoon, under a flag of truce, the Federals removed their dead and wounded from the field on condition that they would not reclaim any of their abandoned equipment.[27]

On December 16, under orders from General Longstreet, Jenkins had Colonel Coward send two companies of the Fifth Regiment, under Major John D. Wylie, into the town on a scouting mission. These were the first armed men in Lee's army to enter the town after the battle, and they quickly discovered that Burnside's troops were gone. Except for stragglers and some of their wounded, they had evacuated the town, retreated back across the river and taken up their pontoon bridges.[28] While on this assignment, Wylie's detail managed to capture 155 prisoners and some small arms and ammunition.[29]

Burnside had been soundly defeated in the fighting at Fredericksburg. He lost more than 12,000 men compared to only about a third that many casualties for Lee.[30] In spite of the glory which the brigades of Cobb and Kershaw had received for the significant part they played in the victory, most of Jenkins' men were delighted they had not been actively engaged. One of his officers wrote later, "[F]or once we did not have to bear the brunt of battle."[31]

Dr. Edward E. Jenkins, the general's brother, acted temporarily as the brigade surgeon at Fredericksburg during the fighting and the days that followed. A week after the battle, however, he returned to South Carolina.[32] At about this same time, Micah Jenkins' father-in-law was beginning a new job. On December 20, fifty-two-year-old David F. Jamison was appointed presiding military judge in South Carolina for General Beauregard's corps.[33]

After the Union retreat at Fredericksburg, the stalemated armies settled into their camps, separated only by the Rappahannock River. Their bands came down to the river banks to play in the evenings; the Northern bands played "Yankee Doodle" and the Southern, "Dixie." They would then join in playing "Home, Sweet Home," moving the men to

---

[27]Foote, *Civil War*, 2:43; Bond and Coward, ed., *South Carolinians*, 73.

[28]Jenkins' Report on Fredericksburg, in Hewett, Trudeau and Suderow, eds., *Supplement to the Official Records*, 3:806; Foote, *Civil War*, 2:44.

[29]Record of Events Cards for the Fifth S.C.V., Company C, November-December 1862. The two companies included in Wylie's detail were Company C, under Captain J. Banks Lyle, and Company F, under Captain James M. Harvey.

[30]Foote, *Civil War*, 2:44.

[31]Coker, *History of Company E, Sixth S.C. Regiment*, 117.

[32]Micah Jenkins to Caroline Jenkins, December 21, 1862, Micah Jenkins Papers, S.C.L.

[33]General Orders, No. 109, December 20, 1862, O. R., series IV, vol. 2, p. 248.

cheers as well as tears.[34] Soldiers on both banks of the river made tiny sailboats, stuffed them with food, newspaper articles or tobacco and floated them to the other side. Even though officers were told to prevent these exchanges, they were allowed to continue.[35]

Shortly before the end of 1862, Jenkins let his ambition get the better of him and ended up damaging his own reputation. In a move primarily designed to gain promotion to major general, he arranged to have his brigade transferred from Pickett's to John B. Hood's division. Jenkins wrote his wife a surprisingly candid explanation:

> I have succeeded in my efforts and [my brigade is] now in Hood's Division. Here I am Senior Brigadier and in Hood's absence command the Division. Where I was before, I was ranked by three Brigadiers. It is painful to break old ties, but I feel satisfied that I have decided to my advantage and that of my Brigade.[36]

Regardless of Jenkins' motives, this transfer suited his troops as well, and one wrote home saying the change was one "which I do not much regret."[37] Another man in the brigade wrote that General Hood was "decidedly preferable" to Pickett.[38] Three weeks later, however, the transfer to Hood's division was completely reversed by General Longstreet. When Jenkins objected, Longstreet became highly irritated and replied:

> Your note of the 18th is received. Just before yours was received I discovered that I was in great trouble with the whole of the three Divisions, all growing out of the same thing. Now if you want to get into trouble with me about the same thing, let me beg of you to wait till I have a little more time to quarrel.[39]

---

[34]Mixson, *Reminiscences of a Private*, 37-38. Private Mixson, in the First South Carolina, stated:
        I do believe that had we not had the river between us that the two armies would
        have gone together and settled the war right there and then.
Ibid., 38.
[35]Anderson and Anderson, *The Generals*, 338.
[36]Micah Jenkins to Caroline Jenkins, December 29, 1862, Micah Jenkins Papers, D.U.L.
[37]H. C. Conner to Ellen O'Leary, December 28, 1862, Henry Calvin Conner Papers.
[38]J. W. McLure to Kate McLure, December 27, 1862, McLure Family Papers.
[39]Longstreet to Jenkins, January 20, 1863, Micah Jenkins Papers D.U.L. Jenkins' note to Longstreet of January 18, 1863, referred to in Longstreet's letter, has not been located.

To this stinging rebuke, Jenkins immediately replied to Longstreet:

> I supposed that as my friend as well as [my] Chief . . .
> you would at once have seen the delicate and injurious
> place the ground of *retransfer* would put me in, and at
> once have relieved me from the same. . . .
>   [However,] I am fully mindful of your kindness in
> [having originally made] the exchange to gratify me . . .
> [and] I am ready in feelings as well as from military
> necessity to obey the order for retransfer.[40]

That was the end of the matter. To Jenkins' bitter disappointment and embarrassment, the transfer was revoked, and his brigade was retransferred back into Pickett's division.[41] In an attempt to rectify the wrong that he apparently felt had been done to Jenkins, General Hood quickly wrote to the War Department in Richmond recommending Jenkins for promotion to major general, in the event such a vacancy existed.[42] Hood's recommendation was warmly endorsed by General Longstreet, who wrote:

> I have heard that a Major General is likely to be
> appointed for South Carolina. If there is a vacancy, or
> command, for such officer, I desire to unite in [General
> Hood's] recommendation of General Jenkins for
> promotion.[43]

---

[40]Jenkins to Longstreet, January 21, 1863, John Jenkins Papers, S.C.L. (emphasis in original). Jenkins' brigade had transferred to Hood's division on December 28, 1862, and Hood inspected the brigade on January 9, 1863. James R. Boulware Diary, December 28, 1862, and January 9, 1863. Thus, by the time Longstreet decided to undo the transfer on about January 18, Jenkins and his men had already been functioning as part of Hood's divisions for three full weeks.

[41]One officer who may have opposed Jenkins' transfer into Hood's division was Brigadier General Evander M. Law, who commanded a brigade in that division, and who was less senior than Jenkins. Jenkins' appointment as brigadier general was dated July 22, 1862; Law's was dated October 3, 1862. This was the same E. M. Law who had served on the faculty at the Kings Mountain Military School under Jenkins, and who had left that position to move to Alabama before the war.

[42]Hood to General Cooper, February 4, 1863, in National Archives, Complied Service Records of Confederate General and Staff Officers and Non-Regimental Enlisted Men, R. G. 109, series M331, Records for Brigadier General Micah Jenkins (referred to hereafter as "Jenkins' Compiled Service Records"). In Hood's letter to Cooper, he stated in part:
> By his great gallantry and ability upon the field of battle and his untiring energy and constant attention to his Command, [Jenkins] has won the admiration of all with whom he has served.
> It is only necessary to witness the condition and manner in which he at all times has his Brigade, to know that he is one of our most able and efficient officers.

[43]Longstreet's endorsement on Hood's letter to Cooper, February 7, 1863, in Jenkins' Compiled Service Records. Longstreet's endorsement also stated:
> General Jenkins has been in every battle fought by our Army (except two missed, whilst he was wounded). He is one of our most distinguished Brigadiers

When the recommendation reached General Lee, he too endorsed it:

> I know nothing of the occasion of [the appointment of a
> major general for South Carolina] and can only positively
> concur in the commendations of Generals Longstreet
> and Hood of the efficiency and gallantry of General
> Jenkins. I would regret to lose his services in this
> Army.[44]

In spite of these high-level efforts to soothe Jenkins' wounded feelings,
the War Department chose to leave him in Pickett's division for the
present, with no chance of promotion.

Jenkins' abortive attempt to have his brigade transferred to Hood's
division, and Longstreet's decision to undo the transfer once it had
already been announced, caused Jenkins to lose some respect among
his men. For example, Palmetto Sharpshooter H. C. Conner,
complaining of Jenkins' "petty ambitions," wrote:

> Jenkins found out he could get into Hood's Division and
> he would be the oldest Brigadier and if Hood resigned or
> be killed [Jenkins] would be promoted to Major
> General. . . .[45]

By the middle of January 1863, the men in Jenkins' brigade had
moved from their camp near the Telegraph Road to a new site at
Hamilton's Crossing, about three miles south of Fredericksburg. There
they constructed their winter quarters with chimneys or flues attached,
and when they could find wood to burn built fires inside to cut the bitter
Virginia chill.[46]

In the second half of the month, several cases of smallpox broke out
in two companies of Coward's Fifth Regiment, and they were temporarily
sent away from the brigade.[47] Fortunately, none of Jenkins' five other
regiments were affected.

At the end of January, the snow around Fredericksburg was almost
twelve inches deep, and some of the men in Longstreet's First Corps got
into an enormous snowball fight. The fight started between regiments

---

on the field of battle, and is the most distinguished for good order, good
management, and good drills, in his Camp.
The "two missed" battles, mentioned in Longstreet's letter, were the Battle of South Mountain on
September 14, 1862, and the Battle of Sharpsburg (Antietam) three days later.
    [44]Lee's endorsement on Hood's and Longstreet's recommendations, February 9, 1863, in Jenkins'
Compiled Service Records.
    [45]H. C. Conner to Ellen O'Leary, March 16, 1863, Henry Calvin Conner Papers.
    [46]Mixson, *Reminiscences of a Private*, 39.
    [47]H. C. Conner to Ellen O'Leary, January 22, 1863, Henry Calvin Conner Papers.

but escalated, and soon four brigades were "engaged": Jenkins', Kershaw's, Anderson's and E. M. Law's.[48]

Describing the fight between Law's brigade and Jenkins' troops, one officer in Lee's army wrote that on the first day of the "battle" Jenkins' men got the worst of it. The next morning, however, Jenkins had his brigade up at dawn, and attacked Law's men just as they were awaking and cooking breakfast. Jenkins' men drove Law's troops from their camp, occupied their huts and ate their breakfasts. Part of the snowball fight took place close to General Lee's headquarters, and it was reported that the army commander was even hit by several balls.[49]

One officer in Jenkins' brigade said that in this snowball battle there were prisoners taken and no quarter was given.[50] A private in the Sixth South Carolina said that they plundered the opposing brigade's camp and that "it was the biggest snowball fight on record."[51] The next day, many of the men in the rival brigades had sore faces where they had been hit by the frozen snowballs.[52]

In late January, Jenkins changed the leadership of the First South Carolina Regiment, which consisted then of some 250 officers and men. When Colonel Glover was killed at Second Manassas, Lieutenant Colonel William Duncan had temporarily assumed command of the regiment, but he was never promoted by the War Department. To fill the vacancy, General Jenkins placed Major F. W. Kilpatrick, of the Palmetto Sharpshooters, in command of the First Regiment, and he was quickly promoted to colonel.[53]

On January 30, General Lee ordered Jenkins to South Carolina to procure conscripts and volunteers for his brigade.[54] He left a few days later on a twenty-five day trip, the first time he had been home since recovering there from the wounds he had received at Second Manassas.

---

[48]*Carolina Spartan*, February 12, 1863. According to one man in the brigade, the snowball battle began on January 29, 1863, and continued into the following day. James R. Boulware Diary, January 29-30, 1863.

[49]Captain Charles M. Blackford to "Little Nancy," February 2, 1863, in Susan L. Blackford, et al., eds., *Letters from Lee's Army* (New York: Charles Scribner's Sons, 1947), 165-166. For a different account of this snowball fight, see the *Carolina Spartan*, February 12, 1863, which indicates that the brigades of Jenkins and Law actually combined to attack the brigades of Kershaw and Anderson.

[50]Lewis, *Camp Life*, 78-79.

[51]Mixson, *Reminiscences of a Private*, 40.

[52]Lewis, *Camp Life*, 78-79. See also, Steven A. Cormier, *The Siege of Suffolk: The Forgotten Campaign, April 11-May 4, 1863* (Lynchburg, Virginia: H. E. Howard, Inc., 1989), 1.

[53]Hagood, *Memoirs*, 101. At the same time, Major Daniel Livingston was promoted to lieutenant colonel and Captain G. M. Grimes was promoted to major of the First South Carolina Volunteers. In the Palmetto Sharpshooters, Captain William W. Humphreys of Company C, was promoted to major, replacing F. W. Kilpatrick. In addition, Colonel Coward had filled the vacancy in his regiment for lieutenant colonel by the promotion of Major John D. Wylie, of Lancaster, South Carolina. This left a vacancy in the position of major in that regiment.

[54]Special Orders No. 30, January 30, 1863, O. R., vol. 25, part 2, p. 600.

Jenkins' senior regimental commander, the Sixth Regiment's John Bratton, was left in command of the brigade.

Meanwhile, Jenkins' men remained in their comfortable winter quarters near Fredericksburg. They were not terribly annoyed by the cold, and one correspondent wrote:

> I was . . . much pleased to see every man of the brigade, with but few exceptions, well and comfortably clad; with good shoes and generally good hats or caps.[55]

They had plenty to eat and received, among other things, a half pound of bacon per day, but no cornmeal, which they craved.[56] The men in the brigade had set up a large tent as a theatre, with calico curtains and candles for footlights, and all money collected for the performances was contributed to a benefit fund for sick and wounded soldiers.[57]

One week after Jenkins left for South Carolina, General Lee received word that the Federals were sending the Ninth Army Corps from Falmouth down to Hampton Roads, at the tip of the Virginia peninsula. As when McClellan had transported his army to the same area in April 1862, this new Federal move posed a serious threat to Richmond and Petersburg. A large Union garrison was already at Suffolk, Virginia, and could now be easily reinforced from Hampton Roads for an advance against the Petersburg and Weldon Railroad, a critical supply line for Lee's army. To counter this new threat, Lee ordered Pickett's division in Fredericksburg to march to Petersburg; Hood's division was told to be in readiness to do likewise.[58]

As part of Pickett's division, Jenkins' men regretfully gave up their warm winter quarters and started their long march toward Richmond on February 15, 1863. The trip on foot was difficult in the extreme, and one officer in the First South Carolina wrote:

> The weather was bitterly cold when [we] began the march. To add to [our] discomfort rain now commenced to fall and rendered the roads almost impassable. The men slept in mud six inches deep each night and this exposure just after leaving the comfortable winter quarters of Fredericksburg caused much suffering and

---

[55]*Carolina Spartan*, February 12, 1863.
[56]Ibid.
[57]Lewis, *Camp Life*, 37-38; Bond and Coward, eds., *South Carolinians*, 74. General Longstreet even escorted his wife to this theatre on the night of February 13, 1863. James R. Boulware Diary, February 13, 1863.
[58]Freeman, *Lee's Lieutenants*, 2:467-468.

sickness. The 1st Regiment had nine deaths from pneumonia; the consequence of this march.[59]

For four days Jenkins' men trudged southward in horrible weather. On February 19, they passed through Richmond and camped near Chester Station, about half way between the capital and Petersburg. The first night there, there was a snowfall which one officer in Jenkins' brigade said "fell . . . so softly that the soldiers under their blankets hardly knew of it until morning."[60]

Jenkins' South Carolinians remained in camp near Chester Station only until February 21 when Pickett's division moved a few miles further south, nearer Petersburg.[61] There, returning from his trip to South Carolina, Jenkins rejoined his men. On March 5 he received some surprising orders. He and his brigade had been transferred to General Samuel G. French's division in the Department of Southern Virginia. Jenkins' orders stated that he was to proceed with his six regiments to the Blackwater River area, roughly forty-five miles southeast of Petersburg, and relieve General Raleigh E. Colston's brigade which was temporarily ordered to take the place of Jenkins' brigade in Pickett's division.[62] Longstreet had developed plans for an offensive against the Union garrison at Suffolk and wanted to use French's division, but not General French himself.[63] One historian has suggested that Longstreet was looking for a way to have Jenkins promoted to the command of that division.[64] When Jenkins' brigade was transferred into French's division, Jenkins became the senior officer in that division in French's absence. Whatever were Longstreet's motives, the transfer had the effect of detaching Jenkins' brigade, not only from Pickett's division, but also from Lee's army. Jenkins never expected, however, that he and his men would be separated from General Lee for any extended period. Unfortunately, they would not be reunited with their beloved army commander for almost fourteen months.

---

[59]Hagood, Memoirs, 105. See also, Cormier, The Siege of Suffolk, 7-9.
[60]Coker, History of Company E, Sixth S.C. Regiment, 119; Cormier, The Siege of Suffolk, 9.
[61]Cormier, The Siege of Suffolk, 298.
[62]Special Orders No. 39, March 5, 1863, O. R., vol. 18, pp. 909-910; Cormier, The Siege of Suffolk, 54.
[63]Cormier, The Siege of Suffolk, 126-127.
[64]Freeman, Lee's Lieutenants, 2:481-482.

Chapter 17

Detached Duty South Of Richmond

Early on a crisp spring morning, a small group of Confederate officers on horseback approached the Blackwater River in southeastern Virginia. Studying the terrain, they trotted down a long country lane edged by budding trees and blooming dogwoods, dappled by sunlight penetrating the lush foliage. They then cut through an open field which was fenced on one side of the road. The party was made up of General Jenkins and several of his officers, including Henry Whitner, a Virginian who had been temporarily assigned to the brigade staff because of his extensive knowledge of the roads in the area. Whitner, unintimidated by the fact that he was the new man in the group, rode a trim little roan mare and boasted to the group that she could out-jump any horse in the army. This stirred the competitive juices in the other officers, especially Colonel Asbury Coward, who was himself light in the saddle and a fine horseman. To prove his point, Whitner and his mare made a run at the roadside fence, clearing the top rail with room to spare.

Coward quickly rose to the challenge, not with his own mount, but with Jenkins' war horse, "Latta." This fine animal had been given to Jenkins by his friend William Latta of Yorkville, for whom the horse was named. Coward spoke briefly to Jenkins, and they both dismounted and exchanged reins. Jenkins gave the small, feisty colonel a look of complete confidence. The deep and lasting friendship between the two men was captured in this warm glance; Jenkins completely trusted his longtime companion.

Coward asked the other officers in the group to set the top bar up another notch on the fence. He shortened Latta's stirrups and walked him close to the fence, where his nose almost touched the bar, giving him a feel for the height. He then mounted and trotted about twenty yards out, wheeled around and rode straight for the fence, easily clearing the top rail. Now it was Whitner's turn. This time his mare jumped and landed nimbly on the other side, but carried the top rail with her as she clipped it with her hind hooves. Coward then had the men raise the bar again, and once more he let the horse nose it before lining up for the jump. Taking him out away from the fence, then turning to it, he patted Latta low on his neck. Coward could feel the animal quiver with excitement as he nudged him with the stirrups and leaned forward in the saddle. Almost instantly, Latta accelerated to a full gallop and, shortening his stride slightly in his last two steps, arched over the bar with unconscious grace. Dr. Joe Foster, the surgeon in Coward's regiment and one of those in the group, exclaimed that Latta had cleared it by more than one foot. As if seeking approval for one more jump, Coward turned toward Jenkins, who now gave him a look of concern. The two men knew each other so well that Coward read exactly what the general was thinking. He dismounted, handed Jenkins the reins, and said sheepishly, "I have a wife and two babies at home. I feel that I have played the fool." Jenkins smiled at his good friend, shook his hand, and with a hearty laugh replied, "We have all been playing the fool." Then the general grew serious again, and climbing back in his saddle, said, "Let's ride on, gentlemen." It had been a fine Virginia spring morning along the Blackwater River, one that Colonel Coward would never forget.[1]

By this time, Jenkins and his brigade had been detached from Lee's army for over a month. They had received orders to proceed to the Blackwater and on March 9, 1863, left Pickett's division in Petersburg and marched southeast in the direction of Suffolk. They followed the Norfolk and Petersburg Railroad for about forty miles to the Blackwater River, then turned due south. Finally, after a march of about four days, they arrived at Franklin, where the Weldon and Suffolk Railroad crossed the Blackwater.[2] Jenkins strategically positioned his six regiments up and down the west bank of the river and began building entrenchments on

---

[1]Bond and Coward, eds., *South Carolinians*, 79-81.
[2]Hagood, *Memoirs*, 105; Coker, *History of Company E, Sixth S.C. Regiment*, 119; J. W. McLure to Kate McLure, March 8 and 13, 1863, McLure Family Papers; J. Banks Lyle to Dora McArthur, March 14, 1863, Joseph Banks Lyle Letters.

the opposite side, facing Suffolk.[3]   On the right of the brigade's line several miles below Franklin was the Hampton Legion, under Colonel Martin W. Gary. The center of the line was in the village of Franklin where the Palmetto Sharpshooters and Colonel Walker were positioned and where Jenkins was headquartered. On the left, up the river a short distance toward Zuni, was the Fifth Regiment, under Colonel Coward. The other three regiments in the brigade were posted a short distance behind the line, held in reserve.[4]

The men in the brigade had barely settled into their camps along the Blackwater when they were attacked. Until Jenkins' men arrived, the Eleventh Pennsylvania Cavalry, led by Colonel Samuel P. Spear, had enjoyed free run of the area and had become well known locally for their bold operations.[5] Three squadrons of Spear's cavalry regiment made a dash at the lines of the Palmetto Sharpshooters, located across the river from Franklin, on the evening of March 17. The Sharpshooters waited until the cavalrymen were at close range before opening fire, causing them to fall back in confused retreat. Spear's men rallied, however, and made four subsequent charges, all of which were repulsed.[6] Following the skirmish, Jenkins reported to General Longstreet that Spear's men had

> carried off four 4-horse ambulances filled with wounded, their legs hanging out in front and rear, and their caisson-boxes were also crowded with wounded. . . . They acknowledged at the time a loss of 70.[7]

In the action, the Palmetto Sharpshooters suffered no casualties, but they killed three Federal troopers, six horses, and captured eleven prisoners, including a first lieutenant.[8]

---

[3] J. Banks Lyle to Dora McArthur, March 28, 1863, Joseph Banks Lyle Letters.

[4] Charleston *Daily Courier*, October 29, 1863. This article gives the locations of the regiments in Jenkins' brigade along the Blackwater in March of 1863. One soldier recalled that the regiments "were camped some four miles apart." Mixson, *Reminiscences of a Private*, 40.

[5] Hagood, *Memoirs*, 105. Spear's regiment was well-regarded by Jenkins' officers, one of whom wrote:
> The enemy has one of the finest regiments of cavalry with which we have to contend, on the continent. It is composed of Pennsylvanians, splendidly mounted, thoroughly equipped and finely officered.
G. L. Strait to his uncle, William Wylie, April 6, 1863, William Wylie Papers, Duke University Library, Durham, North Carolina.

[6] Charleston *Daily Courier*, October 29, 1863.

[7] Jenkins to Longstreet, March 24, 1863, O. R., vol. 18, p. 940-941.

[8] Record of Events Cards of the Palmetto Sharpshooters, Company M, March-April 1863. Spear's own account of the skirmish said that his force consisted of 350 cavalry and four pieces of artillery. Spear's report, March 18, 1863, O. R., vol. 18, pp. 200-201. Spear's report did not include a summary of his casualties.

In his report to Longstreet, Jenkins proposed a plan to ambush and annihilate Spear's cavalry regiment.[9] Jenkins' plan was put into effect toward the end of March at a point midway between Franklin and Suffolk. The success of Jenkins' trap depended entirely on surprise, but, as Captain Lyle in the Fifth Regiment wrote:

> Unfortunately, the [Hampton] Legion (through mistake and contrary to orders) fired upon the advance guard, and the main column [of Spear's cavalry] turned and fled without giving us a fight. . . . Jenkins was outraged at the conduct of the Legion.[10]

Jenkins was indeed furious and said the ambush would have been a complete success had it not been for the excitement of an officer who caused the Hampton Legion to fire prematurely on Spear's advanced guard.[11]

In spite of these skirmishes with Union cavalry, Jenkins' men had settled into a comfortable routine along the Blackwater River by the end of March. The primary objective of the brigade was to hold off the Union troops who were based at Norfolk and Suffolk while food supplies were gathered in southeast Virginia and northeast North Carolina for delivery to Lee's army above Richmond.[12] This work involved very little fighting, and the men took full advantage of the lull. One officer in the brigade wrote:

> We are having a fine time, riding in boats on the river, and a great many amusements to pass off the time pleasantly, and nice comfortable quarters to stay in.[13]

The men of the Palmetto Sharpshooters in the village of Franklin were living in private homes which had been abandoned by the citizens.[14] Some of Jenkins' men had even planted gardens, and they all enjoyed eating fish they caught in the river.[15] General Jenkins took advantage of the relaxed atmosphere to conduct grand reviews of his men who had

---

[9]Jenkins to Longstreet, March 24, 1863, O. R., vol. 18, p. 941.

[10]J. Banks Lyle to Dora McArthur, March 30, 1863, Joseph Banks Lyle Letters. See also, G. L. Strait to his father, March 31, 1863, William Wylie Papers.

[11]Micah Jenkins to Caroline Jenkins, April 2, 1863, Micah Jenkins Papers, S.C.L.; Lewis, Camp Life, 42.

[12]Bond and Coward, eds., South Carolinians, 76.

[13]Lewis, Camp Life, 41.

[14]H. C. Conner to Ellen O'Leary, March 27, 1863, Henry Calvin Conner Papers; G. L. Strait to his parents, March 27, 1863, G. L. Strait Letters.

[15]Lewis, Camp Life, 42; J. W. McLure to Kate McLure, March 13, 1863, McLure Family Papers.

begun calling themselves the "Army of the Blackwater."[16] The only disagreeable part of this assignment along the river was that the men had to spend two days out of every four performing picket duty, but at least there was no drilling.[17]

This easy living was interrupted in early April, when General Longstreet proceeded with his plan to lay siege to the Union garrison at Suffolk, some twenty miles northeast of Jenkins' position on the Blackwater. In spite of the long odds against actually capturing Suffolk, Longstreet reasoned that such a siege would at least allow his commissary officers to freely forage in the Blackwater area, and it would also serve to block any Federal advance on Petersburg from the direction of Suffolk. To implement his plan, Longstreet brought Pickett's and Hood's divisions to the Blackwater from Petersburg to operate jointly with French's division, of which Jenkins' brigade was now a part.[18]

Jenkins' men left the Franklin area on April 10 and marched southeast for several miles until they reached the small village of South Quay. There they combined with General French's only other brigade, commanded by Joseph R. Davis, and prepared to cross the Blackwater on a pontoon bridge the next morning.[19] Joe Davis, the nephew of Jefferson Davis, commanded this brigade of four regiments but had no combat experience. He complained about having to answer to Jenkins, who commanded the division in the absence of French, but French told Davis he would have to do so because Jenkins was the more senior officer.[20]

Colonel Coward, with his own regiment and one other, as well as a section of artillery and a squadron of calvary, crossed the river at dawn on April 11 and served as an advance detachment for French's division. The remainder of the division, under Jenkins' command, crossed the pontoon bridge later that morning and marched up the South Quay Road toward Suffolk.[21]

---

[16]J. W. McLure to Kate McLure, April 3, 1863, McLure Family Papers.

[17]H. C. Conner to Ellen O'Leary, April 5, 1863, Henry Calvin Conner Papers.

[18]Foote, *Civil War*, 2:256; Jeffrey D. Wert, *General James Longstreet, The Confederacy's Most Controversial Soldier – A Biography* (New York: Simon & Shuster, 1993), 234. According to Wert, the purpose of Longstreet's Suffolk expedition was to permit the gathering of supplies in the Blackwater area. Ibid. Jenkins, however, encouraged Longstreet to try and capture the Union garrison at Suffolk and wrote:

> My last estimate of the forces at Suffolk I think [is] correct – say 12,000 to 15,000.
> If you succeed in capturing them it will be the most brilliant affair of the war and
> would be attended by glorious results to the cause.

Jenkins to Longstreet, April 6, 1863, O. R., vol. 18, p. 963.

[19]Lewis, *Camp Life*, 43; Hagood, *Memoirs*, 108; James R. Boulware Diary, April 11, 1863.

[20]Freeman, *Lee's Lieutenants*, 2:490-491 and 711 n. 135; French to Joseph R. Davis, April 17, 1863, O. R., vol. 18, p. 993.

[21]Freeman, *Lee's Lieutenants*, 2:483; Cormier, *The Siege of Suffolk*, 84. Longstreet's two other divisions left the Blackwater for Suffolk also on April 11.

By four in the afternoon, Coward's advance detachment was within two miles of Suffolk and had not yet been detected. Coward's men managed to surprise a Federal outpost near Bethlehem Church on the South Quay Road and captured several cavalrymen, but some escaped and fled into Suffolk to sound the alarm. Coward's men then came to a treetop signal station and fired on the Union signalman who scampered down the tree and fled toward his lines. When the rest of Jenkins' division came up, the Federal batteries in Suffolk opened fire. He then halted his brigades and had the men begin digging entrenchments along the South Quay Road, facing east. His two brigades were positioned in the center of Longstreet's line, and Hood's division was on Jenkins' left. Pickett's division came up the next day and went into position on the right. Longstreet's three divisions had Suffolk besieged from the landward side.[22]

When he moved his divisions to Suffolk, Longstreet kept General French, who was in charge of the Department of Southern Virginia, only minimally informed. Longstreet, French concluded, was attempting to turn his division over to Jenkins, so French left his headquarters in Petersburg and hurried to Suffolk to personally take command of his two brigades.[23]

Once it started on April 11, the siege of Suffolk continued without much activity on the part of Jenkins' men, except that they performed picket duty every five days. Jenkins' pickets were positioned in rifle pits about 800 to 1,000 yards from the Federal works outside the town, and those on picket duty were constantly exposed to enemy sharpshooters and artillery.[24]

On one occasion during April, a detachment of Jenkins' men was sent along the bank of Nansemond River near Suffolk to fire on the Federal boats out in the channel. During this assignment, Captain R. L. Crawford of the First Regiment, who had signed South Carolina's Ordinance of Secession, was decapitated by a cannon shot from a Union gunboat.[25] One officer reported that, while on picket duty, some of Jenkins' men were also fired on by a Federal rocket battery. At first they could not determine what was being fired at them because, unlike cannonfire, the rockets came toward them with no loud report from the

[22]Hagood, *Memoirs*, 108; Cormier, *The Siege of Suffolk*, 84-89.
[23]Freeman, *Lee's Lieutenants*, 2:482-483. French wrote Jenkins on April 23, "I shall assume the immediate command of the division composed of your brigade and that of General [Joseph R.] Davis." French to Jenkins, April 23, 1863, O. R., vol. 18, p. 1018.
[24]Record of Events Cards of the Palmetto Sharpshooters, Company G, March-April 1863. The men were close enough to Suffolk that they could see the church steeples in the town. James R. Boulware Diary, April 15, 1863.
[25]Hagood, *Memoirs*, 108. R. L. Crawford was captain of Company F, First South Carolina Volunteers. According to another account of his death, "a large shell from the [Federal] gunboats exploded near the Captain, and severed his head from his body." Coker, *History of Company E, Sixth S.C. Regiment*, 122.

muzzle blast. These new weapons, however, had little effect on the men outside Suffolk.[26]

By April 17, the Union commander at Suffolk had become annoyed by Jenkins' pickets, and he sent a regiment out to dislodge them.[27] The Fifth South Carolina had at least one company on picket duty when the Union troops came from behind their works and advanced in a heavy skirmish line. Four charges were repulsed before the Federals were finally driven back into their works, and Coward's Fifth Regiment had one man killed in the fight.[28] During this skirmish, as Jenkins was making observations with his field glasses, a Federal sharpshooter fired at him and missed the general by only a foot.[29]

Several days after the skirmish along the picket line, troops in Joe Davis' and E. M. Law's brigades, who were assigned to defend Fort Huger above Suffolk, allowed the fort and Stribling's battery to fall into Federal hands. The reason for the capture of the fort and the five guns became quite controversial, and General French placed the blame squarely upon some of the officers in Hood's division, including E. M. Law.[30] The loss of Stribling's battery came as a bitter disappointment to the men in Jenkins' brigade, and one officer in Coward's Fifth Regiment wrote:

> Our brigade is much downcast at its loss, as it is the battery we took, in June last, at "Frazier's [*sic*] Farm," in which affair we lost about half our members.[31]

Another officer, in the Palmetto Sharpshooters, said that the capture of Stribling's battery was a "sad disaster," since the brigade had paid for it "so dearly at Frazier's [*sic*] Farm."[32]

By the last week of April, Longstreet had concluded there was little more to be gained from continuing operations at Suffolk.[33] Then on April 30, he received information which brought the siege to an abrupt end.

---

[26]Hagood, *Memoirs*, 109.

[27]Cormier, *The Siege of Suffolk*, 134-135.

[28]Benjamin Harris, Company C, from Union, South Carolina, was killed. Micah Jenkins to Caroline Jenkins, April 18, 1863, Micah Jenkins Papers, D.U.L.

[29]Ibid.

[30]Freeman, *Lee's Lieutenants*, 2:485-490. Law, however, blamed the men of the Fifty-fifth North Carolina Regiment, and the incident resulted in a duel between an officer of that regiment and one of Law's officers. Neither officer was seriously wounded in the duel. Ibid., 489.

[31]J. Banks Lyle to Dora McArthur, April 21, 1863, Joseph Banks Lyle Letters. Several of the guns in Stribling's battery were 12-pounder Napoleons captured at Frayser's Farm when Jenkins' men overran A. M. Randol's battery on June 30, 1862.

[32]Lewis, *Camp Life*, 45.

[33]Freeman, *Lee's Lieutenants*, 2:493.

Figure 9
ORGANIZATION OF LONGSTREET'S COMMAND FOR THE SIEGE OF SUFFOLK, APRIL 1863

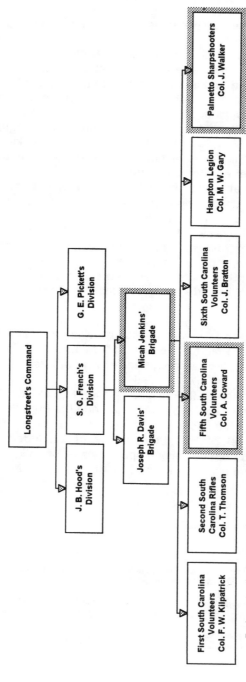

For Longstreet's siege of Suffolk, in the latter part of April and the first three days of May 1863, he used three divisions in the operation. Jenkins' brigade had been detached from Lee's Army of Northern Virginia and was assigned to a division in the Department of Virginia and North Carolina commanded by Major General Samuel G. French. The other brigade in French's division was under the command of Jefferson Davis' nephew, Joseph R. Davis. Jenkins' brigade strength had now been brought up to six full regiments by the addition of Col. Martin W. Gary's Hampton Legion after its merger with the Fourth South Carolina Battalion. The brigade numbered some 4,120 men and officers at this time.

Union troops were crossing the Rappahannock River near Fredericksburg, making it necessary that he and his men immediately return to Lee's army.[34]

On May 3, the day after the Battle of Chancellorsville began, Longstreet's three divisions abandoned the twenty-two day siege and withdrew from Suffolk. Longstreet, with Hood's and Pickett's divisions, marched toward Petersburg where they could board trains for the trip to Fredericksburg. On May 7, as Longstreet made preparations in Richmond to transport his two divisions north to rejoin Lee's army, he received word that there was no need to hurry. Lee and Stonewall Jackson had won the Battle of Chancellorsville without him, but Jackson had been mortally wounded by the mistaken fire of his own men.[35]

LIEUTENANT GENERAL THOMAS JONATHAN "STONEWALL" JACKSON

Jenkins and his brigade pulled away from Suffolk after dark on May 3, but they did not march toward Petersburg with Longstreet. As part of French's division, and still detached from Lee's army, they returned instead to their camps along the Blackwater River. One private in the Palmetto Sharpshooters wrote his wife:

> I am well after a very severe march all night. We marched from Suffolk throw [sic] mud and water up to our neas [sic] to Franklin, 21 miles in the night. I never eat a bight [sic] on the road until we got to Franklin.[36]

By May 6, Jenkins and his six regiments were safely back in their comfortable camps along the Blackwater River, and they had settled

---

[34]Cormier, *The Siege of Suffolk*, 251.

[35]Foote, *Civil War*, 2:261; Lee to Seddon, May 10, 1863, O. R. vol. 25, part 2, p. 791, officially notifying the War Department of Jackson's death. Like Longstreet, Jenkins and his men had missed the Battle of Chancellorsville.

[36]John G. Reeks to his wife, Rebecca M. Reeks, May 8, 1863, John G. Reeks Letters, Georgia Roper Jeter Collection, Powdersville, South Carolina. John G. Reeks was a private in Captain F. L. Garvin's Company I, Palmetto Sharpshooters. From Anderson District he was conscripted in July 1862. He was wounded in the fight at Dandridge, Tennessee, on January 17, 1864, and later paroled at Appomattox.

again into their relaxed routine. According to an assistant surgeon in the brigade, one of the first things the men did on their return was to change into clean clothes, which they had not been able to do for the past twenty-four days.[37] The men quickly resumed their enjoyment of the river, feasting on fresh shad, herring and chub. Searching for ways to avoid boredom, they staged a medieval tournament, complete with knights, horses, lances and jousting. The event was attended by the ladies of nearby villages, and from them a queen was selected. The winner of the tournament, the knight of the Hampton Legion, was given the honor of crowning the queen.[38]

About a week and a half after Jenkins' brigade returned to the Blackwater from Suffolk, several of his regiments were engaged in a skirmish at Carrsville, some sixteen miles away. The Palmetto Sharpshooters and the Fifth South Carolina were involved in this action which lasted for two days.[39] No general engagement developed, however, because the Federals were too well entrenched and would not be lured into the open.[40]

During the Carrsville fight, Jenkins was leading his skirmish line in a charge against the advancing Federals. A Virginia cavalry officer assigned to Jenkins' staff was with him as he led this charge. The officer, T. G. Barham, recalled later that Jenkins was hit by a rifle shot which doubled him over. When Jenkins immediately straightened up and resumed the charge, Barham saw that the ball had hit the general in his belt buckle, which had been nearly flattened.[41]

Several days after the skirmish at Carrsville, Jenkins sent most of his brigade up to the Blackwater Bridge, some fourteen miles above Franklin, where Union troops had been operating, but no fight developed. The same thing happened at Murphreesboro, North Carolina, where the Federals had raided the Confederates' supply base and taken some sixteen thousand pounds of bacon. Jenkins sent the Hampton Legion and the Sixth Regiment to engage them, but the Union troops had left the area by the time the two regiments arrived.[42]

---

[37]James R. Boulware Diary, May 4-5, 1863.

[38]Bond and Coward, eds., South Carolinians, 78; Charleston Daily Courier, October 29, 1863.

[39]Record of Events Cards of the Palmetto Sharpshooters, Companies A, D, and K, May-June 1863, and of the Fifth S.C.V., Companies F and H, May-June 1863.

[40]One of the Palmetto Sharpshooters was killed and eight were wounded. H. C. Conner to Ellen O'Leary, May 18, 1863, Henry Calvin Conner Papers. See also, James Frank Barron to "Jennie," May 20, 1863, James Frank Barron Letters.

[41]"War Record of T. G. Barham," bound volume 138 in the Collection of the Fredericksburg and Spotsylvania National Military Park, Fredericksburg, Virginia, 17. According to Barham, the ball first broke the handle of Jenkins' sword and then ricocheted into his belt buckle. Ibid. Barham felt Jenkins was a man of great character, and they became friends. In his Memoirs, Barham wrote that, in the Army of Northern Virginia, there was "no finer young officer" than Jenkins. Ibid., 10.

[42]H. C. Conner to Ellen O'Leary, May 26, 1863, Henry Calvin Conner Papers.

Before leaving Suffolk, Jenkins had invited Caroline to visit him at his headquarters in Franklin. After Jenkins returned to camp following the Suffolk expedition, she arrived at Franklin and remained with the general for several days.[43]

Meanwhile, General Lee was preparing a new offensive for his army. After his stunning victory at Chancellorsville, he had convinced Jefferson Davis that the time was right for another invasion of the North. Before he embarked on this bold move, however, Lee badly needed to strengthen his army by the return of those detached units of Longstreet's corps, including Jenkins' veteran fighters.[44]

In late May, Jenkins' brigade had been placed within the command of General D. H. Hill, who took over General French's area of operation below Petersburg when French was transferred to the West.[45] Lee wrote to Hill on May 25, ordering him to have Jenkins' brigade rejoin Pickett's division at Hanover Junction and to send Robert Ransom's brigade to Richmond.[46] Jefferson Davis, however, refused to return the detached brigades and, in effect, countermanded Lee's orders to Hill.[47] As Lee's army moved toward the Potomac to begin the invasion, he continued to write letters reiterating his need for the brigades of Ransom and Jenkins. Always diplomatic with the stubborn Davis, Lee wrote him on June 2, saying, "I regret to lose Ransom and Jenkins, both good and tried officers, with veteran troops."[48] In a letter written to Secretary of War Seddon on the same day, Lee used similar language, but he added:

> I . . . dislike to part with officers and men who have been tried in battle and seasoned to the hardships of the campaign in exchange for wholly untried troops.[49]

But the Confederate president had apparently already made up his mind. Instead of returning the detached veteran brigades to Lee, Davis sent him two untried brigades: one under North Carolinian James Johnston Pettigrew and the other under Joseph R. Davis, the president's nephew,

---

[43]Micah Jenkins to Caroline Jenkins, April 18, 1863, Micah Jenkins Papers, D.U.L.; Bond and Coward, eds., *South Carolinians*, 78.

[44]Clifford Dowdey and Louis H. Manarin, eds., *The Wartime Papers of R. E. Lee* (New York: Bramhall House, 1961), 473, 476.

[45]Compare Abstract from Field Return of the troops under French's command as of May 20, 1863, O. R., vol. 18, p. 1067, with Abstract from Monthly Return of the Units in D. H. Hill's Department, as of May 31, 1863, O. R., vol. 18, p. 1086.

[46]Lee to D. H. Hill, May 25, 1863, in Dowdey and Manarin, eds., *Wartime Papers*, 493-494; O. R., vol. 18, p. 1071.

[47]Dowdey and Manarin, eds., *Wartime Papers*, 476.

[48]Lee to Davis, June 2, 1863, O. R., vol. 18, pp. 1088-1089.

[49]Lee to Seddon, June 2, 1863, O. R., vol. 25, part 2, p. 849.

whose Mississippi troops were as green as their well-connected brigadier.[50]

Meanwhile, Jefferson Davis left Jenkins and his battle-hardened veterans to forage and patrol below Petersburg, wasting their valuable fighting experience. By mid-June, Jenkins had become completely frustrated. Sensing that he and his men were about to miss another major engagement, he wrote to General Hill:

> If [the Federal] forces from our department are withdrawn in consequence of General Lee's movements, I beg as a personal and great favor that you will . . . send my brigade, if any is sent, to Lee's army.[51]

But General Hill insisted that he needed to retain Jenkins' brigade below Richmond, because it was the "only force to guard Petersburg and this long line of railroad."[52] Jenkins was not the only man in his brigade who was frustrated by the situation; his officers also yearned for a return to Lee's army. One officer in the Sixth South Carolina wrote later:

> General Jenkins and every commissioned officer of his command, made every effort to prevent the decision which [kept us detached from Lee's Army], but General D. H. Hill . . . had more influence at the War Department than did Jenkins, even though Jenkins was backed by a petition signed by every commissioned officer of his brigade.[53]

After the middle of June, Hill ordered Jenkins' brigade to vacate its position on the Blackwater and move up closer to Richmond. Five of Jenkins' six regiments boarded trains at Franklin and were transported to Petersburg. By June 22, the entire brigade was, according to Jenkins,

---

[50]Dowdey and Manarin, eds., *Wartime Papers*, 476. President Davis wrote Lee saying that since Joe Davis was temporarily absent from the Blackwater, and because Jenkins "was . . . acquainted with the country," he would keep Jenkins there and send Joe Davis' brigade to join Lee's army. Jefferson Davis said he made his decision based on "that and minor reasons." Jefferson Davis to Lee, May 31, 1863, O. R., vol. 25, part 2, p. 842. Davis was aware, however, that his nephew was at least as well acquainted with the Blackwater area as Jenkins.

[51]Jenkins to Hill, June 20, 1863, O. R., vol. 27, part 3, p. 908.

[52]Hill to Seddon, June 21, 1863, O. R., vol. 27, part 3, p. 911.

[53]Coker, *History of Company E, Sixth S.C. Regiment*, 124. See also, J. W. McLure to Kate McLure, June 10, 1863, McLure Family Papers. Exactly why Jefferson Davis so stubbornly refused to allow Jenkins' brigade to rejoin Lee's army prior to Gettysburg is now unclear. Certainly D. H. Hill steadfastly maintained that he could not afford to give up Jenkins' brigade below Richmond. Lee, however, felt equally as strong in the matter as Hill, yet somehow Hill won the argument. One possible explanation is that Davis wanted to give his nephew, Joe Davis, an opportunity to fight under Lee, where the glory was to be had.

"camped close together in a good camp near Petersburg."[54] From this location, Jenkins' six regiments were often separately sent to different points below Petersburg to meet expected enemy advances, but engaged only in minor skirmishing.[55] A weary pattern had now developed for the men: constant marching and changing position to meet threatened Federal advances. They were beginning to complain about what one officer described as

> being kept in a state of uneasiness and suspense all the time, not knowing when we lie down at night . . . that before morning we shall be aroused from our rest and found tugging and sweating along some dusty and sandy road. . . .[56]

Jenkins wrote to General Hill, saying, "From the scattered positions of my regiments during months past, the discipline and *morale* of the brigade has suffered to some extent."[57]

On June 24, General Hill reviewed Jenkins' brigade at the New Market Race Course outside Petersburg. The men had just been issued new uniforms of gray jackets and light blue trousers, and they looked their best. Hill made a stirring speech praising Jenkins and his troops, and all six regiments passed in review to marching music played by the regimental bands of the Sixth Regiment and the Hampton Legion. After the review, Jenkins paraded his men through the streets of Petersburg where thousands of citizens cheered and welcomed them.[58]

The same day that D. H. Hill reviewed Jenkins' brigade in Petersburg, lead elements of Lee's army reached Chambersburg, Pennsylvania, while Longstreet's First Corps crossed the Potomac into Maryland.[59] In spite of all the pomp and pageantry in Petersburg, Jenkins knew that the experienced fighters in his detached brigade should be marching toward Pennsylvania with Pickett's division and Longstreet's First Corps.

Lee's Army of Northern Virginia finally met General George Meade's Union troops at Gettysburg, a quaint village and road hub in southern

---

[54]Micah Jenkins to Caroline Jenkins, June 22, 1863, Micah Jenkins Papers, S.C.L. See also, Hagood, *Memoirs*, 112. The First South Carolina went to Petersburg on foot as an escort for the brigade's wagon train and artillery. Ibid.

[55]Record of Events Cards for the Fifth S.C.V., Field and Staff, May-June 1863; Record of Events Cards for the Palmetto Sharpshooters, Companies B and D, May-June 1863.

[56]Lewis, *Camp Life*, 49. For similar comments, see J. B. Lyle to Dora McArthur, July 3, 1863, Joseph Banks Lyle Letters.

[57]Jenkins to Hill, June 20, 1863, O. R., vol. 27, part 3, p. 908 (emphasis in original).

[58]Yorkville *Enquirer*, July 8 and July 22, 1863; H. C. Conner to Ellen O'Leary, June 25, 1863, Henry Calvin Conner Papers.

[59]Foote, *Civil War*, 2:441.

Pennsylvania, just over the Maryland line. There a momentous battle, one that changed the course of the war, raged fiercely for the first three days in July. It ended with the bloody repulse of a desperate charge, led by General Pickett's division, on July 3 against the center of the Federal lines on Cemetery Ridge. Lee's army was finally defeated, a bitter disappointment for which he took full responsibility.[60]

While Pickett's division and the rest of Longstreet's corps were performing such bloody service at Gettysburg, Jenkins' and Ransom's veteran brigades were involved in an insignificant skirmish with a small body of Federal troops near the Bottom Bridge on the Chickahominy River a few miles northeast of Richmond.[61] One soldier in Jenkins' command later wrote, "We were called 'Davis' Pet Lambs,' but it was not the will of . . . Micah Jenkins. He wanted to go with General Lee and was disappointed when he was detached."[62]

When he received word of the defeat at Gettysburg, along with the reports of the severe losses suffered by Pickett's division, Jenkins stepped up his campaign to return to Lee's army. He wrote directly to the War Department in Richmond:

> I now respectfully beg to be permitted . . . to rejoin [Pickett's] division, and recruit its shattered ranks with my rested brigade. I do not want to be understood as dictating my position to the authorities, but only as representing the natural desire of a soldier to be at the post of honor and danger.[63]

Jenkins' request was formally endorsed by both General Robert Ransom and General Arnold Elzey, commander of the Department of Richmond.[64] In spite of these requests, however, Davis and the War Department still refused to return Jenkins' brigade to Lee's army, perhaps because it was now too late.[65] Several days after Jenkins' request was submitted, orders were issued placing his brigade in

---

[60]Catton, *Centennial History*, 3:189-191.

[61]H. C. Conner to Ellen O'Leary, July 4, 1863, Henry Calvin Conner Papers; Lewis, *Camp Life*, 52.

[62]Captain Peter A. McDavid, "With the Palmetto Riflemen," *Confederate Veteran*, 37 (August 1929):298.

[63]Jenkins to Adjutant General Cooper, July 14, 1863, O. R., vol. 27, part 3, p. 1004.

[64]Ransom, who had now been promoted to the command of the division which included Jenkins' brigade, warmly endorsed Jenkins' request:

> General Jenkins' brigade is in first-rate condition, and if any selection is to be
> made, it is but fair, as he is senior, and formerly belonged to Pickett's division,
> that he be sent to the Army of Northern Virginia.

O. R., vol. 27, part 3, p. 1005. General Elzey's endorsement was stated in similar terms. Ibid.

[65]Apparently Lee himself felt it was too late. There is no further correspondence from Lee to the authorities in Richmond, following Gettysburg, requesting that Jenkins' brigade be ordered to rejoin the Army of Northern Virginia.

Ransom's division, as part of General Elzey's command, to assist in the defense of Richmond.[66] Now completely frustrated, Jenkins wrote directly to General Lee, saying in part:

> Can you not send some shattered brigade to rest and recruit and get the President to allow me to join you with my brigade? I am here temporarily to guard against raiders, but do not think the place in danger.[67]

When he wrote this on July 30, Jenkins was unaware that Lee had already lost this argument with Davis in early June, prior to Gettysburg. Instead of allowing Jenkins' brigade to return to Lee's army, the Confederate president had sent his nephew's untested brigade, which was placed in Major General Harry Heth's division. After this there was little more General Lee could do, other than respond to Jenkins' letter, which he did, by writing:

> I regret exceedingly the absence of yourself and your brigade from the battle of Gettysburg. There is no telling what a gallant brigade, led by an efficient commander, might have accomplished when victory trembled in the balance. I verily believe that the result would have been different if you had been present.[68]

General Lee was no doubt quite sincere when he wrote this note to Jenkins. Had Jenkins' men, rather than Joe Davis' brigade, been at Gettysburg they would certainly have been of greater service to Lee. Joe Davis, because he lacked combat experience, managed to get two of his regiments captured on the first day of the battle.[69] On the third day, what

---

[66]Special Orders No. 170, July 18, 1863, O. R., vol. 27, part 3, p. 1024.

[67]Jenkins to Lee, July 30, 1863, O. R., vol. 51, part 2. p. 745.

[68]Lee to Jenkins, August 1863, in Thomas, *Career and Character*, 8. See also, McDavid, "With the Palmetto Riflemen," 298; Mixson, *Reminiscences of a Private*, 41. In this letter to Jenkins, General Lee may well have been correct. The assistant adjutant and inspector general of Pickett's division wrote after the war:

> With these two brigades [Corse's and Jenkins'], Pickett's Division, in its celebrated charge at Gettysburg, would have been over eight thousand instead of only forty-seven hundred strong. Whether the presence of these two large brigades, of as good and proved fighting material as any in the army, would have materially affected the result of that terrible day – the very turning point of the war – is not for me to say.

Walter Harrison, *Pickett's Men: A Fragment of War History* (New York: D. Van Nostrand, Publisher, 1870), 79.

[69]Freeman, *Lee's Lieutenants, A Study in Command*, vol. 3, *Gettysburg to Appomattox* (New York: Charles Scribner's Sons, 1944), 80.

remained of Davis' brigade also gave way during the bloody charge against Cemetery Ridge.[70]

Regardless of Jenkins' disappointment in being absent from Gettysburg, his men were fortunate to have missed the battle. Had they been there and fought with their old division, no doubt they would have suffered terrible losses, as did the three brigades under Pickett's command.[71] In fact, not all of Jenkins' men appreciated his efforts to return them to Lee's army. Several soldiers in his brigade even wrote disparaging comments about what they felt was his motivation in trying to reunite them with General Lee. One officer in the Palmetto Sharpshooters said that Jenkins would change assignments "as often as possible" in order to be promoted to major general.[72] Another Palmetto Sharpshooter said that after so many Confederate generals had been killed at Gettysburg, Jenkins wanted to return to Lee's army because "[h]e thinks his chance pretty good for promotion."[73]

During July, D. H. Hill was promoted to lieutenant general and sent to Tennessee as a corps commander under General Braxton Bragg.[74] Before leaving for Tennessee, Hill took the time to commend Jenkins and recommend him for promotion, saying, "I know of no Brigadier in this service more worthy of promotion. He has all the qualities necessary to make him a most efficient Division Commander."[75]

One week after Gettysburg, Union troops on the coast of South Carolina mounted the first of several attacks against Battery Wagner, a Confederate defensive fortification on Morris Island in Charleston Harbor. These assaults were repulsed by the Confederate defenders, and in late July the Federals resorted to trying to capture the fortification by siege.[76]

---

[70]Freeman, *Lee's Lieutenants*, 3:166 n. 130.

[71]Ibid., 195-196. In Pickett's three brigades, the staggering losses were reported as follows: Richard B. Garnett's brigade, 941; Lewis A. Armistead's brigade, 1191; James L. Kemper's brigade, 731. Return of Casualties in the Army of Northern Virginia, at the Battle of Gettysburg, July 1-3 (Addenda), O. R., vol. 27, part 2, p. 339. Pickett took 4,600 men into the charge against Cemetery Ridge. Foote, *Civil War*, 2:531.

[72]James M. McFall to his sister, Lucretia McFall Anderson, May 31, 1863, William McFall Papers, Woodruff Library, Emory University, Atlanta, Georgia. McFall was from Anderson, South Carolina, and later became adjutant for the Palmetto Sharpshooters.

[73]H. C. Conner to Ellen O'Leary, July 11, 1863, Henry Calvin Conner Papers. Of the 52 generals Lee took into Pennsylvania, 17 were casualties at Gettysburg. Two of Pickett's brigade commanders were killed (Armistead and Garnett), and the third (Kemper) was seriously wounded and captured. Foote, *Civil War*, 2:577.

[74]Freeman, *Lee's Lieutenants*, 3:230 n. 9.

[75]D. H. Hill to General Cooper, August 13, 1863, in Jenkins' Compiled Service Records. Hill's letter stated, in part:
> In leaving the Department of North Carolina I feel it due to Brigadier General Jenkins that attention should be called to his extraordinary merit. At Seven Pines his brigade was under my immediate notice and by his skillful handling rendered more service than any two engaged. His dispositions on the Blackwater and around Richmond always excited my admiration.

[76]Catton, *Centennial History*, 3:217-222; E. Milby Burton, *The Siege of Charleston: 1861-1865* (Columbia, South Carolina: University of South Carolina Press, 1970), 171.

General Jenkins, who from his service there in the spring of 1861 had some knowledge of the Charleston Harbor fortifications, drew up a plan

for his brigade to be sent to Charleston and attack the Union force threatening Battery Wagner. He wrote that he had submitted his plan to President Davis, but that he told Jenkins his brigade could not be spared from Richmond to carry it out.[77] Jenkins was apparently trying everything possible to get his brigade back into the fighting.

By mid-August, the Union siege was beginning to take a heavy toll on the Confederate defenders of Battery Wagner, and the Federal troops on Morris Island steadily pushed their lines forward and brought up their 300-pounder Parrott guns. It was only a matter of time before the fort, weakened by the siege guns, could be taken by direct assault.[78] Meanwhile, considerable concern had arisen in Charleston for the

WILLIAM PORCHER MILES

safety of the city, and some South Carolinians began requesting that the War Department send troops from Virginia to defend it. William Porcher Miles, a member of the Confederate Congress and prominent South Carolinian who had acted as an aide to General Beauregard during the Battle of Fort Sumter, made one of these requests. On August 15, he wrote to Secretary of War Seddon:

> Can you not now spare us Jenkins' brigade? His coming would be eagerly welcomed by the whole State. . . . In this, our greatest hour of trial, it seems hard that South Carolina cannot have some of her own veteran troops (who have been fighting so long outside of her borders) to strike a blow for their own homes upon their native soil.[79]

---

[77]Micah Jenkins to John Jenkins, August 12, 1863, John Jenkins Papers, S.C.L.; Jenkins to Goree, August 10, 1863, in Cutrer, ed., *Longstreet's Aide*, 112. There is nothing to indicate that Jenkins' plan was ever adopted.

[78]Burton, *The Siege of Charleston*, 174-177.

[79]Miles to Seddon, August 15, 1863, O. R., vol. 28, part 2, p. 282.

Seddon, however, refused the request and told Miles that Jenkins' brigade, along with about 2,000 other troops, constituted the only defense "of the extended line from Fredericksburg to North Carolina."[80]

By the first week in September, the Federal threat to Charleston had become much more acute, and President Davis finally decided to send some of General Lee's troops there as reinforcements. Jenkins, now doubtful that Davis and the War Department would ever return him to Lee's army, felt the chances were good that he and his brigade might at least be sent to Charleston.[81]

Lee and Davis decided to send two brigades from Longstreet's corps to Charleston, and they asked him which two he preferred to send. Longstreet selected George T. Anderson's brigade out of Hood's division and Goode Bryan's brigade out of McLaw's division, but Lee told Davis that, if he preferred, the brigades of Henry A. Wise and Jenkins could be sent to Charleston instead.[82] Davis stated a preference for sending Jenkins' brigade, instead of Anderson's, and notified Lee of this on September 10.[83] When Lee, however, telegrammed Longstreet of Davis' desire to send Jenkins, Longstreet replied that it was too late and stated:

> Anderson's brigade was so far on its way toward Charleston when your telegram got here that it could not be diverted, and fearing that if I sent Jenkins on to take his place that General Beauregard would keep both, I concluded that the wisest and safest plan would be to put Jenkins' brigade in Anderson's place in [John Bell] Hood's division. It has been so arranged.[84]

Thus Longstreet was able to circumvent Lee's orders and Davis' desire that Jenkins and his brigade be sent to Charleston to reinforce Beauregard. Longstreet certainly had strong reasons for ensuring that Jenkins and his men rejoined First Corps, rather than going back to South Carolina. Jenkins was an experienced fighter and his South Carolina troops were well-rested and battle-hardened.[85] Men of that caliber were sorely needed for Longstreet's coming campaign. Regardless of Longstreet's reasons, however, Jenkins' brigade had been

---

[80]Seddon to Miles, August 21, 1863, O. R., vol. 28, part 2, p. 298.
[81]Micah Jenkins to Caroline Jenkins, September 10, 1863, Micah Jenkins Papers, D.U.L.
[82]Lee to Davis, September 10, 1863, O. R., vol. 29, part 2, p. 708.
[83]Davis to Lee, September 10, 1863, O. R., vol. 29, part 2, p. 708.
[84]Longstreet to Lee, September 12, 1863, O. R., vol. 29, part 2, p. 713. Orders were issued on September 11 assigning Jenkins and his brigade to John B. Hood's division in Longstreet's corps. Special Orders No. 216, September 11, 1863, O., R., vol. 29, part 2, p. 713. In Hood's division, Jenkins' men replaced G. T. Anderson's brigade, which Longstreet had sent to Charleston.
[85]Freeman, *Lee's Lieutenants*, 3:223-224.

deprived, at the very last minute, of its only opportunity during the war to fight on South Carolina soil.[86]

As late as September 10, Jenkins still had hopes that he and his men might return to their native state. He wrote his wife that day from his headquarters in Petersburg:

> I think of going over to Richmond this afternoon to [find out] whether there is any determination to send us to Charleston.[87]

Jenkins had strong personal reasons for wanting to serve in South Carolina. There he could see his young wife and four sons more often. Caroline was pregnant with their fifth child, and she needed her husband's help in raising the boys. She was also having to make day-to-day decisions in running their home at a time when South Carolina's economy was beginning to crumble. In addition, Jenkins was trying to sell his three hundred acre farm outside of Yorkville, and this was made all the more difficult with him in Virginia. He desperately needed the sale proceeds to pay his mounting debts. As for his creditors, Jenkins asked Caroline, "Will they take Confederate money for debts – if so let me know at once and what you think about it."[88] Having to ask his pregnant wife to handle these problems by herself was especially frustrating for Jenkins, and he wrote her saying, "I have been very blue at not being able to run home for a few days."[89]

Jenkins finally learned on September 11 that he and his men were not going to Charleston and that they had been assigned instead to John Bell Hood's division. Although not in South Carolina, this new assignment was a bit of good news for Jenkins; it was to Hood's division that Jenkins had sought to transfer his brigade in late 1862 because of his chances for promotion there.[90] There was one problem, however, about the new assignment for Jenkins and his men: they were not being returned to the Army of Northern Virginia. Longstreet had been ordered to take Hood's and Lafayette McLaws' divisions to Tennessee to reinforce General Braxton Bragg's army near Chattanooga. Unfortunately, Jenkins

---

[86]It should be noted, however, that when G. T. Anderson's brigade was sent to Charleston, it remained there only until October 7, 1863, when it was sent to Tennessee to rejoin Longstreet's First Corps. Freeman, *Lee's Lieutenants*, 3:224 n. 40. Thus, even if Jenkins' men had gone to Charleston, instead of Anderson's, presumably their duty in South Carolina would have been only temporary.

[87]Micah Jenkins to Caroline Jenkins, September 10, 1863, Micah Jenkins Papers, D.U.L.

[88]Micah Jenkins to Caroline Jenkins, September 4, 1863, Micah Jenkins Papers, S.C.L.

[89]Micah Jenkins to Caroline Jenkins, September 10, 1863, Micah Jenkins Papers, D.U.L.

[90]After his unsuccessful attempt to have his brigade transferred from Pickett's to Hood's division in January 1863, Jenkins had renewed his efforts. In late April, he wrote Caroline:

> I am trying to get back into Hood's Division as we all prefer it to any other division, and as I will be Senior Brigadier there.

Micah Jenkins to Caroline Jenkins, April 26, 1863, Micah Jenkins Papers, S.C.L.

and his troops would have to remain detached from General Lee for another eight months. J. R. Hagood, an officer in Jenkins' brigade, wrote of "the regretful feelings which [were caused by] the severance of our connection with the grand old Army of [Northern] Virginia. . . ."[91]

---

[91]Hagood, *Memoirs*, 114. James R. Hagood was a captain in the First South Carolina Volunteers at this time. He was later promoted to colonel of that regiment in Jenkins' brigade.

Chapter 18

The Battle Of Lookout Valley

As the general reclined on the army cot in his tent on Lookout Mountain, Tennessee, his hand came up to his face and nose. The gash running from his left eye down across his nose was beginning to heal nicely, and a jagged scab had formed and hardened over the cut. With no prior warning, the explosion had come as a complete surprise as a smoking shell fragment raked across his face. He had felt nothing at impact and realized he had been wounded only when a warm, thick wetness dripped from his nose and chin. Fortunately, the shell fragment had merely cut him, and had not broken any bones or torn the eyeball. He was thinking, on this 25th day of September 1863, how lucky he was when he heard a soldier at the tent fly announce that he had a message for the general. He arose from the cot, accepted the dirty envelope and dismissed the messenger. As Jenkins removed the note from the envelope and read the first words, tears filled his eyes. His youngest son was dead.

Only eight days earlier, General Jenkins had passed through Yorkville, South Carolina, on his way to Tennessee and had spent one night with his four sons and wife who was seven months pregnant. It was a bitter-sweet reunion because he had found two-year-old Whitemarsh quite sick. The day after he left for Tennessee he wrote to Caroline saying how much he hated leaving her alone, in such a condition, to care for their baby boy.[1] With her husband in Tennessee and no possibility of his returning home, Jenkins' young, pregnant wife was having to deal alone with the death of her youngest son. Jenkins had seen hundreds of men die in battle; he had even grown accustomed to it, but the crushing news of the death of Whitemarsh devastated him.

When Jenkins had gathered himself he sat down to compose the most difficult letter he had ever written to Caroline. In it, he said:

> Here amid the rack of arms, I have learned . . . that God has taken from us our beloved child, little Wittie. It fills my heart with sadness, [and] I feel most hard for you my own darling. Let us look to Him for comfort. He has taken our baby to heaven, and to Christ I give him. . . . Ah, how hard and cruel is this war that even in such troubles I cannot be with you to comfort and console you.[2]

Jenkins and his men had been in Tennessee only five days when he wrote this letter.

By the end of August 1863, the military situation in Tennessee had taken an ominous turn against the Confederacy. General W. S. Rosecrans' Federal army had crossed the Tennessee River and on September 9 occupied Chattanooga.[3] Making matters worse, Union troops had occupied Knoxville six days earlier. Unless their eastward advances could be halted, they might be able to cut the Confederacy in half, the ultimate threat to its existence.[4] The only Confederate force in position to stop Rosecrans was the Army of Tennessee under General Braxton Bragg. It had become clear that Bragg's army would soon have to mount an offensive against Rosecrans' force in the area of Chattanooga. It was determined that Bragg must attack once Rosecrans' army pushed east of the mountains around Chattanooga, and Jefferson Davis decided that Bragg's army should be heavily reinforced for the offensive.[5] As part of these reinforcements, the War Department detached Longstreet, along with the First Corps divisions of Lafayette McLaws and J. B. Hood, from Lee's Army of Northern Virginia and ordered them to Bragg in Tennessee.[6] Having just been assigned to

---

[1]Micah Jenkins to Caroline Jenkins, September 18, 1863, Micah Jenkins Papers, S.C.L. Jenkins wrote, "I cannot tell you what hard feelings I had after parting with you, to feel obliged to leave you all sick." Ibid.
[2]Ibid., September 25, 1863.
[3]Foote, *Civil War*, 2:685.
[4]Catton, *Centennial History*, 3:238-239.
[5]Foote, *Civil War*, 2:690.
[6]Freeman, *Lee's Lieutenants*, 2:223, 227.

Hood's division in Longstreet's First Corps, Jenkins and his men began preparing for the move toward Chattanooga.

Longstreet's decision not to send Jenkins' brigade to Charleston in early September had been made in the context of the expedition to Tennessee. Jenkins' veteran soldiers were needed for this operation, and the sending of G. T. Anderson's brigade to Charleston had created an opportunity for Longstreet; he simply removed Anderson's brigade from Hood's division and replaced it with Jenkins'. Since George Pickett's division was still being rebuilt after its losses at Gettysburg, it was not sent with Longstreet to Tennessee, and Jenkins' men would never again serve in that division.[7]

Longstreet's transportation plans for the 12,000 troops in his two divisions quickly ran into a major problem and had to be radically altered. Before September it had appeared that trains could transport Longstreet's men directly from Richmond to Chattanooga by way of Knoxville, a trip expected to take about four days. Ambrose Burnside's Union troops, however, occupied Knoxville on September 2, forcing Longstreet to take a long, circuitous detour through the Carolinas and Georgia by way of Atlanta. This trip had to be made over rail lines of varying track gauges, requiring the troops to change trains several times, and it would take twice as long as the direct route through Knoxville. In spite of the massive transportation problem, Longstreet's men began boarding trains in Virginia on September 8 for the long trip to Tennessee.[8]

When he received the news that his brigade had been assigned to Hood's division and would be traveling with Longstreet to Chattanooga, Jenkins and his men were still camped outside Petersburg where they had spent most of the summer. For four days the crowded troop trains rumbled past them through Petersburg, carrying McLaws' and Hood's divisions toward the Carolinas. Before they left Petersburg, Jenkins' men were called out to witness the execution of two members of their brigade. The two men were privates in the Second South Carolina Rifles and had been sentenced to death by firing squad for having deserted.[9] Jenkins' command, the last of Longstreet's infantry brigades to depart, finally left Petersburg throughout the day on September 14.[10] Five days before their departure, a New York newspaper printed a story outlining the details of

---

[7]Foote, *Civil War*, 2:695.

[8]Freeman, *Lee's Lieutenants*, 3:223, 225.

[9]Linda Sparks Starr, *W. R. Rankin: Manassas to Appomattox* (Norman, Oklahoma: privately printed, 1990), 43. W. R. Rankin, a sergeant (and later lieutenant) in the Palmetto Sharpshooters, identified the two soldiers only as Clark and Taylor and said that they were shot in front of the brigade on September 11, 1863. Ibid. W. H. Clark was a private in Company C, and James Taylor was a private in Company H of the Second South Carolina Rifles.

[10]Hagood, *Memoirs*, 114; Mixson, *Reminiscences of a Private*, 41.

Longstreet's detachment from Lee's army, even including a discussion of whether Jenkins' brigade would be part of the Tennessee expedition.[11]

For seven days Jenkins and his men traveled the rails toward Bragg's army just south of Chattanooga. The trains were made up of all types of rolling stock, including passenger, baggage, mail, box, coal and platform cars. The weather was warm, and the soldiers stripped the side boards off the cars to get fresh air and to see the countryside.[12] The tops of the cars were crowded with men, and some lost their lives when they were knocked off by tree branches extending out over the tracks.[13]

The first major stop on the trip was in Raleigh, North Carolina, where the Raleigh *Standard* had developed a reputation for its harsh criticism of Jefferson Davis. Before Jenkins' men reached Raleigh, men from another brigade in Longstreet's corps had detrained there and had wrecked the office of the *Standard*.[14] As a result, according to one officer in the Fifth Regiment,

> President Davis would not allow our Brigade to be halted within four miles of Raleigh – [I] believe that a riot would have occurred had we stopped in the city.[15]

After passing through Charlotte, the troop trains carrying Jenkins' men made their first South Carolina stop at the village of Chester. Since this town was close to Yorkville, Union, and Spartanburg, many friends and relatives of the men in the Fifth Regiment and the Palmetto Sharpshooters had traveled to Chester to greet the trains. Jenkins' soldiers were under strict orders not to remain in Chester, but to be back on their trains when they pulled out. In fact, according to a soldier in the Palmetto Sharpshooters, they were told that if they were left in Chester, and they missed fighting with their regiment in Tennessee, they would be "court martialed and shot for desertion."[16] In spite of this dire warning, some stayed in South Carolina, catching up with the brigade only after it reached Tennessee.[17] Most of Jenkins' men had not been home for well over a year, and any time with family, however brief, was to be treasured. When the order came to reboard, they sadly climbed back onto the cars, and the trains slowly pulled away. Mothers, daughters, sisters and wives

[11]Freeman, *Lee's Lieutenants*, 3:225.
[12]Ibid., 3:227.
[13]Bond and Coward, eds., *South Carolinians*, 84.
[14]Foote, *Civil War*, 2:650.
[15]J. Banks Lyle to Dora McArthur, September 19, 1863, Joseph Banks Lyle Letters.
[16]H. C. Conner to Ellen O'Leary, September 26, 1863, Henry Calvin Conner Papers.
[17]Ibid. A captain in the Fifth Regiment wrote:
> A good many deserted us by going to their homes – think our Regiment behaved worse in this respect, than any other of the Brigade – five of my Company left.
J. Banks Lyle to Dora McArthur, September 19, 1863, Joseph Banks Lyle Letters.

broke down in tears as their men left them again. Of this emotional scene, Captain Lyle in the Fifth Regiment poignantly wrote of how sad it was to see mothers meet their sons after being separated for so long, only to be forced "to part again in the same moment."[18]

Colonel Coward, who was on furlough in South Carolina at the time his command left Petersburg for Tennessee, was ordered by Jenkins to rejoin the Fifth Regiment as it passed through Chester. There Coward and Jenkins met briefly and discussed the ramifications of his brigade having been assigned to Hood's division. Coward recalled Jenkins saying he regretted that the brigade had not been sent to South Carolina, instead of to Tennessee with Hood's division, because of a potential problem with Brigadier General Evander M. Law. Law had assumed temporary command of that division at Gettysburg after Hood was wounded, but Hood had recovered and resumed his command in mid-September. Jenkins mentioned to Coward that there could be a problem with Law if, for any reason, Hood was not able to continue in command of the division and a successor had to be named. Even though Law had acted as the division commander during Hood's absence, Jenkins was senior in grade to Law by two and a half months, and under normal military practice would take command of the division, which Law might resent. Coward, however, expressed his confidence to Jenkins that there would be no immediate problem since Hood was back in command, and it did not seem likely that he would be wounded again.[19]

It was after this conversation with Coward in Chester that Jenkins had made his side trip to Yorkville, where he found his pregnant wife caring for their extremely sick two-year old son, Whitemarsh. In spite of her need for him at home, however, Jenkins had no choice but to quickly rejoin his men. He left Yorkville on September 17 to meet his brigade in Orangeburg, where the local citizens presented him with a laurel wreath.[20] In the meantime, the brigade's trains rumbled through South Carolina and headed toward Augusta, Georgia, with local citizens turning out along the route to cheer and wave. After passing through Orangeburg, one or two of the trains stopped at the village of Bamberg after midnight. There friends and relatives of the men in the brigade had

---

[18]J. Banks Lyle to Dora McArthur, September 19, 1863, Joseph Banks Lyle Letters.

[19]Bond and Coward, eds., *South Carolinians*, 83. Can Jenkins' statements to Coward be reconciled with the fact that, two months prior to Gettysburg, Jenkins wrote that he was trying to get back into Hood's Division? Micah Jenkins to Caroline Jenkins, April 26, 1863, Micah Jenkins Papers, S.C.L. When Hood was wounded at Gettysburg, Law had led the division in the remainder of that battle and for two months afterwards. Apparently, Jenkins believed that these developments made it more likely that Law would claim the right to command the division in the event Hood was wounded again. This could explain why Jenkins would rather have taken his brigade to South Carolina if given the choice. Another explanation could be that Jenkins' earlier attempts to get into Hood's division were premised on the assumption that it would remain a part of Lee's army in Virginia. Now that the division was detached from General Lee, assignment to it was arguably less desirable for Jenkins and his men.

[20]Micah Jenkins to Caroline Jenkins, September 18, 1863, Micah Jenkins Papers, S.C.L.

been waiting for hours for the trains to arrive. They had lit bonfires and had spread picnic tables with fried chicken, ham, biscuits and boiled eggs. As was the case with the stop in Chester, some of the men saw their families for the first time since 1861, and the trains were held in Bamberg for an hour while the soldiers visited their loved ones and ate their fill. A private in Colonel Kilpatrick's First South Carolina wrote later:

> You may talk of courage and a sense of duty, but when a man pulls up at a station at 1 o'clock at night, finds there his wife and children whom he has not seen for two years, and after about one hour to see them, to be caressed by them . . . then to be hauled off on a freight car . . . *that is manhood*.[21]

After reboarding the trains, the men went on to Augusta, Georgia, where there was a long delay; the entire brigade, with its equipment, had to be unloaded and transferred to a different railroad line for the trip to Atlanta.[22]

The brigade's trains finally reached Atlanta on September 20, where the men changed rail lines again. That afternoon they left on the Western and Atlantic Railroad for Ringgold, Georgia, located southeast of Chattanooga some five miles below the Georgia-Tennessee line.[23] As they were leaving Atlanta, the Battle of Chickamauga was raging a few miles south of Chattanooga, in its second and final day. By sundown, Bragg's army, with the help of Longstreet's corps, had defeated Rosecrans' troops and driven them back into Chattanooga. Only a courageous stand by General George H. Thomas had saved the Union army from being utterly routed at Chickamauga.

Due to the repeated delays during the train trip from Virginia, the main part of Longstreet's corps had arrived on the battlefield too late to participate in the first day of the fighting. Most of his brigades, however, did arrive in time for the second day of the battle on September 20. On this second day at Chickamauga, General Hood was wounded in the thigh, causing his leg to be amputated on the field.[24]

Jenkins and his men completely missed the battle; they were detraining at Ringgold late on the afternoon of September 20 as the battle was winding down some ten miles to the north. As soon as they arrived, the officers were ordered to rush the men to the battlefield in spite of the fact that their teams and baggage had not come with them.

---

[21]Mixson, *Reminiscences of a Private*, 43 (emphasis in original).
[22]Ibid.
[23]Report of Jenkins' movement toward Ringgold, Georgia, September 20, 1863, O. R., vol. 30, part 3, p. 675.
[24]Foote, *Civil War*, 2:741.

Colonel Coward's Fifth Regiment was able to make it up to Chickamauga Creek by sunset, but by then Rosecrans' army had already retreated.[25]

The fact that his brigade had not reached the field until the battle had ended greatly disappointed General Jenkins and some of his men who deplored the lost opportunity to fight. As one proud officer in the brigade later wrote:

> At this period I question if there was a finer body of troops in the service than [our] brigade. Inured by three years of active war to all the vicissitudes of a military life, well [uniformed], well armed, and superbly commanded, it was . . . only necessary to meet the enemy in order to vanquish him.[26]

After the battle at Chickamauga ended on the night of September 20, and the Union troops had withdrawn into Chattanooga, Longstreet urged General Bragg to quickly follow up on the victory and destroy Rosecrans' army, but Bragg refused to budge. Longstreet and most of Bragg's generals felt that by this lack of aggressiveness he had given up all that had been gained at Chickamauga.[27] One of the officers in Jenkins' brigade put it bluntly when he stated that Rosecrans' army had been "saved by [Bragg] from complete dispersion or capture."[28]

LIEUTENANT GENERAL
JOHN BELL HOOD

Meanwhile, the amputation of Hood's leg on the second day of the battle presented exactly the problem Jenkins and Coward had discussed the week before in Chester, South Carolina. A new commander was now needed for Hood's division, and the choice was between the division's two most senior brigadiers,

---

[25]Bond and Coward, eds., *South Carolinians*, 84. Jenkins' brigade was the only one in Longstreet's command to miss the battle, because it was the last one to leave Virginia. That it took nearly seven days for Jenkins' trains to get from Petersburg to Ringgold, Georgia, indicates the steadily deteriorating condition of the rail lines in the Confederacy.

[26]Hagood, *Memoirs*, 115.

[27]Freeman, *Lee's Lieutenants*, 3:233; Foote, *Civil War*, 2:759-762.

[28]Coker, *History of Company E, Sixth S.C. Regiment*, 126.

Jenkins and Law. The day after Hood was wounded, Longstreet put
Jenkins in command of Hood's division. Jenkins again spoke to Colonel
Coward about the anticipated problem with Law, and Coward observed
later that Jenkins was clearly very concerned about the matter.[29]

As Jenkins had expected, Law desperately wanted the command
and quickly took steps to see that he got it. Eleven days after Hood's
amputation, politicians from Alabama, Law's adopted state, were writing
to Jefferson Davis, pressuring him to grant Law's "application for
promotion."[30]

Two days following the Battle of Chickamauga, General Bragg
ordered his divisions to occupy Missionary Ridge and Lookout Mountain,
with the objective of starving the Union army out of Chattanooga; he had
decided to mount a siege. By controlling these heights to the southwest
of the city, Bragg's artillery could reach rail and wagon roads which would
otherwise be used to supply the besieged Federal troops. Instead of
shipping supplies directly into Chattanooga from its base in Bridgeport,
Alabama, the Union army was now forced to use a circuitous sixty-mile
supply route north of the Tennessee River, making its supply trains
vulnerable to attack and subject to bad weather.[31]

Bragg's Army of Tennessee took up positions along an arc facing
Chattanooga from the south, with the left flank anchored on Lookout
Mountain. Hood's division, now under Jenkins' command, was posted
there, and Jenkins' brigade, under the command of Colonel John
Bratton, was on the left of the division.[32] On Lookout Mountain the men
in the Palmetto Sharpshooters were stationed to the left of the brigade,
placing them on the extreme left of Bragg's army.[33]

As Jenkins' brigade prepared to move onto Lookout Mountain on
September 22, Jenkins rode to meet with General Law to discuss the
positioning of the brigades in the division. It was during this meeting with
Law that the shell had exploded near them, a fragment wounding Jenkins
in the face.[34] Three days later Jenkins had received the stunning news
of his son's death.

[29]Bond and Coward, eds., *South Carolinians*, 85.
[30]David Clopton, W. P. Chilton and J. Gill Shorter to Davis, October 2, 1863, in National Archives,
Compiled Service Records of Confederate General and Staff Officers and Non-Regimental Enlisted Men,
R. G. 109, series M331, Records for Brigadier General E. M. Law (referred to hereafter as "Law's
Compiled Service Records"). Apparently, Law was not bashful about directly requesting a promotion. In
April of 1862 he had also "applied for" appointment to brigadier general. E. M. Law to T. H. Watts, April
23, 1862, in Law's Compiled Service Records.
[31]Foote, *Civil War*, 2:761.
[32]Hagood, *Memoirs*, 115.
[33]J. W. McLure to Kate McLure, October 5, 1863, McLure Family Papers.
[34]Bond and Coward, eds., *South Carolinians*, 85. After being wounded, Jenkins told Colonel Coward
about the incident, and said Law was also hit and wounded by a shell fragment, but only slightly. See
also, Charleston *Daily Courier*, October 22, 1863.

By the end of the first week in October, it had become clear that Law and some of his officers resented reporting to Jenkins as division commander. One man in the Palmetto Sharpshooters wrote that because Law had led the division after Hood had been wounded both at Gettysburg and at Chickamauga, many of the officers who had served with Law felt he should be the commander instead of Jenkins, and some of them were circulating petitions to this effect.[35]

Apparently, the possibility of a problem with Law had been fully discussed by Generals Hood and Jenkins prior to Jenkins joining the division, because on October 5, Hood wrote him:

> [I] explained explicitly to General Law your position and the circumstances by which you joined the Division. . . . [W]hen my condition will permit . . . [I] will talk to Generals Benning and Robertson of this business.[36]

The issue of who was to be promoted to major general as Hood's replacement soon became overshadowed by a larger command problem. Before the end of September, Longstreet wrote the secretary of war, urging the removal of General Bragg. Several days later D. H. Hill, Leonidas Polk, and ten other generals in Bragg's army met to discuss the matter. As a result, a petition signed by the generals was sent to President Davis requesting Bragg's removal.[37]

To investigate the mounting sentiment against Bragg by his senior officers, Jefferson Davis left Richmond and made a personal visit to Bragg's headquarters near Chattanooga. On October 9, Davis held a meeting there with Bragg's generals to discuss the matter in Bragg's presence, a curious procedure that Longstreet did not favor. After further conferences, and in spite of what he had heard, Davis decided to retain Bragg in command and relieved D. H. Hill instead.[38]

The following day Davis and Longstreet met privately for several hours, and the discussion became heated over the issue of replacing Bragg. Toward the end of this meeting, the subject was changed to Hood's condition, and Longstreet urged that Jenkins be promoted to replace Hood as division commander. Jenkins had been transferred into

---

[35]J. W. McLure to Kate McLure, October 5, 1863 (portion of letter missing), McLure Family Papers.

[36]Jno. T. Darby (writing for the injured Hood) to Jenkins, October 5, 1863, John Jenkins Papers, S.C.D.A.H. Generals Henry L. Benning and Jerome B. Robertson were brigade commanders in Hood's division.

[37]Freeman, *Lee's Lieutenants*, 3:234; Wert, *General James Longstreet*, 326-327.

[38]Freeman, *Lee's Lieutenants*, 3:236.

the division at Hood's request, and in Longstreet's words, the young South Carolina brigadier

> was a bright, gallant, and efficient officer of more than two years' experience in active warfare, loved by his troops, and all acquaintances as well.[39]

Davis, however, would not agree to promote Jenkins and brought up Law's past service with the division. In spite of his strong feelings that Jenkins, as the senior brigadier, should be given the command,[40] Longstreet finally agreed to promote Law if this was Davis' wish. Longstreet stated that he conceded the matter because he felt that Jenkins was so dedicated to the service he would agree to whatever course seemed to be in its best interests.[41] In spite of this concession, Davis did not state his decision on the matter and, according to Longstreet, "failed to assign a commander."[42] Longstreet, therefore, considered the matter unresolved, and three days later he wrote a formal letter to the War Department recommending Jenkins for promotion to major general in command of Hood's division. His letter outlined Jenkins' distinguished service record, noted that he was the senior brigadier, and said, "His promotion at once will produce greater harmony in the Division."[43] General Hood became involved the next day and wrote a letter on the matter to Robert E. Lee's son, Brigadier General G. W. Custis Lee. In this letter, Hood took the easy approach, recommending both Jenkins and Law for promotion. He suggested that Law be made the commander of his (Hood's) division, and that a new division be formed for Jenkins to command. In his letter Hood recognized that it

---

[39]Longstreet, *From Manassas to Appomattox*, 467. Longstreet stated that Jenkins had been transferred into the division "upon the application of General Hood." Ibid.

[40]Longstreet was clearly bothered by Davis' pressure for the promotion of Law over Jenkins, and recalled:

> I thought it unwise and not military to choose a junior [Law] for assignment to command over his senior officers, and prejudicial to the *esprit de corps* and *morale* of any army, except under most eminent services, and in this instance where service, high military character, and equipment were on the side of the senior [Jenkins] it was more objectionable, but [I] consented that it would be better to have General Law promoted, and the feeling of rivalry put at rest. . . .

Longstreet, *From Manassas to Appomattox*, 467-468 (emphasis in original).

[41]Ibid., 468.

[42]Ibid.

[43]Longstreet to W. W. Mackall, October 13, 1863, in Jenkins' Compiled Service Records. An endorsement on this letter, apparently containing Jefferson Davis' signature and comments as to the recommendation, has been removed from the original.

BRIGADIER GENERAL EVANDER M. LAW, WHO RESENTED LONGSTREET'S NAMING MICAH JENKINS AS THE ACTING COMMANDER OF HOOD'S DIVISION. LONGSTREET BROUGHT CHARGES AGAINST LAW IN LATE 1863, BUT THE CONFEDERATE WAR DEPARTMENT REFUSED TO ENTERTAIN THOSE CHARGES. AFTER BEING WOUNDED AT COLD HARBOR IN JUNE 1864, LAW TRANSFERRED TO THE CAVALRY AND SURVIVED THE WAR.

would not be wise, while Law and Jenkins were in the same division, "to promote General Law, a 'junior Brigadier,' over [Jenkins]."[44]

It appears that Longstreet preferred Jenkins over Law, not only because of seniority, but also on the comparative merits of the two officers. On October 18, Longstreet wrote to General McLaws and explained why he had so "strongly recommended" that Jenkins be promoted to the command of Hood's division. In this letter, Longstreet said, "Of all the Brigadiers in the Army, General Jenkins is my first choice as a most active and zealous officer. Next to him I esteem General Kershaw."[45]

When both Hood's and Longstreet's recommendations were disregarded by the authorities in Richmond, Longstreet left Jenkins in command of the division without his being promoted. Such an arrangement was totally unacceptable to Law, who bitterly resented taking any orders from Jenkins, and who would later reveal a definite talent for crafty political maneuvering within the Confederate military system.[46]

While Longstreet was trying to have Jenkins promoted to the command of Hood's division, the men in Jenkins' brigade occupied their positions on Lookout Mountain throughout the entire month of October. They took turns performing picket duty at the foot of the mountain and were at times close enough to the Union soldiers to hear them coughing and digging rifle pits.[47] Jenkins' men were frequently subjected to enemy shelling, which they endured with good spirits unless their dinner pot was knocked over and a day's meal ruined. During one artillery barrage, a soldier in the Fifth Regiment heard a shell coming in and instead of dodging, he playfully flipped onto his back with his feet in the air. The shell exploded above him and a fragment slammed into the sole of his shoe. The incident was turned into a camp joke, but all knew he had been lucky; his horseplay could easily have cost him his life.[48]

[44]Hood to G. W. C. Lee, October 14, 1863, in Jenkins' Compiled Service Records. Jenkins' son, Robert, recalled discussing the problem with Asbury Coward years after the war. According to Coward, in 1863 Jenkins had asked Hood, before going into his division, how Law would react if something happened to Hood and command of the division devolved upon Jenkins. Hood told Jenkins that Law fully understood that, as senior brigadier, Jenkins would take over command. According to Coward, however, Law claimed that Hood told him the opposite – that the command would go to Law and that Jenkins understood this. Thus, when Longstreet put Jenkins in command, Law felt betrayed. Robert F. Jenkins, "General Micah Jenkins," Charleston News and Courier, November 19, 1934, p. 5.

[45]Longstreet to McLaws, October 18, 1863, Lafayette McLaws Papers, Southern Historical Collection, University of North Carolina, Chapel Hill, North Carolina. See also, Longstreet, From Manassas to Appomattox, 467-468.

[46]Clifford Dowdey, Lee's Last Campaign: The Story of Lee and His Men Against Grant – 1864 (Boston: Little, Brown & Co., 1960), 139.

[47]Journal of Lieutenant James P. Lockwood, Company K, Palmetto Sharpshooters, October 13 and 19, 1863, South Caroliniana Library, University of South Carolina, Columbia, South Carolina.

[48]Charleston Daily Courier, October 20 and 22, 1863.

The only fighting which Jenkins' brigade saw before the last week in October occurred early in the month when the First and Fifth Regiments, under Colonel Coward's command, were sent on a reconnaissance mission across Chattanooga Creek, close to the Federal lines. The men had to cross the creek over a single log, which resulted in a dangerous bottleneck and delay. When they finally got across, one company in the First and two in the Fifth were sent forward as skirmishers, but they quickly ran head on into the Federal lines only a short distance away. The Union troops opened fire and Coward's skirmishers retreated, but several were shot, and another company had to be sent in to remove the wounded. They were finally rescued, but only with great difficulty.[49]

By the middle of October constant rains had made the lives of Jenkins' soldiers' on Lookout Mountain perfectly miserable. They had no shelters and stayed wet and cold in ankle-deep mud. On the nights of October 14 and 15 it rained in torrents, completely flooding the low-lying areas along Chattanooga Creek. The rising water cut off Hood's division, including the men in Jenkins' brigade, from their rations which were supplied from the other side of the creek. The lack of food finally became acute after three days, and some of the men were so hungry they began eating roasted acorns;[50] they had already cut down all the chestnut trees on the mountain to boil and eat the nuts.[51] A private in the First Regiment wrote that some of his fellow soldiers became so hungry they tore down barns to find rats which they boiled and made into a stew.[52]

The soldiers were not the only ones on Lookout Mountain who suffered during that rainy October. A little girl, completely emaciated, came into camp one day begging for food. She told Jenkins' men that she had been hiding for several days, beside the body of her dead mother, in a cave between the opposing armies' picket lines.[53]

After the middle of October the weather finally began to clear, and Jenkins' troops were able to float a timber and plank raft across the creek and return with a load of rations. Some of the men, however, had refused to wait for the rations and had already stolen and eaten livestock belonging to farmers in the area.[54]

---

[49]Hagood, *Memoirs*, 118-119; Lewis, *Camp Life*, 58.

[50]Lewis, *Camp Life*, 60; Charleston *Daily Courier*, October 22, 1863; H. C. Conner to Ellen O'Leary, October 17, 1863, Henry Calvin Conner Papers.

[51]Lewis, *Camp Life*, 57.

[52]Mixson, *Reminiscences of a Private*, 44.

[53]John Bratton to his wife, Bettie, October 23, 1863, Confederate War Letters of General John Bratton, 1861-1865, Private Papers, S.C.D.A.H., Columbia, South Carolina.

[54]Lewis, *Camp Life*, 61-62.

By this time, some of the men in Jenkins' brigade had become highly dissatisfied with General Bragg, and one officer in the Fifth Regiment wrote:

> Everything in Lee's army moves and works like fine machinery newly oiled; while here, everything seems to be ajar and out of joint.[55]

One night in late October, a regimental band on Lookout Mountain played "Carry Me Back to Old Virginia," and the men in Longstreet's corps "raised a yell that was long and loud."[56]

During October, General Ulysses S. Grant went to Chattanooga and relieved Rosecrans, replacing him with General George Thomas. The long, circuitous, sixty-mile supply route from Bridgeport, Alabama, was causing great difficulty for the Union army bottled up in Chattanooga, and Grant clearly saw the need to open up a shorter supply line. He decided to first have Thomas send a Federal force down the river by boat from Chattanooga to capture Brown's Ferry, the important river crossing west of Chattanooga for the road to Bridgeport. Then General Joe Hooker and three Federal divisions would march up from Bridgeport, through Lookout Valley west of Lookout Mountain, and attempt to open up the road all the way from Bridgeport to Brown's Ferry. If successful, this maneuver would solve the Federal supply problem in Chattanooga by creating what was called the "Cracker Line," along which rations and ammunition could be moved quickly and unmolested from Bridgeport through Lookout Valley and across the river at Brown's Ferry into the besieged city.[57]

General Law's troops had been assigned the responsibility of guarding Brown's Ferry and keeping it from falling into Federal hands. As acting division commander, Jenkins pointed out to Law the importance of the Brown's Ferry crossing, but as Colonel Coward wrote later, "I gathered that Law had perhaps resented Jenkins' observation."[58]

In spite of the danger of a Federal attempt to capture Brown's Ferry, Law left that location on October 25 to visit General Hood who was convalescing about thirty miles below Chattanooga. No doubt the purpose of Law's visit was to solicit Hood's help in securing promotion to the command of his division. Law did not return until the night of October 26.[59]

[55]J. Banks Lyle to Dora McArthur, October 14, 1863, Joseph Banks Lyle Letters.
[56]John Bratton to Bettie Bratton, October 23, 1863, Bratton Letters.
[57]Foote, *Civil War*, 2:806-808.
[58]Bond and Coward, eds., *South Carolinians*, 86.
[59]Wert, *General James Longstreet*, 333.

Before daylight the next morning, in a flotilla of small boats, a Federal force silently drifted down the river from Chattanooga, made an amphibious landing and captured the Brown's Ferry crossing. The pickets of Law's regiments were completely surprised, and not being able to hold out against the Union troops, gave up the vital river crossing. Law placed the blame for the loss directly on Jenkins' shoulders, claiming that Jenkins had earlier ordered three of Law's five regiments, which had been posted at Brown's Ferry, to positions on the east side of Lookout Mountain.[60] It has since been suggested, however, that it was Longstreet, not Jenkins, who ordered most of Law's regiments away from Brown's Ferry before the attack.[61] Regardless of who was at fault, Jenkins, Law or Longstreet, the loss of the river crossing was to prove costly for the Confederates. As soon as they had taken Brown's Ferry, Union engineers laid a pontoon bridge across the river and began sending their soldiers across it to establish a firm grip on the bridgehead on the west bank.[62] The next part of the plan was for the three Federal divisions under Hooker to move northeast from Bridgeport through Lookout Valley and link up with the new Union bridgehead at Brown's Ferry.

Until Thomas' troops succeeded in capturing Brown's Ferry, General Bragg had refused to believe that the Federals would take such bold steps to improve their position at Chattanooga. However, once he realized that Brown's Ferry would now be used to shorten and simplify the Union army's supply line, Bragg decided to attempt to retake that strategic river crossing.[63]

On October 28, the day after Brown's Ferry had been captured by the Federals, Longstreet and Bragg conferred on the western side of Lookout Mountain. Gazing down into Lookout Valley, they observed a large Union column moving northeast towards Brown's Ferry from the direction of Bridgeport. This was Hooker's force of three Federal divisions moving to link up with the Union troops holding the bridgehead

---

[60]"Lookout Valley," (undated) Memorandum by General E. M. Law, Box 4, Ezra Ayers Carman Collection, Rare Books and Manuscripts Division, New York Public Library. In this memorandum, Law accused Jenkins of ordering the withdrawal of the three regiments without "rhyme or reason" saying they were not needed where they were ordered. In Law's official report, he states that the three regiments were ordered withdrawn on October 25 "by orders from division headquarters." O. R., vol. 31, part 1, p. 224. If Jenkins ever responded to Law's charges, or explained whether he ordered the regiments withdrawn and for what reason, it is not apparent in the official records or in Jenkins' correspondence.

[61]Wiley Sword, *Mountains Touched with Fire: Chattanooga Besieged,* 1863 (New York: St. Martin's Press, 1995), 119, 124. With regard to the loss of Brown's Ferry, Colonel Coward cryptically stated:

How [the Federals] got possession of this territory, so vitally important to us, I will not discuss. It belongs to the irrevocable past.

Bond and Coward, eds., *South Carolinians,* 88.

[62]Foote, *Civil War,* 2:809.

[63]Freeman, *Lee's Lieutenants,* 3:282.

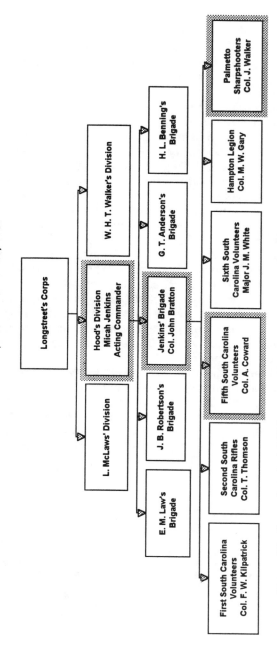

Figure 10
ORGANIZATION OF LONGSTREET'S CORPS (INFANTRY) IN BRAXTON BRAGG'S
ARMY OF TENNESSEE FOR THE NIGHT FIGHT IN LOOKOUT VALLEY
TENNESSEE, OCTOBER 28-29, 1863

Because of Hood's wounds received at Chickamauga, and because Jenkins was the senior brigadier in Hood's division, Longstreet put Jenkins in command of the division, which included five brigades. Jenkins' brigade was under the command of its senior regimental commander, Colonel John Bratton. Of the divisions in Longstreet's corps, only Hood's was engaged during the night fight at Wauhatchie Junction. Of the five brigades in Hood's division, only Jenkins' brigade was sent to attack General John Geary's rear guard at Wauhatchie Junction. The other brigades were used in support of the attack.

on the west bank of the river at Brown's Ferry.[64] Longstreet estimated that Hooker's column numbered about 5,000 men, but soon his rear guard came into view, with another 1,500 troops, artillery, and a large wagon train. This rear guard was part of General John W. Geary's Federal division. It broke off from the main column and settled down for the night only a few hundred yards north of Wauhatchie Junction, where the Trenton Railroad joined the Nashville and Chattanooga line in Lookout Valley. Geary's troops and massive wagon train were now bivouacked about three miles south of Hooker's main force, which had moved on up to Brown's Ferry.[65] Since Hooker's men had combined with their Union comrades holding Brown's Ferry, Bragg's idea of recapturing the river crossing was no longer practical.[66] Longstreet, however, believed he could still surprise and capture Hooker's isolated rear guard and wagon train at Wauhatchie Junction, and reported that he "speedily arranged the plan . . . and ordered the movements."[67] His initial plan called for a rare night attack against Geary's division and wagon train at Wauhatchie Junction, by both Hood's and McLaws' divisions. Through some unfortunate error, McLaws' division did not participate in the operation, and Bragg and Longstreet blamed each other for this critical mistake.[68] In spite of this, Longstreet allowed the night attack to proceed, using only Hood's division under Jenkins' command.[69]

Longstreet's plan called for close cooperation between Generals Law and Jenkins. Because of his knowledge of the terrain around Brown's Ferry, Law was ordered to position his own brigade and Jerome Robertson's brigade between Hooker's main force there and the rear guard near Wauhatchie Junction, three miles to the south. Law's orders were to prevent Hooker's men at Brown's Ferry, once they heard the battle begin at Wauhatchie, from moving to the relief of their rear guard.

The attack against Geary's five regiments, four pieces of artillery, and wagon train was to be made by Jenkins' own brigade of six regiments under command of Colonel John Bratton, with Henry Benning's brigade in support.[70] Three of the brigades in Hood's division had to march from the east to the west side of Lookout Mountain before the attack could

---

[64]Ibid.; Longstreet, *From Manassas to Appomattox*, 474.

[65]Longstreet's [second] report on the fight in Lookout Valley, March 25, 1864, O. R., vol. 31, part 1, p. 217. Wauhatchie Junction is frequently referred to as Wauhatchie Station.

[66]Freeman, *Lee's Lieutenants*, 3:282.

[67]Longstreet's [first] report on fight in Lookout Valley, December 25, 1863, O. R., vol. 31, part 1, p. 219.

[68]Freeman, *Lee's Lieutenants*, 3:284 n. 18; Longstreet, *From Manassas to Appomattox*, 475.

[69]In his memoirs, Longstreet claimed that once he learned McLaws' division had not been sent to participate, Longstreet intended to cancel the attack but admitted "failing to give countermanding orders," and that Jenkins decided, on his own, that the attack would proceed with only Hood's division. Longstreet, *From Manassas to Appomattox*, 476. Longstreet's memory on this point has been the subject of well-reasoned criticism. Freeman, *Lee's Lieutenants*, 3:284 n. 18.

[70]Longstreet, *From Manassas to Appomattox*, 475-476.

MAP 1: BATTLE OF LOOKOUT VALLEY - OCTOBER 28-29, 1863

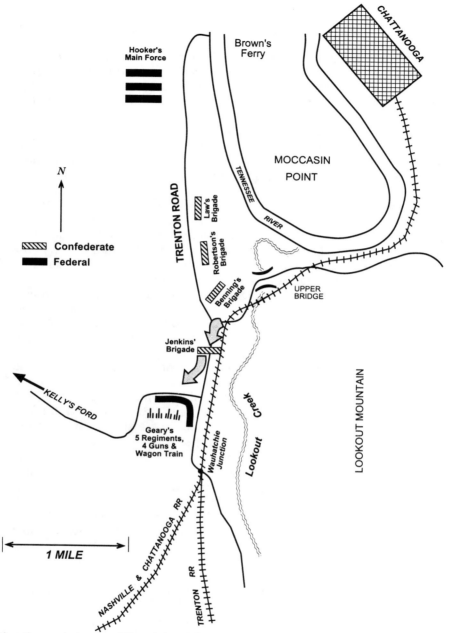

During the early hours of the night of October 28-29, 1863, Jenkins' Brigade crossed from the east to the west side of Lookout Mountain by way of a narrow road at the northern base of the mountain. At about midnight, the brigade, under the command of Colonel John Bratton, turned left on the Trenton Road. About a mile south, near Wauhatchie Junction, was Hooker's Federal rear guard, under the command of General John Geary. The plan called for Jenkins' Brigade to attack Geary's force at Wauhatchie Junction while the Confederate brigades of E. M. Law and Jerome Robertson blocked Hooker's main Federal force at Brown's Ferry from marching south on the Trenton Road to relieve Geary's troops.

begin. Being vulnerable to Federal artillery, however, they could not begin their march until dark, and it was not until about midnight before they were in position to begin the attack.[71]

After crossing Lookout Creek at the lower bridge, Law positioned his two brigades facing west, toward the Trenton Road which ran from Wauhatchie Junction to Brown's Ferry. This position would enable them to intercept Hooker's men when they countermarched south to rescue their rear guard. Shortly after midnight, Longstreet conferred with Jenkins "on the field." Immediately after this conference, Jenkins gave Colonel Bratton the orders to proceed with the operation.[72]

Bratton marched Jenkins' brigade west over Lookout Creek across the upper (or southernmost) bridge shortly before midnight. After the men crossed the creek, they pushed on west for less than a mile to the Trenton Road which ran from Wauhatchie Junction up to Brown's Ferry. When Bratton reached the road, he turned left and began moving four of his regiments south in a line of battle toward General Geary's camp and wagon train at Wauhatchie Junction. Benning's brigade was brought up last, almost to the place where Bratton had turned onto the Trenton Road, and took up a supporting position there between Bratton's troops and Law's two brigades. After Bratton's men had moved about a half mile down the Trenton Road, his skirmishers crossed a small branch and could see the Federal camp about a hundred yards away on the west side of the road.[73]

Bratton halted his regiments to adjust his lines, but his skirmishers failed to receive the order recalling them, and they got too close to

---

[71]O. R., vol. 31, part 1, pp. 217-218.

[72]Longstreet attached his endorsement, dated December 25, 1863, to Jenkins' official report on the night action in Lookout Valley, but a note attached to this endorsement states, "Jenkins' report not found." O. R., vol. 31, part 1, p. 219 n. A handwritten copy of Jenkins' report, dated November 2, 1863, is at the South Caroliniana Library, University of South Carolina, Columbia, South Carolina, and is a part of that library's Micah Jenkins Papers. References hereafter to this document are to "Jenkins' report on Lookout Valley." In this report, Jenkins confirmed that he and Longstreet conferred "on the field" shortly before the attack began. The day after the fight, Longstreet wrote:

> I left [Jenkins] about 1 o'clock [a.m.], and we [had] just got to the [Trenton] road. As there was nothing there, and it was too late to make any move against the main camp, I directed him to see if he could find any wagons behind, and stragglers, and return to camp.

Longstreet to Brent, October 29, 1863, O. R., vol. 31, part 1, p. 223. Since the Federals' main camp was at Brown's Ferry, and their wagons were at Wauhatchie Junction, Jenkins says he followed the "instructions of [General Longstreet]" and attacked "the detachment [at Wauhatchie] . . . to endeavor to capture the accompanying [wagon] trains. . . ." Jenkins' report on Lookout Valley, November 2, 1863, Micah Jenkins Papers, S.C.L.

[73]Colonel Bratton's report on the fight at Lookout Valley, November 1, 1863, O. R., vol. 31, part 1, p. 231. Advancing against the enemy camp were four regiments in Jenkins' South Carolina brigade: the First, the Second Rifles, the Palmetto Sharpshooters and the Fifth. The Sixth was posted north on the Trenton Road and the Hampton Legion was temporarily held in reserve. The five regiments in Geary's camp were the 137th, 149th, and 78th New York Volunteers, and the 109th and 111th Pennsylvania Volunteers, supported by four guns of Knap's battery. Geary's report on the fight at Lookout Valley, O. R., vol. 31, part 1, pp. 112-114.

MAP 2: BATTLE OF LOOKOUT VALLEY - OCTOBER 28-29, 1863

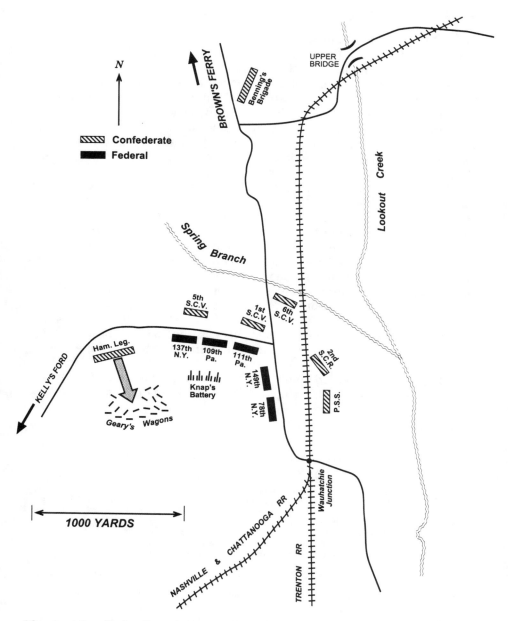

After crossing Spring Branch, Jenkins' Brigade attacked John Geary's Federal troops shortly after midnight. The four guns from Knap's Battery were on high ground and poured grape and canister into the South Carolinians. The Second South Carolina Rifles faltered and fell back. Bratton called forward M. W. Gary's Hampton Legion, which got around the Federals' left flank and captured part of their wagon train. The Palmetto Sharpshooters were on Bratton's left and forced Knap's Battery to change positions. The fight entered its third hour about 2 a.m.

Geary's camp. Unfortunately, the Union sentinels were alerted. One officer in the brigade recalled that there was wild confusion and wrote that, "the Yankee soldiers [were] firing their guns in every direction, not knowing where [Bratton's main body was]. . . ."[74] Instead of taking advantage of the surprise and confusion by quickly attacking, however, Bratton advanced his men slowly and deliberately. As a result of what Captain J. R. Hagood described as "this fatal error," Geary's Union troops were given time to rally and prepare for the attack.[75] Bratton's regiments advanced toward the camp, with the Fifth Regiment on the right under Colonel Coward, and the Palmetto Sharpshooters on the left along the railroad, under Colonel Walker. In the middle were the Second Rifles, under Colonel Thomson, and the First, under Colonel Kilpatrick. As the men ran into heavy fire, Thomson's Second Rifles first halted and then fell back, disrupting the coordinated advance. Bratton then called forward the Sixth Regiment and the Hampton Legion.[76]

The Fifth Regiment continued its advance on the right to the point where Colonel Coward could see that the other regiments had not advanced with him. His men were immediately hit by heavy musketry from Geary's infantry, as well as grape and canister from the four guns in Knap's battery, but even Coward's wounded refused to quit. They crawled to their comrades and bit off the ends of their own paper cartridges to save time, handing them up to the soldiers still able to fire.[77] After advancing past the Federal wagon train, Coward's men remained in their isolated position for some twenty or thirty minutes. He reported:

> [M]y forty rounds per man . . . being exhausted, and my small command weakened by the rapidly increasing casualties, I drew my men back to the gully. . . .[78]

Meanwhile, the Palmetto Sharpshooters moved down the railroad bed and came up on the Federals' right flank. As they pressed forward, they too encountered Geary's artillery which one officer said "was belching forth its iron hail of destruction into the regiments on our right."[79] Colonel Walker's men concentrated their fire on Knap's battery, silencing

---

[74]Hagood, *Memoirs*, 122.

[75]Ibid. General Geary thought he had been attacked by Hood's entire division. He wrote his wife, "They came upon us in three heavy columns . . . with the most demoniacal yell." John Geary to his wife, Mary, November 2, 1863, in William Alan Blair, ed., *A Politician Goes to War: The Civil War Letters of John White Geary* (University Park, Pennsylvania: The Pennsylvania State University Press, 1995), 131.

[76]O. R., vol. 31, part 1, p. 231.

[77]Charleston *Daily Courier*, November 7, 1863.

[78]Colonel Coward's unpublished report on the Battle of Lookout Valley, October 30, 1863, John Jenkins Papers, S.C.D.A.H. See also, October 29, 1863, letter to the Yorkville *Enquirer* from First Lieutenant J. D. McConnell, Company E, Fifth S.C.V., Yorkville *Enquirer*, November 11, 1863.

[79]Lewis, *Camp Life*, 65.

MAP 3: BATTLE OF LOOKOUT VALLEY - OCTOBER 28-29, 1863

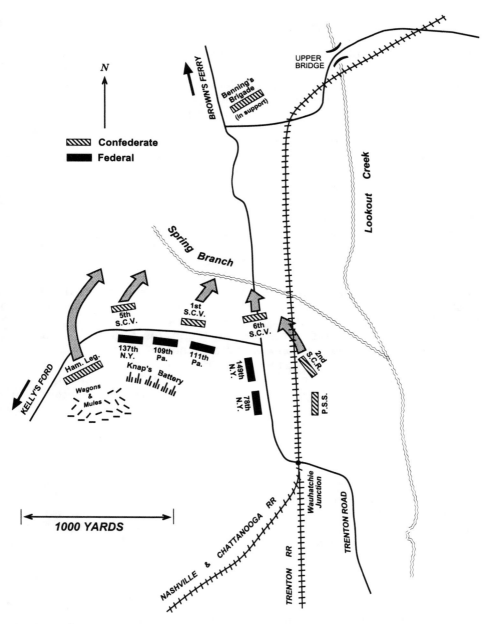

At about 3 a.m. Jenkins learned that the brigades of Law and Robertson had not succeeded in blocking Hooker's main force, which had passed Law's Brigade and was moving down the Trenton Road toward Wauhatchie Junction to rescue Geary's men. Jenkins realized that part of his division was now in danger of being cut off from its only route of withdrawal, back across Lookout Creek. This he could not risk, and he called off the fight at Wauhatchie Junction by ordering his brigade to withdraw back across the Upper Bridge. The night fight at Wauhatchie Junction then sputtered to a halt. General Geary had held his position but at great personal sacrifice: his son, Lieutenant Edward Geary was killed.

it for a brief time and causing the Union artillerymen to move their pieces.[80] The Hampton Legion came up and moved around to the right of the Fifth Regiment and attacked Geary's left flank, driving the Union soldiers through their camp.[81]

While his own brigade, without any artillery, was locked in its desperate fight with Geary's regiments at Wauhatchie Junction, Jenkins received word from Law that he was being pressed hard by Hooker's Federal troops from Brown's Ferry, who were attempting to get past Law's two brigades to relieve Geary's division. Jenkins quickly sent his reply to Law that he must block the Federal advance from Brown's Ferry, even if it meant attacking. Shortly afterward, however, Jenkins was informed that Hooker's troops had managed to get past Law's two blocking brigades and were within one hundred and fifty or two hundred yards of the only road which Bratton could use to retire across Lookout Creek. Once Hooker's soldiers were in position to split Jenkins' division and cut off its retreat, he had no choice but to call off the fight. Jenkins, therefore, reluctantly recalled Bratton, ordering him to break off his attack at Wauhatchie Junction, move back up the Trenton Road and retire across the upper bridge at Lookout Creek.[82] But Bratton's men were a mile away from the bridge and withdrawing them would take some time; accordingly, Jenkins sent Law a message ordering him to "hold his position till I ordered him to retire."[83] In his report, Jenkins stated that he "twice repeated" these orders to Law. In spite of these orders, however, Law prematurely began pulling back his two brigades before Bratton's men had been withdrawn, thus threatening their ability to retire safely across Lookout Creek.[84] Fortunately, by carefully positioning Benning's brigade with two of Bratton's regiments which were coming up the Trenton Road from Wauhatchie Junction, Jenkins was able to get his men back across the creek in good order.

---

[80]Colonel Walker's unpublished report on the Battle of Lookout Valley, October 30, 1863, John Jenkins Papers, S.C.D.A.H. One soldier in Company L of the Palmetto Sharpshooters reported that, in this fight, "the Brigade expended over 40,000 rounds of ammunition." Record of Events Cards for the Palmetto Sharpshooters, Company L, September-October 1863.

[81]Colonel Gary's unpublished report on the Battle of Lookout Valley, October 30, 1863, John Jenkins Papers, S.C.D.A.H.

[82]Jenkins' report on Lookout Valley, November 2, 1863, Micah Jenkins Papers, S.C.L.

[83]Ibid. These orders were delivered in person by John W. Jamison, Jenkins' aide-de-camp, who told Law that Jenkins' instructions were to "hold his position until further orders." Handwritten statement of John W. Jamison, January 15, 1864, John Jenkins Papers, S.C.D.A.H.

[84]Jenkins' report on Lookout Valley, November 2, 1863, Micah Jenkins Papers, S.C.L. In his report on the battle, Law contended that his orders were to hold his position "until [Bratton] could withdraw his troops." He stated that when he received information that Bratton had withdrawn to the creek, he (Law) then withdrew because he believed "the object for which my position was occupied had been accomplished." Law's report on Lookout Valley, November 3, 1863, O. R., vol. 31, part 1, pp. 227-228. Jenkins' report indicates, however, that regardless of where Law thought Bratton was, all of Bratton's regiments had not yet made it back safely to the bridge by the time Law began his withdrawal. Jenkins firmly believed that Law had made his own decision as to when he should withdraw, in spite of his orders that this decision was reserved for Jenkins, as acting division commander.

Believing that Law had endangered the overall withdrawal by not following his orders to hold his position until ordered to retire, Jenkins confronted him the next morning. According to Jenkins,

> I enquired of Gen. Law at his bivouac fire next morning why he had fallen back before my orders, and he said that the enemy was pressing his right flank and that part of his troops acted badly. I mention this as in his report he takes as the grounds of his withdrawing from his position, that it was in accordance with the plan.[85]

There is some indication that Law's conduct on the night of October 28 and 29 was perhaps more sinister than merely a result of the behavior of his troops. As Colonel Coward recalled later:

> Many explanations could be heard from all sides of how the fiasco had happened: misunderstanding of directions . . . mistakes of places on account of darkness . . . and most astounding of all, the statement made by General Longstreet on the authority of a staff officer: that General Law had said in reference to this fight, that he "could not be expected to furnish silver spurs for Jenkins' new uniform as Major General."[86]

Longstreet ordered Jenkins to prepare charges against Law, but when they were ordered to East Tennessee a few days later, Jenkins asked "to have the matter put off to [a] more convenient time."[87] The closest Jenkins ever came to preferring charges was in the cover letter attached to his official report of the battle, in which he stated:

> I should have perhaps taken official notice of the disobedience of General Law, had it not been for my knowledge of his dissatisfied feelings in reference to my having command of this Division as his Senior, and my belief that the contrary course on my part might tend to harmonize this Division and to advance the best interest of the service.[88]

---

[85] Jenkins' report on Lookout Valley, November 2, 1863, Micah Jenkins Papers, S.C.L.
[86] Bond and Coward, eds., *South Carolinians*, 90-91.
[87] Longstreet, *From Manassas to Appomattox*, 477.
[88] Jenkins to Major Osmun Latrobe, January 4, 1864, John Jenkins Papers, S.C.D.A.H.

Law insisted that he had not abandoned his position on the night of October 28 and 29, "except in accordance with the general plan of operations, as indicated to me by [Jenkins]. . . ."[89] With this Longstreet disagreed and stated in his report:

> The brigade under Colonel Bratton claims to have had complete success up to the moment it was recalled. It was recalled in consequence of Law's abandoning his position, which was essential to the safety of Colonel Bratton's command. . . . The loss sustained by the two brigades under General Law was probably one-tenth of the loss sustained by [Bratton's brigade]. As General Law's troops were veterans, I can only attribute the want of conduct with his troops to a strong feeling of jealously among [Jenkins and Law].[90]

Longstreet was fairly accurate on his comparison of casualties. Jenkins' brigade lost 356, killed, wounded or missing, while Law's and Robertson's brigades had only 43 and 9 casualties, respectively.[91] The Palmetto Sharpshooters, under Colonel Walker, lost 7 killed, 34 wounded and 3 missing.[92] By far the most serious losses in Jenkins' brigade, however, were suffered by Colonel Coward's Fifth Regiment. This single regiment lost almost twice as many men as did Law's two brigades combined. Out of 218 men carried into the fight, Coward reported 9 killed, 85 wounded and 8 missing.[93] General Jenkins wrote his wife, "Colonel Coward distinguished himself as did his regiment particularly."[94] One company commander in the Fifth, Captain J. B. Lyle of Company C, wrote:

> I am almost without a company – lost exactly two thirds of all I carried into [the] fight. Lt. [William T.] Norris and

---

[89]Law to Major W. H. Sellers, Nov. 2, 1863, John Jenkins Papers, S.C.D.A.H. In this letter Law indicated he would demand that a court of enquiry be convened, but nothing in the records indicates that such a hearing ever occurred. See also, Law, "Memoranda of Lookout Valley," Ezra A. Carman Papers.

[90]Longstreet's [second] report on Lookout Valley, March 25, 1864, O. R., vol. 31, part 1, p. 218. Indeed, one of the men in Law's own brigade wrote after the night fight, "Law's brigade being but *slightly engaged* lost but few men." Turner Vaughan, "Diary of Turner Vaughan, Co. 'C', 4th Alabama Regiment, C.S.A.," *Alabama Historical Quarterly*, 18 (Winter 1956): 599 (emphasis added).

[91]John Bratton's report on Lookout Valley, November 1, 1863, O. R., vol. 31, part 1, p. 233; Longstreet, *From Manassas to Appomattox*, 477. Geary's division suffered 216 casualties in the fight, and one of those killed was Geary's son, Edward. Sword, *Mountains Touched with Fire*, 144.

[92]Joe Walker's Unpublished Report on Lookout Valley, October 30, 1863, John Jenkins Papers, S.C.D.A.H.; see also, O. R., vol. 31, part 1, p. 233.

[93]Asbury Coward's Unpublished Report on Lookout Valley, October 30, 1863, John Jenkins Papers, S.C.D.A.H.; see also, O. R., vol. 31, part 1, p. 233.

[94]Micah Jenkins to Caroline Jenkins, October 29, 1863, John Jenkins Papers, S.C.L.

I intend to lay aside our swords and take [up] muskets for the present.[95]

Another company commander in the Fifth, Lieutenant J. D. McConnell of Company E, said:

This was the hardest fight in which the Fifth was ever in. . . . Out of the forty men that I carried into the fight, thirty-eight were wounded. Twelve were lost on the field. . . .[96]

While attacking Geary's division, James W. Smith, a private in Company E of the Fifth, was shot as he prepared to fire his musket. Colonel Coward was beside him and grasped the boy's hand as he fell. Coward touched his shoulder and asked if he had been hit. In a gasping voice, the boy replied:

In the neck, Colonel, and its gone plumb through me. Colonel, if you ever get back home, tell my old mammy I died doing my duty for South Carolina.[97]

Colonel F. W. Kilpatrick, leading the First Regiment in the fight, was killed as he rose from his crouching position to continue the charge against Geary's camp.[98] On learning of his death, a stunned Jenkins said:

Sir, it feels like one-half of my heart is gone with the last pulsations of Kilpatrick. Never has a friend been more true and sincere to me, or could one's loss so completely desolate me. . . .[99]

In the aftermath of the night fight in Lookout Valley, called the Battle of Wauhatchie Junction by the Federals, some of Jenkins' men stated that they had been winning the fight against Geary's troops up until the time they were ordered to withdraw. One officer in the Sixth Regiment wrote, "We were driving [Geary's men] back steadily up to the moment when we were called off."[100] A war correspondent with Jenkins' brigade on Lookout Mountain wrote that Colonel Martin W. Gary's Hampton

---

[95]J. Banks Lyle to Dora McArthur, October 31, 1863, Joseph Banks Lyle Letters.
[96]McConnell, "Recollections," 6.
[97]Bond and Coward, eds., *South Carolinians*, 89.
[98]Hagood, *Memoirs*, 125. The command of the First S.C.V. devolved upon Major G. M. Grimes.
[99]Lewis, *Camp Life*, 66.
[100]Coker, *History of Company E, Sixth S.C. Regiment*, 132.

Legion had been progressing nicely against the Federals at Wauhatchie and said, "In ten minutes more [General Geary's] guns would have been ours. . . ."[101] Jenkins himself felt that, had Law held his position, Bratton's brigade could have annihilated Geary's rear guard division. Jenkins wrote to his brother:

> Law's resistance was not considered adequate as he fell back with two brigades without orders and against my orders. . . . Had he prevented the pressure on my active forces, [we] would have captured [Geary's] whole division. . . .[102]

Whether Jenkins' brigade could have prevailed in the fight at Wauhatchie if it had not been recalled is a matter of conjecture. The fact that Geary's infantry was supported by artillery while Jenkins' men had none, together with the fact that the terrain seemed to favor Geary's defensive position, tilted the odds in his favor. It has also been suggested that Jenkins committed a tactical mistake by holding Benning's brigade in support, well away from the fight, rather than sending it with Bratton to join in the attack at Wauhatchie Junction.[103] It appears, however, that the entire operation was flawed from its inception by Longstreet's decision to proceed with only a single (Hood's) division, especially in view of his prior knowledge of Law's bitterness toward Jenkins.[104] In his first report on the fight at Wauhatchie, Longstreet acknowledged what he called "the jealousy between the two brigades" of Law and Jenkins, but said:

> [I] concluded after a moment's hesitation that my troops were so steady that they would hardly require commanders after they were once in position.[105]

After the fight in Lookout Valley, General Hooker concocted a story about a mule stampede which General Grant and the Federals enjoyed telling later. The story was repeated over the years, and it became

---

[101]Charleston *Daily Courier*, November 7, 1863. In fact, General Geary said in his report:
> Our ammunition was now, about 3 a.m., nearly exhausted, and a limited supply was gathered from the hospital and from . . . the dead and wounded of both sides on the field.

O. R., vol. 31, part 1, p. 115.

[102]Micah Jenkins to John Jenkins, November 1, 1863, John Jenkins Papers, S.C.L.

[103]Douglas R. Cubbison, "Midnight Engagement: Geary's White Star Division at Wauhatchie, Tennessee, October 28-29, 1863," *Civil War Regiments*, 3(1993): 99. Cubbison estimates Geary's force at 1,500 infantry and Jenkins' brigade (under Bratton) at about 1,800. Ibid., 70, 82 n.33.

[104]Peter Cozzens, *The Shipwreck of Their Hopes* (Chicago: University of Illinois Press, 1994), 79-83.

[105]O. R., vol. 31, part 1, p. 219.

accepted by some as though it were factual.[106] According to Hooker's version, when Jenkins' men attacked Geary's division and its wagon train, the Federal mules stampeded in the dark and ran toward the Confederate lines causing Jenkins' men to believe they were receiving a cavalry charge and flee in utter panic. This story was embellished into a sort of humorous insult to Jenkins' men by an anonymous poem, "The Charge of the Mule Brigade." While the oft-repeated story may have seemed humorous to some, it appears that Hooker turned the facts around. None of the reports of any of the regimental commanders in Bratton's (Jenkins') brigade concerning the fight on the night of October 28-29 contains any reference whatsoever to stampeding horses or mules.[107] On the contrary, the commander of the Hampton Legion, which overran the mule train and the Federal camp that night at Wauhatchie Junction, said in his report:

> I pressed [the Federals] through [their] camp so fast that
> [they] abandoned everything, leaving [their] colors . . .
> dead, wounded, . . . prisoners, arms, knapsacks, tents,
> wagons, and ambulances and animals belonging
> thereto. . . . [Upon receiving orders to withdraw], I . . .
> passed again through their camp, killing their animals
> and capturing a number of prisoners. I made good my
> withdrawal from the fight in perfect order.[108]

The records of the Palmetto Sharpshooters show likewise that, when they received orders to withdraw, they "fell back in good order. . . ."[109] Colonel Bratton's acting assistant adjutant general on the night of October 28-29, Captain James L. Coker, was wounded during the fight. In rebuttal to Hooker's fabricated mule story, Coker stated that Jenkins' brigade was withdrawn

> on account of [Major] General [O. O.] Howard's advance
> [past Law] threatening Bratton's rear, and not by a

---

[106]Foote, *Civil War*, 2:810-811. Even this respected historian tells the story as though it were factual. More recently, the story has been called both "a myth" and "false." Cozzens, *The Shipwreck of Their Hopes*, 88; Sword, *Mountains Touched with Fire*, 136.

[107]Copies of the unpublished reports of the following regimental commanders on the Battle of Lookout Valley, John Jenkins Papers, S.C.D.A.H.: First Regiment, Major G. M. Grimes; Fifth Regiment, Colonel Asbury Coward; Palmetto Sharpshooters, Colonel Joe Walker; Hampton Legion, Colonel M. W. Gary; Sixth Regiment; Major J. M. White. There was apparently no report for Colonel Thomson's Second Rifles.

[108]Colonel Gary's Unpublished Report on Lookout Valley, October 30, 1863, John Jenkins Papers, S.C.D.A.H. Private Frank Mixson, in Kilpatrick's First Regiment, recalled that Gary's men "got into the [Federal] train before being discovered, and they went to turning loose the mules and raising cain in general." Mixson, *Reminiscences of a Private*, 45.

[109]Record of Events Cards of the Palmetto Sharpshooters, Company B, September-October 1863.

Confederate stampede caused by a "*mule charge*" in the dark. When the order to retire was received, the brigade was withdrawn in good order.[110]

This evidence raises the question of where Hooker got the idea for such a story. Ironically, it appears to have been based on the conduct of his own men.[111] In fact, the commander of the One Hundred and Forty-ninth New York regiment, part of General Geary's rear guard at Wauhatchie Junction that night, gave this account in his report:

> In an instant the mounted men attending [our] generals, forming a cavalcade of some 20 horsemen, became very much scattered and broke to the rear, passing through my regiment in a dozen different places. In addition to those, two or three ambulances and wagon teams, attached to headquarters, also passed through my lines. The regiment was thus entirely broken to pieces and disorganized. . . .[112]

One of Geary's brigade commanders likewise reported:

> The One hundred and forty-ninth New York Volunteers were . . . marching by the left flank when [Bratton's men] opened [fire], which, in connection with the retrograde movements of horses belonging to orderlies, ambulances, and wagons, passing through their lines, created momentary confusion. . . .[113]

Adding to the evidence, the historian for the One Hundred and Eleventh Pennsylvania regiment, which was also a part of Geary's rear guard that

---

[110]Footnote by Captain James L. Coker, annotating Ulysses S. Grant, "Chattanooga," *Battles and Leaders*, 3:690 n (emphasis in original). This is a clear rebuttal by Coker, an eyewitness, to Grant's version of the story.

[111]See, John K. Stevens, "Of Mules and Men: The Night Fight at Wauhatchie Station," *South Carolina Historical Magazine*, 90 (October 1989): 297. This historian concluded that Hooker knew full well it was his men, not Jenkins', who had broken during the mule stampede, and that Hooker changed the story to keep his own troops from appearing foolish. Ibid.

[112]Lt. Colonel Charles B. Randall's report on Lookout Valley, O. R., vol. 31, part 1, p. 133.

[113]Colonel David Ireland's report on Lookout Valley, O. R., vol. 31, part 1, p. 128. Ireland was commanding the Third Brigade, Second Division, of the Federals' XII Corps.

night, described the same incident as follows:

> The One Hundred and Forty-ninth New York was broken
> as it came into line, by a stampede of the dismounted
> officers' horses and the train mules. . . .[114]

These statements, written by men representing General Geary's own units, clearly reveal what really happened that night in Lookout Valley. When Bratton's skirmishers came in contact with the Federal camp and wagon train near Wauhatchie Junction well after midnight, Geary's surprised and confused troops began firing their guns in every direction.[115] This sent their horses and mules stampeding in confusion through the One Hundred and Forty-ninth New York, and not into Bratton's lines, as Hooker had conveniently altered the story. Hooker's crude reversal of the facts, and his calculated implication of cowardice, unfairly insulted Jenkins and his brigade. It has recently been suggested that, now that the truth is known, Hooker's dishonorable tale should never again be used to disparage the combat ability of the men in Jenkins' brigade.[116]

In the pre-dawn hours of October 29, after they had broken off their engagement with the Federal rear guard at Wauhatchie Junction, Jenkins' men withdrew in good order. They then recrossed Lookout Creek and started their long march back to the eastern side of Lookout Mountain, finally reaching their camps at between seven and eight in the morning. One soldier in Company C of the Palmetto Sharpshooters wrote that they were "the most completely broken down set you ever saw," and that "Bill Poe, poor fellow, lost a leg, and I am afraid will lose another one."[117]

The effect of Grant's success in capturing Brown's Ferry and in opening up the short supply route from Bridgeport through Lookout Valley to Chattanooga was not lost on Jenkins' men. H. C. Conner, in the Palmetto Sharpshooters, accurately summed up the situation when he wrote:

> [The Federals] surprised a part of Law's Brigade a few
> days ago and effected a landing [at Brown's Ferry], which
> gives them control of the railroad leading from
> Chattanooga to Bridgeport, and they can get their

[114]John Richards Boyle, *Soldiers True: The Story of the One Hundred and Eleventh Regiment Pennsylvania Veteran Volunteers* (New York: Eaton & Mains, 1903), 163.

[115]Hagood, *Memoirs*, 122.

[116]Stevens, "Of Mules and Men," 297.

[117]Lewis, *Camp Life*, 66. Lieutenant William Poe, Palmetto Sharpshooters, Company C, died of the wounds he received in the fight. Hoyt, *Palmetto Riflemen*, 40-41.

supplies [now] . . . without trouble, which they could not do before and we were in hopes we could starve them out.[118]

In a similar tone, a war correspondent with Jenkins' brigade wrote:

[T]o all intents and purposes, Chattanooga has already thus become a permanent base of operations. The danger [to the Federals] of starvation has passed . . . and they can spend the rest of the winter . . . in "inglorious ease."[119]

By October 31, the Union army had massed some 20,000 bluecoats in Lookout Valley and were finally in a position to begin offensive operations. General Jenkins had only one brigade on the west side of Lookout Mountain to oppose these troops. Concerned about the ability of one brigade to repel an expected attack by several Union divisions, he notified Longstreet's headquarters that "a large division is necessary to insure to any extent the integrity of the line. . . ."[120]

General Bragg's failure to follow up his victory at Chickamauga, and his allowing the Federals to set up a permanent base of operations in Chattanooga, had shifted the advantage in Tennessee to General Grant. Bragg now gave him even more of an advantage by detaching Longstreet's troops and sending them to retake Knoxville from General Ambrose Burnside. When Longstreet's corps pulled out, Bragg's six miles of lines around Chattanooga were left vulnerable to an attack by Grant who was rapidly building up the strength of his army.[121] One officer in Jenkins' brigade, not an admirer of General Bragg, accurately described the problem when he later said, "Strange to say [Bragg] concluded to still further weaken himself by dividing his army. . . ."[122]

Longstreet was to take only 15,000 troops to Knoxville, and he told Bragg that this force was not large enough to evict Burnside's 22,000 Union soldiers from the city.[123] Bragg, however, had made up his mind; Longstreet wrote that when he asked that his force be increased to 20,000, Bragg "intimated that further talk was out of order."[124] Longstreet would have to attempt to retake Knoxville with what he had.

---

[118]H. C. Conner to Ellen O'Leary, November 2, 1863, Henry Calvin Conner Papers.
[119]Charleston *Daily Courier*, November 7, 1863.
[120]Jenkins to Sorrel, October 31, 1863, Micah Jenkins Papers, D.U.L.
[121]Foote, *Civil War*, 2:837-838; Freeman, *Lee's Lieutenants*, 3:285.
[122]Coker, *History of Company E, Sixth S.C. Regiment*, 136.
[123]Longstreet, *From Manassas to Appomattox*, 481-482.
[124]Ibid, 482.

Chapter 19

The Fight For Knoxville

Quartered in a large frame house in Morristown, Tennessee, as his men constructed their winter quarters, the exhausted young brigadier could finally relax. Writing to his wife on this cold Christmas morning in 1863, Jenkins paused for long periods, carefully composing each sentence to avoid any hint of pessimism. He had just turned twenty-eight, but the last three months made him feel much older. He wrote of God, of the warmth of home, and of his love for Caroline and their four little boys. Not once did he mention the discouraging events which had appeared so suddenly in his life.[1]

The train delays which had caused him to miss the Battle of Chickamauga seemed to set the tone for Jenkins' duty in Tennessee. Then had come the crushing news of the death of his son, Whitemarsh, and the frustrating realization that he could not go home to comfort his wife even though she was pregnant and desperately needed him there. A month later his division had failed in its attempt to destroy Geary's rear guard division during the night fight in Lookout Valley. Finally, Longstreet's expedition to retake Knoxville had been a dismal failure. Not

---

[1]Micah Jenkins to Caroline Jenkins, "Christmas Morning, 1863," Micah Jenkins Papers, S.C.L.

much had gone right for either Jenkins or his men since they had left Virginia for Tennessee the previous September.

As Jenkins looked back that Christmas morning over the past three months, no doubt he recalled how, upon learning that his brigade had been assigned to Hood's division, he had anticipated trouble with Evander Law. Jenkins' apprehensions were proven justified when Longstreet assigned him to command the division after Hood lost his leg at Chickamauga. As a result of Law's resentment, and perhaps a similar feeling on the part of some of Law's officers, the fighting effectiveness of Hood's division had been impaired. Longstreet had observed this and had decided not to push further for Jenkins' appointment as commander of the division. In fact, Longstreet had even gone so far as to request that the War Department send in an existing major general to take over Hood's division so that Jenkins' promotion would no longer be an issue.[2] This action by Longstreet was the final disappointment which Jenkins had to swallow in 1863. In spite of this apparent disloyalty from his friend and commander, Jenkins struggled to appear optimistic in his Christmas letter to Caroline.

For his expedition to Knoxville in November 1863, Longstreet took Hood's division of five infantry brigades (including Jenkins'), and McLaws' division of four infantry brigades; to these were added Joe Wheeler's four brigades of cavalry, and E. P. Alexander's and Austin Leydon's artillery. About half of Longstreet's force, including McLaw's division, was pulled out of the Confederate lines around Chattanooga on November 4 and sent northeast to Sweetwater, Tennessee, by train the next day.[3] Jenkins' men, along with the rest of Hood's division, left their camps on Lookout Mountain on the night of November 5 to begin their long trip to Knoxville.[4] On that same day, Jenkins' wife gave birth to their fifth son, John Murray, in Yorkville, South Carolina.

Jenkins and his brigade marched first from Lookout Mountain to the tunnel running through Missionary Ridge, where they expected to board trains for Sweetwater. But the trains never arrived, and the men were ordered to walk northeast along the East Tennessee and Georgia Railroad. Longstreet wrote that they were to keep marching and "find the cars where they might have the good fortune to meet them. . . ."[5] They reached Cleveland, Tennessee, after marching some thirty miles, and on November 8 and 9, finally boarded trains for Sweetwater.[6] The Palmetto

[2]Longstreet to Cooper, December 25, 1863, O. R., vol. 31, part 3, pp. 866-867.
[3]Longstreet, *From Manassas to Appomattox*, 482-483.
[4]J. Banks Lyle to Dora McArthur, December 8, 1863, Joseph Banks Lyle Letters; H. C. Conner to Ellen O'Leary, November 20, 1863, Henry Calvin Conner Papers; Longstreet, *From Manassas to Appomattox*, 483.
[5]Longstreet, *From Manassas to Appomattox*, 483.
[6]Ibid.

Sharpshooters was the last regiment in Jenkins' brigade to leave Cleveland, but according to Second Lieutenant James P. Lockwood, the train's engine then hit "an ox" and was knocked off the track. After some delay, the men reached Sweetwater after dark on November 11.[7]

At Sweetwater the men detrained and marched a few miles north to Loudon, a small village near the railroad bridge which spanned the Tennessee River. The trestle had been destroyed by Burnside's troops, leaving Longstreet no alternative but to lay a pontoon bridge for the river crossing.[8]

Late on the night of November 13, Companies B and D of the Palmetto Sharpshooters, under the command of Captain Alfred H. Foster, were sent across the river in pontoon boats to secure the north bank for the laying of the bridge the next morning. These boats had been brought to Sweetwater on flat cars which the men uncoupled from the train and pushed the last mile to the river's edge after dark, so as not to alert the Union troops on the other side.[9] Each boat was "conveyed quietly by men down to the river and launched, taking an officer and eighteen men aboard. . . ."[10] When Captain Foster's men landed on the north bank, they exchanged a few shots with the Union pickets who quickly abandoned the crossing and made what one officer in the detail described as "a general skedaddling."[11] Later that night the remainder of the Palmetto Sharpshooters crossed the river to defend the bridgehead and to cover the construction of the pontoon bridge.[12] Fortunately, Colonel Walker's men were not attacked that night, and early the next morning the pontoon bridge was laid, planks over boats secured by a chain across the river.[13] The remainder of Jenkins' brigade and Hood's division crossed over the bridge later that morning.[14]

As soon as Jenkins' men had crossed the river, he sent reconnaissance parties ahead to scout the Federals' strength and positions. Late on the afternoon of November 14, Union troops advanced in a line of battle against the pickets protecting the bridgehead, but they were repulsed by skirmishers from Jenkins' brigade who inflicted some

---

[7] James P. Lockwood Journal, November 11, 1863. James P. Lockwood, from Spartanburg, South Carolina, was a second lieutenant in Company K of the Palmetto Sharpshooters. He was wounded at Spotsylvania on May 12, 1864, and died twelve days later.

[8] Bond and Coward, eds., *South Carolinians*, 93.

[9] Longstreet's report on the Knoxville Campaign, January 1, 1864, O. R., vol. 31, part 1, p. 457.

[10] Lewis, *Camp Life*, 69. See also, Record of Events Cards for the Palmetto Sharpshooters, Company B, November-December 1863.

[11] Lewis, *Camp Life*, 69.

[12] Jenkins' report on his operations in East Tennessee, January 13, 1864, O. R., vol. 31, part 1, p. 524.

[13] Mixson, *Reminiscences of a Private*, 52. Mixson recalled that it was so cold that morning "that the ice would cover the chain from end to end and the men suffered much from the cold while at this work." Ibid.

[14] O. R., vol. 31, part 1, p. 524; James P. Lockwood Journal, November 14, 1863.

forty casualties while suffering only a slight loss.[15] After this brief fight at the river crossing, Longstreet's two infantry divisions became involved in a sort of running skirmish with Burnside's troops as they fell back along the north bank of the river toward Knoxville, about thirty miles to the northeast.

The next morning Longstreet's force moved toward Knoxville; Hood's division, commanded by Jenkins, was in the lead. Soon the division's advanced units became hotly engaged with the Federal rear guard which, after a brief skirmish, resumed its retreat toward Knoxville. Burnside's troops were pursued by Longstreet to Lenoir's Station, on the rail line a few miles above where his men had crossed the pontoon bridge. Jenkins and his men arrived outside Lenoir's Station late in the afternoon on November 15, and the Palmetto Sharpshooters and the Fifth Regiment immediately seized two commanding hills, but darkness came before any fighting could take place.[16] That night Longstreet had guides lead certain units to positions where the Federal retreat could be intercepted the next morning, but the guides failed to select the right road and the plan miscarried.[17]

On the morning of November 16, Jenkins advanced his men against the Union troops at Lenoir's Station, only to learn that they had pulled out during the night.[18] They had so quickly abandoned their camps that they set fire to most of the supplies which could not be carried. They had also left behind seventy-three wagons full of all kinds of useful items, but with their wheel spokes cut. Jenkins' men found coffee, sugar, preserved meat and vegetables; shirts, underwear, boots, shoes, and oil cloths; cases of medical instruments and medicines; camp chairs, mattresses and blankets; and three or four regimental flags.[19] Captain J. W. McLure, the quartermaster of the Palmetto Sharpshooters, wrote that "the Yankees had just completed [their] nice winter quarters, [and] no doubt thought themselves very snug until spring."[20] The retreating Union troops were not far away, and Jenkins' men followed in hot pursuit; they could not afford to waste time in the abandoned camps. Regimental commanders had some difficulty, however, keeping their men from breaking ranks to share in the spoils. One officer wrote that when the Fifth Regiment came to the abandoned supplies, "Colonel Coward was behind us shouting 'Forward, Double Quick,' to keep us from scattering

---

[15]O. R., vol. 31, part 1, p. 525.
[16]Ibid.
[17]Longstreet's report, O. R., vol. 31, part 1, p. 458.
[18]Jenkins' report, O. R., vol. 31, part 1, p. 525.
[19]Charleston *Daily Courier*, December 21, 1863.
[20]J. W. McLure to Kate McLure, November 18, 1863, McLure Family Papers. John Wilson McLure was a lieutenant in the Pacolet Guards, Company G, of the original Fifth South Carolina Volunteers. At the reorganization of the Army of Northern Virginia in April 1862, he became a member of Jenkins' Palmetto Sharpshooters. He was later promoted to captain and regimental quartermaster.

and foraging in the camp."[21] As the Hampton Legion passed through the camp, the men began to break ranks to pick up abandoned goods and provisions. According to a soldier in that regiment, its commander, Colonel M. W. Gary,

> drew his pistol and swore the first man who got out of ranks he would shoot right there. That stopped [the] plundering in camp. The Yankees were a short distance away and they could have captured all of us if they had turned back while we were plundering.[22]

Jenkins and his men marched hard to catch the retreating Federals, driving them to Campbell's Station some thirteen miles southwest of Knoxville.[23] There Longstreet attempted to deploy his two divisions in order to bring on a general engagement with the retreating Union troops before they could fall back into the protection of their fortifications around Knoxville. He ordered Jenkins, with Hood's division, to move around and attack the Federals' left flank, while McLaws was instructed to make a frontal attack after Jenkins had become engaged.[24] Jenkins placed his own brigade fronting the left side of the Federal line, with George T. Anderson's in line to the right, while Law's brigade was sent around to attack the Federal left flank. Before the coordinated attack could be mounted, however, the Union troops began falling back again. Jenkins then ordered Law and his brigade to

Brigadier General Martin Witherspoon Gary

move quickly to the right with Anderson's brigade and get in position to strike Burnside's retreating troops on their left flank. Jenkins soon saw that Law had not gone far enough to the right to put Anderson's brigade

[21]McConnell, "Recollections," 6.

[22]"Reminiscences of E. T. Tollison, Company E, Hampton Legion," in Georgia Division of the Daughters of the Confederacy, eds., *Reminiscences of Confederate Soldiers and Stories of the War, 1861-1865*, Georgia Department of Archives and History, Atlanta, Georgia, typescript, 12:230.

[23]Freeman, *Lee's Lieutenants*, 3:288.

[24]O. R., vol. 31, part 1, p. 458.

in position to attack, and that Law's brigade was where Anderson's should have been. Running out of daylight, Jenkins immediately ordered Law to make the attack with his own brigade. A few minutes later, however, Jenkins received a message from Law that no attack had been made because his brigade had "obliqued so much to the left as to have gotten out of its line of attack."[25] Darkness came as the Union troops moved away from Campbell's Station almost unmolested; a golden opportunity to cut the Federals' line of retreat to Knoxville had been lost. In his report, a disappointed and frustrated Jenkins wrote:

> This causeless and inexcusable movement [by Law's brigade] lost us the few moments in which success from this point could be attained.[26]

Law offered the excuse that his "regiment of direction" had made a mistake by moving too close to Anderson's brigade. Jenkins responded by saying in his report:

> I do not conceive that a regiment of direction should have been so instructed as to leave such a change of direction discretionary, and the immediate directing presence of [General Law] . . . should have corrected the mistake in its inception.[27]

Jenkins was not the only officer in Hood's division who was skeptical of the "mistake" of Law's brigade. Colonel Coward wrote later:

> I tried to solve the puzzle of how the experienced troops of General Law could have made a mistake between right and left in broad daylight, knowing too that the enemy in considerable numbers was in a cul-de-sac and we had the drawstrings. We had failed to close the mouth of the sack and the enemy was now racing to Knoxville. . . .[28]

There was no doubt that Law failed to carry out his assignment at Campbell's Station, and again evidence surfaced indicating that he had deliberately refused to cooperate because of his jealousy of Jenkins.[29]

---

[25]Jenkins report, O. R., vol. 31, part 1, pp. 526-527.
[26]Ibid., 527.
[27]Ibid.
[28]Bond and Coward, eds., *South Carolinians*, 97-98.
[29]Wert, *General James Longstreet*, 345.

According to Longstreet, one of his staff officers wrote a memorandum regarding the failed attack at Campbell's Station in which he stated:

> I know at the time it was currently reported that General Law said he might have made the attack successfully, but that Jenkins would have reaped the credit of it, and hence he [Law] delayed until the enemy got out of the way.[30]

General E. P. Alexander, Longstreet's chief of artillery, recalled later that, while he had no personal knowledge in the matter, he understood that "some of Law's company officers wrote letters supporting" the charge that he deliberately botched his assignment to keep Jenkins from being credited with succeeding.[31]

In what little fighting occurred at Campbell's Station on November 16 by the men under Jenkins' command, Law's brigade suffered only about one tenth the casualties of Jenkins' brigade.[32] One bizarre incident occurred during the fighting when a Federal shell landed in the midst of Company E of the Fifth Regiment, tearing off the arm of Robert McKnight. The severed arm then flew through the air, striking Lorraine Swann in the head and killing him instantly.[33]

After withdrawing from Campbell's Station, Burnside's troops completed their retreat into Knoxville, but they continued fighting a series of rear guard skirmishes along the way to impede Longstreet's advance. By noon on November 17, Longstreet's men arrived at the suburbs of Knoxville where the Federals had taken up strong positions protected by the city's fortifications.[34] Longstreet's attempt to cut off and destroy part of Burnside's force before it could reach the safety of Knoxville had been unsuccessful. As a result, the Confederates would have to defeat a much larger force, in strong defensive positions, in order to retake the city.

---

[30]Longstreet, *From Manassas to Appomattox*, 494-495. Longstreet is quoting from a staff officer's memorandum which has not been located.

[31]Gary W. Gallagher, ed., *Fighting for the Confederacy: The Personal Recollections of General Edward Porter Alexander* (Chapel Hill, North Carolina: University of North Carolina Press, 1989), 317.

[32]Jenkins reported that his (Bratton's) brigade had 18 killed and 106 wounded, whereas Law's brigade had 1 killed and 12 wounded. O. R., vol. 31, part 1, p. 527. No separate casualty figures were provided for the regiments in Jenkins' brigade.

[33]McConnell, "Recollections," 6. McConnell wrote:

> [A]t Campbell's Station, [the Federals] shelled us . . . and one shell killed four
> men and tore off Bob McKnight's arm. It struck Swann in the head and tore it to
> pieces scattering his brains on my coat.

Ibid. H. Lorraine Swann and Robert D. McKnight were both privates in Company E. McKnight survived the loss of his arm and received a medical discharge in 1864.

[34]Longstreet, *From Manassas to Appomattox*, 495.

Once Longstreet's soldiers arrived outside Knoxville, he began studying the locations and strengths of Burnside's positions. Jenkins, with Hood's division, occupied the left of the Confederate line, which rested on the Cumberland Gap Road. When they first arrived, it appeared to Jenkins' men that they would merely besiege the Union force in Knoxville, as they had done six months earlier at Suffolk. Captain J. R. Hagood of the First South Carolina wrote:

> Our rifle pits were advanced to within 500 yards of the
> city and it was believed that the enemy could hold out
> but a short time on account of the want of
> provisions. . . .[35]

During this lull in the fighting, they were so close to the Federal positions that Jenkins' men became frequent targets for the enemy sharpshooters. In one incident Major William Humphreys, of the Palmetto Sharpshooters, was nearly hit by a Federal rifle ball while he sat under his tent fly.[36]

According to a war correspondent, Jenkins proposed a plan to break through the enemy lines in his front, push on into Knoxville, then turn and attack the rear of the Federal forts guarding the city. His idea, however, was not adopted, "and the days of the siege wore fruitlessly on."[37]

On the night of November 23, Longstreet received a note from Bragg, saying that he was sending reinforcements to Knoxville. By November 28, having been strengthened with two infantry brigades under General Bushrod Johnson, and two cavalry brigades, Longstreet decided to attack. The point selected for the assault was a bastioned earthwork, called Fort Loudon by the Confederates, at the northwest corner of the Federal defenses around Knoxville.[38] Since this fort was facing the position occupied by General McLaws, his division was selected to lead the attack. Running along the bottom of the fort's earthen parapet walls was a ditch which Longstreet believed was only three feet deep and easily negotiable by McLaws' men.[39]

Jenkins' division was assigned to follow up McLaws' assault against Fort Loudon by advancing against the Federal breastworks beside the fort and, if necessary, taking the fort from the rear. He selected G. T.

---

[35]Hagood, *Memoirs*, 128.
[36]Charleston *Daily Courier*, December 23, 1863.
[37]Ibid.
[38]Freeman, *Lee's Lieutenants*, 3:289-290; Foote, *Civil War*, 2:863. The Federals called it Fort Sanders.
[39]Freeman, *Lee's Lieutenants*, 3:290.

Anderson's brigade to lead the movement of the division, and Jenkins then met with McLaws to coordinate the assault.[40]

In a note to Longstreet written later that day, Jenkins described his meeting with McLaws concerning the depth of the ditch around the fort. Jenkins told Longstreet:

> The depth of the ditch was 4 or 5 feet [according to General Archibald Gracie]. The height of the parapet and cotton-bales [on top of them] will make an ascent [of] 11 or 12 feet from the bottom of the ditch up slippery clay. I suggested to General McLaws that the assailing party carry fascines to fill the ditch; but he said they knew nothing about such things, and they would trust to luck in getting around or over. An attack upon which depends the safety of our army, and perhaps country, should have every advantage that science can give.[41]

Longstreet immediately answered the note with one of his own, stating that the ditch was not that deep and that he had no apprehension about the success of the attack. In this response Longstreet then scolded Jenkins for entertaining any notions of failure, saying that "no men who are determined to succeed can fail."[42] Longstreet, however, was tragically wrong, because the assault did fail, primarily because of the depth of the ditch and the lack of any devices to help McLaws' men scale the fort's slippery clay walls.[43]

A war correspondent wrote that the night before the attack was "the coldest, dreariest, drizzliest eight hours of watching to which our men have been exposed."[44] At first light on November 29, McLaws' division, followed by Anderson's brigade, began the assault. Longstreet had decided to forego the normal artillery preparation against such a fortified position in order to gain the element of surprise.[45] While McLaws' men

[40]O. R., vol. 31, part 1, p. 527-528; Freeman, *Lee's Lieutenants*, 3:291.

[41]Jenkins to Longstreet, November 28, 1863, O. R., vol. 31, part 3, p. 756. According to Asbury Coward, Jenkins even offered to send McLaws some men from the Palmetto Sharpshooters to help make the fascines. Bond and Coward, eds., *South Carolinians*, 100. Jenkins also tried unsuccessfully to enlist the help of E. P. Alexander in convincing Longstreet that ladders or other devices should be provided to McLaws' men because of the ditch. Alexander said that he later "regretted" his decision not to accompany Jenkins to Longstreet's headquarters to argue in favor of Jenkins' suggestions, and added, "I have . . . blamed myself for [it] ever since." Gallagher, ed., *Fighting for the Confederacy*, 326.

[42]Longstreet to Jenkins, November 28, 1863, O. R., vol. 31, part 3, p. 757.

[43]A war correspondent wrote that Jenkins had suggested that McLaws' men use fascines (bundles of fodder or sticks) so that they might be able to scale the walls, but "unfortunately that advice was not heeded. . . ." Charleston *Daily Courier*, December 23, 1863. One of Jenkins' regimental commanders, J. R. Hagood, wrote that, "No fascines or other appliances . . . had been provided, and the ditch was too wide to leap." Hagood, *Memoirs*, 129.

[44]Charleston *Daily Courier*, December 23, 1863.

[45]Foote, *Civil War*, 2:863.

lined up for the advance, Longstreet's sharpshooters, all along the lines, opened fire on every movement they saw above the parapet of Fort Loudon.[46] McLaws' troops also started firing long before they reached the fort. As a witness to the assault, Colonel Coward quickly concluded that this was not the correct way to launch an attack which depended on the element of surprise.[47]

As the assaulting troops approached the fort, some were tripped by telegraph wire which Burnside's men had strung among the stumps to slow the advance. McLaws' men finally encountered the ditch, but it was not shallow as Longstreet had insisted to Jenkins; it was nine feet deep in places. McLaw's troops crowded into the ditch and tried to climb the fort's clay wall which, after a very wet and cold night, was half-frozen and muddy. Climbing the wall was impossible, and McLaws' men were unable to get out of the ditch. The fort's defenders then dropped lighted shells, axes and wood on the unfortunate Confederates below, who were caught in a death trap.[48]

When Longstreet received a report of what was happening, he immediately ordered the men recalled, ending the disaster. Jenkins and Bushrod Johnson asked Longstreet to let them send in their reserves to take Fort Loudon, but Longstreet had already seen enough; the attack was ended.[49] With only 440 men inside the fort, Burnside's men had inflicted 813 casualties on Longstreet's assaulting force, while suffering only 8 killed and 5 wounded themselves.[50] At ten a.m. General Burnside offered Longstreet a flag of truce for the opportunity of removing his wounded and burying his dead, a grim duty which continued until after dark.[51]

None of the men in Jenkins' brigade had been engaged in the actual assault. Some of them, however, were involved as part of the brigade's picket line, which was advanced the night before to drive in or capture the Federal pickets.[52] The Fifth Regiment's Lieutenant J. D. McConnell, of Company E, wrote that his 17 men captured 5, wounded 2, and killed 2 Union soldiers in this preliminary action. They chased the Federal pickets out of their rifle pits and into town in the dark but then had to run back to the Confederate lines. McConnell said, "As we were running [back] . . . the grape shot [was] ripping planks off the fences. . . ."[53] When they were safely back in their lines, Jenkins rode up to McConnell

[46]O. R., vol. 31, part 1, p. 528; Freeman, *Lee's Lieutenants*, 3:293.
[47]Bond and Coward, eds., *South Carolinians*, 101.
[48]Foote, *Civil War*, 2:864; Freeman, *Lee's Lieutenants*, 3:294.
[49]Freeman, *Lee's Lieutenants*, 3:294.
[50]Foote, *Civil War*, 2:865.
[51]Charleston *Daily Courier*, December 23, 1863.
[52]O. R., vol. 31, part 1, p. 528.
[53]McConnell, "Recollections," 7.

and said, "Glad to see you Lieutenant. Thought that I would hear from you next [from] Rock Island."[54]

In the meantime, four days prior to Longstreet's failed assault on Fort Loudon, Grant's army had finally attacked Bragg's Confederates outside Chattanooga. By November 26, the Confederate line there had been broken at Missionary Ridge, and Bragg's army had begun its withdrawal toward Dalton, Georgia.[55] On the night of November 29, a few hours after McLaws' attack on Fort Loudon had been repulsed, Longstreet held a council of war outside of Knoxville which Jenkins and the other commanders attended. The prevailing view was not to attempt to rejoin Bragg's army because Sherman's troops were said to be on their way to relieve Burnside at Knoxville. Longstreet's position at Knoxville had become untenable, and he made the decision to withdraw to the northeast. This brought his Knoxville Campaign to an unsuccessful conclusion, and many in the South felt that he had suffered a humiliating defeat.[56]

Longstreet's infantry, including the men in Jenkins' brigade, left Knoxville after dark on December 4 and made a difficult night march to Blain's Crossroads, some eighteen miles away, which they reached about noon the next day. By December 9, they had marched about forty more miles to Rogersville, Tennessee.[57] Jenkins noted in his report that during this long march from Knoxville, there was "on the part of some, a tendency to straggle and a most disgraceful spirit of plunder. . . ."[58] As a result, General Longstreet issued orders to his division commanders that at every halt on the march, a roll call was to be taken, and those soldiers who were absent without permission were to be arrested and punished.[59]

While Longstreet's troops were in Rogersville, he learned that there were three brigades of Federal cavalry and one of infantry at Bean's Station, a few miles to the east. Hoping to surprise this force, Longstreet marched his men there on December 14. When they reached Bean's Station, a spirited conflict took place between the Union troops and the divisions of McLaws and Bushrod Johnson, but Jenkins and his division were in the rear of the march and came up too late to join in the fighting.[60]

[54]Ibid. Rock Island was a well-known Federal prisoner of war facility in Illinois.
[55]Freeman, *Lee's Lieutenants*, 3:295.
[56]Ibid., 3:297; Foote, *Civil War*, 2:865-866. In the words of one officer in Jenkins' brigade, "an adverse destiny seemed to be suspended over the Confederate affairs at this time." Hagood, *Memoirs*, 129.
[57]E. Porter Alexander, "Longstreet at Knoxville," *Battles and Leaders*, 3:745, 750.
[58]O. R., vol. 31, part 1, p. 530.
[59]Circular issued by command of General Longstreet, December 6, 1863, E. P. Alexander Papers, Southern Historical Collection, University of North Carolina, Chapel Hill, North Carolina.
[60]O. R., vol. 31, part 1, pp. 463-464 and 529.

The next morning, Jenkins and his 2,500 men were in pursuit toward the village of Rutledge when his skirmishers encountered the Union troops about three miles south of Bean's Station. Jenkins estimated the enemy's strength at about 6,000, drawn up in line of battle behind formidable breastworks. At mid-morning, Jenkins and Longstreet decided on a flank attack, but agreed to wait until General Law's two brigades, which were guarding wagon trains some eight miles away, could come up.[61] Jenkins ordered his own brigade into position to attack the Federals' right flank and then halted to await the arrival of Law's brigade. Law and his men, however, did not arrive until two-thirty that afternoon, and by then the Federals had been substantially reinforced, causing Jenkins to call off his attack.[62] In his report, General Longstreet noted his displeasure with Law's slowness in coming to the support of Jenkins, implying that Law could have arrived much earlier.[63]

The next morning, December 16, Longstreet decided to pursue the Federal force at daylight, and he arose early to arrange the movement. Generals Law and McLaws, however, were not anxious to cooperate and a frustrated Longstreet wrote:

> As I rode to the front, General Law preferred a complaint of hardships, etc. General McLaws was not yet fed, and there seemed to be so strong a desire for rest rather than to destroy the enemy, that I was obliged to abandon the pursuit. . . . This was the second time during the campaign when the enemy was completely in our power, and we allowed him to escape us.[64]

Jenkins and his brigade had already pursued the Federals as far as Rutledge, where they received Longstreet's orders to give up the chase and return to camp.[65]

As soon as his men had returned to Rogersville, Longstreet issued orders relieving General McLaws of command and ordering him to proceed to Augusta, Georgia.[66] Two days later Evander Law, unable to accept Jenkins' having been recommended for promotion to command

[61]Ibid., 464, 530.

[62]Ibid., 530.

[63]Ibid., 464. Longstreet later said that if Law had started at six a.m., "he was about eight hours making as many miles." Longstreet, *From Manassas to Appomattox*, 514.

[64]O. R., vol. 31, part 1, p. 464.

[65]Ibid., 530.

[66]Special Orders No. 27, December 17, 1863, O. R., vol. 31, part 1, p. 497; Longstreet, *From Manassas to Appomattox*, 518. Before the end of December, Longstreet filed formal charges and specifications against McLaws. O. R., vol. 31, part 1, p. 503. After a court martial, McLaws was found guilty of not providing a means of crossing the ditch at Fort Loudon, and he was ordered suspended for sixty days. The War Department in Richmond, however, failed to uphold the court and ordered McLaws to rejoin his command in 1864. Freeman, *Lee's Lieutenants*, 3:373.

Hood's division, submitted his resignation to Longstreet.[67] Longstreet was apparently led by Law to believe that his purpose in resigning was to transfer to the cavalry and to obtain a command in that service.[68] While his resignation was still pending, Law requested a leave of absence to go to Richmond, and he asked Longstreet's permission to take along the written resignation so that Law could present it personally. These requests were "cheerfully granted" by Longstreet.[69]

Soon after Law left for Richmond, it was reported to Longstreet that some of Law's officers had signed a petition to the War Department for the transfer of Law's brigade to Alabama. It was also reported that Law had gone to Richmond to try to influence the granting of this petition.[70] An outraged Longstreet drew up charges against Law for "obtaining a leave of absence under false pretenses, and thus deceiving his commanding general as to his real intentions. . . ."[71] When it was later learned that Law had gone to Richmond but had not submitted his resignation, Longstreet filed an additional charge that Law had engaged in "conduct unbecoming an officer and a gentleman." The accompanying specification alleged that Law had given a false reason for taking his written resignation from Longstreet, and that, since Law had not submitted it through proper channels, he had abused the confidence of his commanding general and robbed the War Department of an official record.[72] Longstreet later referred to the missing record as a "pretended resignation" and described Law's involvement with the petition of his men for transfer as "mutinous conduct."[73] Law, however, was able to use General Hood's influence, as well as Longstreet's deteriorating relationship, with the War Department in Richmond to challenge

[67]Longstreet, *From Manassas to Appomattox*, 519. Longstreet stated that "[t]he Law disaffection was having effect, or seemed to be, among some of the officers. . . ." Ibid.
[68]Freeman, *Lee's Lieutenants*, 3:304.
[69]Longstreet, *From Manassas to Appomattox*, 519.
[70]Freeman, *Lee's Lieutenants*, 3:304.
[71]Charge and Specification against Law, December 19, 1863, O. R., vol. 31, part 1, p. 471. The Charge and Specification alleged that Law had

        arranged . . . with officers of his brigade to petition the War Department for
        service for the brigade in Alabama . . . and thus [used] the influence of his high
        official position to create discontent amongst his troops, by encouraging them to
        hope for more pleasant service in some field other than that to which they
        properly belong.

The wording of the Charge and Specification against Law is very similar to that contained in Longstreet's endorsement of the officers' petition, forwarding it to the War Department in Richmond. Endorsement Upon an Application from the Officers of Law's Brigade for Transfer to Other Service, December 30, 1863, National Archives, Letters and Telegrams sent by Longstreet's Command, February 26, 1863-February 23, 1865, R. G. 109, Chapter II, vol. 269.
[72]Additional Charge and Specification against Law (undated), O. R., vol. 31, part 1, p. 472. General Samuel Cooper, the Confederacy's adjutant general, later noted that Law's resignation "never came to the office" and said that it had apparently been "presented by a friend of General Law unofficially to the Secretary of War, and never came through the regular channel as an office paper." Cooper's Endorsement on Longstreet to Cooper, March 22, 1864, O. R., vol. 31, part 1, p. 471.
[73]Longstreet, *From Manassas to Appomattox*, 548-549.

Longstreet's charges.[74] Jefferson Davis and those in his inner circle had become disinclined to listen to Longstreet in such matters, regardless of the merits.

Meanwhile, Jenkins and his brigade left Rogersville with Hood's division on December 23 and proceeded to Long's Ferry on the Holston River where they waited for McLaws' division to cross. With only one boat available, it then took Hood's division until after midnight to complete the river crossing, and the men bivouacked on the other side for the rest of the night. On Christmas Eve morning, Jenkins' men finally reached their destination, Morristown, Tennessee.[75]

The march from Knoxville to Morristown had been especially hard on the troops, but it was torture for those who had no shoes. A war correspondent estimated that there were 3,500 men in Longstreet's force, including some officers, who were barefooted during this march, and wrote:

> The surface of the ground is as hard as rock, and at every step the frozen edges of earth cut into naked feet, until the path of the army may be almost said to have been tracked in blood.[76]

Any time a cow was slaughtered for food, some of the men would take the fresh hide, "reeking with the warm blood," and fashion crude moccasins to get them through the day's march.[77] On occasion the shoeless men would beg a passing horseman to let them ride a few miles for some relief from their agony. The shortage of footwear was finally resolved several weeks later when the Confederate quartermaster general sent Longstreet's divisions some three thousand pairs of shoes.[78]

At Morristown, the men in Longstreet's corps were allowed to begin setting up their winter quarters about a mile east of the village. Jenkins' troops immediately went to work constructing their shanties, joking about who would get theirs built first and offering prizes for the best. Colonel Coward recalled that all of the winter huts were finished in less than a week, in spite of the lack of necessary tools.[79]

---

[74]Dowdey, *Lee's Last Campaign*, 139. Dowdey describes Law's dealings with the authorities in Richmond, in his contest with Longstreet, as "behind-the-scenes Machiavellian tactics. . . ." Ibid.

[75]O. R., vol. 31, part 1, p. 530; Joseph Banks Lyle Journal, December 22, 23 and 24, 1863, Private Collection, Elmer Oris Parker, Columbia, South Carolina.

[76]Charleston *Daily Courier*, December 24, 1863.

[77]Ibid. One soldier in Company K of the Palmetto Sharpshooters said that the condition of the barefoot men "is something bettered by the very poor substitute for shoes – calfskin moccasins." Record of Events Cards for the Palmetto Sharpshooters, Company K, November-December 1863.

[78]General G. Moxley Sorrel, *Recollections of a Confederate Staff Officer* (second edition; New York: The Neale Publishing Co., 1917), 215; Charleston *Daily Courier*, February 16, 1864.

[79]Bond and Coward, eds., *South Carolinians*, 74.

Jenkins' troops spent a quiet Christmas in Morristown, and especially enjoyed the chicken and corn pones they had for dinner.[80] As Jenkins was writing to his wife that morning, Longstreet was sending his second letter to the War Department in Richmond requesting that, instead of appointing Jenkins, an existing major general be sent to Tennessee to take over the command of Hood's division. In this letter Longstreet asked for Major General W. H. Whiting and wrote:

> I found it impossible to use [Hood's] division to great advantage, owing to the jealousy between two of the brigadiers (Jenkins and Law). . . . I regret to say that the efficiency of the division has been much impaired [as a result]. . . .[81]

When Jefferson Davis read Longstreet's letter, he not only refused to send Whiting but he also added a stinging endorsement, saying in part, "If General Jenkins were assigned to another command, the difficulty, long since anticipated, might be overcome."[82] Although he had no way of knowing it, Jenkins was apparently now caught in the crossfire of bitter feelings which had developed between Jefferson Davis and Longstreet since their October meeting in Tennessee over the issue of Braxton Bragg's competency.[83]

It is not clear whether Jenkins ever knew of Longstreet's Christmas letter to Richmond requesting that Whiting take over Hood's division. Had he been advised of it, Jenkins would have undoubtedly taken issue with its wording. By stating that he found it impossible to get the most out of Hood's division due to the jealousy between Law and Jenkins, Longstreet implied that both brigadiers were equally at fault. Being more senior and already in command, however, Jenkins had no reason to be jealous of Law. From Jenkins' perspective, it was Law who had

---

[80]Ibid.

[81]Longstreet to Cooper, December 25, 1863, O. R., vol. 31, part 3, p. 866. In his first letter to the War Department on this subject, Longstreet had requested that Major General Robert Ransom be assigned to the command of Hood's Division. Longstreet to Cooper, November 21, 1863, National Archives, Telegrams and Letters sent by Longstreet's Headquarters, R. G. 109, Chapter II, vol. 277. When he learned that Ransom was unavailable, Longstreet then requested W. H. Whiting. O. R., vol. 31, part 3, pp. 866-867.

[82]Undated endorsement by Jefferson Davis on Longstreet's letter to Cooper, December 25, 1863, O. R., vol. 31, part 3, p. 867.

[83]In Longstreet's memoirs, he recalled suggesting to Davis in their October meeting that Bragg be replaced by General Joe Johnston, which served to aggravate the president's displeasure and caused him to severely "rebuke" Longstreet. When Longstreet and Davis parted, they shook hands and Davis smiled, but Longstreet said there was "a bitter look lurking around its margin." Longstreet, *From Manassas to Appomattox*, 466, 468. To make matters worse, when Bragg later resigned, Davis brought him to Richmond in February to serve as "nominal general-in-chief of the Confederacy." Bragg was now in a perfect position to get even with Longstreet and to further damage the already deteriorating relations between him and Davis. Wert, *General James Longstreet*, 362-363.

deliberately refused to cooperate in a subordinate role, and Law's bitterness and resentment were the cause of the problems in the division.

Meanwhile, after his men were comfortably settled in their winter quarters in Morristown, Longstreet learned that Federal troops were using an area around nearby Dandridge, Tennessee, to supply their provisions. Colonel Coward was sent with his men, along with another regiment and some cavalry, to Dandridge to investigate. On January 2, 1864, with the temperature at only eight degrees, Coward and his men left Morristown and marched to Dandridge.[84] Finding that the Union soldiers had temporarily vacated that area, he returned to Morristown and brought back several wagons loaded with supplies. A few days later, Federal troops moved back into the Dandridge area, and Longstreet decided to engage them there. Jenkins left Morristown with Hood's division on January 15 and was involved in a brief skirmish the next day. On January 17, they found the Union troops on a hill near Dandridge, and Jenkins ordered the division drawn up in a line of battle. Under Colonel Bratton, Jenkins' brigade charged the hill at dusk driving the Federals from it. In this action the brigade lost some 59 men, killed, wounded or missing, but it inflicted about 300 casualties and took over 100 prisoners.[85] Coward's regiment lost most heavily since it had to advance across a mile of open ground.[86] That night Jenkins' men bivouacked on the same hill, but finding the enemy gone the next morning, they returned to their winter quarters at Morristown on January 19.[87] According to one officer in Jenkins' brigade, this skirmish at Dandridge "was the last affair of [Longstreet's] campaign of East Tennessee."[88]

Immediately after the fight at Dandridge, General Jenkins rode by a Union soldier who had been captured. Jenkins stopped to question the prisoner, a sergeant in the One Hundred and Twenty-fifth Ohio, as to the

---

[84]Bond and Coward, eds., *South Carolinians*, 103-104. According to Coward, they were scheduled to leave for Dandridge on New Year's Day, but on the previous night the temperature had dropped to ten degrees below zero. Because of this, their departure was delayed for one day. Ibid., 104.

[85]John Bratton to Bettie Bratton, January 21, 1864, Bratton Letters.

[86]Bond and Coward, eds., *South Carolinians*, 109.

[87]John Bratton to Bettie Bratton, January 21, 1864, Bratton Letters.

[88]Hagood, *Memoirs*, 130. The day after the fight at Dandridge, Longstreet wrote the War Department in Richmond:

> A part of Martin's Cavalry, and a part of the Sharpshooters of Hood's Division,
> Brigadier General Jenkins commanding, had a successful affair near Dandridge
> yesterday.

Longstreet to Cooper, January 18, 1864, National Archives, Letters Sent by Headquarters, Department of East Tennessee, January 1864-February 1865, R. G. 109, Chapter II, vol. 276.

location of his regiment.   When he refused to give Jenkins any
information, Jenkins replied:

> You are a good soldier, sergeant, and I cannot blame
> you for not giving any information about your own troops
> which might be of some disadvantage to them. Good
> day.[89]

The First South Carolina Regiment had been without a commander
since the death of Colonel F. W. Kilpatrick in Lookout Valley the previous
October, and General Jenkins had appointed Captain James R. Hagood
as Kilpatrick's successor. In the latter half of January, when Hagood's
appointment was officially approved, he was promoted to colonel in
command of the regiment.[90]

Meanwhile, there was talk in the brigade of some of the men's
enlistments expiring in April, three months away. Colonel Walker wrote
a letter to the Palmetto Sharpshooters, urging his officers and men to re-
enlist. In the letter Walker asked:

> Will the "Sharp-shooters" reenlist, preserve their name
> and same organization, and the proud distinction of
> being the only entire volunteer regiment in this army
> corps?[91]

During the next month, a majority of the men in each of the six regiments
in the brigade voted to re-enlist "for the war."[92] The men had been told
that if they did not re-enlist, they could not expect to go home but would
have to remain in the service as conscripts, perhaps in a different unit
and serving with strangers.[93]

By the end of January, the men in Jenkins' brigade had vacated their
winter quarters in Morristown and moved down to New Market, about
twenty-seven miles northeast of Knoxville.   Moving came as a
disappointment because they had expected that after the Dandridge
skirmish they would be allowed to enjoy their winter quarters for the rest

[89]J. W. Minnich, "That Affair at Dandridge, Tennessee," *Confederate Veteran*, 30 (August 1922):297.
[90]Hagood, *Memoirs*, 133-134. Prior to his promotion, Captain Hagood had commanded Company K
of the First South Carolina.
[91]Yorkville *Enquirer*, February 3, 1864.
[92]Yorkville *Enquirer*, March 16, 1864. In Company E of the Fifth Regiment, for example, 22 of the 26
present for duty voted to re-enlist "for the war."
[93]Yorkville *Enquirer*, February 3, 1864.

of the season.[94]   H. C. Conner, in the Palmetto Sharpshooters, wrote to his new wife about the move to New Market:

> [T]he only thing I regret is leaving our winter quarters after going to the trouble of building them, but it seems as if we are doomed to disappointments. . . .[95]

Like his men, Jenkins had faced his own disappointments since arriving in Tennessee, and on February 12, 1864, he was given yet another: the War Department promoted Charles W. Field to major general and ordered him to Tennessee as commander of Hood's division.[96] Captain J. B. Lyle, in Coward's Fifth Regiment, noted in his journal:

> General Longstreet informs General Jenkins that his chances for promotion are over for the present – that General [Charles W.] Field, of Kentucky, has been promoted and ordered to duty with this Command. Longstreet seemed to be much annoyed by the fact, while Jenkins bore it well.[97]

Longstreet was so annoyed, in fact, that he sought to circumvent the orders by assigning Field to command a different division, but the War Department was adamant. Refusing to give in, the stubborn Longstreet then demanded an explanation from the War Department of exactly why Field was being forced on him, a demand which Jefferson Davis considered to be a direct challenge to his presidential authority. Longstreet quickly received a stern reply from the War Department, saying that his demand for an explanation was "considered highly insubordinate and demands rebuke."[98] Longstreet had not only lost the argument, but he had further offended the War Department and Jefferson Davis in the process and was forced to assign Field to

---

[94]John Bratton to Bettie Bratton, January 28, 1864, Bratton Letters.

[95]H. C. Conner to his wife, Ellen O'Leary Conner, February 12, 1864, Henry Calvin Conner Papers. H. C. Conner had married Ellen O'Leary on January 12, 1864.

[96]Freeman, *Lee's Lieutenants*, 3:310. Charles W. Field was a graduate of West Point who had lost a leg at Second Manassas. Since then he had served in Richmond as superintendent of the Bureau of Conscription. Foote, *Civil War*, 3:166.

[97]Joseph Banks Lyle Journal, February 19, 1864.

[98]Cooper to Longstreet, April 2, 1864, O. R., vol. 32, part 3, p. 738. See also, Freeman, *Lee's Lieutenants*, 3:311-312. In addition, Longstreet wrote to General A. R. Lawton, under whom Field had served in Richmond, to inquire about Field's qualifications to command Hood's Division. In this letter, Longstreet said that Field's assignment to Hood's Division "ignores the claims of all the General Officers of my command, and my own recommendations. . . ." Longstreet to Lawton, March 7, 1864, National Archives, Letters and Telegrams sent by Longstreet's Command, February 26, 1863-February 23, 1865, R. G. 109, Chapter II, vol. 269.

command Hood's division. Field's assignment, however, was met with some skepticism by certain officers in Jenkins' brigade who felt that their own general should have been promoted and assigned the command. As Colonel Hagood put it,

> General Field was a very gallant officer and worthy man but he compared unfavorably with Jenkins' superb military tact and talent, whose promotion to the command of [Hood's] Division would have been but a just acknowledgment of his past important services.[99]

Not only had Jenkins been denied the particular promotion he felt so qualified to fill,[100] but his chances for a future appointment to major general appeared to be jeopardized by Longstreet's steadily deteriorating relationship with Davis and the War Department. By now, the discouraged Jenkins must have felt much like Lieutenant Richard Lewis in the Palmetto Sharpshooters, who wrote:

> This has been one of the hardest and most fruitless campaigns of the war with us, and is causing a sad, dispiriting feeling among our troops, all wishing . . . that we may return to [Lee's] army in Virginia. . . .[101]

On February 21, Jenkins left his men in East Tennessee and went on furlough to South Carolina.[102] Colonel Coward was also on furlough, and they were in Yorkville together for a short time about the first of March.[103] The conditions in Yorkville were much worse than either man had expected, and food shortages had become a serious problem. Those living in the village were forced to go out of town to local farmers

---

[99]Hagood, *Memoirs*, 137. Hagood went on to state:
> I have understood, and I have reason to believe with a considerable degree of truth, that Jenkins was *not* promoted because that event would have given dissatisfaction to a rival Brigadier [E. M. Law] in the Division. The question was consequently settled by bringing to the command an officer whom nobody knew anything about. . . .

Ibid. (emphasis in original).

[100]Jenkins was not the only one who felt he was well-qualified to command a division. In addition to the earlier recommendations of Generals Longstreet, D. H. Hill, Elzey, Ransom and Hood, one historian has written that Jenkins clearly had the ability to lead a division and that he was one of the Confederacy's most "admired" brigadier generals. Dowdey, *Lee's Last Campaign*, 139.

[101]Lewis, *Camp Life*, 74. Another cause of poor morale, at least in the Palmetto Sharpshooters, was that some of the men had not been paid for months. John G. Reeks, a private in Company I, wrote:
> I haven't drawed any money since I left Petersburg. I have got five months wages due me and a hundred and thirty-five dollars clothing money. . . .

John G. Reeks to Rebecca M. Reeks, February 2, 1864, John G. Reeks Letters.

[102]Lewis, *Camp Life*, 82.

[103]Yorkville *Enquirer*, March 2, 1864.

to find food to eat, and there was not even enough fodder in the stables to feed the horses.[104]

Jenkins was still in South Carolina when he received word that his mother had died on the night of March 18.[105] For this reason he was granted an extension of his furlough, and he remained in South Carolina until the end of April.[106]

While Jenkins was on furlough, Longstreet's corps had moved from New Market to Bull's Gap, Tennessee, at the last of February. Longstreet had decided to retire to safer lines of defense and areas of better foraging after it became clear that he would not be furnished additional reinforcements with which to attack the Union troops in Knoxville. At Bull's Gap his troops were deployed in comfortable camps near the Holston River.[107] According to an officer in the Fifth South Carolina, there the men in Jenkins' brigade "did a lot of picket duty but very little fighting."[108]

During March 1864, Colonel Martin W. Gary of the Hampton Legion succeeded in having his regiment re-equipped and designated as mounted infantry. The regiment was then removed from Jenkins' brigade and sent to South Carolina to obtain horses and recruit additional men.[109] This left Jenkins' brigade with five South Carolina regiments: the First, the Second Rifles, the Fifth, the Sixth and the Palmetto Sharpshooters.

At the end of March, Hood's division, now under Charles W. Field's command, left Bull's Gap and marched to Zollicoffer, Tennessee, some ten miles below Bristol.[110] During the march, the men in Jenkins' brigade passed through Greeneville, Tennessee, the home of Andrew Johnson, who would later become president.[111] The quartermaster of the Palmetto Sharpshooters wrote that the town's citizens "are pretty thoroughly Union, and hence do not look with much affection on rebel soldiers."[112] The sixty-five mile march to Zollicoffer was particularly difficult because it was made in a snow storm. Captain J. B. Lyle wrote that he had to "wade, plunge and drag – awful – never more exhausted. . . ."[113] The men were on the march for four days and finally reached Zollicoffer on April 1. Longstreet's headquarters were in Bristol, some nine miles away, and his

---

[104]Bond and Coward, eds., *South Carolinians*, 122.

[105]Edward E. Jenkins to John Jenkins, March 18, 1864, John Jenkins Papers, S.C.L.

[106]*Carolina Spartan*, April 28, 1864.

[107]Longstreet, *From Manassas to Appomattox*, 540-541.

[108]McConnell "Recollections," 8.

[109]Freeman, *Lee's Lieutenants*, 3:549. When Gary had recruited enough men to constitute a small brigade, he was promoted to brigadier general in June 1864.

[110]J. Banks Lyle to Dora McArthur, April 1, 1864, Joseph Banks Lyle Letters.

[111]Joseph Banks Lyle Journal, March 28, 1864.

[112]J. W. McLure to Kate McLure, January 27, 1864, McLure Family Papers.

[113]Joseph Banks Lyle Journal, March 28, 1864.

men were camped all along the rail line running between the two towns.[114]

On March 3 Ulysses S. Grant was ordered to Washington to receive, from Lincoln personally, his commission as lieutenant general in charge of all Federal forces. General William T. Sherman then met with Grant in mid-March to take over command of the Federal armies in the West and to listen to Grant's plan for two massive, coordinated campaigns against the Confederates. The plan was simple: Grant was to go after Lee's army in Virginia, and Sherman was to take on Bragg's (now Joe Johnston's) army which had retreated into North Georgia.[115]

At the time Grant assumed overall command, his Army of the Potomac was headquartered at Brandy Station, Virginia, about midway between Culpepper and Rappahannock Station. Twenty miles due south, Lee's Army of Northern Virginia was drawn up in defensive positions behind the Rapidan River. The ranks of Lee's army had been dangerously thinned, and his men were low on ammunition; now they faced a force twice their size.[116] Lee could do nothing more than wait for Grant to make the first move.

Certain that the Union army would advance across the Rapidan as soon as the roads were dry, Lee began appealing to Jefferson Davis to return all detached troops to the Army of Northern Virginia, including Longstreet and his men in Tennessee. By now it had become apparent to Davis that no meaningful offensive could be mounted in Tennessee by the Confederates, and there was no longer any reason to hold Longstreet's force there. Orders were then issued to move his men from East Tennessee back to Virginia, and Longstreet received these orders in Bristol on April 11.[117] That same day, Longstreet ordered General Field to make the necessary "preparations to move your Division by rail to Charlottesville, Virginia."[118]

After more than a year of separation, Jenkins and his men were finally being returned to General Lee and his army. One soldier in the Palmetto Sharpshooters said, "I assure you we feel greatly relieved in getting away from East Tennessee, for all agree that it is a hard place."[119] No man could have been more relieved than Jenkins for whom the entire Tennessee expedition had been a thoroughly unpleasant experience.

---

[114]J. W. McLure to Kate McLure, April 2, 1864, McLure Family Papers.

[115]Foote, *Civil War*, 2:962-966.

[116]Shelby Foote, *The Civil War, A Narrative*, vol. 3, *Red River to Appomattox* (New York: Random House, 1974), 9.

[117]Freeman, *Lee's Lieutenants*, 3:336.

[118]Sorrell to Field, April 11, 1864, National Archives, Letters Sent by Headquarters, Department of East Tennessee, January 1864-February 1865, R. G. 109, Chapter II, vol. 276.

[119]H. C. Conner to Ellen Conner, April 23, 1864, Henry Calvin Conner Papers.

Chapter 20

The Battle Of The Wilderness,
Part One

J enkins stared at the passing North Carolina countryside, lost in his thoughts of home. Leaving his mother buried in Summerville, South Carolina, he felt a deep sadness that she could not be laid to rest on Edisto Island next to his father. But Edisto was still under control of Federal troops, and he pondered this new irony: the war had even managed to separate his parents.

The long train ride from South Carolina back to Virginia was painful for Jenkins, and he could not make himself comfortable, no matter how he shifted his weight on the hard seats. The carbuncles on his back were tender to the slightest touch, and the salves his brother had prescribed for him were giving only minor relief. The train was filled with soldiers: some new recruits and conscripts going to war for the first time, and some scarred veterans dutifully returning to their units after their wounds had healed at home. It was a boisterous and bumpy journey, and the young general got no sleep because of both the noise and pain. He had made this same train trip to Virginia many times since June 1861, when he had led the men of the Fifth South Carolina Volunteers to the plains of Manassas for their first battle. The war was brand-new then and full of excitement. As he headed back to it now, he felt as if the conflict had started ten years ago, instead of only three.

Desperately needing rest, Jenkins detrained in Petersburg and found a hotel room near the depot. In utter exhaustion he lay down on the squeaky bed, turning carefully onto his stomach. His thoughts drifted back to his years growing up on Edisto Island, his days at the Citadel, the Kings Mountain Military School and the beginnings of the war. He recalled his past battles with absolute clarity, even the minor details. He saw himself leading his brigade again, as part of General Lee's army, preparing and positioning his men for an engagement about to begin. Mounted on Latta, he led his men into battle amid the sounds of cannon, the rattle of musketry and the noise of hard-driven wagons. He plainly heard wounded horses bellowing, soldiers cursing and his own orders being given. Then the dream went completely blank.

Jenkins arose feeling strangely uneasy, and he emptied the ceramic pitcher into the wash basin by his bed. As he splashed cold water onto his face, the dream came back to him as clearly as if he had lived it within the last hour. But he felt troubled by its conclusion, or more accurately, its lack of conclusion. It was as if one person had been reading to another from a book and slammed it shut before finishing a chapter, leaving the listener in confusion and frustration. Realizing that he had no more time to analyze this strange dream, he dressed in his uniform, made his way to the depot and boarded the next train for Richmond. There he changed lines and rode on to Gordonsville where he rejoined his brigade which had already been in Virginia for almost two weeks.[1]

Within a week after they had received orders on April 11, 1864, to rejoin Lee's army, Longstreet and his men had begun moving from Tennessee back to Virginia. His wagons, artillery and officers' horses left first and traveled overland since only the infantry could be carried by rail.[2]

The men in Jenkins' brigade received their orders on April 12, while they were still camped at Zollicoffer, to prepare for the train trip to Virginia.[3] For the next four days they made their preparations, finally boarding the trains for Charlottesville, Virginia, on April 17. Their first stop was at nearby Bristol, where they had an all-night layover, and the next day they crossed the state line into Virginia, which delighted the men.[4] When Palmetto Sharpshooter H. C. Conner reached Virginia, he said it was "almost next to home with us. . . ."[5]

---

[1]Bond and Coward, eds., *South Carolinians*, 133. Jenkins recounted this dream to Asbury Coward when they met later on Jenkins' return to his brigade in April 1864. Minor details have been added to Coward's account of the incident, based on the author's best estimate of how it probably occurred.

[2]Hagood, *Memoirs*, 138.

[3]*Carolina Spartan*, April 28, 1864.

[4]Joseph Banks Lyle Journal, April 12-18, 1864.

[5]H. C. Conner to Ellen Conner, April 23, 1864, Henry Calvin Conner Papers.

The trip by rail from Bristol to Charlottesville was a distance of some three hundred miles. Prior to this journey, Colonel John Bratton, commander of the Sixth South Carolina, wrote:

> I always dread these long rides with troops more than long marches. Soldiers are crowded on cars like so many hogs and I am always surprised at the end of the journey that half of them are not dead.[6]

At Lynchburg, Jenkins' men were delayed by having to unload and reload onto other trains because of the difference in track gauges.[7] Late on the afternoon of April 19, lead elements of the brigade finally reached their destination.[8] Colonel Coward recalled that the men were completely worn out by the time they rolled into Charlottesville.[9] That night the brigade camped in an open field within sight of the University of Virginia.[10]

Left in Tennessee was E. M. Law's brigade, with its commander still under arrest on the charges Longstreet had filed against him. General Lee, however, needed all the manpower he could muster for the coming campaign and requested that Law and his troops be ordered to join Field's (Hood's) division in Virginia. The War Department granted the request and also ordered Law restored to his command, stating that the charges against him would "not be further entertained."[11] Infuriated, Longstreet wrote directly to Lee complaining of the War Department's refusal to court-martial Law. In his letter, Longstreet stated:

> [O]ur failures at Lookout Mountain . . . and at Campbell's Station . . . were due to a want of conduct on the part of . . . Law. In addition to this, charges of a very grave character have been preferred against [him], which, if established, must dismiss him from the service.[12]

Longstreet even threatened to resign unless Law was made to stand trial, and said he had ordered Law to be rearrested.[13] On April 30, General Lee wrote to the War Department, forwarding Longstreet's ultimatum.

---

[6]John Bratton to Bettie Bratton, April 12, 1864, Bratton Letters. The Palmetto Sharpshooters were lucky on this trip. Instead of being crowded into box cars like the other men, they went to Virginia in passenger coaches. Lewis, *Camp Life*, 92.
[7]Bond and Coward, eds., *South Carolinians*, 132.
[8]Joseph Banks Lyle Journal, April 19 and 20, 1864.
[9]Bond and Coward, eds., *South Carolinians*, 132.
[10]Ibid.
[11]Cooper to Buckner, April 18, 1864, O. R., vol. 31, part 1, p. 472,
[12]Longstreet to Lee, April 27, 1864, O. R., vol. 31, part 1, p. 475.
[13]Ibid. Longstreet told Lee:
> It is necessary, therefore, that General Law should be brought to trial upon the charges . . . or that I be relieved from duty in the Confederate States service.

Lee stated that he felt that a court should be convened to investigate Longstreet's charges against Law, which Lee himself acknowledged were "of a very grave character."[14] Jefferson Davis, however, refused to hear of it and took the opportunity to clearly display his hard feelings toward Longstreet. Davis rebuked Longstreet for rearresting Law without any new offense having been alleged and said, "General Longstreet has seriously offended against good order and military discipline, in rearresting [Law]. . . ."[15] By the time Lee finally learned of Davis' strong feelings against Longstreet and his charges, Lee was facing a military crisis, and he chose to drop the matter and restore Law to his command.[16]

Meanwhile, after arriving in Virginia during the third week in April, Jenkins' men remained encamped at Charlottesville where they awaited their wagons, artillery and horses which were still in transit from Tennessee.[17] On April 26, they moved up to within seven miles of Gordonsville, where they set up a new camp.[18] Three days later, Longstreet's men, in an emotional reunion with their old army commander, were reviewed by General Lee and his staff near Gordonsville. At this time, Longstreet's corps consisted of two infantry divisions, Field's and McLaws', plus its artillery. Their ranks had been reduced to only about 10,000 men, but each soldier worked especially hard to be presentable to Lee.[19] The men passed in review, with the artillery preceding the infantry. Captain J. B. Lyle, in Coward's Regiment, described the spectacle in his journal, saying:

> [It was] the most grand affair of the kind I ever witnessed. When the old General [Lee] appeared on the field, a shout arose that made the hills resound – the air was filled with hats – his physical appearance was fine, but he has become quite gray since we last saw him.[20]

---

[14]Lee to Cooper, April 30, 1864, O. R., vol. 31, part 1, p. 473. In addition, Lee said, "There have been instances of officers obtaining indulgences on not the true grounds, which I think discreditable and prejudicial to military discipline, and should be stopped." Ibid. Longstreet had charged Law with, among other things, obtaining a leave of absence under false pretenses. O. R., vol. 31, part 1, p. 471.

[15]Davis' endorsement, May 18, 1864, on Lee to Cooper, April 30, 1864, O. R., vol. 31, part 1, pp. 473-474; Freeman, Lee's Lieutenants, 3:337-338.

[16]Lee to Seddon, May 24, 1864, O. R., vol. 52, part 2, p. 672. Presumably, Lee learned of Davis' position in the Law controversy almost three weeks after Grant had launched his spring offensive in northern Virginia.

[17]Hagood, Memoirs, 138.

[18]Joseph Banks Lyle Journal, April 26, 1864. McLaws' division was under the temporary command of its senior brigadier, South Carolinian Joe Kershaw, while McLaws' case was pending. Freeman, Lee's Lieutenants, 3:343.

[19]Freeman, Lee's Lieutenants, 3:342.

[20]Joseph Banks Lyle Journal, April 29, 1864. Another officer in the Palmetto Sharpshooters wrote that "it has been a long time since we have been graced by [Lee's] noble and majestic appearance." Lewis, Camp Life, 93.

General E. P. Alexander, Longstreet's chief of artillery, described the review as a sort of "military sacrament" by which the men in First Corps renewed their loyalty to General Lee.[21] Lee was so moved that tears traced down his cheeks; many of the men wept with him.[22] One of Jenkins' regimental commanders said that as the men passed by Lee they "respectfully and reverently [saluted] the great chieftain who had directed their destinies so long."[23] Colonel Coward led the Fifth Regiment during the review; he too noticed that General Lee had aged a great deal in the past year. As for Traveller, Coward wrote:

> He took the cheering of the men as a matter of course. This fat, sleek horse had heard cheering of soldiers so often that he had become convinced the cheers were for him. And I believe the men would have cheered him if they met him without his rider.[24]

During the review, Dr. William E. Boggs, a chaplain in Jenkins' brigade, turned to Colonel Charles Venable, one of Lee's staff officers, and asked if it made the old general proud to see how he was loved by his men. Venable replied, "Not proud. It awes him."[25]

Three days after Lee's grand review, Field's division moved forward again to the northeastern side of Gordonsville about seven miles from General Lee's headquarters. Colonel Bratton, sensing the nearness of the coming battle, wrote to his wife, "[this] closing towards the front indicates something. . . ."[26]

Jenkins arrived in camp on May 1 from his extended furlough in South Carolina. Upon his return, in a conversation with Colonel Coward, Jenkins described the troubling dream he had during the stopover at Petersburg a few nights earlier. Coward recalled Jenkins saying, "Why have I not forgotten this dream, as I have all the dreams I've had before? It's as clear and the details as sharp as though I had actually lived it."[27]

By the time Jenkins rejoined his men outside Gordonsville on May 1, General Grant had massed 122,000 Federal troops on the north side of

---

[21]Gallagher, ed., *Fighting for the Confederacy*, 346. A soldier in Jenkins' brigade said it seemed as though the men wanted to touch General Lee, or his horse or bridle, because "anything that Lee had was sacred to us fellows. . . ." Mixson, *Reminiscences of a Private*, 64.

[22]Mixson, *Reminiscences of a Private*, 64; Dowdey, *Lee's Last Campaign*, 138; Foote, *Civil War*, 3:122.

[23]Hagood, *Memoirs*, 139.

[24]Bond and Coward, eds., *South Carolinians*, 133.

[25]Gallagher, ed., *Fighting for the Confederacy*, 346. Boggs was a chaplain in the Sixth South Carolina Volunteers. Ibid., 595 n.3.

[26]John Bratton to Bettie Bratton, May 3, 1864, Bratton Letters. Actually, the move was designed to meet an expected advance by the Federals at Liberty Mills which did not materialize. Longstreet's report, March 23, 1865, O. R., vol. 36, part 1, p. 1054.

[27]Bond and Coward, eds., *South Carolinians*, 133.

the Rapidan River. Lee's army, drawn up along a twenty mile front south of the river, numbered only about 62,000. Grant decided to cross the Rapidan beyond Lee's right flank and then march his army through an area some twelve miles long and eight miles wide known as "the Wilderness." Grant planned for his men to speed through this area of difficult terrain and thick vegetation, pushing to get into the open country where they could maneuver their superior numbers and use their massive artillery. Predicting Grant's move, Lee began making plans to strike the Federals' flank soon after they crossed the Rapidan. That was when Grant would be the most vulnerable, while his ponderous blue columns were still struggling through the Wilderness.[28]

The army which Lee took into this campaign was made up of three corps: Longstreet's First, Richard Ewell's Second and A. P. Hill's Third. Lee's plan was for each of his three corps to move eastward along separate roads and mount a coordinated attack against Grant's troops as they moved south through the Wilderness.[29] Awaiting Grant's river crossing, Hill's and Ewell's two corps were drawn up near Orange Court House on the turnpike which ran east to Fredericksburg. Longstreet's First Corps was still positioned outside of Gordonsville, a two days' march away.

At dawn on May 4, the massive Army of the Potomac began moving toward Germanna and Ely's fords to cross the Rapidan in an attempt to turn the Confederate right. Now certain of Grant's strategy, Lee began moving Hill's and Ewell's two corps eastward from their camps near Orange Court House to intercept the Union troops. Lee, however, hoped to avoid a general engagement until Longstreet's corps could come up from Gordonsville to join Hill and Ewell. First Corps was ordered to begin its march to the Wilderness at four in the afternoon on May 4 and to arrive there on the morning of May 6.[30] Jenkins' brigade, as part of Field's division, left Gordonsville and marched northeast for about sixteen miles on May 4 before stopping to bivouac at Brock's Bridge on the Orange County line.[31]

The next morning, May 5, Longstreet's men resumed their long march toward the Wilderness while Ewell's corps continued its eastward

---

[28]Foote, *Civil War*, 3:132-134, 144-145.
[29]Ibid., 3:150-151.
[30]Dowdey, *Lee's Last Campaign*, 134; Freeman, *Lee's Lieutenants*, 3:345-346.
[31]Longstreet's report, March 23, 1865, O. R., vol. 36, part 1, p. 1054.

Figure 11
ORGANIZATION OF LONGSTREET'S CORPS FOR THE BATTLES OF THE WILDERNESS,
SPOTSYLVANIA, NORTH ANNA, AND COLD HARBOR - MAY 5–JUNE 3, 1864

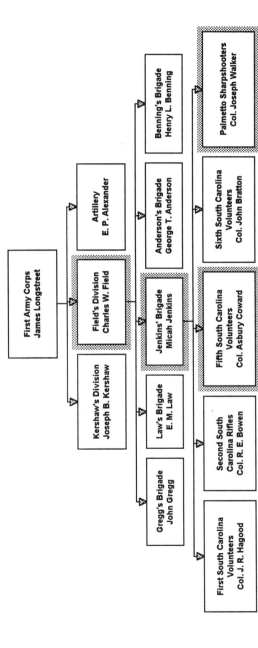

Before returning to Virginia from Tennessee, Hood's Division was put under the command of Major General Charles W. Field. When Longstreet was wounded and Micah Jenkins was killed at The Wilderness on May 6, 1864, the temporary command of First Corps was assumed by Richard H. Anderson. The command of Jenkins' brigade was assumed by Colonel (later Brigadier General) John Bratton, who remained the brigade's commander until the end of the war. In addition, the make-up of Jenkins' brigade had changed before it left Tennessee. Colonel Martin W. Gary's Hampton Legion had transferred to the cavalry in March 1864. This left the brigade with the same five full regiments which had fought together since the Second Battle of Manassas in August 1862. These five regiments made up Jenkins' (Bratton's) brigade until its surrender at Appomattox.

Shop until one o'clock on the morning of May 6; they were then approximately twelve miles from the battlefield.[39]

Longstreet's men were still several miles away from Hill's corps on the Plank Road as dawn broke and the Union assault began. Not properly deployed to receive the attack, Hill's two divisions were hammered and began falling back. Longstreet, riding east on the Plank Road about a mile in front of his men, learned that Hill's troops were in trouble and rode back to quickly bring up his two divisions.[40] While Longstreet was speeding his troops forward, the situation on the Plank Road grew desperate. Hancock's Federal corps was threatening a major breakthrough of Hill's lines on the south side of the Plank Road while James C. Wadsworth's Federal division was pushing back Hill's Confederates north of the road. As the crisis intensified, Longstreet and his two divisions came up the Plank Road in parallel columns; they had double-quicked for almost four miles hurrying to Hill's relief.[41]

As Hill's troops were being thrown back, Longstreet's men came up and re-established a line, with Kershaw's (McLaws') division forming on the right of the road and Field's (Hood's) on the left. Field and Kershaw slowly pushed back Wadsworth's and Hancock's troops, and then there came a lull in the fighting which Longstreet used to his advantage. He sent his assistant adjutant general, Colonel G. Moxley Sorrel, into the woods on the right of the Plank Road to gather the scattered Confederate brigades there and attack the exposed Federal left flank. Longstreet planned for Field and Kershaw to attack parallel to the Plank Road after Sorrel had begun his flanking movement on the right. It took Sorrel about an hour to reform four brigades, along the cut of an unfinished rail line which ran south of the Plank Road, and begin his flank attack back toward the road. As Sorrel's four brigades began their flanking movement from the unfinished railroad, Longstreet advanced Field's and Kershaw's divisions on both sides of the Plank Road. Longstreet's two-pronged counterattack was an immediate success, and Hancock's bluecoats began to fall back, finally breaking for the rear. By this time it was approaching noon and the prospect of Longstreet routing Hancock's corps appeared quite good.[42]

[39]Edward Steere, *The Wilderness Campaign* (Harrisburg, Pennsylvania: The Stackpole Company, 1960), 314-316.
[40]Foote, *Civil War*, 3:165-168; Freeman, *Lee's Lieutenants*, 3:356.
[41]Joseph Banks Lyle Journal, May 6, 1864; Rhea, *The Battle of the Wilderness*, 283-285, 298; Steere, *The Wilderness Campaign*, 315.
[42]Freeman, *Lee's Lieutenants*, 3:358-362; Foote, *Civil War*, 3:175-178; Dowdey, *Lee's Last Campaign*, 159-163; Steere, *The Wilderness Campaign*, 389. It has been suggested that had Longstreet's Corps not arrived on the field when it did, the Army of Northern Virginia might have been destroyed on May 6, 1864. Rhea, *The Battle of the Wilderness*, 446; Wert, *General James Longstreet*, 385.

MAP 2: BATTLE OF THE WILDERNESS - MAY 6, 1864

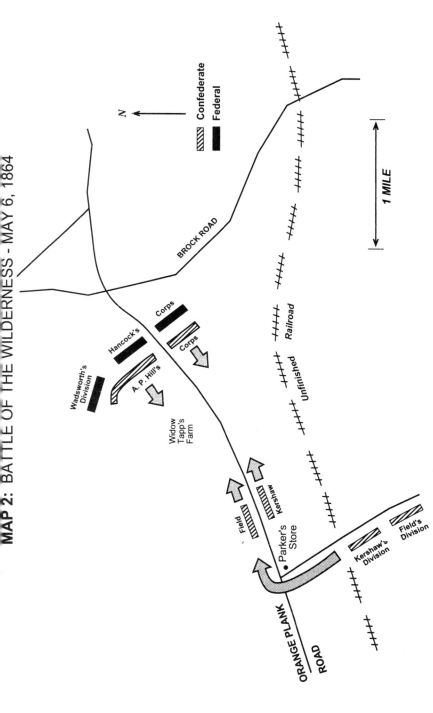

BEFORE 8 A.M., SECOND DAY: As dawn broke on May 6, 1864, Union troops from Hancock's Corps and Wadsworth's Division charged A. P. Hill's Confederates on both sides of the Orange Plank Road. Hill's men began to fall back while Longstreet double-quicked his two fresh divisions (Field's and Kershaw's) east along the Orange Plank Road toward Hill's crumbling lines. Longstreet's men crashed into the Federal troops near the Widow Tapp's Farm, stopping their advance, and saved Lee's right flank from destruction.

With the Union troops having been pushed all the way back behind their temporary breastworks along the Brock Road, which ran perpendicular to the Plank Road, Longstreet saw a great opportunity. He decided to push the attack east along both sides of the Plank Road to where it intersected the Brock Road, break through the Union breastworks there, then turn north and roll up the left flank of the entire Federal army.[43]

During the morning, most of Field's division had been fighting on the north side of the Plank Road, advancing in the general direction of the Brock Road. Except for some minor skirmishing, Jenkins' brigade had been held in reserve, and he was anxious to get into the fight. After the success of his morning counterattack, Longstreet immediately began preparing for his follow-up assault, and he called for Jenkins' fresh brigade. Riding forward shortly before noon to confer with Longstreet, Jenkins stopped to speak to his long-time companion, Asbury Coward. Jenkins reached down and shook Coward's hand, and with great affection said:

> Old man, we are in for it today. . . . Your regiment is the
> Battalion of Direction. Tell your men that South Carolina
> is looking for every man to do his duty to her this day.[44]

As he rode ahead to find General Longstreet, Jenkins was followed by his men, marching in column, ready for battle and wearing their new dark gray uniforms that looked almost blue.[45] Jenkins' men came up while he was conferring with Longstreet on the Plank Road, and Jenkins called for a cheer for their corps commander, which they enthusiastically gave. Longstreet's party, including Jenkins, then turned and started riding east toward the Brock Road. One of Jenkins' regimental commanders wrote:

> I cannot forget the grand appearance of General Jenkins
> on this morning. Elegantly dressed (as he always was),
> superbly mounted and his face lit up with a martial fire
> such as I have never seen in anyone else, he realized all
> that I had ever dreamed of in the true soldier. His words
> shot life into the hearts of everyone, and my men's faces

[43]Dowdey, *Lee's Last Campaign*, 163-164; Freeman, *Lee's Lieutenants*, 3:362.
[44]Bond and Coward, eds., *South Carolinians*, 134.
[45]Freeman, *Lee's Lieutenants*, 3:363. In fact, one eyewitness said the dark gray uniforms appeared "almost black." Gilbert E. Govan and James W. Livingood, eds., *The Haskell Memoirs: John Cheves Haskell* (New York: G. P. Putnam's Sons, 1960), 65.

wore proud and happy smiles as they listened to his commendations on their recent gallant action.[46]

Then Moxley Sorrel, fresh from his highly successful flanking movement against Hancock's left flank, rode up to the party of officers on the Plank Road. Jenkins congratulated him, saying, "Sorrel, it was splendid; we shall smash them now."[47] In his youthful exuberance, Jenkins then turned to Longstreet and said to him:

> I am happy; I have felt despair of the cause for some months, but am relieved, and I feel assured that we will put the enemy back across the Rapidan before night.[48]

Longstreet explained to Jenkins that his brigade was to play a major role in the next move. Kershaw's division was to push through the woods on the right of the Plank Road as Field's division advanced on the left. Between Kershaw and Field, Jenkins was to advance his brigade directly along the Plank Road. Once they overran the Federal breastworks at the Brock Road, Kershaw's division would pivot on Jenkins' brigade and they would all turn north and "roll up" the Federals' left flank.[49]

MAJOR GENERAL
JOSEPH B. KERSHAW

Longstreet then began riding forward on the Plank Road while Jenkins and Kershaw rode a few yards behind to coordinate the details of their combined advance. In the meantime, some men from Sorrel's flanking force had followed the retreating Federals across the Plank Road. Two or three shots rang out from the north side of the road as these Confederates straggled across

---

[46]Hagood, *Memoirs*, 143. See also, Steere, *The Wilderness Campaign*, 405. One of the officers in the Palmetto Sharpshooters wrote that, earlier that morning,

> Jenkins came down our lines, with a smile on his face, saying, "now, my boys, don't get scared before you are hurt."

Lewis, *Camp Life*, 94.

[47]Sorrel, *Reflections of a Confederate Staff Officer*, 238.

[48]Longstreet, *From Manassas to Appomattox*, 563. See also, Freeman, *Lee's Lieutenants*, 3:363.

[49]Dowdey, *Lee's Last Campaign*, 165.

MAP 3: BATTLE OF THE WILDERNESS - MAY 6, 1864

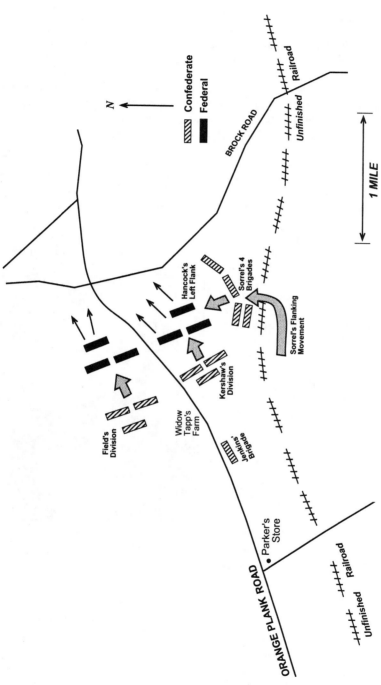

LATE MORNING: After Longstreet's Corps had stopped Hancock's and Wadsworth's Federals and restored the Confederate line on both sides of the Orange Plank Road, Longstreet then sent Moxley Sorrel and four Confederate brigades east, along the unfinished railroad, to surprise Hancock's unprotected left flank. At the same time, Field's and Kershaw's Divisions mounted a frontal assault against the Federals on each side of the Orange Plank Road. Longstreet's two-pronged counterattack was a brilliant success, and it sent the Union troops reeling back to their breastworks along the Brock Road. Up to this point, Jenkins and his brigade had been held in reserve beside the Plank Road and had engaged only in some minor skirmishing.

it to rejoin their comrades on the south side. There, after having fought as part of Sorrel's flanking movement, William Mahone's brigade of Virginians was still drawn up in a line of battle, parallel to and facing the Plank Road. Apparently confused as to the identity of the stragglers, and mistaking Longstreet and his mounted party for the enemy, some of Mahone's men started firing at the officers on the road. According to one witness, Jenkins rose in his stirrups and shouted, "Steady men! For God's sake, steady!"[50] But it was too late. Longstreet and Jenkins were hit, along with two men on Kershaw's staff. Seeing Jenkins fall from his horse, his men on the Plank Road immediately faced to the right, cocked their rifles, and were about to return the fire. General Kershaw, realizing what was about to happen, dashed his horse into their ranks and screamed "They are friends!" at the top of his voice. Jenkins' men then lowered their rifles as Mahone's troops, realizing their horrible mistake, came running out of the woods voicing their regret and trying to help.[51]

There was nothing that could be done. Longstreet was on the ground, seriously wounded in the neck and shoulder; Jenkins lay dying with a terrible wound in his head. His men looked on, in stunned disbelief. Coward rushed to Jenkins' side, took his hand and asked, "Jenkins . . . Mike, do you know me?"[52] All Coward felt was a gripping pressure from the hand of his dying commander, his whole body now convulsed. Coward and the other officers in the brigade watched helplessly as Jenkins was gently placed in an ambulance and taken to the rear. A few minutes later, the devastated Colonel Coward returned to his regiment; he was weeping.[53]

As Jenkins was taken away from the lines to the field hospital, Reverend James McDowell, chaplain of the Palmetto Sharpshooters, rode in the ambulance with him. McDowell tried to speak to him but could see that the ball had pierced his forehead; he could not respond. He was completely paralyzed on one side, but his hand on the other side "he repeatedly lifted to the wound and then laid it down again."[54]

When Jenkins arrived at the field hospital he was still alive, although not conscious. His head wound was so serious it was obvious to those

---

[50]Francis W. Dawson, *Reminiscences of Confederate Service, 1861-1865*, edited by Bell I. Wiley (Baton Rouge, Louisiana: Louisiana State University Press, 1980), 115.

[51]Kershaw's report on the Battle of the Wilderness (undated), O. R., vol. 36, part 1, pp. 1061-1062; Dowdey, *Lee's Last Campaign*, 166-167; Freeman, *Lee's Lieutenants*, 3:365; Foote, *Civil War*, 3:178; Longstreet, *From Manassas to Appomattox*, 564; Wert, *General James Longstreet*, 387; Gallagher, ed., *Fighting for the Confederacy*, 360.

[52]Bond and Coward, eds., *South Carolinians*, 135. Coward said, "I knelt by the friend of my life since I entered The Citadel, my alter ego." Ibid.

[53]McConnell, "Recollections," 8.

[54]The Reverend James McDowell to John P. Thomas, September 16, 1903, in Thomas, *Career and Character*, 9.

MAP 4: BATTLE OF THE WILDERNESS - MAY 6, 1864

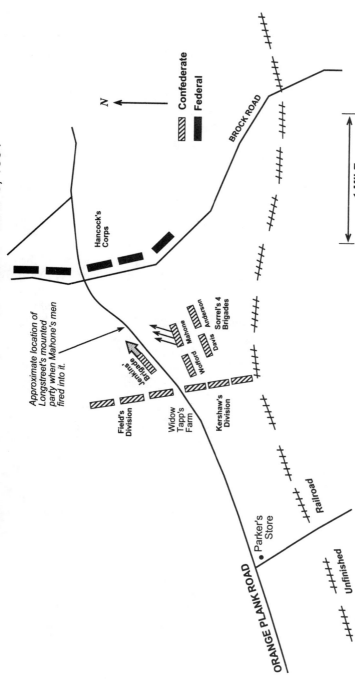

Confederate

Federal

N

Hancock's Corps

Approximate location of Longstreet's mounted party when Mahone's men fired into it.

Field's Division

Widow Tapp's Farm

Jenkins' Brigade

Wofford

Mahone

Davis

Anderson

Sorrel's 4 Brigades

Kershaw's Division

BROCK ROAD

ORANGE PLANK ROAD

Parker's Store

Railroad

unfinished

1 MILE

AROUND NOON: With Hancock's Federals driven back to the Brock Road, Longstreet moved to press his counterattack. He planned to overrun Hancock's breastworks along the Brock Road, then swing north and "roll up" the Federal left. For the renewed attack, Longstreet planned for Jenkins' fresh brigade to attack directly along the Orange Plank Road, with the rest of Field's Division on the left and Kershaw's on the right. Sorrel's four brigades, including Mahone's Virginians, had halted short of, and roughly parallel to, the Orange Plank Road after their flanking movement. Longstreet, Jenkins, Kershaw and several staff officers had ridden toward the Brock Road, as Longstreet explained to Jenkins the role his brigade was to play in the next phase. As Longstreet's mounted party was riding along the Orange Plank Road, men from Mahone's Brigade mistakenly fired into the group of officers, seriously wounding Longstreet and mortally wounding Jenkins.

LIEUTENANT GENERAL JAMES LONGSTREET, BORN IN EDGEFIELD DISTRICT, SOUTH CAROLINA, WAS CALLED "OLD PETE" BY HIS MEN. HE WAS SEVERELY WOUNDED ON MAY 6, 1864, IN THE SAME INCIDENT WHEN MICAH JENKINS WAS MORTALLY WOUNDED BY MAHONE'S VIRGINIANS DURING THE SECOND DAY OF THE BATTLE OF THE WILDERNESS. LONGSTREET WROTE THAT, OF ALL THE BRIGADIERS IN THE ARMY, MICAH JENKINS WAS HIS "FIRST CHOICE."

present that "[p]rofessional aid was useless."[55] He lived for only five or six hours, dying that Friday afternoon about an hour before sunset. According to one of the surgeons present, at the moment Jenkins stopped breathing, "a bright, happy, trusting smile lit up his face. Those around watched it; we thought, we felt, he was with his God."[56] Then his body was washed, and he was dressed in his finest uniform and his flag draped over him.[57]

That evening, Colonel Coward, himself wounded in the arm during the day's fighting, rode back to the field hospital for one final visit with his dead friend. As he knelt beside the hospital cot and leaned forward to kiss Jenkins on the head, Coward broke down, unable to control his emotions. He wrote later that he felt a "bitterness at the thought of this fine, gentle man being cut off from his life in his twenties, because of stupid blunderers."[58]

The next day, Jenkins' body was placed in a coffin and loaded into an ambulance for transportation to the train station and the trip to Richmond. As the coffin was gently lifted into the back of the wagon, the regimental band of the Sixth South Carolina

JOHN W. JAMISON, MICAH JENKINS' AIDE-DE-CAMP AND BROTHER-IN-LAW.

Volunteers played "Old Hundred," followed by a solemn funeral dirge, while the horses slowly drew the ambulance out of sight.[59] When his body arrived in Richmond, members of the Confederate House and

---

[55]Dr. Francis L. Parker (the surgeon who tended to Jenkins at the field hospital) to Caroline Jenkins, May 29, 1864, in Thomas, *Career and Character*, 21. Parker said, "I could do nothing but join with other friends in lamenting a fatality we could not help, a blow we tried to be resigned to."

[56]Ibid. See also, Yorkville *Enquirer*, June 29, 1864.

[57]Mary P. McDowell to Caroline Jenkins, June 21, 1864, Micah Jenkins Papers, S.C.L.

[58]Bond and Coward, eds., *South Carolinians*, 138. Colonel Coward later became furious when General Mahone, whose men had made the fatal mistake, allowed "his newspaper to announce that Jenkins' own men, in their excitement, did the killing." Ibid., 138. Coward felt that Mahone should have admitted that his men, not Jenkins', had made the mistake. According to Coward, "All agreed that it was Mahone's men who did the firing." Ibid., 140 n.3.

[59]Reverend James McDowell to Caroline Jenkins, July 11, 1864, in Thomas, *Career and Character*, 20.

Senate escorted the coffin to the Capitol and attended a memorial service at six o'clock on Monday afternoon, May 9.[60]

After the services in Richmond, Jenkins' body, accompanied by his aide-de-camp and brother-in-law, Captain John W. Jamison, was taken by train to Columbia, arriving there at dawn on May 11. With solemn martial music, a military escort conveyed his coffin from the train depot to the Arsenal Academy, accompanied only by the Presbyterian minister who had married Jenkins and Caroline eight years before.[61] There he lay in state, with cadets of the South Carolina Military Academy, under the command of Captain John P. Thomas, serving as a guard of honor.[62] Afterward, his coffin was taken by train to Summerville, South Carolina, where he was buried on May 15 beside the still-fresh grave of his mother.[63]

CAPTAIN JOHN PEYRE THOMAS, WHO WROTE AND COMPILED *CAREER AND CHARACTER OF GENERAL MICAH JENKINS*, PUBLISHED IN 1903.

The news of Jenkins' death was received with deep sorrow throughout South Carolina. The General Assembly adopted a resolution mourning "the loss of one of [the state's] noblest, most patriotic and

[60]The record of the Proceedings of the Confederate House of Representatives, May 9, 1864, states:
> Mr. Marshall, of Kentucky, introduced a resolution that the members attend the funeral of Brigadier General Jenkins at six o'clock, p.m., and attend it as an escort to the Capitol.

Frank E. Vandiver, ed., "Proceedings of the Second Confederate Congress," *Southern Historical Society Papers*, 51 (1958):49. The Senate's record for the same day states:
> The President *pro tem.* laid before the Senate an invitation from the South Carolina Delegation to attend the funeral of General M. Jenkins, to take place that evening at six o'clock, p.m., from Blevin's block, on Bank street.

Ibid., 46.

[61]The Reverend Benjamin M. Palmer to Caroline Jenkins, May 25, 1864, in Thomas, *Career and Character*, 22.

[62]John P. Thomas had been superintendent of the Arsenal Academy until the war began, and was a close friend of Micah Jenkins. He later authored *Career and Character of General Micah Jenkins*. Upon Jenkins' death, Thomas wrote to Caroline Jenkins:
> It was my melancholy privilege to [post] . . . military honors to your husband's remains as they passed through [Columbia].

John P. Thomas to Caroline Jenkins, June 1864, Micah Jenkins Papers, S.C.L.

[63]Yorkville *Enquirer*, May 11, 1864. Jenkins' body was removed to Magnolia Cemetery in Charleston in 1881 and a monument was placed there by the Association of Citadel Cadets to mark his grave.

accomplished citizens. . . ."[64] When General Longstreet had sufficiently recovered from his wound, he wrote to the governor of South Carolina that Jenkins was a Christian hero who had left a "noble legacy in his dauntless heroism and spotless life" to the youth of the state. Longstreet concluded by saying, "I trust that his memory will be cherished and his noble example will be felt for generations to come."[65] The adjutant of the Palmetto Sharpshooters put it more simply when he wrote:

> I tell you [Jenkins' death] was a hard blow on us. We did not know the value of him until now.[66]

Caroline Jenkins was in Yorkville when she learned of her husband's death. The residents of that village regularly received the latest news of the war from the Chester train, which they always eagerly awaited. According to the local custom, if the news was good, the train's whistle sounded in short, rapid blasts; for bad news it blew long and slow. On the day after Jenkins died, the whistle, wailing its notice of bad news, could be heard for miles as the train moved up the Kings Mountain Railroad toward Yorkville. Local citizens, among them Caroline Jenkins and her sons, rushed to the depot that Saturday morning to learn the bad news. As they waited anxiously in their carriage, the train screeched and hissed to a stop, and the news filtered through the crowd that her husband had been killed the day before.[67] The twenty-six year old mother of four was devastated. She and Micah had been married for only seven years and ten months. Their four young sons had barely gotten to know their father.

The terrible mistake of Mahone's men the day before had not only taken the life of a young husband and father of four, it had also robbed General Lee of the services of Longstreet and one of his most capable brigadiers at the very moment when Hancock's corps had been rocked back on its heels. As Longstreet and Jenkins were taken to the rear shortly after noon on May 6, Jenkins' dazed and saddened men stood beside the Plank Road, wondering about the next move. One thing they knew: there was more fighting to be done before dark.

---

[64] Joint Resolution adopting the Report of the House Committee on the Military, concerning the death of Brigadier General Micah Jenkins, December 13, 1864, "Reports of the Various Standing Committees Adopted at the Session of 1864," in *Reports and Resolutions of the General Assembly of the State of South Carolina, 1864-1865* (Columbia, South Carolina: Julian A. Selby, Printer to the State, 1866), 32. See also, Thomas, *Career and Character*, 7.

[65] Longstreet to Governor M. L. Bonham, July 16, 1864, and Bonham's reply to Longstreet, September 1, 1864, in Thomas, *Career and Character*, 7. Longstreet also said of Jenkins in this letter:
> His brigade was worthy of such a commander, and the mutual trust and confidence between them was beautiful to behold.

Ibid.

[66] James McFall to his sister, Lucretia McFall Anderson, May 25, 1864, William McFall Collection.

[67] Smith, "K.M.M.S., a York Institution," 2-C.

Chapter 21

The Battle Of The Wilderness, Part Two, And Spotsylvania

W ith the wounding of Longstreet on the Plank Road shortly after noon on May 6, his proposed follow-up attack against the Union troops on the Brock Road came to an abrupt standstill. He had not yet issued final orders for the next phase of the assault; all he had done was merely give Kershaw and Jenkins their assignments. Bleeding profusely as he waited for the ambulance, Longstreet turned the movement over to Charles Field, telling him to press on and take the Brock Road. The wounded corps commander then sent word to General Lee describing the success First Corps was having on the Plank Road.[1] According to Colonel J. R. Hagood in Jenkins' brigade, Field declined the assignment due to his inexperience, and General R. H. Anderson had to be summoned. Meanwhile, the troops waited, without moving a step.[2]

Another major problem contributed to the long delay in resuming the attack: Longstreet's brigades were at right angles to each other. Sorrel's

---

[1]Dowdey, *Lee's Last Campaign*, 167-168; Foote, *Civil War*, 3:179-180.
[2]Hagood, *Memoirs*, 144.

flanking force was parallel to and facing the Plank Road, while the remaining brigades were perpendicular to it.[3]

When Generals Lee and Anderson finally arrived at the scene, Lee decided to execute Longstreet's plan for the follow-up attack. First he had to realign Longstreet's brigades for the frontal assault against the Federal breastworks along the Brock Road a few hundred yards to the east.[4] It was not until about four in the afternoon that Lee finally ordered First Corps, with the help of some of R. H. Anderson's brigades, to resume the attack.[5] Four precious hours had been lost, however, and General Hancock's Union troops had wisely used this lull in the fighting to strengthen their positions along the Brock Road and to bring up reinforcements.[6]

The command of Jenkins' brigade had now been assumed by its senior colonel, John Bratton of the Sixth Regiment.[7] He was ordered to advance on the right of G. T. Anderson's brigade, which was slightly north of the Plank Road, and to penetrate the Union breastworks along the Brock Road. Within Jenkins' brigade, the regiments were posted in the following order from left to right: the Fifth (Colonel Coward); the First (Colonel Hagood); the Second Rifles (Colonel Bowen); and on the far right, the Palmetto Sharpshooters (Colonel Walker). The Sixth (Lieutenant Colonel Steedman) was held in reserve.[8]

As the men in Jenkins' (now Bratton's) brigade began their advance, Hancock's pickets, some three hundred yards west of the Brock Road, opened fire and then fell back behind their breastworks.[9] As Bratton's men drew closer, they saw that the Union troops had cleared everything in front of their works to a width of about one hundred yards, leaving the fallen trees and limbs on the ground to obstruct the advance.[10] The regiments in Bratton's brigade had advanced in a rough line to within about two hundred yards of the breastworks when Hancock's soldiers opened what Colonel J. R. Hagood described as "a furious blaze of musketry [which] illuminated the dismal forest, tearing off the limbs of trees."[11] Next came the Union artillery, which included a deadly mixture of grape and canister. To avoid being slaughtered, the men in the Fifth

---

[3]This dangerous alignment had been a major factor in the wounding of Jenkins and Longstreet by Mahone's troops.

[4]Dowdey, *Lee's Last Campaign*, 168; Foote, *Civil War*, 3:180.

[5]Joseph Banks Lyle Journal, May 6, 1864; Foote, *Civil War*, 3:180.

[6]Freeman, *Lee's Lieutenants*, 3:366; Foote, *Civil War*, 3:180.

[7]Bratton had been a colonel since April 1862, when he was elected to command the Sixth South Carolina Volunteers. Capers, *South Carolina*, 6:378-380. The next colonel, in order of seniority, was Joe Walker, of the Palmetto Sharpshooters.

[8]Hagood, *Memoirs*, 145.

[9]Joseph Banks Lyle Journal, May 6, 1864.

[10]Hagood, *Memoirs*, 146.

[11]Ibid. Captain J. B. Lyle described this phase of the attack simply as "terrible." Joseph Banks Lyle Journal, May 6, 1864.

Regiment lay down on the ground for a moment, causing those in the First Regiment, on the right, to hesitate. Then they saw Coward and his men get up and charge the breastworks. As his color bearer was hit, Coward grabbed the flag; Colonel Hagood watched him "advancing ahead of his troops, bearing his regimental colors and beckoning his men to follow."[12] When he saw Coward charging, Hagood pushed the First Regiment forward, but he wrote that the Second Rifles, on his right, "never budged after receiving the enemy's first fire."[13]

Coward and his men finally managed to mount the log breastworks, parts of which were in flames. He was shot in the arm just as he planted the staff of his colors into the top of the parapet.[14] But he fought on, and his men followed him over the breastworks with loud cheers as Hancock's Union troops, from David B. Birney's and Gershom Mott's divisions, melted into the trees east of the Brock Road. When he noticed one of his men, Sergeant Isaac F. Gregory, standing on the breastworks cheering, Coward yelled for him to get down. The lad replied, "Just one more cheer for South Carolina," and was killed instantly by an enemy bullet.[15]

The men in Hagood's regiment also reached the breastworks about the same time as Coward's troops, jumped the trench and helped chase the Union troops into the woods. The rest of Bratton's brigade, however, never made it to the breastworks. Once the men in the Second Rifles stopped their advance, the Palmetto Sharpshooters were unwilling to expose their left flank and did not advance with the Fifth and the First. Thus the only two regiments in the brigade to penetrate the Federal breastworks on the Brock Road were the First and the Fifth.[16]

Once the First and Fifth Regiments had occupied their section of the breastworks, they were then exposed to an enfilading fire from the Union troops farther north on the Brock Road. To make matters worse, the Federals quickly began bringing up artillery and infantry reinforcements for a counterattack. After holding a section of breastworks for about a

---

[12]Hagood, *Memoirs*, 146.

[13]Ibid., 147.

[14]Bond and Coward, eds., *South Carolinians*, 136; Joseph Banks Lyle Journal, May 6, 1864; Foote, *Civil War*, 3:180.

[15]Union *Daily Times*, December 6, 1960. Gregory, from Union District, South Carolina, was a sergeant in Company D, Fifth South Carolina.

[16]Bond and Coward, eds., *South Carolinians*, 136; Hagood, *Memoirs*, 147; Joseph Banks Lyle Journal, May 6, 1864. In fact, these were apparently the only regiments in Longstreet's corps to penetrate a portion of the breastworks on the Brock Road. See, Foote, *Civil War*, 3:180; Rhea, *The Battle of the Wilderness*, 393-396. It has been suggested that the only reason these two regiments were able to penetrate the Federal line is that the breastworks were on fire at that point, and many of the Union defenders had already abandoned the flaming works. Rhea, *The Battle of the Wilderness*, 394. Such a suggestion is of doubtful validity, however, because the flames and smoke were not so intense as to keep Coward's and Hagood's men from occupying the works once they were penetrated.

MAP 5: BATTLE OF THE WILDERNESS - MAY 6, 1864

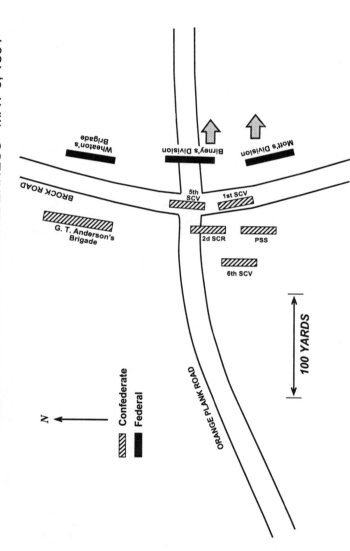

N

Confederate
Federal

BROCK ROAD

G. T. Anderson's Brigade

Wheaton's Brigade

Birney's Division

Mott's Division

5th SCV

1st SCV

2d SCR

PSS

6th SCV

ORANGE PLANK ROAD

100 YARDS

BETWEEN 5 AND 6 P.M.: In the final advance of the day by Longstreet's men, Lee attempted to take the Federal breastworks along the Brock Road. Apparently, the only two Confederate regiments to actually penetrate the Federal works there were Colonel Asbury Coward's Fifth South Carolina Volunteers and Colonel James Hagood's First South Carolina Volunteers, both regiments of Jenkins' Brigade which was under the command of Colonel John Bratton. Coward was wounded as he planted his regimental colors on the parapet of the breastworks, parts of which were on fire, near the intersection of the Brock Road and the Orange Plank Road. With the help of their artillery the Federals counterattacked, driving Coward's and Hagood's South Carolinians out of the works and restoring Hancock's lines along the Brock Road.

half hour, and not being joined by any other men from the attacking force, Coward and Hagood finally withdrew their regiments.[17] As the men began their withdrawal, they first had to slowly pick their way back through the fallen trees and limbs in front of the breastworks.[18] Colonel Hagood described what happened when they finally reached the open woods:

> We then fled at the top [of] our speed while the crash of shot about us, strewing whole trees in our pathway, sounded like the fury of some hell-born passion. Brave men who . . . would have *faced* undaunted a legion of foes, shuddered at the thought of [taking] a bullet in the back.[19]

Colonel Coward's regiment had suffered 111 casualties out of 213 men he had taken into the battle, and his colors had been shot down five times while planted on the Federal works.[20] Colonel Hagood's regiment lost two-thirds of its men, while the Second Rifles, the Sixth South Carolina and the Palmetto Sharpshooters were comparatively unhurt.[21]

When Coward was safely back to his lines and the battle had sputtered to a halt, he attended to his wounded arm. Even though he had lost some blood, he had no pain and could move the arm; luckily it was not broken. He removed his coat, cut off the bloody sleeve of his undershirt and put bandages where the bullet had entered and where it had exited. After dark, he mounted his horse, Celeste, and rode to the field hospital to see the body of Micah Jenkins for the last time. All was quiet except for an occasional boom of artillery and the rumbling of Union wagons along the Brock Road.[22]

General Lee's effort to follow up with First Corps on Longstreet's successes of the morning had failed, and the attack by the Confederate right wing had been repulsed by Grant's troops along the Brock Road.[23] Late on the afternoon of May 6, General Lee authorized a flanking movement on the Confederate left, near the Orange Turnpike some three miles north of Longstreet's men, by General John B. Gordon of Ewell's corps. Gordon's men were able to roll up the Federal right flank for more than a mile, but then darkness set in, ending the two-day Battle

---

[17]Joseph Banks Lyle Journal, May 6, 1864; Hagood, *Memoirs*, 147.

[18]Bond and Coward, eds., *South Carolinians*, 137.

[19]Hagood, *Memoirs*, 148 (emphasis in original).

[20]Bond and Coward, eds., *South Carolinians*, 137; Report of Captain Edwin B. Dow, Sixth Maine Battery, O. R., vol. 36, part 1, p. 514.

[21]Hagood, *Memoirs*, 148. Apparently, Colonel Bratton filed no report on the action of May 6, 1864.

[22]Bond and Coward, eds., *South Carolinians*, 137.

[23]Freeman, *Lee's Lieutenants*, 3:366.

of the Wilderness.[24] Grant had lost almost 18,000 men compared to about 8,000 for the Confederates; in terms of numbers, Lee had soundly beaten him in their first head-to-head contest.[25] In spite of the casualty comparisons, however, Lee realized that his counteroffensive in the Wilderness had failed.[26] Unlike the Federal commanders who had preceded him, Grant would not pull back to regroup. Instead, he was determined to push on, maintaining the initiative no matter what the cost.[27]

By the close of the second day of the battle, Longstreet's brigades had pulled back to the same positions they occupied when they began the afternoon attack against the Federal breastworks. Along both sides of the Plank Road, Longstreet's troops shifted to the defensive. That night the men in Bratton's brigade hastily completed their own line of trenches in case they were attacked the following day. Unlike some other parts of the Wilderness battlefield, the woods where Bratton's men were positioned did not catch fire.[28]

The next day, May 7, there was only picket skirmishing between the opposing armies because neither side elected to renew the attack. That day General Lee named R. H. Anderson acting commander of First Corps, temporarily replacing the wounded Longstreet. During the first half of 1862, "Dick" Anderson had commanded what later became Jenkins' (now Bratton's) brigade.[29] The men in the brigade still had great affection for Anderson, a fellow South Carolinian. As he had ridden past them the day before to take over for the wounded Longstreet, the men rose to their feet and cheered Anderson. They were quickly silenced, however, because they could be heard in the Federal lines, so then they quietly tossed their hats in the air. Anderson came to a stop, removed his hat and thanked his old brigade; he and some of Bratton's men were moved to tears.[30]

Throughout May 7, General Lee received reports indicating that Grant was preparing to move his troops toward Spotsylvania Court House, some ten or twelve miles southeast of the Confederate right wing. To meet Grant's movement, Lee ordered Anderson to pull the men of First Corps out of their lines astride the Plank Road in the Wilderness

---

[24]Ibid., 3:371-372; Foote, *Civil War*, 3:182-184.

[25]Foote, *Civil War*, 3:188.

[26]Dowdey, *Lee's Last Campaign*, 174.

[27]Foote, *Civil War*, 3:189.

[28]Hagood, *Memoirs*, 149, 150 n.

[29]Although the brigade had undergone some changes, its nucleus was much as it had been in late 1861 under D. R. Jones. R. H. Anderson then took over from Jones at the beginning of 1862 and was in command of the brigade until he was promoted in July 1862. Micah Jenkins then led the brigade from that time until his death on May 6, 1864. From that date to Appomattox, the brigade was under the command of John Bratton.

[30]Freeman, *Lee's Lieutenants*, 3:374-375. Anderson had been born and raised in Sumter District, South Carolina.

and march them to Spotsylvania. Both Field's and Kershaw's divisions were to move after nightfall to a position in the rear where their men could rest for a few hours. They would then begin their march before three o'clock the next morning in order to beat Grant's infantry to Spotsylvania.[31] All during the day, Lee had his "pioneers" cut a two-mile road through the woods from the Plank Road due south to the Catharpin Road. This shortcut was designed to give Anderson's First Corps a chance to win the race for Spotsylvania.[32]

At about nine o'clock on the evening of May 7, after spending all day behind their earthworks on the north side of the Plank Road, Bratton's men received the order to pull back.[33] They were not, however, allowed the rest which Lee had planned for them. When Anderson saw the rough condition of the newly cut road through the woods, he decided to forego the rest period and start his two divisions immediately for Spotsylvania Court House. This wise decision turned out to be the chief reason that Lee was able to beat Grant to Spotsylvania the next day.[34]

Anderson started his two divisions, with Kershaw in the lead, down the newly cut road at eleven o'clock on the night of May 7.[35] Colonel Hagood, commanding the First Regiment in Bratton's brigade, wrote that the men were marched "at their utmost speed" all during the night and the pre-dawn hours of May 8.[36] An officer in the Palmetto Sharpshooters said Bratton's men were so exhausted that when the column halted to rest they would fall fast asleep and could hardly be awakened to resume the march.[37]

At sunrise on May 8, when Anderson and his two divisions were only about three miles from Spotsylvania Court House, he allowed his column to halt for breakfast and a short rest. After about an hour, the men fell in again and resumed their march, with Field's division still behind Kershaw's. About a mile and a half west of Spotsylvania Court House, Anderson was notified that General Fitzhugh Lee and his Confederate cavalry were being pressed hard by Federal infantry moving toward the village down the Brock Road; two of Kershaw's brigades were immediately dispatched to meet the threat. First Corps soon received word that a different Confederate cavalry unit, under General Thomas L. Rosser, was outnumbered and under attack by Federal cavalry at Spotsylvania Court House, where Anderson quickly sent Kershaw's two remaining brigades. By this time, Field's division was coming up, and

---

[31]Ibid., 3:378-379.
[32]Ibid., 3:377-378; Foote, *Civil War*, 3:192.
[33]Bratton's report, January 1, 1865, O. R., vol. 36, part 1, p. 1065.
[34]Dowdey, *Lee's Last Campaign*, 183; Foote, *Civil War*, 3:194; Freeman, *Lee's Lieutenants*, 3:380.
[35]Diary of First Corps, May 7, 1864, O. R., vol. 36, part 1, p. 1056.
[36]Hagood, *Memoirs*, 149.
[37]Lewis, *Camp Life*, 94.

Anderson divided it as well, sending one part to join the fight up the Brock Road and the other down to Spotsylvania Court House.[38]

Bratton's brigade was one of those dispatched by Anderson to Spotsylvania Court House to meet the Union cavalry. According to Bratton, he and his men arrived there at about ten that morning. In his report, Bratton wrote:

> [T]he enemy's cavalry [was] in possession of and between us and the Court House. My brigade formed on the right of the road and moved down to the Court House, the enemy retiring before us and abandoning the place without a fight.[39]

Bratton's men were given a hearty welcome by Rosser's outnumbered Confederate troopers who had been struggling to hold the village.[40] It was later learned that the Federal cavalrymen had been abruptly recalled, which explained why they abandoned the village. After the Union troopers had withdrawn, Anderson felt safe in ordering Bratton's men at Spotsylvania Court House to march some two miles northwest and reinforce Field's and Kershaw's other brigades which were fighting astride the Brock Road.[41]

Bratton quickly moved his brigade up the Brock Road and joined Anderson's other brigades in the line they had already established during the fighting that morning. When Bratton's men arrived, they took up positions on the right of Kershaw's brigade and were given a much needed rest of about two or three hours.[42] Their line was then subjected to a limited probing action by a Union reconnaissance force which was easily repulsed. According to Bratton, his troops inflicted about forty to fifty casualties while he lost only two or three men.[43]

At about five that afternoon, after marching down the Brock Road from the Wilderness, Federal troops began massing in front of the right part of Anderson's lines in preparation for a determined advance toward

[38]Freeman, *Lee's Lieutenants*, 3:380-384.
[39]Bratton's report on Spotsylvania, January 1, 1865, O. R., vol. 36, part 1, p. 1065.
[40]Bond and Coward, eds., *South Carolinians*, 141.
[41]Freeman, *Lee's Lieutenants*, 3:384-385; O. R., vol. 36, part 1, p. 1065.
[42]O. R., vol. 36, part 1, p. 1065. There has been some question as to whether Bratton's brigade went on the right of Kershaw's brigade, as Bratton states, or on the left. Freeman, *Lee's Lieutenants*, 3:384 n. 41. It appears from Captain Joseph Banks Lyle's Journal that Bratton is correct, and that the brigade was first put "on Kershaw's right" and was not moved to the left until the next morning "to take its place in our own [Field's] division – had been in McLaws' [Kershaw's]." Joseph Banks Lyle Journal, May 8-9, 1864. Bratton states the same thing in his report. O. R., vol. 36, part 1, p. 1066. It should be noted that, while Kershaw was in temporary command of McLaws' division, Kershaw's own brigade continued to fight in that division under Colonel J. W. Henagan. Kershaw's report on the Wilderness, O. R., vol. 36, part 1, p. 1061.
[43]O. R., vol. 36, part 1, p. 1065.

Spotsylvania.[44] The bluecoats then attacked in two lines, directing their main thrust toward the right part of Bratton's brigade "where they supposed there was no force to oppose them."[45] This was at the right end of the Confederate line, and the Union troops threatened to turn this flank and get behind Anderson's First Corps. Just then, however, Ewell's Second Corps arrived from the Wilderness. His lead division was immediately positioned on Bratton's right, along with one of Kershaw's brigades, in time to repulse this final Federal advance of the day.[46] After being repulsed, the Federals broke and began retreating to their lines. They were hotly pursued by Bratton's skirmishers, who succeeded in capturing some 125 prisoners.[47]

The only regiment in Bratton's brigade involved in this final Union assault on May 8 was Colonel Walker's Palmetto Sharpshooters, because his men were posted on the extreme right of the brigade. The Fifth South Carolina was not involved in fending off the final advance, but the regiment's pickets were kept busy all afternoon. After sundown, the regiment was moved to fill a gap between Kershaw's and Benjamin G. Humphrey's brigades.[48] Colonel Coward had been forced to leave the regiment because of the wound he had received two days earlier. Fearing possible gangrene if Coward remained in the less-than-sanitary conditions of the active battlefield, a surgeon had ordered him to a hospital in Richmond. Coward's man-servant, Charles, had packed a small trunk for the colonel and made up his own bundle for the trip, and the two men had taken the next train to Richmond.[49] Before he left, however, Coward had turned over the temporary command of the Fifth Regiment to Captain J. Banks Lyle, the senior captain.[50]

On the morning of the second day at Spotsylvania, May 9, Bratton's brigade was shifted to the left, across the Brock Road. It was put in the line on the right of Field's division, with the brigade's right resting on the road itself, while the left stretched toward the Po River.[51] The regiments were posted in line from right to left as follows: Palmetto Sharpshooters, Second Rifles, Sixth Regiment, First Regiment, and Fifth Regiment. The two left regiments, the Fifth and the First, were in the woods while the three on the right faced an open field.[52]

[44]Freeman, *Lee's Lieutenants*, 3:386.
[45]O. R., vol. 36, part 1, pp. 1065-1066.
[46]Ibid., 1065-1066; Freeman, *Lee's Lieutenants*, 3:386-387.
[47]O. R., vol. 36, part 1, p. 1066; Joseph Banks Lyle Journal, May 8, 1864.
[48]Joseph Banks Lyle Journal, May 8 and 9, 1864.
[49]Bond and Coward, eds., *South Carolinians*, 142.
[50]J. Banks Lyle to M. S. McArthur, May 11, 1864, Joseph Banks Lyle Letters; O. R., vol. 36, part 1, p. 1066. Lyle remained in command from May 6 to May 22, when Major Thomas C. Beckham returned to the regiment. Joseph Banks Lyle Journal, May 22, 1864.
[51]O. R., vol. 36, part 1, p. 1066.
[52]Ibid.

Bratton's men quickly constructed breastworks of pine trees, some so large that it took a whole company of men to lift them into place. A hundred yards in front of these log works, they dug rifle pits in which men from different companies took their turns at picket duty.[53] Late that afternoon, a line of Union troops advanced toward the brigade, but they were turned back several times by Bratton's pickets.[54]

When General Ewell's Second Corps had arrived from the Wilderness the day before, his troops began fortifying a large salient on the right of Anderson's First Corps. This salient, called the "Mule Shoe" because of its shape, had an apex which pointed roughly northeast, toward the Union lines, and was almost 1,200 yards wide at its base.[55] It was located several hundred yards to the right of Bratton's brigade which was drawn up on the immediate left of the Brock Road. On May 10, Grant's troops attacked the northwest side of the salient and broke the Confederate defenses there, but the lines were quickly restored.[56] Union soldiers also made several advances that day against the left and right parts of the lines held by Anderson's First Corps, southwest of the salient, but as Captain Lyle in the Fifth Regiment wrote:

> Our brigade was not heavily engaged [on May 10] and lost but lightly. Think that this arises from the fact that we have an open field in our front which the enemy are afraid to attempt to cross.[57]

Bratton's men spent the morning of May 11 improving the earthworks along their line.[58] While everyone expected to be attacked at any moment, there was no significant action anywhere along Lee's lines.[59] Bratton reported that while "the sharpshooting was incessant, nothing of importance transpired" until the next day.[60]

At dawn on May 12, thousands of bluecoats attacked the apex of the Mule Shoe, and the fighting raged in that area all day. At about nine that morning, between the Mule Shoe and the Po River, Warren's Corps of Federal infantry mounted a full-scale assault against Anderson's First Corps.[61] In his report, Bratton said, "The enemy assaulted us heavily, advancing beautifully in two lines of battle."[62] As the Union troops

---

[53]Mixson, *Reminiscences of a Private*, 74-75.
[54]Joseph Banks Lyle Journal, May 9, 1864.
[55]Freeman, *Lee's Lieutenants*, 3:393-394.
[56]Ibid.
[57]J. Banks Lyle to Dora McArthur, May 11, 1864, Joseph Banks Lyle Letters.
[58]Joseph Banks Lyle Journal, May 11, 1864.
[59]Freeman, *Lee's Lieutenants*, 3:397.
[60]O. R., vol. 36, part 1, p. 1066. See also, Joseph Banks Lyle Journal, May 11, 1864.
[61]Foote, *Civil War*, 3:222.
[62]O. R., vol. 36, part 1, p. 1066.

advanced closer, Bratton's pickets first formed a skirmish line and held the ground as long as possible. Then, as the pressure increased, they fell back from tree to tree, firing as they withdrew. Finally they heard the welcomed order, "Skirmishers, into the works," and they climbed over their breastworks with the enemy close behind.[63] Meanwhile, the rest of Bratton's men knelt behind their breastworks and waited in silence, watching the Federals advance. He said that he let the attackers get to within fifty yards before opening fire, and with the first volley, "a line of their dead was laid down across the entire front of my brigade."[64] The slaughter was terrible; according to Colonel Hagood, as soon as Bratton gave the signal to fire,

> our whole line blazed right away into the faces of the Yankee soldiers, shivering their regiments to atoms and hurling them back upon their own ground.[65]

At about noon the Federals attacked again along Anderson's front. This second assault was a little more to Bratton's left and was repulsed more quickly than the first. Men in Bratton's Fifth and First Regiments then leaped from behind their works and charged the broken bluecoat line, driving the Union troops in confusion.[66] Many of the retreating Union soldiers massed behind the crest of a hill which was several hundred yards in front of Bratton's brigade. When the South Carolinians from the First and Fifth Regiments got to the crest, they charged the Yankees with a yell. Bratton wrote that this "routed and put the whole mass to flight most precipitate and headlong" and resulted in the capture of "some 40 prisoners."[67]

As the Fifth Regiment rounded up the captured soldiers, Captain Lyle refused to allow his men to confiscate the prisoners' personal property. They responded by expressing their appreciation to Lyle and shook his hand; one prisoner told him:

> We like to meet gentlemen [and] are not ashamed to be captured by such men. Our best wishes Captain, and [we] truly hope you will come through safely.[68]

---

[63]Mixson, *Reminiscences of a Private*, 77.
[64]O. R., vol. 36, part 1, p. 1066.
[65]Hagood, *Memoirs*, 151.
[66]Joseph Banks Lyle Journal, May 12, 1864.
[67]O. R. vol. 36, part 1, p. 1066. Colonel Hagood's report of December 20, 1864, states that he and Captain Lyle advanced their skirmishers and captured some 17 or 18 Federals. O. R., vol. 36, part 1, p. 1069. Captain Lyle put the figure at 35 or 40 prisoners. Joseph Banks Lyle Journal, May 12, 1864.
[68]Joseph Banks Lyle Journal, May 12, 1864. The prisoners were from General George Syke's brigade of Federal regulars.

When the Union troops behind the crest were routed by the charge, those who had evaded capture panicked and ran across a portion of the open field directly in front of the remainder of Bratton's brigade. Completely exposed, the fleeing Federals were cut down by the South Carolinians, littering the field with dead and wounded.[69] In his report, Colonel Bratton wrote:

> In this battle [on May 12] I had about 1,250 muskets, and lost in killed and wounded not more than 15; prisoners none. We destroyed of the enemy in killed, wounded, and prisoners, in my judgment, at least 3,000. They left about 500 dead in my front, and it is known that they took many dead from the field.[70]

This last repulse ended the day's fighting along Bratton's section of the Confederate line, where the Union troops had clearly taken a beating.

Grant's massive assault at the apex of the Mule Shoe salient that same day was much more successful. His soldiers not only penetrated the Confederate works there, but they also got behind the famous "Stonewall" brigade, capturing almost that entire command. Once Grant's troops had broken the line, his reinforcements poured through the break and continued to press southward in an attempt to destroy all the Confederates in the salient.[71] Realizing the danger, General Lee quickly ordered a line of entrenchments prepared at the base of the Mule Shoe, where his men in the salient could be withdrawn to safety.

Shortly before sunset, Bratton and his brigade were pulled out of the lines on the left of the Brock Road and moved to the salient to relieve the exhausted troops of Ewell's Second Corps. Captain Lyle, leading the Fifth Regiment, recorded in his journal:

> About 5 p.m. we are double-quicked to our right – find this part of the field much confused – stragglers hunting their commands and telling of their deeds of valor, while at the same time they were singing the stragglers' wail. . . .[72]

The regiments in the brigade were immediately positioned to support the withdrawal of Ewell's troops from the upper part of the salient. Bratton's men then spent the night in trenches almost filled with water because it

---

[69]O. R., vol. 36, part 1, p. 1067.
[70]Ibid.
[71]Freeman, *Lee's Lieutenants*, 3:401-404.
[72]Joseph Banks Lyle Journal, May 12, 1864.

had rained all of the day and the night. Lieutenant Richard Lewis, in the Palmetto Sharpshooters, wrote:

> The Yankees [charged] us about 9 o'clock in the night, and I was wounded about that time. It was raining all night and I had an awful time – so dark I could not find the hospital. . . . [A] minie-ball . . . had passed through my wrist and lodged. The bone is terribly fractured, and I'm afraid I am ruined.[73]

Most of Bratton's men could see very little and did not even fire a shot, but they were under constant enemy fire. During the night they lost about 70 men, killed or wounded. Sergeant Frank Mixson, in Hagood's First South Carolina, recalled that the men all had dirty faces, and explained:

> Our hands and faces would get wet, and taking our cartridges out and biting off the stem we would get the powder on our hands and faces.[74]

At about daybreak Bratton's men withdrew to the new defensive line which had been constructed during the night at the base of the salient, about four hundred yards to the rear.[75]

On the morning of May 13, the brigade left the base of the Mule Shoe and returned to the rear of its former position on the Confederate left, where it was briefly held in reserve.[76] A few hours later, Bratton's men were moved forward into their old position in the line to the left of the Brock Road, but there was no fighting except by the pickets.[77] That night the men, many of whom had not taken off their accoutrements or shoes since the Battle of the Wilderness a week earlier, finally got some sleep.[78]

Bratton's men remained behind their breastworks for most of the next day, which was fairly quiet up until about three in the afternoon. Then they heard that the Union troops had withdrawn from their front. To test the reliability of this information, Bratton's skirmishers went forward and fired on the Federal works, provoking only a feeble reply. The

---

[73]Lewis, *Camp Life*, 93-94. Lieutenant Richard Lewis, from Anderson, South Carolina, recovered and returned to duty with Company B of the Palmetto Sharpshooters in September 1864. Three weeks later he was wounded and captured in a fight on the Darbytown Road outside of Richmond, and it became necessary to amputate his leg. He survived and was released at the end of the war.

[74]Mixson, *Reminiscences of a Private*, 79. Frank M. Mixson was a sergeant in Company E, First South Carolina Volunteers. He entered the war at age fourteen as a private. Ibid., 130.

[75]O. R., vol. 36, part 1, p. 1067.

[76]Ibid.; Joseph Banks Lyle Journal, May 13, 1864.

[77]Joseph Banks Lyle Journal, May 13, 1864.

[78]Mixson, *Reminiscences of Private*, 81.

skirmishers then charged the Federal line and found it only lightly defended by a few sentinels. As was suspected, the Union troops had withdrawn from this portion of the lines. According to Captain Lyle, the men in Bratton's brigade then proceeded to

> plunder the field. . . . Knapsacks, blankets, canteens, haversacks, etc., cover the ground – boys are loaded with "Yankee tricks" – think every man in our Brigade is supplied with a "tent shelter" – none of their dead had been buried, and the stench was becoming very offensive.[79]

That evening around midnight, the men were abruptly awakened and dispatched to the extreme right of the Confederate lines below Spotsylvania Court House. The following day, Sunday May 15, all was quiet along the lines as both armies took a day of rest. In the pre-dawn hours of the following day, Bratton's brigade again moved to the right about two or three miles where they erected earthworks but engaged in no fighting.[80]

Grant ordered another assault against the Confederate line at the Mule Shoe on May 18, but his troops were completely repulsed.[81] By then Anderson's First Corps was far to the right of the Mule Shoe, below Spotsylvania Court House, and was not involved in that action, although Bratton's men could clearly hear the fighting on their left.[82] J. D. McConnell, a first lieutenant in the Fifth Regiment, was in command that night of two companies which were digging a rifle pit in front of their lines. Whenever his men stopped work for a moment, they could hear Union soldiers in the dark, also digging close by. McConnell later wrote:

> Since our pit was nearly finished, I ordered Company "E" to fire [in the direction of the sound of digging] and Company "D" to fire at the flash of their return fire. We killed five, all in Zouave uniform.[83]

After that, there was no more fighting by Bratton's men, who left the area three days later.[84] Fortunately, most of their fighting had been done from behind protective breastworks, and their casualties had been very light.

---

[79]Joseph Banks Lyle Journal, May 14, 1864.
[80]Ibid., May 14, 15, and 16, 1864; O. R., vol. 36, part 1, p. 1067.
[81]Freeman, *Lee's Lieutenants*, 3:437-439.
[82]Joseph Banks Lyle Journal, May 18, 1864.
[83]McConnell, "Recollections," 9. McConnell was first lieutenant in command of Company E, Fifth S.C.V.
[84]Joseph Banks Lyle Journal, May 19, 20, and 21, 1864.

Grant's losses at Spotsylvania were estimated to have been more than 18,000, a substantial total by any standard, but especially so in light of his similar casualties at the Wilderness only a few days before.[85] At this time, Lee's army at Spotsylvania was in a strong defensive position behind protective breastworks, and it was obvious that repeated Union assaults against such heavily-defended positions had little or no chance of success. For Grant to retain the initiative, he would have to draw Lee's men out of their entrenchments at Spotsylvania and into the open. Grant decided to pull one corps out of his lines at Spotsylvania and start it south with orders to drive towards Richmond. If Lee followed with his army, Grant planned to attack before the Confederates had time to entrench.[86]

By May 21, it was apparent that Grant was again attempting to sideslip around Lee's right and get between the Army of Northern Virginia and Richmond.[87] Thus began another race between the two armies. Lee believed that Grant's next objective was Hanover Junction, some twenty-five miles to the south, where the railroad from Richmond to Fredericksburg connected with the Virginia Central Railroad, linking the capital city with the Shenandoah Valley. The Confederate commander fully intended to beat the Federals to Hanover Junction and quickly put his army in motion.[88]

The troops in Anderson's First Corps pulled out of their lines near Spotsylvania late on the afternoon of May 21. When they left, they moved to the Telegraph Road and then turned due south toward Hanover Junction.[89] Bratton and his men, assigned as the rear guard for First Corps, were again on the march, heading for their next battle. Unfortunately, they were being drawn ever closer to Richmond.[90]

---

[85]Dowdey, *Lee's Last Campaign*, 214. The Federals had suffered over 36,000 casualties at the Wilderness and Spotsylvania combined. William F. Fox, *Regimental Losses in the American Civil War, 1861-1865* (reprint; Dayton, Ohio: Morningside Bookshop, 1974), 541, 546. Lee had lost about half that many: 8,000 at the Wilderness and 10,000 at Spotsylvania. Foote, *Civil War*, 3:182-184; Dowdey, *Lee's Last Campaign*, 214.

[86]Grant to Meade, May 18, 1864, in John Y. Simon, ed., *The Papers of Ulysses S. Grant*, volume ten, January 1, 1864 to May 31, 1864 (Carbondale, Illinois: Southern Illinois University Press, 1982), 464.

[87]Freeman, *Lee's Lieutenants*, 3:496.

[88]Ibid.; Foote, *Civil War*, 3:241.

[89]Diary of First Corps, May 21, 1864, O. R., vol. 36, part 1, p. 1058.

[90]O. R., vol. 36, part 1, p. 1067.

Chapter 22

Falling Back Toward Richmond

A s Bratton and his brigade were heading toward Hanover Junction on the Telegraph Road, Colonel Coward was in his second week of furlough at home in Yorkville, trying to regain the use of his left arm. During his long train trip to Yorkville, Coward had plenty of time to ponder the events of the first two weeks in May. He had always been one to look forward to the next day, no matter how dark things seemed to be at the time. Now, however, he was having real doubts about what the future might bring; the prospects for the Confederacy did not seem good. He tried to attribute this despondency to his fever, but even when it abated, his gloom only began to intensify. Somehow, the Battle of the Wilderness had changed him; years later he wrote that the events of May 6 had robbed him of his youth.[1]

By the time Coward arrived in Yorkville, everyone in the village was still in a state of shock and grief over the death of Micah Jenkins. After a few days at home, Coward's arm began to improve but was still in a sling. The only information he could get on the movement and welfare of his men came from news reports in the Yorkville *Enquirer*. These indicated that Lee's Army of Northern Virginia, although vastly

---

[1]Bond and Coward, eds., *South Carolinians*, 141.

outnumbered by Grant, was holding its own but falling back toward Richmond. Coward sensed that this might be the final campaign of the war, and he was anxious to return to his men.[2]

Bratton's brigade, along with the rest of First Corps, had left Spotsylvania on May 21 and was hurrying south in the direction of Richmond. Colonel J. R. Hagood, commander of the First South Carolina, wrote:

> Hanover Junction was the goal for which the rival combatants now directed their course. . . . All the night of the 21st of May, and the best part of the next day, [we] toiled upon the arduous march before reaching the North Anna River, which was designed as our next defensive position.[3]

It was indeed a difficult march for Bratton's men; they walked almost continuously for nearly twenty-four hours, covering a distance of about the same number of miles. They acted as the rear guard for Anderson's First Corps, following the same route as Ewell's corps which had started earlier. The Union cavalry followed the column closely, but according to Bratton's report, "did not molest anybody; they rather aided us in driving stragglers before us."[4]

Lead elements of First Corps reached the North Anna River shortly after noon on May 22.[5] At sunset Bratton's brigade crossed the river over the Chesterfield Bridge, about two miles north of Hanover Junction. After crossing, his men marched on for about a mile and finally bivouacked for the night along the roadside about halfway between the railroad junction and the river.[6]

As was the case at Spotsylvania, Lee's army had won the race, arriving outside of Hanover Junction almost a day ahead of Grant. Anderson's First Corps was positioned in the center of Lee's lines, from the Chesterfield Bridge to Ox Ford, about a mile and a half up the North Anna.[7] Federal troops reached the Chesterfield Bridge on May 23 and, rather than attempting to cross, brought up their artillery and began shelling Anderson's corps on the opposite side.

Earlier that day Bratton had sent Colonel Hagood and the First Regiment back up to the North Anna to perform picket duty at the

---

[2]Ibid., 145-146.
[3]Hagood, *Memoirs*, 153.
[4]Bratton's report, January 1, 1865, O. R., vol. 36, part 1, p. 1067.
[5]Diary of First Corps, May 21-22, 1864, O. R., vol. 36, part 1, p. 1058.
[6]Hagood, *Memoirs*, 154.
[7]Freeman, *Lee's Lieutenants*, 3:497.

railroad bridge.[8] Hagood said that his men were shelled at about three in the afternoon but that very little damage was done. That night his men helped destroy the bridge and then rejoined the other four regiments in Bratton's brigade which had remained by the road just north of Hanover Junction.[9] The men in the brigade had already begun digging earthworks, using axes, boards and whatever tools they could find.[10]

Federal units were able to cross the North Anna on May 23 at Jericho Mills, several miles upriver from the Chesterfield Bridge, and A. P. Hill's corps could not force them back across the river. By the next morning, Union soldiers of Hancock's corps had also crossed the North Anna downriver from the Chesterfield Bridge.[11] Lee then arranged his lines into a large inverted "V," with the apex at Ox Ford; Hill's corps was on the left, Anderson's corps in the center, and Ewell's corps on the right. That section of the line along the south bank of the river at Ox Ford, held by part of Anderson's corps, was high ground where Lee had concentrated his artillery.[12]

After crossing the North Anna below the Chesterfield Bridge, Union troops began to probe the right part of Anderson's lines, and heavy skirmishing erupted in front of Bratton's brigade throughout the evening of May 24.[13] Men of different companies in the brigade took their turns on picket duty between their lines and the river. While Major Thomas C. Beckham was marching two companies of the Fifth Regiment out to picket duty during a blinding rainstorm, they arrived at a little bluff. The men in the front ranks could barely make out two regiments of bluecoats standing only about thirty yards away. Beckham had not yet seen them when he commanded "Forward," but his men in front quickly signaled the trouble to him. Beckham finally saw the enemy regiments, and one officer in Company E later wrote:

> [H]e waved his hand and we crawled back a little way, got to our feet again and made a run [for it]. We expected to be fired on, but the Yanks never saw us. . . . They might have mistook us for some of their own men because they were standing in the rainstorm.[14]

---

[8]Ibid; O. R., vol. 36, part 1, p. 1067.
[9]Hagood, *Memoirs*, 154.
[10]Joseph Banks Lyle Journal, May 23, 1864.
[11]Foote, *Civil War*, 3:269-270.
[12]Ibid., 3:272-273.
[13]Joseph Banks Lyle Journal, May 24, 1864.
[14]McConnell, "Recollections," 9. Beckham had returned to the regiment on the evening of May 22, 1864, and had taken temporary command in Coward's absence. Joseph Banks Lyle Journal, May 22, 1864.

By this time, the men in Bratton's brigade were exhausted from constant fighting and a lack of sleep. James S. Wingard, a private in Company F of the Palmetto Sharpshooters, wrote his brother on May 25:

> We have had but two nights' sleep in twenty-one, so you can imagine the state we are in. We have been almost fighting every day since the 6th of May. . . . We have undergone the most arduous and toilsome duties for the past twenty-five days that ever the human race was exposed to.[15]

The two wings of Grant's massive army were now on the south side of the river but were separated by Lee's inverted "V" alignment. For one Union wing to have gone to the aid of the other, it would have had to cross the North Anna twice; Grant reluctantly had to concede that Lee held the advantage. Captain J. B. Lyle's company was on picket duty at daylight on May 27, and he soon discovered that the Union troops to his front had withdrawn to the other side of the river.[16] Grant had corrected his mistake; in fact, the entire Union army had moved back to the north bank of the river.[17]

Grant then began another in his series of flanking movements around the Confederate right in an attempt to position his army between Lee's troops and Richmond. As Grant's force was moving southeast, along the opposite bank of the North Anna River, Lee once again began shifting his three corps to cover the approaches to Richmond.[18] Colonel J. R. Hagood concisely described the situation when he wrote that "the Army of Northern Virginia was now drawn back for the immediate defense of the Southern Capital."[19]

Bratton's men were pulled away from their lines outside Hanover Junction on the morning of May 27 and marched due south toward Richmond, which was only about twenty-two miles away.[20] They walked down the Richmond and Fredericksburg Railroad to a point about six miles below Ashland where they camped for the night. Late that afternoon some of Bratton's men saw General Lee ride by in his ambulance, and they learned that the general was not well.[21]

---

[15]J. S. Wingard to his brother, Simon Wingard, May 25, 1864, Simon P. Wingard Correspondence.
[16]Joseph Banks Lyle Journal, May 27, 1864.
[17]Foote, *Civil War*, 3:274-276; Freeman, *Lee's Lieutenants*, 3:498.
[18]Freeman, *Lee's Lieutenants*, 3:499.
[19]Hagood, *Memoirs*, 155.
[20]O. R., vol. 36, part 1, p. 1067.
[21]Joseph Banks Lyle Journal, May 27, 1864. Lee was so ill with an intestinal ailment that he had been unable to direct any offensive against Grant's army when it was divided and vulnerable on the south side of the North Anna River. Freeman, *Lee's Lieutenants*, 3:497.

Early the following morning, Anderson's corps was on the march again, with Field's division in the lead, headed east towards Atlee's Station on the Virginia Central Railroad. That night Bratton's brigade finally stopped to bivouac two miles east of Atlee's Station and some four miles south of the Pamunkey River.[22]

By this time, General Lee had positioned his three corps to block the approaches to Richmond from the Pamunkey River where he expected Grant would cross.[23] Anderson's First Corps was bivouacked between Hundley's Corners and Walnut Grove Church, in the vicinity of Totopotomoy Creek.[24] All during the afternoon and evening of May 28, Grant's infantry was crossing the Pamunkey River,[25] and Lee decided to strike before Grant could extend his left flank.[26]

On May 30, Lee ordered Ewell's Second Corps, led by Jubal Early, to attack Grant's left near Bethesda Church.[27] As Early's men moved to the right for the attack, Anderson's corps was shifted into their place. At about noon, Bratton's men moved into the Confederate line which ran a few hundred yards northeast of Gaines' Mill, within a cannon shot of where General Lee had won his first victory as commander of the Army of Northern Virginia two years before.[28] Bratton reported that after his brigade was put into position, the "[s]kirmishing on this line was severe, and [the] loss [in the brigade] was greater than usual."[29] Later that afternoon, when they attacked Grant's troops near Bethesda Church, the men in Early's Second Corps suffered a bloody repulse.[30] However, Anderson's First Corps, on Early's left, was not involved.

When Early's attack failed to prevent Grant from extending his lines to his left, it became obvious to Lee that the village of Cold Harbor, because of its converging roads, was Grant's next objective.[31] By this time both Lee and Grant were seeking reinforcements for the impending battle. Grant expected to gain some 16,000 troops coming up by boat from below Richmond, while Lee hoped to acquire 7,000 soldiers under the command of Major General Robert Hoke, who were coming up by rail from the area between Petersburg and Richmond. The question was which reinforcements would arrive at Cold Harbor first.[32]

---

[22]Joseph Banks Lyle Journal, May 28, 1864; O. R., vol., 36, part 1, p. 1067.
[23]Freeman, *Lee's Lieutenants*, 3:499. The North Anna merged with the South Anna about five miles southeast of Hanover Junction and became the Pamunkey River. Thus the Pamunkey was the next river between Grant's army and Richmond.
[24]Diary of First Corps, May 28, 1864, O. R., vol. 36, part 1, p. 1058.
[25]Foote, *Civil War*, 3:276-277.
[26]Ibid., 3:278-279; Freeman, *Lee's Lieutenants*, 3:502.
[27]Freeman, *Lee's Lieutenants*, 3:502.
[28]Joseph Banks Lyle Journal, May 30, 1864.
[29]O. R., vol. 36, part 1, p. 1067.
[30]Freeman, *Lee's Lieutenants*, 3:502.
[31]Ibid.
[32]Ibid., 3:504-505.

The Confederate reinforcements won the race; Hoke's division reached the Cold Harbor area on May 31, and Lee designed an offensive movement around Hoke's fresh troops.[33] That afternoon, Anderson's corps was pulled out of the lines above Gaines' Mill and shifted to the right until his men were on the immediate left of Hoke's division, which was aimed directly at the Cold Harbor crossroads. Exhausted by the previous day's fighting, Early's corps was now relieved by Anderson's men; the two corps simply swapped positions. Within Anderson's corps, Kershaw's division was on the right, connecting with Hoke, Pickett's division was in the center, and Field's division was on the left.[34]

With this shifting along the lines, Bratton's brigade was on the march most of the night, and he wrote:

> On the evening of May 31 we began to slide to the right, and continued to do so until we arrived upon what was afterward known as the Cold Harbor line. My position on this line covered the road from Mechanicsville to Old Church.[35]

When they reached their position on the extreme right of Field's division, a mile and a half west of New Cold Harbor, Bratton's men "immediately proceeded to entrench [their] position."[36]

Kershaw's division mounted an attack the next morning, June 1, and was supposed to be joined by Hoke's division. Hoke and his troops never joined in the attack, however, and it was completely repulsed.[37] Later in the day, after his reinforcements had finally arrived, Grant launched a furious counterattack, penetrating the Confederate line between Kershaw's and Hoke's divisions.[38] Kershaw desperately requested assistance from Field, who quickly sent three of his five brigades. Benning's and Bratton's brigades, however, were left in position to hold the lines.[39] By late in the day, the breach in the line had been repaired and the fighting had stopped.

---

[33]Ibid., 3:505-506; Dowdey, *Lee's Last Campaign*, 284-285.

[34]Dairy of First Corps, May 31, 1864, O. R., vol. 36, part 1, p. 1058; Freeman, *Lee's Lieutenants*, 3:506. Pickett's division had rejoined First Corps at Hanover Junction a few days before. Diary of First Corps, May 21-22, 1864, O. R., vol. 36, part 1, p. 1058.

[35]O. R., vol. 36, part 1, p. 1067.

[36]Hagood, *Memoirs*, 157.

[37]Freeman, *Lee's Lieutenants*, 3:506.

[38]Diary of First Corps, June 1, 1864, O. R., vol. 36, part 1, p. 1059.

[39]Field said that when Kershaw requested assistance, he was sent only the brigades of Law, Anderson and Gregg. Major General C. W. Field, "Campaign of 1864 and 1865," *Southern Historical Society Papers*, 14 (1886): 548-549. Thus Bratton's and Benning's were the two brigades which Field left in position to hold the lines.

The next day, June 2, no coordinated Federal attack was mounted, but heavy skirmishing continued along the lines of First Corps.[40] Grant's troops made several attempts against Bratton's section of the lines, and one of his regimental commanders wrote:

> These were in every instance repulsed with ease. . . .
> Half a dozen times a day these attacks were made which
> . . . made rest or composure impossible. The same
> programme was continued during the night until our want
> of sleep made us suffer anguish. . . .[41]

For several reasons, Grant was becoming impatient. If the war was allowed to drag on, an anti-war candidate might unseat Lincoln in the November election and end the conflict short of victory. In addition, many of Grant's troops served under enlistments which were due to expire in July, and Grant hated to risk losing these veterans before the conflict was ended. Finally, he was convinced that Lee's Confederates were suffering from lack of food and rest, and that their morale was low. Grant concluded that the time was right for a showdown engagement with Lee; he had Lee outnumbered by 109,000 to 59,000.[42]

At dawn on June 3, Grant launched a full-scale attack along the entire line at Cold Harbor. The main thrust of the Federal assault was at the Confederate right; especially hard hit were the men in what was called "Kershaw's salient," where the line had been breached two days earlier.[43] There were fourteen reported Union charges at Kershaw's salient that morning, each one repulsed with severe losses to the attackers.[44] The fighting on June 3 at Cold Harbor resulted in a massive defeat for Grant who had completely misjudged the status of Confederate morale, and who later expressed regret for having ordered the final charge.[45] During the battle, E. M. Law, leading his brigade at the Kershaw salient, was wounded just above his eye and was sent home to recuperate.[46] The "young Machiavelli" would never again return to Lee's Army of Northern Virginia.[47]

---

[40]Diary of First Corps, June 2, 1864, O. R., vol. 36, part 1, p. 1059.

[41]Hagood, *Memoirs*, 157.

[42]James M. McPherson, *Battle Cry of Freedom: The Civil War Era* (New York: Oxford University Press, 1988), 733-735.

[43]Freeman, *Lee's Lieutenants*, 3:508; Diary of First Corps, June 3, 1864, O. R., vol. 36, part 1, p. 1059.

[44]Diary of First Corps, June 3, 1864, O. R., vol. 36, part 1, p. 1059.

[45]Freeman, *Lee's Lieutenants*, 3:508; McPherson, *Battle Cry of Freedom*, 735.

[46]Field, "Campaign of 1864 and 1865," 549.

[47]Dowdey, *Lee's Last Campaign*, 157, 302. Orders were issued on January 7, 1865, relieving Law from duty with the Army of Northern Virginia at his request. Special Orders No. 5, O. R., vol. 46, part 2, p. 1019. On March 4, 1865, he was assigned to the cavalry under General Wade Hampton's command. Special Orders No. 53, O. R., vol. 47, part 2, p. 1320. Although he was recommended by Generals Hampton and Johnston for promotion, this apparently was never acted upon by Jefferson Davis or the

Grant's army lost some 7,000 men on June 3, compared to Confederate casualties of less than 1,500.[48] While the major part of the fighting was done along Kershaw's salient, the regiments in Bratton's brigade, several hundred yards to Kershaw's left, were engaged in heavy skirmishing along their lines. To his wife, Bratton wrote:

> On [June 3] Grant made a very stubborn and persistent attack on several points of our line, but was repulsed with great slaughter. . . . They did not attack our Brigade front . . . but we have been skirmishing pretty heavily for three days and our casualties are greater than those of any Brigade that was in the fight. . . .[49]

Company C of the Fifth Regiment was on picket duty in front of the lines at daylight on June 3, and the company's captain recorded in his journal:

> The enemy [was] upon us before we [were] aware of his approach – turned our right by driving the Virginians – fought him for a while hand to hand – swung back to save our flank – a hard picket fight.[50]

After the massive and repeated Federal assaults ended on June 3, there was only sporadic skirmishing along the lines. Grant's troops made a somewhat feeble assault, which was easily repulsed, on the Confederate left after dark on June 4.[51]

Following this fighting at Cold Harbor, which had even rattled windows in nearby Richmond, Grant decided to rest his demoralized men while he considered his next move.[52] Since the opening gun at the Wilderness on May 5, the Federals had lost some 65,000 men, killed, wounded or missing, and the competing armies had fought their way some fifty miles to the southeast during the full month of almost continuous combat.[53] They were like two old bull elk, their antlers locked

---

Confederate Congress. Johnston to Lee (Johnston's endorsement on Hampton's recommendation), April 1, 1865, O. R., vol. 47, part 3, p. 737. General Hampton addressed a note to "Brig. Gen. E. M. Law" on April 28, 1865, indicating that Law was never promoted to major general. O. R., vol. 47, part 3, p. 852. Additionally, there is nothing in Law's Compiled Service Records to show that he was ever promoted to major general. In spite of this, however, he was occasionally addressed after the war as though he had attained the rank of major general.

[48]Freeman, *Lee's Lieutenants*, 3:508; McPherson, *Battle Cry of Freedom*, 735.

[49]John Bratton to Bettie Bratton (undated), from the "Trenches near Mechanicsville, Tenn.," Bratton Letters. This letter, of course, was mailed from Virginia, not Tennessee, and was apparently written on June 5, 1864.

[50]Joseph Banks Lyle Journal, June 3, 1864.

[51]Ibid., June 4, 1864.

[52]Dowdey, *Lee's Last Campaign*, 298; Freeman, *Lee's Lieutenants*, 3:508.

[53]McPherson, *Battle Cry of Freedom*, 742.

in mortal combat with neither one being able to finish off the other; both were being gradually worn down.

The men in Bratton's brigade, like the other soldiers on both sides, badly needed a rest. Bratton himself wrote that he had not removed his boots but two nights since the Battle of the Wilderness.[54] During the lull in the fighting, some men in the brigade visited the old battlefield near Gaines' Mill where they had fought to victory two long years before. On June 9, one officer in Coward's regiment wrote:

> All day quiet – nothing from any section. Visited the old battlefield of Gaines' Mill – looked familiar, somewhat – the graves of our dead neglected, oats growing over them.[55]

With this time for reflection, no doubt Bratton's men pondered the irony of having to repeatedly fight in the same Virginia locations. If the soldiers did not consider it, surely the unfortunate local citizens who lived in those desolate areas anguished over it.

---

[54] John Bratton to Bettie Bratton (undated), apparently written June 5, 1864, Bratton Letters. A soldier in Bratton's brigade said, "We had not made down our beds nor even [taken] off our accoutrements. . . since the night before the Wilderness." Mixson, *Reminiscences of a Private*, 81.

[55] Joseph Banks Lyle Journal, June 9, 1864.

Chapter 23

Under Siege At Petersburg

A fter the failure of his massed assault at Cold Harbor, Grant realized the futility of trying to go through Lee's army to capture Richmond. The Union general then changed his strategy and decided to take Petersburg instead, thus cutting off the Confederate capital from its supply lines to the south.[1] In the face of Grant's vastly superior numbers, all Lee could do was await his adversary's next move; it came in only a matter of days. An officer in Coward's Fifth South Carolina at Cold Harbor wrote in his journal on June 13, 1864:

> Soon after day-break it is discovered that the enemy have left our entire front – are reported to be crossing the Chickahominy at Long Bridge and other bridges and fords far to our right. . . .[2]

The officer's report was accurate. Grant had secretly pulled his troops out of their lines at Cold Harbor on the night of June 12-13 and crossed the Chickahominy River on pontoon bridges. As had become his pattern

---

[1]Dowdey, *Lee's Last Campaign*, 314; Foote, *Civil War*, 3:300-301.
[2]Joseph Banks Lyle Journal, June 13, 1864.

in this campaign, Grant once again sideslipped his army to the southeast, around Lee's right.[3]

The next morning, when it was discovered that the Grant's army had disappeared from Cold Harbor, General Lee reacted quickly. According to the Diary of First Corps, "The troops are at once put in motion."[4] The three divisions of First Corps moved out early, crossing the Chickahominy River about three miles southwest of Gaines' Mill.[5]

The men in Bratton's brigade crossed over the river on "McClellan's Bridge" and then marched south through Seven Pines. Upon seeing the old battlefield, Captain Lyle, who had fought there with the Fifth Regiment in May 1862, wrote:

> Many places look familiar – McClellan's old works and ours peeping at each other, suspiciously, through the bushes – many parts of the field covered with bones, human and horse. . . .[6]

Bratton's troops then marched down the Charles City Road and bivouacked on June 13 near Frayser's Farm.[7] The next morning some of the men were allowed to walk over the old Frayser's Farm battleground. Captain Lyle recalled what had happened there two years earlier, and wrote:

> It was on this field that [R. H.] Anderson and [Micah] Jenkins won their batons. Here, our Brigade captured a fine six-gun battery, considered the finest in our service. You will remember that we lost four of the guns before Suffolk. . . . The little mounds, which are scattered everywhere over the field and which mark the graves of our dead, show at what price that battery was purchased.[8]

By now it appeared likely to the Confederates that Grant was moving his army to the south side of the James River for an attack against either Richmond or Petersburg. Not being certain of Grant's plan, however,

---

[3]Dowdey, *Lee's Last Campaign*, 317; Foote, *Civil War*, 3:314.
[4]Diary of First Corps, June 13, 1864, O. R., vol. 36, part 1, p. 1059. R. H. Anderson was still in temporary command of First Corps while Longstreet recuperated from his wound.
[5]Ibid.
[6]Joseph Banks Lyle Journal, June 13, 1864.
[7]Diary of First Corps, June 13, 1864, O. R., vol. 36, part 1, p. 1060; Hagood, *Memoirs*, 162.
[8]J. B. Lyle to Dora McArthur, June 14, 1864, Joseph Banks Lyle Letters. Lyle was referring to the capture of A. M. Randol's battery on June 30, 1862, at Frayser's Farm.

Lee could not commit his army until he was sure that the Federals would not turn due west and attack Richmond without crossing the James.[9]

On June 15, Lee began to receive more information on Grant's movements. His army had begun crossing the James on the night of June 14-15, and Hancock's entire corps was across by dawn. During the next two days, three other Federal corps crossed the river on a pontoon bridge at Wilcox's Landing.[10] Lee reacted by ordering Pickett's and Field's divisions across the James on June 16, but he kept about half his troops on the north side of the river in case they were needed to protect Richmond.[11]

Bratton and his men did not cross the James with Field's division on June 16. At Frayser's Farm the previous day, they were ordered to separate from the division, move down near the James River, and picket toward the river from the vicinity of Deep Bottom. They arrived at their designated position at about ten o'clock that evening and found no Union troops in the area except, in Bratton's words, "squads from [enemy] gunboats lying in the river."[12]

Pickett's division, followed by Field's, crossed the James before dawn on June 16.[13] They were ordered to clear the turnpike and railroad between Petersburg and Richmond, and to retake the "Howlett Line," a line of Confederate works across the Bermuda Neck which General Beauregard had been forced to abandon a few hours earlier when he pulled back to defend Petersburg.[14] By nightfall on June 16, Field and Pickett had reopened the roads between Petersburg and Richmond, but General Benjamin F. Butler's Union soldiers were still in control of the Howlett Line.[15]

Bratton's men finally crossed the river about midday on June 16 at Drewry's Bluff and rejoined Field's division late that afternoon.[16] They found Field's and Pickett's troops drawn up near the turnpike, preparing to advance against the Howlett Line. Bratton's men were put in the line near Kingsland Creek on the right of Field's division, east of and parallel to the turnpike, but by then it was dark. All Bratton could do was advance a line of skirmishers, but they did manage to take back a part of the line that evening.[17]

The next day, June 17, Pickett's and Field's divisions carried out a coordinated attack to retake the Howlett Line. They had little trouble in

---

[9]Foote, *Civil War*, 3:316-317; Freeman, *Lee's Lieutenants*, 3:529-530.
[10]Foote, *Civil War*, 3:427.
[11]Freeman, *Lee's Lieutenants*, 3:531.
[12]Bratton's report, January 1, 1865, O. R., vol. 40, part 1, p. 766.
[13]Diary of First Corps, June 16, 1864, O. R., vol. 40, part 1, p. 760.
[14]Foote, *Civil War*, 3:434-435; Freeman, *Lee's Lieutenants*, 3:531.
[15]Foote, *Civil War*, 3:435.
[16]O. R., vol. 40, part 1, p. 766.
[17]Ibid.; Joseph Banks Lyle Journal, June 16, 1864.

regaining most of the line until they came to a Union strongpoint at Mrs. Clay's Farm. Acting First Corps commander R. H. Anderson then ordered Field and Pickett to assault the position, but, for engineering reasons, Lee felt an attack unnecessary and issued countermanding orders. Only Field received the countermand, however, and Pickett's men proceeded with the assault. In spite of their orders, many of the men in Field's division could not resist getting into the fray as well.[18] Bratton reported that some, but not all, of his men had joined in the attack:

> About the middle of the day, the division made a sort of spontaneous charge, in which my skirmish line participated, and recovered and reoccupied the [Howlett] line that had been abandoned on the morning before.[19]

By mid-afternoon Field's and Pickett's divisions had retaken the entire Howlett Line, prompting Lee to send his congratulations to General Anderson.[20]

As darkness fell on June 17, the men in Bratton's brigade could hear heavy fighting from the direction of Petersburg, and they knew that the city was in grave danger.[21] Early that night, General Lee ordered Kershaw's and Field's divisions to Petersburg to reinforce the city's defenders.[22] Colonel Hagood of Bratton's brigade wrote:

> [Field's] Division marched about half the night [of June 17-18] and then went into bivouac. The next morning at daylight we were again on the road and at noon reached [Petersburg].[23]

When Bratton's men reached the city on June 18, they found the local citizens confused and afraid; however, they became increasingly hopeful with the arrival of each fresh Confederate unit. While under Jenkins' command, the men in the brigade had spent much of the previous summer in Petersburg before leaving for Tennessee, and they had made

---

[18]Freeman, *Lee's Lieutenants*, 3:532.
[19]O. R., vol. 40, part 1, p. 766.
[20]Freeman, *Lee's Lieutenants*, 3:532.
[21]Joseph Banks Lyle Journal, June 17, 1864.
[22]Foote, *Civil War*, 3:438.
[23]Hagood, *Memoirs*, 165.

many friends in the city. Colonel Hagood wrote that when they arrived on June 18,

> Jenkins' brigade was recognized by its old friends, [and] cheer after cheer was sent up whilst men and women rushed into [the] ranks to grasp by the hands their old acquaintances who had come back so opportunely to defend [their city]. . . .[24]

After passing through Petersburg, Bratton's troops marched south on the Jerusalem Plank Road until they reached the old line of fortifications called the Dimmock Line. They then moved several hundred yards to the right (west) of the road and were "put in position on the line [at] about Battery No. 34."[25] Bratton's men remained in this position until nightfall on June 18. He wrote:

> At dark we moved to the left and relieved [Bushrod Johnson's division] on the new line covering the Baxter Road, my left resting on the battery under which the enemy afterward sprung a mine.[26]

In the course of moving to this new line, which was done under the light of a moon, they were spotted by the Federals who opened fire with their artillery, wounding Lieutenant William T. Norris of the Fifth South Carolina.[27]

The new line was already laid out nearer the city, but almost nothing had been done to construct the works there until the arrival of Bratton's men.[28] Fully expecting the Union troops to mount an attack at any moment, the men labored the entire night digging earthworks. As they dug in the darkness, rifle fire broke out along the lines, leading them to believe the Federals were advancing, but no assault was made.

At daylight on June 19 all work had to be stopped because of enemy sharpshooters, but by that time Bratton's men had already completed a shallow trench.[29] In his report, he wrote:

> The enemy was found next morning well intrenched close to our front, and could sharpshoot us from two

---

[24]Ibid.

[25]Ibid.; O. R., vol. 40, part 1, p. 766.

[26]O. R., vol. 40, part 1, p. 766; see also, Joseph Banks Lyle Journal, June 18, 1864.

[27]Joseph Banks Lyle Journal, June 18, 1864. Norris was first lieutenant in Company C.

[28]Hagood, *Memoirs*, 166.

[29]Ibid., 166-167.

lines. We suffered for the first two days from this
advantage over us, losing heavily.[30]

That morning the Federal sharpshooters picked off Bratton's men with
deadly accuracy, and Colonel Hagood later wrote:

> [N]o man dared to show his head without an imminent
> risk of getting his brains shot out and all we could do was
> to lay upon our arms and await the return of night.[31]

By noon Hagood's regiment had lost two of its sentinels and a third had
been wounded.[32] All day Bratton's men were pinned down in their
trenches. Cramped and unable to move, they much preferred fighting in
an open field engagement.[33] Grant's troops did not advance upon this
section of the line that day, and the only fighting was between opposing
sharpshooters. By dark, however, Bratton's brigade had already lost
about 20 men killed and about half that number wounded.[34]
     That part of the defensive works occupied by Bratton's men extended
about a half mile on either side of Baxter Road, roughly several hundred
yards northeast of the Jerusalem Plank Road.[35] Constantly subjected to
enemy sharpshooting, they dug their trench deeper and deeper, until
finally it was six or seven feet deep in places.[36] By June 21, they had
settled into a torturing routine, trapped in their trench during the day
without even a tree for shade along the entire brigade line.[37] Not only
were they extremely confined, they were constantly exposed to the
broiling Virginia sun. They became accustomed to enemy shells and rifle
fire knocking dirt off the parapet onto their heads and backs, and they
were only really annoyed when the dirt fell into their dinner.[38] They had
very little water, most of it not fit to drink. Each day this trench duty
became more unbearable. Colonel Hagood described the unsanitary
conditions in detail:

> All the filth and offal, inseparable from a large collection
> of men, was here suffered to remain right in the lines
> because the enemy's fire prevented its removal, and

---

[30]O. R., vol. 40, part 1, p. 766.
[31]Hagood, *Memoirs*, 167.
[32]Ibid.
[33]Joseph Banks Lyle Journal, June 19, 1864.
[34]Ibid.
[35]O. R., vol. 40, part 1, p. 766; Hagood, *Memoirs*, 169. Baxter Road was also called Sussex Road.
Freeman, *Lee's Lieutenants*, 3:539.
[36]Hagood, *Memoirs*, 169-170.
[37]John Bratton to Bettie Bratton, July 2, 1864, Bratton Letters; Hagood, *Memoirs*, 172.
[38]John Bratton to Bettie Bratton, July 2, 1864, Bratton Letters.

> myriads of flies and other vermin . . . infested the neighborhood. . . . Day after day we remained in this miserable situation . . . until our energies and spirits lost their vigor and our very lives were regarded with indifference. Men who had been cautious in exposing themselves heretofore now grew reckless and hardly an hour elapsed during the day in which the enemy's sharpshooters did not bring down some unfortunate soldier.[39]

The Federal sharpshooters used "globe-sighted" rifles which were so accurate that they hardly ever missed. One of these marksmen shot a pig to the rear of Bratton's trenches, and when Private John Lambert jumped out to retrieve it, he was narrowly missed several times by long-range rifle fire.[40] So many of his men were shot by sharpshooters that Bratton wrote in his report, "There is the chill of murder about the casualties of this month. . . ."[41]

To make matters worse, the Union artillerymen also began lobbing mortar shells into the Confederate trenches. One captain in the Fifth South Carolina dreaded the Federal mortars, and wrote, "These [mortar shells] are lofted, and often fall immediately in our trenches, throwing men, guns . . . in every direction."[42] Colonel Coward, who by now had recovered from his wound and rejoined the Fifth Regiment at Petersburg, recalled that to avoid these mortar shells, the men dug small caves in the trench walls.[43]

The men could actually see a mortar shell once it was fired, and special lookouts were appointed to warn the men in that section of the trenches where the projectile was heading. In one incident, a mortar shell fell in the trench between the legs of Frank Mixson, a sergeant in Hagood's First South Carolina. Mixson was sitting on his oilcloth, which prevented the shell from burying in the dirt. The astonished sergeant picked up the shell, with its fuse burning, and threw it out of the trench.[44]

One night in late June, as Bratton's men were manning the trenches near the Baxter Road, a party of ten men, one from each company in the Fifth Regiment, slipped over the parapet to construct an abatis of

---

[39]Hagood, *Memoirs*, 172.

[40]Mixson, *Reminiscences of a Private*, 90, 93. Lambert, from Orangeburg, South Carolina, was a private in Company E of Hagood's First South Carolina. Frank Mixson, a member of Lambert's company, said, "It was one of the most marvelous feats, besides the most daring, of anything that I recollect happening." Ibid., 93.

[41]O. R., vol. 40, part 1, p. 767.

[42]J. B. Lyle to Dora McArthur, July 14, 1864, Joseph Banks Lyle Letters.

[43]Bond and Coward, eds., *South Carolinians*, 149.

[44]Mixson, *Reminiscences of a Private*, 100. Mixson said that it took him "a day or two to recover from the fright." Ibid., 101.

sharpened tree limbs in front of the line. Lieutenant Colonel John D. Wylie, who was leading the detail, decided that ten more men were needed to finish the job quickly. After the ten additional men came out to help, Union troops heard the noise in the darkness and fired on Wylie's detail, mortally wounding two men.[45]

Because of the extreme discomfort of extended trench duty, a system of periodic relief was arranged. Each brigade in Field's division was relieved every four days and allowed two days of rest.[46] The first relief of Bratton's men came on June 24 when they were pulled back about half a mile to a ravine behind the lines and were allowed to bathe in the nearby Appomattox River. One of Bratton's regiments, however, did not get much rest. The Palmetto Sharpshooters were sent to General Hoke to reinforce a part of his lines against which an assault was expected. Fortunately, no such assault occurred, and Walker's men were allowed to rejoin the brigade. On June 28, Bratton's men reluctantly resumed their duty in the trenches at their old position astride the Baxter Road.[47]

By the end of June, thirty-three-year-old Colonel John Bratton had finally received his appointment to brigadier general.[48] The make-up of his command did not change; his brigade still included the same five South Carolina regiments which had

BRIGADIER GENERAL JOHN BRATTON, SHOWN HERE BEFORE HIS PROMOTION TO COLONEL IN 1862.

fought together continuously under Jenkins and Bratton since the summer of 1862: the First South Carolina (Colonel J. R. Hagood), the Second Rifles (Colonel R. E. Bowen), the Fifth (Colonel A. Coward), the Sixth (Colonel J. M. Steedman) and the Palmetto Sharpshooters (Colonel J. Walker).[49]

---

[45]McConnell, "Recollections," 9; J. B. Lyle to Dora McArthur, June 22, 1864, Joseph Banks Lyle Letters. The two men were J. C. Jennings and Oliver Goudelock of Company C. Joseph Banks Lyle Journal, June 21 and 22, 1864.

[46]Hagood, *Memoirs*, 171.

[47]O. R., vol. 40, part 1, p. 766; Joseph Banks Lyle Journal, June 24, 1864.

[48]John Bratton to Bettie Bratton, July 2, 1864, Bratton Letters; Freeman, *Lee's Lieutenants*, 3:549-550; Special Orders No. 151, June 27, 1864, O. R., vol. 40, part 2, p. 694.

[49]The only change in the brigade since 1862 was that Colonel Gary's Hampton Legion had transferred to the cavalry in March, 1864, while Jenkins was still in command. Freeman, *Lee's Lieutenants*, 3:549.

On the evening of July 1, Captain J. B. Lyle was asleep in the Petersburg trenches when he heard shouting above him. He found that several men from the Palmetto Sharpshooters were talking with Union soldiers across the lines. Lyle wrote that some of the men even "exchanged papers" with the enemy, and he added:

> Captain Moore [was] arrested for the act – our [men were] ordered down from the parapet and we [were] soon "popping away" again. . . .[50]

July 4 came on a Monday, and the Federals put on a big celebration which was clearly visible from the Confederate lines.[51] Four days later General Lee ordered the troops all along his lines to make what the First Corps' diarist described as, "something of a Chinese demonstration in the way of shooting and artillery firing to ascertain the enemy's strength."[52] After the artillery bombardment stopped, the Confederate troops gave a cheer as though they were going to attack. General Bratton wrote that this demonstration "created quite a commotion in the Yankees' lines. . . ."[53] Afterwards, he found that a Federal shell, which had failed to explode, had landed in his tent.[54]

By mid-July it had become clear that Grant was reluctant to risk a conventional frontal assault against Lee's defensive works around Petersburg. Union soldiers, however, had begun digging a mine shaft all the way from their lines to beneath the Confederate trenches. By July 21 the Federal digging could be heard under the portion of the Confederate line then occupied by General Stephen Elliott's South Carolina brigade, which was a part of Bushrod Johnson's division.[55] Elliott's and Bratton's brigades rotated in relief of each other along this portion of the lines during part of June and most of July.[56] Grant planned to blow the mine and assault the Confederate lines at that point, taking advantage of the confusion caused by the explosion.

As a diversion for his mine attack at Petersburg, Grant assembled certain units of his infantry on the north bank of the James River, creating a new threat to Richmond. This left General Lee no choice but to

---

[50]Joseph Banks Lyle Journal, July 1, 1864. Captain James P. Moore, commanding Company H, Palmetto Sharpshooters, was the officer arrested. There is no indication in the records of how the matter was resolved.

[51]Joseph Banks Lyle Journal, July 4, 1864.

[52]Diary of First Corps, July 8, 1864, O. R., vol. 40, part 1, p. 761.

[53]John Bratton to Bettie Bratton, July 9, 1864, Bratton Letters.

[54]Ibid.

[55]Freeman, *Lee's Lieutenants*, 3:541.

[56]O. R., vol. 40, part 1, p. 767.

transfer several of his divisions from Petersburg to the north side of the James.[57]

Field's division was one of those dispatched toward Richmond, and Bratton's men were pulled out of the Petersburg trenches on July 28. The next morning they were taken by train from Petersburg to Rice's Station just south of Richmond, and that afternoon they marched across the James River at Drewry's Bluff. Bratton reported that on the morning of July 30 they were sent to the vicinity of Fussell's Mill to meet an expected Federal advance which did not materialize. Later that day the brigade moved up to the Confederate line of works at New Market Heights, east of Richmond, where it was put into position, "with its right resting on Four-Mile Creek."[58]

When Grant learned that several Confederate divisions had been shifted to north of the James, he knew that his diversion had worked; the time was right to blow the mine and assault the weakened Confederate lines at Petersburg.[59] The mine shaft ran for almost 500 feet from the Federal lines to directly underneath the Confederate trenches, where Union soldiers had dug a huge chamber and filled it with 320 kegs of black powder.[60]

The mine exploded with devastating effect shortly before five o'clock on the morning of July 30, only a day and a half after Bratton's brigade had pulled out of the section of the Confederate line where the explosion occurred.[61] At the time of the explosion, the trenches immediately above it were occupied mainly by the South Carolina troops in Stephen Elliott's brigade. General Bushrod Johnson reported that in Elliott's brigade,

> five companies of the Twenty-second South Carolina . . .
> were blown up. The Eighteenth South Carolina [also]
> . . . had four companies blown up or destroyed by the
> falling earth.[62]

Colonel Hagood, in Bratton's Brigade, wrote that the explosion occurred only 100 yards from where his regiment had been positioned before it was shifted to north of the James River.[63] Colonel Coward recalled later

---

[57]McPherson, *Battle Cry of Freedom*, 759; Freeman, *Lee's Lieutenants*, 3:542.
[58]O. R., vol. 40, part 1, p. 767. Bratton reported that his brigade lost 53 men killed and 72 wounded in the trenches at Petersburg before leaving on July 28, 1864. Ibid.
[59]Foote, *Civil War*, 3:533.
[60]Freeman, *Lee's Lieutenants*, 3:542-543.
[61]Foote, *Civil War*, 3:535.
[62]Report of General Bushrod Johnson on the Battle of the Crater, August 20, 1864, O. R., vol. 40, part 1, p. 788. Elliott's brigade was in General Johnson's division. Johnson said the mine exploded "about 200 yards north of the Baxter Road." Ibid., 787. This is where the left part of Bratton's brigade had been positioned for much of June and July 1864. O. R., vol. 40, part 1, p. 766.
[63]Hagood, *Memoirs*, 173.

that prior to being moved, his Fifth Regiment had been in position "directly over the mine."[64]

The explosion ripped a huge crater, almost thirty feet deep, which created a break in the Confederate lines.[65] Grant's troops, however, were unable to fully exploit the breach. By one o'clock in the afternoon, Lee's troops around the breach had evicted the bluecoats from the works, restored the line and won the Battle of the Crater. Grant lost some 3,500 men killed or wounded, compared to Confederate casualties of about 1,500.[66] Of the Confederate losses, 698 were in Elliott's brigade alone.[67] Had Bratton's men been left in position in the Petersburg trenches rather than being sent north of the James, it is likely that they would have suffered similar casualties from the explosion.

The Federals' overall strategy for the battle[68] was accurately described several days later by a member of the Palmetto Sharpshooters, who wrote:

> The Yankees made a demonstration [on the north side of the James on July 27 and 28], and our Division, and others, were brought over to meet them, but I think it was only a feint to draw our forces from Petersburg and enable them to carry our works there. . . .[69]

Grant was extremely disappointed with his army's failure to break the Petersburg defenses and felt that a golden opportunity to destroy Lee's army had been wasted.[70]

While other Confederate divisions north of the James River had returned to Petersburg by August 1,[71] Field's division remained in its position at New Market Heights, between Deep Bottom and the old Frayser's Farm battlefield.[72] For the first two weeks in August, the men in Bratton's brigade were posted on the extreme left of Field's division, performing rotating picket duty without Federal interference. Colonel Hagood said:

> These were the first days of anything approaching a state of rest which it had been our privilege to enjoy

[64]Bond and Coward, eds., *South Carolinians*, 156.
[65]O. R., vol. 40, part 1, p. 788.
[66]Freeman, *Lee's Lieutenants*, 3:542-543; Foote, *Civil War*, 3:535-537.
[67]O. R., vol. 40, part 1, p. 793.
[68]See Foote, *Civil War*, 3:533.
[69]H. C. Conner to Ellen Conner, August 4, 1864, Henry Calvin Conner Papers.
[70]McPherson, *Battle Cry of Freedom*, 760.
[71]Field, "Campaign of 1864 and 1865," 551; Hagood, *Memoirs*, 173.
[72]O. R., vol. 40, part 1, p. 767.

Richards, of Coward's Company D, was shot through the head.
Lieutenant McConnell described what happened:

> [Richards'] hat was knocked off but he reached down and
> clapped it back on his head, although he was dead when
> Captain [James T.] Douglas[s] grabbed him by the arm an
> instant later.[87]

For a short time the fighting was desperate as Coward's men charged
headlong into the bluecoats' fire. Before his troops reached the works,
their regimental colors went down twice, but they were never captured.
The men finally reached the works, jumped over and started after the
fleeing Federals, but Coward alertly called his troops back.[88] Lieutenant
McConnell recalled that Private Tate McDaniel picked up an abandoned
Yankee haversack and was showing off its contents, "when a cannon ball
took his head off."[89] Coward saw it happen and said that he witnessed
McDaniel crumple to the ground with his entire head gone except for his
bottom teeth.[90] After the shooting finally stopped at White's Tavern on
August 16, the men in the Fifth Regiment saw a horrifying sight,
described later by Lieutenant McConnell:

> I saw a wounded Yankee stark naked with his bowels
> protruding from his wound. He must have stripped
> himself in his agony. He asked me to have him taken
> back.[91]

That night, as Coward's regiment was returning to Bratton's brigade
through a pine thicket, a Federal shell exploded in Company H, "cutting
off the legs of Captain Comer. . . ."[92] According to Colonel Coward,
during this Battle at White's Tavern, which some called the Battle of
Fussel's Mill,[93] the Fifth Regiment lost 7 killed and 20 wounded in the
day's fighting.[94]

---

[87]Ibid. From Union, South Carolina, Hiram Richards had once been a cadet at the Kings Mountain
Military School. Bond and Coward, eds., *South Carolinians*, 152.

[88]McConnell, "Recollections," 10.

[89]Ibid. The soldier was Private William Tate McDaniel of Company E, Fifth Regiment. Salley, *South
Carolina Troops, Fifth S.C.V.*, 3:153.

[90]Bond and Coward, eds., *South Carolinians*, 152.

[91]McConnell, "Recollections," 10.

[92]Ibid. This was Captain Thomas Comer, of Company H, Fifth Regiment, whom Coward called "my
big man." He had just returned from home, where he had recovered from being injured by a falling tree
at Bean's Station, Tennessee, the previous December. Bond and Coward, eds., *South Carolinians*, 152.

[93]J. F. J. Caldwell, *The History of a Brigade of South Carolinians, Known First as "Gregg's," and
Subsequently as "McGowan's Brigade"* (Philadelphia: King & Baird, Printers, 1866; reprint, Marietta,
Georgia: Continental Book Co., 1951), 178.

[94]Record of Events Cards for the Fifth S.C.V., Field and Staff, July-August 1864.

While the Fifth Regiment and the Second Rifles were fighting at White's Tavern, the other three regiments in Bratton's brigade remained behind to defend the lines which had been formerly occupied by Field's entire division. So many of Field's troops had been taken out and sent to the fight near White's Tavern that the line was left too thinly manned. Colonel Hagood described trying to defend the line with such a small force:

> [I]t was . . . necessary to double-quick incessantly up and down the works in order to keep opposite to the parties of the enemy which quite as incessantly attacked us. Fortunately these parties consisted only of skirmishers and we were, therefore, enabled to hold our ground until the return of the troops which had been sent to our left.[95]

When his line was broken on August 16, the situation had looked so bleak to Field that he thought nothing but a miracle could save his men. By the end of the day, however, the breach had been repaired and the Confederate works retaken. Coward and his Fifth Regiment had played a significant part in restoring the broken line. Field said later that not many people realized how much danger Richmond was in that day, and that too few appreciated the importance of the Battle at White's Tavern.[96]

After the fighting on August 16 there was only minor skirmishing along Bratton's part of the lines from New Market Heights down to Chafin's Bluff, and the next four days were passed in relative quiet. Then on the night of August 20, most of the Union troops facing Field's lines pulled out and recrossed the James River.[97]

While Field's division was still manning the Richmond outer defenses north of the James River, Grant's army succeeded in capturing a section of the vital Weldon Railroad, about two or three miles south of Petersburg. In battles at Globe Tavern on August 21, and at Ream's Station on August 24, the Confederates failed to reopen the railroad line.[98] Being forced to fight on both sides of the James had simply spread Lee's army too thin.

At about noon on August 24 Bratton's brigade received orders to return to Petersburg, along with one other brigade in Field's division. They crossed the James later that afternoon at Drewry's Bluff, boarded trains at Rice's Station about sunset, and arrived at Petersburg well after

---

[95]Hagood, *Memoirs*, 175-176.
[96]Field, "Campaign of 1864 and 1865," 553, 555. In his report Bratton said that he had been informed that the Fifth and the Second Rifles had "rendered most effective assistance in driving the enemy away and recovering our line." O. R., vol. 42, part 1, p. 878.
[97]Hagood, *Memoirs*, 176; Joseph Banks Lyle Journal, August 20, 1864.
[98]Freeman, *Lee's Lieutenants*, 3:588-589.

dark.[99] Most of the men mistakenly believed that they had been sent
back there to help drive Grant's troops from the Weldon Railroad,[100] but
the brigade was merely held in reserve near "the lead works" at
Petersburg for several days.[101] Afterwards, instead of returning to duty
in the trenches outside the city, the brigade was employed in the
construction of defensive works on Indian Town Creek between the
Weldon Railroad and the Boydtown Plank Road.[102]

Meanwhile, the National Democratic Convention, which had met in
Charleston four years earlier, convened in Chicago on August 29, 1864,
and the delegates selected General George McClellan as the party's
presidential nominee. He ran on a peace platform, suggesting that the
North's war effort had been a failure. Southerners' hopes for McClellan's
election, as a possible avenue toward a negotiated peace, were dashed
two days after the convention adjourned when Sherman captured
Atlanta.[103] This news came as a blow to the men in Bratton's brigade,
prompting an officer in the Palmetto Sharpshooters to write, "Atlanta has
gone at last, which is decidedly discouraging. . . ."[104] Similarly, Captain
Lyle in the Fifth Regiment, wrote:

> [It is] rumored that [General John B.] Hood has been
> forced to fall back from Atlanta – gave me the blues. . . .
> [A]ll are satisfied that we are not to have peace without
> much more fighting.[105]

While working on the fortifications at Indian Town Creek, the men in
Bratton's brigade were frequently shelled by Grant's artillery. On one
occasion a shell exploded near a group of men in Company E of the Fifth
Regiment, and one of them later wrote:

> Snoddy Lowry was sleeping in the shade of the works
> one day when a mortar shell burst so near that he was
> buried. He got mad when the boys [who dug him out]
> said that they were resurrecting him.[106]

[99]Joseph Banks Lyle Journal, August 24, 1864; Hagood, *Memoirs*, 177; H. C. Conner to Ellen Conner, August 26, 1864, Henry Calvin Conner Papers. Bratton, in his report, erroneously states that he moved back across the James on August 22. O. R., vol. 42, part 1, p. 879.
[100]Joseph Banks Lyle Journal, August 24, 1864.
[101]O. R., vol. 42, part 1, p. 879.
[102]Hagood, *Memoirs*, 177.
[103]Catton, *Centennial History*, 3:382-383; McPherson, *Battle Cry of Freedom*, 772-773.
[104]J. W. McLure to Kate McLure, September 5, 1864, McLure Family Papers.
[105]Joseph Banks Lyle Journal, September 4, 1864.
[106]McConnell, "Recollections," 11. The soldier buried was apparently Private James Lowry, a conscript in Company E, Fifth Regiment. Salley, *South Carolina Troops, Fifth S.C.V.*, 3:152.

In the middle of September, General Wade Hampton's cavalry raided a group of Grant's men herding the Union army's cattle south of the James River. Hampton's troopers won the skirmish and took some 2,500 head of cattle back to Petersburg to feed the hungry Confederate soldiers there. The cows arrived in Petersburg on September 18, much to the delight of the men in Bratton's brigade.[107] Palmetto Sharpshooters' Lieutenant Richard Lewis wrote that the men in the regiment had bountiful rations, and said they had been "feasting lately on some of the fine beeves Hampton drove in from Grant's range. . . ."[108]

LIEUTENANT GENERAL
WADE HAMPTON

By this stage of the war, desertion was becoming a problem for the Confederate army, and Bratton's brigade was not immune. The army generals felt that strong measures were needed to deter further desertions. On September 19, Bratton's brigade was called out to witness the execution by firing squad of Private J. J. Strickland, a deserter from Company K of Colonel Hagood's First Regiment. Captain Lyle, who witnessed the execution, wrote that it was "badly done," because Strickland "was not killed by the first volley, and the reserve . . . had to finish the work."[109]

Bratton's men remained camped at Petersburg on Whitworth's farm until September 29, working on the defensive fortifications along the Squirrel Level Road and constantly marching to different locations to meet anticipated Federal movements.[110] They did not engage in any real fighting, however, and on September 25, one soldier in the Palmetto Sharpshooters wrote that "everything is remarkable [*sic*] quiet here at this time. . . ."[111]

During the waning days of that summer of 1864, Colonel Coward had begun to notice a distinct change in the men in his Fifth Regiment. No longer did they sit around their night fires and joke; they had become

---

[107]Joseph Banks Lyle Journal, September 18, 1864.
[108]Lewis, *Camp Life*, 97.
[109]Joseph Banks Lyle Journal, September 19, 1864.
[110]Hagood, *Memoirs*, 178; O. R., vol. 42, part 1, p. 879.
[111]H. C. Conner to Ellen Conner, September 25, 1864, Henry Calvin Conner Papers.

quieter.[112] As October approached, morale was indeed slipping for the men in Bratton's brigade, and for good reason. They had been under siege at Petersburg for almost three months, except for the time they spent defending Richmond's outer line, and siege warfare was enough to dampen even hardy spirits. By cutting the Weldon Railroad, Grant had tightened his grip on Petersburg, and his well-supplied army was growing in numbers each day. Atlanta had just fallen to Sherman, and there was very little to stop his troops from marching into South Carolina. Simply stated, the Confederate military situation was not one to cause optimism, and Lee's men, from privates to generals, knew it. One of the officers in the Palmetto Sharpshooters captured the mood of the men as he wrote to his wife, "A mantle of darkness for the present overhangs our beloved Confederacy."[113]

---

[112]Bond and Coward, eds., *South Carolinians*, 153.
[113]J. W. McLure to Kate McLure, September 25, 1864, McLure Family Papers.

Chapter 24

Virginia: The Fall Of 1864

I n late September of 1864, General Grant continued to take full advantage of his army's numerical superiority. He planned a massive one-two punch, with one blow to be landed a few miles east of Richmond, and the other against the Southside Railroad, southwest of Petersburg. Employing the same diversionary tactic as he had used in setting up the mine attack two months earlier, Grant first struck north of the James River. This move caused Lee to strip a part of his defensive lines below Petersburg and send troops north to meet the new threat to the Confederate capital.[1]

Grant initiated the operation by sending General Benjamin F. Butler's Union troops to the north side of the James River on September 28 to attack Forts Harrison and Gilmer. These were two important defensive fortifications on Richmond's outer line, and they also protected Lee's works at Chafin's Bluff on the James River, only eight miles southeast of the city.[2] The surprise attack of September 29 against Fort Harrison, held only by a small Confederate garrison, was a success, and Butler's men quickly occupied the fort. They then moved almost two miles north and attacked Fort Gilmer, which they failed to capture.

---

[1] Foote, *Civil War*, 3:560-561.
[2] Ibid., 3:560; Freeman, *Lee's Lieutenants*, 3:590.

Once Fort Harrison fell into Union hands, it became an immediate threat to Lee's works at Chafin's Bluff, considered the "watergate" of Richmond.[3] The Confederate War Department quickly decided that the fort would have to be retaken. Both Field's and Hoke's divisions, along with one of Pickett's brigades and a division of cavalry, were sent to the north side of the James to mount the attack.[4]

On the same day that Butler's troops captured Fort Harrison, Lee summoned General Field to headquarters and showed him the telegram stating that the fort had fallen. Under Lee's orders to proceed immediately to Chafin's Bluff, Field pulled his division away from Petersburg and began moving his troops to the north side of the James.[5] As part of Field's division, Bratton's men left Petersburg on the morning of September 29 and by three that afternoon had crossed the James.[6] Once across the river, Field's division, including the men in Bratton's brigade, marched not to Fort Harrison but to Fort Gilmer, which was still under attack.[7] They did not reach Fort Gilmer until sunset, however, and by then the Federal attack there had already been repulsed.[8]

That night General Field decided to attack Fort Harrison, some two miles away, and he moved Bratton's, William F. Perry's and G. T. Anderson's brigades into position for the assault.[9] Captain Lyle, of Coward's regiment, wrote:

> After dark, Anderson's and our brigades are moved back to the rear of Fort Harrison – are arranged for an assault on the Fort about 2 a.m. – when just ready to move on the work, the movement is stopped, and we return to the left and rest in the immediate rear of [Fort Gilmer].[10]

The night attack had been called off by acting First Corps commander R. H. Anderson. Field said later that he believed the attack should have been allowed to proceed that night.[11] He may well have been right.

[3]Freeman, *Lee's Lieutenants*, 3:590.
[4]Ibid.
[5]Field, "Campaign of 1864 and 1865," 555.
[6]Joseph Banks Lyle Journal, September 29, 1864.
[7]Hagood, *Memoirs*, 179. In his report Bratton said that they crossed the James at Drewry's Bluff, got on the Osborn Turnpike, and marched north towards Fort Gilmer. Bratton's report, January 1, 1865, O. R., vol. 42, part 1, pp. 879-880.
[8]Field, "Campaign of 1864 and 1865," 556.
[9]Ibid. Colonel William Flank Perry was in command of E. M. Law's brigade after Law was wounded at Cold Harbor on June 3, 1864.
[10]Joseph Banks Lyle Journal, September 29, 1864. In Bratton's report, he stated, "We . . . were [already] making dispositions to attack [Fort Harrison] when orders came to move [back] to the rear of Fort Gilmer and rest." O. R., vol. 42, part 1, pp. 879-880.
[11]Field, "Campaign of 1864 and 1865," 556.

The assault on Fort Harrison was then scheduled for the following day, September 30. The plan called for a coordinated attack at two o'clock that afternoon, with portions of Hoke's and Field's divisions making up separate assaulting columns; Hoke's men were to attack one face of the fort, and Field's men another. The attack was to be preceded by a thirty-minute artillery bombardment, after which Hoke's and Field's men were to rush the fort. Hoke's column, attacking on Field's right, would be led by a brigade, with a second brigade one hundred yards to the rear. Field's column was to be led by G. T. Anderson's brigade, with Bratton's brigade following at the same interval. It was critical to the success of the attack that the two Confederate columns assault the fort simultaneously. Unfortunately, this did not happen.[12]

A few minutes before two o'clock, Hoke's lead brigade was already in position to begin its assault, only about a hundred yards from the fort. Field's lead brigade, G. T. Anderson's, was much farther from the fort and had a greater distance to cover than Hoke's brigades. To correct this problem, Field ordered Anderson to move his men closer to the fort, and have them lie down to await the signal to begin the simultaneous assault. Anderson, however, failed to explain this preliminary movement to his men, and when they were told to move forward, merely to get into position, they thought they were being ordered to start the attack. Thus, instead of stopping to await the signal to begin the assault, Anderson's men began the attack on their own.[13]

When he saw that Anderson's men were going in prematurely, Field immediately ordered Bratton's brigade to join the assault by attacking in line behind Anderson. Bratton's men, however, were still several hundred yards away from the fort. Anderson's failure to halt his men before beginning the assault had deprived Bratton's troops of the time they needed to move up in support. Bratton had no choice but to rush his men forward, and in his report, he complained:

> To give my promised support . . . it was necessary for my brigade to file out at the double-quick, and, without halting, or even moderating to quick time, to move by the right flank in line against the enemy. I deplored this and felt that my men were not having a fair chance, but it was too late to give new orders. . . .[14]

[12]Ibid., 557; Joseph Banks Lyle Journal, September 30, 1864.
[13]Field, "Campaign of 1864 and 1865," 557.
[14]O. R., vol. 42, part 1, p. 880.

Meanwhile, Hoke's assault column on the right refused to budge, as he stubbornly awaited the agreed-upon attack time.[15] This meant that instead of the fort being attacked simultaneously on two sides, it was assaulted on only one, and by a column which had been allowed to attack before it was ready.

In order to assist Anderson's brigade, Bratton's men had to quickly cover almost six hundred yards of open ground while under heavy fire from the fort.[16] The men in the right regiment, Walker's Palmetto Sharpshooters, were running but were still unable to keep up with the rest of the brigade. Bratton finally halted his men, closed their ranks, and sent the Palmetto Sharpshooters to the left to take "a little redan on the line a short distance in front of the enemy's retrenchments."[17] Walker's regiment did capture the redan, and because of its proximity to Fort Harrison, this forced the Federals to abandon one side of the fort.[18]

The other four regiments in Bratton's brigade then continued their assault, with Colonel Coward's Fifth Regiment on the left, coming up behind Anderson's brigade. As the men advanced over the open ground, the fort's artillerymen blasted them first with shell; then came the grape and canister. Finally, when the Confederates were only about two hundred yards from the fort, its defenders unleashed savage volleys of musket fire. Colonel Hagood, leading the First Regiment in Bratton's brigade, said, "The noise sounded like the magnified roar of a thousand kettle drums."[19] He described what then happened:

> Anderson's brigade, which received the first shock, came
> at once to a dead halt and then, as the fire increased,
> wheeled and, panic-stricken to a man, rushed through
> Bratton's line to the rear. This, of course, threw us into
> a great deal of confusion. . . .[20]

In this confusion, most of the men in Bratton's brigade fell back and took positions behind log huts, which stood outside the fort walls and had served as the Confederate militia's winter quarters before the fort was captured. There Bratton's troops were subjected to a vicious crossfire from the Union troops inside the fort. Colonel Hagood and some of his men, along with a small contingent from Steedman's Sixth Regiment, then moved forward and got to within forty yards of the fort walls. At this point, however, only about 30 men were following Hagood, and they were

---

[15]Field, "Campaign of 1864 and 1865," 557.
[16]Hagood, *Memoirs*, 181.
[17]O. R., vol. 42, part 1, p. 880.
[18]Ibid.
[19]Hagood, *Memoirs*, 181.
[20]Ibid., 182.

soon forced to withdraw.[21]   A sergeant in Hagood's regiment later described the intensity of the fire from the Federal defenders. He said that as they got closer to the fort, a lieutenant in his company was first shot in the thigh. A moment later the lieutenant was "shot clear through on the right side, the ball entering about the nipple." The same officer turned to go to the rear and "another ball hit him in the back, about an inch below where the other ball had come out. . . ." Two men put him on a litter, and "[a]s they raised him up another ball knocked off two of his toes. . . ."[22]

General Hoke, who had failed to attack when he saw Anderson's premature assault begin, finally started his column forward, and Bratton's men were quickly reformed and moved up to join in Hoke's assault. In his report Bratton wrote:

> General Hoke assaulted, but so feebly, and was so quickly repulsed, that I did not put my regiments in again, but took up a position to support the [Palmetto Sharpshooters] in the redan in case they were assailed by the enemy.[23]

Noting the fact that the Palmetto Sharpshooters had been able to capture the redan facing the fort, Bratton said that this had distracted the Union troops in the fort and saved the lives of many of his men as they withdrew.[24]

The attempt to retake Fort Harrison was a dismal failure for Field as well as Hoke and did not help the reputation of either man.[25] After the debacle, the Fifth Regiment's Captain J. B. Lyle wrote a letter saying, "Fortune seems to be against us just now, but all will be well again."[26] Bratton's brigade suffered moderately heavy losses in the failed effort to retake the fort; out of 1,294 men he took into the battle, he reported that 377 were killed or wounded.[27]

During the assault at Fort Harrison on September 30, Lieutenant J. D. McConnell, of the Fifth Regiment, was knocked to the ground by a rifle shot. As he lay still, he felt a warm wetness saturating his clothes on the side where he had been hit. Instinctively, he felt for the bullet hole but

---

[21]Ibid., 182-186. When Bratton was promoted to brigadier general, the command of the Sixth South Carolina Volunteers devolved upon Lt. Colonel (later Colonel) J. M. Steedman.

[22]Mixson, *Reminiscences of a Private*, 104. The officer, Lieutenant J. R. B. Best, miraculously survived his wounds at Fort Harrison. Ibid.

[23]O. R., vol. 42, part 1, p. 880.

[24]Ibid.

[25]Field, "Campaign of 1864 and 1865," 557; Freeman, *Lee's Lieutenants*, 3:591.

[26]J. Banks Lyle to Dora McArthur, October 2, 1864, Joseph Banks Lyle Letters.

[27]O. R., vol. 42, part 1, p. 880. Bratton reported that "some of the wounded are prisoners." Ibid. No separate casualty figures were provided for Bratton's five regiments.

could find none. To his relief, the ball had hit his canteen; it was warm water, not blood, he felt on his side. He later recalled:

> I had a sore side with a lump on it as big as a goose egg
> for some days. The bullet had fallen in my breeches
> pocket.[28]

The next day Bratton's men were inactive until evening when they moved to a line some three quarters of a mile from the fort. There they constructed and strengthened the earthworks until the night of October 6, when they were relieved by the Richmond Militia and were marched to the Darbytown Road, roughly three or four miles north of Fort Harrison.[29] Following the Battle of Fort Harrison, the Federals had extended their lines to that road, and General Lee decided to attempt the next day to turn his adversary's right flank at that point.[30]

As was the case at Fort Harrison, the October 7 attack was to be carried out by the divisions of Field and Hoke; to this force had been added General Martin W. Gary's dismounted cavalry and a brigade from Florida.[31] The plan called for Gary's men to circle around the Federal right, anchored on the Darbytown Road, and to attack the Union troops from the rear. Drawn up in a line perpendicular to the Darbytown Road, extending beyond the Federal right flank, was Field's division. His men were to make a frontal assault, pivot on their right, and drive the bluecoats into Hoke's division, positioned to the right of Field.[32]

Bratton's brigade was in a line of battle on the north side of the Darbytown Road facing east, and Field's other brigades extended the line on Bratton's right. Bratton deployed the men in Coward's Fifth Regiment as skirmishers, and his remaining regiments were positioned as follows: the Second Rifles on the extreme left of the brigade; next, the First Regiment; then the Sixth; and the Palmetto Sharpshooters on the right, next to the Darbytown Road. After the regiments were in position, Coward's men advanced first, parallel to the road.[33] Colonel Coward wrote: "With bugle calls, I soon had my men in groups twenty paces apart deployed as skirmishers and [we advanced] firing. The enemy [pickets] gave way."[34]

After Coward's men had driven the pickets back to their lines, Bratton started the rest of his brigade toward the Union works, some six to eight

[28]McConnell, "Recollections," 11.
[29]O. R., vol. 42, part 1, pp. 880-881.
[30]Hagood, *Memoirs*, 188.
[31]Freeman, *Lee's Lieutenants*, 3:592; Hagood, *Memoirs*, 189.
[32]Hagood, *Memoirs*, 189.
[33]Ibid.
[34]Bond and Coward, eds., *South Carolinians*, 159.

hundred yards away. He reported that when his brigade began advancing, G. T. Anderson's brigade of Georgians, on Bratton's immediate right, also moved forward.[35] On the extreme right of the Union line, Bratton's two left regiments attacked a redoubt and evicted its defenders while the Sixth Regiment and the Palmetto Sharpshooters drove the Union troops from their works in front.[36] Meanwhile, to Bratton's right, Anderson's brigade had been abruptly stopped by the fire from another enemy redoubt, and General Field quickly sent Hagood's First Regiment and Bowen's Second Rifles to assist. Those two regiments crossed an abatis and charged the redoubt, driving the bluecoats from it and capturing almost 100 prisoners. After it had already been taken by Hagood's and Bowen's regiments, the Georgians in Anderson's brigade ran up and planted their colors on the redoubt as if they had captured it. According to Hagood, his men "took no pains to conceal the fact that [they were] not deceived by the bombast of the Georgians."[37]

As Bratton's men reached the main works, General Gary's cavalry came up on the Federal right flank and threw the Union troops into confusion. Colonel Hagood wrote that "Gary's cavalry [came up and] cooperated with Field's division and the two forces attacked with a splendid spirit."[38] This simultaneous frontal and flank attack completely routed August V. Kautz's Federal cavalry division and led to the capture of ten pieces of artillery and about one hundred artillery and cavalry horses.[39]

Once Bratton and Gary had pushed Kautz's cavalry toward the right, they fully expected to hear the sounds of Hoke's division picking up the pursuit, as had been planned. After more than an hour of waiting in vain for Hoke to attack, however, Field decided to pursue the retreating Federals with only his division.[40]

Bratton's brigade then shifted to its right, across a tangled swamp, and joined the remainder of Field's division in the pursuit. The retreating Union cavalrymen had taken refuge behind a log breastworks, protected by a line of abatis near the New Market Road, some two miles to the rear of where they had been routed.[41] By then, however, they had been substantially reinforced with artillery and fresh units of infantry, while Hoke had delayed in bringing his division up.[42] Hoke's men finally

---

[35]O. R., vol. 42, part 1, p. 881.
[36]Ibid.; Hagood, *Memoirs*, 189-190.
[37]Hagood, *Memoirs*, 191.
[38]Ibid.
[39]Field, "Campaign of 1864 and 1865," 557.
[40]Hagood stated that Field also sent a messenger "to ascertain what had become of Hoke." Hagood, *Memoirs*, 192.
[41]Field, "Campaign of 1864 and 1865," 557.
[42]Hagood, *Memoirs*, 192.

appeared and formed a line of battle on the right of Field, who assumed that the two divisions would then attack simultaneously.[43]

When the assault began, Field's division moved forward across a cleared field, breaking through the abatis. Bratton's brigade drove back the Union skirmishers and captured a number of them before they could reach the safety of their breastworks. Finally, as Bratton's men got to within about one hundred yards of the breastworks, the Federal troopers opened fire with their highly-effective Spencer repeating rifles. Colonel Hagood, describing the effect these rifles had on the attack, wrote:

> The most infernal fire of musketry imaginable now greeted us and brought our column to a dead halt, every man throwing himself on the ground to seek protection from the leaden storm which roared through the woods. We remained [there] about fifteen minutes in the hope that some pause in the firing would open an opportunity to get up and charge but, none such occurring, we finally retreated pell-mell. . . .[44]

Unfortunately, Field's division was repulsed with heavy losses; Field noted that once again Hoke's division, for some unexplained reason, had failed to join in the assault.[45] Colonel Hagood expressed his frustration by stating:

> The causes of Hoke's dereliction, on which hinged the whole catastrophe, I have never been able to understand; but it was much to be deplored, since it prevented our reaping results of great importance to us.[46]

This was the second time in eight days that Field's men had made an assault, with the understanding that they were to be supported by Hoke's division, only to find that Hoke had failed to advance.[47]

The casualties in Bratton's brigade during the two fights (at Darbytown Road and at New Market Road) on October 7 amounted to

---

[43]Field, "Campaign of 1864 and 1865," 557-558.

[44]Hagood, *Memoirs*, 193. The Spencer repeating rifle used a metallic cartridge with the primer already built in, making a percussion cap unnecessary. It also had a magazine which allowed seven shots to be taken simply by moving a lever and cocking the hammer each time the rifle was fired. The Spencer's rate of fire made it the rifle-of-choice for the Union cavalry after 1863, when it was first introduced in quantity.

[45]Field, "Campaign of 1864 and 1865," 558.

[46]Hagood, *Memoirs*, 193.

[47]Freeman, *Lee's Lieutenants*, 3:592-593.

190 men, about half of whom were in the Palmetto Sharpshooters.[48] One officer in that regiment, Lieutenant Richard Lewis of Company B, wrote from a Federal prison five days later:

> I was wounded in the left leg on [October] 7th . . . charging the enemy's entrenchments, and fell into their hands. They sent me . . . to the hospital . . . where I had to suffer the amputation of my leg, just below the knee, from its being so badly fractured. I was then sent to Point of Rocks [prison] where I remain.[49]

Bratton himself was wounded in the left shoulder on October 7 at the New Market Road, just before he ordered his men to fall back, and he was sent home two days later to recuperate.[50] One of the Palmetto Sharpshooters' most experienced and capable officers, Captain Joab Quattlebaum of Company F, was killed as he led his men against the Federal breastworks.[51]

In the Fifth Regiment, Colonel Coward's brother, James, was wounded, but Coward was able to reach him and have him taken to the rear.[52] He died at the Winder Hospital in Richmond a few days later.[53] In addition, Lieutenant William T. Norris of Company C was wounded and left on the field, and Captain J. B. Lyle organized a skirmish party to rescue him. They were prevented from doing so when they saw that Union troops had taken possession of the part of the field where Norris had fallen.[54] Norris, who was captured, died about a month later in a Federal prison.[55]

After the fighting ended on October 7, Bratton's men returned to the Darbytown Road and in the next few days erected a series of earthworks.[56] His brigade was on the extreme left of Field's division, resting on the Darbytown Road, and Hoke's division was on Field's right.[57] Sensing that his left flank was vulnerable, General Field soon moved another brigade across the Darbytown Road to the left of Bratton's brigade. This was a timely move, because on October 13 the Federals unsuccessfully attacked Field's lines several times before withdrawing

---

[48]O. R., vol. 42, part 1, p. 881.

[49]Lewis, *Camp Life*, 97; see also, O. R., vol. 42, part 1, p. 882. Lewis had also been wounded at Spotsylvania in May 1864. Lewis, *Camp Life*, 93.

[50]O. R., vol. 42, part 1, pp. 881-882; Field, "Campaign of 1864 and 1865," 558. Bratton was replaced temporarily as brigade commander by Colonel Joe Walker, of the Palmetto Sharpshooters.

[51]O. R., vol. 42, part 1, pp. 881-882.

[52]Bond and Coward, eds., *South Carolinians*, 159.

[53]Ibid., 162.

[54]Joseph Banks Lyle Journal, October 7, 1864.

[55]Salley, *South Carolina Troops, Fifth S.C.V.*, 3:86.

[56]Hagood, *Memoirs*, 193.

[57]Joseph Banks Lyle Journal, October 11, 1864.

that evening. One of these assaults was made against Bratton's left, but was easily repulsed.[58] A soldier in Company G of the Palmetto Sharpshooters wrote:

> We had [a] heavy fight here yesterday, but my regiment was not engaged except in sharpshooting, and we did not lose any men. The Fifth and Second [Rifles] was under pretty heavy fire. . . . The enemy attempted to flank us out of our works, but failed.[59]

The losses in Bratton's brigade during this attack were light, but many Union dead were left upon the field.[60]

By October 17, Bratton's men were in the process of executing a general order to remove all able-bodied men on detail in the rear and place them in the front ranks, replacing them with men who were disabled.[61] Those men on detail performed such jobs as clerks, attendants, butchers and teamsters in the quartermaster and commissary departments. They were called "bomb-proof" by the men in ranks, some of whom were quite happy with the new order.[62] One soldier in the Palmetto Sharpshooters welcomed the change with some skepticism, saying, "[w]e now need every effective man, and they should at once be pushed to the front regardless of favoritism, but I fear it will not be done. . . ."[63]

General Longstreet, who had finally recovered from the wound he received from Mahone's men in the Wilderness some five months earlier, returned to the command of First Corps on October 19. One week later, on October 27, long columns of Federal troops were observed moving north in the direction of the Charles City Road. Field's division had already moved up to this vicinity, about a mile from the Darbytown Road, ten days before.[64] The Federal plan was to create a diversion in front of Field's lines, while Godfrey Weitzel's two divisions of Union infantry and Kautz's cavalry division moved farther north, to attack the thinly-manned Confederate works on the Williamsburg Road. Weitzel and Kautz hoped to break Longstreet's lines there and then roll up his left flank.[65] Longstreet, however, was not fooled by the Federal feint and accurately predicted where the real attack was to be made.[66] He immediately

[58]Ibid., October 13, 1864.
[59]H. C. Conner to Ellen Conner, October 14, 1864, Henry Calvin Conner Papers.
[60]Joseph Banks Lyle Journal, October 13, 1864; Field, "Campaign of 1864-1865," 558.
[61]Joseph Banks Lyle Journal, October 17, 1864.
[62]J. B. Lyle to Dora McArthur, October 16, 1864, Joseph Banks Lyle Letters.
[63]H. C. Conner to Ellen Conner, October 18, 1864, Henry Calvin Conner Papers.
[64]Joseph Banks Lyle Journal, October 17, 20, and 27, 1864.
[65]Field, "Campaign of 1864 and 1865," 559.
[66]Freeman, *Lee's Lieutenants*, 3:615.

ordered Field's division to pull out of its lines and march north to the Williamsburg Road near the old battlefield at Seven Pines. Field was instructed to leave only a strong skirmish line to guard the Darbytown Road lines that he was vacating.[67]

Holding the defensive works at the Williamsburg Road on October 27, when the Union troops began to advance, was a small group of the Virginia Home Guard. This minuscule force had courageously managed to hold off the Federal skirmishers and was about to be attacked by the divisions of Charles A. Heckman and Gilman Marston when the lead elements of Field's division arrived, just in time.[68] In the race for the works at the Williamsburg Road, Field had beaten the Federals by only about five minutes.[69] General Field later recalled that he hardly had time to form his lines before the bluecoats came out of the woods to his front.[70] Two brigades of Union infantry, in lines of battle on either side of the Williamsburg Road, quickly charged across an open field toward Field's men behind the works. The Confederate fire completely shattered the Union line, however, and the assault quickly sputtered to a stop.[71]

About two hundred yards in front of Bratton's troops, running parallel to their line, were two depressions in the topography which afforded the only protection from the Confederate rifles. When their charge was stopped cold, a huge group of Union troops took cover in the depression closest to Bratton's line.[72] Serving temporarily on Bratton's staff at the time was Captain J. B. Lyle of the Fifth South Carolina, who had led that regiment in Colonel Coward's absence at Spotsylvania. Observing that the mass of enemy troops was pinned down in the depression, the thirty-five-year-old captain determined that they might just surrender if such a demand was made.

Lyle, who had already been slightly wounded in the day's fighting,[73] went to the men in the brigade's skirmish line but could get no volunteers to accompany him out to the trapped Federals, so he started toward

---

[67]Field, "Campaign of 1864 and 1865," 559.

[68]J. W. Trowbridge, "Conspicuous Feats of Valor," *Confederate Veteran* 24 (January 1916):25; Elmer O. Parker, "Captain Lyle: Forgotten Hero of the Confederacy," *Prologue: The Journal of the National Archives* 4 (Fall 1972):166.

[69]Joseph Banks Lyle Journal, October 27, 1864.

[70]Field, "Campaign of 1864 and 1865," 560.

[71]Ibid. See report of Charles A. Heckman, October 29, 1864, O. R., vol. 42, part 1, p. 807. It states that he advanced Colonel H. S. Fairchild's brigade on the left of the Williamsburg Road, in conjunction with Colonel Edgar M. Cullen's brigade on the other side of the road, but found the Confederate works "too strongly defended by artillery and infantry to be carried." Ibid.

[72]General Charles A. Heckman's report confirms this fact, and states:

> To avoid a raking fire from the enemy, [Colonel H. S. Fairchild's brigade] took shelter in a gully or ditch and held their position until ordered to retire.

O. R., vol. 42, part 1, p. 808.

[73]Lyle wrote in his journal at the end of the day that he had been "wounded on the shoulder and head by a grapeshot." Joseph Banks Lyle Journal, October 27, 1864.

them by himself. After he had moved out a few paces, he was joined by two men from the skirmish line, and the three started walking cautiously toward the enemy troops in the depression. Lyle then decided not to subject these two brave men to such a risk and he proceeded alone, leaving them on the crest of a hill overlooking the depression. As Lyle approached the mass of Union soldiers, one of their officers began shouting at his men to continue the fight. Lyle immediately yelled to his two volunteers on the hill to fire on the officer unless he stopped his harangue.[74]

Lyle then walked on to the depression alone, but the men in Field's other brigades mistook him for a Union officer and opened fire on him. The rifle balls kicked up a cloud of dust around him until the word finally spread along the entire line that he was an officer from the Fifth South Carolina; then the firing ceased. The troops throughout Field's division were filled with admiration for Lyle's courage, and the question was repeated all along the line, "Who is he?" When Lyle finally reached the depression, he firmly demanded that the entire body of about 500 or 600 Union troops throw down their arms and surrender. They promptly did so, and began filing out of the depression toward Bratton's lines. After about half of them had filed out, one officer among them began to berate his soldiers for yielding to a single man and demanded that they kill or capture Captain Lyle. General Bratton later wrote:

> Throwing down his trophies and picking up a [Spencer] carbine which had been lost in the retreat of cavalry . . . [Lyle then] advanced promptly and directly on the officer, presenting the carbine and threatening to blow his brains out if he did not surrender. He yielded [and] the capture was completed without further trouble.[75]

Lyle himself captured three stands of colors, along with several swords and small arms.[76] General Longstreet later recounted the incident and wrote that Lyle had "picked up about six hundred prisoners."[77] Those troops who did not surrender that afternoon made

---

[74]Trowbridge, "Conspicuous Feats of Valor," 25-26.

[75]Ibid. For similar accounts of Lyle's achievement, see Parker, "Captain Lyle," 165-172; Longstreet, *From Manassas to Appomattox*, 578; Field, "Campaign of 1864 and 1865," 560; Hagood, *Memoirs*, 195; Bond and Coward, eds., *South Carolinians*, 163.

[76]Joseph Banks Lyle Journal, October 27, 1864.

[77]Longstreet, *From Manassas to Appomattox*, 578. Longstreet's account states as follows:
> Meanwhile . . . many [Federals] got away down the dry ditch on their left, until Captain Lyle, of the Fifth South Carolina Regiment, got a force out on the flank and secured the surrender of the remainder. He picked up about six hundred prisoners.

Ibid. In Longstreet's official report, he used the same number of prisoners and said that "most of [them] were taken through the personal exertions of Captain Lyle. . . ." O. R., vol. 42, part 1, p. 872.

their way back to the Federal lines, leaving their dead on the field. Unofficially, about 2,000 Union soldiers were killed, wounded or captured in the day's fighting, and five of their standards were taken.[78] General Field later recalled that the day after the battle on the Williamsburg Road his men buried nearly 100 dead Federal troops on the battlefield.[79]

Three months later, Captain Lyle was granted a furlough and returned home to be married. Before Lyle left, General Bratton permitted him to take the same Spencer carbine, which he had picked up on the field on October 27 and used in his capture of the Union troops, as a wedding present to his bride.[80]

Several days after the battle on the Williamsburg Road on October 27, General Field wrote to the War Department in Richmond recommending that Captain Lyle be promoted to major for his "conspicuously gallant conduct."[81] Unfortunately, because of delays and technicalities, Lyle never received his promotion. He had gained, however, the complete admiration and respect of General Field and every soldier in his division.

At the end of October, Field's defensive line, which ran between the Charles City Road and the Williamsburg Road, was moved back toward Richmond a short distance. There his men began constructing works along the new line.[82] The troops got a one-day respite from their work when President Davis declared November 16 a day of prayer and thanksgiving, and all Confederate duties and operations not deemed absolutely necessary were suspended.[83]

General Bratton, who had been on leave due to the shoulder wound he had received in early October, returned to his command near the Williamsburg Road on November 20.[84] By that time his men had almost

---

[78]Hagood, *Memoirs*, 194. It is impossible to get an accurate account from the Federal after-action reports of the actual number of men captured by Lyle. Not surprisingly, none of those reports admits that any troops were captured by a single man. General Heckman's report admitted to having 6 officers and 380 enlisted men missing in Fairchild's brigade. O. R., vol. 42, part 1, p. 808. General Marston's report stated that Cullen's brigade lost "many brave officers and men and three stands of colors. . . ." O. R., vol. 42, part 1, p. 803. The One Hundred and Forty-eighth New York, one of Heckman's regiments, admitted having 64 men missing. O. R., vol. 42, part 1, p. 811. The Eighty-ninth New York admitted losing "many . . . prisoners." O. R., vol. 42, part 1, p. 813. The commander of another Federal regiment which made the charge, the Nineteenth Wisconsin, claimed that "[a]bout 5 p.m. the enemy charged out from their line of works and captured nearly all of the command and regimental colors." O. R., vol. 42, part 1, p. 814.

[79]Field, "Campaign of 1864 and 1865," 56C.

[80]Trowbridge, "Conspicuous Feats of Valor," 26.

[81]Field to Cooper, November 6, 1864, in Parker, "Captain Lyle," 169. In his letter, Field said that Captain Lyle deserved to be made a colonel, "but as the only vacancy in his brigade is that of Major, I limit my recommendations to that." One source states that, during the war, Lyle "was nine times wounded with balls, shell and saber. . . ." Trowbridge, "Conspicuous Feats of Valor," 26.

[82]Joseph Banks Lyle Journal, October 31, 1864.

[83]Ibid., November 16, 1864.

[84]O. R., vol. 42, part 1, p. 882.

completed their new defensive works, which Colonel Hagood described as including

> [t]wo lines of impassable "abatis" . . . the first forty yards, the second eighty yards – in front of the outer ditch, while some 300 yards ahead of the main defenses was an entrenched picket line, quite sufficient to turn any but the most determined attack.[85]

By the end of November cold weather had set in, and Bratton's men were allowed to begin constructing their winter quarters behind the main line. In addition, they constructed a military road well to the rear of the line. The colonel of the First South Carolina wrote that it was concealed from the Federals' view so that large bodies of Lee's troops could be moved "from one wing of the army to the other with perfect secrecy."[86] It was primarily in constructing these defensive works, winter quarters and roads, that Bratton's men spent the remainder of 1864. They were, however, involved in two additional but relatively minor offensive operations.

The first of these operations was on December 10, after a full night of freezing rain. The men in Field's division left their comfortable quarters and moved first down the Charles City Road. They then crossed over to the Darbytown Road and pushed southeast for about two miles toward the New Market Road, with the Fifth South Carolina in the lead. The men in the Fifth drove the enemy's pickets back into their works on New Market Heights, but there was no attack against the Federal line. After dark, Bratton's men returned to their winter quarters and learned that their movement had been merely a demonstration to divert the enemy's attention from another Confederate operation elsewhere.[87] The day's work, however, was very rough on Bratton's troops, and one soldier in the Palmetto Sharpshooters wrote:

> We did not get in a regular engagement, but skirmished with them most of the day. We had quite a severe time of it as the ground was covered with sleet and the men could not keep themselves warm. . . .[88]

---

[85]Hagood, *Memoirs*, 196.
[86]Ibid. See also, H. C. Conner to Ellen Conner, December 6, 1864, Henry Calvin Conner Papers.
[87]Joseph Banks Lyle Journal, December 10, 1864.
[88]H. C. Conner to Ellen Conner, December 11, 1864, Henry Calvin Conner Papers.

General Bratton described this operation as a "reconnaissance of the enemy's line [near] Deep Bottom," and reported that he had 1 officer and 11 men killed, wounded or missing.[89]

Colonel Coward missed the skirmishing on December 10 because he was on furlough in Yorkville, South Carolina. His wife was expecting a baby, and he had rushed home but had arrived too late for the baby's birth. The child was born on December 1, which was also the birthday of Coward's longtime friend, Micah Jenkins. The baby boy was named for Jenkins, but Coward wrote that the child "died a few weeks later, before he learned what [his] name stood for."[90]

On the anniversary of South Carolina's secession from the Union, a young lady from Charlottesville sent down a load of food for the men in Bratton's brigade. Since it was not enough for all the men, each regiment drew lots for it, and Hagood's First Regiment was the winner.[91]

Two days later the men in Bratton's brigade were called out to witness the execution of Private J. G. Mack, in Hagood's regiment, for having deserted.[92] Mack had apparently received some distressing news from his wife back in Orangeburg, South Carolina. When Mack was denied a furlough, he left for home anyway and was caught. After a court martial, he was convicted of desertion and sentenced to be shot. Twelve men were selected to form the shooting detail, six of whom were furnished rifles with only blank cartridges. A wagon rode in front of the entire corps, carrying Private Mack; he was sitting on his coffin, as a regimental band played the death march. After being blindfolded, Mack was made to kneel down and was tied to a stake. The execution detail was marched up and, after being given several orders, heard "Ready-aim-fire!" The shots rang out and Mack's head dropped to his chest as his body went limp. Sergeant Frank Mixson was part of the execution detail; he remarked later that this sickening lesson for desertion "was hard to see, but such had to be."[93]

The final military movement of 1864 for Bratton's men began three days before Christmas, after the Confederate War Department learned of a planned raid on Gordonsville by a Federal force thought to number some 6,000 men. To meet this expected attack, Bratton's troops, along

---

[89]O. R., vol. 42, part 1, p. 882.
[90]Bond and Coward, eds., *South Carolinians*, 165.
[91]Hagood, *Memoirs*, 202.
[92]Joseph Banks Lyle Journal, December 22, 1864. Private J. G. Mack was in Company K, Hagood's First South Carolina.
[93]Mixson, *Reminiscences of a Private*, 114.

with another brigade from Longstreet's command, were pulled out of their winter quarters near Richmond and sent to Gordonsville.[94]

Bratton left his winter quarters near the Williamsburg Road shortly before midnight on the night of December 22 with Bowen's Second Rifles and Coward's Fifth Regiment; the other three regiments in the brigade followed a few hours later.[95] The men were marched to Richmond where they boarded trains for Gordonsville, the first train leaving at four o'clock the next morning, and the last leaving about nine a.m.[96] When Bratton arrived in Gordonsville at mid-morning, he quickly deployed Bowen's and Coward's regiments on either side of the Madison Turnpike and set out a company of sharpshooters, fully expecting the Union troops to charge at any moment. One of Bratton's regiments, however, opened fire prematurely, alerting the Federals to the arrival of the Confederate infantry reinforcements. Instead of advancing, the Union troops then elected to withdraw without a fight.[97] By the time Bratton's other three regiments arrived in Gordonsville on December 23, they found that the place was no longer in any danger of attack.[98]

The next afternoon, December 24, Bratton's men began boarding trains for the return trip to Richmond, but the last part of the brigade did not leave until after dark. Once the trains left Gordonsville, there were lengthy delays due to the poor condition of the railroad, and most of the men in the brigade did not reach Richmond until Christmas day.[99] To make matters worse, the men then had to march back to their winter quarters on the Williamsburg Road, a distance of a least five miles. General Bratton described the Gordonsville operation as "a most unsuccessful [and] very horrid trip."[100] Palmetto Sharpshooter Henry C. Conner also wrote:

> [W]e were glad to get back, for we suffered from cold . . .
> and we slept but little in five nights, as . . . the cars were
> so badly crowded that we could not sleep on them.[101]

---

[94]Freeman, *Lee's Lieutenants*, 3:617. On December 22, 1864, Field was ordered to have "Bratton's Brigade . . . prepare three days' cooked rations at once" and to have the men marched "to the Central Rail Road Depot, in Richmond, to take the cars for Gordonsville." Latrobe to Field, December 22, 1864, National Archives, Letters Sent by Headquarters, Department of East Tennessee, January 1864-February 1865, R.G. 109, Chapter II, vol. 276.

[95]O. R., vol. 42, part 1, p. 882.

[96]Joseph Banks Lyle Journal, December 23, 1864.

[97]O. R., vol. 42, part 1, pp. 882-883.

[98]Joseph Banks Lyle Journal, December 23, 1864.

[99]O. R., vol. 42, part 1, p. 883.

[100]John Bratton to Bettie Bratton, December 25, 1864, Bratton Letters.

[101]H. C. Conner to Ellen Conner, December 25, 1864, Henry Calvin Conner Papers.

Indeed, it had been so bitterly cold on the trip that an officer in Coward's Fifth Regiment described how he had slept in the snow at Gordonsville "without even a blanket" and said, "My clothes froze to the ground."[102]

As the year 1864 drew to a close, the men in Bratton's brigade received a bit of good news. They were told that the women of Richmond were preparing a lavish dinner for the Confederate troops which would be delivered to their camps on New Year's day. The men built up this expected dinner in their minds and waited eagerly for its delivery on January 1, 1865. When it finally arrived in the pre-dawn hours of the next day, the dinner consisted of only ham sandwiches, but most of the men refused to complain.[103] According to Captain Lyle, while it was a scanty meal, "all the same, we equally appreciated the intention."[104] A soldier in the Palmetto Sharpshooters wrote that, even though the expected feast was somewhat of a failure, it had gone a long way "to show the generosity of Virginia's people."[105]

Thus ended a rough year for Bratton and the men in his brigade. Since returning to Virginia from Tennessee in April, they had found little to cheer about, and they had suffered greatly. Ironically, the failed dinner at the end of 1864 symbolized the primary problem for the Confederacy: it was running out of troops and supplies while its opponent grew stronger by the day. Gone were the opportunities for General Lee to put his Army of Northern Virginia on the offense. Facing a foe of overwhelming numbers, the aging general was now restricted to a static defense which, as he himself had admitted, would number the days of his army.[106] As of January 1, 1865, that number of days would in fact turn out to be only ninety-nine.

---

[102]McConnell, "Recollections," 12.
[103]Freeman, *Lee's Lieutenants*, 3:620.
[104]Joseph Banks Lyle Journal, January 2, 1865.
[105]H. C. Conner to Ellen Conner, January 4, 1865, Henry Calvin Conner Papers.
[106]Dowdey, *Lee's Last Campaign*, 368; Foote, *Civil War*, 3:442; McPherson, *Battle Cry of Freedom*, 743.

Chapter 25

A sbury Coward had gone without food all day, but he had no appetite; he could only watch as his hungry men devoured the rations provided by the Federal troops. There was no joking around the fires of the Fifth South Carolina this night, and not a single song was heard. The silence and gloom completely pervaded the camp of exhausted men.

In the dim light of his fire, Coward saw one of his sergeants approaching. The old veteran of four years of war, omitting all formalities, handed Coward a small package. He said that the men wanted Coward to have it, but that he was not to open it until he reached Yorkville. Near Appomattox Court House the next morning, along with the remaining regiments in Lee's army, the men of the Fifth South Carolina stacked their arms and furled their flag, which was then placed in the center of the stack. But it was not the battle flag of the regiment. It was not the flag that they had carried into all the fights from Fredericksburg to Farmville while Coward was the regiment's colonel. Instead, they furled a new regimental flag that had seen no battle, an unused one that had remained, until now, in General Bratton's headquarters wagon. The real battle flag, riddled with bullet holes, had been cut up the night before and the pieces divided among Coward's men; each man had been given a swatch as a sacred memento of his companions and the regiment. The small package which the sergeant had presented to Coward the night before contained the flag's center star. It was good that he had not opened it that same night; the little colonel with the big heart would have surely broken down in front of his devoted men.[1]

The year 1865 had begun quietly and peacefully for the 1,500 men in Bratton's brigade, and they quickly shook off the disappointment of the "feast" they never received on New Year's day. It had just snowed, and they were still enjoying their winter huts near Richmond behind the defensive works between the Darbytown and Williamsburg roads on the north side of the James River.[2]

In Bratton's brigade, chapels had been constructed between the regiments. These structures were used on weekdays for officers' schools, court martial proceedings and lectures. On Sundays they were used for church services, and there were some indications of a religious revival in the brigade.[3] In addition to the chapels, the men in Field's division had constructed a theater. In the first week of January, one officer in the Fifth Regiment wrote that he had just attended the "Field's Varieties" but gave it low marks.[4] By this stage of the war, some of the men in Lee's army had begun to jokingly refer to themselves as "Lee's Miserables."[5]

Of this winter of 1865, General Field wrote that the most unpleasant duty his men faced was picketing, and that otherwise they were fairly comfortable.[6] Occasionally, however, the men would fail to take their picketing duty seriously enough. According to Captain J. B. Lyle, on January 7 General Bratton discovered his picket line "in a loose, lax condition" and had Lieutenant J. C. I. Wannamaker of Hagood's First Regiment arrested for neglect of duty.[7] Two days later, Bratton put Lieutenant Colonel John D. Wylie of the Fifth Regiment under arrest on

---

[1]Bond and Coward, eds., *South Carolinians*, 179-180.

[2]Joseph Banks Lyle Journal, January 1, 1865. The Inspection Report for Bratton's brigade for February 1865 showed the following totals of men and officers present in each of the five regiments: Hagood's First, 219; Bowen's Second Rifles, 312; Coward's Fifth, 273; Steedman's Sixth, 342; and Walker's Palmetto Sharpshooters, 382. This gave the brigade a total of men present for duty of 1,534, including Bratton and his staff. Inspection Report of A. A. and I. G. Sorrel, February 25, 1865, in National Archives, Confederate Inspection Reports, R. G. 109, series M935. This report also indicates that there were a total of 1,394 guns in the brigade, all .58 caliber Enfield rifles, with 155,760 rounds of ammunition on hand.

[3]Bond and Coward, eds., *South Carolinians*, 167.

[4]Joseph Banks Lyle Journal, January 3, 1865.

[5]Freeman, *Lee's Lieutenants*, 3:619.

[6]Field, "Campaign of 1864 and 1865," 560.

[7]Joseph Banks Lyle Journal, January 7, 1865. Wannamaker was a first lieutenant in Company B of Hagood's First South Carolina Volunteers.

similar charges.[8] Wylie, perhaps upset over Bratton's action, retired from the service three weeks later.[9]

After Savannah fell in December of 1864, General William T. Sherman turned his army north toward South Carolina. His men marched in two primary columns, feinting at both Charleston and Augusta, with Columbia as their real objective.[10] Sherman's vengeful entry into the state which had led the secession movement, following his devastating march from Atlanta to Savannah, caused great concern among the South Carolina troops in Bratton's brigade. Serving in Virginia, they were far away from their families and property and powerless to protect them. One man in the Palmetto Sharpshooters wrote home expressing his worry that Sherman would "overrun the State. . . ."[11] Captain J. B. Lyle, on leave to be married in South Carolina at the time, wrote on February 7 that there was great excitement in South Carolina as Sherman moved toward Columbia.[12] By then, rumors about Sherman's army were rampant among the soldiers in Bratton's brigade.[13] All of this worry, combined with what most of them could see was an almost impossible military situation, led some of Bratton's men to have, what Colonel Hagood described as, "an undefined feeling of hopelessness."[14]

On February 17, the city of Columbia surrendered to the Federals, and two-thirds of the state capital was destroyed by a fire which Sherman blamed General Wade Hampton and his men for having started.[15] The next day the city of Charleston was occupied by the Federal troops of General John G. Foster, prompting Captain J. B. Lyle to write from South Carolina that he saw "a gloomy state of things – great despondency – many crying out whipped! whipped!"[16]

The mens' apprehensions concerning affairs at home and the general decline of morale in the camps in Virginia led to a marked increase in the number of desertions in Lee's army. Initially, Longstreet's First Corps had fewer of these problems than the other corps.[17] By March, however, desertions from Longstreet's brigades had become more numerous, and Bratton was having his share. When Captain Lyle returned to the Fifth Regiment's camp from leave on March 3, he learned

---

[8]Ibid., January 9, 1865.
[9]Wylie retired from the service on January 28, 1865. Salley, *South Carolina Troops, Fifth, S.C.V.*, 3:6.
[10]Foote, *Civil War*, 3:751.
[11]H. C. Conner to Ellen Conner, February 4, 1865, Henry Calvin Conner Papers.
[12]Joseph Banks Lyle Journal, February 7, 1865.
[13]Bond and Coward, eds., *South Carolinians*, 167.
[14]Hagood, *Memoirs*, 206.
[15]Foote, *Civil War*, 3:795.
[16]Joseph Banks Lyle Journal, January 26 to March 3, 1865. See also, Foote, *Civil War*, 3:800.
[17]Freeman, *Lee's Lieutenants*, 3:624-625.

that "a good many of [his] Brigade [had] been deserting."[18] Six men in Company K of the Fifth Regiment deserted on the night of March 14 and apparently went over to the Federals.[19] The next day, Lieutenant James S. Ballenger, of Company D in the Palmetto Sharpshooters, was arrested and relieved of duty for allowing his men to converse with the Union pickets.[20]

With a few exceptions, there was little fighting around Richmond and Petersburg during the winter, but General Grant never relaxed his siege.[21] After Sherman destroyed Columbia in mid-February, he headed for North Carolina. There he proposed to link up in Goldsboro with General Schofield's Federal troops who were moving inland from the coast. Sherman could then march the combined force into southern Virginia, destroy Lee's railroad lines and mount a coordinated attack with Grant to overwhelm Lee's army. This made it clear to Lee and Davis that Sherman had to be stopped before he could reach Virginia.[22] To accomplish this difficult task, General Joe Johnston was placed in command of all Confederate troops in the Carolinas. Johnston fully realized that if Schofield's force was allowed to combine with Sherman's in North Carolina, there was little his army could do to prevent them from marching into Virginia.[23]

As the winter came to an end, Lee concluded that there was no way Johnston's army in North Carolina would be able to stop Sherman and Schofield without help. It appeared that the only hope was for Lee's army to join Johnston in North Carolina, defeat Sherman, and then return to Virginia to meet Grant. The problem with this strategy was that, while Lee's men were combining with Johnston's in North Carolina, only a thinly-defended line would be left to protect Richmond and Petersburg against Grant. A way had to be devised to hold Grant in place in Virginia while the bulk of Lee's army was in North Carolina joining with Johnston to defeat Sherman and his 90,000 man combined force.[24]

The plan adopted by Lee called for a surprise attack to break through the Federals' line at Petersburg, and once in their rear to sweep down their works forcing them to abandon a portion of their line. If Grant could be compelled to shorten his lines, less of Lee's army would be

---

[18]Joseph Banks Lyle Journal, March 3, 1865.
[19]Ibid., March 14, 1865.
[20]Ibid., March 15, 1865.
[21]Freeman, *Lee's Lieutenants*, 3:627.
[22]Ibid., 3:638; Foote, *Civil War*, 3:800-801.
[23]Freeman, *Lee's Lieutenants*, 3:644.
[24]Ibid., 3:644-645. Sherman reached Goldsboro, North Carolina, on March 23, and Schofield's men were already there. This gave Sherman a combined force of almost 90,000 men. Foote, *Civil War*, 3:817.

needed to defend Petersburg, freeing up most of his troops to march to North Carolina to join Johnston.[25]

Lee selected Major General John B. Gordon and his men for the attack which was made at Fort Stedman, about two miles due east of Petersburg, on March 25. While Gordon's men, along with Pickett's division, were successful in taking the fort, they were unable to effect the necessary breakthrough to get behind the Federal lines. The Confederate attack was then called off, Gordon and his force withdrew and gave up the fort, and a great many of his men were captured.[26]

Once Gordon's last-ditch effort had failed, General Lee concluded that his army could not much longer remain in its position to protect Richmond and Petersburg. His men would have to be evacuated soon so that they could join with Johnston's army in North Carolina.[27] The only practicable way to get Lee's army there was to move them by railroad southwest to Danville. The one line to Danville from Petersburg was the Southside Railroad which ran from Petersburg to Burkeville, joining there with the Richmond and Danville. Any movement by rail of Lee's men west, away from Petersburg toward Danville, was contingent on keeping the Southside Railroad clear of Union troops. Well aware of this fact, Grant planned his strategy which focused on blocking this vital railroad line.[28]

Grant began his move on March 29 by sending his troops southwest, around Lee's right at Petersburg.[29] The next day Federal soldiers were at Dinwiddie Court House, only six or eight miles below the Southside Railroad. General Pickett was immediately sent with his division to the area to protect the railroad and drive off Grant's troops. On April 1, however, Pickett's men were attacked and defeated at Five Forks, only three miles below the railroad, by a Federal force three times their size.[30] This defeat meant that Lee no longer had the ability to keep the Southside Railroad open from Petersburg to Burkeville.[31]

As soon as he learned the news of Pickett's disaster at Five Forks, Lee ordered General Longstreet to leave his lines east of Richmond and travel to Petersburg with Field's division to restore the Confederate right.[32] The rail cars could transport only one brigade at a time, and Benning's brigade left Richmond first, arriving in Petersburg about two o'clock on the afternoon of April 2.[33] Bratton's brigade arrived a little later

---

[25]Freeman, *Lee's Lieutenants*, 3:645.

[26]Ibid., 3:646-650; Foote, *Civil War*, 3:841-843.

[27]Foote, *Civil War*, 3:844; Freeman, *Lee's Lieutenants*, 3:655.

[28]Freeman, *Lee's Lieutenants*, 3:655.

[29]Ibid., 3:657; Foote, *Civil War*, 3:857.

[30]Foote, *Civil War*, 3:862-873.

[31]Catton, *Centennial History*, 3:443.

[32]Freeman, *Lee's Lieutenants*, 3:675; Foote, *Civil War*, 3:877.

[33]Field, "Campaign of 1864 and 1865," 560.

that day and had to detrain on the north side of the Appomattox River, cross over a bridge and march through the city.[34] Commanding the First South Carolina, Colonel Hagood said that when they arrived in Petersburg, they were immediately "pushed right off to the front, where the enemy was furiously assaulting our lines."[35] Bratton's regiments then joined Benning's brigade along the old inner line of works, between Battery 45 to the south and the Appomattox River to the north, on Indian Town Creek.[36]

A lieutenant in Company E of the Fifth Regiment described an incident which occurred just as the men reached their position on the inner works:

> As we were going into the works, marching by fours, a shell burst in front of where [my] brother . . . was marching with three Rawls brothers. A lone man went down and I thought it was [my brother]. I stopped an instant intending to go to him [but heard the command] "Close Up." The two remaining Rawls boys brushed away their tears [for it was their brother], and closed up with the others.[37]

Throughout the remainder of the day, Bratton's men skirmished with Grant's troops; all afternoon the opposing sharpshooters kept up a continual fire.[38]

While Bratton's men were hurrying from Richmond on April 2, Grant had unleashed a massive offensive, with some 60,000 troops, against the Confederate lines at Petersburg held by General A. P. Hill's corps. Not only were Hill's lines broken, but he himself was killed in the morning's battle. When Lee learned of the magnitude of Grant's success, he quickly determined that he must pull out of Petersburg and get his army back across the Appomattox River before it could be cut off.[39] Colonel Hagood summarized the situation when he wrote:

> We knew that the defense of Petersburg must be given up and that it was only nightfall that General Lee awaited before giving the signal to abandon [the city] to the enemy.[40]

---

[34]Bond and Coward, eds., *South Carolinians*, 169; Joseph Banks Lyle Journal, April 2, 1865.
[35]Hagood, *Memoirs*, 209.
[36]Freeman, *Lee's Lieutenants*, 3:682-683; Hagood, *Memoirs*, 209.
[37]McConnell, "Recollections," 13. Wounded by the shell was J. B. Rawls, who was captured but released at the end of the war. His two brothers, Martin and William, were later paroled at Appomattox. Salley, *South Carolina Troops, Fifth S.C.V.*, 3:156.
[38]Bond and Coward, eds., *South Carolinians*, 170.
[39]Foote, *Civil War*, 3:878-880.
[40]Hagood, *Memoirs*, 211.

Captain J. B. Lyle stated the problem in similar terms when he said, "[it was] evident to us all that the evacuation of the place was now a necessity."[41] In fact, General Lee had already advised the War Department and President Davis that Petersburg was about to be abandoned and that they too should prepare to evacuate Richmond that night.[42]

Under the cover of darkness on April 2, the Confederates began pulling out of both Petersburg and Richmond, after what Captain Lyle described as "the darkest day that the [Confederacy] has known."[43] Lee's evacuation order called for his artillery to move out first, at eight o'clock that night, followed by the infantry.[44]

LIEUTENANT GENERAL
AMBROSE POWELL HILL

Field's division acted as the rear guard for the Petersburg evacuation; his brigades crossed the Appomattox River over a pontoon bridge about eleven that night.[45] Colonel Coward's regiment covered the division's withdrawal, and as soon as Field's men had crossed the river, oil was poured on the bridge and it was set on fire.[46]

As Bratton's men quietly evacuated Petersburg, most of the inhabitants of the city were already asleep, unaware that by morning they would be in Federal hands. Colonel J. R. Hagood was gripped by the sadness of having to abandon these civilians and wrote:

> All the glorious recollections which encompassed [Petersburg] arose with a melancholy distinctness which made it impossible to view this step without profound emotion.[47]

---

[41] Joseph Banks Lyle Journal, April 2, 1865.

[42] Foote, *Civil War*, 3:880-881.

[43] Joseph Banks Lyle Journal, April 2, 1865.

[44] Foote, *Civil War*, 3:884.

[45] Field, "Campaign of 1864 and 1865," 561; Joseph Banks Lyle Journal, April 2, 1865.

[46] Bond and Coward, eds., *South Carolinians*, 170-171; Field, "Campaign of 1864 and 1865," 561; Mixson, *Reminiscences of a Private*, 116.

[47] Hagood, *Memoirs*, 211. Hagood was referring to his recollections of the summer of 1863, when the brigade, then under Jenkins' command, had been treated so warmly by the people of Petersburg.

Finally, in the pre-dawn hours of April 3, the Confederate ammunition supplies in the city were exploded by Lee's retreating army, and the people of Petersburg, "as well as the enemy, knew then for the first time that the retreat had commenced."[48] The only hope for Lee's army was to unite with Joe Johnston's troops in North Carolina. General Grant, however, had Lee's army vastly outnumbered and was determined to bring it to bay long before any such union could be effected.

During the night of April 2-3, Lee and his 12,500 troops from Petersburg marched steadily towards Amelia Court House, a rail station thirty-nine miles southwest of Richmond and thirty-six miles northwest of Petersburg. There they would unite with the Confederate soldiers who had evacuated the capital city. The men were told that trains had been ordered to deliver food and ammunition to Amelia Court House, and they expected to receive these needed supplies the following day.[49]

Bratton's exhausted and hungry men engaged in a brief skirmish with Federal cavalry northwest of Petersburg at dawn on April 3, suffering only light casualties.[50] The march toward Amelia Court House was quickly resumed, but, as Colonel J. R. Hagood wrote:

> [Because of] the immense trains which accompanied the Army, the march was necessarily slow although the troops were not suffered to rest except when some obstruction in the road delayed the wagons.[51]

During the day, Bratton's men crossed back over the Appomattox River about eight miles east of Amelia Court House, and they soon learned that their brigade quartermaster wagons had been captured.[52] The men finally reached Amelia Court House at about two o'clock in the afternoon the next day, April 4.[53] According to Colonel Hagood, Bratton's brigade

> reached Amelia Court House without accident . . . and halted in the expectation of finding supplies of rations which had been ordered to be accumulated there for just this emergency.[54]

---

[48]Ibid., 212.
[49]Freeman, *Lee's Lieutenants*, 3:681, 687.
[50]Bond and Coward, eds., *South Carolinians*, 171-172.
[51]Hagood, *Memoirs*, 212.
[52]Joseph Banks Lyle Journal, April 3, 1865.
[53]Ibid., April 4, 1865.
[54]Hagood, *Memoirs*, 212.

By some horrible mistake, however, there were no supplies or rations waiting there, and nobody seemed to know why.[55] Bratton's men had left Petersburg two days before with only one day's rations in their haversacks; they had not eaten for at least a day.[56] To make matters worse, the supply wagons in Field's division had taken a different road and were lost.[57]

When Lee's army reached Amelia Court House on the afternoon of April 4, it held only a one-day lead on Grant's troops. However, because no rations were there for the men, Lee had no choice but to delay the retreat to give his men time to forage. They foraged in the Amelia Court House vicinity until the following day and found some food, but their one-day head start had been lost. The Federal infantry was closing fast.[58]

On April 5, Lee moved his troops southwest out of Amelia Court House, with Longstreet's column in the lead. After marching only five miles, they ran into Federal cavalry at Jetersville, indicating to Lee that Grant now blocked the rail line to Burkeville where the Southside Railroad crossed the Richmond and Danville. Burkeville was the last remaining rail station where Lee could have been sent supplies by train from Danville. With Burkeville blocked, Lee decided to turn his army toward Farmville, twenty-three miles to the west, where he could receive desperately needed rations and supplies by rail from Lynchburg.[59]

Bratton's men skirmished with Grant's cavalry at Jetersville until late in the afternoon on April 5 and resumed their march towards Farmville after dark.[60] All night they trudged westward, completely exhausted and famished.[61] At daylight on April 6, they reached Rice's Station on the Southside Railroad, about seven miles southeast of Farmville.[62] Captain Lyle described in his journal what happened that afternoon:

> [The] enemy move upon us in pretty heavy force about 2 p.m. – [our] skirmish line and artillery checks and drives back a line of battle – pretty heavy skirmishing until dark. . . . Reported that Longstreet's Headquarters wagon was sacked and destroyed – also, Bratton's Headquarters wagon. . . .[63]

---

[55]Freeman, *Lee's Lieutenants*, 3:689-690.

[56]Hagood, *Memoirs*, 212.

[57]Field, "Campaign of 1864 and 1865," 561. Field said that he did not see his wagons again until he got to Appomattox Court House.

[58]Freeman, *Lee's Lieutenants*, 3:691; Foote, *Civil War*, 3:910.

[59]Freeman, *Lee's Lieutenants*, 3:692-694; Foote, *Civil War*, 3:911-912.

[60]Hagood, *Memoirs*, 212; Joseph Banks Lyle Journal, April 5, 1865.

[61]Foote, *Civil War*, 3:912-913.

[62]Joseph Banks Lyle Journal, April 6, 1865; Freeman, *Lee's Lieutenants*, 3:698.

[63]Joseph Banks Lyle Journal, April 6, 1865.

After dark, they continued on toward Farmville, marching some two or three miles to the west and halting near the High Bridge over the Appomattox River.[64]

While Longstreet's corps was leading the retreat on April 6, disaster struck the rear of Lee's army. Except for some 200 men, General Ewell's and General Anderson's corps were captured by Federal troops. This meant the loss to Lee of two of his four corps, and in effect, the destruction of half his army.[65] This day was known afterward as the Black Thursday of the Confederacy.[66]

With what was left of his army, General Lee pushed on toward Farmville that night, crossing to the north bank of the Appomattox River well after dark. Lee then had only Longstreet's and Gordon's corps, or a total of six divisions, four of which had been shattered. Only Field's and Mahone's divisions remained sufficiently intact to mount a defense against the onslaught of the 100,000 Federal troops ready to come up for the attack.[67]

Field's division did not cross the river on April 6 with Lee and the rest of the army. According to Colonel Hagood in Bratton's brigade,

> Our Division, which brought up the rear, was, owing to the sudden irruption [*sic*] of the enemy on our flank, staved off from the High Bridge where the main body, under Lee, had crossed. We did not until the next morning [April 7], after a running fight of two hours, reach Farmville, five miles above, where we effected a passage and rejoined our comrades.[68]

There was no bridge where the Fifth Regiment crossed the Appomattox, but only two river boats tied up side by side, which took up most of the width of the river.[69] Coward's men crossed at this point by walking across the decks of the two boats and made their way into Farmville with the rest of Bratton's men on the morning of April 7.[70] Rations had finally arrived there for Lee's famished army, and what was left of the food supply was in rail cars on sidings in the town.[71] Those men who had marched into Farmville the night before were lucky; they had been issued two days' rations. Unfortunately, Bratton's men were part of the rear guard and

---

[64]Ibid.
[65]Freeman, *Lee's Lieutenants*, 3:706-707.
[66]Foote, *Civil War*, 3:915.
[67]Freeman, *Lee's Lieutenants*, 3:712.
[68]Hagood, *Memoirs*, 213.
[69]Bond and Coward, eds., *South Carolinians*, 173.
[70]Ibid. The horses and wagons crossed at a ford some eighty yards away.
[71]Foote, *Civil War*, 3:921.

found the food almost gone by the time they arrived the next morning.[72] For Bratton's disappointed troops, all that was left was a little hardtack.[73] Even this had to be eaten quickly because they were soon ordered to rush to the front.[74] According to Colonel Hagood, "[We were] hurrying through Farmville, with Sheridan's [Federal] cavalry right on our heels. . . ."[75] General Mahone, the same officer whose men had fired the mistaken volley at Jenkins and Longstreet in the Wilderness, had failed to destroy the High Bridge across the Appomattox after Lee's army was in Farmville.[76] As a result, Grant's cavalry had crossed quickly and was attacking Lee's troops on both flanks.[77]

When General Lee became aware of this new threat, he quickly put his army on the march northwest toward Lynchburg. He sent Mahone's division ahead to a position about three miles north of Farmville to cover the army's line of retreat. The Union troops, pouring across the High Bridge, were expected to attack there.[78] As the Federals bore down on Mahone's position on the afternoon of April 7, Longstreet's men arrived from Farmville and were hastily drawn up in a line of battle on Mahone's right.[79] There was brisk skirmishing along their front until the Federals finally made an attempt to turn Mahone's left flank. Field quickly sent both G. T. Anderson's and Bratton's brigades to Mahone's assistance, and they were able to repulse the Federal attack. In the process, they managed to take several hundred enemy prisoners.[80] Colonel Hagood, leading the First South Carolina in Bratton's brigade, described the April 7 fight north of Farmville as "an action of some magnitude," and wrote:

> Suddenly the enemy fell upon our left flank and we were hastily moved to that point. On arriving on the ground, we boldly charged his line, driving it back and capturing one or two hundred prisoners.[81]

These were the last shots fired in the war by Field's division, including the men in Bratton's brigade.[82] As he had done on so many occasions since assuming command of Hood's division in early 1864, Charles Field had sent Bratton's troops where the fighting was the thickest. In this their last

---

[72]Field, "Campaign of 1864 and 1865," 561.
[73]Bond and Coward, eds., *South Carolinians*, 173; Freeman, *Lee's Lieutenants*, 3:715-716.
[74]Bond and Coward, eds., *South Carolinians*, 173.
[75]Hagood, *Memoirs*, 213.
[76]Freeman, *Lee's Lieutenants*, 3:714-716; Foote, *Civil War*, 3:922.
[77]Joseph Banks Lyle Journal, April 7, 1865.
[78]Freeman, *Lee's Lieutenants*, 3:716; Foote, *Civil War*, 3:923-924.
[79]Foote, *Civil War*, 3:924; Field, "Campaign of 1864 and 1865," 561.
[80]Field, "Campaign of 1864 and 1865," 561.
[81]Hagood, *Memoirs*, 213-214; see also, Joseph Banks Lyle Journal, April 7, 1865.
[82]Field, "Campaign of 1864 and 1865," 561.

battle, without food or rest, they had attacked the Union lines and had taken hundreds of prisoners: a fitting, final display of their fighting spirit.

After the battle ended on the afternoon of April 7, Bratton's men, along with the rest of Lee's dwindling army, again resumed their march in the direction of Lynchburg.[83] The retreat, which had begun six nights before at Petersburg, was like torture for the men. Captain J. B. Lyle said that the only rations he had been issued since leaving Petersburg were one pint of meal and one-fourth pound of bacon, and he wrote, "I have lived pretty much on the corn which cavalrymen [had been issued for their horses and] gave me. . . ."[84] So many teams of horses and mules had starved to death that Lee's men burned over one hundred wagons rather than let them fall into Federal hands.[85] Colonel J. R. Hagood described what Bratton's men witnessed:

> The smoke and flames of burning wagons which had to be abandoned . . . [and] dead and dying horses at every step – added the scenic effects to this horrid drama in which our soldiers were the actors.[86]

It was amid this scene of disaster that Lee ordered another night march, the third in a row for his hungry and exhausted troops.[87] Bratton's men marched all night on April 7 and into the pre-dawn hours of the next day, but they covered only a few miles, finding it almost impossible to keep their wagons moving.[88] Lee was trying to reach Appomattox Station, some twenty-five miles west of Farmville on the Southside Railroad where eight Confederate supply trains were supposed to be waiting for his arrival.[89]

Lee's troops trudged toward Appomattox Station all day on Saturday, April 8, with Longstreet's men acting as rear guard.[90] Captain Lyle wrote that the soldiers in Lee's army seemed to be "completely demoralized – guns scattered along the way. . . ."[91] On the previous afternoon, Grant had sent General Lee a note requesting him to surrender, but Longstreet, when asked for his advice, told his old commander, "Not yet."[92]

Except for the cavalry, which was protecting the rear of his army, Lee's men were not harassed by the Federals during this long march on

[83]Hagood, *Memoirs*, 214.
[84]Joseph Banks Lyle Journal, April 8, 1865.
[85]Hagood, *Memoirs*, 213.
[86]Ibid., 214.
[87]Foote, *Civil War*, 3:925.
[88]Joseph Banks Lyle Journal, April 8, 1865.
[89]Foote, *Civil War*, 3:926; Freeman, *Lee's Lieutenants*, 3:720.
[90]Freeman, *Lee's Lieutenants*, 3:722.
[91]Joseph Banks Lyle Journal, April 8, 1865.
[92]Foote, *Civil War*, 3:929; Freeman, *Lee's Lieutenants*, 3:724.

April 8.[93] The critical question was whether Lee and his men would make it to Appomattox Station, and the eight supply trains there, before Grant's troops. If they failed to win this race, it would mean the end of Lee's army.[94] After marching all day undisturbed by the enemy, Bratton's men halted about dark.[95] By then, the head of Lee's column approached Appomattox Court House, some three miles short of Appomattox Station.[96] That night Lee received another note from Grant, this one suggesting a meeting to discuss the surrender of the Army of Northern Virginia. Lee responded by saying he did not propose to surrender, but he did agree to a meeting the next day to discuss steps necessary to restore the peace.[97]

Later on the night of April 8, Lee held a council of war with his commanders. The consensus was to try to break through the Union lines the next morning toward Lynchburg.[98] Lee's cavalry would initiate the attack, supported by Gordon's Second Corps, while Longstreet held his position as rear guard.[99] Longstreet's men, including those in Bratton's brigade, received their orders to resume the march about midnight on April 8, and by the next morning had reached a point some two miles from Appomattox Court House.[100]

Palm Sunday, April 9, began with Gordon's corps and Fitzhugh Lee's cavalry successfully clearing the Lynchburg Road so that Lee's army could resume its westward retreat. Within hours, however, the situation had deteriorated, with some 30,000 Federal cavalry and infantry threatening Gordon's front and flanks. He badly needed the help of First Corps, but at this time, Grant's troops were coming up on Longstreet's men from the rear. The situation for Lee's army had clearly become desperate.[101] As Colonel J. R. Hagood so succinctly wrote:

> [W]e reached a point two miles from Appomattox Court House, [and] we found the enemy drawn up across the road ahead of us, while simultaneously, another force closed upon our rear. The game was now decided.[102]

All morning the men in Field's division, including those in Bratton's brigade, continued their work felling trees and throwing up earthworks,

---

[93]Freeman, *Lee's Lieutenants*, 3:722.
[94]Foote, *Civil War*, 3:931.
[95]Joseph Banks Lyle Journal, April 8, 1865; Hagood, *Memoirs*, 215.
[96]Foote, *Civil War*, 3:932.
[97]Ibid., 3:932-933.
[98]Ibid., 3:934; Freeman, *Lee's Lieutenants*, 3:724.
[99]Freeman, *Lee's Lieutenants*, 3:724-725.
[100]Hagood, *Memoirs*, 215; Joseph Banks Lyle Journal, April 8, 1865.
[101]Foote, *Civil War*, 3:941; Freeman, *Lee's Lieutenants*, 3:729-730.
[102]Hagood, *Memoirs*, 215.

preparing to make a stand against the Union troops pressing them from the rear. They were unaware that General Lee was about to leave his headquarters to meet with Grant.[103] Colonel Coward, looking through his field glasses, saw what appeared to be a white flag passing between the opposing armies.[104]

General Lee had arisen that morning to the cold realization that what was left of his army was about to be destroyed, and he had dressed in his finest uniform for the momentous and humiliating occasion that he knew he must now face.[105] Shortly after noon, the beloved army commander mounted Traveller and rode to meet Grant at Appomattox Court House.[106] Colonel Coward recalled that as Lee rode by the men in Bratton's brigade, they let out a cheer as a token of their affection.[107] Lee was gone for more than three hours, working out the terms of the surrender.[108]

Bratton's men, who had ceased their labors on the earthworks, were resting beside the road to Appomattox Court House that afternoon when they first heard the news from a fast-riding courier. Colonel Hagood described their reaction, saying:

> The emotion which the news produced can only be imagined – I cannot describe it. We looked in each other's faces, where blank and fathomless despair was written, nor said one word – our hearts were too full for language.[109]

Finally, as he returned from his meeting with Grant, Lee rode toward the men in Bratton's brigade and those in First Corps. As he came among them, he had his hat in his hand and tears in his eyes. The men surged toward him, trying to touch him or his famous horse.[110] Colonel Coward recalled that Lee, surrounded by his devoted troops, spoke a few emotional words and asked them to return to their homes and "obey the laws of [their] several states."[111] With this, the distinguished general bowed his head and bid the men good-bye. Looking straight ahead, he then rode off; Coward never saw him again.[112] Sergeant Frank Mixson

---

[103]Freeman, *Lee's Lieutenants*, 3:730-731.
[104]Bond and Coward, eds., *South Carolinians*, 177.
[105]Foote, *Civil War*, 3:939.
[106]Ibid., 3:945; Freeman, *Lee's Lieutenants*, 3:739.
[107]Bond and Coward, eds., *South Carolinians*, 177.
[108]Freeman, *Lee's Lieutenants*, 3:739.
[109]Hagood, *Memoirs*, 215.
[110]Foote, *Civil War*, 3:952.
[111]Bond and Coward, eds., *South Carolinians*, 178.
[112]Ibid.

recalled the emotional scene as Lee rode away from the men in Bratton's brigade that April 9:

> The old man pulled off his hat, and, with tears streaming down his cheeks, without a word, he rode through us. . . . We knew he had done for the best and we had more confidence in him . . . than we ever had before, and we loved him more.[113]

An hour later, General Field saw Asbury Coward; according to Field, there were "tears streaming down the face of the chivalrous Colonel [from] South Carolina."[114]

That afternoon, following the surrender, General Grant sent wagons loaded with food over to the starving Confederates.[115] Many of the men ate so quickly that they became sick to their stomachs.[116] Darkness finally ended the saddest of all days for the Confederacy, and Bratton's men went to sleep feeling the profound humiliation of the vanquished.

The two days following the surrender were spent by the officers in Bratton's five regiments preparing and checking their rolls and determining which of their troops still had their rifles.[117] The Confederate troops were not belittled or heckled by their Federal counterparts after the surrender. In fact, one soldier in Bratton's brigade even wrote:

> *And they, the Yankees*, acted with much consideration, and like good soldiers, and good Americans can only act, did not show that exultation they must have felt.[118]

When all the numbers were tallied, General Lee had surrendered 28,231 men, a mere remnant of his once-powerful Army of Northern Virginia.[119] The largest Confederate infantry brigade at Appomattox was made up of the 1,548 South Carolinians commanded by General John Bratton.[120] The Palmetto Sharpshooters, with 356 men and 29 officers, was the largest infantry regiment surrendered, a tribute to their devotion,

---

[113]Mixson, *Reminiscences of a Private*, 119.

[114]Field, "Campaign of 1864 and 1865," 562.

[115]Freeman, *Lee's Lieutenants*, 3:741.

[116]Bond and Coward, eds., *South Carolinians*, 179.

[117]Ibid.; Freeman, *Lee's Lieutenants*, 3:741.

[118]Mixson, *Reminiscences of a Private*, 121 (emphasis in original).

[119]Freeman, *Lee's Lieutenants*, 3:744.

[120]R. A. Brock, ed., "Paroles of the Army of Northern Virginia, R. E. Lee, Gen., C.S.A., Commanding, Surrendered at Appomattox C. H., Va., April 9, 1865," *Southern Historical Society Papers*, 15 (1887):144. See also, Tabular Statement of Officers and men of the Confederate Army paroled at Appomattox Court House, O. R., vol. 46, part 1, p. 1277.

determination and tenacity.[121] The Fifth South Carolina Volunteers was not far behind, with 19 officers and 263 men in the regiment at the time it surrendered, more than some of the brigades at Appomattox.[122]

The formal surrender ceremony for Lee's infantry divisions occurred on Wednesday, April 12, when each Confederate solider was required to lay down his arms.[123] The Second Corps, led by General John B. Gordon, surrendered first, while Longstreet and his First Corps came last.[124]

When Field's division marched to the surrender ceremony, Bratton's brigade was in the lead. The men of the Palmetto Sharpshooters, commanded by Captain A. H. Foster, were at the front of Bratton's brigade.[125] They marched some three miles to a hill near Appomattox Court House; as they came up, opposite the Federal divisions, they halted, turned and faced their adversaries.[126] Bratton's men stepped forward and silently stacked their rifles, bayonets and cartridge belts.[127] Grant's troops were in full uniform with flags flying, and the ceremony was formal and somber.[128] Sergeant Frank Mixson recalled:

> We suffered no insult from any of our enemies. *No other army in the world would have been so considerate* of a foe that it had taken so long . . . to overwhelm. General Grant had acted nobly towards General Lee. His men acted considerately towards us.[129]

Ironically, the men in the Palmetto Sharpshooters stacked their arms in front of the Sixteenth Michigan. It had been almost three years since the "duel" between these men at Gaines' Mill had nearly destroyed the Michigan regiment. After the arms were stacked and the ceremony was ended, several men in the Sixteenth Michigan asked, "What Regiment is that?" At Gaines' Mill, such questions had gone unanswered, but now the

---

[121]Brock, ed., "Paroles of the Army of Northern Virginia," 144. See also, Hoyt, "Anderson's Brigade at Gaines' Mill," 226.

[122]Brock, ed., "Paroles of the Army of Northern Virginia," 144. For example, two brigades in Kershaw's division, Humphrey's and Simms', surrendered only 251 and 190, respectively. O. R., vol. 46, part 1, p. 1277.

[123]Foote, *Civil War*, 3:954; Freeman, *Lee's Lieutenants*, 3:745.

[124]Freeman, *Lee's Lieutenants*, 3:750.

[125]Captain A. H. Foster was in command, because none of the regiment's field officers were present. Colonel Walker and Lt. Colonel Goss were both apparently on leave in South Carolina. Major Humphreys, who had been wounded in August 1864, was apparently still on furlough.

[126]Royce G. Shingleton, ed., "South From Appomattox: The Diary of Abner R. Cox," *The South Carolina Historical Magazine*, 75 (1974):240-241. Cox commanded Company L of the Palmetto Sharpshooters at the war's end.

[127]Bond and Coward, eds., *South Carolinians*, 179.

[128]Shingleton, ed., "South From Appomattox," 240-241.

[129]Mixson, *Reminiscences of a Private*, 122-123 (emphasis in original).

response was "Palmetto Sharpshooters." One veteran of that regiment wrote that, on hearing this response,

> the Michigan boys broke ranks again, but [this time] it was to rush across the line that was no longer to divide them and press the hands of the South Carolinians, the remnant of the command that bore off [the Sixteenth Michigan's] flag nearly three years before. . . . Haversacks and canteens were then opened to the famished "Rebs" by the Michigan soldiers. . . .[130]

Also surrendered during the formal ceremony were the Confederates' regimental flags. When the color sergeant of the Fifth South Carolina placed the regiment's furled flag on his regiment's stack of arms, Colonel Coward took understandable pride in knowing that his men had cut up their battle flag so that each man could keep a piece, and had turned in an extra flag instead.[131] Later in the day, when he went to say goodbye to his corps commander, Colonel Coward received a written commendation signed by Longstreet and endorsed by General Lee, who said, "I have always considered [Colonel Coward] one of the best officers of this Army."[132]

There were some men in Bratton's brigade who refused to surrender, preferring to escape instead. One of these was Captain J. B. Lyle of the Fifth South Carolina, whose daring action the previous October had directly led to the capture of so many Union troops east of Richmond.[133]

The officers in Lee's army were not required to surrender their swords, but by the time Lieutenant J. D. McConnell in the Fifth Regiment learned of this, he had already broken his sword between two trees.[134]

The humiliating day, April 12, finally ended, and with it, Lee's Army of Northern Virginia. The men in Bratton's brigade could console themselves only with the following words in General Lee's farewell order:

> You will take with you the satisfaction that proceeds from the consciousness of duty faithfully performed. . . .[135]

---

[130]Hoyt, "Anderson's Brigade at Gaines' Mill," 226.
[131]Bond and Coward, eds., *South Carolinians*, 179-180.
[132]Ibid., 181.
[133]McConnell, "Recollections," 13. In the Fifth, S.C.V., Captain James M. Harvey, of Company F, also refused to surrender and escaped.
[134]McConnell, "Recollections," 13.
[135]Lee's Order (General Orders No. 9) read:
> After four years of arduous service marked by unsurpassed courage and fortitude, the Army of Northern Virginia has been compelled to yield to overwhelming numbers and resources.
> I need not tell the brave survivors of so many hard fought battles, who have remained steadfast to the last, that I have consented to this result from no distrust

Whatever else had been lost, the men in Coward's Fifth Regiment and in Walker's Palmetto Sharpshooters had Lee's respect and admiration. They knew that General Lee was right; they had indeed faithfully performed their duty. For them the war was over, and they were going home.

---

of them; but feeling that valor and devotion could accomplish nothing that could compensate for the loss that must have attended the continuance of the contest, I determined to avoid the useless sacrifice of those whose past services have endeared them to their countrymen. . . . You will take with you the satisfaction that proceeds from the consciousness of duty faithfully performed, and I earnestly pray that a Merciful God will extend to you His blessing and protection. With an unceasing admiration of your constancy and devotion to your Country, and a grateful remembrance of your kind and generous consideration for myself, I bid you all an affectionate farewell.

R. E. Lee
General

Foote, *Civil War*, 3:955-956; Freeman, *Lee's Lieutenants*, 3:752.

Chapter 26

The Journey Home

T he day that Bratton's men finally started home followed a cold night of steady Virginia rain.[1] On the morning of April 13, they left their camp near Appomattox Court House as a group, accompanied by a Federal cavalry officer. He was assigned to assure that Federal cavalry scouting parties, still active in the area, did not molest Bratton's column which was headed for Danville.[2] Colonel Coward recalled that after having had four nights of rest, the men started out in good spirits, and while a few jokes were heard, the sporadic laughter had a hollow ring.[3] On that first day of their journey home, the men marched some twenty-four miles before bedding down for the night.[4]

At sunrise the following day, Bratton's men arose to a breakfast of beef, parched corn and coffee, after which they were finally issued their paroles. They then walked south to Campbell Court House where they were befriended by a local farmer who offered them an acre of his onions. The men stopped and ate a hearty lunch of onions and potato

---

[1]Shingleton, ed., "South From Appomattox," 241 n. 11.
[2]Bond and Coward, eds., *South Carolinians*, 180; McConnell, "Recollections," 13.
[3]Bond and Coward, eds., *South Carolinians*, 180-181.
[4]Shingleton, ed., "South From Appomattox," 241.

soup and then resumed the march toward Danville. They finally stopped to make camp at around three in the afternoon, having covered some fifteen miles that day. The next morning, April 15, the men trudged steadily southward in a cold drizzle which soaked them to the skin; they reached the Staunton River at McIvers Ferry late that afternoon.[5]

According to Colonel Coward, Bratton's men crossed the river on a flat-bottomed scow operated by a young lad of about eighteen who delighted in using extremely foul language.[6] Sunday, April 16, marked the end of the first full week since the surrender at Appomattox. Under clear skies, Bratton's former soldiers marched some twenty-two miles and camped near Pittsylvania Court House, Virginia.[7] That night the mayor of Pittsylvania invited Bratton's men to a welcoming ceremony to be held the next day, followed by a picnic prepared by the ladies of village. The men arose early on Monday and tried to spruce themselves up for the welcome they were to receive. It was everything they had hoped for, with an abundance of ham, fried chicken, breads and several different kinds of deserts.[8] Following this feast, Coward was informed by General Bratton that all mounted men in the column would return home by one route, while the enlisted men, who were on foot, would go by a different route. Bratton requested that Coward lead the latter group to Danville where they would be able to take a train to Greensboro and then to Charlotte.[9]

Before reaching Danville on April 18, Colonel Coward spoke to the men and told them how a mob of rowdy civilians and paroled Confederate soldiers had destroyed government and private property in that town. He told the men that he knew them too well to think that they would do such a thing. According to one account, they then marched through Danville in perfect order and stopped some three miles southeast of the town where they enjoyed the rations which Coward had been able to procure for them there.[10]

Later that same day, Bratton's men walked down the railroad tracks toward Greensboro, North Carolina, for a distance of some eight miles to Pelham Station.[11] When the train of empty boxcars came up from Greensboro, the engineer was discovered to have been a cadet at the

---

[5]Ibid.

[6]Bond and Coward, eds., *South Carolinians*, 181.

[7]Shingleton, ed., "South From Appomattox," 241.

[8]Bond and Coward, eds., *South Carolinians*, 181-182.

[9]Ibid., 182.

[10]Shingleton, ed., "South From Appomattox," 242. At least one other account, however, indicates that some of Bratton's men joined in the rowdy conduct in Danville. Sergeant Frank Mixson, in Hagood's First South Carolina, recalled that he and some other men decided to "charge" a store which contained some government goods. Mixson said, "It did not take long to batter down the doors and get in, [and] then the scramble began [for] bacon, meal, molasses, clothes, blankets and everything else." Mixson, *Reminiscences of a Private*, 125-126.

[11]Shingleton, ed., "South From Appomattox," 242.

Citadel in the class before Colonel Coward's. Coward prevailed upon him to transport Bratton's men down to Greensboro, which he did by running the train backwards.[12]

Coward set off on horseback after seeing the men pull away from Pelham Station, and he rejoined them in Greensboro. That afternoon he learned that the next train for Charlotte was not scheduled until the following morning, so he and the men spent the night near the depot in Greensboro. While there, they were able to draw a half month's pay in gold or Federal currency, or a full month's pay in Confederate money, and they were issued shoes, blankets and clothes.[13]

The next morning, April 20, Bratton's worn-out veterans set out south again, in the direction of Charlotte. They attempted to flag down a train at the Yadkin River crossing, a few miles north of Salisbury, but the engineer merely passed them by. Colonel Coward then concluded that they would all get home quicker if they divided up in pairs.[14] It was there that the men in the Bratton's brigade, who had fought beside each other for so long, finally split up to get home the best way they could. According to Colonel Coward, as he rode away from these men "they raised a feeble cheer [and] I found myself choking and unable to speak."[15] All of them realized that they were leaving each other for the last time. They had endured four years of extreme hardship together, from the glory of First Manassas to the heartbreaking surrender at Appomattox. In all of their time together, they had always done honor to their state, and they had never let down their beloved Confederacy.

Traveling alone, Asbury Coward finally reached South Carolina several days later. When he crossed the Catawba River below Charlotte and rode into York District, he saw first hand how the country had been desolated and the people drained by the war. He even briefly considered moving his family to another country but discarded the thought. Brick-by-brick, he would rebuild in South Carolina.[16]

Years later, Asbury Coward vividly recalled how he had felt immediately after Lee's surrender to Grant at Appomattox on that Palm Sunday afternoon in 1865. He remembered thinking of the great men in Lee's army who had given their lives for a lost cause, and especially of Micah Jenkins, in Coward's words, "the friend of my life."[17] There was a profound irony in the fact that the promising young general, so noted for

---

[12]Bond and Coward, eds., *South Carolinians*, 182.
[13]Ibid., 183; Shingleton, ed., "South From Appomattox," 242.
[14]Bond and Coward, eds., *South Carolinians*, 184. Coward mistakenly placed this incident at the Tar River crossing, but that is well north of Greensboro. He no doubt meant the Yadkin River crossing between Greensboro and Salisbury, North Carolina.
[15]Ibid.
[16]Ibid., 186.
[17]Ibid., 135.

his dedication to the service, had been killed on a beautiful spring morning in Virginia by the mistaken fire of his fellow Confederates. As he struggled to resign himself to the senseless death of Micah Jenkins, Coward said:

> I thought of Byron's bitter diatribe of the [struck] eagle, who, stretched upon the plain, views the feather from his own wing that has guided the arrow that pieced his heart.[18]

---

[18]Ibid., 177-178. Coward's paraphrase is from Byron's "English Bards, and Scotch Reviewers; a Satire," in volume one of *The Works of Lord Byron*, ed., Ernest Hartley Coleridge (New York: Octagon Books, Inc., 1966), lines 841-848 at p. 364.

Epilogue

<u>Caroline Jamison Jenkins</u>

During the war, Caroline Jenkins learned to endure hardship, the same as so many other young wives of Confederate soldiers. Her most painful time was from September 1863 to September 1864. During those twelve months, she lost her two-year-old son, her mother-in-law, her husband, and her father. Although considered delicate and fragile when she first married, the war forced her to develop a quiet inner strength. In February 1865, as Sherman made his way toward Orangeburg, South Carolina, the word spread that his troops planned to dig up the body of Caroline's father buried there. Sherman's men apparently wanted to desecrate the body of D. F. Jamison because he had served as the President of South Carolina's Secession Convention. Although not documented, the story exists that she and a servant went to Orangeburg, disinterred her father's body and temporarily reburied it in a nearby swamp to keep it out of the hands of Sherman's troops. Perhaps she got the idea from the citizens of Charleston who had taken similar steps, at about the same time, to protect the body and grave of John C. Calhoun. Jamison's body was reburied in the Presbyterian cemetery in Orangeburg after the war.

When Caroline received the news that the war had finally ended, she was only twenty-seven-years-old. Left alone with four small boys, ages eighteen months to eight years, she faced the daunting task of raising her family with practically no income. Her world completely shattered, she first moved to Summerville, South Carolina, where some of her own family had located during the war. There she became a tutor to young ladies and operated a boarding house. Each of her four sons was educated in Yorkville at the Kings Mountain Military School. Before the turn of the century, Caroline moved to Charleston, where she continued her work as a tutor.

In late January 1902, she visited her youngest son at the United States Military Academy where he had graduated and had later become an instructor. In early February, she had completed her visit and was returning to Charleston. There she had been invited to attend a ceremony in which President Theodore Roosevelt was to present an engraved sword to her oldest son who had been an officer in the "Rough Riders" under Roosevelt's command. Shortly after leaving West Point, she was stricken with pneumonia and had to detrain in Washington, D.C., where she died on February 9, 1902. Her body was taken on to Charleston, and she was laid to rest in an unmarked grave next to her husband in Magnolia Cemetery. She was sixty-four years old and had never remarried.

David Flavel Jamison

D. F. Jamison, Caroline's father, was fifty years old when elected president of the South Carolina Secession Convention and named South Carolina's secretary of war. Because of his age, he did not take a commission in the Provisional Army of the Confederate States of America. He continued as South Carolina's secretary of war until April, 1861, when that office was no longer needed. Later he was appointed as the presiding judge of the Military Court within General P. T. G. Beauregard's command. While performing this work in Charleston, he died of yellow fever on September 14, 1864, at age fifty-three. He was buried in a small cemetery in the heart of Orangeburg, South Carolina. Five months after his death, Jamison's plantation home, Burwood, was destroyed by the troops of General William T. Sherman as they marched toward Columbia.

Major Micah John Jenkins

Micah Jenkins' oldest son, Micah John, received an appointment to the United States Military Academy at West Point and graduated with a commission in the United States Army in 1879. He later served as a captain in Lieutenant Colonel Theodore Roosevelt's "Rough Riders" during the Spanish-American War, and distinguished himself during the Battle of San Juan Hill in Cuba in 1898. He was promoted to major for his bravery during the fighting in Cuba. On April 11, 1902, after Roosevelt became president of the United States, he visited Charleston, South Carolina, and presented Major Jenkins with a hand-crafted cavalry saber on

MICAH JOHN JENKINS

behalf of Jenkins' friends and admirers. Major Jenkins died ten years later in Charleston.

Robert Flavel Jenkins

The second son of Micah Jenkins worked in South Carolina all of his life. He became assistant collector for the Internal Revenue Service and served in that capacity in four different regions of the state. During his later years, he frequently wrote letters to newspapers on the subject of his famous father's Civil War campaigns. He died at Meggett, South Carolina, on May 26, 1936, and is buried at nearby St. Paul's Episcopal Church beside his wife.

ROBERT FLAVEL JENKINS

William Edward Jenkins

William, the third son of Micah and Caroline Jenkins, went into retailing in Charleston and continued this line of work until about 1893. Then he moved his family to Goldsboro, North Carolina, where he engaged in the importing business. Later he operated the Hotel Morgan in Morganton, North Carolina, after which he retired in Florida. He died in Goldsboro in 1930.

Major General John Murray Jenkins

Micah Jenkins' youngest son graduated from the Citadel in 1883 and from the United States Military Academy at West Point in 1887, where he later served for four years as an instructor. In 1893, he was assigned to the Citadel as commandant, where he remained for four years. During World War One, he commanded an infantry brigade in the Meuse-Argonne offensive, and he was gassed on three separate occasions. For his service in France, he was awarded the Distinguished Service Cross and the Purple Heart. Following that war, he returned home

JOHN MURRAY JENKINS

to recuperate from internal gas burns, after which he was promoted to brigadier general. In 1927, he retired from the Army as a major general and lived in Washington, D.C. There he died in 1958, at age ninety-four.

Evander M. Law

After being wounded at Cold Harbor, Law never returned to General Lee's Army of Northern Virginia. He was transferred to General Wade Hampton's command in early 1865 and became the commander of a Confederate cavalry brigade until he was paroled in May 1865 as a brigadier general. Following the war, he lived briefly in Yorkville, the home of his wife, Jane Latta, and became the administrator of her father's substantial estate. In the late 1860's, Law returned to his adopted state, Alabama, where he engaged in farming and in organizing the Alabama Grange movement. In 1893, he moved to Bartow, Florida, where he was superintendent of the South Florida Military Institute until 1903. He later edited the Bartow *Courier-Informant* until 1915 and died on October 31, 1920, at age eighty-four.

Asbury Coward

Asbury Coward returned to Yorkville, South Carolina, in April 1865, to find his home town economically devastated. His financial condition was such that his wife had to give music lessons to support the family. In the year following Appomattox, Coward reopened the Kings Mountain Military School, which he operated until 1886. During that period, he educated each of Micah Jenkins' four sons at the school; Coward and Jenkins had agreed during the war that if either of them was killed, the other would shoulder the responsibility for educating his slain friend's sons. In 1882, Coward became South Carolina's superintendent of education, a position he held for four years. In 1890, he was named the superintendent of the Citadel in Charleston and remained in this position until his retirement in 1908. He died in Rock Hill, South Carolina, in April 1925, at age eighty-nine. After his death, a bronze plaque was

ASBURY COWARD, AS SUPERINTEN-
DENT OF THE CITADEL.

dedicated in his memory at the Kings Mountain National Battlefield near York. Micah Jenkins' youngest son, Major General John M. Jenkins, delivered the main address. In it, Jenkins praised the memory of the man who had been his father's closest friend and referred to the fine tribute given to Coward at the end of the Civil War by General Robert E. Lee. Asbury Coward had devoted almost forty-five years of his distinguished career to the instruction of young men, both at the Kings Mountain Military School and at the Citadel. Upon his death, the flag of South Carolina, flying over the State House in Columbia, was lowered to half staff in his honor.

The Kings Mountain Military School

The Kings Mountain Military School, closed from 1861 through 1865, was reopened by Asbury Coward in January 1866. He struggled to make the school a success, but the Federal government would not let his cadets use rifles, and there was a lingering indebtedness on the "Garrison." In post-war South Carolina, not many families could afford to send their sons to a boarding school, and Coward was forced to close the academy's doors in 1886. Various sponsors attempted to operate schools on the premises for several years afterwards, but these efforts proved unsuccessful. The buildings and grounds were finally purchased by the Church Home Orphanage, later known as the Episcopal Home for Children, which moved its operations from Charleston to York in 1909. In 1966, the one hundred and nine-year-old Garrison building was razed to make room for a more modern structure. The Episcopal Home for Children, now called "York Place," thrives today on what was the old Kings Mountain Military School campus.

Brigadier General Micah Jenkins

One can only surmise how Micah Jenkins, before he was killed at the Wilderness, felt about the war and its effect on him and his family; there is very little in his correspondence on the subject. It is logical to assume that he was frustrated with the politics of the Confederate military system, which arguably kept him from reaching his goal of promotion to major general. It also appears that he had lost some of his optimism about the probable outcome of the conflict. No doubt he would have been deeply troubled had he known he was to leave Caroline alone to raise their four boys in desolate post-war South Carolina. One thing is clear: he was born to be an army officer and was doing what he most wanted to do. As Longstreet noted in his memoirs, "General Jenkins' heart was in the service, and [he] could submit to anything that seemed best for its interest."[1]

---

[1]Longstreet, *From Manassas to Appomattox*, 468.

APPENDIX ONE

FACTS CONCERNING THE PALMETTO SHARPSHOOTERS

Based primarily on the National Archives' Compiled Service Records of Confederate soldiers,[1] at least 1,410 men and officers served in the Palmetto Sharpshooters from the regiment's formation in April 1862, to its surrender at Appomattox.[2] Of this total of 1,410, the overwhelming majority were volunteers; only 75 were conscripts, and only 5 were substitutes.

Approximately 476 (34%) of the Palmetto Sharpshooters lost their lives during the war. Of these, 322 (23%) were killed or mortally wounded in combat. If the Compiled Service Records were more accurate and complete, no doubt these figures would be higher.

The incomplete records of the wounded show that at least 573 (41%) of the Palmetto Sharpshooters suffered combat wounds that were not mortal. (A more accurate figure would probably exceed 50%). Of the 573, 125 were wounded twice; 12 were wounded three times; and 4 were wounded in four separate battles. One man in Company C, Private R. M. Jenkins (no relation to Micah Jenkins), was wounded on five occasions.

During the one-month period from May 31 through June 30, 1862, the men in the regiment fought three major battles: Seven Pines, May 31; Gaines' Mill, June 27; and Frayser's Farm, June 30, 1862. In these three battles alone, the regiment had 161 men killed or mortally wounded. In addition, approximately 400 were wounded and survived.

The Battle of Frayser's Farm was by far the most deadly for the Palmetto Sharpshooters. Out of 375 men who entered the engagement, 84 were killed or mortally wounded, and approximately 170 were wounded. Not quite 125 men were available for duty the following morning, and even some of them had been slightly wounded.

After the fighting at Seven Pines, Gaines' Mill and Frayser's Farm, the regiment never fully recovered its strength. At Appomattox, however, the Palmetto Sharpshooters was the largest single Confederate regiment to be surrendered, with 356 men and 29 officers.

---

[1] National Archives, Compiled Service Records of the Confederate Soldiers who served in Organizations from the State of South Carolina, R. G. 109, series M267, microfilm rolls 382-390 (Jenkins' Palmetto Sharpshooters).

[2] The following other sources were relied upon for information regarding the deaths during the war of soldiers who served in the Palmetto Sharpshooters: Judith M. Andrews, ed., *Roll of the Dead: South Carolina Troops* (Columbia, South Carolina: South Carolina Department of Archives and History, 1995); John B. O. Landrum, *History of Spartanburg County* (reprint; Spartanburg, South Carolina: The Reprint Co., 1985); Jo Roberts Owens and Ruth Dickson Thomas, *Confederate Veterans Enrollment Book of York County, South Carolina - 1902* (Clover, South Carolina: Westmoreland Printers, Inc., 1983). See also, Randolph W. Kirkland, Jr., *Broken Fortunes: South Carolina Soldiers, Sailors and Citizens who Died in the Service of Their Country and State in the War for Southern Independence* (Charleston, South Carolina: South Carolina Historical Society, 1995).

APPENDIX TWO

LIST OF PALMETTO SHARPSHOOTERS
ENGAGEMENTS/SKIRMISHES

PLACE	NO. DEAD	DATE(S)
Williamsburg (Virginia)	9	May 5, 1862
Seven Pines (Virginia)	53	May 31, 1862
Gaines' Mill (Virginia)	24	June 27, 1862
Frayser's Farm (Virginia)	84	June 30, 1862
Second Manassas (Virginia)	25	August 30, 1862
South Mountain (Maryland)	1	September 14, 1862
Sharpsburg (Maryland)	14	September 17, 1862
Fredericksburg (Virginia)	1	December 13, 1862
Franklin (Virginia)	not known	March 17, 1863
Suffolk (Virginia)	1	April 11-May 3, 1863
Carrsville (Virginia)	not known	May 16-17, 1863
Lookout Valley (Tennessee)	12	October 29, 1863
Loudon (Tennessee)	0	November 13-14, 1863
Campbell's Station (Tennessee)	8	November 16, 1863
Knoxville (Tennessee)	1	November 20-29, 1863
Bean's Station (Tennessee)	not known	December 15, 1863
Dandridge (Tennessee)	6	January 17, 1863
The Wilderness (Virginia)	14	May 6, 1864
Spotsylvania (Virginia)	5	May 8-21, 1864
Hanover Junction (Virginia)	1	May 23-25, 1864
Cold Harbor (Virginia)	3	June 1-3, 1864
Bermuda Neck (Virginia)	2	June 16-17, 1864
Petersburg (Virginia)	19	June 19-July 28, 1864
Deep Bottom (Virginia)	7	August 14, 1864
Fort Harrison (Virginia)	13	September 30, 1864
Darbytown Road (Virginia)	14	October 7, 1864
Williamsburg Road (Virginia)	not known	October 27, 1864
Retreat from Petersburg to Appomattox (Virginia)	1	April 3-8, 1865

APPENDIX THREE

ROSTER OF PALMETTO SHARPSHOOTERS[3]

I. <u>Generally</u>. This Appendix lists, and furnishes data on, almost all of the men who served in the Palmetto Sharpshooters from its formation in April 1862 until the regiment's surrender at Appomattox on April 9, 1865. Three main sources were used to compile this Appendix: (1) National Archives, Compiled Service Records of the Confederate Soldiers Who Served in Organizations from the State of South Carolina, R. G. 109, series M267, microfilm rolls 382-390 (Jenkins' Palmetto Sharpshooters); (2) R. A. Brock, ed., "Paroles of the Army of Northern Virginia . . . Surrendered at Appomattox C. H., April 9, 1865," *Southern Historical Society Papers*, Volume 15 (1887), pp. 123-132; and Judith M. Andrews, ed., *Roll of the Dead: South Carolina Troops*.[4]

II. <u>Data Furnished</u>. On each solider listed, the following information, if available, is given:

Column 1: The soldier's name (last name first).
Column 2: The soldier's final rank during the war, followed by his Company designation (in parenthesis).
Column 3: The date of the soldier's original enlistment, appointment or entry into the service. Since the Palmetto Sharpshooters was not formed until April 1862, many of the solders who joined that regiment had originally enlisted in various South Carolina regiments (especially the Fourth, Fifth and Ninth South Carolina Volunteers) at the beginning of the war in 1861. These original dates of entry or enlistment are the ones furnished. If the soldier was a conscript or a substitute, his date of entry is preceded by a "c" or an "s."
Column 4: The name of the South Carolina town where the soldier originally enlisted or entered the service. If the soldier entered service in a state other than South Carolina, the name of the state is furnished rather than the town.
Column 5: How and when the soldier ended his service in the Palmetto Sharpshooters or for the Confederacy. To conserve space, a set of abbreviations, listed and explained below, has been used.

---

[3]For a roster of men in the Fifth South Carolina Volunteers, see A. S. Salley, *South Carolina Troops in Confederate Service*, vol. 3, *Fifth South Carolina Volunteers* (Columbia, South Carolina: The State Company, 1930).
[4]Other sources include those listed in footnote 2 to Appendix One.

Column 6: Whether the soldier suffered combat-related wounds that were not mortal in nature, and the number of separate battles or skirmishes in which he was wounded.

III. Explanation of Abbreviations.

Disp. Un.	Disposition Unknown. The sources used do not adequately indicate how the soldier ended his service.
KIA	Killed in action.[5]
MW	Mortally wounded. The date furnished is for the date wounded, not the date the soldier died.
Died Un.	Died while still in service, but the cause is not indicated.
DOD	Died of disease.
DOA	Died of accident.
DPOW	Died while a prisoner of war.
Med. D.	Medical discharge, medical retirement or medical resignation.
Sub. D.	Discharged by furnishing a substitute.
Enl. D.	Discharged when enlistment term expired.
Age D.	Discharged due to age.
Unk. D.	Discharged, but the reason is not indicated.
Res.	Resigned.
Des.	Deserted to the enemy or to home.
Tran.	Transferred to another unit and remained in service.
Par.	Paroled at the end of the war. Where the date given is 4/9/65, the soldier surrendered at Appomattox.
RPOW	Released or paroled from a Federal prison at the end of the war.
LOA	On leave of absence at the time the war ended.
W-1	Wounded in one battle or skirmish, but wound not mortal.

IV. Summary

There are 1,410 names listed in this Appendix as having served for some period of time in the Palmetto Sharpshooters. Of course, more men served in the regiment than are listed, but because of poor recordkeeping during the war, a completely accurate listing of those men is not feasible.

---

[5]If an entry under "Final Disposition" indicates that a soldier was killed or mortally wounded, the date of the battle or skirmish is also furnished. To determine in which battle or skirmish the soldier was killed or mortally wounded, compare the date to those given in Apendix Two. For example, if the Final Disposition entry shows "MW 6/30/62," reference to Appendix Two shows that the soldier was mortally wounded in the Battle of Frayser's Farm in Virginia on June 30, 1862.

NAME	LAST RANK (COMPANY)	DATE ENTERED	PLACE ENTERED	FINAL DISPOSITION	NO. TIMES WOUNDED
Abbott, Hamilton H.	Pvt. (K)	4/14/62	Spartanburg	KiA 6/30/62	W-1
Abbott, Henry T.	1st Lt. (E)	4/12/61	Sumter	Par. 4/9/65	
Abbott, John T.	Pvt. (B)	6/3/61	Columbia	MW 6/27/62	
Abbott, Robert R.	Pvt. (K)	4/13/61	Spartanburg	MW 6/30/62	
Able, A. R.	Pvt. (F)	3/2/64	Lexington	DOD 7/19/64	
Acker, Joseph M.	Cpl. (L)	4/14/61	Anderson	Par. 4/9/65	W-1
Adams, Joseph A.	Pvt. (G)	4/13/61	Yorkville	Par. 4/9/65	W-1
Addison, Wm. D. (see Attison, W.D.)					
Adams, J. M.	Sgt. (G)	4/13/61	Yorkville	Disp. Un	W-1
Adkerson, B. (see Atkerson, Burges)					
Adkins, James E. (see Atkins, James E.)					
Alexander, John W.	Pvt. (M)	4/13/61	Limestone Spr.	Disp. Un.	
Alexander, Wm. S.	2d Lt. (M)	4/13/61	Limestone Spr.	Par. 4/9/65	W-1
Allen, James	Pvt. (K)	4/13/61	Spartanburg	DOD 2/27/62	
Allen, James W.	Pvt. (M)	5/7/62	Limestone Spr.	Disp. Un.	W-2
Allen, John	Pvt. (M)	9/18/64	Virginia	Par. 4/9/65	
Allen, John W.	Pvt. (F)	7/12/61	Graniteville	Disp. Un.	W-1
Allen, Wiley	Pvt. (B)	c. 7/1/62	Pickens	Par. 4/19/65	W-1
Allgood, Wm. B.	Sgt. (I)	4/14/61	Pendleton	Par. 4/9/65	W-1
Allison, D. M.	Pvt. (G)	4/13/61	Yorkville	Disp. Un.	W-1
Allison, James L.	Pvt. (M)	4/13/61	Limestone Spr.	Disp. Un.	
Allison, J. R., Jr.	Pvt. (M)	6/10/61	Summerville	DOD 8/12/62	
Altman, Dempsey	Pvt. (F)	7/8/61	Ridgeville	MW 5/31/62	
Altman, S.	Pvt. (F)	9/8/61	Virginia	DOD 1862	
Altman, W. B.	Pvt. (F)	4/14/62	Lexington	Disp. Un.	
Ames, Edward S. (see Armes, Ed. S.)					
Amos, Charles M.	Pvt. (H)	3/11/62	Spartanburg	Par. 4/9/65	W-3
Anderson, Frank L.	Pvt. (K)	4/13/61	Spartanburg	Sub. D. 4/13/62	
Anderson, John F.	Pvt. (F)	7/4/61	Sumter	Disp. Un.	W-1
Anderson, W. B.	Pvt. (F)	7/1/63	Lexington	KIA 5/23/64	
Anderson, William	Major (F&S)	4/14/61	Anderson	MW 6/30/62	

374

NAME	LAST RANK (COMPANY)	DATE ENTERED	PLACE ENTERED	FINAL DISPOSITION	NO. TIMES WOUNDED
Anderson, William D.	2d Lt. (K)	4/13/61	Spartanburg	KIA 11/16/63	
Armes, Edward S.	Pvt. (E)	4/17/61	Kingstree	MW 5/5/62	
Armstrong, J. Bryant	Pvt. (K)		Union	DOD 7/21/62	
Arnold, John	Pvt. (I)		Pickens	DOD 7/20/62	
Arnold, M. M.	Pvt. (I)	3/15/62	Pendleton	Disp. Un.	
Arnold, Ruben	Pvt. (I)	2/8/64	Pickens	Par. 4/9/65	
Arnold, Silas	Pvt. (I)	3/15/62	Pendleton	DOD 7/19/62	
Ashley, John H.	Pvt. (L)	4/14/61	Anderson	Des. 3/31/64	
Atkerson, Burges	Pvt. (F)	7/12/61	Ridgeville	Disp. Un.	W-1
Atkins, James E.	Pvt. (E)	3/8/62	Sumter	Disp. Un.	W-1
Atkinson, Burges (see Atkerson, Burges)					
Atkinson, W. H.	Pvt. (B)	c. 7/1/62	Darlington	DOD 1/6/63	
Attison, W. D.	Pvt. (B)	1/15/64	Tennessee	Disp. Un.	W-1
Atwater, Wm. H.	Pvt. (E)	7/4/61	Ridgeville	Disp. Un.	
Austell, Joseph	Pvt. (A)	5/6/62	Union	Disp. Un.	W-1
Babb, Thomas	Pvt. (M)	c. 7/20/62	Columbia	Disp. Un.	W-1
Babel, Thomas (see Babb, Thomas)					
Bailey, A. W.	Surg. (F&S)			Disp. Un.	
Bailey, John M.	Pvt. (C)	c. 7/ /62	Columbia	DOD 1/30/63	
Bailey, R.	Pvt. (K)			KIA 6/24/64	
Ballenger, A. R.	Pvt. (D)	3/ /62	Spartanburg	Par. 4/9/65	W-1
Ballenger, James S.	1st Lt. (D)	4/13/61	Spartanburg	Par. 4/9/65	
Ballenger, O. P.	Pvt. (D)	3/ /62	Spartanburg	Par. 4/9/65	W-1
Ballenger, Richard D.	2d Lt. (D)	4/13/61	Spartanburg	MW 5/6/64	W-1
Ballenger, Wm. H.	Pvt. (D)	4/13/61	Spartanburg	Par. 4/9/65	W-1
Barclay, Robert H.	Pvt. (E)	3/15/62	Sumter	MW 6/30/62	
Barfield, H. M.	Pvt. (E)	6/4/61	Ridgeville	KIA 6/30/62	
Barker, D. C.	Cpl. (I)	4/14/61	Greenville	Par. 4/9/65	W-2
Barnett, Isaac C.	Pvt. (A)	12/17/61	Columbia	Par. 4/9/65	
Barnett, John W.	Pvt. (A)	8/27/61	Spartanburg	RPOW 1865	W-1
Barnett, Warren	Pvt. (A)	4/13/61	Union	Par. 4/9/65	

NAME	LAST RANK (COMPANY)	DATE ENTERED	PLACE ENTERED	FINAL DISPOSITION	NO. TIMES WOUNDED
Barr, D. T.	Sgt. (F)	7/8/61	Ridgeville	Par. 4/9/65	W-1
Barron, J. P.	Pvt. (G)	7/5/61	Virginia	MW 5/31/62	
Barton, W. J. N.	Pvt. (I)	4/14/61	Pendleton	Par. 4/9/65	W-3
Bates, Daniel	Pvt. (B)	7/12/63	Pendleton	DOD 10/12/64	
Beacham, H. L.	Pvt. (B)	8/22/61	Georgia	Disp. Un.	
Beacham, Thomas L.	Pvt. (B)	8/22/61	Georgia	RPOW 1865	W-1
Beacham, Wm. V.	Pvt. (B)	3/18/62	Anderson	DOD 6/10/62	
Bearden, David T.	Pvt. (K)	4/22/62	Spartanburg	KIA 8/30/62	W-1
Bearden, Eliphas	Pvt. (A)	4/13/61	Union	Par. 4/9/65	
Beaty, Christopher L.	Capt. (A)	4/13/61	Union	MW 8/14/64	W-1
Becknell, C. W.	Pvt. (I)	3/8/64	Columbia	Par. 4/9/65	W-1
Becknell, J. W.	Pvt. (I)	4/14/61	Greenville	DOD 1/9/64	W-1
Bedon, W. Z.	A. Surg. (F&S)			Disp. Un.	
Bedor, William Z. (see Bedon, W. Z.)					
Bellinger, Martin	Surg. (F&S)	4/17/62		Par. 4/9/65	W-1
Bellotte, Wm. M.	Pvt. (L)	6/3/61	Pendleton	Disp. Un.	W-1
Benson, Thomas P.	Capt. (C)	4/14/61	Anderson	Par. 4/9/65	
Berdine, R. H.	Pvt. (B)			MW 5/5/62	
Berry, R. S.	Pvt. (E)	2/14/64	Sumter	RPOW 1865	W-1
Bethune, John B.	Pvt. (K)	7/1/62	Spartanburg	Unk. D.	
Bibbs, Samuel R.	Pvt. (B)	4/14/61	Pendleton	MW 10/7/64	
Bishop, C. C.	Pvt. (D)	7/20/62	Spartanburg	DOD 6/18/63	
Bivings, James M.	Pvt. (K)	4/13/61	Spartanburg	Disp. Un.	
Black, David M.	Pvt. (K)	9/18/63	Union	DOD 12/9/64	
Black, James	2d Lt. (G)	4/13/61	Yorkville	MW 5/31/62	
Black, John	Pvt. (H)	3/11/62	Spartanburg	Par. 4/9/65	
Black, John H.	Pvt. (L)	4/14/61	Wolf Creek	MW 6/30/62	
Black, Templeton T.	Pvt. (K)	2/21/63	Spartanburg	Med. D. 4/30/63	
Black, Thomas P.	Pvt. (E)	3/5/62	Sumter	DOD 10/10/64	W-1
Black, William	Pvt. (M)	s. 9/5/62		KIA 9/17/62	
Blackwell, Berry	Pvt. (I)	4/14/61	Pendleton	Disp. Un.	W-1

NAME	LAST RANK (COMPANY)	DATE ENTERED	PLACE ENTERED	FINAL DISPOSITION	NO. TIMES WOUNDED
Blackwell, Jason	Pvt. (H)	3/11/62	Spartanburg	Disp. Un.	
Blackwell, T.	Pvt. (H)	3/11/62	Spartanburg	Med. D. 10/ /62	
Blakely, B. F.	Pvt. (I)	4/14/61	Anderson	Disp. Un.	
Blanton, C. D.	Pvt. (H)	3/11/62	Spartanburg	DOD 10/21/62	
Blanton, James, Jr.	Pvt. (M)	3/16/62	Virginia	Disp. Un.	W-2
Blanton, James, Sr.	Pvt. (M)	5/4/62	Limestone Spr.	KIA 6/30/62	
Blanton, John	Pvt. (M)	4/13/61	Limestone Spr.	Des. 3/ /65	W-1
Blanton, Joseph	Pvt. (M)	10/1/63	Limestone Spr.	DOD 4/ /65	
Blanton, Mike	Pvt. (M)	10/1/63	Limestone Spr.	DOD 1864	W-1
Blanton, Wm. Henderson	Pvt. (M)	12/25/64	Limestone Spr.	RPOW 6/5/65	
Blassingame, John H.	Capt. (K)	4/13/61	Spartanburg	Par. 4/9/65	W-2
Boatright, James A.	Pvt. (G)	2/29/64	Tennessee	Par. 4/9/65	W-2
Boggs, J. Thomas	Pvt. (I)	2/10/64	Pendleton	Des. 3/ /65	
Boling, J. M.	Pvt. (I)	2/21/63	Pendleton	KIA 6/20/64	W-1
Bolling, Joseph T.	Pvt. (I)	2/21/63	Pendleton	Par. 4/9/65	W-1
Bomar, L. D.	Pvt. (K)	2/16/65	Spartanburg	Par. 4/9/65	
Bomar, Thomas A.	Pvt. (D)	4/13/61	Spartanburg	DOD 5/2/62	
Bond, B. T.	Pvt. (E)			Par. 5/8/65	
Bonner, Benjamin F.	Sgt. (M)	4/13/61	Limestone Spr.	Disp. Un.	W-1
Bonner, George W.	Sgt. (M)	4/13/61	Limestone Spr.	Par. 4/9/65	W-1
Bonner, Luther	3d Lt. (M)	4/13/61	Limestone Spr.	MW 6/30/62	
Bonner, Pinckney	Pvt. (M)	4/13/61	Limestone Spr.	KIA 5/31/62	
Booker, T. P.	Pvt. (D)	1/5/63	Spartanburg	Par. 4/9/65	
Booker, Thomas W.	Pvt. (D)	4/13/61	Spartanburg	MW 5/6/64	W-1
Booker, W. S.	Pvt. (D)	3/9/64	Spartanburg	Par. 4/9/65	
Booth, James	Pvt. (E)	6/24/61	Ridgeville	Disp. Un.	
Boroughs, E. P.	Pvt. (I)	3/15/62	Pendleton	MW 8/30/62	W-1
Boroughs, G. W.	Pvt. (I)	4/14/61	Pendleton	Par. 4/9/65	W-1
Bowden, Samuel L.	Sgt. (B)	6/3/61	Pendleton	Disp. Un.	W-2
Bowen, John M.	Pvt. (K)	4/30/62	Spartanburg	Par. 4/9/65	
Bowie, Andrew	Pvt. (K)	7/9/62	Spartanburg	DOD 1/22/63	

377

NAME	LAST RANK (COMPANY)	DATE ENTERED	PLACE ENTERED	FINAL DISPOSITION	NO. TIMES WOUNDED
Bowling, Berry	Pvt. (I)			Des. 3//65	
Boyce, B. E.	Pvt. (E)	4/5/64	Sumter	Par. 4/9/65	
Boyce, H. W.	Pvt. (E)	4/5/64	Sumter	DOD 12/21/64	
Boyle, W. C.	Pvt. (M)	c. 7/20/62	Columbia	KIA 10/29/63	W-1
Bratcher, Thomas J.	Pvt. (L)	4/14/61	Anderson	Disp. Un.	
Brawley, J. B.	2d Lt. (H)	4/13/61	Spartanburg	Disp. Un.	
Bridges, William	Pvt. (M)	4/13/61	Limestone Spr.	Med. D. 3/6/63	W-1
Bright, C.	Pvt. (D)	c. 11/26/64	Spartanburg	Par. 4/9/65	
Bright, Orlay	Pvt. (M)	4/13/61	Limestone Spr.	Disp. Un.	
Bright, Thomas B.	Pvt. (K)	4/13/61	Spartanburg	DPOW	
Brock, J. F.	Pvt. (I)	3/15/62	Pendleton	MW 6/30/62	
Brogden, Robert	Pvt. (F)	7/8/61	Ridgeville	Disp. Un.	W-1
Brown, Albert	Pvt. (K)	4/13/61	Spartanburg	KIA 6/30/62	
Brown, C. W.	Pvt. (B)	3/26/62	Townville	Disp. Un.	
Brown, Caleb P.	1st Lt. (H)	6/28/61	Spartanburg	Par. 4/9/65	W-1
Brown, Charles W.	Pvt. (H)	3/11/62	Spartanburg	Med. D. 11//64	W-1
Brown, E. G.	Pvt. (E)	10/28/63	Sumter	Par. 4/9/65	
Brown, Green	Pvt. (M)	4/13/61	Limestone Spr.	Med. D. 7/12/62	
Brown, H. H.	Pvt. (D)	6/3/61	Spartanburg	Par. 4/9/65	W-1
Brown, J. A.	Pvt. (G)	4/13/61	Yorkville	RPOW 6/14/65	W-2
Brown, James Nardin	Pvt. (C)	4/15/61	Donaldsonville	KIA 8/30/62	W-1
Brown, John J.	Capt. (H)	6/28/61	Spartanburg	Res. 2/3/63	W-1
Brown, Joseph C.	Pvt. (K)	3/28/64	Spartanburg	Med. D. 1864	W-1
Brown, M. M.	Sgt. (E)	4/12/61	Morris Is.	Par. 4/9/65	W-2
Brown, Newton J.	Pvt. (K)	3/28/64	Spartanburg	Par. 4/9/65	W-1
Brown, Samuel G.	Pvt. (E)	3/19/62	Sumter	Disp. Un.	
Brown, T. Cicero	1st Sgt. (H)	6/28/61	Spartanburg	Par. 4/9/65	
Brown, William L.	Pvt. (H)	3/11/62	Spartanburg	Med. D. 4/19/63	W-1
Brunson, W. E.	Pvt. (E)	4/13/61	Sumter	MW 9/30/64	
Bryson, Marsh S.	Pvt. (K)	3/20/62	Spartanburg	KIA 5/31/62	
Buchanan, George G.	Pvt. (A)	4/13/61	Union	RPOW 6/24/65	W-1

NAME	LAST RANK (COMPANY)	DATE ENTERED	PLACE ENTERED	FINAL DISPOSITION	NO. TIMES WOUNDED
Buchanan, Jesse B.	Pvt. (A)	4/13/61	Union	Med D. 1/5/63	W-1
Bulling, Mattison	Pvt. (I)		Pickens	KIA 6/21/64	
Bullington, Jesse H.	Pvt. (K)	4/13/61	Spartanburg	Par. 4/9/65	
Bullock, George B.	Pvt. (K)	8/18/61	Virginia	Disp. Un.	W-1
Bulman, George J.	Cpl. (K)	4/13/61	Spartanburg	Par. 4/9/65	W-1
Bulman, William M.	Pvt. (K)	4/13/61	Spartanburg	Par. 4/9/65	
Burk, Alfred	Pvt. (H)	6/28/61	Spartanburg	Par. 4/9/65	
Burk, Matthew	Pvt. (H)	3/2/63	Spartanburg	Disp. Un.	W-1
Burkett, B. F.	Pvt. (E)	6/28/62	Virginia	Par. 4/ /65	
Burkett, W. E.	Pvt. (M)	c. 7/20/62	Columbia	Disp. Un.	W-1
Burnett, Granville	Pvt. (D)	4/30/62	Spartanburg	Par. 4/9/65	
Burnett, James B.	Pvt. (D)	3/19/62	Spartanburg	MW 9/17/62	
Burnett, Joseph	Pvt. (D)	5/8/62	Spartanburg	DOD 3/14/63	W-2
Burnett, Richard	Pvt. (D)	3/28/62	Spartanburg	MW 8/30/62	
Burns, Andrew	Pvt. (L)	3/17/62	Anderson	Disp. Un.	
Burns, David S.	Pvt. (D)	4/13/61	Spartanburg	KIA 6/19/64	W-1
Burris, T. B.	Pvt. (C)	c. 1/15/64	Tennessee	Par. 4/9/65	W-1
Bush, Govan	Pvt. (K)	4/13/61	Spartanburg	KIA 6/19/64	
Butler, Allen	2d Lt. (B)	4/14/61	Pendleton	KIA 11/16/63	
Butler, Obadiah	Pvt. (B)	4/14/61	Pendleton	KIA 6/30/62	W-1
Byars, Nathan	Pvt. (H)	4/13/61	Spartanburg	Par. 4/9/65	W-1
Byrum, B. P.	Pvt. (C)	4/12/61	Anderson	Par. 4/9/65	
Byrum, J. N.	Pvt. (C)	2/18/64	Anderson	Par. 4/9/65	
Calbert, Augustus	Pvt. (H)	4/13/61	Spartanburg	Disp. Un.	
Caldwell, Thomas E.	Pvt. (G)	4/13/61	Yorkville	Died Un. 1864	
Caminade, John C.	Pvt. (B)	6/1/61	Pendleton	DPOW 1863	
Camp, George H.	Pvt. (K)		Spartanburg	Med. D. 1/28/63	W-1
Camp, John Joseph	2d Lt. (M)	4/13/61	Limestone Spr.	Par. 4/9/65	W-2
Camp, William E.	Sgt. (M)	4/13/61	Limestone Spr.	KIA 4/5/65	W-1
Campbell, James L.	Pvt. (C)	s. 7/1/62	Columbia	Disp. Un.	
Campbell, T. A. F.	Cpl. (C)	4/16/62	Anderson	RPOW 6/5/65	W-1

379

NAME	LAST RANK (COMPANY)	DATE ENTERED	PLACE ENTERED	FINAL DISPOSITION	NO. TIMES WOUNDED
Canley, James F.	Pvt. (B)	10/10/61	Greenville	Disp. Un.	W-2
Cannon, Elkanah	Pvt. (M)	c. 7/20/62	Columbia	Des. 3/65	
Cannon, Enoch	Pvt. (M)	c. 7/20/62	Columbia	Disp. Un.	W-1
Cannon, Lewis M.	Pvt. (K)	4/28/62	Spartanburg	Par. 4/9/65	
Cannon, Nahum	Pvt. (K)	3/18/62	Spartanburg	Des. 3/65	W-1
Cannon, Owen	Sgt. (F)	7/8/61	Ridgeville	Disp. Un.	W-1
Cantrell, J. B.	Pvt. (I)	4/14/61	Pendleton	Disp. Un.	W-1
Cantrell, J. T.	Pvt. (H)	c. 6/10/63	Spartanburg	RPOW 6/26/65	
Cantrell, Jackson A.	Pvt. (H)	5/10/62	Spartanburg	Disp. Un.	
Capers, T. L.	Pvt. (K)	7/7/62	Spartanburg	KIA 8/30/62	
Carden, C. J.	Cpl. (B)	6/3/61	Anderson	MW 10/7/64	W-1
Carpenter, Jacob Q.	Capt. (M)	4/13/61	Limestone Spr.	KIA 5/31/62	
Carpenter, James B.	Pvt. (C)	4/14/61	Anderson	Tran. 12/20/62	W-1
Carpenter, M. M.	Pvt. (A)	4/13/61	Union	Disp. Un.	
Carr, P. J.	Pvt. (A)	4/13/61	Union	Disp. Un.	
Carraway, J. A. M.	Sgt. (E)	4/8/61	Sumter	Med. D. 1/10/63	W-1
Carroll, D. H.	Pvt. (G)	4/23/63	Yorkville	Disp. Un.	W-2
Carroll, James	Pvt. (A)	4/13/61	Union	MW 8/14/64	W-2
Carroll, Joseph W.	1st Lt. (G)	4/13/61	Yorkville	Disp. Un.	W-2
Carroll, T. L.	Pvt. (G)	12/1/63	Columbia	Par. 4/9/65	
Cash, A. F.				Des. 3/65	
Cash, Alexander W.	Pvt. (H)	1/6/64	Spartanburg	Par. 4/9/65	
Cash, Andrew M.	Pvt. (H)	3/11/62	Spartanburg	Des. 3/65	
Cash, Dillard	Pvt. (H)	6/28/61	Spartanburg	Disp. Un.	W-1
Cash, Marvel	Pvt. (H)			Des. 3/65	W-1
Cash, Smith	Pvt. (H)	3/11/62	Spartanburg	Des. 3/65	
Cash, T. Gaines	Pvt. (H)			Disp. Un.	W-1
Castles, Barnet	Pvt. (G)	5/8/62	Yorkville	KIA 6/30/62	
Caughman, G. E.	Pvt. (F)	5/7/62	Columbia	DOD 7/2/62	
Chamblin, W. W.	Pvt. (D)	11/20/63	Spartanburg	DOD 3/30/64	
Champion, R.	Pvt. (H)	3/11/62	Spartanburg	MW 6/30/62	

NAME	LAST RANK (COMPANY)	DATE ENTERED	PLACE ENTERED	FINAL DISPOSITION	NO. TIMES WOUNDED
Chapman, James	Pvt. (I)	3/15/62	Pendleton	Med. D. 9/15/62	
Chapman, W. A.	Pvt. (I)	3/15/62	Pendleton	KIA 1/17/64	
Cheatham, W. W.	Pvt. (L)	4/14/61	Anderson	KIA 8/30/62	
Clanton, Levi	Pvt. (D)	4/13/61	Spartanburg	Tran. 1864	
Clary, Olvey (see Clery, Obey)					
Clayton, F. V.	Pvt. (I)	3/15/62	Pendleton	Disp. Un.	W-2
Clayton, S. W.	Pvt. (I)	4/14/61	Pendleton	Disp. Un.	W-2
Clayton, W. C.	Sgt. (I)	4/14/61	Pendleton	MW 6/30/62	
Clery, Obey	Pvt. (M)	4/13/61	Limestone Spr.	DOD 6/2/63	
Cleveland, B. F.	Pvt. (B)	4/14/61	Pendleton	Par. 4/9/65	
Cleveland, E. J.	Pvt. (B)	4/14/61	Pendleton	Disp. Un.	W-1
Cleveland, H. A.	Pvt. (B)			Par. 1865	
Cleveland, J. R.	Pvt. (B)	4/14/61	Fair Play	Par. 4/9/65	
Cleveland, L. C.	1st Lt. (B)	4/14/61	Pendleton	Disp. Un.	W-1
Cleveland, Wm. T.	Pvt. (L)	4/14/61	Fair Play	Par. 1865	W-1
Clifford, Patrick	Pvt. (L)	6/3/61	Pendleton	Med. D. 5/27/63	W-1
Clinkscales, B. T.	Pvt. (C)	11/5/62	Virginia	Par. 4/9/65	W-1
Clinkscales, John F.	Cpl. (C)	4/16/62	Virginia	Par. 4/9/65	
Clinkscales, L. N.	Pvt. (M)	c. 7/20/62	Columbia	Disp. Un.	W-1
Clinkscales, R. L.	Pvt. (C)	5/16/64	Anderson	Par. 4/9/65	
Clinkscales, R. M.	Pvt. (C)	4/14/61	Anderson	Par. 4/9/65	W-1
Cobb, J. A.	Pvt. (G)	8/13/61	Yorkville	Par. 4//65	W-1
Cobb, Lem	Pvt. (M)	5/4/62	Limestone Spr.	Med. D. 10/21/64	W-1
Cochran, H.	Pvt. (F)	6/30/61	Ridgeville	KIA 6/30/62	
Colbert, A. G.	Pvt. (H)	4/13/61	Spartanburg	Par. 4/9/65	
Colbert, A. W.	Pvt. (M)	4/13/61	Limestone Spr.	Unk. D. 7/20/62	
Colbert, E. M.	Pvt. (H)	4/13/61	Spartanburg	Par. 4/9/65	
Colbert, Earls	Pvt. (H)	3/2/63	Spartanburg	Med. D. 1863	
Colclough, Alexander	Capt. (E)	4/16/61	Sumter	Disp. Un.	W-1
Collins, D. B.	Pvt. (M)	4/13/61	Limestone Spr.	DOD 10/22/63	W-1
Collins, G. W.	Pvt. (E)	2/13/63	Charleston	Disp. Un.	

382

NAME	LAST RANK (COMPANY)	DATE ENTERED	PLACE ENTERED	FINAL DISPOSITION	NO. TIMES WOUNDED
Crawford, E. D.	Pvt. (G)	7/14/61	Yorkville	Disp. Un.	W-1
Crawford, J. D.	Pvt. (C)	4/14/61	Anderson	Par. 4/9/65	W-1
Crawford, J. K.	Pvt. (A)	6/1/62	Union	Disp. Un.	
Crawford, W. D.	Pvt. (L)	4/14/61	Anderson	DOD 12/15/63	W-1
Crawley, James	Pvt. (B)		Spartanburg	Died Un.	
Crenshaw, Newton	Pvt. (M)	c. 7/20/62	Columbia	Disp. Un.	W-1
Crittenden, Richard T.	Pvt. (K)	4/13/61	Spartanburg	DOD 12/19/63	
Crocker, Alexander	Pvt. (H)	6/28/61	Spartanburg	Des. 3/ /65	
Crocker, J. A.	Pvt. (H)	5/10/62	Spartanburg	KIA 6/27/62	
Crocker, M.	Pvt. (H)	6/28/61	Spartanburg	KIA 9/17/62	
Crow, Thomas	Pvt. (L)	6/3/61	Pendleton	Disp. Un.	W-1
Crumpton, J. Thaddeus	Pvt. (L)	9/4/64	Virginia	Par. 4/9/65	
Cudd, John C.	Pvt. (H)	6/28/61	Spartanburg	Tran. 7/ /63	W-1
Cudd, W. H.	Pvt. (H)	c. 10/20/64	Spartanburg	Par. 4/9/65	
Cullum, S. F.	Pvt. (F)	7/8/61	Ridgeville	Par. 4/9/65	
Culp, Green B.	1st Sgt. (K)	4/13/61	Spartanburg	Disp. Un.	W-1
Cunningham, A. C.	Pvt. (D)	3/12/62	Spartanburg	Med. D. 1/17/63	W-1
Cunningham, James	Pvt. (K)	2/12/62	Spartanburg	DOD 5/20/62	
Cusac, J. W.	Pvt. (M)	c. 7/20/62	Columbia	Par. 4/9/65	
Cushman, J.	Pvt. (F)	6/30/61	Ridgeville	Disp. Un.	
Dalton, Bradley	Pvt. (D)	6/3/61	Spartanburg	Par. 4/9/65	
Daniel, Columbus A.	Sgt. (L)	6/3/61	Pendleton	KIA 9/30/64	
Daniels, John W.	Capt. (L)	1861	Pendleton	Med. D. 4/24/64	W-1
Daniels, Julius A.	Pvt. (L)	9/11/63	Columbia	RPOW 5/13/65	
Darlington, J. T.	Pvt. (C)	4/14/61	Anderson	Tran. 1/31/63	W-1
Darracott, J. C.	Pvt. (C)	4/14/61	Anderson	Par. 4/9/65	
Darracott, T. B.	Pvt. (C)	9/1/63	Abbeville	Par. 4/ /65	
Davidson, E. N.	Pvt. (G)	1/1/64	Columbia	Par. 4/9/65	
Davidson, John C.	Pvt. (H)	c. 7/19/62	Spartanburg	Disp. Un.	W-1
Davis, B. Franklin	Pvt. (H)	3/11/62	Spartanburg	Des. 3/ /65	W-1
Davis, D. Sumter	Pvt. (A)	2/1/64	Union	Par. 4/9/65	

383

NAME	LAST RANK (COMPANY)	DATE ENTERED	PLACE ENTERED	FINAL DISPOSITION	NO. TIMES WOUNDED
Davis, G. M.	Pvt. (D)	3/13/62	Spartanburg	Med. D. 12/23/63	W-1
Davis, J. F. M.	Pvt. (A)	4/13/61	Union	Par. 4/9/65	
Davis, Jacob N.	Pvt. (H)	3/8/62	Spartanburg	Disp. Un.	W-1
Davis, R. T.	Sgt. (A)	4/13/61	Union	Disp. Un.	W-1
Davis, Robert	A. Surg. (F&S)			Par. 4/9/65	
Davis, Robert	Pvt. (D)	4/27/62	Spartanburg	DOD 12/10/63	W-1
Davis, Wm. R.	Pvt. (M)	4/13/61	Limestone Spr.	KIA 5/31/62	
Davison, E. N. (see Davidson, E. N.)					
Dawson, Jerome W.	Cpl. (H)	6/28/61	Spartanburg	Med. D. 1/20/65	W-2
Dawson, Stephen	Pvt. (I)	6/28/61	Greenville	KIA 1/17/64	
Day, F. M.	Pvt. (L)	7/30/61	Anderson	MW 5/6/64	W-1
Dean, A. F.	Pvt. (E)	3/19/62	Sumter	DOD 5/1/62	
Dean, Edward J.	Pvt. (D)	4/13/61	Spartanburg	Disp. Un.	
Dean, P. L.	Pvt. (B)	12/20/62	Virginia	Par. 4/9/65	
DeLorne, John F.	Pvt. (E)	3/15/62	Sumter	DOD 5/1/62	
DeLorne, T. M.	Pvt. (E)	3/26/62	Sumter	DOD 1862	
Dempsey, Elisha	Pvt. (M)	10/1/64	Virginia	Par. 4/9/65	
Derrick, D. W.	Pvt. (F)	5/7/62	Columbia	DOD 3/25/63	
Derrick, J. S.	Sgt. (F)	7/8/61	Ridgeville	Disp. Un.	W-1
Derrick, T. H.	Cpl. (F)	7/8/61	Ridgeville	Par. 4/9/65	W-3
Dick, Thomas M.	Pvt. (E)	10/1/61	Sumter	KIA 6/30/62	
Dick, W. Edward	Capt. Com. (F&S)	7/12/61	Virginia	Disp. Un.	
Dickison, Isaac	Pvt. (F)	3/14/62	Lexington	Med. D. 10/5/62	
Dickison, Wiley	Pvt. (F)	3/14/62	Lexington	Med. D. 10/9/62	
Dickson, J. L.	Pvt. (B)	5/10/62	Walhalla	DOD 6/28/62	
Dickson, J. L.	Pvt. (L)	6/3/61	Pendleton	Tran. 1/1/63	W-1
Dickson, J. W. (see Dixon, J. W.)					
Dickson, John R.	Pvt. (D)	4/28/62	Spartanburg	Par. 4/9/65	
Dickson, W. B.	1st Sgt. (B)	4/14/61	Pendleton	Par. 4/9/65	
Dixon, J. D.	Pvt. (G)	6/4/61	Orangeburg	Par. 4/9/65	W-1
Dixon, J. W.	Cpl. (E)	7/4/61	Sumter	Par. 4/9/65	

384

NAME	LAST RANK (COMPANY)	DATE ENTERED	PLACE ENTERED	FINAL DISPOSITION	NO. TIMES WOUNDED
Dixon, Zimmerman	Cpl. (E)	3/15/62	Sumter	MW 6/30/62	
Dobbins, W. P.	Pvt. (H)	3/11/62	Spartanburg	DOD 1862	
Dodd, William P.	Pvt. (I)	4/14/61	Pendleton	Par. 4/9/65	W-1
Donalds, J. F.	Pvt. (E)	2/14/64	Sumter	Disp. Un.	
Donalds, W. M.	Pvt. (E)	2/14/64	Sumter	Disp. Un.	
Donigan, J. J.	Pvt. (K)	5/25/62	Spartanburg	Disp. Un.	W-1
Dorr, Charles W.	Pvt. (L)	3/17/62	Belton	Med. D. 1864	
Driggers, Alex	Pvt. (B)	c.		Disp. Un.	
Driggers, William	Pvt. (M)	c. 7/20/62	Columbia	Par. 4/9/65	W-1
Drummond, W. S.	1st Sgt. (D)	4/13/61	Spartanburg	MW 11/16/63	W-1
Duke, H. M.	Pvt. (B)	4/14/61	Pendleton	Par. 4/9/65	W-2
Duke, John T.	Pvt. (B)	4/14/61	Pendleton	Par. 4/9/65	W-1
Dunaway, Abram	Pvt. (A)		Union	KIA 8/14/64	
Dunaway, Joseph	Pvt. (A)	3/1/64	Union	KIA 8/14/64	
Dunaway, Stephen	Pvt. (A)	4/12/62	Union	MW 9/30/64	
Dunaway, William	Pvt. (A)	3/20/62	Union	Par. 4/9/65	
Duncan, T. W.	Pvt. (F)	3/12/62	Lexington	Par. 4/9/65	W-1
Duncan, Thomas C.	1st Sgt. (K)	4/13/61	Spartanburg	KIA 6/30/62	
Dunlap, R. D.	Cpl. (A)	4/13/61	Union	Par. 4/9/65	W-2
Dunlap, William S.	Sgt. (A)	4/13/61	Union	Med. D. 12/13/62	W-1
Dunn, Silas Y.	Cpl. (A)	4/13/61	Union	MW 6/27/62	
Dupree, R. F.	Pvt. (A)	4/13/61	Union	KIA 6/30/62	
Dupriest, John	Pvt. (K)	4/19/62	Spartanburg	KIA 6/30/62	W-1
Durant, Andrew S.	Pvt. (K)	8/1/63	Spartanburg	DOD 7/2/64	
Durant, E. C.	S. Maj. (F&S)	7/9/61	Ridgeville	Par. 4/9/65	W-2
Durant, J. S.	Sgt. (E)	3/18/62	Sumter	Par. 4/9/65	W-1
Durant, John	Pvt. (K)	4/13/61	Spartanburg	MW 10/7/64	
Durant, R. M.	2d Lt. (E)	7/4/61	Sumter	Par. 4/9/65	W-1
Durant, W. J.	Sgt. (E)	6/4/61	Clarendon	Med. D. 7/20/63	W-1
Dye, W. F.	Pvt. (G)	6/4/61	Orangeburg	Par. 4/9/65	W-1
Eagan, D. G.	Sgt. (F)	7/8/61	Ridgeville	KIA 9/30/64	

NAME	LAST RANK (COMPANY)	DATE ENTERED	PLACE ENTERED	FINAL DISPOSITION	NO. TIMES WOUNDED
Eagan, J. S.	Pvt. (F)	2/16/63	Lexington	DOD 7/3/63	
Earle, George W.	Pvt. (C)	4/14/61	Anderson	Med. D. 12/13/63	W-1
Earnhart, James B.	Pvt. (K)	4/13/61	Spartanburg	DPOW 5/9/65	
East, William W.	Cpl. (G)	4/13/61	Yorkville	MW 5/31/62	
Elliott, E. H.	Pvt. (B)	4/14/61	Pendleton	KIA 5/11/64	W-1
Elliott, E. J.	Pvt. (B)	9/8/63	Virginia	Par. 4/9/65	W-2
Elliott, John L.	Pvt. (B)	5/6/62	Pendleton	MW 10/29/63	
Elliott, Lee M.	Pvt. (G)	4/13/61	Yorkville	Par. 4/9/65	
Elrod, Andrew W.	Pvt. (C)	9/21/63	Anderson	Par. 4/9/65	
Emerson, E. N.	Pvt. (C)	3/4/63	Anderson	Par. 4/9/65	
Emerson, J. H.	Pvt. (I)	4/14/61	Pendleton	MW 6/30/62	
Enloe, J. N.	Pvt. (G)	4/13/61	Yorkville	Disp. Un.	W-1
Erskine, Hugh C.	Pvt. (L)	4/14/61	Anderson	Par. 4/9/65	
Erskine, J. Sidney	Pvt. (L)	4/14/61	Anderson	Disp. Un.	W-2
Erwin, Hazel H.	Pvt. (G)	3/19/62	Yorkville	MW 5/5/62	
Erwin, W. R.	Pvt. (G)	4/13/61	Yorkville	KIA 1/17/64	
Eskew, W. T.	Pvt. (L)	4/14/61	Anderson	Med. D. 3/5/63	W-1
Eubanks, Joseph	Pvt. (A)	s. 7/3/62	Union	Par. 4/9/65	W-1
Eubanks, Thomason	Pvt. (A)	4/13/61	Union	Disp. Un.	
Evins, John H.	Capt. (K)	4/13/61	Spartanburg	Med. D. 6/3/63	W-1
Ezell, Landrum C.	Sgt. (H)	6/28/61	Spartanburg	Par. 4/9/65	W-2
Fallow, Aeil	Pvt. (F)	7/8/61	Ridgeville	KIA 6/30/62	
Fant, J. M.	Cpl. (A)	4/13/61	Union	Par. 4/9/65	
Fant, W. A.	Pvt. (C)	4/14/61	Anderson	Par. 4/9/65	
Farmer, C. J.	Pvt. (H)			Disp. Un.	
Featherston, E. B.	Pvt. (C)	4/14/61	Anderson	DOD 6/7/62	
Featherston, T. C.	Pvt. (C)	5/9/61	Columbia	Disp. Un.	W-1
Felton, A.	1st Lt. (C)	4/14/61	Anderson	MW 5/31/62	
Felts, J. W.	Pvt. (G)	4/13/61	Yorkville	DOD 3/16/63	
Fennell, F. G.	Pvt. (I)	8/1/62	Pendleton	MW 5/6/64	
Fennell, W. J.	Pvt. (I)	4/14/61	Pendleton	Par. 4/9/65	

NAME	LAST RANK (COMPANY)	DATE ENTERED	PLACE ENTERED	FINAL DISPOSITION	NO. TIMES WOUNDED
Ferguson, W. J. M.	Pvt. (I)	4/14/61	Pendleton	Par. 4/9/65	W-1
Fewell, W. A.	Pvt. (G)	4/13/61	Yorkville	MW 5/31/62	
Fincher, C. P.	Pvt. (A)	4/13/61	Union	Par. 4/9/65	
Fincher, John M.	Cpl. (A)	3/20/62	Union	Par. 4/9/65	
Fincher, T. D.	Pvt. (A)	3/1/64	Union	Par. 4/9/65	W-1
Finley, G. W.	Cpl. (H)	4/13/61	Spartanburg	KIA 9/17/62	W-1
Flanigan, James	Pvt. (A)	4/13/61	Union	KIA 9/17/62	
Floyd, J. J.	Pvt. (H)	5/9/62	Spartanburg	KIA 6/30/62	
Floyd, James C.	Pvt. (H)	5/20/62	Spartanburg	Des. 3/ /65	W-1
Floyd, M.	Pvt. (E)	7/16/61	Ridgeville	MW 11/16/63	W-1
Floyd, N.	Pvt. (E)	7/13/61	Ridgeville	Med. D. 7/ /62	
Foister, J. M. (see Foster, J. M.)					
Ford, A. W.	Cpl. (L)	6/3/61	Pendleton	KIA 5/31/62	
Forrester, James	Pvt. (L)			DOD 1862	
Foster, A. A.	Pvt. (D)	4/13/61	Spartanburg	Par. 4/9/65	
Foster, A. C.	Pvt. (M)	4/13/61	Limestone Spr.	KIA 6/30/62	
Foster, A. J.	Pvt. (D)	12/16/62	Spartanburg	DPOW 4/27/65	
Foster, Alfred H.	Capt. (D)	4/13/61	Spartanburg	Par. 4/9/65	W-1
Foster, Asa	Pvt. (K)	4/13/61	Spartanburg	KIA 6/30/62	
Foster, John A.	Pvt. (D)	6/3/61	Spartanburg	KIA 6/30/62	
Foster, J. J.	Cpl. (D)	4/13/61	Spartanburg	MW 5/31/62	
Foster, J. M.	Pvt. (L)	7/30/61	Anderson	MW 5/31/62	
Foster, Joseph H.	Pvt. (D)	4/13/61	Spartanburg	DOD 5/16/63	W-1
Foster, L. L.	Pvt. (D)	4/29/64	Spartanburg	Par. 4/9/65	W-1
Foster, Moses	Cpl. (D)	4/13/61	Spartanburg	Par. 4/9/65	
Foster, Richard	Pvt. (K)	4/28/62	Spartanburg	Med. D. 9/ /62	W-1
Foster, Thomas T.	Pvt. (D)	4/28/62	Spartanburg	KIA 6/30/62	
Foster, W. J.	Pvt. (D)	5/5/62	Spartanburg	MW 9/14/62	
Foster, William M.	Cpl. (D)	4/13/61	Spartanburg	Par. 4/9/65	W-2
Fowler, Charles	Pvt. (H)	4/13/61	Spartanburg	Des. 3/ /65	W-1
Fox, J. S.	Pvt. (F)	7/8/61	Ridgeville	RPOW 6/5/65	W-1

NAME	LAST RANK (COMPANY)	DATE ENTERED	PLACE ENTERED	FINAL DISPOSITION	NO. TIMES WOUNDED
Frasier, J. J.	Pvt. (L)	3/15/62	Pendleton	Med. D. 12/15/62	W-1
Frasier, Ransom A. (see Frasier, Robt. A.)					
Frasier, Robert A.	Pvt. (L)	4/14/61	Fair Play	Disp. Un.	W-2
Freeman, J. T.	(B)			Disp. Un.	
Frey, F. M. (see Fry, F. M.)					
Fricks, D. H.	Pvt. (B)	6/1/61	Pendleton	Tran. 1862	
Fry, F. M.	Pvt. (E)	3/14/62	Sumter	Par. 4/9/65	
Gable, E. M.	Pvt. (L)	4/14/61	Anderson	MW 6/27/62	
Gable, H. N.	Pvt. (F)	1/20/64	Tennessee	Par. 4/9/65	
Gable, Henry	Pvt. (F)	8/1/63	Lexington	Disp. Un.	
Gable, William	Pvt. (F)	4/19/64	Lexington	Par. 4/9/65	
Gaffney, Thomas	Pvt. (M)	4/13/61	Limestone Spr.	Disp. Un.	
Gaillard, C. D.	Pvt. (C)	4/14/61	Anderson	KIA 10/7/64	W-1
Gaines, H. M.	Pvt. (L)	4/14/61	Anderson	DOD 6/10/62	
Galloway, J. D.	Pvt. (B)	c. 1862		Disp. Un.	
Gambrell, Almon R.	Pvt. (L)	4/14/61	Anderson	Par. 4/9/65	W-1
Gantt, J. P.	Pvt. (F)	7/8/61	Ridgeville	Disp. Un.	
Gantt, R. V.	Cpl. (F)	9/8/61	Virginia	Par. 4/9/65	
Gantt, S. C.	Pvt. (F)	7/8/61	Ridgeville	Med. D. 12/31/62	W-1
Gardner, George W.	Pvt. (M)	c. 7/20/62	Columbia	DOD 4/1/63	
Gardner, J. M.	Pvt. (E)	7/12/61	Ridgeville	Disp. Un.	W-1
Garvey, J.	Pvt. (F)	6/30/61	Ridgeville	KIA 5/31/62	
Garvin, Frederick L.	Capt. (I)	4/14/61	Pendleton	Par. 4/9/65	W-1
Garvin, J. J.	Pvt. (I)	3/15/62	Pendleton	Par. 4/9/65	
Garvin, W. T.	Pvt. (I)	4/14/61	Pendleton	Disp. Un.	
Gassaway, C. I.	Sgt. (A)	4/13/61	Union	Par. 4/9/65	W-1
Gassaway, Caleb	Cpl. (A)	4/13/61	Union	Disp. Un.	W-1
Gassaway, Charles M.	Pvt. (A)	4/13/61	Union	KIA 6/30/62	
Gaston, A. L.	Pvt. (D)	10/15/63	Spartanburg	Par. 4/9/65	
Gaston, W. D.	Pvt. (D)	4/13/61	Spartanburg	Par. 4/9/65	
Gee, Andrew J.	Pvt. (H)	6/28/61	Spartanburg	DOD 7/19/64	W-2

388

NAME	LAST RANK (COMPANY)	DATE ENTERED	PLACE ENTERED	FINAL DISPOSITION	NO. TIMES WOUNDED
Gentry, Elias L.	Pvt. (K)	10/25/61	Spartanburg	Med. D. 7/2/64	W-1
Gentry, Hamilton	Pvt. (K)	3/20/62	Spartanburg	Tran. 1862	
Gentry, L. W.	Pvt. (C)	c. 3/25/63	Columbia	Disp. Un.	
Gentry, W. H.	Cpl. (H)	2/24/62	Spartanburg	Par. 4/9/65	
George, J. W.	Pvt. (C)	4/18/64	Anderson	Par. 4/9/65	
George, William IV	Pvt. (C)	4/14/61	Anderson	Par. 4/9/65	
Gibson, John H.	Pvt. (K)	4/15/63	Spartanburg	Par. 4/9/65	
Gibson, Thomas L.	Pvt. (B)	4/14/61	Pendleton	Par. 4/9/65	
Gibson, William M.	Pvt. (K)	7/10/61	Spartanburg	Par. 4/9/65	W-2
Gilchrist, Daniel E.	Pvt. (K)	7/1/62	Spartanburg	Tran. 4/18/64	
Gilfilen, R. A.	Pvt. (G)	5/10/62	Yorkville	Par. 4/9/65	
Gillespie, J. B.	Cpl. (G)		York	DOD 1862	
Gillespie, R. T.	Pvt. (I)	7/9/61	Summerville	Par. 4/9/65	W-1
Gilstrap, J. W.	2d Lt. (C)	4/14/61	Pendleton	KIA 5/31/62	
Gleason, Joel H.	Pvt. (D)	4/14/61	Anderson	KIA 6/30/62	
Glenn, William M.	Pvt. (F)	6/3/61	Spartanburg	Par. 4/9/65	
Goff, James E.	2d Lt. (M)	8/1/63	Lexington	DOD 1864	W-1
Goforth, John	Pvt. (M)	4/13/61	Limestone Spr.	Disp. Un.	W-1
Goforth, William	Pvt. (D)	8/31/63	Virginia	KIA 1/17/64	
Goins, N. G.	Pvt. (D)	5/8/62	Spartanburg	Med. D. 10/10/62	
Goins, W. Mitchell	Pvt. (D)	4/1/62	Spartanburg	DOD 4/12/62	
Golightly, Jacob	Pvt. (D)			DOD 11/27/63	
Golightly, Z. D.	Pvt. (A)	4/13/61	Spartanburg	KIA 5/5/62	
Goss, H. L.	Lt. Col. (F&S)	7/3/62	Union	Sub. D. 1862	
Goss, John Wesley	Pvt. (A)	4/13/61	Union	LOA	
Gowing, William H.	Cpl. (A)	6/4/61	Union	Med. D. 9/24/62	
Grady, H. P.	Pvt. (E)	4/13/61	Union	Par. 4/9/65	
Graham, J. A.	Pvt. (G)	7/4/61	Sumter	Disp. Un.	
Graham, John	Pvt. (A)	3/20/64	Tennessee	Par. 4/9/65	
Graham, O. B. H.	Pvt. (A)	4/13/61	Union	Age D. 7/15/62	W-1
Graveley, James W.	Pvt. (B)	c. 7/1/62		MW 9/17/62	

NAME	LAST RANK (COMPANY)	DATE ENTERED	PLACE ENTERED	FINAL DISPOSITION	NO. TIMES WOUNDED
Gray, William H.	Pvt. (K)	4/13/61	Spartanburg	Des. 3/65	
Green, Drury	Pvt. (M)	5/13/64	Virginia	Par. 4/9/65	
Green, H. A.	Pvt. (D)	3/13/62	Spartanburg	MW 10/7/64	W-1
Green, L. J.	Pvt. (D)	4/13/61	Spartanburg	Med. D. 12/28/64	
Greer, B. H.	Pvt. (D)	4/13/61	Spartanburg	Disp. Un.	
Greer, R. H.	Pvt. (A)	5/6/62	Union	Par. 4/9/65	W-1
Gregory, E. H.	Pvt. (A)	4/14/62	Union	DOD 6/62	W-2
Gregory, J. J. E.	Pvt. (A)	3/13/62	Union	Med. D. 10/10/64	
Gregory, James A.	Pvt. (D)	4/13/61	Spartanburg	Par. 4/9/65	W-1
Grier, Joseph R.	Pvt. (G)	7/28/63	Yorkville	Disp. Un.	
Grier, Thomas	Ord. Sgt. (F&S)	4/13/61	Yorkville	Tran. 1/31/63	
Griffin, James	Pvt. (A)	4/10/62	Union	Par. 4/9/65	
Gunn, James D.	Pvt. (G)	c. 7/1/62	Yorkville	DOD 2/27/64	W-1
Gunnell, W. H.	Pvt. (F)	7/7/61	Summerville	Disp. Un.	W-1
Gunter, E.	Pvt. (F)	7/8/61	Ridgeville	Disp. Un.	W-2
Gunter, J. L.	Pvt. (F)	7/8/61	Ridgeville	KIA 6/20/64	W-1
Gunter, Jackson	Pvt. (I)	2/24/62	Greenville	Disp. Un.	
Gunter, Joshua	Pvt. (F)	3/18/62	Lexington	Par. 5/26/65	W-1
Gunter, M.	Pvt. (F)	7/8/61	Ridgeville	Par. 4/9/65	W-1
Gunter, M. R.	Pvt. (F)	1/1/63	Lexington	Par. 5/19/65	W-1
Gunter, Tilman	Capt. (F)	7/8/61	Ridgeville	RPOW 6/17/65	W-1
Guyton, Nathaniel	Pvt. (M)	3/1/64	Tennessee	Par. 4/9/65	W-2
Gwinn, Chesly D.	Pvt. (G)	1/1/64	Columbia	RPOW 6/26/65	
Gwinn, Henry J.	Pvt. (G)	1/20/64	Tennessee	MW 7/27/64	
Gwinn, J. Henry	Pvt. (G)	7/28/63	Yorkville	Disp. Un.	
Gwinn, L. Hart	Pvt. (G)	4/13/61	Yorkville	Par. 4/9/65	W-1
Gwinn, O. J.	Sgt. (G)	4/13/61	Yorkville	Par. 4/9/65	W-1
Gwinn, T. A.	Pvt. (G)	10/4/63	Tennessee	Disp. Un.	
Hackett, W. K.	Pvt. (G)	6/4/61	Orangeburg	MW 5/31/62	W-1
Hair, J. R. P.	Pvt. (E)	2/11/64	Columbia	Par. 4/9/65	W-1
Hair, W. W.	Pvt. (E)	7/4/61	Sumter	RPOW 6/27/65	W-1

390

NAME	LAST RANK (COMPANY)	DATE ENTERED	PLACE ENTERED	FINAL DISPOSITION	NO. TIMES WOUNDED
Hall, A. O. N.	Sgt. (C)	4/14/61	Anderson	KIA 6/17/64	
Hall, E. M.	Cpl. (L)	6/3/61	Pendleton	DOD 12/6/62	W-1
Hall, J. T.	Cpl. (G)	6/22/61	Yorkville	Par. 4/9/65	W-1
Hall, Leitner	Pvt. (K)	3/1/62	Spartanburg	Med. D. 10/14/62	
Hall, P. C.	Pvt.(C)	4/14/61	Anderson	Par. 4/9/65	W-1
Hallman, D. J.	Pvt. (F)	4/14/62	Lexington	Disp. Un.	W-1
Hallman, Davis	Pvt. (F)	c. 9/16/63	Columbia	Par. 6/24/65	
Hallman, G. R.	Pvt. (F)	2/23/64	Lexington	DOD 5/1/64	
Hallman, G. W.	Pvt. (F)	4/20/63	Columbia	Par. 5/3/65	W-1
Hallman, J. F.	Pvt. (F)	7/8/61	Ridgeville	RPOW 5/23/65	W-2
Hallman, Lewis	Pvt. (F)	7/8/61	Ridgeville	Par. 4/9/65	W-2
Hallman, Noah	Pvt. (F)	7/8/61	Ridgeville	Par. 4/9/65	
Hambright, J. M.	Pvt. (G)	8/10/63	Yorkville	DOD 12/13/63	
Hambright, J. P.	Cpl. (G)	6/4/61	Orangeburg	Par. 4/9/65	W-1
Hames, L. A.	Pvt. (A)	3/1/64	Union	Par. 4/9/65	
Hamilton, William W.	1st Sgt. (L)	6/3/61	Pendleton	Par. 4/9/65	
Hammett, A. A.	Pvt. (K)			Des. 1865	
Hammett, John J.	Cpl. (I)	4/14/61	Pendleton	RPOW 6/12/65	
Hammett, William D.	Pvt. (K)	4/13/61	Spartanburg	DPOW 1865	
Hammitt, J. C.	Pvt. (D)	3/8/62	Spartanburg	Med. D. 9/26/62	
Hammond, H. S.	Pvt. (C)	3/17/62	Pendleton	KIA 8/30/62	
Hankins, J. Wyatt (see Hawkins, J. W.)					
Harbin, A. P.	Cpl. (B)	4/14/61	Pendleton	Par. 5//65	W-1
Harbin, B. Whitner	Pvt. (L)	3/19/62	Pendleton	RPOW 4//65	W-3
Harbin, D. Sanford	Pvt. (L)	4/14/61	Anderson	RPOW 4//65	W-3
Harbin, John A.	Pvt. (L)	3/17/62	Anderson	Disp. Un.	W-1
Harbin, Nat W.	Capt. (B)	4/14/63	Pendleton	MW 9/17/62	
Harbin, Samuel V.	Pvt. (B)	9/18/61	Pendleton	Disp. Un.	W-1
Harbin, William J.	Sgt. (B)	4/14/61	Pendleton	Disp. Un.	W-1
Harrington, Dwight W.	2d Lt. (E)	7/4/61	Sumter	MW 6/30/62	
Harris, Benjamin	Pvt. (F)	3/10/62	Lexington	MW 10/7/64	

NAME	LAST RANK (COMPANY)	DATE ENTERED	PLACE ENTERED	FINAL DISPOSITION	NO. TIMES WOUNDED
Harris, Jonas W.	1st Sgt. (M)	4/13/61	Limestone Spr.	Disp. Un.	W-3
Harris, L. S.	Pvt. (G)	6/4/61	Orangeburg	KIA 8/14/64	
Harris, Noah	Pvt. (F)	6/20/64	Tennessee	Disp. Un.	
Harris, Rice H.	Pvt. (M)	4/13/61	Limestone Spr.	KIA 5/31/62	
Harris, T. D.	Pvt. (G)	4/13/61	Yorkville	Disp. Un.	
Harris, W. P.	Cpl. (B)	4/14/61	Pendleton	MW 5/31/62	
Harrison, John A.	Pvt. (C)	4/14/61	Anderson	KIA 10/29/63	W-1
Harshaw, R. S.	Cpl. (G)	5/10/62	Yorkville	DOD	
Hartin, J. L.	Pvt. (G)	4/13/61	Yorkville	Disp. Un.	
Hartley, J. Benjamin	Pvt. (F)	5/10/62	Lexington	DOD 3/ /64	
Hartley, L.	Pvt. (F)	7/8/61	Ridgeville	Disp. Un.	
Harvin, Arthur	Pvt. (K)	7/1/62	Spartanburg	Disp. Un.	
Hatfield, C. W.	Pvt. (E)	6/24/61	Ridgeville	MW 6/27/62	
Hause, Andrew J.	Pvt. (K)	4/13/61	Spartanburg	Med. D. 2/19/63	W-1
Hawkins, J. Caldwell	Pvt. (K)	5/8/62	Spartanburg	MW 5/31/62	
Hawkins, J. L.	Pvt. (D)	3/1/64	Spartanburg	Disp. Un.	
Hawkins, J. W.	Cpl. (D)	4/13/61	Spartanburg	Par. 4/9/65	
Hawkins, Jabez	Pvt. (C)	4/14/61	Greenville	KIA 10/29/63	
Hawkins, Paschal	Sgt. (D)	7/1/61	Spartanburg	Par. 4/9/65	W-1
Hawthorne, Jasper N.	1st Lt. (I)	4/14/61	Pendleton	KIA 6/30/62	
Hayes (see Hays)					
Haynes, John W.	Pvt. (K)	3/19/62	Spartanburg	MW 6/30/62	
Haynes, Joseph F.	Pvt. (K)	1/21/63	Spartanburg	Par. 4/9/65	W-1
Haynes, R. Elias	Pvt. (K)	4/30/62	Spartanburg	Disp. Un.	
Haynes, Thomas J.	Pvt. (K)	4/13/61	Spartanburg	Par. 4/9/65	
Haynes, W. S.	Pvt. (K)	3/19/62	Spartanburg	MW 5/31/62	
Hays, B. R.	Pvt. (I)	1/14/64	Tennessee	RPOW 7/3/65	
Hays, Robert	Pvt. (D)	3/3/63	Spartanburg	DOD 4/11/63	
Hemphill, R. L.	Pvt. (G)	6/4/61	Orangeburg	KIA 5/5/62	
Henderson, A. Thomas	Pvt. (M)	8/10/63	Limestone Spr.	Par. 4/9/65	
Henderson, James T.	Pvt. (M)	8/10/63	Limestone Spr.	KIA 5/6/64	

NAME	LAST RANK (COMPANY)	DATE ENTERED	PLACE ENTERED	FINAL DISPOSITION	NO. TIMES WOUNDED
Henderson, Thomas	Pvt. (K)	9/3/62	Spartanburg	Disp. Un.	W-1
Hendricks, William A.	Cpl. (L)	7/1/61	Anderson	Par. 4/9/65	W-2
Henry, Patrick L. N.	Sgt. Maj. (F&S)	4/13/61	Spartanburg	Disp. Un.	W-2
Hensly, James D.	Pvt. (K)	4/13/61	Spartanburg	RPOW 6/27/65	W-1
Henson, T. C.	Pvt. (M)	c. 7/20/62	Columbia	Disp. Un.	
Herbison, William	Pvt. (A)	4/13/61	Union	Disp. Un.	W-1
Herndon, D. J.	Pvt. (C)	4/14/61	Anderson	MW 6/30/62	
Herndon, W. C.	Cpl. (C)	4/14/61	Anderson	MW 10/29/63	W-1
Hicks, C. R.	Pvt. (L)	6/3/61	Pendleton	KIA 5/31/62	
Hinds, W. D.	Cpl. (E)	3/18/62	Sumter	Disp. Un.	
Hix, Berry	Pvt. (B)	4/28/64	Anderson	Des. 2/27/65	
Hodge, M. E.	Pvt. (E)	7/4/61	Sumter	Disp. Un.	W-3
Holkins, B. P.	Pvt. (A)	4/13/61	Union	KIA 6/27/62	
Holland, D. D.	Cpl. (A)	4/13/62	Anderson	Med. D. 3/5/63	W-1
Holland, E. M.	Pvt. (B)	9/19/61	Pendleton	Age D. 1862	
Holland, Elijah M.	Pvt. (L)	4/14/61	Anderson	Par. 4/9/65	W-1
Holland, Francis M.	Pvt. (L)	4/14/61	Anderson	Par. 4/9/65	W-1
Holleyman, Wiley F.	Pvt. (K)	5/1/63	Spartanburg	Disp. Un.	
Holmes, William	Pvt. (M)	4/13/61	Limestone Spr.	Unk. D. 7/12/62	
Holt, James T.	Cpl. (K)	4/13/61	Spartanburg	KIA 6/30/62	
Holt, John C.	Pvt. (K)	4/13/61	Spartanburg	DOA 6/22/63	W-1
Holt, Peter A.	Pvt. (K)	4/13/61	Spartanburg	Par. 4/9/65	W-1
Hooks, John H.	Pvt. (E)	7/4/61	Sumter	Par. 4/9/65	W-1
Hope, D. M.	Cpl. (G)	6/10/61	Virginia	MW 9/30/64	W-1
Hope, J. A.	Pvt. (G)	4/13/61	Yorkville	Disp. Un.	
Hopkins, John W.	Pvt. (L)	6/3/61	Pendleton	Med. D. 1864	W-1
Hopkins, William A.	Pvt. (L)	3/13/62	Anderson	Disp. Un.	W-2
Horton, Joel	Pvt. (K)	3/18/62	Spartanburg	DOD 5/25/62	
Howard, S. H.	Sgt. (F)	7/8/61	Ridgeville	Par. 4/9/65	
Howe, D. J.	Pvt. (G)	4/13/61	Yorkville	Par. 4/9/65	
Howe, John M.	Pvt. (G)	4/13/61	Yorkville	Par. 4/9/65	

393

NAME	LAST RANK (COMPANY)	DATE ENTERED	PLACE ENTERED	FINAL DISPOSITION	NO. TIMES WOUNDED
Howell, D. A.	Pvt. (F)	4/13/61	Lexington	KIA 6/27/62	
Howell, G. W.	Cpl. (D)	7/8/61	Spartanburg	MW 8/30/62	
Howell, Ira	Pvt. (F)		Ridgeville	Disp. Un.	W-1
Howell, J. P.	Pvt. (D)	3/8/62	Spartanburg	KIA 11/16/63	
Howell, R. B.	Pvt. (D)	3/8/62	Spartanburg	Med. D. 8/30/64	W-1
Howell, Richard A.	Pvt. (D)	3/8/62	Spartanburg	MW 5/1/63	W-1
Howell, Samuel	Pvt. (G)	8/15/63	Yorkville	Par. 4/9/65	
Howerton, J. F.	Pvt. (D)	4/13/61	Spartanburg	DOD 2/20/65	
Hoyt, James A.	1st Lt. (C)	4/14/61	Anderson	Med. D. 1864	W-2
Hudson, J. M.	Pvt. (M)	c. 7/20/62	Columbia	MW 8/30/62	
Hughes, H. Thomas	1st Lt. (F&S)	4/13/61	Union	Par. 4/9/65	W-2
Hughes, John T.	Pvt. (I)	11/24/63	Tennessee	Par. 4/9/65	
Hughes, Toliver H.	Pvt. (L)	7/30/61	Anderson	Par. 5/18/65	W-1
Hughes, William G.	Pvt. (A)	4/16/64	Union	Par. 4/9/65	
Hughes, William N.	Pvt. (I)	4/14/61	Pendleton	Par. 4/9/65	W-2
Hughston, Elisha	Pvt. (K)	3/11/62	Spartanburg	MW 5/31/62	
Hughston, George N.	Pvt. (K)	4/13/61	Spartanburg	KIA 5/31/62	
Hughston, Thomas F.	Pvt. (K)	4/22/62	Spartanburg	Par. 4/9/65	W-1
Hughston, Thomas M.	Pvt. (K)	3/30/62	Spartanburg	Par. 4/9/65	W-1
Hughston, William P.	Pvt. (K)	4/13/61	Spartanburg	Par. 4/9/65	
Humphreys, William W.	Maj. (F&S)	4/14/61	Anderson	Disp. Un.	W-1
Humphries, Clayton	Pvt. (H)	c. 7/19/62	Spartanburg	Med. D. 4/15/64	
Humphries, J. M.	Pvt. (M)	4/13/61	Limestone Spr.	Disp. Un.	
Humphries, John W.	Pvt. (A)	4/13/61	Union	Med. D. 8/18/62	W-1
Humphries, M. M.	Pvt. (A)	4/16/64	Union	Par. 4/9/65	
Humphries, Marion	1st Sgt. (A)	5/5/62	Union	KIA 6/19/64	W-1
Humphries, Simpson	Pvt. (H)	4/13/61	Spartanburg	DOD 11/8/62	
Hunsucker, A. L.	Pvt. (A)	4/13/61	Union	Par. 4/9/65	W-2
Hunt, William	Pvt. (B)	9/18/61	Pendleton	Age D. 7/21/62	
Hunt, William H. H.	Cpl. (B)	6/1/61	Pendleton	Par. 4/9/65	W-3
Huskey, A.	Pvt. (M)	4/13/61	Limestone Spr.	Disp. Un.	W-1

394

NAME	LAST RANK (COMPANY)	DATE ENTERED	PLACE ENTERED	FINAL DISPOSITION	NO. TIMES WOUNDED
Hutchenson, W. K.	Pvt. (D)	4/1/62	Spartanburg	DOD 1862	
Hutto, B. A.	Pvt. (F)	10/27/63	Georgia	RPOW 6/28/65	
Ingraham, George	Pvt. (L)	4/14/61	Pickens	Par. 4/9/65	
Isbell, Robert	Pvt. (B)	4/14/61	Pendleton	Par. 4/9/65	
Isbell, William J.	Pvt. (B)	4/14/61	Pendleton	KIA 6/30/62	
Ison, Wm. F. McS.	Pvt. (A)	3/14/62	Union	DOD 7/3/62	
Jackson, D. H.	Cpl. (G)	4/13/61	Yorkville	DOD 5/9/63	
Jackson, H. H.	Pvt. (F)	7/8/61	Ridgeville	MW 5/31/62	
Jackson, H. M.	Cpl. (F)	7/8/61	Ridgeville	MW 5/31/62	
Jackson, John O.	Pvt. (G)	4/13/61	Yorkville	DOD 6/5/64	
James J. A.	Pvt. (M)	c. 7/20/62	Columbia	Des. 8/25/62	
James, J. L.	Pvt. (A)	4/14/62	Union	MW 6/30/62	
James, William	Pvt. (M)	4/14/61	Limestone Spr.	Des. 1864	W-2
Jameson,	Sgt. Maj. (F&S)			Disp. Un.	W-1
Jameson, John W.	Capt. (F&S)	6/62	Charleston	Tran. 8/23/64	W-1
Jamison, Thomas	Pvt. (A)	4/13/61	Union	DOD 7/12/62	
Jefcoat, R.	Pvt. (F)	5/1/64	Lexington	Des. 10/16/64	
Jefcoat, V. V. R.	Pvt. (F)	7/1/62	Lexington	Disp. Un.	
Jefferson, J. F.	Pvt. (L)	4/14/61	Anderson	DOD 6/19/63	
Jefferys, F. G.	Pvt. (G)	4/17/62	Yorkville	DOD 7/1/63	
Jenkins, J. R.	Pvt. (G)	6/26/61	Virginia	DOD 8/1/63	W-1
Jenkins, Micah	Col. (F&S)	4/13/61	Yorkville	KIA 5/6/64	
Jenkins, R. M.	Pvt. (C)	3/7/62	Pendleton	Par. 1865	W-5
Jenkins, Thomas O.	Sgt. (C)	3/6/62	Pendleton	Par. 4/9/65	W-2
Jenkins, W. G.	Pvt. (C)	6/3/61	Pendleton	Med. D. 6/30/63	W-1
Jennings, John J.	Pvt. (E)	3/2/62	Sumter	KIA 10/7/64	W-1
Jennings, S. D.	Cpl. (E)	3/2/62	Sumter	KIA 6/19/64	W-1
Johns, E. H.	Pvt. (B)	9/18/61	Pendleton	MW 1/17/64	
Johnson, B. H.	Pvt. (M)	c. 7/20/61	Columbia	KIA 8/30/62	
Johnson, C.	Pvt. (F)			KIA 6/27/62	
Johnson, Daniel	Pvt. (D)	2/13/64	Spartanburg	DOD 1863	

NAME	LAST RANK (COMPANY)	DATE ENTERED	PLACE ENTERED	FINAL DISPOSITION	NO. TIMES WOUNDED
Johnson, E.	Pvt. (M)	c. 7/20/61	Columbia	Disp. Un.	
Johnson, G. W.	Pvt. (A)		Union	KIA 6/29/62	
Johnson, J. M.	Cpl. (F)	7/8/61	Ridgeville	Par. 5/19/65	W-1
Johnson, Levi	Pvt. (F)	3/26/62	Virginia	KIA 6/27/62	
Johnson, R. L.	A. Surg. (F&S)			Disp. Un.	
Johnson, Richard C.	Capt. (A)	4/13/61	Union	Par. 4/9/65	W-1
Johnson, S. R.	Pvt. (B)	9/18/61	Pendleton	Disp. Un.	
Johnson, W. J.	Pvt. (E)	7/17/61	Florence	Age D. 7/8/62	
Johnson, W. W.	Pvt. (E)	7/15/61	Ridgeville	MW 6/27/62	
Johnson, William	Pvt. (K)	5/6/62	Spartanburg	Disp. Un.	
Johnson, William L.	Cpl. (K)	4/13/61	Spartanburg	Par. 4/14/65	
Johnson, William M.	Pvt. (F)	11/15/64	Lexington	Par. 4/9/65	
Johnston, James T.	Pvt. (B)	9/18/61	Pendleton	Disp. Un.	W-1
Jolley, Thomas F.	Sgt. (B)	4/14/61	Pendleton	Disp. Un.	W-2
Jolly, J. Knott	Pvt. (H)	4/1/62	Spartanburg	MW 1864	
Jolly, R. M.	Pvt. (M)	4/13/61	Limestone Spr.	Disp. Un.	W-1
Jolly, W. N.	Pvt. (H)	8/1/63	Spartanburg	MW 10/7/64	
Jonakan, Charles	Pvt. (F)	9/1/63	Aiken	Unk. D. 11/13/64	
Jones, Hampton R.	Pvt. (L)	3/7/62	Pendleton	Par. 4/19/65	W-2
Jones, John A. H.	Pvt. (B)	7/16/62	Anderson	Disp. Un.	W-2
Jones, Newton	Pvt. (A)	4/13/61	Union	Disp. Un.	W-2
Jones, Thomas J.	Pvt. (E)	4/15/62	Sumter	Med. D. 6/3/62	
Jordan, Francis	Pvt. (E)	7/4/61	Sumter	Disp. Un.	
Jordan, Moses	Pvt. (B)	c. 7/1/62	Columbia	DOD 12/11/62	
Julien, John	Cpl. (B)	4/14/61	Pendleton	Disp. Un.	W-1
Kaney, John	Pvt. (F)	7/12/61	Ridgeville	MW 5/5/62	
Kasler, Andrew	Pvt. (D)	8/20/63	Spartanburg	Par. 4/9/65	
Kay, Charles A.	Pvt. (L)	4/14/61	Anderson	Par. 4/9/65	
Kay, William S.	Pvt. (L)			Disp. Un.	W-1
Keasler, D. A.	Pvt. (C)	3/2/62	Pendleton	Disp. Un.	W-1
Keasler, David C.	Pvt. (L)	6/3/61	Pendleton	KIA 9/30/64	

NAME	LAST RANK (COMPANY)	DATE ENTERED	PLACE ENTERED	FINAL DISPOSITION	NO. TIMES WOUNDED
Keasler, Henry C.	Pvt. (L)	3/7/62	Pendleton	Disp. Un.	
Keese, Thomas B.	Pvt. (B)	4/14/61	Pendleton	Par. 4/9/65	W-2
Kell, Samuel A.	Hosp. (F&S)	4/13/61	Yorkville	Par. 4/9/65	
Kennedy, James	Pvt. (A)	4/10/62	Union	Disp. Un.	
Keown, C. D.	Pvt. (C)	6/20/63	Columbia	MW 5/6/64	
Keown, James T.	Pvt. (C)	4/14/61	Anderson	Disp. Un.	W-2
Keown, W. M., Jr.	Pvt. (C)	4/14/61	Anderson	KIA 8/30/62	W-1
Kersey, John	Pvt. (G)	6/22/61	Yorkville	RPOW 1865	W-1
Keys, P. A.	Pvt. (C)	5/31/61	Anderson	Disp. Un.	W-1
Keys, Robt. L.	Cpl. (C)	5/31/61	Anderson	Par. 4/9/65	W-1
Kilbey, J. T.	Pvt. (B)	4/14/61	Pendleton	Par. 4/9/65	W-1
Killian, A. A.	Pvt. (A)	4/13/61	Union	Par. 4/9/65	
Killian, D. E.	Pvt. (A)	4/13/61	Union	Par. 4/9/65	W-2
Kilpatrick, F. W.	Maj. (F&S)	4/14/61	Pendleton	Tran. 1/31/63	
King, John B.	Pvt. (I)	4/14/61	Greenville	Par. 4/9/65	W-2
King, W. J.	Cpl. (I)	4/14/61	Pendleton	Par. 4/9/65	W-2
Kinnett, G. M.	Sgt. (H)	6/28/61	Spartanburg	KIA 6/27/62	
Kirby, C. C.	Pvt. (M)	5/7/62	Limestone Spr.	Med. D. 10/9/63	W-1
Kirby, Jonas	Pvt. (M)	4/13/61	Limestone Spr.	DOD 7/7/62	
Kirby, P. Govan	Pvt. (K)	c. 6/20/63	Spartanburg	Disp. Un.	
Kirkland, George A.	Pvt. (K)	6/23/62	Spartanburg	Par. 4/9/65	W-1
Kirkland, William	Pvt. (F)	7/8/61	Ridgeville	Disp. Un.	
Kirkpatrick, E. M.	1st Sgt. (G)	4/13/61	Yorkville	KIA 6/30/62	W-1
Kitchens, John T.	1st Lt. (A)	4/13/61	Union	Par. 4/9/65	
Kneece, V.	Pvt. (F)	5/1/64	Lexington	Par. 4/9/65	
Knight, W. C.	Pvt. (D)	6/20/61	Spartanburg	Par. 4/9/65	W-1
Knox, James M.	Sgt. (B)	6/13/61	Pendleton	MW 6/30/62	W-1
Lamb, Francis M.	Pvt. (H)	3/11/62	Spartanburg	Unk. D. 1/31/63	W-1
Laminack, William	Pvt. (F)	7/8/61	Ridgeville	Par. 4/9/65	W-1
Lancaster, David M.	Pvt. (K)	11/21/61	Spartanburg	Disp. Un.	W-1
Land, W. L.	Pvt. (C)	4/14/61	Anderson	Disp. Un.	W-3

NAME	LAST RANK (COMPANY)	DATE ENTERED	PLACE ENTERED	FINAL DISPOSITION	NO. TIMES WOUNDED
Land, William H.	Pvt. (M)	c. 7/20/62	Columbia	RPOW 6/14/65	
Landford, T. P.	Pvt. (D)	4/26/62	Spartanburg	MW 9/30/64	
Landrum, F. V.	Sgt. (D)	4/13/61	Spartanburg	Par. 4/9/65	W-2
Langston, W. N.	Pvt. (C)	10/20/62	Anderson	KIA 10/29/63	
Lanier, R.	Pvt. (G)	6/22/62	Yorkville	Des. 9/17/62	
Lark, William F.	Pvt. (C)	4/14/61	Greenville	MW 10/29/63	W-2
Latham, Frederick G.	Capt. (M)	4/13/61	Limestone Spr.	Res. 3/16/65	W-2
Lawson, E. A.	Pvt. (I)	5/20/62	Pendleton	Par. 4/9/65	
Lawson, E. L.	Pvt. (B)	10/31/62	Pendleton	Disp. Un.	
Lawson, F. L.	Pvt. (I)	4/14/61	Pendleton	KIA 5/31/62	
Lawson, H. S.	Pvt. (I)	4/1/64	Tennessee	RPOW 6/26/65	W-1
Lawson, J. L.	Pvt. (I)	3/15/62	Pendleton	Des. 1865	
Lawson, Joseph	Pvt. (A)	3/1/62	Union	Med. D. 9/23/64	W-1
Lawson, William	Pvt. (A)	3/11/62	Union	Med. D. 8/11/63	
Layton, Maynard C.	Pvt. (K)	6/23/62	Spartanburg	DOD 10/19/63	W-1
League, J. M.	Pvt. (B)	4/14/62	Pendleton	MW 6/30/62	W-1
Lee, D. M.	Pvt. (E)	7/4/61	Sumter	Disp. Un.	
Lee, H. J.	Pvt. (C)	4/2/62	Anderson	MW 5/31/62	
Lee, J. Dozier	1st Lt. (E)	7/4/61	Sumter	KIA 6/30/62	
Lee, Joseph E.	Capt. (F)	7/8/61	Ridgeville	KIA 9/17/62	
Lee, R. L.	Pvt. (B)			Disp. Un.	
Lee, William	Pvt. (C)	4/14/61	Anderson	Par. 4/9/65	
Lemaster, William E.	Pvt. (A)	4/13/61	Union	RPOW 6/26/65	W-2
Lemmon, D. D.	Pvt. (E)	4/8/61	Sumter	Med D. 3/15/64	
Leneer, James M.	Pvt. (L)	3/15/62	Pendleton	KIA 10/7/64	
Lester, John	Pvt. (B)	11/1/64	Pickens	Par. 4/9/65	
Lester, Thomas H.	Pvt. (B)	6/1/61	Pendleton	Disp. Un.	W-1
Leverett, F. P.	A. Surg. (F&S)			Tran. 4/10/64	
Lewis, D. S.	Pvt. (B)	3/5/62	Pendleton	DOD 6/24/62	
Lewis, E. H.	Pvt. (F)	7/8/61	Ridgeville	Tran. 2/18/65	W-1
Lewis, Earle S.	Pvt. (B)	6/15/62	Pendleton	DOD 1/19/63	

398

NAME	LAST RANK (COMPANY)	DATE ENTERED	PLACE ENTERED	FINAL DISPOSITION	NO. TIMES WOUNDED
Lewis, James O.	Pvt. (K)	2/24/63	Pendleton	Disp. Un.	
Lewis, James W.	Pvt. (B)	5/31/61	Anderson	Disp. Un.	W-2
Lewis, John E.	Pvt. (B)	4/14/61	Anderson	Sub. D. 1862	W-2
Lewis, R. L.	Capt. (B)	4/25/61	Columbia	Disp. Un.	W-2
Lewis, Richard	1st Lt. (B)	4/14/61	Anderson	RPOW 5/8/65	W-1
Lewis, Samuel D.	Pvt. (C)	5/3/61	Columbia	KIA 8/14/64	W-1
Liles, D. S.	Pvt. (B)	5/10/62	Walhalla	Par. 4/9/65	
Liles, J. W.	Pvt. (B)	4/14/61	Pendleton	Par. 4/9/65	W-1
Linder, J. M.	Pvt. (H)	6/28/61	Spartanburg	MW 6/30/62	
Linder, Lee	Pvt. (H)	3/11/62	Spartanburg	Disp. Un.	W-1
Linson, Jesse	Pvt. (E)	6/24/61	Ridgeville	DOD 12/7/64	W-2
Linton, J. W.	Pvt. (M)	c. 7/20/62	Columbia	DOD 1862	
Lipscomb, M.	Pvt. (M)	4/13/61	Limestone Spr.	KIA 5/31/62	W-1
Lipscomb, Nathan	Pvt. (H)	5/10/62	Spartanburg	Tran. 1862	W-1
Lipsey, Ira	Pvt. (D)	4/13/61	Spartanburg	Des. 1/65	W-2
Lipsey, Newton	Pvt. (A)	4/13/61	Union	Disp. Un.	
Lipsey, William	Pvt. (A)	4/16/64	Union	Disp. Un.	
Little, W. E.	Pvt. (D)			KIA 9/17/62	
Lloyd, J. G.	Pvt. (A)	4/13/61	Union	DOD 4/5/63	
Lockhart, Smith	Pvt. (M)	4/13/61	Limestone Spr.	Disp. Un.	
Lockwood, James P.	2d Lt. (K)	4/13/61	Spartanburg	MW 5/12/64	
Loftin, J. E.	Pvt. (L)	4/14/61	Anderson	Med. D. 1/10/63	W-1
Logan, H. W.	Pvt. (E)	4/8/61	Sumter	DOD 5/23/62	
Lominac, J. T.	Pvt. (G)	8/15/63	Yorkville	DOD 1864	
Long, George	Pvt. (F)	c. 5/14/64	Lexington	Par. 4/9/65	
Long, J. B.	Pvt. (F)	3/10/62	Lexington	DOD 6/25/62	
Long, J. H.	Pvt. (E)	4/28/62	Virginia	KIA 7/22/64	W-1
Long, Joseph	Pvt. (E)		Sumter	KIA 9/30/64	
Long, M. T.	Pvt. (M)	c. 7/20/62	Columbia	Par. 4/9/65	
Long, W. E.	Pvt. (E)	7/4/61	Sumter	RPOW 6/16/65	W-1
Looney, J. T.	Pvt. (B)	4/14/61	Pendleton	MW 5/5/62	

NAME	LAST RANK (COMPANY)	DATE ENTERED	PLACE ENTERED	FINAL DISPOSITION	NO. TIMES WOUNDED
Love, W. E.	Pvt. (G)	4/13/61	Yorkville	Tran. 1863	
Lovelace, N. Langdon	Pvt. (H)	5/5/62	Spartanburg	KIA 5/6/64	W-1
Lowry, James W.	Sgt. (E)	7/4/61	Sumter	Disp. Un.	W-2
Lowry, Samuel	Pvt. (E)	3/18/62	Sumter	Disp. Un.	
Lucas, C. D.	Pvt. (M)	c. 7/20/62	Columbia	Disp. Un.	
McAbee, J. J.	Pvt. (D)	4/13/61	Spartanburg	MW 6/30/62	
McArthur, Wm. F.	Sgt. (K)	7/10/61	Summerville	Par. 4/9/65	W-2
McCaw, Robert	Pvt. (G)	4/13/61	Yorkville	MW 5/31/62	
McClellan, John M.	Pvt. (B)	7/20/61	Pickens	KIA 11/24/63	W-2
McCombs, M.	Pvt. (H)	4/13/61	Spartanburg	Disp. Un.	
McConnell, A. F.	Pvt. (G)	4/13/61	Yorkville	Par. 4/9/65	
McCormick, George	Pvt. (A)	4/13/61	Union	Tran. 6/15/62	
McCowen, T. A. (see McKeown, T. A.)					
McCoy, J. W.	Pvt. (E)	7/9/61	Ridgeville	KIA 6/30/62	W-4
McCully, N. A.	2d Lt. (C)	4/14/61	Anderson	Par. 4/9/65	W-1
McCully, Samuel	Pvt. (C)	4/14/61	Anderson	Par. 4/9/65	
McDaniel, B. F.	Pvt. (B)	11/2/61	Pickens	DOD 4/20/64	
McDaniel, Lemuel	Pvt.(A)	4/13/61	Union	Par. 4/9/65	
McDavid, G. W.	Pvt. (L)	4/14/61	Anderson	Enl. D. 7/22/62	
McDonald, Alfred M.	Pvt. (K)	7/10/61	Summerville	Disp. Un.	W-1
McDonald, B. F. (see McDaniel, B. F.)					
McDow, W. A.	Pvt. (I)	4/14/61	Pendleton	MW 5/31/62	
McDowell, Henry F.	Sgt. (K)	4/13/61	Spartanburg	Par. 4/9/65	
McDowell, James	Chapl. (F&S)	7/7/62		Par. 4/9/65	
McElveen, J. L.	Cpl. (G)	6/4/61	Orangeburg	KIA 9/17/62	W-1
McElveen, Major L.	Pvt. (E)	6/4/61	Clarendon	RPOW 6/5/65	W-1
McFall, James M.	Adjut. (F&S)	5/31/61	Anderson	Par. 4/9/65	W-2
McFall, W. C.	Pvt. (C)	4/14/61	Anderson	Par. 4/9/65	
McFarland, William	Pvt. (K)	s. 6/10/62	Virginia	DOD 7/8/62	
McIson, Wm. F. (see Ison, Wm. F.)					
McJunkin, S. P.	Cpl. (B)	4/14/61	Pendleton	KIA 6/30/62	

NAME	LAST RANK (COMPANY)	DATE ENTERED	PLACE ENTERED	FINAL DISPOSITION	NO. TIMES WOUNDED
McKay, G. W.	Sgt. (L)	6/3/61	Pendleton	MW 5/31/62	
McKelvey, W. F.	Pvt. (H)	5/1/64	Spartanburg	KIA 6/17/64	
McKenny, D. C. (see McKinny, D. C.)					
McKenzie, N. R.	Pvt. (E)	6/4/61	Ridgeville	KIA 5/11/64	W-1
McKeown, T. A.	Pvt. (G)	8/10/63	Yorkville	Par. 4/9/65	W-2
McKeown, W. F.	Sgt. Maj. (F&S)	7/22/62	Virginia	MW 12/13/62	W-1
McKern, John	Pvt. (L)	4/14/61	Anderson	Par. 4/9/65	W-2
McKinney, D. C.	Sgt. (G)	6/10/61	Virginia	Par. 4/9/65	W-1
McKinney, J. H.	Pvt. (G)	11/1/61	Virginia	MW 6/4/64	W-1
McKinney, James C.	1st Sgt. (E)	4/8/61	Sumter	Par. 4/9/65	
McKnight, A. C.	Pvt. (G)	7/28/63	Yorkville	Par. 4/9/65	
McLure, J. Wm.	Capt. QM (F&S)	4/13/61	Limestone Spr.	Disp. Un.	
McPherson, Wm. D.	Pvt. (M)	4/13/61	Limestone Spr.	Par. 4/9/65	W-1
McSkelly, John	Pvt. (G)	8/15/63	Yorkville	Par. 4/9/65	
McSwain, Eldridge T.	Pvt. (K)	2/25/62	Spartanburg	Tran. 1863	
McSwain, Horace A.	1st Sgt. (K)	4/13/61	Spartanburg	KIA 8/30/62	
McVay, J. B.	Pvt. (D)	4/13/61	Spartanburg	Disp. Un.	
McWhorter, G. W.	Pvt. (I)	4/14/61	Pendleton	Par. 4/9/65	W-1
Mabry, Harvey	Pvt. (A)	12/17/61	Columbia	Par. 4/9/65	W-1
Madden, B. F.	Pvt. (I)	4/14/61	Pendleton	Par. 4/9/65	W-1
Madden, E. M.	Pvt. (I)	3/15/62	Pendleton	MW 5/6/64	
Madden, Thomas E.	Pvt. (I)	3/15/62	Pendleton	Par. 4/9/65	
Maddox, John P.	Pvt. (C)	3/15/62	Pendleton	Disp. Un.	W-1
Magill, Thomas	Pvt. (C)	4/14/61	Anderson	KIA 6/30/62	
Major, Daniel N.	Pvt. (L)	4/14/61	Anderson	Disp. Un.	W-2
Major, William N.	2d Lt. (L)	4/13/61		Res. 7/24/63	W-1
Malone, John	Pvt. (A)	4/20/62	Union	Disp. Un.	
Malone, Marion	Pvt. (A)	4/13/61	Union	Par. 4/9/65	
Mann, A. A.	Pvt. (I)	5/27/64	Virginia	DOD 7/19/64	
Mann, Thomas	Pvt. (I)	5/27/64	Virginia	Par. 4/9/65	
Manning, John M.	Pvt. (C)	4/14/61	Anderson	MW 6/30/62	

401

NAME	LAST RANK (COMPANY)	DATE ENTERED	PLACE ENTERED	FINAL DISPOSITION	NO. TIMES WOUNDED
Manning, P. C.	Pvt. (G)	1/1/64	Tennessee	Par. 4/9/65	W-1
Maret, Wiley H.	Pvt. (B)	8/8/63	Pendleton	KIA 10/29/63	
Marett, W. A. (see Merritt, W. A.)					
Marsh, H.	Pvt. (F)	7/8/61	Ridgeville	Disp. Un.	W-1
Marsh, John	Pvt. (C)			Disp. Un.	
Marsh, R. H.	Pvt. (F)	6/30/61	Ridgeville	MW 6/27/62	
Marshall, J. Sidney	Pvt. (L)	6/3/61	Pendleton	DOD 5/20/64	
Marshall, M. L.	Pvt. (L)			Disp. Un.	
Martin, B. J.	Cpl. (H)	6/28/61	Spartanburg	Med. D. 1/20/63	W-2
Martin, Benson B.	Pvt. (H)	7/7/61	Spartanburg	Par. 4/9/65	
Martin, Berry T.	Pvt. (L)	7/27/63	Columbia	Par. 4/9/65	
Martin, D. J. V.	1st Lt. (H)	6/28/61	Spartanburg	MW 8/30/62	
Martin, G. H.	Pvt. (M)		Spartanburg	DOD 6/15/65	
Martin, George	Pvt. (C)	4/14/61	Anderson	KIA 9/30/64	W-1
Martin, Green	Pvt. (M)	c. 7/28/63	Columbia	RPOW 6/14/65	W-1
Martin, J. Micah	Pvt. (H)	3/11/62	Spartanburg	Par. 4/9/65	W-2
Martin, J. Welles	Pvt. (H)	3/11/62	Spartanburg	Par. 4/9/65	W-1
Martin, John M.	Capt. (H)	6/28/61	Spartanburg	MW 6/30/62	
Martin, John V.	Pvt.			Disp. Un.	
Martin, M. Lafayette	Cpl. (H)	3/11/62	Spartanburg	Disp. Un.	W-1
Martin, Newton T.	Pvt. (L)	6/13/61	Pendleton	Par. 4/9/65	W-1
Martin, S. G.	Pvt. (A)	4/13/61	Union	Med D. 6//62	W-1
Martin, T. C.	Pvt. (L)	4/14/61	Anderson	DOD 9/18/62	
Martin, Thomas W. A.	2d Lt. (H)	6/28/61	Spartanburg	Par. 4/9/65	W-2
Mason, John	Pvt. (G)	3/19/62	Yorkville	Med. D. 7/18/62	
Massengill, J. G.	Pvt. (I)	3/15/62	Pendleton	KIA 5/31/62	
Massengill, W. L.	Pvt. (I)	3/14/64	Pickens	Par. 4/9/65	
Massey, J. B.	Pvt. (E)			Par. 4/9/65	
Massey, Ross	Pvt. (H)	3/11/62	Spartanburg	Med. D. 1//65	
Massey, William	Pvt. (H)	3/11/62	Spartanburg	Disp. Un.	W-1
Mathis, Martin	Pvt. (D)	4/18/62	Spartanburg	Disp. Un.	

402

NAME	LAST RANK (COMPANY)	DATE ENTERED	PLACE ENTERED	FINAL DISPOSITION	NO. TIMES WOUNDED
Mathis, William	Pvt. (M)	c. 7/1/62	Columbia	Par. 4/19/65	W-1
Mauldin, Rucker	Pvt. (I)	3/15/62	Williamston	Disp. Un.	W-1
Mauldin, William	Pvt. (I)	3/15/62	Williamston	Unk. D. 5/ /62	W-1
Mauldin, William E.	Pvt. (K)	4/13/61	Spartanburg	Par. 4/9/65	
Maxwell, D. S.	Pvt. (B)	12/22/62	Virginia	Disp. Un.	
Mayberry, D. Z.	Cpl. (M)	4/13/61	Limestone Spr.	RPOW 6/21/65	W-1
Mayes, W. S.	Sgt. (E)	4/8/61	Sumter	MW 6/27/62	
Mazeke, L. H.	Pvt. (K)			Des. 1864	
Medlin, Chesley D.	Pvt. (B)	c. 7/1/62	Pendleton	DOD 1864	
Medlin, Joseph B.	Pvt. (I)	3/15/62	Williamston	KIA 9/17/62	
Medlin, R. S.	Sgt. (I)	4/14/61	Pendleton	Par. 4/9/65	
Medlin, Samuel H.	Pvt. (B)	4/14/61	Pendleton	Par. 4/9/65	W-1
Meeks, J. B.	Pvt. (G)	8/15/63	Yorkville	DOD 1864	
Merritt, A. L.	Pvt. (F)	6/16/62	Virginia	Disp. Un.	
Merritt, G. A.	Pvt. (F)	6/16/62	Lexington	Disp. Un.	
Merritt, G. B.	Pvt. (F)	7/8/61	Ridgeville	MW 5/8/64	
Merritt, W. A.	Pvt. (C)	5/3/61	Columbia	Par. 4/9/65	W-1
Merritt, William L.	1st Sgt. (F)	7/8/61	Ridgeville	Par. 4/9/65	
Messer, Lewis H.	Cpl. (B)	4/14/61	Pendleton	MW 8/30/62	W-1
Miller, Andrew H.	Pvt. (K)	4/27/62	Spartanburg	DOD 2/1/63	
Miller, J. Abner	Pvt. (F)	3/10/62	Lexington	MW 6/30/62	
Miller, J. Augustus	Pvt. (F)	4/8/61	Charleston	MW 5/31/62	
Miller, J. J.	Pvt. (G)	6/4/61	Orangeburg	Par. 4/9/65	
Miller, Jesse	Pvt. (I)	4/14/61	Pendleton	KIA 6/30/62	
Miller, P. O.	Pvt. (D)	5/5/63	Spartanburg	Disp. Un.	
Miller, Robert P.	1st Lt. (K)	5/7/62	Spartanburg	KIA 11/16/63	
Miller, Samuel W.	Pvt. (K)	2/25/62	Spartanburg	KIA 6/30/62	
Miller, Wm. Thomas	Ord. Sgt. (F&S)	4/13/61	Spartanburg	Par. 4/9/65	W-1
Mills, Daniel	Pvt. (I)	3/15/62	Pendleton	Par. 4/9/65	W-2
Milwee, James A.	Sgt. (L)	4/14/61	Anderson	Des. 1865	
Mims, G. W.	Pvt. (E)	6/24/61	Ridgeville	Par. 4/9/65	W-1

NAME	LAST RANK (COMPANY)	DATE ENTERED	PLACE ENTERED	FINAL DISPOSITION	NO. TIMES WOUNDED
Mims, Pinckney W.	Pvt. (E)	6/24/61	Ridgeville	Disp. Un.	
Minus, Joseph	Sgt. (K)	4/13/61	Spartanburg	Med. D. 12/28/64	W-1
Mitchell, Abe	Pvt. (F)	6/30/61	Ridgeville	Med. D. 1864	W-2
Mitchell, Daniel	Pvt. (L)	4/24/62	Anderson	Disp. Un.	W-1
Mitchell, Edward	Pvt. (L)	4/16/62	Virginia	Disp. Un.	W-1
Mitchell, Frazier G.	Sgt. (M)	4/30/61	Charleston	Par. 4/9/65	
Mitchell, Hiram H.	2d Lt. (K)	4/13/61	Spartanburg	Res. 6/3/63	W-1
Mobley, D.	Pvt. (M)	c. 7/20/62	Columbia	Disp. Un.	W-1
Mobley, O. R.	Pvt. (M)	c. 7/1/62	Columbia	DOD 1/5/64	
Montgomery, Robert F.	1st Lt. (M)	4/13/61	Limestone Spr.	Par. 4/9/65	W-1
Moody, Peter	Pvt. (I)	c. 7/14/62	Darlington	Disp. Un.	
Moody, W. Dudley	Pvt. (D)		Spartanburg	KIA 7/7/64	
Moore, A. A.	Sgt. (C)	4/8/62	Virginia	Tran. 1863	
Moore, C. R.	Pvt. (G)	3/19/62	Yorkville	MW 6/30/62	
Moore, David	Pvt. (D)	6/3/61	Spartanburg	KIA 8/30/62	
Moore, H. H.	Pvt. (G)	6/26/61	Virginia	KIA 5/31/62	
Moore, Hugh	Pvt. (H)	2/24/64	Spartanburg	Par. 4/9/65	W-2
Moore, J. A.	Pvt. (F)	3/10/62	Lexington	MW 6/27/62	
Moore, James Alex.	Cpl. (K)	4/13/61	Spartanburg	KIA 5/31/62	
Moore, James P.	Capt. (H)	4/13/61	Spartanburg	Par. 4/9/65	W-1
Moore, Jesse N.	2d Lt. (G)	4/13/61	Yorkville	KIA 5/6/64	
Moore, John	Pvt. (K)	5/25/64	Spartanburg	Des. 7/23/64	
Moore, Joseph B.	Sgt. (L)	4/14/61	Anderson	Par. 4/9/65	W-2
Moore, R. S.	Pvt. (E)	3/19/62	Sumter	Med. D. 8/9/62	W-1
Moore, S. C.	Pvt. (E)	6/24/61	Ridgeville	Unk. D. 7/23/62	
Moore, Samuel	Pvt. (B)	s. 1862		KIA 8/30/62	
Moore, T. A.	Pvt. (E)	4/8/61	Sumter	KIA 9/30/64	W-2
Moose, A. W.	Pvt. (D)	4/13/61	Spartanburg	Des. 12/10/64	W-2
Moree, J. A.	Pvt. (E)	7/15/61	Ridgeville	Par. 4/9/65	W-1
Morehead, Robert	Pvt. (C)	7/1/62	Columbia	Par. 4/9/65	
Morgan, Arthur	Pvt. (M)	4/13/61	Limestone Spr.	Tran. 1862	

NAME	LAST RANK (COMPANY)	DATE ENTERED	PLACE ENTERED	FINAL DISPOSITION	NO. TIMES WOUNDED
Morgan, Jesse M.	Pvt. (D)	4/13/61	Spartanburg	DOD 3/24/62	W-2
Morgan, Peter	Pvt. (M)	c. 7/20/62	Columbia	Par. 4/9/65	W-2
Morris, M. J.	Pvt. (E)	4/8/61	Sumter	Disp. Un.	
Morris, William T.	Pvt. (K)	5/10/62	Spartanburg	DOD 9/19/62	
Moseley, William D.	Pvt. (H)	3/11/62	Spartanburg	DOD 11//62	
Moss, Hiram	Pvt. (G)	8/10/63	Yorkville	Par. 4/9/65	W-2
Mott, J. C.	Pvt. (A)	4/16/64	Union	Par. 4/9/65	W-1
Muller, J. G.	Pvt. (D)	4/1/62	Spartanburg	RPOW 4/18/65	
Mulliken, James H.	Pvt. (C)	4/14/61	Anderson	MW 6/30/62	
Mullinax, E. K.	2d Lt. (I)	4/14/61	Pendleton	KIA 5/31/64	
Mullinax, Francis M.	Pvt. (I)	7/3/61	Georgia	Des. 1865	
Mullinax, James L.	Pvt. (I)	3/15/62	Pendleton	DPOW 2/12/64	
Mullinax, Joshua	1st Lt. (A)	4/13/61	Union	Par. 4/9/65	W-1
Nalley, C. M.	Pvt. (L)	7/30/61	Anderson	Par. 4/9/65	W-1
Nance, T. D.	Pvt. (A)	8/14/63	Union	KIA 5/6/64	
Neal, H. R.	Pvt. (G)	6/12/61	Virginia	Med. D. 9/28/62	W-1
Neal, John B.	Pvt. (I)	3/15/62	Pendleton	DOD 2/26/63	
Neal, S. M.	Pvt. (I)	4/14/61	Pendleton	Des. 1865	W-2
Neal, W. A.	Pvt. (G)	4/13/61	Yorkville	KIA 10/29/63	
Neely, Benjamin	2d Lt. (F)	4/8/61	Camp Butler	Res. 12/6/62	W-1
Neice, V.	Pvt. (F)	4/20/62	Virginia	Par. 5/22/65	
Neil, John Calhoun	Pvt. (G)		York	KIA 8/30/62	
Nesbitt, A. J.	Sgt. (D)	6/3/61	Spartanburg	Par. 4/9/65	
Nesbitt, Alex. J.	Pvt. (D)	4/13/61	Spartanburg	MW 9/30/64	
Nesbitt, J. R.	Pvt. (D)	4/13/61	Spartanburg	Disp. Un.	
Nesbitt, Wilson	Pvt. (D)	4/13/61	Spartanburg	KIA 6/30/62	
Nethers, James V.	Pvt. (A)	3/11/62	Union	Med. D. 2/6/63	
Nettles, J. M.	Pvt. (F)	7/4/61	Sumter	Par. 4/9/65	
Nevitt, R. C.	Sgt. (C)	4/14/61	Anderson	KIA 5/31/62	
Nichols, E. W. P.	Pvt. (D)	3/8/62	Spartanburg	KIA 6/30/62	
Nichols, J. S. E.	Pvt. (D)	4/13/61	Spartanburg	Par. 4//65	W-2

405

NAME	LAST RANK (COMPANY)	DATE ENTERED	PLACE ENTERED	FINAL DISPOSITION	NO. TIMES WOUNDED
Nichols, James A.	Pvt. (E)	7/19/61	Florence	Des. 12/15/63	
Nichols, W. P.	Pvt. (E)			Des. 12/ /63	
Norman, T. F.	Pvt. (A)	4/13/61	Union	KIA 6/30/62	
Norris, J. A. E.	Pvt. (C)	10/19/64	Anderson	Par. 4/9/65	
Norris, John R.	Pvt. (B)	2/1/64	Pickens	Par. 4/9/65	
Nun, I.	Pvt. (G)	6/1/64	Columbia	Disp. Un.	
O'Farrell, G. H.	Sgt. (G)	4/13/61	Yorkville	MW 5/6/64	W-2
O'Leary, G. H.	Pvt. (G)	c. 11/10/64	Columbia	Par. 4/9/65	
Osborne, A. H.	Pvt. (C)	4/14/61	Anderson	Par. 4/9/65	W-2
Owen, James J.	Pvt. (L)	7/4/62	Columbia	Par. 4/9/65	
Owen, Joshua	Pvt. (L)	4/14/61	Anderson	Disp. Un.	W-2
Owens, David	Pvt. (H)	6/28/61	Spartanburg	KIA 1/17/64	W-1
Owens, David	Sgt. (L)	4/14/61	Anderson	Par. 4/9/65	
Owens, Robert D.	Pvt. (K)	8/13/63	Spartanburg	Par. 5/13/65	
Palmer, J. P.	Pvt. (G)	4/13/61	Yorkville	Unk. D. 11/7/62	W-1
Palmer, James J.	Cpl. (K)	4/8/61	Charleston	KIA 8/30/62	
Parker, H. J.	Pvt. (G)	4/13/61	Yorkville	KIA 6/30/62	
Parker, John W.	Pvt. (C)	4/14/61	Anderson	DPOW 5/9/65	W-1
Parris, G. B.	Pvt. (H)	3/11/62	Spartanburg	DOD 1862	
Parris, J. W.	Pvt. (A)	4/13/61	Union	MW 6/27/62	
Parris, James T.	Pvt. (H)	5/10/62	Spartanburg	DOD 1862	
Parris, P. G.	Pvt. (A)	4/13/61	Union	RPOW 5/12/65	W-2
Parris, P. P.	Pvt. (H)	7/7/61	Spartanburg	KIA 6/30/62	
Parrish, D. F.	Pvt. (G)	7/1/62	Yorkville	DPOW 8/6/64	W-1
Parrish, R. R.	Pvt. (G)	4/13/61	Yorkville	Par. 5/3/65	
Parsons, J. T. J.	Pvt. (I)	3/15/62	Pendleton	DOD 8/21/62	
Parsons, T. J.	Pvt. (E)	3/19/62	Sumter	DOD 6/1/62	
Patrick, John L.	Pvt. (F)	6/30/61	Ridgeville	Des. 1862	
Patterson, John S.	Pvt. (B)	c. 7/1/62	Columbia	Par. 5/ /65	W-1
Patterson, William S.	Pvt. (K)	6/22/62	Spartanburg	KIA 9/30/64	
Pearce, Martin	Pvt. (M)	c. 7/1/62	Columbia	Par. 4/9/65	W-1

NAME	LAST RANK (COMPANY)	DATE ENTERED	PLACE ENTERED	FINAL DISPOSITION	NO. TIMES WOUNDED
Pearson, Perry P.	Pvt. (M)	5/7/62	Limestone Spr.	Disp. Un.	W-1
Pearson, William	Sgt. (M)	5/7/62	Limestone Spr.	KIA 6/22/64	W-2
Perry, E. A.	Sgt. (I)	4/14/61	Pendleton	Par. 4/9/65	W-1
Perry, S. A.	Pvt. (I)	4/14/61	Pendleton	Des. 1865	
Perry, Silas M.	Pvt. (I)	2/21/63	Pendleton	Par. 4/9/65	W-1
Perry, William H.	Pvt. (I)	3/15/62	Pendleton	Par. 4/9/65	
Pettit, Henry	Pvt. (H)	5/10/62	Spartanburg	KIA 6/30/62	
Petty, Joseph	Pvt. (K)	3/17/62	Spartanburg	DOD 5/30/62	
Petty, Lee	Pvt. (M)	c. 7/20/62	Columbia	Par. 4/9/65	W-2
Petty, M. T.	Pvt. (E)			Par. 5/8/65	
Petty, N.	Pvt. (M)	c. 7/20/62	Columbia	KIA 9/17/62	
Petty, William	Pvt. (M)	6/10/61	Summerville	Disp. Un.	W-4
Philips, T.	Pvt. (M)	c. 7/20/62	Columbia	DOD 11/14/62	
Phillips, R. Wesley	Pvt. (I)	4/14/61	Belton	Par. 4/9/62	
Phillips, Ruben	Pvt. (I)	3/15/62	Williamston	DOD 6/24/62	
Phillips, Toliver	Pvt. (H)	3/11/62	Spartanburg	Des. 8/13/62	
Phillips, W. H.	Pvt.(I)	5/20/62	Virginia	DOD 6/11/62	
Pilgrim, Samuel	Pvt. (I)	4/14/61	Pendleton	Par. 4/9/62	W-1
Pitts, William	Pvt. (B)	4/14/61	Pendleton	MW 5/5/62	
Poe, William	1st Lt. (C)	4/14/61	Anderson	MW 10/29/63	W-1
Pollard, John R.	Cpl. (D)	4/13/61	Spartanburg	MW 11/16/63	
Poole, John T. L.	Pvt.(H)	c. 7/19/62	Columbia	Par. 4/9/65	W-1
Poole, Robert L.	Capt. (K)	4/13/61	Spartanburg	Res. 9/12/63	
Post, William M.	Surg. (F&S)			Tran. 1864	
Potter, J. R.	Pvt. (M)	2/1/64	Tennessee	Disp. Un.	W-1
Powell, James F.	Pvt. (A)	4/13/61	Union	Par. 4/9/65	W-1
Power, W. K.	Pvt. (I)	3/15/62	Pendleton	Par. 4/9/65	W-2
Prater, Mattison	Pvt. (L)	10/1/63	Columbia	DOD 8/18/64	
Prather, Henry	Pvt. (G)		Lexington	KIA 5/28/64	
Prather, W. J.	Pvt. (I)	1/1/64	Tennessee	Disp. Un.	W-1
Prather, William	Pvt. (B)		Abbeville	KIA 10/7/64	

NAME	LAST RANK (COMPANY)	DATE ENTERED	PLACE ENTERED	FINAL DISPOSITION	NO. TIMES WOUNDED
Presley, T. B.	Pvt. (A)	4/13/61	Union	Disp. Un.	
Prichard, Alfred	Cpl. (M)	5/7/62	Limestone Spr.	Par. 4/9/65	W-2
Prichard, James	Pvt. (H)	c. 10/20/64	Spartanburg	Par. 4/9/65	
Pridmore, George G.	Pvt. (A)	4/13/61	Union	Disp. Un.	W-2
Prince, J. E. F.	Pvt. (I)	4/14/61	Pendleton	Par. 4/9/65	W-1
Puckett, Calvin	Pvt. (A)	12/17/61	Columbia	Par. 4//65	
Puckett, John	Pvt. (A)	4/13/61	Union	Des. 2/21/65	
Purgason, James	Pvt. (K)	2/24/62	Spartanburg	Med. D. 8/28/62	
Qualls, W. B.	Pvt. (C)	4/14/61	Anderson	Par. 4/9/65	W-2
Quattlebaum, J. D.	Pvt. (F)	3/10/62	Lexington	Par. 4/9/65	W-1
Quattlebaum, J. H.	Pvt. (F)	7/8/61	Ridgeville	Par. 4//65	W-1
Quattlebaum, Joab	Capt. (F)	7/8/61	Ridgeville	KIA 10/7/64	W-1
Quinn, J. Franklin	Pvt. (H)	1/15/63	Spartanburg	Des. 1865	W-1
Quinn, James W.	Sgt. (H)	3/11/62	Spartanburg	Par. 4/9/65	W-1
Quinn, O. J. (see Gwinn, O. J.)					
Rackley, J. H.	Pvt. (B)	10/9/61	Pendleton	DOD 6/1/63	W-1
Rackley, William B.	Pvt. (B)	6/28/62	Pendleton	DPOW	
Rainey, John L.	Pvt. (G)	5/26/64	Columbia	Par. 4/9/65	W-1
Ramsaur, Pinckney A.	Pvt. (K)	4/26/62	Spartanburg	Tran. 1862	
Ramsey, Calvin	Cpl. (M)	6/10/61	Summerville	MW 6/30/62	
Ramsey, David	Pvt. (M)	5/18/62	Limestone Spr.	Disp. Un.	W-2
Ramsey, John	Pvt. (M)	6/10/61	Summerville	KIA 8/30/62	W-1
Ramsey, W. Harvey	Pvt. (G)	6/5/61	Chester	KIA 8/30/62	W-2
Rankin, George A.	1st Lt. (L)			Med. D. 2/17/64	W-1
Rankin, George W.	Pvt. (L)	11/12/64	Columbia	Par. 4/9/65	
Rankin, W. Robertson	2d Lt. (L)	5//61		Par. 4/9/65	
Rawls, Ansel	Pvt. (F)	5/1/64	Lexington	Par. 4/9/65	
Rawls, Cary E.	Pvt. (F)	4/24/62	Lexington	Par. 5/20/65	
Rawls, E. J.	Pvt. (F)	2/23/64	Lexington	Par. 4/9/65	
Rawls, H. A.	Pvt. (F)	7/8/61	Ridgeville	KIA 7/15/64	
Rawls, J. E.	1st Lt. (F)	7/8/61	Ridgeville	Res. 7/29/63	

NAME	LAST RANK (COMPANY)	DATE ENTERED	PLACE ENTERED	FINAL DISPOSITION	NO. TIMES WOUNDED
Rawls, M.	Pvt. (I)			Par. 5/22/65	
Ray, Elijah	Sgt. (A)	4/13/61	Union	DPOW 7/18/62	W-1
Ray, Hugh	Pvt. (M)	5/7/62	Limestone Spr.	Disp. Un.	
Read, William (see Reed, William)					
Reams, William	Cpl. (L)	6/3/61	Pendleton	MW 5/31/62	
Reaves, Burrell F.	Pvt. (H)	5/10/62	Spartanburg	Des. 1865	
Reed, William	Pvt. (F)	9/2/63	Aiken	Par. 4/9/65	W-2
Reeks, John G.	Pvt. (I)	c. 7/14/62		Par. 4/9/65	
Reid, Christopher L.	Pvt. (C)	6/3/61	Pendleton	Disp. Un.	W-2
Reid, J. P.	Pvt. (C)	4/10/63	Anderson	Disp. Un.	
Reid, T. G.	Pvt. (B)	5/12/62	Pendleton	DOD 8/16/62	
Reynolds, John	Pvt. (M)	6/10/61	Summerville	Par. 4/21/65	W-1
Reynolds, Joseph	Pvt. (M)	6/10/61	Summerville	Unk. D. 7/13/62	
Rice, E. B.	Sgt. (C)	4/14/61	Anderson	Par. 4/9/65	
Rice, H. F.	Pvt. (C)	4/28/62	Anderson	Par. 4/9/65	
Rice, J. L.	Pvt. (C)	5/31/61	Anderson	MW 6/30/62	
Richard, H. (see Rickard, Henry)					
Richardson, B. F.	Pvt. (D)	1/19/63	Spartanburg	DOD 3/29/63	
Richardson, C. P.	Pvt. (I)	6/12/61	Williamston	DOD 1864	W-1
Richardson, T. W.	Pvt. (D)	4/13/61	Spartanburg	RPOW 6/26/65	W-1
Richardson, W. E. M.	Sgt. (I)	4/14/61	Pendleton	MW 6/30/62	
Richardson, W. H. H.	Sgt. (D)	4/13/61	Spartanburg	Par. 4/9/65	W-2
Richardson, Wm. F. S.	Pvt. (K)	4/13/61	Spartanburg	MW 6/30/62	
Richey, John	Pvt. (C)	4/14/61	Anderson	KIA 5/6/64	
Rickard, Henry	Pvt. (F)	c. 9/16/64	Columbia	Par. 4/9/65	
Rickster, E.	Pvt. (M)	c. 7/1/62	Columbia	Disp. Un.	
Riogell, J. D.	(F)			Disp. Un.	
Robberson, Jason	Pvt. (B)	9/12/64	Pickens	Par. 4/9/65	
Robbins, J. S.	Pvt. (H)	c. 10/20/64	Spartanburg	DPOW 6/7/65	
Robbs, A. C.	Cpl. (M)	4/13/61	Limestone Spr.	Disp. Un.	W-2
Roberson, H.	Pvt. (E)	c. 3/14/64	Spartanburg	Disp. Un.	W-1

409

NAME	LAST RANK (COMPANY)	DATE ENTERED	PLACE ENTERED	FINAL DISPOSITION	NO. TIMES WOUNDED
Roberts, C. C.	Pvt. (G)	4/13/61	Yorkville	Disp. Un.	W-1
Robertson, C.	Pvt. (L)	4/10/62	Pendleton	KIA 6/30/62	
Robinson, Jason (see Robberson, Jason)					
Robinson, T. J.	Pvt. (E)	3/19/62	Sumter	MW 7/ /64	
Robison, R. R.	Cpl. (G)	4/13/61	Yorkville	KIA 6/19/64	
Rochester, W. D.	Pvt. (B)	7/1/62	Columbia	Par. 4/9/65	
Rogers, W. Edgar	Pvt. (H)	4/13/63	Spartanburg	Par. 4/9/65	W-2
Rollins, Wm. L. D.	Pvt. (H)	6/28/61	Spartanburg	Des. 1/25/65	W-1
Roper, Taliafero	Pvt. (I)	4/14/61	Pendleton	Par. 4/9/65	W-1
Rose, E. M.	Pvt. (G)	10/8/61	Virginia	Age D. 1862	W-1
Rush, John M.	Pvt. (E)	6/4/61	Clarendon	MW 11/16/63	W-1
Russell, D. M.	Capt. (B)	4/14/61	Pendleton	Med. D. 2/9/63	W-1
Russell, J. S.	Pvt. (C)	11/2/64	Anderson	Par. 4/9/65	
Russell, James S.	Pvt. (H)	3/11/62	Spartanburg	Disp. Un.	
Rutledge, J. B.	Sgt. (B)	6/3/61	Columbia	KIA 6/30/62	
Sadler, S. C.	Pvt. (G)	9/13/61	Yorkville	Tran. 4/15/64	W-2
Sadler, William B.	Pvt. (G)	9/13/61	Virginia	Age D. 1862	W-1
Sanders, William H.	Pvt. (A)	4/13/61	Union	Tran. 5/15/63	W-1
Sanderson, J. C.	Pvt. (M)	c. 7/20/62	Columbia	Des. 8/18/62	
Sargent, Ephraim	Pvt. (I)	3/15/62	Pendleton	Unk. D. 7/21/62	
Sarratt, F. C.	Pvt. (M)	4/13/61	Limestone Spr.	MW 6/27/62	
Sarratt, H. J.	Pvt. (G)	4/13/61	Yorkville	Par. 4/ /65	W-1
Sarratt, J. M.	Pvt. (M)	4/13/61	Limestone Spr.	Age D. 4/13/62	
Sarratt, O. C.	Pvt. (M)	4/13/61	Limestone Spr.	Unk. D. 11/5/62	W-1
Sarratt, W. A.	Pvt. (M)	4/13/61	Limestone Spr.	Disp. Un.	
Sartor, Lawrence	Cpl. (A)	4/13/61	Union	KIA 8/14/64	
Sawyer, D. C.	Pvt. (F)	9/8/61	Virginia	Disp. Un.	W-1
Sawyer, W. E.	Pvt. (F)	7/8/61	Ridgeville	Par. 4/ /65	
Scates, J. Pinckney	Pvt. (H)	7/10/61	Summerville	Disp. Un.	W-2
Scates, Stewart	Pvt. (M)	5/7/62	Limestone Spr.	MW 8/30/62	
Scates, W. H.	Pvt. (H)	6/28/62	Spartanburg	Disp. Un.	

410

NAME	LAST RANK (COMPANY)	DATE ENTERED	PLACE ENTERED	FINAL DISPOSITION	NO. TIMES WOUNDED
Scates, William J.	Pvt. (M)	7/10/61	Summerville	DOD 1/10/63	W-1
Schappaul, A.	Pvt. (D)	6/3/61	Spartanburg	Disp. Un.	W-1
Schrimp, G. L.	Pvt. (C)	4/14/61	Anderson	Par. 4/9/65	W-1
Scott, Berry B.	Pvt. (M)	3/18/62	Spartanburg	DPOW 2/4/64	W-1
Scott, Thomas C.	Pvt. (K)	3/19/62	Spartanburg	Des. 2/25/62	W-1
Scruggs, A. M.	2d Lt. (H)	6/28/61	Spartanburg	KIA 6/30/62	
Scruggs, J. P.	Pvt. (H)	3/11/62	Spartanburg	Disp. Un.	
Scruggs, J. W.	Pvt. (H)	3/11/62	Spartanburg	Disp. Un.	
Scruggs, W. D.	Pvt. (M)	4/13/61	Limestone Spr.	Par. 4/9/65	W-1
Seaborn, William R.	Pvt. (B)	4/14/61	Pendleton	KIA 5/31/62	
Seabrook, Cato A.	Adju. (F&S)		Yorkville	KIA 8/30/62	
Sears, J. N.	Pvt. (L)	6/3/61	Pendleton	KIA 6/30/62	
Sellars, George B.	Pvt. (M)	7/10/61	Spartanburg	Disp. Un.	
Sellars, Henry	Pvt. (M)	5/7/62	Limestone Spr.	MW 5/6/64	
Sellars, Michael	Pvt. (M)	12/25/64	Limestone Spr.	Par. 4/9/65	
Settle, G. F.	Pvt. (D)	2/13/64	Spartanburg	Tran. 7/8/64	W-1
Settle, John L.	Pvt. (D)	7/15/62	Spartanburg	Par. 4/9/65	
Settle, William	Pvt. (D)	4/13/61	Spartanburg	KIA 9/17/62	W-1
Settlemyer, J. A.	Pvt. (D)	6/3/61	Spartanburg	Par. 4/19/65	W-2
Settlemyer, M. E.	Pvt. (D)	6/3/61	Spartanburg	Disp. Un.	
Sexton, J. C.	Pvt. (D)	7/28/62	Spartanburg	Disp. Un.	W-1
Shands, R. C.	Pvt. (D)	3/15/62	Spartanburg	RPOW 6/26/65	
Sharp, Henry N.	Pvt. (M)	c. 7/20/62	Columbia	DOD 5/22/63	
Shealy, J. J.	Pvt. (F)	3/14/62	Lexington	Par. 4/9/65	
Shealy, Paul	Sgt. (F)	7/8/61	Ridgeville	Disp. Un.	W-2
Shealy, T.	Pvt. (F)	3/10/62	Lexington	DOD 5/17/62	
Sherrard, D. J.	Pvt. (C)	4/14/61	Anderson	Par. 4/9/65	
Shettlesworth, D. D.	Pvt. (B)	5/6/62	Pendleton	Disp. Un.	
Shields, A. L.	Pvt. (E)	4/8/61	Sumter	Par. 4/9/65	
Shouse, Wiley	Cpl. (B)			Disp. Un.	
Shurley, W. M.	Pvt. (L)	4/14/61	Anderson	KIA 5/31/62	

411

NAME	LAST RANK (COMPANY)	DATE ENTERED	PLACE ENTERED	FINAL DISPOSITION	NO. TIMES WOUNDED
Simmons, C. J.	Pvt. (B)	6/1/61	Pickens	Par. 4/9/65	
Simmons, Charles	Pvt. (K)	5/7/62	Spartanburg	MW 5/31/62	
Simmons, D. L.	Pvt. (B)	6/1/61	Pendleton	KIA 6/30/62	
Simmons, James N.	Pvt. (B)	1/15/64	Tennessee	Disp. Un.	
Simmons, John A.	Cpl. (B)	4/14/61	Pendleton	Disp. Un.	W-2
Simmons, W. T.	Pvt. (B)	8/17/61	Pickens	Disp. Un.	W-2
Simpson, W. J.	Pvt. (B)	c. 7/1/62	Anderson	DOD 1/25/64	
Sims, J. K. S.	Pvt. (G)	4/13/61	Yorkville	DOD 4/15/63	W-1
Singleton, George W.	Pvt. (B)	10/9/61	Greenville	RPOW 5/31/65	W-1
Singleton, William O.	Pvt. (B)	10/9/61	Greenville	Par. 4/9/65	W-1
Sitton, Augustus J.	Q.M.S. (F&S)	4/14/61	Pendleton	Par. 4/9/65	
Sitton, Frank L.	Pvt. (B)	5/12/62	Pendleton	Par. 4/9/65	W-1
Skelton, J. Thomas	Sgt. (C)	4/14/61	Anderson	Par. 4/9/65	W-2
Skipper, James	Pvt. (M)	c. 7/20/62	Columbia	DOD 1863	
Sloan, David B.	Pvt. (C)	4/14/61	Anderson	Unk. D. 6/28/62	
Sloan, Robert E.	1st Sgt. (C)	4/14/61	Anderson	Par. 4/9/65	W-1
Smith, Ambrose	Pvt. (I)	4/14/61	Pendleton	KIA 6/27/62	W-1
Smith, B. S.	Cpl. (C)	4/14/61	Anderson	MW 6/30/62	
Smith, G. A.	1st Sgt. (I)	4/14/61	Pendleton	Par. 4/9/65	W-1
Smith, Gambrell	Pvt. (L)	4/14/61	Anderson	Med D. 7/20/63	W-1
Smith, H. S.	Pvt. (F)	4/14/62	Lexington	MW 6/30/62	
Smith, Isaiah	Pvt. (G)	6/17/62	Greenville	Disp. Un.	
Smith, J. B.	Pvt. (G)	4/17/62	Yorkville	KIA 6/30/62	
Smith, J. D.	Pvt. (A)	4/13/61	Union	Par. 4/9/65	W-2
Smith, J. L. N.	Pvt. (C)	6/3/61	Pendleton	KIA 5/31/62	
Smith, J. M.	Pvt. (D)	4/19/62	Spartanburg	MW 5/31/62	
Smith, John J.	Pvt. (G)	3/19/62	Yorkville	Par. 4/9/65	W-1
Smith, Joseph W.	Pvt. (I)	4/14/61	Pendleton	DOD 1862	
Smith, L. C.	Pvt. (I)	3/15/62	Pendleton	RPOW 4/15/65	W-2
Smith, M. T.	1st Lt. (I)	4/14/61	Pendleton	Par. 4/9/65	W-1
Smith, Martin	Pvt. (M)	6/3/61	Spartanburg	KIA 5/31/62	

412

NAME	LAST RANK (COMPANY)	DATE ENTERED	PLACE ENTERED	FINAL DISPOSITION	NO. TIMES WOUNDED
Smith, R. B.	Sgt. (G)	7/4/61	Virginia	MW 9/17/62	
Smith, R. P.	Pvt. (G)	4/13/61	Yorkville	Par. 4/9/65	
Smith, R. S.	Pvt. (I)	3/15/62	Pickens	RPOW 6/26/65	W-1
Smith, Reuben	Pvt. (I)	3/15/62	Pendleton	Par. 4/9/65	
Smith, Stephen	Pvt. (I)	3/15/62	Pendleton	Par. 4/9/65	
Smith, T. J.	Pvt. (B)	5/14/61	Grove Sta.	Disp. Un.	W-1
Smith, T. Jesse	Pvt. (E)	4/8/61	Kingstree	KIA 6/30/62	W-1
Smith, Thomas G.	Pvt. (K)	4/14/61	Pendleton	MW 6/30/62	
Smith, W. A.	Pvt. (I)	3/15/62	Pendleton	MW 6/30/62	
Smith, W. Beaty	Capt. (G)	4/13/61	Yorkville	Par. 4/9/65	W-1
Smith, W. G.	Pvt. (I)	3/15/62	Pendleton	Disp. Un.	W-1
Smith, Whitehead	Pvt. (K)	8/7/61	Spartanburg	KIA 8/30/62	
Smith, William	Pvt. (A)	3/20/62	Union	Par. 4/9/65	W-1
Smith, William	Pvt. (D)	4/13/61	Spartanburg	KIA 6/27/62	W-1
Smith, William C.	Pvt. (I)	6/5/61	Pendleton	Par. 4/9/65	W-1
Snoddy, J. A.	Pvt. (D)	8/1/63	Spartanburg	Par. 4/9/65	
Snoddy, Robert A.	1st Lt. (D)	4/13/61	Spartanburg	MW 10/29/63	
Solsbee, James E.	Pvt. (K)	2/25/62	Spartanburg	Disp. Un.	W-1
Spann, J. F.	1st Lt. (F)	7/8/61	Ridgeville	KIA 6/20/64	W-1
Spann, J. W.	Pvt. (F)	2/16/63	Lexington	Par. 4/9/65	W-1
Spence, W. J.	Pvt. (C)	4/16/64	Anderson	Disp. Un.	W-1
Spencer, W. H.	Pvt. (H)	6/28/61	Spartanburg	KIA 5/5/62	
Spencer, W. T.	Pvt. (I)	4/14/61	Pendleton	Disp. Un.	
Spradly, B. F.	Pvt. (F)	7/1/63	Lexington	DPOW 1864	
St. Amand, A. W.	Pvt. (A)	7/1/64	Union	Par. 4/9/65	W-1
Stacey, W. R.	Pvt. (M)	4/13/61	Limestone Spr.	Disp. Un.	
Stansell, Robert L.	Cpl. (L)	4/14/61	Anderson	Par. 4/9/65	
Starnes, R.	Pvt. (F)	7/8/61	Ridgeville	Disp. Un.	
Steading, G. F.	Cpl. (D)	4/13/61	Spartanburg	MW 10/7/64	W-1
Steedman, J. G.	Cpl. (F)	7/8/61	Ridgeville	Disp. Un.	
Steedman, Napoleon B.	Pvt. (F)	7/8/61	Ridgeville	Par. 4/9/65	W-1

413

NAME	LAST RANK (COMPANY)	DATE ENTERED	PLACE ENTERED	FINAL DISPOSITION	NO. TIMES WOUNDED
Steedman, W. D.	Pvt. (F)	7/8/61	Ridgeville	Disp. Un.	
Steedman, W. L.	2d Lt. (F)	7/8/61	Ridgeville	Par. 4/9/65	W-1
Steele, C. S.	Sgt. (B)	6/2/61	Pendleton	Par. 4/9/65	
Steele, William	2d Lt. (B)	6/2/61	Pendleton	Par. 4/9/65	W-2
Stephens, J. B.	Pvt. (I)	4/14/61	Pendleton	Par. 4/9/65	W-1
Stevens, Calvin	Pvt. (K)	3/19/62	Spartanburg	Tran. 5//63	W-1
Stevens, E. B.	Pvt. (L)	6/3/61	Pendleton	Med. D. 12/19/62	W-1
Stevenson, Henry C.	Pvt. (K)	4/13/61	Spartanburg	Med. D. 9/5/63	W-1
Stevenson, R. C.	Sgt. (G)	4/13/61	Yorkville	Par. 4/9/65	W-1
Stevenson, T. W.	Pvt. (G)	6/4/61	Orangeburg	DOD 10/13/62	
Stevenson, William H.	Cpl. (L)	6/3/61	Pendleton	Par. 4/9/65	W-2
Stewart, E. W.	Pvt. (C)	4/14/61	Anderson	Par. 4/9/65	W-2
Stone, P. A.	Pvt. (D)	5/2/62	Spartanburg	DOD 7/13/62	
Stone, Thomas R.	Pvt. (L)	4/22/62	Anderson	MW 6/27/62	
Strait, G. Lafayette	A. Surg. (F&S)		York	DOD 10/18/63	
Strange, William	Sgt. (A)	4/13/61	Union	RPOW 5/14/65	
Stribling, J. W.	Sgt. (B)	9/18/61	Pendleton	Disp. Un.	W-1
Strong, M. J.	Pvt. (A)	4/13/61	Union	RPOW 5/3/65	
Sullivan, John P.	Sgt. (C)	4/14/61	Anderson	Par. 4/9/65	W-1
Summey, P. W.	Pvt. (L)	4/14/61	Anderson	Med D. 1/23/63	W-1
Surratt, A. J.	Pvt. (D)	4/13/61	Spartanburg	Par. 4/9/65	W-2
Surratt, John	Pvt. (D)	4/11/62	Spartanburg	Par. 4/9/65	W-1
Tate, James	Pvt. (M)	5/7/62	Limestone Spr.	Des. 1864	
Taylor, James	Pvt. (F)	c. 5/10/64	Lexington	Par. 4/9/65	
Taylor, R. G.	Pvt. (M)	4/13/61	Limestone Spr.	MW 6/27/62	
Taylor, Samuel J.	Cpl. (L)	4/14/61	Anderson	DOD 5/8/64	
Taylor, Thomas	Pvt. (A)	4/13/61	Union	Disp. Un.	
Teague, G. W. L.	Sgt. (A)	4/13/61	Union	Par. 4/9/65	W-1
Telford, Edwin M.	Pvt. (L)	3/14/64	Tennessee	Par. 4/9/65	
Telford, William B.	Pvt. (L)	4/14/61	Anderson	RPOW 5/14/65	W-1
Templeton, D. H.	Cpl. (I)	4/14/61	Pendleton	Par. 4/9/65	W-2

414

NAME	LAST RANK (COMPANY)	DATE ENTERED	PLACE ENTERED	FINAL DISPOSITION	NO. TIMES WOUNDED
Tennison, Wm. P.	Pvt. (H)	6/28/61	Spartanburg	Disp. Un.	
Thames, J. P.	Pvt. (E)	7/17/61	Kingstree	KIA 6/3/64	W-2
Thames, W. S.	Pvt. (E)	7/9/61	Ridgeville	MW 6/30/62	
Thomas, D. A.	Pvt. (A)	7/12/62	Union	Par. 4/9/65	W-1
Thomas, P. G.	Pvt. (A)	4/13/61	Union	Par. 4/9/65	W-1
Thompson, George M.	Pvt. (I)	4/14/61	Pendleton	Med. D. 12/3/62	
Thompson, J. W.	Pvt. (E)	7/4/61	Sumter	Disp. Un.	
Thompson, Waddy	A. Surg. (F&S)	2/6/62	Virginia	Tran. 12/ /64	
Thomson, Henry H.	1st Lt. (K)	4/13/61	Spartanburg	Med. D. 1/15/63	W-1
Thomson, James A.	Cpl. (C)	6/3/61	Columbia	MW 10/29/63	W-1
Thomson, John S. R.	Sgt. (K)	4/13/61	Spartanburg	Disp. Un.	
Thornkill, J. W.	Pvt. (E)	6/4/61	Clarendon	Des. 1864	W-1
Thrift, Allen	Pvt. (M)	6/10/61	Summerville	RPOW 6/21/65	W-3
Thrift, L. D.	Pvt. (I)	4/14/61	Pendleton	Par. 4/9/65	
Thrift, Pleasant	Pvt. (M)	4/13/61	Limestone Spr.	Disp. Un.	W-2
Timmons, William M.	Pvt. (D)	2/23/62	Spartanburg	Par. 4/9/65	W-1
Tims, P. W.	Pvt. (C)	9/21/63	Anderson	Disp. Un.	W-1
Tinsley, Jesse G.	Pvt. (D)	4/22/62	Spartanburg	MW 5/31/62	
Tinsley, Thomas J.	Pvt. (D)	4/22/62	Spartanburg	KIA 6/30/62	W-1
Tisdale, D. M.	Cpl. (E)	6/24/61	Ridgeville	Par. 4/9/65	W-1
Todd, H. C.	Pvt. (C)	4/14/61	Anderson	Med. D. 3/25/63	W-1
Todd, James T.	Pvt. (C)	4/14/61	Anderson	MW 5/31/62	
Todd, Robert F.	Cpl. (I)	4/14/61	Pendleton	MW 6/30/62	
Todd, S. D.	Pvt. (M)	c. 7/20/62	Columbia	DOD 1864	
Tolleson, A. J.	Sgt. (K)	4/13/61	Spartanburg	Disp. Un.	
Tolly, G. F.	Pvt. (C)	3/17/62	Pendleton	Disp. Un.	W-1
Trammel, B. E. W.	Pvt. (I)	4/14/61	Pendleton	Disp. Un.	
Treadway, Geo. T.	Pvt. (B)		Pickens	DOD 1863	
Tuck, J. Armstrong	Pvt. (K)	3/18/62	Spartanburg	DOD	
Tuck, Robert E.	Pvt. (K)	3/18/62	Spartanburg	Par. 4/9/65	W-2
Tuck, Samuel	Pvt. (K)		Spartanburg	MW 5/31/62	

415

NAME	LAST RANK (COMPANY)	DATE ENTERED	PLACE ENTERED	FINAL DISPOSITION	NO. TIMES WOUNDED
Tucker, Henry	Pvt. (D)	4/13/61	Spartanburg	Age D. 7/15/62	
Tucker, J. B.	Pvt. (A)	4/13/61	Union	Disp. Un.	W-1
Tucker, Wm. B.	Pvt. (K)		Spartanburg	DOD	
Turner, C. J.				Des. 1865	
Turner, John L.	Pvt. (A)	4/13/61	Union	KIA 6/30/62	
Turner, R.	Pvt. (D)			Par. 4/9/65	
Vandiver, Thomas E. C.	Pvt. (I)	11/4/64	Columbia	Par. 4/9/65	
Vassey, John	Pvt. (M)	4/13/61	Limestone Spr.	Disp. Un.	W-1
Vassey, Jonas	Pvt. (M)	10/16/64	Virginia	Disp. Un.	
Vaughan, R. N. C.	Pvt. (A)	4/13/61	Union	KIA 10/7/64	W-2
Vickery, G. W.	Pvt. (M)	c. 7/20/62	Columbia	Par. 4/9/65	
Vickery, J. W.	Pvt. (M)	c. 7/20/62	Columbia	Disp. Un.	
Walden, Fielden	Sgt. (K)	4/13/61	Spartanburg	Par. 4/9/65	W-3
Walden, William A.	Pvt. (K)	4/30/62	Spartanburg	Par. 4/9/65	W-1
Waldrup, A. B.	Pvt. (D)	1/7/62	Spartanburg	DOD 1/26/63	
Walker, Absalom	Pvt. (K)	4/13/61	Spartanburg	Disp. Un.	W-1
Walker, Felix	Pvt. (K)	9/19/61	Spartanburg	MW 5/31/62	
Walker, J. D.	Pvt. (H)	5/10/62	Spartanburg	Med. D. 9/8/62	
Walker, James J.	Pvt. (A)	4/13/61	Union	Par. 4/9/65	W-1
Walker, John E.	Pvt. (K)	11/13/61	Spartanburg	KIA 7/18/64	W-1
Walker, John T.	1st Lt. (K)	7/24/61	Spartanburg	Par. 4/9/65	W-2
Walker, Joseph	Col. (F&S)	4/13/61	Spartanburg	LOA	
Walker, M. T.	Pvt. (K)	4/3/64	Spartanburg	Disp. Un.	
Wallace, David	Pvt. (G)	4/13/62	Virginia	Disp. Un.	
Wallace, James	Pvt. (G)	10/10/63	Yorkville	DOD 2/19/64	
Walsh, James	Pvt. (G)	4/13/61	Yorkville	Med. D. 1863	W-2
Warr, J. W.	Pvt. (M)	c. 7/20/62	Columbia	Par. 4/9/65	W-1
Warren, G. W.	Pvt. (F)	7/8/61	Ridgeville	Disp. Un.	
Warren, S. J.	Pvt. (F)	7/8/61	Ridgeville	KIA 8/30/62	
Washburn, A. C.	Pvt. (H)	6/7/61	Spartanburg	KIA 6/27/62	
Waters, Hosea M.	Pvt. (H)	12/25/61	Spartanburg	MW 5/8/64	

NAME	LAST RANK (COMPANY)	DATE ENTERED	PLACE ENTERED	FINAL DISPOSITION	NO. TIMES WOUNDED
Waters, J. E.	Pvt. (F)	7/8/61	Ridgeville	Par. 4/9/65	
Watkins, J. C.	Pvt. (I)	3/15/62	Pendleton	Par. 4//65	W-1
Watkins, Judson	3d Lt. (F)	7/8/61	Ridgeville	DOD 8/18/64	W-1
Watson, Irvin	Pvt. (M)	3/13/63	Virginia	Par. 4/9/65	
Watson, James J.	Pvt. (H)	6/28/61	Spartanburg	RPOW 6/21/65	
Watson, Jesse	Pvt. (E)	4/22/64	Sumter	KIA 10/7/64	
Watson, John W.	Pvt. (M)	c. 7/20/62	Columbia	Par. 4/9/65	
Watson, R. W.	Pvt. (K)	6/2/62	Spartanburg	KIA 8/30/62	
Webb, J. M.	Pvt. (C)	4/14/61	Anderson	Par. 4/9/65	
Webb, J. T.	Pvt. (C)	4/14/61	Anderson	MW 5/31/62	
Webster, C. W.	Pvt. (E)	3/19/62	Sumter	Disp. Un.	
Webster, J. W.	Pvt. (E)	3/22/62	Marion	Disp. Un.	W-1
Welch, R. L.	Cpl. (E)	4/8/61	Sumter	Disp. Un.	W-1
Wells, David A.	Pvt. (L)	6/3/61	Pendleton	RPOW 5/10/65	W-1
Wells, David E.	Sgt. (E)	4/8/61	Sumter	KIA 6/30/62	
Wells, James	Pvt. (E)	7/4/61	Sumter	KIA 6/30/62	
Werner, T. J.	Pvt. (C)	11/2/64	Anderson	Par. 4/9/65	
West, William J.	Pvt. (H)	c. 8/19/62	Spartanburg	Par. 4/9/65	W-1
White, Elias	Sgt. (L)	4/14/61	Pendleton	Par. 4/9/65	W-2
White, George W.	Pvt. (B)	4/14/61	Pendleton	RPOW 1865	
White, Henry	Pvt. (L)	7/29/62	Pickens	Par. 4/9/65	
White, James W.	Pvt. (L)	6/3/61	Pendleton	Par. 4/9/65	
White, John W.	2d Lt. (K)	4/13/61	Spartanburg	Med. D. 11/6/62	W-1
White, John W.	Cpl. (K)	9/20/63	Spartanburg	MW 9/30/64	
White, Joseph B.	Pvt. (B)	4/14/61	Pendleton	Disp. Un.	
White, L. A.	1st Sgt. (E)	4/18/61	Sumter	MW 6/3/64	W-1
White, Rufus	Pvt. (K)	4/13/61	Spartanburg	MW 6/30/62	W-1
White, W. A.	Pvt. (I)	4/14/61	Pendleton	Med. D. 2/3/63	
White, W. R.	Pvt. (D)	4/13/61	Spartanburg	Med. D. 7/17/64	W-1
White, William	Cpl. (E)	7/4/61	Sumter	MW 6/30/62	W-1
White, William	Pvt. (K)	3/19/62	Spartanburg	DOD 6/2/62	

NAME	LAST RANK (COMPANY)	DATE ENTERED	PLACE ENTERED	FINAL DISPOSITION	NO. TIMES WOUNDED
Whitesides, W. T.	Pvt. (G)	8/10/63	Yorkville	Par. 4/ /65	
Whitlock, D. G.	Pvt. (H)	1/21/64	Union	Par. 4/9/65	
Whitner, J. H.	Pvt. (C)	10/10/63	Virginia	Tran. 1/2/65	
Whitten, John B.	Pvt. (B)	3/15/62	Pendleton	Disp. Un.	W-1
Wilder, Josiah M.	2d Lt. (E)	7/4/61	Sumter	Res. 4/22/64	W-2
Wilkerson, W. S.	Pvt. (G)	1/1/64	Tennessee	Disp. Un.	
Wilkes, Warren D.	1st Lt. (L)		Anderson	Par. 4/9/65	
Wilkins, James	Pvt. (H)	c. 7/19/62	Spartanburg	DOD 11/16/62	
Wilkins, William	Pvt. (A)	4/13/61	Union	Disp. Un.	W-1
Wilkinson, C. C.	1st Sgt. (I)	4/14/61	Pendleton	Disp. Un.	W-1
Willard, Caleb Y.	Pvt. (A)	4/13/61	Union	Par. 4/9/65	
Willard, Cary W.	Pvt. (A)	12/13/61	Cross Keys	Par. 4/9/65	W-1
Willard, Cornelius	Pvt. (A)	4/22/62	Union	Disp. Un.	
Willard, Drayton D.	Pvt. (A)	4/14/62	Union	Par. 4/9/65	W-1
Willard, James	Pvt. (A)	4/13/61	Union	Disp. Un.	W-1
Willard, L. B.	Sgt. (A)	4/14/62	Union	Par. 4/9/65	W-2
Willard, Mabry	Pvt. (A)	4/13/61	Union	DOD 2/ /63	
Williams, Alexander	Pvt. (M)	c. 7/20/62	Columbia	Des. 1865	
Williams, Andrew J.	Pvt. (K)	4/13/61	Spartanburg	Par. 4/9/65	
Williams, Andy	Pvt. (G)	5/8/62	Yorkville	DOD 5/28/62	
Williams, C. K.	Pvt. (G)			Disp. Un.	
Williams, G. F.	Pvt. (I)	4/14/61	Pendleton	DOD 11/28/63	W-1
Williams, J. Alex	Pvt. (K)	2/25/62	Spartanburg	Par. 4/9/65	
Williams, Jack	Pvt. (K)	3/19/62	Spartanburg	Des. 1865	
Williams, Jesse C.	Pvt. (D)	4/14/62	Spartanburg	Par. 4/9/65	
Williams, John C.	Pvt. (D)	4/13/61	Spartanburg	Par. 4/9/65	
Williams, P. E. A.	Sgt. (I)	4/14/61	Pendleton	Disp. Un.	W-2
Williams, R. O.	Pvt. (I)	4/14/62	Pendleton	Par. 4/9/65	
Williams, Richard L.	Pvt. (L)	4/14/61	Anderson	Disp. Un.	W-2
Williams, T. C.	Pvt. (G)	7/14/61	Yorkville	Par. 4/9/65	W-1
Williams, T. J.	Pvt. (D)			Disp. Un.	

NAME	LAST RANK (COMPANY)	DATE ENTERED	PLACE ENTERED	FINAL DISPOSITION	NO. TIMES WOUNDED
Williams, Thomas H.	2d Lt. (I)	4/14/61	Pendleton	Par. 4/9/65	W-1
Williams, W. B.	Pvt. (G)	6/4/61	Orangeburg	Med. D. 9/28/62	W-1
Williamson, John B.	Pvt. (K)	2/21/62	Spartanburg	Tran. 1864	W-1
Willis, D. Rice	Pvt. (H)	c. 7/19/62	Spartanburg	Disp. Un.	W-2
Willis, John	Pvt. (H)	3/11/62	Spartanburg	DOD 8/17/62	
Willis, William	Pvt. (H)	3/11/62	Spartanburg	MW 6/30/62	
Wilson, B. E.	Pvt. (E)	10/19/61	Sumter	Par. 4/9/65	
Wilson, D. W.	Pvt. (M)	c. 7/20/62	Columbia	DOD 10//62	
Wilson, J. A.	Pvt. (C)	4/14/61	Greenville	KIA 5/31/62	
Wilson, L. N.	Pvt. (M)	c. 7/20/62	Columbia	DOD 9/23/62	
Wilson, William	Pvt. (L)	7/15/62	Greenville	MW 6/27/62	
Winebrener, Solomon	Pvt. (A)	4/13/61	Union	Age D. 7/15/62	
Wingard, A. E.	Pvt. (F)	7/8/61	Ridgeville	Par. 5/24/65	W-4
Wingard, J. S.	Pvt. (F)	7/8/61	Ridgeville	Par. 4/9/65	W-1
Wingard, J. T.	Pvt. (F)	c. 11/1/64	Columbia	Par. 4/9/65	
Wingo, M. C.	Pvt. (D)	4/13/61	Spartanburg	Par. 4/9/65	W-1
Winkles, L. D.	Pvt. (E)	3/15/62	Sumter	Med. D. 5/14/62	
Winkles, William	Pvt. (E)	7/24/61	Ridgeville	DOD 4//62	
Withers, J. Newton	Capt. (G)	4/13/61	Yorkville	Tran. 10/21/63	W-1
Witherspoon, J. R.	Pvt. (G)	4/13/61	Yorkville	Disp. Un.	
Wix, Hiram	Pvt. (A)	4/13/61	Union	MW 5/31/62	
Wix, J. T.	Pvt. (A)	4/13/61	Union	Age D. 7/15/62	
Wofford, J. T. H.	Pvt. (D)	7/1/62	Spartanburg	Par. 4/9/65	
Wood, J. R.	Pvt. (D)	6/3/61	Spartanburg	MW 6/27/62	
Wood, James	Pvt. (G)	6/4/61	Orangeburg	MW 5/31/62	
Wood, W. A.	Pvt. (D)	11/2/64	Spartanburg	Par. 4/9/65	
Woods, Robert	Pvt. (L)	3/1/64	Tennessee	DOD 5/12/64	
Woody, N. J.	Pvt. (D)	4/13/61	Spartanburg	Tran. 1864	W-1
Woody, W. D.	Pvt. (D)	4/13/61	Spartanburg	KIA 7/12/64	W-1
Wooley, G. W.	Pvt. (F)	6/30/61	Ridgeville	KIA 5/31/62	
Wooten, George H.	Pvt. (L)	10/28/63	Tennessee	Par. 4/9/65	W-1

NAME	LAST RANK (COMPANY)	DATE ENTERED	PLACE ENTERED	FINAL DISPOSITION	NO. TIMES WOUNDED
Wooten, W. R.	Pvt. (I)	8/2/62	Virginia	Des. 1865	
Workman, P.	Pvt. (D)	6/3/61	Spartanburg	KIA 7/14/64	W-1
Wrightson, S. C.	Pvt. (D)	4/19/62	Spartanburg	RPOW 4/14/65	W-2
Wyatt, Henry M.	Pvt. (K)	7/23/63	Spartanburg	DPOW 2/3/64	
Wyatt, Monroe W.	Pvt. (K)	4/13/61	Spartanburg	Par. 4/9/65	
Young, Alexander M.	Pvt. (L)	11/14/62	Pocataligo	DOD 11/21/63	
Young, Robert	Pvt. (L)	3/12/62	Pendleton	Par. 4/9/65	
Zimmerman, John M.	Pvt. (K)	6/23/62	Spartanburg	KIA 6/30/62	
Zimmerman, L. C.	1st Sgt. (D)	4/13/61	Spartanburg	Par. 4/9/65	

420

PHOTOGRAPH CREDITS

Dust Cover	Palmetto Sharpshooters Flag	Ron Weaver; Emmaus, Pennsylvania
Frontispiece	Micah Jenkins	Library of Congress
p. 4	Captain John Jenkins (portrait)	Marianne Jenkins Rutledge; Greenville, South Carolina
p. 18	Kings Mountain Military School	S. C. State Museum; Columbia, South Carolina
p. 26	Sergeant William Jasper (print)	South Caroliniana Library; Columbia, South Carolina
p. 29	David Flavel Jamison	South Caroliniana Library
p. 34	Asbury Coward	David J. Rutledge; Greenville, South Carolina
p. 43	Colonel Micah Jenkins	Library of Congress
p. 48	Edward Byers Clinton	Elmer Oris Parker; Columbia, South Carolina
p. 68	Major General David R. Jones	Eleanor S. Brockenbrough Library, The Museum of the Confederacy; Richmond, Virginia
p. 78	Lieutenant General Richard Heron Anderson	Library of Congress
p. 82	General P. T. G. Beauregard	South Caroliniana Library
p. 112	Colonel John R. R. Giles	S. C. Confederate Relic Room and Museum; Columbia, South Carolina
p. 116	General Joseph E. Johnston	South Caroliniana Library
p. 180	Lieutenant Colonel John W. Goss	S. C. Confederate Relic Room and Museum
p. 199	Lieutenant General Stonewall Jackson	South Caroliniana Library
p. 207	William Porcher Miles	South Caroliniana Library
p. 217	Lieutenant General John Bell Hood	South Caroliniana Library
p. 221	Brigadier General Evander M. Law	Shaw Collection, The Virginia Historical Society; Richmond, Virginia
p. 246	Brigadier General Martin W. Gary	Library of Congress
p. 275	Major General Joseph B. Kershaw	South Caroliniana Library
p. 279	Lieutenant General James Longstreet	Eleanor S. Brockenbrough Library, The Museum of The Confederacy
p. 280	John W. Jamison	Albert L. Jamison; Boerne, Texas
p. 281	Captain John Peyre Thomas	John Earle Jones; Greenville, South Carolina
p. 314	Brigadier General John Bratton	South Caroliniana Library
p. 323	Lieutenant General Wade Hampton	South Caroliniana Library
p. 348	Lieutenant General Ambrose Powell Hill	South Caroliniana Library

p. 366	Micah John Jenkins	Frances Jenkins Turnipseed; Bowling Green, Kentucky
p. 366	Robert Flavel Jenkins	David J. Rutledge; Greenville, South Carolina
p. 367	John Murray Jenkins	United States Military Academy Archives; West Point, New York
p. 368	Asbury Coward	The Citadel Archives; Charleston, South Carolina

Photographic Consultant: David J. Rutledge

SELECT BIBLIOGRAPHY

MANUSCRIPTS, LETTERS AND
OTHER UNPUBLISHED MATERIALS

The Citadel Archives, Charleston, South Carolina
Official Register of Officers and Cadets.

Fredericksburg and Spotsylvania National Military Park, Fredericksburg, Virginia
T. G. Barham's War Record.
James Frank Barron Letters.

Georgia Department of Archives and History, Atlanta, Georgia
Abner R. Cox Diary.
"Reminiscences of E. T. Tollison, Company E, Hampton Legion." In
Reminiscences of Confederate Soldiers and Stories of the War, Volume
Twelve, compiled by the Georgia Division of the United Daughters of the
Confederacy.

Manassas National Battlefield Park Library, Manassas, Virginia
William Choice. "Memoirs of My Four Years in the War Between the States."

New York Public Library, Division of Rare Books and Manuscripts, New York, New York
Ezra Ayers Carman Collection, Astor, Lenox and Tilden Foundations.
"Lookout Valley," Memorandum by E. M. Law (undated).

Private Collections
Georgia Roper Jeter Collection, Powdersville, South Carolina
John G. Reeks Letters.
Elmer Oris Parker Collection, Columbia, South Carolina
Joseph Banks Lyle and Edward Byers Clinton Papers.
Emily Wilson Taylor Collection, Fountain Inn, South Carolina
Elizabeth Jenkins LaRoche and Micah Jenkins Letters.
Dr. W. Frank Strait Collection, Rock Hill, South Carolina
G. L. Strait Letters.

South Carolina Confederate Relic Room and Museum, Columbia, South Carolina
John Wesley Goss Letter.

South Carolina Department of Archives and History, Columbia, South Carolina

Private Papers:
Confederate War Letters of General John Bratton, 1861–1865.
John Jenkins Papers.

South Caroliniana Library, University of South Carolina, Columbia, South Carolina

Alexander Colclough Diary.
Henry Calvin Conner Papers.
Colonel James R. Hagood. "Memoirs of the First South Carolina Regiment of Volunteer Infantry in the Confederate War."
John Jenkins Papers.
Micah Jenkins Papers.
James P. Lockwood Journal.
McLure Family Papers.
Papers of the Tarrant, Reese and Radcliffe Families.

Southern Historical Collection, University of North Carolina, Chapel Hill, North Carolina

E. M. Law Papers.
E. P. Alexander Papers.
Lafayette McLaws Papers.

Special Collections Department, University of Virginia Library, Charlottesville, Virginia

William Anderson Collection.

Special Collections Library, Duke University, Durham, North Carolina

Micah Jenkins Letters.
Simon P. Wingard Correspondence.
William Wylie Papers.

Virginia State Library and Archives, Richmond, Virginia

James R. Boulware Diary.

Winthrop Archives and Special Collections, Winthrop University, Rock Hill, South Carolina

J. D. McConnell. "Recollections of the Civil War."

Robert W. Woodruff Library, Special Collections, Emory University, Atlanta, Georgia

William McFall Papers.

BOOKS

Anderson, Nancy Scott and Dwight. *The Generals: Ulysses S. Grant and Robert E. Lee*. New York: Random House, 1987.

Andrews, Judith M., ed. *Roll of the Dead: South Carolina Troops, Confederate States Service*. Columbia, South Carolina: South Carolina Department of Archives and History, 1995.

Bailey, N. Louise, Mary L. Morgan and Carolyn R. Taylor, eds. *Biographical Directory of the South Carolina Senate, 1776–1985*, Volume Two. Columbia, South Carolina: University of South Carolina Press, 1986.

Bates, Samuel P. *History of Pennsylvania Volunteers, 1861–5*, Volume Four. Reprint; Wilmington, North Carolina: Broadfoot Publishing Co., 1993.

Blackford, Susan L., comp., Charles Minor Blackford, III, ed. *Letters from Lee's Army*. New York: Charles Scribner's Sons, 1947.

Blair, William Alan, ed. *A Politician Goes to War: The Civil War Letters of John White Geary*. University Park, Pennsylvania: The Pennsylvania State University Press, 1995.

Bond, Natalie Jenkins, and Osmun Latrobe Coward, eds. *The South Carolinians: Colonel Asbury Coward's Memoirs*. New York: Vantage Press, 1968.

Bond, O. J. *The Story of the Citadel*. Richmond, Virginia: Garrett and Massie, Publishers, 1936.

Boyle, John Reynolds. *Soldiers True: The Story of the One Hundred and Eleventh Pennsylvania Volunteers, and of its Campaigns in the War for the Union 1861–1865*. New York: Eaton & Mains, 1903.

Bratton, Theodore DuBose. *An Apostle of Reality: The Life and Thought of Reverend William Porcher DuBose*. New York: Longmans, Green and Co., 1936.

Buell, Clarence C., and Robert U. Johnson, eds. *Battles and Leaders of the Civil War*. Four Volumes.

_____. Volume Two, *The Struggle Intensifies*. Reprint; Secaucus, New Jersey: Castle Books, 1982.

_____. Volume Three, *The Tide Shifts*. Reprint; Secaucus, New Jersey: Castle Books, 1982.

Burton, E. Milby. *The Siege of Charleston: 1861–1865*. Columbia, South Carolina: University of South Carolina Press, 1970.

Byron, George Gordon. "English Bards, and Scotch Reviewers; a Satire." In *The Works of Lord Byron,* ed., Ernest Hartley Coleridge, Volume One. New York: Octagon Books, Inc., 1966.

Caldwell, J. F. J. *The History of a Brigade of South Carolinians, Known First as "Gregg's" and Subsequently as "McGowan's Brigade."* Reprint; Marietta, Georgia: Continental Book Co., 1951.

Capers, Ellison. *South Carolina*, Volume Six of *Confederate Military History*, Clement A. Evans, ed. Extended edition; Wilmington, North Carolina: Broadfoot Publishing Co., 1987.

Catton, Bruce. *The Centennial History of the Civil War*. Three Volumes.

_____. Volume One, *The Coming Fury*. Garden City, New York: Doubleday and Co., 1961.

_____. Volume Two, *Terrible Swift Sword*. Garden City, New York: Doubleday and Co., 1963.

_____. Volume Three, *Never Call Retreat*. Garden City, New York: Doubleday and Co., 1965.

Cauthen, Charles Edward. *South Carolina Goes to War, 1860–1865*. Chapel Hill, North Carolina: University of North Carolina Press, 1950.

Channing, Steven A. *Crisis of Fear: Secession in South Carolina*. New York: Simon & Schuster, Inc., 1970.

Coker, James Lide. *History of Company G, Ninth S.C. Regiment, Infantry, and of Company E, Sixth Regiment, Infantry, S.C. Army*. Reprint; Greenwood, South Carolina: The Attic Press, 1979.

Cormier, Steven A. *The Siege of Suffolk: The Forgotten Campaign, April 11, 1863–May 4, 1863*. Lynchburg, Virginia: H. E. Howard, Inc., 1989.

Cozzens, Peter. *The Shipwreck of Their Hopes*. Chicago: University of Illinois Press, 1994.

Cutrer, Thomas W. *Longstreet's Aide: The Civil War Lettrs of Major Thomas J. Goree*. Charlottesville, Virginia: University Press of Virginia, 1995.

Dawson, Francis W. *Reminiscences of Confederate Service, 1861–1865*, Bell I. Wiley, ed. Baton Rouge, Louisiana: Louisiana State University Press, 1980.

Dowdey, Clifford. *The Seven Days: The Emergence of Lee*. Boston: Little, Brown and Co., 1964.

_____. *Lee's Last Campaign, The Story of Lee and His Men Against Grant–1864*. Boston: Little, Brown and Co., 1960.

Dowdey, Clifford and Louis H. Manarin. *The Wartime Papers of R. E. Lee*. New York: Bramhall House, 1961.

Edmunds, John B., Jr. *Francis W. Pickens and the Politics of Destruction*. Chapel Hill, North Carolina: University of North Carolina Press, 1986.

Elliott, Joseph Cantey. *Lieutenant General Richard Heron Anderson: Lee's Nobel Soldier*. Dayton, Ohio: Morningside House, Inc., 1985.

Ellis, Richard E. *The Union at Risk: Jacksonian Democracy, States' Rights, and the Nullification Crisis*. New York: Oxford University Press, 1987.

Foote, Shelby. *The Civil War, A Narrative*. Three Volumes.

_____. Volume One, *Fort Sumter to Perryville*. New York: Random House, 1958.

_____. Volume Two, *Fredericksburg to Meridian*. New York: Random House, 1963.

_____. Volume Three, *Red River to Appomattox*, New York: Random House, 1974.

Ford, Lacy K., Jr. *Origins of Southern Radicalism: The South Carolina Upcountry, 1800–1860*. New York: Oxford University Press, 1988.

Fox, William F. *Regimental Losses in the American Civil War, 1861–1865*. Reprint; Morningside Bookshop, 1974.

Fraser, Walter T., Jr. *Charleston! Charleston! The History of a Southern City*. Columbia, South Carolina: University of South Carolina Press, 1989.

Freeman, Douglas Southall. *Lee's Lieutenants, A Study in Command.* Three Volumes.
_____. Volume One, *Manassas to Malvern Hill.* New York: Charles Scribner's Sons, 1942.
_____. Volume Two, *Cedar Mountain to Chancellorsville.* New York: Charles Scribner's Sons, 1943.
_____. Volume Three, *Gettysburg to Appomattox.* New York: Charles Scribner's Sons, 1944.
Freeman, Douglas Southall, ed. *Lee's Dispatches: Unpublished Letters of Lee to Davis, 1862-1865.* New York: The Knickerbocker Press, 1915.
Gallagher, Gary W., ed. *Fighting for the Confederacy: The Personal Recollections of General Edward Porter Alexander.* Chapel Hill, North Carolina: University of North Carolina Press, 1989.
Govan, Gilbert E. and James W. Livingood, eds. *The Haskell Memoirs: John Cheves Haskell.* New York: G. P. Putnam's Sons, 1960.
Graydon, Nell S. *Tales of Edisto.* Columbia, South Carolina: R. L. Bryan Co., 1955.
Greenberg, Kenneth S. *Masters and Statesmen: The Political Culture of American Slavery.* Baltimore: The Johns Hopkins University Press, 1985.
Harrison, Walter. *Pickett's Men: A Fragment of War History.* New York: D. Van Nostrand, Publisher, 1870.
Hart, Joseph E., Jr. *The Church of the Good Shepherd, York, South Carolina: A Centennial History, 1855–1955.* York, South Carolina: privately printed, 1955.
Hennessy, John J. *Return to Bull Run: The Campaign and Battle of Second Manassas.* New York: Simon and Schuster, 1993.
Hewett, Janet B., Noah Andre Trudeau and Bryce A. Suderow, eds. *Supplement to the Official Records of the Union and Confederate Armies*, Part One (Battle Reports) in twelve volumes. Wilmington, North Carolina: Broadfoot Publishing Co., 1994—.
Hoyt, James A. *The Palmetto Riflemen: Co. B, Fourth Regiment S. C. Volunteers and Co. C, Palmetto Sharpshooters: Historical Sketch.* Greenville, South Carolina: Hoyt and Keys, Printers, 1886.
Kirkland, Randolph W., Jr. *Broken Fortunes: South Carolina Soldiers, Sailors and Citizens who Died in the Service of their Country and State in the War for Southern Independence, 1861–1865.* Charleston, South Carolina: The South Carolina Historical Society, 1995.
Landrum, John B. O. *History of Spartanburg County.* Reprint; Spartanburg, South Carolina: The Reprint Co., 1985.
Law, John Adger, ed. *Citadel Cadets, The Journal of Cadet Tom Law.* Clinton, South Carolina: P. C. Press, 1941.
Lewis, Richard. *Camp Life of a Confederate Boy of Bratton's Brigade, Longstreet's Corps, C.S.A.: Letters Written by Lieutenant Richard Lewis, of Walker's Regiment, to His Mother, During the War.* Charleston, South Carolina: The News and Courier Book Presses, 1883.
Longstreet, James. *From Manassas to Appomattox, Memoirs of the Civil War in America*, James I. Robertson, Jr., ed. Reprint; Bloomington, Indiana: University of Indiana Press, 1960.

Malone, Dumas, ed. *Dictionary of American Biography*, Volume Five, Part Two. New York: Charles Scribner's Sons, 1932.

May, John Amasa, and Joan Reynolds Faunt. *South Carolina Secedes*. Columbia, South Carolina: University of South Carolina Press, 1960.

McPherson, James M. *What They Fought For: 1861–1865*. Baton Rouge, Louisiana: Louisiana State University Press, 1994.

_____. *Battle Cry of Freedom: The Civil War Era*. New York: Oxford University Press, 1988.

McWhiney, Grady and Perry D. Jamieson. *Attack and Die: Civil War Military Tactics and the Southern Heritage*. Tuscaloosa, Alabama: University of Alabama Press, 1982.

Mikell, I. Jenkins. *Rumbling of the Chariot Wheels*. Columbia, South Carolina: R. L. Bryan Co., 1923.

Mixson, Frank M. *Reminiscences of a Private: Company "E", 1st S.C. Volunteers (Hagood's), Jenkins' Brigade, Lee's Army, 1861–1865*. Columbia, South Carolina: The State Company, 1910.

Oliphant, Mary Simms, Alfred O'dell Taylor and T. C. Duncan Eaves, eds. *The Letters of William Gilmore Simms*, Volume Three. Columbia, South Carolina: University of South Carolina Press, 1954.

Owens, Jo Roberts and Ruth Dickson Thomas. *Confederate Veterans Enrollment Book of York County, South Carolina – 1902*. Clover, South Carolina: Westmoreland Printers, Inc., 1983.

Priest, John Michael. *Before Antietam: The Battle for South Mountain*. Shippensburg, Pennsylvania: White Mane Publishing Co., 1992.

_____. *Antietam: The Soldiers' Battle*. New York: Oxford University Press, 1989.

Ramsay, David. *Ramsay's History of South Carolina, From its First Settlement in 1670 to the Year 1808*. Charleston, South Carolina: Walker, Evans & Co., 1858.

Reid, J. W. *History of the Fourth Regiment of S.C. Volunteers from the Commencement of the War Until Lee's Surrender*. Greenville, South Carolina: Shannon and Co., 1892.

Rhea, Gordon C. *The Battle of the Wilderness, May 5–6, 1864*. Baton Rouge, Louisiana: Louisiana State University Press, 1994.

Salley, A. S. *South Carolina Troops in the Confederate Service*, Volume Three, *Fifth South Carolina Volunteers*. Columbia, South Carolina: The State Company, 1930.

Sanger, Donald Bridgman and Thomas Robson Hay. *James Longstreet*. Baton Rouge, Louisiana: Louisiana State University Press, 1952.

Sears, Stephen W. *Landscape Turned Red: The Battle of Antietam*. New York: Ticknor and Fields, 1983.

_____. *To the Gates of Richmond: The Peninsula Campaign*. New York: Ticknor and Fields, 1992.

Simon, John Y., ed. *The Papers of Ulysses S. Grant*, Volume Ten. Carbondale, Illinois: Southern Illinois University Press, 1982.

Smith, Gustavus W. *The Battle of Seven Pines*. New York: C. G. Crawford, Printer, 1891.

Smith, Roy McBee. *Vardry McBee, 1775–1864: Man of Reason in an Age of Extremes*. Columbia, South Carolina: R. L. Bryan Co., 1992.

Snowden, Yates, ed. *History of South Carolina*, Volume Two. Chicago: The Lewis Publishing Co., 1920.

Sorrel, G. Moxley. *Recollections of a Confederate Staff Officer*. Second Edition; New York: Neale Publishing Co., 1917.

Starr, Linda Sparks. *W. R. Rankin: Manassas to Appomattox*. Norman, Oklahoma: privately printed, 1990.

Steere, Edward. *The Wilderness Campaign*. Harrisburg, Pennsylvania: The Stackpole Company, 1960.

Sword, Wiley. *Mountains Touched with Fire: Chattanooga Besieged, 1863*. New York: St. Martin's Press, 1995.

Thomas, Emory M. *The Confederate Nation 1861-1865*. New York: Harper and Row, Publishers, 1979.

Thomas, John Peyre. *The Career and Character of General Micah Jenkins, C.S.A.* Columbia, South Carolina: The State Company, 1903.

_____. *The History of the South Carolina Military Academy*. Reprint; Columbia, South Carolina: Palmetto Bookworks, 1991.

Wert, Jeffrey D. *General James Longstreet: The Confederacy's Most Controversial Soldier – A Biography*. New York: Simon and Shuster, 1993.

Woodward, C. Vann, ed. *Mary Chesnut's Civil War*. New Haven: Yale University Press, 1981.

Wyatt–Brown, Bertram. *Southern Honor: Ethics and Behavior in the Old South*. New York: Oxford University Press, 1982.

COMPILATIONS OF CIVIL WAR REMINISCENCES AND RECOLLECTIONS

Recollections and Reminiscences, 1861–1865 through World War One. Three Volumes. Complied and published by the South Carolina Division of the United Daughters of the Confederacy.

Reminiscences of Confederate Soliders and Stories of the War. Fourteen Volumes. Compiled by the Georgia Division of the United Daughters of the Confederacy. Georgia Department of Archives and History.

NEWSPAPERS

Carolina (Spartanburg, South Carolina) *Spartan*	1860–1865
Charleston (South Carolina) *Daily Courier*	1853–1865
Charleston (South Carolina) *News and Courier*	1964
Charleston (South Carolina) *Evening Post*	1964
Charleston (South Carolina) *Mercury*	1853–1865
The (Columbia, South Carolina) *State*	1951–1960
The (Columbia, South Carolina) *Daily Southern Guardian*	1861
Yorkville (South Carolina) *Enquirer*	1854–1870

U. S. GOVERNMENT SOURCES

National Archives

Compiled Records Showing Service of Military Units in Confederate
Organizations, R. G. 109, series M861.

Compiled Service Records (and Unit Record of Events Cards) of the
Confederate Soldiers Who Served in Organizations from the State of
South Carolina, R. G. 109, series M267.

Compiled Service Records of Confederate General and Staff Officers and
Non–Regimental Enlisted Men, R. G. 109, series M331.

Confederate Inspection Reports, R. G. 109, series M935.

Letters Received by the Confederate Adjutant and Inspector General's Office,
R. G. 109, series M410.

Telegrams and Letters Sent by Longstreet's Headquarters, R. G. 109, Chapter
II, Volume 277.

Unfiled Papers and Slips Belonging in Compiled Service Records, R. G. 109,
series M347.

United States War Department

*The War of the Rebellion: A Compilation of the Official Records in the Union
and Confederate Armies.* Four Series, Seventy Volumes in One Hundred
and Twenty–eight Parts. Washington, D.C.: Government Printing Office,
1880–1901.

STATE AND LOCAL SOURCES

South Carolina Department of Archives and History

Court of Equity Record Book, March 6, 1855 to June 16, 1856 for Charleston
District.

Inventory Appraisement and Sales, 1854–1857, for Charleston District.

Records of the Confederate Historian. Rolls of South Carolina Volunteers in
the Confederate States Provisional Army, 1861–1865. Five volumes.

South Carolina State Library, Columbia, South Carolina

*Reports and Resolutions of the General Assembly of the State of South
Carolina, 1864–1865.* Columbia, South Carolina: Julian A. Selby, Printer
to the State, 1866.

ARTICLES APPEARING IN JOURNALS
OR OTHER PERIODICAL PUBLICATIONS

Brock, R. A., ed. "Paroles of the Army of Northern Virginia, R. E. Lee, Gen.,
C.S.A., Commanding, Surrendered at Appomattox C. H., Va., April 9, 1865, to

Lieutenant General U. S. Grant, Commanding Armies of the U. S." *Southern Historical Society Papers*, Volume 15 (1887).

Carson, E. Scott. "Hampton's Legion and Hood's Brigade." *Confederate Veteran* 16 (July 1908): 342.

Crowson, E. T. "Jenkins, Coward and the Yorkville Boys." *Sandlapper Magazine* 7 (December 1974): 32–36.

Cubbison, Douglas R. "Midnight Engagement: Geary's White Star Division at Wauhatchie, Tennessee, October 28-29, 1863." *Civil War Regiments* 3 (1993): 70–101.

Field, Major General C. W. "Campaign of 1864 and 1865." *Southern Historical Society Papers* 14 (1886), 542–563.

Hill, D. H. "Address by General D. H. Hill on October 22, 1885." *Southern Historical Society Papers* 13 (July–December 1885): 259–276.

Hoyt, James A. "Anderson's Brigade at Gaines' Mill." *Confederate Veteran* 7 (May 1899): 224–227.

McDavid, Peter A. "With the Palmetto Riflemen." *Confederate Veteran* 37 (August 1929): 298–300.

Minnich, J. W. "That Affair at Dandridge, Tennessee." *Confederate Veteran* 30 (August 1922): 294–297.

Murray, Chalmers S. "Edisto Island and its Place Names." *Names in South Carolina* 7 (Winter 1960): 73–74.

Nye, W. S. "Action North of Bull Run an Often Overlooked Phase of Battle of First Manassas." *Civil War Times Illustrated* 4 (April 1965): 48–49.

Parker, Elmer O. "Captain Lyle: Forgotten Hero of the Confederacy." *Prologue: The Journal of the National Archives* 4 (Fall 1972): 165–172.

Salley, A. S. "A Career Built in Friendship." *The State Magazine*, a supplement to *The* (Columbia, South Carolina) *State*, August 5, 1951, pp. 14–15.

Salley, Marion. "Sixty-seven Years of Married Life." *Confederate Veteran* 32 (July 1924): 259.

Shingleton, Royce G., ed. "South From Appomattox: The Diary of Abner R. Cox." *South Carolina Historical Magazine* 75 (1974): 238–244.

Stevens, John K. "Of Mules and Men: The Night Fight at Wauhatchie Station." *South Carolina Historical Magazine* 90 (October 1989): 282–298.

Trowbridge, J. W. "Conspicuous Feats of Valor." *Confederate Veteran* 24 (January 1916): 25–26.

Vandiver, Frank E., ed. "Proceedings of the Second Confederate Congress." *Southern Historical Society Papers*, Volume 51 (1958).

Vaughan, Turner. "Diary of Turner Vaughan, Co. 'C', 4th Alabama Regiment, C.S.A." *Alabama Historical Quarterly* 18 (Winter 1956): 573–601.

Index

Mayre's Heights, 182-83
Mattison, C. S.
Fourth S.C. Battalion, 87, 87n. 33,
93, 145n. 64, 151, 154, 165
Hampton's Legion, assigned to,
179, 179n. 6
Second Manassas, Battle of,
157n. 40
Williamsburg, Battle of, 94
See also, Fourth South Carolina
Battalion
McArthur, Medora Caroline
J. B. Lyle, married to, 84n. 22
McCall, George A., 72, 72n. 10 and
n. 13
on bayonet fight, 136
Frayser's Farm, Battle of, 134-36
McClellan, George B., 87
Maryland Campaign, 162-64, 166-
67, 170-71, 176n. 51
Peninsular Campaign, 89, 91-92,
99, 102, 111, 117-19, 127-
28, 130, 132, 141-42, 142n.
49, 145
president, runs for, 322
relieved of command, 177
McConnell, J. D.
Appomattox, surrender at, 358
Company E, Fifth S.C.V., 113,
113n. 26
describing scenes of battle, 320
Hiram Richards, death of, 319-20
with Jenkins at Knoxville, 251-52
Lee at Darbytown Road, 319
Lookout Valley, Battle of, 236,
231n. 78
at North Anna River, 300n. 14
shot at Fort Harrison, 329-30
Spotsylvania, Battle of, 296,
296n. 83
See also, Company E, Fifth South
Carolina Volunteers
McCravy, Hartwell A.
killed, 66n. 70
McDaniel, William Tate
death, description of, 320, 320n.
89
McDowell, Irvin, 54-56, 65n. 66, 66-
67, 87, 89, 99, 102, 145, 154

McDowell, James
describing Jenkins death, 277
McFall, James M., 206n. 72
on Jenkins' death, 282n. 66
McKeown, W. F.
killed, 183, 183n. 22
McKnight, Robert D.
loss of arm, 248, 248n. 33
McLaws, Lafayette, 165
at Campbell's Station, 246
Fort Loudon, attack on, 249-51
Fredericksburg, Battle of, 182
Jenkins on depth of ditch, 250,
250n. 41 and n. 43
Kershaw, replaced by, 266n. 18
Knoxville, division sent to, 243
Longstreet's letter to, praising
Jenkins, 222
Lookout Valley, 226-27
relieved of command, 253, 253n.
66
to Tennessee, 209, 212-13
McLean's Ford
Fifth S.C.V., camped at, 73
First Manassas, Battle of, 54-58, 68
McLure, Jane Catherine (Kate), 82n.
10
McLure, John W.
Company G, Fifth S.C.V., 82n10
in Greeneville, Tennessee, 261
Lenoir's Station, Federals
abandon, 245, 245n. 20
on R. H. Anderson, 82
McSwain, Horace A.
killed, 160, 160n. 43
Meacham, Samuel Banks
Company E, Fifth S.C.V., 87n. 31,
88
elected lieutenant, Jasper Light
Infantry, 37n. 21
Seven Pines, Battle of, 113, 113n.
26
See also, Company E, Fifth South
Carolina Volunteers
See also, Jasper Light Infantry
Meade, George Gordon, 203-4
Metts, W. B.
elected lieutenant, 25
See also, Jasper Light Infantry